*The Fourth Review of Special Education*

# The Fourth Review
## of
# Special Education

Editors

**LESTER MANN, Ph.D.**
*Professor*
*Pennsylvania State University*
*Radnor Center*
*Radnor, Pennsylvania*

**DAVID A. SABATINO, Ph.D.**
*Professor and Chairperson*
*Department of Special Education*
*Southern Illinois University*
*Carbondale, Illinois*

GRUNE & STRATTON
*A Subsidiary of Harcourt Brace Jovanovich, Publishers*
New York  London  Toronto  Sydney  San Francisco

*Grune & Stratton, Inc.*
*111 Fifth Avenue*
*New York, New York 10003*

Distributed in the United Kingdom by
*Academic Press, Inc. (London) Ltd.*
*24/28 Oval Road, London NW 1*

Library of Congress Catalog Number 73-645036
International Standard Book Number 0-8089-1263-1
Printed in the United States of America

# CONTENTS

# PREFACE

The Fourth Review of Special Education reflects, as have our earlier Reviews, the state of opinion and practice in special education in both Europe and the United States.

Readers who have been following our Reviews from their inception will note that a rather short period of time (from the first to the present volume) has seen considerable change in the perspectives of special education. Learning disabilities is no longer its old process-oriented self; the examination of its issues in the current Review is in orientation a far cry from those in the first and other early Reviews. Behavior modification is no longer a matter of novelty within the provenance of special education. Rather, it is now seen as a major (and familiar) tool of intervention for which we seek ever broadened horizons of use. In particular, behavioral modification appears to be replacing traditional psychodynamic interventions as can be seen in the papers in the Fourth Review on the education and treatment of behaviorally disturbed and autistic children.

If behavior modification is a familiar tool, biofeedback is yet a novel one. Our article reviewing its applications with handicapped children and youth will serve as a valuable introduction to the topic for some of our readers and a timely update for those familiar with the topic.

The Fourth Review also offers state-of-the-art articles on visual handicaps and giftedness. The latter is an area of inquiry that earlier Reviews had neglected to cover; we are pleased to be able to provide a discussion of this field for interested readers.

Our update on technology in special education should be especially appreciated by readers of the Fourth Review. Given the current explosion of new technologies that special educators are faced with, there is an urgent need for thoughtful assessment of what is new and what is still needed in these special education technologies.

No current examination of special education, dealing with either the cutting edge or state-of-the-art of inquiries in the field, can afford to ignore those articles in the Fourth Review that discuss nondiscriminatory assessment, labels and expectancies, mainstreaming, career and vocational education, and personnel preparation.

Of critical importance in the present Review is a look at the important professional interface of special education and school psychology. Much of the misunderstanding about the school psychologists' role in special education should be resolved by the insightful examination of key issues in special education/school psychology vis-a-vis the exceptional pupil, that the reader will obtain from our Review.

Finally, the Fourth Review is able to present again our traditional review of Eastern European special education, which our readers have come to anticipate. This, we are delighted to note, is now supplemented with an examination of special education in Western Europe and Scandinavia.

In closing we would like to express our appreciation to our authors who have waived their royalties to facilitate publication of this volume.

*Lester Mann, Ph.D.*
*David A. Sabatino, Ph.D.*

# CONTRIBUTORS

Marty Abramson, Ph.D.
Assistant Professor
Department of Educational
    Psychology
Texas A&M University
College Station, Texas


Robert Algozzine
Associate Professor of Special
    Education
University of Florida
Gainesville, Florida


Sandra Alper, Ph.D.
Department of Special Education
University of Missouri
Columbia, Missouri


Richard Baer, Ph.D.
Autism Project
University of Arkansas
Little Rock, Arkansas


A. Edward Blackhurst, Ph.D.
Professor
Department of Special Education
University of Kentucky
Lexington, Kentucky


Anthony A. Cancelli, Ed.D.
Department of Educational
    Psychology
University of Arizona
Tucson, Arizona


Douglas Cullinan, Ed.D.
Department of Learning and
    Development
Northern Illinois University
DeKalb, Illinois


Calvin O. Dyer, Ph.D.
Professor of Education, and
Director of School Psychology
    Program
Combined Program in Education
    and Psychology
University of Michigan
Ann Arbor, Michigan


Andrew L. Egel, Ph.D.
Assistant Professor
Department of Special Education
College of Education
University of Maryland
College Park, Maryland


Michael H. Epstein, Ed.D.
Department of Learning and
    Development
Northern Illinois University
DeKalb, Illinois


Norma J. Ewing
Department of Special Education
Southern Illinois University
Carbondale, Illinois


Barbara G. Ford, Ph.D.
Assistant Professor
Northern Illinois University
DeKalb, Illinois

*Amanda P. Hall, Ph.D.*
Director
Assessment Center for the Visually
   Impaired
California School for the Blind
Berkeley, California

*Daniel P. Hallahan, Ph.D.*
Associate Professor, and Director
Learning Disabilities Research
   Institute
University of Virginia
Charlottesville, Virginia

*Philip H. Hatlen, Ed.D.*
Professor of Special Education
San Francisco State University
San Francisco, California

*Alan M. Hofmeister, Ph.D.*
Dean, School of Graduate Studies, and
Associate Vice-President for Research
Utah State University
Logan, Utah

*Ivan Z. Holowinsky, Ed.D.*
Professor and Coordinator
Special Education Programs
Department of Educational
   Psychology
Rutgers University
New Brunswick, New Jersey

*Reva C. Jenkins, Ph.D.*
Department of Educational
   Psychology
University of Kansas
Lawrence, Kansas

*Kristen D. Juul*
Department of Special Education
Southern Illinois University
Carbondale, Illinois

*James M. Kauffman, Ed.D.*
Associate Professor
Department of Special Education
University of Virginia
Charlottesville, Virginia

*Robert L. Koegel, Ph.D.*
Social Process Research Institute
University of California
Santa Barbara, California

*Thomas R. Kratochwill, Ph.D.*
Department of Educational
   Psychology
University of Arizona
Tucson, Arizona

*M. Stephen Lilly*
Professor and Chairman
Department of Special Education
University of Illinois
Urbana-Champaign, Illinois

*John Lloyd, Ph.D.*
Assistant Professor
Learning Disabilities Research
   Institute
University of Virginia
Charlottesville, Virginia

*Cecil D. Mercer*
Professor of Special Education
University of Florida
Gainesville, Florida

*Sidney R. Miller*
Department of Special Education
Southern Illinois University
Carbondale, Illinois

*Ted L. Miller, Ph.D.*
Department of Special Education and
   Counseling
University of Tennessee
Chattanooga, Tennessee

**L. Allen Phelps**
University of Illinois
Urbana, Illinois

**Terry L. Rose, Ph.D.**
Department of Learning and
  Development
Northern Illinois University
DeKalb, Illinois

**Richard C. Schofer**
Professor and Chairman
Department of Special Education
University of Missouri
Columbia, Missouri

**Laura Schreibman, Ph.D.**
Psychology Department
Claremont Men's College
Claremont, California

**Sebastian Striefel, Ph.D.**
Professor, Psychology Department, and
Director, Division of Services
Exceptional Child Center
Utah State University
Logan, Utah

**Dean Tuttle, Ph.D.**
Professor
Department of Special Education
University of Northern Colorado
Greeley, Colorado

# EDUCATION OF THE VISUALLY HANDICAPPED: AN OVERVIEW AND UPDATE

Philip H. Hatlen
*San Francisco State University*

Amanda P. Hall
*California School for the Blind*

Dean Tuttle
*University of Northern Colorado*

Visually handicapped students are proportionately fewer in number than other handicapped populations. Therefore, one might assume that the historical development of educational services for the visually handicapped is of minor importance to the field of special education. However, as this chapter will illustrate, educators, parents, and the visually handicapped themselves have made significant contributions to all of special education. Quality education for the blind was made possible many years ago by the establishment of residential schools. Successful placement of visually handicapped students in regular classrooms occurred long before recent legislation affecting the education of the handicapped. Educators of the visually handicapped were among the early pioneers in attempting to provide appropriate educational services for the multihandicapped.

## WHO ARE THE VISUALLY HANDICAPPED?

The terms "visually handicapped," "visually impaired," and "visually disabled," are used interchangeably to define a similar population. Regardless of the term used, the reference is to persons who have a visual loss significant to the extent that they require alternative or adapted methods of learning. The visually handicapped are generally divided into two groups, the blind and the partially seeing.

1

A legal definition of blindness was first established by the Social Security Act of 1935, which set into law certain privileges for the blind, such as an extra tax deduction. This definition reads as follows: "Visual acuity for distant vision of 20/200 or less in the better eye with best correction, or widest diameter of visual field subtending an angle of less than 20 degrees" (Vaughan & Ashbury, 1977, p. 304). This is an important definition as it is used for eligibility for a variety of social, rehabilitative, and educational services.

Partially seeing individuals are defined as "persons with a visual acuity greater than 20/200, but not greater than 20/70 in the better eye after correction" (National Society for the Prevention of Blindness, 1966, p. 10).

For some time these legal definitions were used to make educational decisions regarding services to visually handicapped students (Jones, 1962). However, as the medical profession developed better techniques for measuring remaining vision and for predicting the prognosis of further visual loss, and as educators began to question the need for children with substantial usable vision to learn to utilize tactual and auditory modes, the definitions came into serious question. In the 1950s and 1960s it was gradually recognized and accepted that many legally blind students had remaining vision sufficient to function primarily as visual learners with no resulting damage to their vision. The result has been a gradually evolving functional definition of blindness. Widely accepted in the United States at the present time is a functional definition which assumes that if the visually handicapped person can utilize vision as his or her primary avenue of learning, then he or she is functionally partially seeing. It is estimated that as much as two-thirds to three-fourths of the legally blind persons in the United States are functionally partially seeing. This fact has profound implications for educational placement and services for visually handicapped students. It is generally accepted that no longer should the student with 20/300 vision who is capable of using it effectively automatically be a braille reader.

The educational or functional definition of partially seeing is also currently in the process of revision. Teachers have found that there are students with better than 20/70 vision who seem to need some assistance in the learning process. Therefore, some states have revised their definition of eligibility for services from a teacher of the visually handicapped to include students with better than 20/70 vision who are identified both educationally and medically as in need of special education services.

Genensky (1978) has developed the following definition:

A person is functionally blind if he/she is either totally blind or has at most light perception or light projection. A person is partially sighted and legally blind if he or she is legally blind, but not functionally blind. A person is partially sighted if the acuity in his better eye even with ordinary corrective lenses does not exceed 20/70 or if the maximum diameter of his visual field does not exceed 20 degrees and if he is not functionally blind. (p. 177)

The prevalence of visual loss among citizens of the United States is difficult to determine. One estimate is that by 1980 the rate of legal blindness in the United States will be 2.14 per 1000 population, or a total of 519,200 citizens (National Society for the Prevention of Blindness, 1966). Genensky (1978) states that in 1970 there were at least 420,000 legally blind Americans and an additional 1.28 million who could not read newspaper type, even with corrective lenses. He estimates that in 1977 there were 141,200 legally partially seeing and 14,800 functionally blind children and youth between the ages of 5 and 19, or approximately school age. Thus it is readily apparent that the functionally partially seeing represent a much larger population for educational purposes.

Causes of visual handicaps in the school-age population is again difficult to determine. It is generally accepted that diabetic retinopathy is becoming a more serious cause of visual loss in adults. In the school-age population cataracts, optic nerve damage, glaucoma, and myopia appear to be among the major causes.

In summary, the visually handicapped children who are the responsibility and concern of educators of the visually handicapped are a very heterogenous population whose vision ranges from total blindness to better than 20/70, with the major population of students capable of using vision as their primary avenue of learning. The school-age population represents a relatively small proportion of the total population of visually handicapped persons in the United States; the highest proportion are over 65 years old. The major causes of visual handicaps in the school-age population are impairments to vision that only occasionally result in total blindness.

## RESIDENTIAL SCHOOLS FOR THE BLIND IN THE UNITED STATES—THEIR HISTORY AND PRESENT ROLE

Formal education for blind children in the United States began in 1829 with the founding of the New England Asylum for the Blind. Establishment of this school, later to be called Perkins School for the Blind in

Watertown, Massachusetts, was the result of Dr. John D. Fisher's recommendation that services for the blind be provided in the Boston area similar to those he observed at Huay's School in France. Samuel Gridley Howe was chosen to serve as its first director. Two more private schools were to follow shortly thereafter, the New York Institution for the Education of the Blind in New York City in 1831 and the Overbrook School for the Blind in Philadelphia in 1883 (Frampton & Kerney, 1953).

Upon returning from Europe, Howe spent considerable time addressing state legislatures urging them to create other schools. His efforts led to the establishment of the first two state-supported schools for the blind in Ohio in 1837 and in Kentucky in 1842. By 1870 there were 23 residential schools, largely due to Howe's efforts and influence (Farrell, 1956).

Today there are approximately 50 residential schools in the United States. Enrollments in these schools vary from 20–30 pupils in the smaller ones to as many as 250–300 in the larger programs (Lowenfeld, 1971). Residential schools can be found in all states except Delaware, Maine, Nevada, New Hampshire, New Jersey, Rhode Island, Vermont, and Wyoming (Lowenfeld, 1973).

In 11 states, blind and deaf children are educated in "dual schools," i.e., a single school serving both populations. Educators contine to agree that such arrangements are not ideal and are a "source of friction and compromise" (Farrell, 1956, p. 55).

Initially the student body of the residential schools was made up of students who were totally blind. Gradually, in the 1900s low vision and partially seeing children became enrolled in residential programs. For this reason, the word "blind" was dropped from the name of many schools (Farrell, 1956).

Until the early 1900s residential schools were the only educational setting available to blind children. Day programs, established first in Chicago in 1900, provided an alternative to residential programs (Farrell, 1956).

The factors that contributed to the establishment of day classes — increasing integration of the blind into society, high regard for public school education, and the importance of family life — also influenced the policies and practices of residential schools. As a result, these schools have turned from "closed" to "open" programs in terms of involvement with the community (Lowenfeld, 1971).

Bledsoe (1971) indicates that these factors influenced residential programs and discerns three types of present-day patterns: (1) the *classic type,* which although modernized its approach, remains traditional in its basic emphasis on educating blind children in grades K–12 on the school's campus; (2) the *center type,* which has evolved as a nucleus for services to blind children who are functioning in the community; and (3) the *hospital type,* which serves primarily the multihandicapped blind.

Residential schools in recent years have made noteworthy changes in their programs. In the past these schools were placed in various departments of state government, such as departments of institutions and asylums or public welfare. More recently residential programs have been reassigned, more appropriately, to state departments of education (Lowenfeld, 1973). In 1975, Lowenfeld reported that approximately 33% of the legally blind school-age population was receiving instruction in residential programs.

Other widespread changes, as pointed out by Taylor (1973), are that children enrolled in residential programs now have more opportunities for (1) regular attendance in classes in nearby public schools, (2) living at home and attending residential schools on a day school basis, (3) regularly scheduled weekend transportation home; and (4) contact with more specialized ancillary staff such as consulting psychiatrists, full-time psychologists, speech therapists, social workers, physical therapists, etc.

Taylor additionally indicates that residential programs have established (1) regular and better communication with the child's family, (2) preschool, college prep, specialized summer remedial, and "special help" programs; (3) "outreach" programs providing educational materials and diagnostic and consultant services to local districts; and (4) more comprehensive programs to meet the needs of multihandicapped visually impaired children.

Public Law (PL) 94-142, the Education for All Handicapped Children Act of 1975, has generated discussion involving the future of residential schools in light of the "least restrictive environment" concept. Hapeman (1977) expressed fear that implementation of the law would cause "increased avoidance of employment of residential schools as an integral part of the system." Bischoff (1977) contends that the residential school is the "least restrictive educational program appropriate to the needs of many visually handicapped students." Maron (1978), in a response to this controversy, concluded that residential schools still represent a viable educational alternative for many visually handicapped individuals. PL 94-142 will not eliminate this alternative, nor will there be a sudden influx of students into public school programs.

## PUBLIC DAY SCHOOL EDUCATION

In 1900, Chicago opened the first day school class for blind students. Boston is credited with beginning the first class for partially seeing children in 1913. For many years thereafter, these classes in local school districts were established primarily in urban areas and were, with few exceptions, self-contained. By 1948 less than 50 local school districts reported having programs for blind students and about 250 districts had programs for the partially seeing. In 1958 these numbers had increased to 500 and 340, respectively (Jones, 1963).

In the early 1950s public day school programs for the visually handicapped began a very rapid and dramatic transformation. Blind and partially seeing children were enrolled in regular classrooms throughout the country and a new and sophisticated pattern of support services was developed. There were a number of causes for this significant change over a relatively short period of time: (1) The number of children congenitally blinded from retrolental fibroplasia reached epidemic proportions and literally thousands of these children were being enrolled in local school programs. Communities found themselves with a large population of school-age blind children and could therefore justify a full-time teacher of blind children. (2) Parents of blind children began to demand local school services as an alternative to sending their children sometimes hundreds of miles from home to a residential school. Parental pressure was placed on school boards and administrations throughout the country. (3) Leading educators of the blind began to promote placement of blind children in regular classrooms. Leaders such as Georgie Lee Abel, Josephine Taylor, Florence Henderson, and Berthold Lowenfeld were among the strongest advocates for the development of local education services for blind children. (4) Nationally respected organizations advocated the placement of blind children in local school programs. In particular, the American Foundation for the Blind, through its publications and traveling consultants, assisted states and local districts in the development of appropriate local educational services. These individuals and organizations promoted new service delivery systems to ensure that each child received the best available in regular classrooms plus a support service from competent teachers of the visually handicapped.

The three most common service delivery systems advocated were as follows (American Foundation for the Blind, 1954):

1. *The Cooperative Plan:* This plan is one in which the blind child is enrolled with

a teacher of blind children in a special room from which he goes to the regular classroom teachers.

2. *The Integrated Plan:* This plan is one in which the blind child is enrolled in the regular classroom. Available to him and his regular teachers is a full-time qualified teacher of blind children and also a resource room. The regular teachers turn to the teacher of blind children for assistance in planning the child's program, for guidance in adapting the classroom procedures, and for providing, as necessary, specialized instruction appropriate to the child's needs.

3. *The Itinerant Teacher Plan:* This plan is one in which the blind child is enrolled in the regular class in his home school where his needs are met through the cooperative efforts of the regular teacher and those of the itinerant teacher qualified to offer this special service.

It is important to stress that these definitions were first published in 1954 and that, as models for service delivery for visually handicapped children and perhaps for many other exceptional children, they remain as valid as when they were first developed.

Because of these dramatic changes in both the population and availability of services, the number of blind students enrolled in day schools surpassed the number in residential schools in 1958 (Jones, 1963). With some exceptions, the itinerant teacher plan became most often used with partially seeing students who it was felt required less daily support from the teacher of the visually handicapped. The integrated (resource room) plan was most often used for functionally blind children whose needs for the services of a teacher of the visually handicapped were more intense.

Long before PL 94-142, the concept of "least restrictive environment" was initiated for the education of visually handicapped students. The profession of education of the visually handicapped had, for more than 20 years, proven the desirability and the success of offering many educational options for visually handicapped students.

As retrolental fibroplasia students began graduating from high school in the late 1960s, another gradual change began in public day school programs for the visually handicapped. More emphasis was placed on the educational needs of partially seeing children, and the result has been that more partially seeing children have been identified as needing special education services. Because this population is viewed as needing less intensive services, many integrated plan programs have changed into itinerant programs. At the present time the itinerant teacher plan is the most widely used model for education of blind and partially seeing children in the United States.

As day school programs evolved and were successful in providing appropriate experiences for blind and partially seeing students, a complementary role with residential schools developed. Residential schools for the blind began serving primarily multihandicapped visually impaired children who were more difficult to serve in local day schools; residential schools continued to serve visually handicapped students from remote geographical areas where local services were not economically feasible.

The success of public day schools in providing appropriate educational services for visually handicapped students depends on a number of factors. The local school district must have a commitment to the provision of such services and must administratively support the concept of the visually handicapped child in the regular classroom. Regular classroom teachers must be amenable to the idea of including a visually handicapped student in their classrooms. This should mean some inservice preparation of the regular classroom teacher. The successful placement of visually handicapped students in regular classrooms is dependent on a support system for the classroom teacher and the child which includes a competent, well-prepared teacher of the visually handicapped.

The adoption of an itinerant teacher plan by a school district must be considered carefully. If the age range and geographical spread of children results in a minimum amount of time for the teacher of the visually handicapped to function in a teacher role, it must be determined whether the visually handicapped student will receive the support services that he/she needs.

Ideally, a full range of support systems will be available in any given school district. There is no one best program for the education of visually handicapped students. There is a best program for a particular child at a particular time in his/her life. This means that the options of a self-contained class, a cooperative plan, a resource room plan, an itinerant teacher plan, and a residential school should be available to any child at any time. None of these should be viewed as being the only "least restrictive environment." Each will be least restrictive to certain children at certain times in their educational lives.

## INFANT AND PRESCHOOL SERVICES

In the late nineteenth and early twentieth centuries, most very young blind children were either cared for by parents in the home or sent to residential nursery schools for the blind (Norris, 1965; Wood, 1947). Certain isolated programs may have provided preschool blind children with other special services, such as home counseling (Totman, 1947). With the large increase in the blind population caused by retrolental fibroplasia during the mid-1940s to mid-1950s, formalized programs emerged for the purpose of educating parents of young blind children. Parents attended lectures and discussion groups while their blind children were observed by nursery school teachers (Scholl, 1973). These parent education programs declined in number when the retrolental fibroplasia preschool population decreased.

Since the late 1950s there has been a gradual increase in direct educational services to preschool visually handicapped children for three major reasons: (1) research findings have indicated developmental needs and anomalies caused by loss of sight which require special intervention measures (Fraiberg, 1977; Norris, Spaulding, & Brodie, 1957); (2) an increase in the population of young multihandicapped blind children has necessitated a corresponding growth in services to meet these needs; and (3) federal legislation has been passed related to early childhood education for the handicapped and federal funds have been committed to these services (Felix & Spungin, 1978). A survey of existing preschool programs conducted by the American Foundation for the Blind indicated that 74 percent of the programs surveyed were established after 1966 and about one-half were initiated after 1972 (Felix & Spungin, 1978).

Many educators of the visually handicapped once operated under the assumption that the developmental needs of blind and low vision children were the same as those of sighted children. It was assumed that the only difference between a congenitally blind child and a normally sighted child was that the blind child could not see. Research investigations during the past three decades have cast doubt upon that assumption. Norris et al. (1957), in a longitudinal study of 66 young visually handicapped children, found that the development of intelligence and social maturity of blind children can follow an orderly progression without serious retardation only if appropriate early experiences were provided that fostered motor skills and an interest in the world. Later, Fraiberg (1977) and her associates concluded that there were developmental differences between blind and sighted children from a longitudinal study of 10 congenitally blind infants.

One area of difference found by Fraiberg's group was in gross motor development involving locomotion. A comparison of gross motor development milestones of the blind infants in the Fraiberg study and the children in the Norris et al. study (1957) showed that the children in the Fraiberg group exhibited earlier ages for many gross motor achievements and that this age advantage increased over time (Adelson & Fraiberg, 1974).

The children in the Fraiberg longitudinal study had been exposed

9

to comprehensive guidance that involved a close working relationship with parents. This finding indicated that training would have a positive effect on gross motor development. Development differences caused by vision loss have been postulated in the areas of cognition (Stephens, 1972), precision in gross motor skills (DuBose, 1976), self concept development (Fraiberg & Adelson, 1976), spatial awareness (Cratty & Sams, 1968), and attachment relationships (Fraiberg, 1977), to name a few. For a full review of the research see Warren (1977).

Comprehensive programs must address the particular needs of visually handicapped children from infancy to school age in order to promote optimum development in the context of a potentially different developmental pattern so that permanent social, emotional, motor, or cognitive problems can be prevented. A parental guidance program that trains parents in the developmental needs of their young children and provides counseling to allay parental fears and problems is considered essential (Maloney, 1966; O'Brien, 1975). Curriculum areas in programs for young visually handicapped children can include self-concept development, language development, gross and fine motor development, sensory stimulation and discrimination training (including vision training for low vision children), social skills, and cognitive development, as well as creativity in art, music, and movement (Hull & McCarthy, 1973; O'Brien, 1976). Chase (1975) proposes the use of a variety of assessment techniques in developing an accurate profile of a young visually handicapped child's abilities, strengths, and weaknesses.

There are many possible program placements for visually handicapped preschool children. Brown (1974) stresses that when considering placement alternatives, every child must be treated as an individual with appropriate educational strategies tailored to meet each child's needs. One area of concern has been the need to provide instruction specific to the handicapping condition of vision loss while also providing the dual experience of both sighted and blind associations in the right proportion and at the right times. Some of the successful alternatives that have provided appropriate instruction as well as contact with normally sighted children have included programs involving the integration of visually handicapped children into classes for normally sighted children (Moore, 1952; Tait, 1974), programs involving the integration of normally sighted children into classes for visually handicapped children (O'Brien, 1975), and programs involving both the integration of visually handicapped children into classes for the normally sighted and attendance in self-contained preschool classes for the visually handicapped on alternate days (Hull & McCarthy, 1973).

## EDUCATION OF MULTIHANDICAPPED
## VISUALLY IMPAIRED

Educational services for multihandicapped children who were mentally retarded became available when public and residential schools began admitting these children into their programs. However, only a relatively small number of programs were in existence for blind mentally retarded children in the 1960s (Tretakoff, 1977). It is generally agreed that the rapid growth in both the quality and quantity of services available to visually impaired children with additional handicaps can be attributed to efforts made to meet the needs of the large number of multihandicapped children born as a result of the rubella epidemic of 1963–1965 (Barraga, 1976; Hatlen, 1973).

Another factor related to the increase in services was the contention that many conditions contributing to the delayed development or the bizarre behavior patterns of visually handicapped children who were mentally retarded were preventable through early intervention, parental counseling, and a greater understanding by professionals of roadblocks to normal development (Elonen & Zwarensteyn, 1964). Intervention strategies designed to deal with the cognitive, social, emotional, and motor requirements of the multihandicapped visually impaired were developed, and improved services were extended to the multihandicapped visually impaired who were orthopedically handicapped, emotionally disturbed, and neurologically handicapped (Cicenia, Belton, & Meyers, 1965; Graham, 1968; Winn, 1968). Services are now being refined and extended to the increasing proportion of individuals with severe sensory deficits who are served by mental retardation facilities (Rogow & Rodriguez, 1977), but these efforts are only beginning.

A team approach with members from different disciplines has evolved as the best means of achieving a comprehensive assessment of multihandicapped children for determining both program placement and instructional plans (Barraga, 1976; Elonen, 1970; Hatlen, 1973). Hatlen (1973) emphasizes the need to place children according to the handicapping condition most closely related to problems in learning and suggests periodic assessments to accommodate changing placement needs. A model comprehensive service delivery system for multiply handicapped children whose primary handicap is visual involves cooperation among schools and agencies serving students from early childhood to young adulthood and emphasizes individual instruction and ongoing diagnosis (Bourgeault, Harley, & DuBose, 1977).

A survey of organizations serving multihandicapped blind individ-

11

uals (Leach, 1971) indicated that communication skills, self-care and daily living skills, and orientation and mobility skills were the most significant educational concerns, in that order. Other instruction areas were cognitive skills, sensory development, and self-concept formation. The curriculum for the multihandicapped child was considered to be more experience oriented and concrete than curriculum for the visually handicapped child, with an emphasis on language and communication skills as well as the use of a great deal of repetition. Factors that most hindered learning were nonattending behavior, emotional disturbance, experiential deprivation, and communication and language problems.

Behavior modification techniques have been successfully applied to the instruction of multiply handicapped visually impaired children (Gallagher & Heim, 1974; Hayes & Weinhouse, 1978; Sklar & Rampulla, 1973). Rogow and Rodriguez (1977) caution that the use of behavior modification programs to eliminate stereotyped behaviors (e.g., rocking, twirling, eyepoking) must be complemented with rich programs of alternative activities since the elimination of stereotyped behaviors without substitute activities can have serious psychological consequences.

A developmental scale of orientation and mobility for multiply impaired blind children has been developed along with programmed instruction for teaching the skills on the scale (Harley, Wood, & Merbler, 1975). Another program of instruction in orientation and mobility for multiply impaired low vision children is also available (Harley, Merbler, & Pupke, 1978). The effectiveness of both sets of programmed instruction was demonstrated in systematic field tests (Harley et al., 1975; Harley et al., 1978).

Programs for multihandicapped children whose primary handicap is visual loss are still in the developmental stage. It is expected that improved services will be available in the next few years as interdisciplinary team efforts become more efficient and effective.

## CURRICULUM ADAPTATIONS

Sepcial education is "special" when handicapped children require modification or adaptation in one or more of the following areas: curriculum, methodology, materials, and equipment and/or facilities (Gearheart, 1972). The education of visually handicapped children has primarily involved the use of adapted materials and equipment along with appropriate instruction in their use and some specific methodological techniques to handle problem situations. Rarely is it necessary to alter the facilities, the buildings and grounds, in order to accommodate visually handicapped children.

With respect to the curriculum, there has been a general assumption that visually handicapped children can and should handle the same curriculum offered sighted children since their cognitive abilities are not impaired. Barraga (1976) stated,

> The general practice in educational programming for visually handicapped children, especially in local schools, has been to parallel the academic curriculum of the sighted, although providing different materials, equipment, and teaching devices. The assumption that this enabled children to learn the same academic subjects that their sighted peers learned was not based on an objective appraisal of functional achievement. The tendency to parallel the regular school curriculum has been less prevalent in residential school programs.

Since the majority of visually handicapped students are integrated into the regular curriculum with sighted peers, a cooperative effort between the regular classroom teacher and the special teacher for visually handicapped children ensures maximal learning. Understandably, the regular classroom teacher who has had little or no experience with visually impaired children frequently has many management or procedural questions. "How will the visually handicapped child obtain his books?" "How will the visually handicapped child get around?" Is the blind child safe on the playground?" "How will the visually handicapped child handle boardwork or ditto worksheets?" etc. These and other questions are answered in the following pamphlets:

*Handbook for Teachers of the Visually Handicapped* (American Printing House for the Blind, 1974)
*Mainstreaming the Visually Impaired Child* (Calovini, 1977)
*Supporting Visually Impaired Students in the Mainstream* (Martin & Hoben, 1977)
*When You Have a Visually Handicapped Child in Your Classroom: Suggestions for Teachers* (Corn & Martinez, 1977)

These pamphlets also define the role of the regular classroom teacher and the role of the resource or itinerant teacher for the visually handicapped. In general, the regular classroom teacher is responsible for integrating the visually handicapped child, whenever possible, into class activities; to that extent, this teacher is responsible for curriculum planning for all children in her class, including the blind child. On the other hand, the resource or itinerant teacher is responsible for providing consultative service to the classroom teacher, teaching specific compensatory skills to the visually handicapped child, obtaining appropriate texts and other instructional materials and equipment, etc. Optimum integration occurs when these two educators work efficiently and smoothly together on behalf of the visually handicapped child.

The most critical area of curriculum adaptation is to provide access to printed materials and providing an alternative writing tool, in other words, the development of effective communication skills (Henderson, 1973; Napier, 1973). Braille as a system of reading and writing for the blind was founded by Louis Braille in France in 1829. However, its adoption and subsequent revisions in the United States were slow, laborious, and controversial (Lowenfeld, Abel, & Hatlen, 1969). Although braille is slow and bulky, "braille is the most effective graphic tool in existence for communication by individuals who are blind" (Henderson, 1973, p. 193). Unlike braille, the Optacon provides direct access to the printed page by converting printed symbols into tactile vibrating images (Bliss & Moore, 1974). However, it too is slow and requires the use of an expensive, complicated electronic device.

Audio reading is the process of obtaining printed information after it has been read aloud onto disc or tape (Tuttle, 1974). Good listening skills do not develop automatically. A systematic sequential program must be designed to foster aural learning and study skills (Bishop, 1971; Hanninen, 1975; Stoker, 1973).

Typewriting enables visually handicapped persons to communicate directly with the sighted:

> The visually limited child should, at some time during his educative process, add the skill of typing to his personal resources. The blind child especially needs to learn to type simply as a means of communication, but the partially sighted child should have this additional skill at his disposal as well. The visually limited child's handwriting is often poor, and, though he needs to learn to write legibly enough for his own purposes, there is no reason why classwork and homework cannot be typed rather than laboriously handwritten. (Bishop, 1971, p. 111)

Curriculum adaptations required in specific subject areas such as arithmetic, science, social studies, physical education, art, and music can be described as special techniques, materials, and devices rather than content alterations (Bishop, 1971; Hanninen, 1975; Napier, 1973). For example, after reviewing a number of computational devices available to blind persons, Tuttle (1976) concluded that the abacus is potentially the most useful tool for learning arithmetic in the elementary grades. Tactile maps and globes, while helpful to sighted children in social studies, are difficult for visually handicapped children to understand conceptually (Napier, 1973). In regard to yet another subject, "physical fitness is the single most important contribution that physical activity can, on its own merit, make toward the child's development" (Kratz, 1973, p. 33).

Recent curriculum adaptations appear to represent an emerging trend toward more content-oriented modifications. *Science Activities for the Visually Impaired,* developed at Lawrence Hall of Science, Berkeley, California, is specifically designed for visually handicapped children ages 9–12. The Social Science Education Consortium in Boulder, Colorado, is currently sponsoring a project entitled "Materials Adapted for Visually Impaired Students in Social Studies." Stephens, Smith, Fitzgerald, et al. (1977), have designed a program to remediate reasoning deficits in blind children, entitled *Training Manual for Teachers of the Visually Handicapped, a Piagetian Perspective.* The American Printing House for the Blind, Louisville, Kentucky, is in the process of developing a beginning braille reading program. Whether or not this trend continues, curriculum adaptations will still be required to fully meet the educational needs of visually handicapped children.

## CURRICULUM IN NONACADEMIC AREAS

"One of the most serious losses to the blind child or the child with limited vision is lack of opportunity for learning through visual observation. Equally important is his loss of the ability to control many of the problems in social relationships" (American Foundation for the Blind, 1957). This statement, contained in an early publication advocating the placement of visually handicapped students in regular classrooms, is evidence that educators had concerns regarding the specialized needs of visually handicapped students. Jones (1963) and the Pinebrook Report (American Foundation for the Blind, 1954) verify this concern that visually handicapped students require educational experiences in addition to those provided in the regular classroom. However, the early stress on successful academic experiences in the regular classroom seemed to cause a deemphasis in the importance of specialized learning experience for the visually handicapped student. It is the observation of some educators that the capability of many postsecondary visually handicapped young adults to readily and easily be assimilated into the general community has been affected by this deemphasis (Hatlen, LeDuc, & Canter, 1975; Morrison, 1974).

In the late 1960s and the early 1970s, as hundreds of retrolental fibroplasia blinded young adults began leaving school, concern for their functioning as adults began to grow. Many continued their educational experience in colleges and universities, using the relatively undemanding life style of dormitory living to postpone their acquisition of independent living skills. A few found competitive employment but continued to live with their parents, and many others continued to live at home with no educational or vocational goals. Why was this happening?

Educators of the visually handicapped had assumed that placement of students in regular classrooms with sighted contemporaries would ease the transition from school to adult life. It was assumed that social skills, living skills, personal hygiene and grooming skills, etc. would be the natural outcome of local day school programs which provided children with the opportunity to continue to live with their families and to learn with their sighted contemporaries. For many visually handicapped students these assumptions proved true. There are congenitally visually handicapped adults living in their own homes and apartments, working in competitive employment, and sharing their leisure time with sighted neighbors and friends. There are many others, however, more than were expected, who have not been able to make this transition. Rehabilitation workers, social workers, educators, and parents are voicing an increasing concern regarding this unexpected outcome in view of the advances made in educational services.

Little has been written concerning the area of the nonacademic needs of visually handicapped students, other than illustrations of poor preparation for adult life (Hatlen et al., 1975; Morrison, 1974). During the academic year 1977–1978, a group of teachers and administrators in Northern California met and attempted to develop a statement of the role of the teacher of the visually handicapped which would include the teaching of nonacademic skills (Committee on Assessment of Visually Handicapped Children, 1978). It was felt that this is a necessary task, considering the movement toward more and more itinerant teaching services resulting in less and less face-to-face teaching time between the teacher of the visually handicapped and the visually handicapped student. For the present, with little literature available, this statement is the most concise document available outlining potential areas of need that must be specifically addressed by the teacher of the visually handicapped. These areas of responsibility include the following:*

*This list is reprinted with permission from: Committee on Assessment of Visually Handicapped Children. The role of the teacher of the visually handicapped—A self definition. In The International Council for Education of the Visually Handicapped: *The Educator*. 1978, *1*(2), p. 2.

1. *Psychomotor development:* It is recognized that many visually handicapped students have potential problems with motor development in the areas of body image, spatial awareness, and visual–motor skills (Cratty, 1971). Also included under psychomotor development are physical education experiences, including physical fitness and orientation and mobility skills.

2. *Independent living skills:* The teacher of the visually handicapped shares the responsibility for a gradual and sequential growth in such independent living skills as personal grooming and hygiene, homemaking, awareness of community services, and financial management.

3. *Social skills:* It is generally recognized that exposure to sighted children does not ensure the acquisition of appropriate social skills for visually handicapped students. Some specific efforts must be made by teachers, parents, and others to ensure the acquisition of appropriate social skills.

4. *Listening skills:* Both partially seeing and functionally blind students need to learn good listening skills. It is necessary for the visually handicapped child to begin a sequential course of study to develop listening skills as early in the grades as possible. Listening skills are used not only for an alternative reading system, but are also important in social conversation, in mobility, and in interpreting a variety of auditory signals received from the environment. It cannot be assumed that a program in development of listening skills offered in the regular classroom will be appropriate for the visually handicapped student.

5. *Tactual skills:* The development of tactual skills for the functionally blind student is not confined to the reading of braille. Students must be taught to use their fingers and hands in order to explore, identify, and appreciate all tangible materials in their environment.

6. *Visual efficiency:* This underlies achievement skills, self-help, and vocational and social skills. The use of residual vision is fundamental. Training of the child in the best use of vision is one of the most important aspects of the curriculum offered by the teacher of the visually handicapped.

7. *Career education:* A curriculum that has been developed for sighted children may require supplementary instruction from the teacher of the visually handicapped. At the career exploration level this could well mean field trips into the community, so that the visually handicapped student will have exposure to people and work situations.

8. *Concept development:* The teacher of the visually handi-

capped shares with others the responsibility for the development of basic concepts by students. Future learning is dependent upon the student's thorough understanding of basic concepts such as association, discrimination, and relationships. Because the ability to reason in the abstract depends upon concept development, visually handicapped students often require special instruction or assistance from the teacher of the visually handicapped.

9. *Human sexuality:* Teachers of the visually handicapped, parents, and others share the responsibility of gradual, sequential instruction in human sexuality for visually handicapped students. Because programs in sex education for sighted children assume that much visual information has been previously obtained, the visually handicapped student may need a specific curriculum taught by appropriate, well-prepared professionals.

10. *Leisure and recreation:* The teacher of the visually handicapped, parents, and community agencies share a responsibility to expose the student to, and provide learning experiences in, a wide variety of leisure time activities that have carry-over value to adult life.

11. *Study skills:* Skimming braille or large-print materials, outlining in braille or large print, searching for significant information in recorded materials, and other study skills may need to be taught by the teacher of the visually handicapped.

12. *Parental involvement:* It is the responsibility of the teacher of the visually handicapped to attempt to intimately involve parents in the educational planning and attainment of all objectives beyond the level of involvement required to develop the Individualized Education Programs. Parents may often need assistance in understanding the growth and development patterns of their visually handicapped child. Teachers must help parents to provide opportunities for their child, as a responsible member of the family, to grow in independence, to acquire concrete experiences, to make and live with decisions and choices, and to attain goals that are realistically set.

13. *Counseling and guidance:* The teacher of the visually handicapped may need to assist counseling and guidance personnel in understanding the similarities and differences of visually handicapped students relative to all students. When necessary, the teacher should be prepared to counsel the students in areas related to their visual loss, such as learning to cope with occasional frustration and failure.

14. *Securing materials:* The teacher of the visually handicapped must be prepared to work with and train volunteers in order to provide materials needed by the students but not available through other sources.

15. *School and community involvement:* The teacher of the visually handicapped should be prepared to interpret the program to school personnel, the board of education, and other groups within the community.

The above list is included in this chapter to illustrate that, although a high degree of success has been achieved through the placement of visually handicapped students in regular classrooms, a number of areas of potential need for each visually handicapped student remains which must be met by a qualified, appropriately prepared special teacher. The partially sighted or functionally blind child has developmental and educational needs which are the direct result of his/her visual handicap. The responsibility of meeting these needs cannot be placed on the classroom teacher because successful placement of visually handicapped children in the regular classroom depends in large part on assuring the teacher that these children will not require an inordinate amount of attention. The identification of this lengthy list of potential needs of the visually handicapped child brings into question the feasibility of itinerant programs, if such programs result in a service which is primarily or exclusively consultative. There appears to be a clear need to investigate new, imaginative, and creative service delivery systems that can ensure that visually handicapped students receive the best of regular classroom experiences and the specialized instruction that may be necessary.

## ORIENTATION AND MOBILITY

A vital component of the education of visually handicapped children and youth is orientation and mobility. Orientation is the process by which an individual establishes his or her position or relationship to significant objects in the environment. Mobility is the ability to move from a fixed position to another desired position (Lydon & McGraw, 1973). Competence in orientation and mobility skills enables safe, efficient, and effective travel.

Orientation and mobility specialists first taught long-cane technique to blinded war veterans after World War II. Their role has expanded to include the training of visually handicapped children in orientation and mobility as well as premobility skills. This training is considered an essential part of the curriculum for many visually handicapped students. In a survey of 50 State Departments of Education, all respondents indicated that orientation and mobility services were needed to meet the guidelines in PL 94-142 for a portion of their visually handicapped students, and that some 400 additional orientation and mobility specialists will be needed to provide the required services (Smith, Dickerson, & Liska, 1978).

Formal training in cane travel now begins in the late elementary to high school grades, depending upon the student. This training involves a sequential program going from simple to complex travel situations. Prior to any formal long-cane training, precane skills are taught at an early age as the foundation for more advanced training (Suterko, 1973). Students with low vision are trained to use their vision more effectively for travel purposes (Allen, 1977).

In addition to travel with the conventional long cane, the mobility student is taught to use sighted guides, low vision distance aids (if usable vision is present), and, most recently, newly developed electronic mobility aids. The use of dog guides, an alternate means of mobility, is not generally taught in the educational setting, and interested students are referred to organizations that have special training programs for that purpose.

Independent travel is the ultimate goal of orientation and mobility training. While an orientation and mobility specialist must carry out formal mobility training, teachers of the visually handicapped are now performing a complementary function by helping to prepare their students for this training (Olsen, 1978). This preparation includes instruction in common environmental relationships such as rooms in a house, orientation to familiar and unfamiliar places, instruction in basic concepts needed prior to formal orientation and mobility training (Cratty & Sams, 1968; Hapeman, 1967; Hill, 1971), sensory training to improve discrimination and interpretation abilities, and physical education to improve posture, coordination, and movement skills (Siegel, 1965), as well as fostering attitudes conducive to safe, independent travel (Olsen, 1978). Teachers also encourage low vision students to use low vision aids and to maximize the use of their available vision (Richterman, 1966). Since many of the premobility functions of the teacher of the visually handicapped and orientation and mobility specialist overlap, coordination of the two specialties is necessary to achieve a successful overall program for the student.

Coordination of services is especially important since it has been found that students with acceptable travel skills may not use these skills unless they have a need to travel (Lord & Blaha, 1968). A team effort, including parent participation, is desirable to generate social, recreational, and vocational interests in the community for visually handicapped students so that they are motivated to use the orientation and mobility skills they possess.

Most of the literature related to orientation and mobility is of a descriptive rather than an analytical nature. A major reason for this situation is that the field is relatively new. Its growth and direction were prescribed by the immediate needs of the visually handicapped population, and the training techniques were developed and refined through trial and error in practice.

Attempts have been made to examine particular components of mobility tasks such as veering and gradient (Cratty, 1967). The systematic assessment of orientation and mobility concepts in children (Hill, 1971), and the assessment of orientation and mobility readiness in adults (Menzel, Shapiro, & Dreifuss, 1967) has also been considered. Developmental scales for the measurement of orientation and mobility in young children were prepared by Lord (1969), and the assessment of actual orientation and mobility performance was conducted by Brown and Jessen (1972). A review of factors which may play a role in successful mobility performance was conducted by Warren and Kocon (1974).

The evaluation of orientation and mobility performance has become an issue which must be addressed (Leonard, 1973). One of the major problems in mobility evaluation has been the comparability of conditions of testing since the infinite variability in rooms, sidewalks, and streets, etc., makes standardization difficult (Lord, 1969). Another problem in standardized assessment is in the identification, definition, and measurement of those skills in a complex behavior that are either predictive or indicative of successful mobility performance. Different solutions to these evaluations problems are discussed by De L'Aune (1978).

## EDUCATIONAL IMPLICATIONS OF LOW VISION

From an educational point of view, there is a need to differentiate those children who are primarily visual and those who are primarily tactile learners. Toward this end, many terms have been used in the literature to describe the former group: partially blind, partially sighted, severely visually impaired, and having residual, limited, subnormal, useful, travel, or guiding vision. Colenbrander (1976, p. 3) describes yet another term as follows: "In between the normally sighted and the blind is another group of people with distinct problems of their own. These people have been characterized as having low vision." In an effort to avoid confusion, low vision will, for purposes of this chapter, refer to an uncorrectable visual loss that interferes with normal functioning of the child. Consequently, "acuity in low vision may range from nearly normal to nearly blind and visual field defects may range from small central depression to true contractions of the peripheral field'' (Faye, 1976 p. 7).

Barraga's research (1964) was the first to demonstrate improvement in functional vision among low vision children through appropriate intervention strategies. A replication by Ashcroft, Halliday, and Barraga (1965) found similar results among secondary students. Although these early studies used subjects with vision ranging from light perception to a visual acuity of 8/200, it is now estimated that 79 percent of legally blind children have sufficient residual vision to potentially profit from a vision stimulation program (Kederis & Ashcroft, 1970).

The theoretical rationale for a vision stimulation program is given by Barraga, Collings, and Hollis (1977, p. 387) "Even when severe visual impairment is present at birth or is diagnosed early in life, there is sufficient evidence to infer that the development of vision both optically and perceptually generally follows a sequence similar to that found in children with no impairments." They also summarize the available literature on the early development of normal vision. Neurophysiologically, visual acuity improves from birth to about three years of age, whereupon any subsequent gain in visual efficiency is due to a learning process (Jan, Freeman, & Scott, 1977). In visually impaired children, the lack of adequate visual stimulus inhibits development of the visual system, particularly in the visual receiving area of the brain, as its development depends on visual experiences (Woodruff, 1973). Hence, the range and scope of visual functioning is restricted without extensive intervention to develop maximal use of residual vision (Barraga, 1976).

The only thing that low vision children have in common is their restricted visual capabilities, and even this manifests itself in a variety of ways: central and/or peripheral loss, near and/or distance vision loss, blind spots, sensitivity to light, uncontrollable eye movements, inability to attach appropriate meaning to a visual experience, etc. In general, however, low vision persons have the most difficulty with the visual tasks that are related to depth, movement, objects with minimal contrasting background, objects in poor illumination, distinctive features in forms, and body movements in others (Apple & May, 1970). Factors influencing seeing, as reported by Jan et al., (1977), include the judgment and experience of the observer, the region of the retina stimulated, the intensity and distribution of the illumination, the special nature of the light, the time of exposure, and the effects of the movements of the objects. The needs of low vision persons can be summarized as follows: (1) services for the detection of eye diseases; (2) optical services; and (3) psychological, educational, and rehabilitative services (Colenbrander, 1976).

The first need is met by the medical profession, in particular the ophthalmolgist. [If the reader is interested in a description of the structure and function of the eyes and the effects of common disorders written by an ophthalmologist for laymen, *Your Eyes* by Chalkley (1974) is suggested.] In addition, "a general knowledge of educational implications of eye conditions can be helpful to the teacher of visually impaired children" (Harley & Lawrence, 1977, p. 93). After the low vision child has received comprehensive medical attention and possibly a corrective prescription, a medical report is sent to the school upon request. It provides critical information for planning an individualized educational program (Dennison, 1974).

Meeting the second need of optical services requires a group of professionals "interacting in an effort to give an individual the opportunity to function at his or her highest level of visual performance irrespective of the extent of the loss of visual function" (Jose, 1974–1975, p. 52). It has been estimated that there are 2.5 million low vision persons (Jose, 1974–1975) in the United States, of whom 180,000 are school-age children who could potentially profit from low vision aids service (Genensky, 1978). It has been recommended that these children, aged 5–13, be evaluated by a low vision specialist or clinic for possible use of valuable optical aids in the educational setting (Friedman, Tallman, and Asarkoff, 1974–1975). The optical aid service, which includes evaluation, prescription, training, and follow-up, is optimized when it is provided by an interdisciplinary team (Carter and Carter, 1975; Jose, 1975; Jose, Cummings, and McAdams, 1975; Taylor, 1978). As a member of this team, "teacher should be able to teach the use of low vision aids and residual vision" (Carter and Carter, 1975, p. 260).

For the school-age child, the third need identified by Colenbrander is met primarily by the specially trained teacher of the visually impaired. One should begin to learn to use one's vision as early as possible (Ashcroft et al., 1965). Preschool programs to enhance readiness for school through vision stimulation activities have been demonstrated to be successful (Hull & McCarthy, 1973; O'Brien, 1976; Wilson, McVeigh, McMahan, Bauer, & Richardson, 1976). For the low vision children in school, many program alternatives are available, primarily the resource and itinerant plans (Stephens and Birch, 1969). Factors to be considered when making decisions regarding the educational placement of low vision children include medical, psychological, and social considerations, educational background, level of visual functioning, and the nature and extent of the required adaptations or specialized instruction (Martin & Hoben 1977; Sibert, 1966).

One of the most critical problems in servicing low vision children in school is obtaining printed material in the appropriate medium. There are four basic ways to enlarge print images on the retina: (1) hold the page closer to the eye; (2) enlarge the size of the print; (3) use a lens or lens systems for magnification; and (4) use a projection device or electronic aid, such as a closed-circuit television reader (Faye, 1976; Jan et al., 1977; Stokes, 1976). Research to date has not been able to demonstrate a significant relationship among the following variables: visual acuity, reading speed or comprehension, type size, and reading with or without magnification (Bateman, 1964; Bateman & Wetherell, 1967; Bock, 1971; McLaughlin, 1974; Sykes, 1971). This implies that there are other more important determinants of reading proficiency, such as interest, motivation, and/or self-concept.

Finally, the adequate social–emotional development of low vision children is another critical problem for the educator. "As the low vision child matures, social problems may outweigh academic problems" (Faye, 1976, p. 329). Low vision children seem to demonstrate poorer self-concept and adjustment when compared with either the totally blind or the sighted (Bateman & Wetherell, 1967; Cowen, Underberg, Verrillo, & Benham, 1961). The poor self-concept is illustrated by the fact that low vision children more frequently conform to peer pressure (LaDuke, 1978). Educators thus have a responsibility to assist in the adequate affective as well as cognitive development of low vision children to more nearly approximate that of sighted children.

## TECHNOLOGICAL INNOVATIONS IN THE EDUCATIONAL SETTING

Technologically advanced reading machines and environmental sensing devices for the visually handicapped have been incorporated into the curriculum of visually handicapped students. By far the most widely used and discussed device is the Optacon (Optical-to Tactile-Converter), an electronic inkprint reading machine developed by Telesensory Systems, Inc. This device enables a visually handicapped reader to read print directly without its conversion into braille. When an electronic camera is scanned across a line of print with one hand, the index finger of the reader's free hand is placed on a panel that carries a vibrating tactile impression of each printed symbol as it is scanned. Optacon training takes about 50 hours and has been reported successful for children of elementary school age and older (American Foundation for the Blind, 1976; Weihl, 1971; Weisgerber, Everett, Rodabaugh, Shanner, & Crawford, 1974). Considered a supplement to braille, recorded materials, and live readers (Bliss and Moore, 1974), The Optacon has also been used successfully by deaf–blind individuals (Thurman & Weiss-Kapp, 1977).

Two evaluations of the Optacon have been performed with school-age children. Both were conducted immediately after initial Optacon training. One study concluded that the device has merit for some blind students, but not all (Weisgerber et al., 1974). The second evaluation recommended that Optacon training become a standard part of any educational and or rehabilitative program (American Foundation for the Blind, 1976). A systematic study of the effects of Optacon use by school-age children who have had long-term access to the device has not been performed to date.

A speech output component that converts print directly into speech is being developed for the Optacon (Telesensory Systems, Inc., 1978). A speech output reading machine currently in operation is the Kurzwell Reading Machine; this device, a technological breakthrough in reading for the blind, is now being evaluated in educational settings (Kurzwell Computer Products, 1978).

Closed-circuit television (CCTV) systems are widely used to magnify print and illustrations for students with low vision (Robinson, 1974–1975). The camera of the CCTV unit can also be directed at a blackboard or at the teacher so that students with low vision can discern, via greater magnification, events at a distance. An extension of the CCTV system is the interactive television system (ICTS), which includes several television monitors, a room-viewing camera, a master control unit, a videotape recorder, and a color television monitor/receiver (Genensky, Peterson, Clewett, & Yoshimura 1978). This system, tried on a limited basis, permits partially sighted students to be in continuous visual contact with their teachers. In order to take advantage of the ICTS in its present form, partially sighted children must be in a special classroom separate from normally sighted peers.

## ELECTRONIC ENVIRONMENTAL SENSING DEVICES

Electronic environmental sensing devices are currently being used as part of the orientation and mobility training of elementary and high school students; they are also being used experimentally with infants and preschool children. The laser cane is a long cane that sends out three laser beams in different directions. When one of the beams hits an object, a high-pitched sound or a vibrating tactile signal is triggered. The sonicguide is an ultrasonic sensing device housed in a spectacle frame. Similar in principle to the sonar of bats, it provides complex auditory information about the distance and composition of detected objects (Mims, 1973). Other electronic mobility aids include the Mowat Sensor (Telesensory Systems, Inc., 1977) and the Russel Pathsounder (Freiberger, 1974).

Electronic sensing devices are being used as orientation and mobility aids (Baird, 1977; Goldie, 1977; Newcomber, 1977) and as aids in concept development programs (Scione, 1978). Various head-mounted versions of the sonicguide have been successfully used by infants for object detection (Bower, 1976; Strelow, Kay, & Kay, 1978). Case studies of the few very young children who have used an ultrasound echolocation device are provocative. However, the small number of subjects and the lack of systematic follow-up over a long period point to the need for further research before general recommendations can be made about the application of these devices for very young visually handicapped children.

## FEDERAL AND STATE LEGISLATION

Legislation that has dramatically affected educational services for visually handicapped students includes HR 42-28, "the Act to Promote the Education of the Blind," passed by the 45th Congress. This legislation established and appropriated funds for the American Printing House for the Blind, located in Louisville, Kentucky. This facility provides textbooks, recreational reading materials, and educational aids for legally blind students at no cost to schools. Various ammendments to this law provide additional funding and support for the continued operation of the American Printing House for the Blind. PL 787, approved by the 71st Congress in 1931, established the Division for the Blind in the Library of Congress and appropriated funds for the production and distribution of reading materials for the blind through regional libraries. These materials are primarily in the form of talking books and braille.

The most significant legislation affecting the education of exceptional children in the United States is PL 94-142. However, after reading this chapter it should be apparent to the reader that many of the percepts of this relatively new legislation have been in practice in the education of the visually handicapped for years. The concept of the "least restrictive environment" has been put into practice extensively by educators of the visually handicapped for more than 20 years. The inclusion of parents as educational partners in planning educational experiences for their children may be new for some teachers of the visually handicapped, and it will take time for teachers and parents to become comfortable in their shared role in providing appropriate educational experiences for visually handicapped students.

PL 94-142 did cause some concern about the future role of schools for the blind. Bischoff, 1977–1978; Maron, 1977–1978). Hapeman (1977) expresses concern that the concept of "least restrictive environment" will result in schools for the blind being considered "most restrictive" because they do not provide for regular and extensive contact with sighted students. Bischoff (1977) aggressively defends the role of the school for the blind by pointing out that such schools have much more control over curriculum and experiences, and therefore can provide appropriate experiences for visually handicapped students that are not currently available in public school programs. Maron (1977) suggests that such discussions are counterproductive and revive old hostilities and controversies that date back to the early days of the establishment of public day school programs.

The authors of this chapter support the position that residential schools are indeed necessary in order to ensure that all visually handicapped students will have opportunities for education in the "least restrictive environment." It is therefore our position that compliance with PL 94-142 requires that every visually handicapped child have available to him or her all options of educational programs.

# References

Adelson, E., & Fraiberg, S. Gross motor development in infants blind from birth. *Child Development*, 1974, *45*, 114–126.

Allen, D. Orientation and mobility for persons with low vision. *Journal of Visual Impairment and Blindness*, 1977, *71*, 13–15.

American Foundation for the Blind. *The Pinebrook report*. New York: Author, 1954.

American Foundation for the Blind. *Itinerant teaching service for blind children*. New York: Author, 1957.

American Foundation for the Blind. *Final report on the Richard King Mellon Foundation Optacon training and purchase subsidy program*. (Pittsburgh City Area). New York: Author, 1976.

American Printing House for the Blind. *Handbook for teachers of the visually handicapped*. Louisville, Ky.: Author, 1974.

Apple, L., & May, M. *Distance vision and perceptual training*. New York: American Foundation for the Blind, 1970.

Ashcroft, S. C., Halliday, C., & Barraga N. *Study II: Effects of experimental teaching on the visual behavior of children educated as though they had no vision*. Grant 32-52-0120-1034. Nashville, Tenn.: George Peabody College, 1965.

Baird, A. Electronic aids: Can they help blind children? *Journal of Visual Impairment and Blindness*, 1977, *71*, 97–101.

Barraga, N. *Increased visual behavior in low vision children*. New York: American Foundation for the Blind, 1964.

Barraga, N. *Visual handicaps and learning: A development approach*. Belmont, Calif.: Wadsworth, 1976.

Barraga, N. C., Collings, M., & Hollis, J. Development of efficiency in visual functioning: Literature analysis. *Journal of Visual Impairment and Blindness*, 1977, *71*, 387–391.

Bateman, B. *Reading and psycholinguistic processes of partially seeing children*. Reston, Va.: The Council of Exceptional Children, 1964.

Bateman, B., & Wetherell, J. L. Some educational characteristics of partially seeing children. *The International Journal for the Education of the Blind*, 1967, *17*, 33–40.

Bischoff, R. W. The least restrictive educational program: The residential school. *Education of the Visually Handicapped*, 1977, *9*, 106–108.

Bishop, V. E. *Teaching the visually limited child*. Springfield, Ill.: Thomas, 1971.

Bledsoe, C. W. The family of the residential schools. *Blindness, American Association of Workers for the Blind Annual*, 1971, 19–73.

Bliss, J. C., & Moore, M. W. The Optacon reading system. *Education of the Visually Handicapped*, 1974, *6*, 98–102.

Bock, J. Reading performance of visually impaired print readers. Unpublished doctoral dissertation, University of Michigan, 1971.

Bourgeault, S. E., Harley, R. K., & DuBose, R. F. The model vision project: A conceptual framework for service delivery. *Journal of Visual Impairment and Blindness*, 1977, *71*, 16–22.

Bower, T. G. R. Repetitive processes in child development. *Scientific American*, 1976, *235*, 38–47.

Brown, G. D., & Jessen, W. E. Preliminary performance test battery of orientation, mobility, and living skills. *Research Bulletin, American Foundation for the Blind*, 1972, *24*, 1–20.

Brown, J. N. New directions in service to young visually handicapped children. Paper presented at 32nd annual conference of the Association for the Education of the Visually Handicapped, 1974.

Calovini, G. (Ed.). *Mainstreaming the visually impaired child*. Chicago: Illinois Office of the Superintendent of Public Instruction, 1977.

Carter, K. D., & Carter, C. A. Itinerant low vision services. *The New Outlook for the Blind*, 1975, *69*, 255–261; 265.

Chalkley, T. *Your eyes: A book for paramedical personnel and the lay reader*. Springfield, Ill.: Thomas, 1974.

Chase, J. B. Developmental assessment of handicapped infants and young children: With special attention to the visually impaired. *The New Outlook for the Blind*, 1975, *69*, 345–349.

Cicenia, E. F., Belton, J. A., Myers, J. J., & Mundy, F. The blind child with multiple handicaps: A challenge. *International Journal of the Education of the Blind*. Part I, 1965, *14*, 65–71; Part II, 1965, *14*, 105–112.

Colenbrander, A. Low vision: Definition and classification. In E. E. Faye (Ed.), *Clinical low vision*. Boston: Little, Brown, 1976.

Committee on Assessment of Visually Handicapped Children. The role of the teacher of the visually handicapped—A self definition. In The International Council for Education of the Visually Handicapped: *The Educator*. 1978, *1*(2), 1–5.

Corn, A. L., & Martinez, I. *When you have a visually handicapped child in your classroom: Suggestions for teachers*. New York: American Foundation for the Blind, 1977.

Cowen, E. L., Underberg, R. P., Verrillo, R. T., & Benham, F. G. *Adjustment to visual disability in adolescence*, New York: American Foundation for the Blind, 1961.

Cratty, B. J. The perception of gradient and the veering tendency while walking without vision. *Research Bulletin, American Foundation for the Blind*, 1967, *14*, 31–51.

Cratty, B. J. *Movement and spatial awareness in blind children and youth*. Springfield, Ill. Thomas, 1971, 240.

Cratty, B. J., & Sams, T. A. *The body image of blind children*. New York: American Foundation for the Blind, 1968.

De l'Aune, W. R. Research and the mobility specialist. *Journal of Visual Impairment and Blindness*, 1978, *72*, 267–272.

Dennison, A. L. The eye report points the way. In American Printing House for the Blind (Ed.), *Handbook for teachers of the visually handicapped*. Louisville, Ky.: Editor, 1974.

DuBose, R. Developmental needs in blind infants. *The New Outlook For the Blind*, 1976, *70*, 49–52.

Elonen, A. S. Assessment of the nontestable blind child. *Proceedings of a conference on new approaches to the evaluation of blind persons*. New York: American Foundation for the Blind, 1970.

Elonen, A. S., & Zwarensteyn, S. B. Appraisal of developmental lag in certain blind children. *Journal of Pediatrics*, 1964, *65*, 599–600.

Farrell, G. *The study of blindness*. Cambridge, Mass.: Harvard University Press, 1956.

Faye, E. E. *Clinical low vision*. Boston: Little, Brown, 1976.

Felix, L., & Spungin, S. J. Preschool services for the visually handicapped: A national survey. *Journal of Visual Impairment and Blindness*, 1978, *72*, 59–66.

Fraiberg, S. *Insights from the blind: Comparative studies of blind and sighted infants*. New York: Basic Books, 1977.

Fraiberg, S., & Adelson, E. Self-representation in young blind children. In Jastrzembska, Z. S. (ed.), *The Effects of Blindness and Other Impairments on Early Development*. New York: American Foundation for the Blind, 1976, 136–147.

Frampton, M. E., & Kerney, E. *The residential school: Its history, contributions, and future*. New York: Gould, 1953.

Freiberger, H. Mobility aids for the blind. *Bulletin of Prosthetics Research*, Fall 1974 (BPR-10-22), 73–78.

Friedman, D. B., Tallman, C. B., & Asarkoff, J. E. Comprehensive low vision care. *New Outlook for the Blind*, Part I, 1974, *68*(3), 97–103; Part II, 1975, *69*(5), 207–211.

Gallagher, P. A., & Heim, R. E. The classroom application of behavior modification principles for multiply handicapped blind students. *The New Outlook for the Blind,* 1974, *68,* 447–453.

Gearheart, B. R. (Ed.). *Education of the exceptional child: History, present, practices, and trends.* Scranton: Intext, 1972.

Genensky, S. M. Data concerning the partially sighted and the functionally blind. *Journal of Visual Impairment and Blindness,* 1978, *72,* 177–180.

Genensky, S. M., Peterson, H. E., Clewett, R. W., & Yoshimura, R. I. A second generation interactive classroom television system for the partially sighted. *Journal of Visual Impairment and Blindness,* 1978, *72,* 41–45.

Goldie, D. Use of the C-5 laser cane by school-age children. *Journal of Visual Impairment and Blindness,* 1977, *71,* 346–348.

Graham, M. D. *Multiply-impaired blind children: A national problem.* New York: American Foundation for the Blind, 1968.

Hanninen, K. A. *Teaching the visually handicapped.* Columbus, Ohio: Merrill, 1975.

Hapeman, L. Developmental concepts of blind children between the ages of 3 and 6 as they relate to orientation and mobility. *International Journal for the Education of the Blind,* 1967, *17,* 41–48.

Hapeman, L. Reservations about the effect of PL 94-142 on the education of visually handicapped children. *Education of the Visually Handicapped,* 1977, *9,* 33–36.

Harley, R. K., & Lawrence, G. A. *Visual impairment in the schools.* Springfield, Ill.: Thomas, 1977.

Harley, R. K., Merbler, J. B., & Pupke B. *The development of a program in orientation and mobility for multiply impaired low vision children* (Final report, Grant G007-60-5199). Nashville, Tenn.: George Peabody College for Teachers, 1978.

Harley, R. K., Wood, T. A., & Merbler, J. B. The development of the scale in orientation and mobility for multiply impaired blind children. *Education of the Visually Handicapped,* 1975, *7,* 1–4.

Hatlen, P. H. Visually handicapped children with additional problems. In B. Lowenfeld (Ed.), *The visually handicapped child in school.* New York: Day, 1973.

Hatlen, P. H., LeDuc, P., Canter, P. The blind adolescent life skills center. *The New Outlook for the Blind,* 1975, *69,* 109–115.

Hayes, C. S., & Weinhouse, D. Application of behavior modifications to blind children. *Journal of Visual Impairment and Blindness,* 1978, *72,* 139–146.

Henderson, F. Communication skills. In B. Lowenfeld (Ed.), *The visually handicapped child in school.* New York: Day, 1973.

Hill, E. W. The formation of concepts involved in body position in space. *Education of the Visually Handicapped,* 1971, *3,* 21–25.

Hull, W. A., & McCarthy, D. G. Supplementary program for pre-school visually handicapped children. *Education of the Visually Handicapped,* 1973, *5,* 97–104.

Jan, J. E., Freeman, R. D., & Scott, E. P. *Visual impairment in children and adolescents.* New York: Grune & Stratton, 1977.

Jones, J. W. Problems in defining and classifying blindness. *The New Outlook for the Blind,* 1962, *56,* 115–121.

Jones, J. W. *The visually handicapped child at home and school.* Washington, D.C.: U.S. Government Printing Office, 1963.

Jose, R. T. What is low vision service? *Blindness, American Association of Workers for the Blind Annual,* 1974–1975, 49–52.

Jose, R. T. Low vision clinics: The need, the organization, the manpower. In *Vision.* Springfield, Ill.: Thomas, 1975, pp. 215–219.

Jose, R. T., Cummings, J., & McAdams, L. The model low vision clinical service: An interdisciplinary vision rehabilitation program. *The New Outlook for the Blind,* 1975, *69,* 249–254.

Kederis, C., & Ashcroft, S. C. The Austin conference on utilization of low vision. *Education of the Visually Handicapped,* 1970, *2,* 33–38.

Kratz, L. E. *Movement without sight.* Palo Alto, Calif.: Peek, 1973.

Kurzweil Computer Products. The KRM: the idea, the company, and the future. *The Kurzweil Report,* 1978, *1,* 1–2.

LaDuke, R. A comparative study of the conformity behavior of low vision and normal children. Unpublished doctoral dissertation, University of Northern Colorado, 1978.

Leach, R. Multihandicapped visually impaired children: Instructional material needs. *Exceptional Children,* 1971, *38,* 153–156.

Leonard, J. A. The evaluation of blind mobility. *Research Bulletin, American Foundation for the Blind,* 1973, *26,* 73–76.

Lord, F. E. Development of scales for the measurement of orientation and mobility of young blind children. *Exceptional Children,* 1969, *36,* 71–81.

Lord, F. E., & Blaha, L. E. *Demonstration of home and community support needed to facilitate mobility instruction for blind youth* (Rehabilitation Services Administration Grant DG-RD-1784-S). Los Angeles: California State College, 1968.

Lowenfeld, B. *Our blind children.* Springfield, Ill.: Thomas, 1971.

Lowenfeld, B. (Ed.). *The visually handicapped child in school.* New York: Day, 1973.

Lowenfeld, B. *The changing status of the blind: From separation to integration.* Springfield, Ill.: Thomas, 1975.

Lowenfeld, B., Abel, G. L., & Hatlen, P. H. *Blind children learn to read.* Springfield, Ill.: Thomas, 1969.

Lydon, L. T., & McGraw, M. L. *Concept development for visually handicapped children.* New York: American Foundation for the Blind, 1973.

Maloney, E. Philosphy and goals of a pre-school program. Paper presented at Biennial Conference of the American Association of Instructors for the Blind, Washington, D.C., 1966.

Maron, S. PL94-142 and the residential school—a rebuttal to Dr. Hapeman. *Education of the Visually Handicapped,* 1977, *9,* 121–122.

Martin, G. L., & Hoben, M. *Supporting visually impaired students in the mainstream.* Reston, Va.: Council for Exceptional Children, 1977.

McLaughlin, W. J. Reading attainment of blind and partially sighted children: A comparative study. *The Teacher of the Blind,* 1974, *62,* 98–106.

Menzel, R., Shapiro, G., & Dreifuss, G. A proposed test for mobility-training readiness. *The New Outlook for the Blind,* 1967, *61,* 33–40.

Mims, F. M. Sensory aids for blind persons. *The New Outlook for the Blind,* 1973, *67,* 407–414.

Moore, P. M. *A blind child, too, can go to nursery school.* New York: American Foundation for the Blind, 1952.

Morrison, M. The other 128 hour a week: Teaching personal management to blind young adults. *The New Outlook for the Blind,* 1974, *68,* 454–459.

Napier, G. Special subject adjustments and skills. In D. Lowenfeld (Ed.), *The visually handicapped child in school.* New York: Day, 1973.

National Society for the Prevention of Blindness. *Estimated statistics on blindness and vision problems.* New York: Author, 1966.

Newcomber, J. Sonicguide: Its use with public school blind children. *Journal of Visual Impairment and Blindness,* 1977, *71,* 268–271.

Morris, M. *What affects blind children's development?* Paper presented at the National Conference on Pre-school Services for Visually Handicapped Children and Their Families, American Association of Instructors for the Blind, 1965.

Norris, M., Spaulding, P. J., & Brodie, F. H. *Blindness in children.* Chicago: University of Chicago Press, 1957.

O'Brien, R. Early childhood services for visually impaired children. A model program. *The New Outlook for the Blind*, 1975, *69*, 201–206.

O'Brien, R. *Alive . . . aware . . . a person: A developmental model of early childhood services*. Rockville, Md.: Montgomery County Public Schools, 1976.

Olsen, M. R. Orientation and mobility instruction for blind children in rural areas—Whose responsibility? *Journal of Visual Impairment and Blindness*, 1978, *72*, 21–24.

Richterman, H. Mobility instruction for the partially seeing. *The New Outlook for the Blind*, 1966, *60*, 236–238.

Robinson, D. P. The use of closed circuit television for partially sighted pupils. *Teacher of the Blind*, 1974–1975, *63*, 43–46.

Rogow, S., & Rodriguez, M. *Their special needs*. Ontario, Canada: Ministry of Community and Social Services, Mental Retardation Residential and Consulting Services Branch, 1977.

Scholl, J. T. Understanding and meeting developmental needs. In B. Lowenfeld (Ed.), *The visually handicapped child in school*. New York: Day, 1973.

Scione, N. W. Electronic sensory aids in a concept development program for congenitally blind young adults. *Journal of Visual Impairment and Blindness*, 1978, *72*, 88–93.

Sibert, K. N. The legally blind child with useful residual vision. *International Journal for the Education of the Blind*, 1966, *16*, 33–45.

Siegel, I. M. The expression of posture in the blind. *International Journal for the Education of the Blind*, 1965, *15*, 23–24.

Sklar, M. J., & Rampulla, J. Decreasing inappropriate classroom behavior of a multiply handicapped blind student. *Education of the Visually Handicapped*, 1973, *5*, 71–74.

Smith, T. E. C., Dickerson, L. R., & Liska, J. S. Availability of orientation and mobility services in public schools. *Journal of Visual Impairment and Blindness*, 1978, *72*, 173–180.

Stephens, B. Cognitive processes in the visually impaired. *Education of the Visually Handicapped*, 1972, *4*, 106–111.

Stephens, B., Smith, R. E., Fitzgerald, J. R., Grube, C., Hitt, J., & Daly, M. *Training manual for teachers of the visually handicapped, a Piagetian perspective*, Richardson, Tex.: University of Texas, 1977.

Stephens, T. M., & Birch, J. W. Merits of special class resource and itinerant plans for teaching partially seeing children. *Exceptional Children*, 1969, *35*, 481–484.

Stoker, C.S. *Listening for the Visually Impaired*. Springfield, Ill.: Thomas, 1973.

Stokes, L. Educational considerations for the child with low vision. In E. E. Faye (Ed.), *Clinical low vision*. Boston: Little, Brown, 1976.

Strelow, E. R., Kay, N., & Kay, L. Binaural sensory aid: Case studies of its use by two children. *Journal of Visual Impairment and Blindness*, 1978, *72*, 1–9.

Suterko, S. Life adjustment. In B. Lowenfeld (Ed.), *The visually handicapped child in school*. New York: Day, 1973.

Sykes, K. C. A comparison of the effectiveness of standard print and large print in facilitating the reading skills of visually impaired students. *Education of the Visually Handicapped*, 1971, *3*, 97–105.

Sykes, K. C. Print reading for visually handicapped children. *Education of the Visually Handicapped*, 1972, *3*, 71–75.

Tait, P. E. Believing without seeing: Teaching the blind child in a regular kindergarten. *Childhood Education*, 1974, *50*, 285–291.

Taylor, D. Multidisciplinary work in low vision. *Division for the Visually Handicapped Newsletter, Council for Exceptional Children*, 1978, *22*, pp. 5; 11.

Taylor, J. L. Education programs. In B. Lowenfeld (Ed.), *The visually handicapped child in school*. New York: Day, 1973.

Telesensory Systems, Inc. *TSI Newsletter*, 1977, No. 15.

Telesensory Systems, Inc. *TSI Newsletter*, 1978, No. 17.

Thurman, D., & Weiss-Kapp, S., Optacon instruction for the deaf-blind. *Education of the Visually Handicapped,* 1977, *9,* 47–50.

Totman, H. E. Training problems and techniques. In B. Lowenfeld (Ed.), *The blind pre-school child.* New York: American Foundation for the Blind, 1947.

Tretakoff, N. J. The evaluation of programs for blind mentally retarded children in residential facilities. *Journal of Visual Impairment and Blindness,* 1977, *71,* 29–33.

Tuttle, D. Audio reading: An effective alternative. In American Printing House For the Blind (Ed.), *Handbook for teachers of the visually handicapped.* Louisville, Ky.: Editor, 1974.

Tuttle, D. Computation devices with focus on the Cranmer abacus. *Proceedings of a conference.* Sydney, Australia: Australian and New Zealand Association of Teachers of the Visually Handicapped, 1976.

Vaughan, D., & Asbury, T. *General ophthalmology.* Los Altos, Calif.: Lange, 1977.

Warren, D. H. Blindness and early childhood development. New York: American Foundation for the Blind, 1977.

Warren, D. H., & Kocon, J. A. Factors in the successful mobility of the blind: A review. *Research Bulletin, American Foundation for the Blind,* 1974, *28,* 191–218.

Weihl C. The Optacon reading program at the Monroe Public School. *The New Outlook for the Blind,* 1971, *65,* 155–162.

Weisgerber, R. A., Everett, B. C., Rodabaugh, B. J., Shanner, W. H., & Crawford, J. J. *Educational evaluation of the Optacon (optical-to-tactile converter) as a reading aid to blind elementary and secondary students.* (Final report, Contract OEC-O-72-5780). Palo Alto, Calif.: American Institutes for Research, 1974.

Wilson, J. D., McVeigh, N. M., McMahon, J. F., Bauer, A. M., & Richardson, P. C. Early intervention: The right to sight. *Education of the Visually Handicapped,* 1976, *1,* 83–90.

Winn, R. J. Two year program analysis of project for multi-handicapped visually impaired children at the Texas School for the Blind. *International Journal for the Education of the Blind,* 1968, *18,* 99–107.

Wood, M. L. The special nursery school. In B. Lowenfeld (Ed.), *The blind pre-school child.* New York: American Foundation for the Blind, 1947.

Woodruff, M. E. The visually at risk child. *Journal of the American Optometric Association,* 1973, *44,* 130–133.

# LEARNING DISABILITIES: A REVIEW OF SELECTED TOPICS

John Lloyd
Daniel P. Hallahan
James M. Kauffman

*University of Virginia*

Many reviews of learning disabilities (LD) are available: Bateman (1966) described the current state of knowledge at a time when the field had not received wide or legislative recognition. Wiederholt (1974) contributed a historical review, tracing ideas from the early 1800s into the 1960s and 1970s. Torgesen (1975) presented a review of research on the psychological characteristics of LD children, with particular reference to those who have reading difficulties. Arter and Jenkins (1977), Haring and Bateman (1977, chap. 4), Tarver and Dawson (1978), and Ysseldyke (1973) have all reviewed the evidence bearing on reading instruction differentiated on the basis of modality strengths. Lahey (1976) and Lovitt (1975a, 1975b) have both discussed the literature where behavior modification and LD intersect. Adelman and Compas (1977) and Sroufe (1975) have reviewed psychopharmacology studies, while Kauffman and Hallahan (1979) have examined studies in which there were direct comparisons of behavior modification and chemotherapy. Hammill and Wiederholt (1973) and Klesius (1972), among others, have evaluated the evidence for the effectiveness of perceptual–motor treatments of LD. Hammill and Larsen (1974), among others, have reviewed the literature regarding

Preparation of this manuscript was supported in part by Contract 300-77-0495 from the Bureau of Education for the Handicapped for the University of Virginia Learning Disabilities Research Institute. The manuscript was prepared while J. M. Kauffman was a Sesquicentennial Associate of the Center for Advanced Studies of the University of Virginia and a Postdoctoral Scholar at the University of California at Los Angeles.

the effectiveness of psycholinguistic training, arriving at conclusions with which not everyone agrees (e.g., Lund, Foster, & McCall-Perez, 1978). These areas will not be addressed here since they have been discussed in the cited sources. Furthermore, we shall not attempt to review the current state of knowledge about effective procedures for teaching LD children.

In this chapter we shall discuss several current topics. Perhaps restricting ourselves illustrates a want of confidence in wrestling with difficult issues. However, we think that it reflects (1) the fact that many other areas have been reviewed recently, (2) the often noted growth of the LD field, and (3) our editors' insistence on receiving a chapter rather than a book from us. In any case, we shall focus on (1) definition, (2) information processing, and (3) social–behavioral characteristics of children with LD. Because only a limited amount of evidence is available regarding secondary school-age LD students, our comments are based upon, and should be viewed as referring to, elementary school-age LD children.

## DEFINITION

In the early 1960s, before they became known as such, children with LD were an unserved minority. They were not among the mentally retarded, emotionally disturbed, or so-called normal. The professional appelations given them included developmentally aphasic, dyslexic, neurologically impaired, perceptually handicapped, psychoneurologically disordered and at least 20 (McDonald, 1968) if not 40 (Cruickshank, 1972) others. Disagreement on definition is virtually as old as the Kirk and Bateman (1962) description of the field. Kirk's (1963) speech is widely credited with affecting the initial adoption of the term "learning disabilities," but there were disagreements at that meeting. There were further disagreements only a few years later when (1) Cruickshank convened a meeting of scholars to discuss issues in the investigation of brain injury (reported in Hallahan & Cruickshank, 1973), (2) Task Force I (Clements, 1966) and Task Force II, Part I (Haring, 1969) tried to deal with terms applied to these children, (3) an Institute for Advanced Study confronted the definition question (Kass & Myklebust, 1969), and (4) the Issues in the Classification of Children group (Wepman, Cruickshank, Deutsch, Morency, & Strother, 1975) made their recommendations. At present, it seems that we have come to fairly uniformly call them "children with learning disabilities," but we still do not seem to uniformly agree about to whom we refer when we use the term.

Many factors may have contributed to the confusion. (1) The

population probably is heterogeneous, and as the heterogeneity increases, so too does the difficulty of establishing a clear definition. (2) The study of LD is influenced by many disciplines (e.g., for years the *Journal of Learning Disabilities* has claimed multidisciplinary status), and one result of this is the kind of disciplinary territoriality observed during hearings on the Administrative Rules proposed as a result of the Education for All Handicapped Children Act of 1975 (PL 94-142). (3) The American Association on Mental Deficiency revision of its definition of mental retardation (Grossman, 1973), so that subaverage intellectual functioning is represented by scores two or more standard deviations below the mean, exposed another 13 to 14 percent of the population to possible LD services. (4) The reluctance of the Association for Children with Learning Disabilities to accept a broad definition and parents' influence on legislation and program development (Richards & Clark, 1968) have probably contributed to some degree to maintenance of the status quo. Whatever the reasons for the problems in definition—and the above are not presented as comprising an exhaustive catalog—we see the central issue as one of determining whether the focus of the field should be narrow or broad and, consequently, whether LD should be defined in a categorical or generic fashion.

### The evidence

There have been several reports of surveys of professional opinion regarding definition. McDonald (1968) asked postdoctoral level special educators (for the most part) how they would describe LD children, while Vaughn and Hodges (1973) asked special education service personnel (teachers, program directors, psychologists, social workers, speech therapists, and nurses) in Northern Colorado to rank order several definitions on the basis of acceptability. McDonald noted that many of the responses he received treated the terms "learning disabilities" and "learning disorders" as synonyms, that some used the terms generically while others used them categorically, and that underachievement was the major component of the generic, if not of all views. By contrast, Vaughn and Hodges reported that their respondents found specific definitions more acceptable than generic ones. Of interest in this regard, however, is that Vaughn and Hodges drew many of their definitions from McDonald, but classified as specific some that he had considered generic.

Another pair of surveys yielded more easily reconcilable results. Gillespie, Miller, and Fiedler (1975) and Mercer, Forgnone, and Wolking (1976) surveyed 49 and 42 state departments of education, respectively, as to how each defined LD in its laws, rules, and regulations. The results were not substantively different and so we shall report only the one with the more complete sample (i.e., Gillespie et al., 1975), although some points from Mercer et al. (1976) will be discussed. In general the data obtained indicated that over 50 percent of the states had adopted the PL 91-230 definition or a slight variant of it, while no more that 8 percent were reported to have no specific definition or to be in the process of formulating one. With allowance for the use of cutoff scores on certain tests or a requirement of certification of minimal brain dysfunction, nearly two-thirds of the states can be considered to be using the PL 91-230 definition.

Although it is not independent of the fact that so many states have adopted the PL 91-230 definition, one point of the analysis reported by Mercer et al. (1976) deserves serious note. As the authors commented, there was no clear consensus among the various states as to which students could be considered learning disabled. As they noted, it is interesting that academic deficiencies were mentioned less frequently in definitions than process and language deficits. This is particularly intriguing when one tries to imagine certifying as learning disabled, children who have atypical processing abilities but normal academic achievement.

Although there appears to be agreement among the various states in respect to their general definitions of LD, there also appear to be some inconsistencies and disagreements. One might suspect that this state of affairs would be accompanied by some discrepancies in the selection of children to whom LD services are rendered. Unfortunately, we do not have much state-by-state data beyond the Mercer et al. (1976) report that prevalence figures suggested by 10 of the responding states ranged from 1 to 7 percent. In a survey of restricted populations as opposed to legislated limits, Kirk and Elkins (1975) reported prevalence figures ranging from 1 to 26 percent (the 26 percent was disregarded) with a median of 4 percent overall and, for teacher-judged severe learning disability, 2.5 percent. These figures are interesting in light of the 2 percent "cap" used in the interim between passage of PL 94-142 and adoption of the final rules for evaluating specific learning disabilities.

We do, however, know something about the characteristics of over 3000 children served in federally funded Child Service Demonstration Centers (CSDCs) as a result of the Kirk & Elkins (1975) survey. Some of these data make interesting commentary on the topic of definition. Of particular concern is the fact that when the mean IQ for children in each of the 24 CSDCs surveyed was considered, the median of these data was 93 (range: 83–105). Further analyses indicated that children with IQs below 90 were overrepresented in comparison with the general population. Another interesting consideration is the discrepancy between expected and actual achievement. When evaluated by comparing median *chronological age*-based grade expectancy with achievement, the students in the responding CSDCs were retarded in reading, arithmetic, and spelling by 1.7, 1.2, and 1.8 grade levels, respectively. When evaluated by comparing *mental age*-based grade expectancy with achievement, the students were not as severely retarded. Kirk and Elkins interpreted this and other evidence as indicating that many of the children enrolled in CSDCs suffer from simple underachievement rather than LD. One further finding of this study germane here was that teachers in these model programs placed the greatest remedial emphasis on the major academic skill areas.

Other evidence bearing on this topic may be garnered from studies considering children having behavior disorders or mental retardation. For example, in an evaluation of children with behavior disorders, Wright (1974) found that 70 percent of the sample manifested reading problems according to a .90 Johnson-Myklebust (1967) reading performance index and that 98 percent manifested frank or borderline deficits on tests commonly used to identify children with LD. Certainly, it is difficult to determine whether learning disabilities precede or follow behavior disorders, and as we discuss later, many LD children have social behavior problems. But this study clearly indicates that, given children with school problems, it is difficult to discriminate operationally between children with LD and children with behavior disorders. With regard to distinguishing between children with LD and those considered mentally retarded, similar difficulties obtain. Some studies suggest that one way to make the distinction is to consider race or socioeconomic status, (e.g., Burke, 1975; Kappelman, Kaplan, & Ganter, 1969).

An often mentioned solution to the definition problem has been the application of a quantified discrepancy as a discriminant variable (e.g., Bateman, 1965; Gaddes, 1976). The proposed rules mandated by PL 94-142 (Department of Health, Education and Welfare, 1976) incorporated the discrepancy concept by adopting a "severe discrepancy level" formula. As Salvia and Clark (1973) had pointed out well before the proposed rulemaking, measurement error associated with the test scores entered into such formuli creates a lack of reliability in the resulting deficit scores. The proposed formula was attacked on these grounds (e.g., Lloyd, Sabatino, Miller, & Miller, 1977; Sulzbacher & Kenowitz, 1977), among others, and was dropped from the final procedures (Department of Health, Education and Welfare, 1977). Further discussion of the formula-based LD definition has been offered by Danielson and Bauer (1978).

## The issue

To say that there has not been much consensus about defining LD is to understate the case. There are continued calls for an operational-izable, categorical definition (e.g., Chalfant & King, 1976; Senf, 1977) and there are repeated arguments that (1) we need no new definition (Haring & Bateman, 1977), (2) that all areas of mild handicap should be merged (Hallahan & Kauffman, 1977; Lilly, 1977), and (3) that LD should be treated as a concept rather than a category (Hallahan & Kauffman, 1976). It appears that about the only point of agreement among the various arguments is that there are slightly atypical students to whom we all feel an obligation to provide specialized services designed directly or indirectly to improve their academic skills. The issue is not so much whether we need to distinguish these students from other types of children as it is whether we need to distinguish among them, i.e., identify subpopulations.

Probably the greatest benefit of categorically discriminating among these children will accrue to research. As has been pointed out by people too numerous to cite, a reliable designation of a target population is likely to increase the chances of obtaining replicable and generalizable results. However, as we see it, efforts to identify and evaluate marker variables (e.g., Keogh, Major, Reid, Gándara, & Omori, 1978) will further the needs of research far more clearly than would some new and presumably more precise definition of LD.

As Hammill (1972), among others, has demonstrated, the definition adopted in PL 91-230 and essentially unchanged by PL 94-142 is not an unambiguously operationalizable one. It allows great latitude in identi-fying a given student as LD. Assuming that LD services are of value to students, it then appears that the principle beneficiaries of the current state of affairs are the very children to whom we should provide services.

It should come as no surprise that there have been problems in defining LD such that it is distinguishable from other mild handicaps. The areas of LD, mild behavior disorders, and educable mental retar-dation have been described as having common histories and the children classified under them have been shown to have similar characteristics and etiologies and to benefit equally from virtually identical teaching procedures (Adelman, 1971; Hallahan & Kauffman, 1976; 1977; Kauff-man, 1977; Lilly, 1977; Neisworth & Greer, 1975). When coupled with the work on marker variables (Keogh, et al., 1978), we think these arguments indicate that there is little reason to redefine LD as such. The need to have homogeneous subpopulations of mildly handicapped learners for research purposes can be met by work with marker variables. The provision of specialized services to LD children can best be met by treating LD as a generic concept referring to students manifesting learning and behavior problems.

## INFORMATION PROCESSING

The study of information processing is the study of thinking or cognition. As Hall (1980) has noted, the field of cognitive psychology includes a wide variety of research areas, e.g., perception, memory, attention, and problem solving. The 1960s and 1970s have witnessed a burgeoning interest in the cognitive development of normal children. Following closely behind the study of information processing in the normal child has come a concern for how exceptional children develop or do not develop cognitive abilities. The following section focuses on three areas—memory, selective attention, and cognitive tempo—that have, perhaps, received the most intensive study in LD children.

### Memory

The 1970s have seen a rapid proliferation of studies of the memory capabilities of LD children. Much of this work has emanated from the laboratories of few investigators (e.g., Perfetti, Swanson, Torgesen, and Vellutino). Virtually all of the work in this area has been laboratory based and in the domain of short-term memory. Although relatively limited in scope, this research has advanced our understanding of the memory processing deficiencies of LD children. The research on memory of the previous decade was rather simplistic and generally restricted to comparing LD children's and normal controls' performance on standardized tests or subtests [e.g., digit span from the Wechsler Intelligence Scale for Children (WISC); visual sequential memory from the Illinois Test of Psycholiguistic Abilities (ITPA)]. The research of this decade, however, has borrowed extensively from the paradigms of experimental child psychology and has begun to advance beyond merely documenting differences between LD and normal children's memory performance; investigators are now beginning to focus their efforts on determining the specific ways LD pupils differ and do not differ from normal controls. Toward this end, many researchers have designed experimental studies in which LD children have been instructed in ways to improve their memory performance.

41

While the authors of most studies have concluded that LD children (or retarded readers) are deficient in memory performance compared to normal children (Cummings & Faw, 1976; Farnham-Diggory & Gregg, 1975; Kail, Chi, Ingram, & Danner, 1977; Leslie, 1975; Parker, Freston, & Drew, 1975; Perfetti & Goldman, 1976; Ring, 1976; Senf, 1969; Senf & Feshback, 1970; Swanson, in press; Torgesen, 1977a; Torgesen & Goldman, 1977; Waller, 1976; Vellutino, Harding, Phillips, & Steger, 1975; Vellutino, Steger, Harding, & Phillips, 1975), many of the same studies, and others too, have found no differences between LD children and normal peers (Leslie, 1975; Perfetti & Goldman, 1976; Swanson, in press; Vellutino, Harding, Phillips, & Steger, 1975; Vellutino, Steger, De Setto, & Phillips, 1975; Vellutino, Steger, Harding, & Phillips, 1975; Waller, 1976). Rather than concluding that the results are contradictory, some investigators (e.g. Perfetti, Swanson, and Vellutino) have cited specific reasons when differences have not been found (e.g., the stimuli used were not verbal in nature). Strengthening their case, the reader will note in the following pages that most of these conclusions have not come as post hoc explanations for nonsignificant findings. Most of these studies found differences on some tasks but not on others, and both sets of findings were consistent with hypothesized results. In other words, when nonsignificant differences obtained, they were usually in line with pre-dicted results.

There have generally been two different explanations offered for the differences in memory functioning that have been found between LD and normal children. Some investigators have posited a deficiency in language skills that places children at a disadvantage on tasks requiring verbal encoding of the stimuli to be remembered (Perfetti & Goldman, 1976; Vellutino, Harding, Phillips, & Steger, 1975; Vellutino, Steger, De Setto, & Phillips, 1975; Vellutino, Steger, Harding, & Phillips, 1975), while Torgesen (1977b) has hypothesized a more general deficiency regarding the management of learning strategies.

Vellutino and his colleagues, in a series of studies using either a memory recognition or a paired-associate format, have found that poor readers are equal to good readers except when verbal stimuli are used. For example, Vellutino, Steger, De Setto, and Phillips (1975) visually presented normal and poor readers with Hebrew letters and then asked them to recognize them from among alternatives. Finding no differences in recognition recall, they noted the fact that the stimuli were visually presented, and concluded that reading disabled children do not exhibit visual memory dificits. In other studies Vellutino has found LD children to perform more poorly than normal children on tasks involving verbal material, but in an equally adequate fashion with nonverbal material (either visually or auditorially presented). For example, Vellutino, Harding, Phillips, and Steger (1975) compared poor and normal readers on a paired-associated task consisting of cards depicting either nonsense words and geometric figures (verbal–visual) or geometric figures and geometric figures (visual–visual). As hypothesized, the reading disabled group scored lower relative to the normal children on the verbal–visual but not on the visual–visual paired associates. Vellutino et al. liken the verbal–visual task to that of reading and state that poor readers have difficulties in the process of associating graphic symbols and sounds.

In agreement with Vellutino's conclusions are the results of Swanson (in press), who presented LD and normal children with pictures of nonsense shapes in one of two conditions. In one condition children were trained to label the stimuli, while in the other one they were not. Differences between LD and normal groups favoring the normal groups obtained in the nonlabeling condition. However, the learning disabled children profited from the labeling condition such that their performance came to equal that of the normal controls.

Perfetti, too, has reached conclusions essentially similar to those of Vellutino. Comparing good and poor readers on a short-term memory task involving the auditory presentation of stories or digits, Perfetti and Goldman (1976) found differences on the former only. They therefore concluded that poor readers do not have a general memory deficit, but rather one that is specific to the encoding of linguistic information.

Torgesen has reached conclusions similar to those of Vellutino and Perfetti in that he notes that LD children have difficulties in using verbal mediation to help them on memory tasks. His research, however, points to a broader based deficit than that relating only to linguistic skills. Torgesen (1977b) has conceptualized the LD child as an inactive or passive rather than an active learner. He, along with Hallahan (Hallahan & Reeve, 1980; Kauffman & Hallahan, 1979), posits that many LD children lack the necessary strategies for problem solving. Torgesen and Kail (1980) state that the memory problems encountered by LD children are not due merely to deficits in basic linguistic knowledge or verbal skills, but to the management of capacities. They maintain that if the deficits were due merely to the lack of basic verbal skills, it would not be so easy to reduce them by training LD children in learning strategies. In this vein, Torgesen and Goldman (1977) presented normal and poor readers with familiar pictures and told them that they would be asked to remember their serial order. After presentation of the stimuli, observers recorded lip movements and other indications that the subjects were engaging in verbal rehearsal. Not only did the normal readers recall more stimuli, but they also engaged in more rehearsal than poor readers. Furthermore, under instructions to point to the pictures and name them during presentation, the performance differences between the two groups were eliminated.

There are findings suggesting that LD children also lack the ability to use another type of mnemonic device—categorization. A common feature of the short-term memory literature is the finding that older children and adults will recall items in categorical groups (e.g., animals, foods, objects, etc.). In other words, if presented with a number of stimuli from a few categories, mature learners often adopt the strategy of grouping items into their respective categories in order to reduce the memory load. Torgesen (1977a) presented good and poor readers with 24 pictures of common objects and told them that after two minutes of study time they would be asked to remember them. The experimenter specifically told the children that they could move the pictures around or do anything else with them that they wished. Compared with the poor readers, the good readers recalled more of the pictures, and, (more interestingly), they sorted more of the pictures into categories during the study period. In addition, when Torgesen trained the poor readers to sort the pictures into categories during the study period their recall performance equaled that of good readers.

Two other studies, however, have not obtained such clear-cut results on the issue of whether LD children can take advantage of categorization as a mnemonic device (Freston & Drew, 1974; Parker et al. 1975). Freston and Drew presented LD children with spoken words in either an unorganized or organized (grouped into conceptual categories of animals, geometric shapes, flowers, and foods) fashion. They found no differences in memory between the two conditions, and thus concluded that LD children are unable to take advantage of conceptual categorizations. Parker et al. (1975), however, using the same task, failed to find an interaction between list type (unorganized versus organized) and subject classification (normal versus LD children).

## Selective attention

The research on the selective attention abilities of LD children parallels that on memory performance in several important respects. First, LD children are found to perform less capably than their normal peers. Second, one of the reasons for this discrepancy appears to be LD children's use of inefficient strategies. Third, LD children, when trained in the application of appropriate strategies, perform similarly to normal children.

The bulk of the research on the selective attention ability of LD children has been done using a central–incidental learning paradigm developed by Hagen (Hagen, 1967; Maccoby & Hagen, 1965). In the typical procedure, the experimenter presents the child with a series of pictures, each containing two line drawings—one of an animal and one of a household object. The same animal and household object are always paired together. The child is told to pay attention to the serial order of the animals. Each card is presented for about two seconds and then turned face down. After each trial (about four to seven cards in length), the experimenter shows the child a probe card containing one of the animals and asks the child to point to its corresponding position in the face-down array. The child's number correct over a series of these trials (about 12–14) is referred to as central, or relevant, recall. After all of the trials are completed, the experimenter gives the child a set of pictures, half of which contain the same animals and half of which contain the same household objects that had been paired with the animals. The child is requested to match up each animal with the particular household object with which it had always been paired. The number of correct pairings is termed incidental, or irrelevant, recall. It is incidental in the sense that the child is not instructed to pay attention to the household objects during the earlier central learning trails.

For normal children the results on the Hagen central–incidental task have been consistently clear cut (Hagen & Kail, 1975): with age, normal children do better on central, but not incidental, recall. In fact, some studies have found a decline in incidental learning at about 12–13 years of age. Furthermore, correlations between central and incidental learning are positive at younger ages, but shift to negative at about 12–13 years of age. Hagen hypothesizes that older children have adopted the strategy of abandoning the processing of incidental information so that they may perform better on central recall.

In a series of studies Hallahan and his colleagues (Dawson, Hallahan, Reeve, & Ball, 1978; Hallahan, Gajar, Cohen, & Tarver, 1978; Hallahan, Kauffman, & Ball, 1973; Hallahan, Tarver, Kauffman, & Graybeal, 1978; Mercer, Cullinan, Hallahan, & La Fleur, 1975; Tarver, Hallahan, Cohen, & Kauffman, 1977; Tarver, Hallahan, Kauffman, & Ball, 1976) and Ross (Pelham & Ross, 1977) have investigated the selective attention performance of LD children. The following five conclusions can be drawn from this literature:

1. LD children, compared to normal peers, are deficient in selective attention performance. They score lower in central recall, but their incidental recall is at least equal, and sometimes superior, to that of normal children. In addition, compared to normal children there tends to be a higher positive correlation between central and incidental recall for LD children, suggesting that the latter are less likely to adopt a strategy of giving up the processing of incidental in favor of central information.

2. LD children exhibit a "developmental lag" in selective attention performance in that they respond similarly to normal children who are about 2–3 years younger. This effect has been found in LD children across a relatively broad age range (about 8–15 years of age). Thus, it appears that the differences between the selective attention performance of LD and normal children are more quantitative than qualitative.

3. The poorer selective attention performance of LD children can be linked to their not using efficient learning strategies such as cumulative verbal rehearsal. Again, this effect is developmentally based in that LD children do eventually adopt such strategies, but at a later age than normal children.

4. The selective attention performance of LD children can, through training, be made similar to that of their normal peers. This can be accomplished through instructing them in the use of cumulative verbal rehearsal strategies or by providing reinforcement for correct responses on central recall. The former is more effective than the latter, although there is some evidence that a combination of both types of training is the most effective procedure of all.

5. All of the training studies have been of short duration and the assessments of their effects have been in terms of immediate rather than long-term results. Not only has there been no research on the durability of attention training effects in LD children, but there has been no research on the generalization of such training. Similar literature in the area of mental retardation would suggest that such effects will be difficult to achieve—particularly the generalization of training from one task to another (Brown, Campione, & Murphy, 1974; Campione & Brown, 1977).

### Cognitive tempo

Although we shall not discuss it in great detail here, a factor related to information-processing skills is cognitive tempo, a construct that refers to the manner in which children approach certain problem-solving situations. In order to classify learners as to whether they consider alternative responses for relatively longer or shorter times and whether they make relatively more or fewer errors in a choice situation, Kagan, Rosman, Day, Albert, & Phillips (1964) developed the Matching Familiar Figures (MFF) test. On each trial of the test a subject is asked to select from among an array of six variants, one that is identical to a standard. If a choice is incorrect, the subject is directed to continue selecting. The test yields two dependent measures: "time," which is the mean time, across trials, elapsed from presentation of the stimulus display to the subject's first choice; and "errors," which is the total number of incorrect choices across all trials. When a subject's time score is below and error score is above the sample medians for each measure, the child is considered *impulsive,* while the opposite scores (i.e., time above and errors below the median, relative to the sample tested) result in a label of *reflective.* Test–retest reliabilities of the time and error scores of LD children have been assessed and found to be weak to moderate for both time ($r$ = .24–.72) and errors ($r$ = .36–.55) (Becker, Bender, & Morrison, 1978; Epstein, Cullinan, & Lloyd, 1977; Smith & Rogers, 1978); internal consistency coefficients of .69 for time and .54 for errors have been reported (Smith & Rogers, 1978).

Consistent with earlier suggestions (e.g., Clements, 1966), LD children are more likely to be classified as impulsive in samples that include LD and normal learners (Hallahan et al., 1973; Keogh & Donlon, 1972). Additionally, boys considered to be severely LD are more impulsive than those considered mildly LD, who, in turn, are more impulsive than normals (Epstein, Cullinan, & Sternberg, 1977).

In line with criticisms of the scoring procedure described above, more sophisticated means of combining the time and error scores have been developed (see Salkind & Wright, 1977). Using this model, Cullinan, Epstein, Lloyd, and Noel (1980) have reported that LD boys at two age levels do not differ from younger normal boys but have significantly higher scores on the impulsivity dimension than older normals. Furthermore, on the efficiency dimension in the scoring model, a dimension that appears to be related to intelligence (Salkind, 1975), the LD children do not differ from the normals. In contrast to these various findings of differences between LD and normal children, Becker (1976) reported that children judged by other means to be at risk of developing learning disabilities did not differ from normals.

Of greater interest than the fact that LD and normal children differ on the MFF is the possibility that poor performance on it also reflects a lack of strategic skills. Although some attempts to modify impulsive cognitive tempo have involved the manipulation of response consequences (e.g., Briggs & Weinberg, 1973; Hemry, 1973), a number of

47

other studes have accomplished modification by providing subjects with more reflective attack strategies. Particular techniques have included teaching scanning of the alternatives (e.g., Egeland, 1974; Heider, 1971; Zelnicker, Jeffrey, Ault, & Parsons, 1972), requiring subjects to repeat instructions to themselves (e.g., Meichenbaum & Goodman, 1969), modeling a reflective strategy (e.g., Debus, 1970), and combinations of these (e.g., Cullinan, Epstein, & Silver, 1977; Meichenbaum & Goodman, 1971; Ridberg, Parke, & Hetherington, 1971). (For a comprehensive review, see Digate, Epstein, Cullinan, & Switzky, 1978). The similarities of these procedures, and their effects, to procedures used to modify memory and selective attention performance are compelling.

## Some conclusions based on the information processing literature

Researchers in the areas of memory, selective attention, and cognitive tempo have reached essentially similar conclusions. Many children with LD apparently do not use appropriate learning strategies. They are passive rather than active learners. It is not that they are deficient learners per se, but that they are deficient in applying task approach skills. To use the terminology of Flavell (Flavell, Beach, & Chinsky, 1966), the LD child exhibits a production deficiency. He or she is capable of remembering and selectively attending, but needs to be trained to use learning strategies at the appropriate time. When so trained, the LD child performs similarly to the normal child on these tasks. The fact that LD children exhibit problems in the spontaneous use of strategies suggests that they have difficulties in what some researchers (Atkinson & Shiffrin, 1968; Butterfield & Belmont, 1977; Flavell, 1970) have referred to as "control or executive functions." In contrast to "structural" features of cognition that are built-in and invariant from one situation to another, executive functions are optional activities that an individual can use to enhance cognitive performance within different contexts (Torgesen & Kail, 1980).

The constructs of "production deficiency," "executive function," and the like are closely related to yet another aspect of cognitive processing—"metacognition." The 1970s have seen the emergence of interest in how children develop ideas about what is needed to engage in cognitive acts, e.g., knowing that some tasks are more difficult than others, knowing that certain strategies such as rehearsal can help one to remember things (Brown, 1975; Flavell & Wellman, 1977). Children's awareness of cognitive processing along these lines has been studied almost exclusively with regard to memory, although there has been some interest in metaattention (Loper, 1980; Miller & Bigi, 1976). As yet no studies of metacognition have been undertaken with LD subjects and only a few have involved retarded children (Brown & Barclay, 1976; Brown, Campione, & Murphy, 1976). Given LD children's difficulties in engaging in control processes, it is obviously important to determine if they are aware that such strategies are available to them.

### Educational implications of the research on information processing

Very little direct application of the laboratory research on information processing has been made to classroom settings. Hallahan and his colleagues (Hallahan & Reeve, 1980; Kauffman & Hallahan, 1979), however, note that this body of literature indirectly suggests that LD children are in need of instruction in task approach skills. They state that training in the use of strategies such as mnemonic aids is warranted. They further suggest that teaching techniques that generally fall under the rubric of cognitive behavior modification (Mahoney, 1974; Meichenbaum, 1977) hold a great deal of promise for LD children. Noting such techniques as self-instruction, self-monitoring, and self-reinforcement, they point out that some cognitive behavior modification techniques attack the strategy deficits revealed by information-processing research. Furthermore, and perhaps most importantly, they suggest that cognitive behavior modification, almost by definition, requires the active participation of children in their own treatment. Thus, if it is true as Torgesen (1977b) claims that LD children generally possess passive learning styles, cognitive behavior modification may be of benefit in helping them become more self-reliant learners.

Some unresolved questions about teaching attack strategies are (1) whether children learn attack strategies as a by-product of adequate academic instruction, (2) whether teaching attack strategies on nonacademic tasks will transfer to academic performance, and (3) whether training in attack strategies on specific tasks will transfer to "executive control." The first question revolves around the possibility that children at risk for LD may not develop such problems when taught by teachers and through instructional programs that virtually ensure success. There is some preliminary evidence indicating that early successful educational experiences have lasting effects (Pedersen, Faucher, & Eaton, 1978) and may counteract risk factors for potential LD pupils (Hall & Keogh, 1978). The second question revolves around the previously mentioned and often encountered problem of transfer. Training in attack strategies per se may have little effect on academic skills. A more productive approach would probably be to teach academic skills by training attack strategies suitable to them. Many, if not most, academic skills admit to the application of attack strategies. By teaching LD children to use efficient, effective attack strategies in approaching academic tasks we may be able to overcome their principle presenting problem—academic retardation—as well as lead them to apply attack strategies in general (Lloyd, 1980).

## SOCIAL BEHAVIOR

In addition to increased interest in information processing, the 1970s witnessed growing concern about the characteristics and effects of LD children's social behaviors (Bryan & Bryan, 1977, 1977a). On the basis of the literature reviewed in this section, it is clear that the notion that LD children have deficits only in academic performance is erroneous. Unfortunately, however, aside from the literature on hyperactivity (see Ross & Ross, 1976), there have been few attempts to evaluate how and to what extent the social behaviors of LD children are problems. In the following sections we consider sociometric analyses, interactional analyses, and other comparisons of the social behaviors of LD children.

### Sociometric analyses

Five recent studies have employed sociometric techniques to assess LD children's social status in their classrooms. In each of the studies the children were identified as LD by the school system and were placed in regular elementary classes. Bryan (1974b) initially found that LD children received fewer positive or accepting responses and more negative or rejecting responses from classmates than did their normal peers. In a subsequent study conducted one year later (Bryan, 1976), she replicated her earlier findings with some of the same children. In addition, she found that LD children remained low in social status even though they had entered a new class and had a new peer group. Bryan and Bryan (1978b) replicated the original finding that LD children are rejected by their classmates in sociometric choices. Siperstein, Bopp, and Bak (1978) reported that LD children were underrepresented among children chosen as most well liked by their peers but were not overrepresented among social isolates. Bruininks (1978) also found that LD children were rejected, but in addition she found the LD children to have a significantly distorted notion of how they were viewed by their classmates: they did not perceive that their classmates viewed them so negatively.

What little research is available clearly indicates that LD children's classmates do not like them, that their rejection by their classmates is persistent, and that they seem unaware that they are rejected. It is apparent that inquiries into the reasons for LD children's low social status should be conducted.

## Interactional analyses

Bryan and her associates have conducted several investigations into how LD children interact with their peers and teachers. The studies (Bryan, 1974a; Bryan & Wheeler, 1972, 1976), have shown that LD children attend to their work less, and engage in irrelevant, off-task behavior more than their nondisabled peers. However, the LD children were much more attentive to their work with a special education teacher than with their regular class teacher. Regular class teachers gave them about the same amount of positive attention to LD and normal children, but they gave much more negative attention to LD children, and their interactions with LD children tended to be around academic tasks, whereas their interactions with normal children tended to be nonacademic. In addition, LD children tended to be ignored by their peers and teachers much more often than normal children when they attempted interactions. On the other hand, the amount of language stimulation which occurs in self-contained LD classrooms was greater than occurs in regular classrooms; and teacher–student interactions were more likely to be carried through to completion in special classes. The picture emerging from these studies is one of LD children being inattentive in regular classes and ignored or criticiized by other children and their regular class teachers, and behaving more positively in special classes. These data suggest interesting questions about service delivery schemes.

In other studies (Bryan & Bryan, 1978b; Bryan & Pflaum, 1978; Bryan, Wheeler, Felcan, & Henek, 1976), the language interactions of LD children have been examined. Compared to nondisabled peers, LD children have been found to emit and receive more negative and fewer positive statements, to emit more competitive statements, and (for males only) to use less complex linguistic constructions. Apparently, the language interactions of LD children are often offensive (as such children seem to give and receive negative statements) and ineffective. Clearly, the communication patterns of LD children deserve a closer look.

## Other analyses and comparisons

The nonverbal communication of LD children has been examined by Bryan (1977). She found that LD children were less able than normals to comprehend nonverbal messages having affective content. There is the suggestion in these data that LD children may acquire low social status and negative patterns of interaction because they misconstrue or misinterpret the nonverbal behavior of others.

Bryan (1978) has also reported that college students are able to identify accurately LD and normal children based on the children's social interactions. Given brief video- or audiotapes of interactions or even transcriptions of the tapes, untrained observers who did not know the children could correctly sort them into LD and normal groups. Evidently, there are clear characteristics of LD children and/or such children's interactions with their peers that, "give them away." LD children apparently were seen as less attractive, less academically capable, less able to express themselves, and less thoughtful. Aside from that, little is known about the characteristics that distinguished the LD children.

## Summary

The available research, which is little, indicates that LD children have serious problems in the area of social–emotional behavior: they (1) are unpopular with their peers, (2) do not realize how unpopular they are, (3) are often ignored or responded to negatively by regular class teachers and their peers, (4) tend to give and receive negative verbal statements in interactions with peers, (5) are poor interpreters of non-verbal communication, and (6) are easily identifiable on the basis of their interactions by untrained observers. It is quite clear now that LD children cannot be assumed to have only academic deficits. Bryan's work provides strong evidence that LD children's interpersonal problems include difficulties in verbal and nonverbal communication. This evidence reinforces our previous arguments that it is extremely difficult to distinguish types of mildly handicapped learners.

Programs for teaching social–interpersonal skills to LD children are clearly needed. Whether such programs should differ from programs for teaching the same social skills to other mildly handicapped learners remains to be seen. It would seem that if three different children need to be taught the same skills, their categorical labels should have little to do with whether and in what way those social skills should be built. Given the paucity of evidence suggesting that different social-learning programs are needed for different categories of children, perhaps the most sensible approach would be to develop teaching procedures for specific social deficits regardless of special education categories.

Programs for training teachers of LD children need to include instruction in identifying, measuring, and teaching social as well as academic skills. In spite of the probability that successful remediation of academic deficits may improve children's self-concepts, teachers who also teach school-appropriate social skills will have accomplished a more complete remediation. The obligation to do this may be even more serious for resource teachers consulting with regular class teachers because (1) LD children will probably be spending an increasing amount of time in regular classrooms and (2) there is evidence indicating that the frequent reprimands and criticisms which are common in classes (e.g., Walker & Buckley, 1973) may be the very teacher actions which sometimes exacerbate social interaction problems.

Finally, regardless of the resolution of the definitional issue discussed earlier, it is apparent that many children served by special education exhibit problems in the area of development called "social," "emotional," "social–emotional," "behavioral," etc. There is no dispute that such difficulties involve getting along with others and feelings about oneself. Quibbles about terminology should not obscure the fact that these children need help in learning to relate well with others and to develop and maintain realistic and positive self-appraisals, just as quibbles about terminology should not deter us from providing powerful academic instruction to children who need it.

## CONCLUSION

Of the many topics in LD we have discussed three: definition, information processing, and social behavior. With regard to the first of these, we have suggested that the present state of affairs is not as terrible as it might seem. Evidence bearing on information processing has led us to suspect that LD children have not learned efficient attack strategies. In the realm of social behavior, we have seen that LD children often have frank deficits that deserve remedial attention. In all of these areas the obligatory call for further research has been implied or actually made, as well it should be, given the still tenuous nature of our knowledge in these areas.

As evidence inevitably accumulates, we expect that it will shed further light on the areas we have discussed, as well as on others. Ultimately, we hope that what is learned will be translated into programs and procedures for obviating and ameliorating LD. Perhaps the major impediment to such a turn of events would be renewed factionalization of people working in this area. Outcomes are very unlikely to favor the position of Camp A while cutting Camp B at the knees. It would be a cruel irony if children were to fail while champions of factions argued over who should teach them what and how.

# References

Adelman, H. S. The not so specific learning disability population. *Exceptional Children,* 1971, *37,* 528–533.

Adelman, H. S., & Compas, B. E. Stimulant drugs and learning problems. *Journal of Special Education,* 1977, *11,* 377–416.

Arter, J. A., & Jenkins, J. R. Examining the benefits and prevalence of modality considerations in special education. *Journal of Special Education,* 1977, *11,* 281–298.

Atkinson, R. C., & Shiffrin, R. M. Human memory: A proposed system and its control processes. In K. W. Spence & J. T. Spence (Eds.), *The psychology of learning and motivation* (Vol. 2). New York: Academic Press, 1968.

Bateman, B. An educator's view of a diagnostic approach to learning disorders. In J. Hellmuth (Ed.), *Learning Disorders* (Vol. 1). Seattle: Special Child, 1965.

Bateman, B. Learning disorders. *Review of Educational Research,* 1966, *36,* 93–119.

Becker, L. D. Conceptual tempo and the early detection of learning problems. *Journal of Learning Disabilities,* 1976, *9,* 433–442.

Becker, L. D., Bender, H. H., & Morrison, G. Measuring impulsivity-reflection: A critical review. *Journal of Learning Disabilities,* 1978, *11,* 626–632.

Briggs, C., & Weinberg, R. Effects of reinforcement in training children's conceptual tempo. *Journal of Educational Psychology,* 1973, *65,* 383–394.

Brown, A. L. The development of memory: Knowing, knowing about knowing, and knowing how to know. In H. W. Reese (Ed.), *Advances in child development and behavior* (Vol. 10). New York: Academic Press, 1975.

Brown, A. L., & Barclay, C. R. The effects of training specific mnemonics on the metamnemonic efficiency of retarded children. *Child Development,* 1976, *47,* 71–80.

Brown, A. L., Campione, J. C., & Murphy, M. D. Keeping track of changing variables: Long-term retention of a trained rehearsal strategy by retarded adolescents. *American Journal of Mental Deficiency,* 1974, *78,* 446–453.

Brown, A. L., Campione, J. C., & Murphy, M. D. *Maintenance and generalization of trained metamnemonic awareness by educable retarded children: Span estimation.* Unpublished manuscript, University of Illinois, 1976.

Bruininks, V. L. Actual and perceived peer status of learning-disabled students in mainstream programs. *Journal of Special Education,* 1978, *12,* 51–58.

Bryan, T. H. An observational analysis of classroom behaviors of children with learning disabilities. *Journal of Learning Disabilities,* 1974a, *7,* 26–34.

Bryan, T. H. Peer popularity of learning disabled children. *Journal of Learning Disabilities,* 1974b, *7,* 621–625.

Bryan, T. H. Peer popularity of learning disabled children: A replication. *Journal of Learning Disabilities,* 1976, *9,* 307–311.

Bryan, T. H. Learning disabled children's comprehension of nonverbal communication. *Journal of Learning Disabilities,* 1977, *10,* 501–506.

Bryan, T. H. Social relationships and verbal interactions of learning disabled children. *Journal of Learning Disabilities,* 1978, *11,* 108–115.

Bryan, T. H., & Bryan, J. H. The social-emotional side of learning disabilities. *Behavioral Disorders,* 1977, *2,* 141–145.

Bryan, T. H., & Bryan, J. H. *Understanding learning disabilities* (2nd ed.). Sherman Oaks, Calif.: Alfred, 1978a.

Bryan, T. H., & Bryan, J. H. Social interactions of learning disabled children. *Learning Disability Quarterly,* 1978b, *1*(1), 33–38.

Bryan, T. H., & Pflaum, S. Social interactions of learning disabled children: A linguistic, social, and cognitive analysis. *Learning Disability Quarterly,* 1978, *1*(3), 70–79.

Bryan, T. H., & Wheeler, R. Perception of learning disabled children: The eye of the observer. *Journal of Learning Disabilities,* 1972, *5,* 484–488.

Bryan, T. H., & Wheeler, R. Teachers' behaviors in classes for severely retarded–multiply trainable mentally retarded, learning disabled and normal children. *Mental Retardation*, 1976, *14*(4), 41–45.

Bryan, T. H., Wheeler, R., Felcan, J., & Henek, T. "Come on dummy": An observational study of children's communications. *Journal of Learning Disabilities*, 1976, *9*, 661–669.

Burke, A. A. Placement of black and white children in educable mentally handicapped classes and learning disability classes. *Exceptional Children*, 1975, *41*, 438–439.

Butterfield, E. C., & Belmont, J. M. Assessing and improving the executive cognitive functions of mentally retarded people. In I. Bialer & M. Stermlicht (Eds.), *Psychological issues in mental retardation*. New York: Psychological Dimension, 1977.

Campione, J. C., & Brown, A. L. Memory and metamemory development in educable retarded children. In R. V. Kail & J. W. Hagen (Eds.), *Perspectives on the development of memory and cognition*. Hillsdale, N.J.: Erlbaum, 1977.

Chalfant, J. C., & King, F. S. An approach to operationalizing the definition of learning disabilities. *Journal of Learning Disabilities*, 1976, *9*, 228–243.

Clements, S. D. *Minimal brain dysfunction in children: Phase 1* (NINDS Monograph No. 3, U.S. Public Health Service Publication No. 1415). Washington, D.C.: U.S. Government Printing Office, 1966.

Cruickshank, W. Some issues facing the field of learning disabilities. *Journal of Learning Disabilities*, 1972, *5*, 380–388.

Cullinan, D., Epstein, M. H., Lloyd, J., & Noel, M. Development of cognitive tempo of learning disabled and normal children. *Learning Disability Quarterly*, 1980, *3*, 46–53.

Cullinan, D., Epstein, M. H., & Silver, L. Modification of impulsive cognitive tempo in learning disabled pupils. *Journal of Abnormal Child Psychology*, 1977, *5*, 437–444.

Cummings, E. M., & Faw, T. T. Short-term memory and equivalence judgments in normal and retarded readers. *Child Development*, 1976, *47*, 286–289.

Danielson, L. C., & Bauer, J. N. A formula-based classification of learning disabled children: An examination of the issues. *Journal of Learning Disabilities*, 1978, *11*, 163–176.

Dawson, M. M., Hallahan, D. P., Reeve, R. E., & Ball, D. W. *The effect of reinforcement and verbal rehearsal on selective attention in learning disabled children*. Unpublished manuscript, University of Virginia, 1978.

Debus, R. L. Effects of brief observation of model behavior on conceptual tempo of impulsive children. *Developmental Psychology*, 1970, *2*, 22–32.

Department of Health, Education and Welfare. Education of handicapped children: Assistance to states: Proposed rulemaking. *Federal Register*, 1976, *41*, 52404–52407.

Department of Health, Education and Welfare. Assistance to states for education of handicapped children: Procedures for evaluating specific learning disabilities. *Federal Register*, 1977, *42*, 65082–65085.

Digate, G., Epstein, M. H., Cullinan, D., & Switzky, H. N. Modification of impulsivity: Implications for improved efficiency in learning for exceptional children. *Journal of Special Education*, 1978, *12*, 459–468.

Egeland, B. Training impulsive children in the use of more efficient scanning techniques. *Child Development*, 1974, *45*, 165–171.

Epstein, M. H., Cullinan, D., & Lloyd, J. Reliability of the Matching Familiar Figures test scores of learning disabled children. *Perceptual and Motor Skills*, 1977, *45*, 56–58.

Epstein, M. H., Cullinan, D., & Sternberg, L. Impulsive cognitive tempo in severe and mild learning disabled children. *Psychology in the Schools*, 1977, *14*, 290–294.

Farnham-Diggory, S., & Gregg, L. W. Short-term memory function in young readers. *Journal of Experimental Child Psychology*, 1975, *19*, 279–298.

Flavell, J. H. Developmental studies of mediated memory. In H. W. Reese & L. P. Lipsitt (Eds.), *Advances in child development and behavior* (Vol. 5). New York: Academic Press, 1970.

Flavell, J. H., Beach, D. R., & Chinsky, J. M. Spontaneous verbal rehearsal in a memory task as a function of age. *Child Development,* 1966, *37,* 283–299.

Flavell, J. H., & Wellman, H. M. Metamemory. In R. V. Kail & J. W. Hagen (Eds.), *Perspectives on the development of memory and cognition.* Hillside, N.J.: Erlbaum, 1977.

Freston, C. W., & Drew, C. J. Verbal performance of learning disabled children as a function of input organization. *Journal of Learning Disabilities,* 1974, *7,* 424–428.

Gaddes, W. H. Prevalence estimates and the need for definition of learning disabilities. In R. M. Knights & D. J. Bakker (Eds.), *The neuropsychology of learning disorders.* Baltimore: University Park Press, 1976.

Gillespie, P. H., Miller, T. L., & Fiedler, V. D. Legislative definitions of learning disabilities: Roadblocks to effective service. *Journal of Learning Disabilities,* 1975, *8,* 659–666.

Grossman, H. J. (Ed.). *Manual on terminology and classification in mental retardation* (Rev. ed.). Washington, D.C.: American Association on Mental Deficiency, 1973.

Hagen, J. W. The effect of distraction on selective attention. *Child Development,* 1967, *38,* 685–694.

Hagen, J. W., & Kail, R. V. The role of attention in perceptual and cognitive development. In W. M. Cruickshank & D. P. Hallahan (Eds.), *Perceptual and learning disabilities in children* (Vol. 2): *Research and theory.* Syracuse, N.Y.: Syracuse University Press, 1975.

Hall, R. J. An information-processing approach to the study of exceptional children. In B. K. Keogh (Ed.), *Advances in special education* (Vol. 2). Greenwich, Conn.: JAI Press, 1980.

Hall, R. J., & Keogh, B. K. Qualitative characteristics of educationally high-risk children. *Learning Disability Quarterly,* 1978, *1*(2), 62–68.

Hallahan, D., & Cruickshank, W. *Psychoeducational foundations of learning disabilities.* Englewood Cliffs, N.J.: Prentice-Hall, 1973.

Hallahan, D. P., Gajar, A. H., Cohen, S. B., & Tarver, S. G. Selective attention and locus of control in learning disabled and normal children. *Journal of Learning Disabilities,* 1978, *11,* 231–236.

Hallahan, D. P., & Kauffman, J. M. *Introduction to learning disabilities: A psychobehavioral approach.* Englewood Cliffs, N.J.: Prentice-Hall, 1976.

Hallahan, D. P., & Kauffman, J. M. Categories, labels, behavioral characteristics: ED, LD, and EMR reconsidered. *Journal of Special Education,* 1977, *11,* 139–149.

Hallahan, D. P., Kauffman, J. M., & Ball, D. W. Selective attention and cognitive tempo of low achieving and high achieving sixth grade males. *Perceptual and Motor Skills,* 1973, *36,* 579–583.

Hallahan, D. P., & Reeve, R. E. Selective attention and distractibility. In B. K. Keogh (Ed.), *Advances in special education* (Vol. 1). Greenwich, Conn.: JAI Press, 1980.

Hallahan, D. P., Tarver, S. G., Kauffman, J. M., & Graybeal, N. J. A comparison of the effects of reinforcement and response cost in the selective attention of learning disabled children. *Journal of Learning Disabilities,* 1978, *11,* 430–438.

Hammill, D. D. Learning disabilities: A problem in definition. *Prise Reporter,* Pennsylvania Resources and Information Center for Special Education, No. 4, 1972.

Hammill, D. D., & Larsen, S. The effectiveness of psycholinguistic training. *Exceptional Children,* 1974, *41,* 5–14.

Hammill, D. D., & Wiederholt, J. L. Review of the Frostig visual perception test and the related training program. In L. Mann & D. Sabatino (Ed.), *First review of special education* (Vol. 1). New York: Grune & Stratton, 1973.

Haring, N. G. (Ed.). *Minimal brain dysfunction in children: Phase 2* (U.S. Public Health Service Publication No. 2015). Washington, D.C.: U.S. Government Printing Office, 1969.

Haring, N. C., & Bateman, B. *Teaching the learning disabled child.* Englewood Cliffs, N.J.: Prentice-Hall, 1977.

Heider, E. R. Information processing and the modification of an "impulsive cognitive tempo." *Child Development,* 1971, *42,* 1276–1281.

Hemry, F. P. Effect of reinforcement conditions on a discrimination learning task for impulsive versus reflective children. *Child Development,* 1973, *44,* 657–660.

Johnson, D. J., & Myklebust, H. R. *Learning disabilities: Educational principles and practices.* New York: Grune & Stratton, 1967.

Kagan, J., Rosman, B., Day, D., Albert J., & Phillips, W. Information processing in the child: Significance of analytic and reflective attitudes. *Psychological Monographs,* 1964, *78*(1, Whole No. 578).

Kail, R. V., Chi, M. T. H., Ingram, A. L., & Danner, F. W. Constructive aspects of children's reading comprehension. *Child Development,* 1977, *48,* 684–688.

Kappelman, M., Kaplan, E., & Ganter, R. A study of learning disorders among disadvantaged children. *Journal of Learning Disabilities,* 1969, *2,* 261–268.

Kass, C. E., & Myklebust, H. R. Learning disability: An educational definition. *Journal of Learning Disabilities,* 1969, *2,* 377–379.

Kauffman, J. M. *Characteristics of children's behavior disorders.* Columbus, Ohio: Merrill, 1977.

Kauffman, J. M., & Hallahan, D. P. Learning disability and hyperactivity (with comments on minimal brain dysfunction). In B. B. Lahey & A. E. Kazdin (Eds.), *Advances in clinical child psychology* (Vol. 2). New York: Plenum Press, 1979.

Keogh, B. K., & Donlon, G. Field dependence, impulsivity, and learning disabilities. *Journal of Learning Disabilities,* 1972, *5,* 331–336.

Keogh, B. K., Major, S. M., Reid, H. P. Gándara, P., & Omori, H. Marker variables: A search for comparability and generalizability in the field of learning disabilities. *Learning Disability Quarterly,* 1978, *1*(3), 5–11.

Kirk, S. A. Behavioral diagnosis and remediation of learning disabilities. *Proceedings of the Conference on Exploration into the Problems of the Perceptually Handicapped Child* (Vol. 1), Chicago, April 1963.

Kirk, S. A., & Bateman, B. Diagnosis and remediation of learning disabilities. *Exceptional Children,* 1962, *29,* 73–77.

Kirk, S. A., & Elkins, J. Characteristics of children enrolled in the child service demonstration centers. *Journal of Learning Disabilities,* 1975, *8,* 630–637.

Klesius, S. E. Perceptual–motor development and reading: A closer look. In R. Aukerman (Ed.), *Some persistant questions on beginning reading.* Newark, DE: International Reading Association, 1972.

Lahey, B. B. Behavior modification with learning disabilities and related problems. In M. Hersen, R. M. Eisler & P. M. Miller (Eds.), *Progress in behavior modification* (Vol. 3). New York: Academic Press, 1976.

Leslie, L. Susceptibility to interference effects in short-term memory of normal and retarded readers. *Perceptual and Motor Skills,* 1975, *40,* 791–794.

Lilly, M. S. A merger of categories: Are we finally ready? *Journal of Learning Disabilities,* 1977, *10,* 115–121.

Lloyd, J. Academic instruction and cognitive-behavior modification: The need for attack strategy training. *Exceptional Education Quarterly,* 1980, *1,* 59–69.

Lloyd, J., Sabatino, D., Miller, T., & Miller, S. Proposed federal guidelines: Some open questions. *Journal of Learning Disabilities,* 1977, *10,* 69–71.

Loper, A. B. Metacognitive development: Implications for cognitive training of exceptional children. *Exceptional Education Quarterly,* 1980, *1,* 1–8.

Lovitt, T. C. Applied behavior analysis and learning disabilities: Part 1. *Journal of Learning Disabilities,* 1975a, *8,* 432–443.

57

Lovitt, T. C. Applied behavior analysis and learning disabilities: Part 2. *Journal of Learning Disabilities*, 1975b, *8*, 504–518.

Lund, K., Foster, G. E., & McCall-Perez, F. C. The effectiveness of psycholinguistic training: A reevaluation. *Exceptional Children*, 1978, *44*, 310–319.

Maccoby, E. E., & Hagen, J. W. Effects of distraction upon central versus incidental recall: Developmental trends. *Journal of Experimental Child Psychology*, 1965, *2*, 280–289.

Mahoney, M. J. *Cognition and behavior modification*. Cambridge, Mass.: Ballinger, 1974.

McDonald, C. W. Problems concerning the classification and education of children with learning disabilities. In J. Hellmuth (Ed.), *Learning disorders* (Vol. 3). Seattle: Special Child, 1968.

Meichenbaum, D. *Cognitive-behavior modification*. New York: Plenum Press, 1977.

Meichenbaum, D., & Goodman, J. Reflection-impulsivity and verbal control of motor behavior. *Child Development*, 1969, *40*, 785–797.

Meichenbaum, D. H., & Goodman, J. Training impulsive children to talk to themselves: A means of developing self-control. *Journal of Abnormal Psychology*, 1971, *77*, 115–126.

Mercer, C. D., Cullinan, D., Hallahan, D. P., & La Fleur, N. K. Modeling and attention–retention in learning disabled children. *Journal of Learning Disabilities*, 1975, *8*, 444–450.

Mercer, C. D., Forgnone, C., & Wolking, W. D. Definitions of learning disabilities used in the United States. *Journal of Learning Disabilities*, 1976, *9*, 376–386.

Miller, P. H., & Bigi, L. *Children's understanding of attention, or "You know I can't hear you when the water's running."* Unpublished manuscript, University of Michigan, 1976.

Neisworth, J. T., & Greer, J. G. Functional similarities of learning disability and mild retardation. *Exceptional Children*, 1975, *42*, 17–21.

Parker, T. B., Freston, C. W., & Drew, C. J. Comparison of verbal performance of normal and learning disabled children as a function of input organization. *Journal of Learning Disabilities*, 1975, *8*, 386–393.

Pedersen, E., Faucher, T. A., & Eaton, W. W. A new perspective on the effects of first-grade teachers on subsequent adult status. *Harvard Educational Review*, 1978, *48*, 1–31.

Pelham, W. E., & Ross, A. O. Selective attention in children with reading problems: A developmental study of incidental learning. *Journal of Abnormal Child Psychology*, 1977, *5*, 1–8.

Perfetti, C. A., & Goldman, S. R. Discourse memory and reading comprehension skill. *Journal of Verbal Learning and Verbal Behavior*, 1976, *14*, 33–42.

Richards, L. J., & Clark, A. D. Learning disabilities: A national survey for existing public school programs. *Journal of Special Education*, 1968, *2*, 223–226.

Ridberg, E. H., Parke, R. D., & Hetherington, E. M. Modification of impulsive and reflective cognitive styles through observation of film-mediated models. *Developmental Psychology*, 1971, *5*, 369–377.

Ring, B. C. Effects of input organization on auditory short-term memory. *Journal of Learning Disabilities*, 1976, *9*, 591–595.

Ross, D. M., & Ross, S. A. *Hyperactivity: Research, theory, action*. New York: Wiley, 1976.

Salkind, N. J. *Errors and latency on the MFFT: A reassessment of classification strategies*. Paper presented at the Annual Convention of the Society for Research in Child Development, Denver, April 1975.

Salkind, N. J., & Wright, J. C. The development of reflection-impulsivity and cognitive efficiency: An integrated model. *Human Development*, 1977, *20*, 377–387.

Salvia, J., & Clark, J. Use of deficits to identify the learning disabled. *Exceptional Children*, 1973, *39*, 305–308.

Senf, G. Development of immediate memory for bisensory stimuli in normal children and children with learning disorders. *Developmental Psychology Monograph*, 1969, *1*(pt 2), 6.

Senf, G. M. A perspective on the definition of LD. *Journal of Learning Disabilities*, 1977, *10*, 537–539.

Senf, G., & Feshback, S. Development of bisensory memory in culturally deprived, dyslexic, and normal readers. *Journal of Educational Psychology*, 1970, *61*, 461–470.

Siperstein, G. N., Bopp, M. J., & Bak, J. J. Social status of learning disabled children. *Journal of Learning Disabilities*, 1978, *11*, 98–102.

Smith, M. D., & Rogers, C. M. Reliability of standardized assessment instruments when used with learning disabled children. *Learning Disability Quarterly*, 1978, *1*(3): 23–31.

Sroufe, L. A. Drug treatment of children with behavior problems. In F. D. Horowitz (Ed.), *Review of child development research* (Vol. 4). Chicago: University of Chicago Press, 1975.

Sulzbacher, S., & Kenowitz, L. At last, a definition of learning disabilities we can live with? *Journal of Learning Disabilities*, 1977, *10*, 67–69.

Swanson, L. Verbal coding effects on learning disabled and normal readers' visual short-term memory. *Journal of Educational Psychology*, in press.

Tarver, S. G., & Dawson, M. M. Modality preference and the teaching of reading: A review. *Journal of Learning Disabilities*, 1978, *11*, 5–17.

Tarver, S. G., Hallahan, D. P., Cohen, S. B., & Kauffman, J. M. The development of visual selective attention and verbal rehearsal in learning disabled boys *Journal of Learning Disabilities*, 1977, *10*, 491–500.

Tarver, S. G., Hallahan, D. P., Kauffman, J. M., & Ball, D. W. Verbal rehearsal and selective attention in children with learning disabilities: A developmental lag. *Journal of Experimental Child Psychology*, 1976, *22*, 375–385.

Torgesen, J. K. Problems and prospects in the study of learning disabilities. In E. M. Hetherington (Ed.), *Review of child development research* (Vol. 5). Chicago: University of Chicago Press, 1975.

Torgesen, J. K. Memorization processes in reading-disabled children. *Journal of Educational Psychology*, 1977a, *69*, 571–578.

Torgesen, J. K. The role of non-specific factors in the task performance of learning disabled children: A theoretical assessment. *Journal of Learning Disabilities*, 1977b, *10*, 27–34.

Torgesen, J. K., & Goldman, T. Verbal rehearsal and short-term memory in reading-disabled children. *Child Development*, 1977, *48*, 56–60.

Torgesen, J. K., & Kail, R. V. Memory processes in exceptional children. In B. K. Keogh (Ed.), *Advances in special education* (Vol. 1). Greenwich, Conn.: JAI Press, 1980.

Vaughn, R. W., & Hodges, L. A statistical survey into a definition of learning disabilities: A search for acceptance. *Journal of Learning Disabilities*, 1973, *6*, 658–664.

Vellutino, F. R., Harding, C. J., Phillips, F., & Steger, J. A. Differential transfer in poor and normal readers. *Journal of Genetic Psychology*, 1975, *126*, 3–18.

Vellutino, F. R., Steger, J. A., De Setto, L., & Phillips, F. Immediate and delayed recognition of visual stimuli in poor and normal readers. *Journal of Experimental Child Psychology*, 1975, *19*, 223–232.

Vellutino, F., Steger, J., Harding, C., Phillips, F. Verbal vs. non-verbal paired-associates learning in poor and normal readers. *Neuropsychologia*, 1975, *13*, 75–82.

Walker, H., & Buckley, N. Teacher attention to appropriate and inappropriate classroom behavior: An individual case study. *Focus on Exceptional Children*, 1973, *5*, 5–11.

Waller, T. G. Children's recognition memory for written sentences: A comparison of good and poor readers. *Child Development*, 1976, *47*, 90–95.

Wepman, J. M., Cruickshank, W. M., Deutsch, C. P., Morency, A., & Strother, C. R. Learning disabilities. In N. Hobbs (Ed.), *Issues in the Classification of Children* (Vol. 1). San Francisco: Jossey-Bass, 1975.

Wiederholt, J. L. Historical perspectives on the education of the learning disabled. In L. Mann & D. Sabatino (Eds.), *Second review of special education.* New York: Grune & Stratton, 1974.

Wright, L. S. Conduct problem or learning disability. *Journal of Special Education,* 1974, *8,* 331–336.

Ysseldyke, J. Diagnostic–prescriptive teaching: The search for aptitude–treatment interactions. In L. Mann & D. Sabatino (Eds.), *First review of special education.* New York: Grune & Stratton, 1973.

Zelnicker, T., Jeffrey, W. E., Ault, R., & Parsons, J. Analysis and modification of search strategies of impulsive and reflective children on the Matching Familiar Figures Test. *Child Development,* 1972, *43,* 321–335.

# APPLIED BEHAVIOR ANALYSIS AND BEHAVIORALLY DISORDERED PUPILS: SELECTED ISSUES

Michael H. Epstein
Douglas Cullinan
Terry L. Rose
*Northern Illinois University*

Within the past 20 years the behavioral model for understanding and improving human functioning has had substantial impact upon the various helping professions, including medicine (Williams & Gentry, 1977), psychiatry and psychiatric nursing (O'Neil, McLaughlin, & Knapp, 1977), psychological counseling and therapy (Agras, 1978), social case work (Tharp & Wetzel, 1969), school counseling (Krumboltz & Thoresen, 1976), and regular and special education (Becker, 1973; Gardner, 1977; Haring, 1978). This development stems from operant conditioning research into basic learning and behavior processes of animals and humans in the laboratory. By the late 1950s and early 1960s, well-established operant conditioning principles were being applied to produce therapeutic behavior changes in severely handicapped people. Many of these studies employed single-case research methodologies associated with the experimental analysis of behavior (again out of the operant tradition)—research strategies that enable a demonstration of cause–effect relationships between environmental events (e.g., therapeutic procedures) and behavior changes. As a result, the 1960s saw the

Preparation of this manuscript was supported in part by Grant G00-7700642 from the Bureau of Education for the Handicapped to the Department of Learning and Development, Northern Illinois University.

The authors are grateful to Heather Vye Reding and Barbara Kober for their assistance with this manuscript.

emergence of a new area of behavior change technology which came to be called *applied behavior analysis.*

Applied behavior analysis may be defined as the application and experimental evaluation of procedures for modifying significant human behaviors in practical situations (Baer, Wolf, & Risley, 1968; Kazdin, 1978). Stated another way, applied behavior analysis permits examination of the effects of intervention procedures upon carefully defined and reliably recorded behaviors of immediate concern to the behaver and/or society. There is every indication that applied behavior analysis is becoming the basis for an individually oriented, scientific technology of human behavior modification. This is attested to by the appearance of numerous experimentally verified techniques for changing quite a large variety of human behaviors (Kazdin, 1978; Kazdin & Wilson, 1978).

Concurrent with the evolution of applied behavior analysis, the behavioral model was exerting its influence upon the education of handicapped children and, in particular, special education for behaviorally disordered pupils. Precursors of some aspects of the current behavioral approaches to special education can be found in early accounts of step-wise teaching methodologies, token or other incentive systems for performance, highly structured and predictable educational programs for handicapped children, and so on (see Cullinan, Epstein, & Kauffman, in press; Kazdin, 1978). Growing dissatisfaction with the psychodynamic model coupled with the availability of the behavioral model as an alternative approach to child treatment has produced a sharp decline in the popularity of the psychodynamic model. Because education for behaviorally disordered pupils has historically been closely tied to psychiatry and clinical psychology, this paradigm shift profoundly affected special education as well. Thus, an increasing number of reports of successful applications of behavioral principles to behavior disorders of pupils began to appear in the 1960s. While these applications were usually carried out by persons trained in psychology, and the reports were often anecdotal, a serious scientific foundation was being built for education and special education. A few large-scale special educational applications of the behavioral model did surface during this period (e.g., Hewett, 1968; Quay, Werry, McQueen, & Sprague, 1966).

The current decade has seen an ever-expanding impact of the behavioral model in general, and applied behavior analysis in particular, upon special education for the behaviorally disordered. For example, a large number of available "behavior modification methods" texts (e.g., Axelrod, 1977) deal predominantly or solely with behavioral teaching practices designed to remediate school behavior problems, and introductory textbooks on behavior disorders of pupils often reflect a behavioral focus (e.g., Kauffman, 1977). Similarly, university training programs for teachers of behaviorally disordered pupils are quite commonly aligned to the behavioral model (Fink, Glass, & Guskin, 1975). This popularity of the behavioral model may be attributable both to the attractiveness of intervention procedures supported by experimental results rather than mere expert testimony, and to the relative ease with which many behavioral teaching practices can be learned and implemented.

Available applied behavior analysis research on educative procedures for behavior problems of children clearly provides a substantial foundation on which to base a technology of special education for the behaviorally disordered. However, there are important gaps in this literature which must be addressed in order to advance this technology. For example, relatively few studies have been carried out with pupils specifically identified as behaviorally disordered. Perhaps this is a consequence of one assumption of the behavioral model, which holds that quantitative rather than qualitative differences exist between behaviorally disordered and nonidentified individuals (Kauffman, 1977; Quay, 1972; Ross, 1974); that is, behaviorally disordered pupils are thought to exhibit the same behaviors as normal pupils but exhibit them excessively (e.g., too much unpermitted talking, offtask movement, aggression toward peers, and so on) or deficiently (too little interaction with classmates, work on assignments, compliance with teacher instructions, assertiveness, and so on).

Such a view suggests that an intervention shown to be successful in improving the behavior of a pupil *not* identified for special education is likely to apply as well to one identified as behaviorally disordered. However, several factors may limit the validity of this assumption. For example, a particular behavior problem to be modified is typically but one facet of a pattern of maladjustment exhibited by a behaviorally disordered pupil. Such pupils often have a limited repertory of appropriate behaviors that the teacher can encourage as alternatives to undesired excessive behaviors which need to be reduced or eliminated. Particularly in special classrooms for the behaviorally disordered, classmates may support disturbed behavior and discourage appropriate behavior. Furthermore, educational provisions for behaviorally disordered pupils frequently can be discriminated from "regular" education on the basis of factors such as physical setting, classroom climate, and so on. For these and perhaps other reasons, it cannot necessarily be assumed that interventions shown to be effective for behavior problems of nonidentified pupils will produce identical results with the behaviorally disordered.

The generalized applicability of educative procedures should be experimentally established for behaviorally disordered pupils in special education settings.

In order to review what has already been done along these lines, behavioral intervention studies were selected if (1) the subjects were identified as "behaviorally disordered" or some equivalent term (e.g., "emotionally maladjusted"), as delinquent, or as receiving education in a placement for such pupils; and (2) the treatment setting for such individuals was an educational one (classroom, tutorial session, etc.). Studies of children with profound levels of disorder (e.g., autistic, psychotic) were not reviewed.

Two areas of great concern to special education practitioners but, ironically, of apparently less interest to researchers, are academic remediation, and interventions for adolescent-age pupils. Of the small body of behavioral research directly pertaining to the education of behaviorally disordered pupils, the major part has been focused on improving the classroom conduct of elementary-age pupils; there has been considerably less emphasis on procedures to enhance academic functioning of the behaviorally disordered and on applying behavioral techniques to secondary-age behaviorally disordered students. Thus, for review of these two areas, selection of studies was further narrowed to those in which (1) academic skills or subject areas were a main intervention target, or (2) pupils were identified as adolescents or the equivalent (e.g., secondary school pupils, age fell within the 12–19 range). Some studies (e.g. academic improvement for delinquents attending school) were relevant to both reviews. Table 1 describes all studies in these two reviews. Finally, a most relevant approach to the issues raised in these reviews is careful experimentation in the relevant educational situation. Therefore, some broad recommendations are offered regarding how such issues might be investigated through the single-case experimental methodology that characterizes applied behavior analysis.

## MODIFYING ACADEMIC RESPONSES

Poor academic achievement is often associated with school behavior problems and is a major characteristic of pupils labeled as behaviorally disordered (Kauffman, 1977; Rose, Epstein, Cullinan, & Lloyd, in press; Swift & Spivack, 1969, 1973). Over the past few years, several applications of applied behavior analysis have been used to modify the academic skills of behaviorally disordered pupils. In this section, the use of social, activity, and consumable reinforcers, token reinforcers and self-control programs are considered.

## Social, activity, and consumable reinforcers

Social, activity, and consumable reinforcers have been used in an attempt to improve academic functioning of behaviorally disordered students. In one of the earliest classroom investigations, Zimmerman and Zimmerman (1962) used differential attention to improve the spelling performance of an emotionally disturbed student. Preliminary observations of student–teacher interactions had indicated that the teacher frequently coaxed a correct response after the pupil had made an error, and thus allocated considerable social attention to inaccurate responding. During treatment, teacher attention (smiling, talking, and physical proximity) was made contingent on correct responses; incorrect responses and inappropriate social behavior were ignored. Although the authors reported no data, they did indicate that this procedure was effective in increasing spelling performance. Similarly, Chan, Chiu, and Mueller (1970) used consumable and social reinforcement to produce increases in the amount, rate, and comprehension of reading for an 11-year-old behaviorally disordered pupil. In this case study, the pupil's continued performance increases also appeared to be dependent on the addition of a peer "competitor" to further motivate improvement. Unfortunately, the research design used did not permit analysis of the functions of the various intervention components.

In one study that was well designed, Marholin, McInnis, and Heads (1974) studied the effects of free-time reinforcement on the reading, English, and mathematics performance of three students attending a class in an institution for emotionally disturbed children. During baseline, the students earned a period of free activity if they had not been timed out for disruption or rule breaking during any of three academic periods. In treatment phase one, free time was contingent on meeting or surpassing the baseline median for reading accuracy. In phase two, free time was contingent upon meeting or surpassing baseline median accuracy in one of the three subjects that day; the specific subject was determined by a blind draw just before the free-time period (thus students could not predict which academic subject they had to do well in). Results showed that free time reinforced accuracy in reading when contingent upon that behavior, and reinforced accuracy in all three subjects when the academic subject upon which it was contingent was unpredictable to the students. During phase one, generalized improve-

## TABLE 1
## REVIEW OF SELECTED APPLIED BEHAVIOR ANALYSIS RESEARCH:
## INTERVENTIONS FOR ACADEMIC DEFICITS AND FOR ADOLESCENT-AGE PUPILS

| Identifying Number | Authors and Date | Subjects | N | Setting | Behavior(s) | Treatment(s) |
|---|---|---|---|---|---|---|
| 1 | Bailey et al. (1970) | Predelinquent boys | 9 | Community home | Study behavior, rule following | Home-based token reinforcement |
| 2 | Bailey et al. (1971) | Predelinquent boys | 2 | Community home | Articulation errors | Token program managed by peers |
| 3 | Bednar et al. (1970) | Delinquent boys | 32 | School for delinquents | Reading and word comprehension, standard reading achievement test, student attitudes, teacher ratings | Token reinforcement |
| 4 | Brigham et al. (1972) | Elementary age boys | 13 | Adjustment class | Composition writing | Token reinforcement |
| 5 | Broden et al. (1970) | Adolescent boys and girls | 13 | Self-contained junior high classroom | Study behavior, nonstudy behavior | Differential attention, token reinforcement |
| 6 | Chan et al. (1970) | Elementary-age boy | 1 | Tutorial setting | Reading rate and comprehension, reading at home | Consumable reinforcers, social praise, peer competition |
| 7 | Clark et al. (1975) | Delinquent boys and girls | 6 | Community home | Writing biographical information | Instructional package, token reinforcement |
| 8 | Cohen & Filipczak (1971) | Delinquent boys | 25 | Correctional institution | Standard achievement scores, IQ score | Token reinforcement |
| 9 | Cotler et al. (1972) | Adolescent boys | 8 | Psychiatric hospital | Study behavior, quantity of academic work, quality of academic work | Token reinforcement, consumable reinforcers |

| | Study | Subjects | N | Setting | Target behavior | Intervention |
|---|---|---|---|---|---|---|
| 10 | Graubard (1969) | Adolescent boys | 8 | Residential | Appropriate classroom behavior, inappropriate classroom behavior, reading grade level | Individual and group token reinforcement |
| 11 | Grimm et al. (1973) | Elementary-age boys | 2 | Demonstration class | Arithmetic problem solving | Task sequencing, token reinforcement, teacher attention, self-verbalization |
| 12 | Hall et al. (1971) | Adolescent boy | 1 | Self-contained junior high classroom | Talk-outs | Differential attention |
| 13 | Harris et al. (1975) | Delinquent boys | 5 | Community home | Academic assignments completed, semester grade averages | Home token reinforcement program |
| 14 | Haubrich & Shores (1976) | Elementary-age boys | 5 | Residential treatment center | Attend to task, reading comprehension | Environmental restructuring, token reinforcement |
| 15 | Heaton et al. (1976) | Adolescents | 14 | Junior high special class | Reading, arithmetic, and spelling standard scores, school suspensions and expulsions, disruptive behavior | Token reinforcement |
| 16 | Hundert et al. (1976) | Elementary-age boys | 5 | Psychiatric hospital | Arithmetic rate and accuracy, appropriate classroom behavior | Token reinforcement |
| 17 | Hundert & Batstone (1978) | Elementary-age boys | 5 | Psychiatric hospital | Arithmetic performance, accuracy of self-reports | Token reinforcement, self-evaluation |
| 18 | Kaufman, & O'Leary (1972) | Adolescent boys | 16 | Psychiatric hospital | Disruptive behavior, academic assignments completed, standard reading achievement test | Token reward, token cost, self-evaluation |

*(continued)*

**TABLE 1** (continued)

| Identifying Number | Authors and Date | Subjects | N | Setting | Behavior(s) | Treatment(s) |
|---|---|---|---|---|---|---|
| 19 | Lovitt (1973) | Elementary-age boys and girls | 7 | Demonstration class, regular class | Rate and accuracy of academic work, classroom deportment | Self-management |
| 20 | Lovitt & Curtiss (1968) | Elementary-age boy | 1 | Demonstration class | Arithmetic rate and accuracy | Self-verbalization |
| 21 | Lovitt & Curtiss (1969) | Elementary-age boy | 1 | Demonstration class | Academic response rate | Student- versus teacher-determined scheduling |
| 22 | MacDonald et al. (1970) | Adolescent boys, chronic truants | 6 | Special motivation classroom in junior high school | School attendance | Community-based token reinforcement |
| 23 | Marholin & Steinman (1977) | Elementary-age boys | 8 | Special class | Arithmetic response rate and accuracy, ontask, disruptive behaviors | Token reinforcement, teacher presence or absence |
| 24 | Marholin et al. (1974) | Preadolescent and adolescent boys | 3 | Residential treatment center | Academic accuracy | Activity reinforcement |
| 25 | Marholin et al. (1975) | Preadolescent and adolescent boys and girls | 6 | Residential treatment center | Academic accuracy, disruptive behaviors, ontask | Token reinforcement, teacher presence or absence |
| 26 | McCarty et al. (1977) | Adolescents | 4 | Psychiatric hospital | Multiplication facts | Group oriented token reinforcement |
| 27 | Meichenbaum et al. (1968) | Delinquent girls | 10 | Remedial classroom in a training school | Inappropriate classroom behavior, appropriate classroom behavior | Token reinforcement |

| | | | | | |
|---|---|---|---|---|---|
| 28 | Minkin et al. (1976) | Delinquent girls | 4 | Community home | Conversational skills | Instructional package, token reinforcement |
| 29 | Phillips (1968) | Predelinquent boys | 3 | Community home | Homework | Token reinforcement |
| 30 | Phillips et al. (1971) | Predelinquent boys | 4 | Community home | Watching news program, current events quiz | Token reward, token response cost |
| 31 | Polirstok & Greer (1977) | Adolescent girl | 1 | Junior high school | Approval and disapproval statement of teacher, approval and disapproval statements of student | Students as change agents |
| 32 | Quay et al. (1972) | Elementary-age boys and girls | 69[a] 48[b] | Resource class | Academic achievement, ontask | Token reinforcement |
| 33 | Rickard et al. (1970) | Elementary-age and preadolescent boys | 5 | Remedial class in a summer camp | Arithmetic accuracy | Token reinforcement |
| 34 | Rickard et al. (1973) | Elementary-age and preadolescent boys and girls | 32 | Remedial class in a summer camp | Academic rate and accuracy | Token reinforcement |
| 35 | Rosenberg & Graubard (1975) | Adolescent boys | 7 | Junior high school | Praise rates, negative comments, and punishing statements of teachers | Students as change agents |
| 36 | Santogrossi et al. (1973) | Adolescent boys | 9 | Psychiatric hospital | Disruptive behavior | Self-evaluation, teacher-determined versus student-determined token reinforcement |
| 37 | Schumaker et al. (1977) | Adolescent boys | 3 | Junior high school | Rules followed, classroom work completed, teacher | Home-based token reinforcement |

(continued)

**TABLE 1** *(continued)*

| Identifying Number | Authors and Date | Subjects | N | Setting | Behavior(s) | Treatment(s) |
|---|---|---|---|---|---|---|
| | | | | | satisfaction, semester grade average | |
| 38 | Seymour & Stokes (1976) | Delinquent girls | 4 | Vocational class in institution | Work behavior, production units completed, positive verbal statements of students, and staff praise | Self-recording, token reinforcement |
| 39 | Staats & Butterfield (1965) | Delinquent boy | 1 | High school | Number of words read, reading comprehension, number of stories read, reading grade level, and school behavior | Token reinforcement |
| 40 | Staats et al. (1967) | Adolescent boys and girls | 11 | Special class | Number of words read, reading comprehension, reading grade level | Token reinforcement |
| 41 | Thomas et al. (1969) | Elementary-aged boy | 1 | Regular class | Oral reading, reading comprehension, disruptive behavior | Token reinforcement |
| 42 | Tyler (1967) | Delinquent boy | 1 | Residential treatment center | Classroom "effort" | Token reinforcement |

| 43 | Tyler & Brown (1968) | Delinquent boys | 15 | Residential treatment center | Current events quiz | Token reinforcement |
| 44 | Zimmerman & Zimmerman (1962) | Elementary-age boy | 1 | Residential treatment center | Spelling responses | Differential reinforcement |

[a]Experimental.
[b]Control.

ments in the other academic subjects were also noted, even though free time was contingent only upon reading. As a result, phase one and phase two treatment procedures did not differentially affect academic improvement, although both were superior to baseline.

Social attention from the teacher and access to preferred activities are resources that pervade educational situations for the behaviorally disordered and can readily be made contingent upon desired academic or other behavior of pupils. Experimental analyses have repeatedly shown that these two resources can reinforce academic improvement of normal and deviant children (e.g., Evans & Oswalt, 1968; Kirby & Shields, 1972; Lovitt, Guppy, & Blattner, 1969; Patterson, 1965). Therefore, research is needed to explore applications and variations of social and activity reinforcement programs to enhance the academic skills of behaviorally disordered pupils.

**Token reinforcers**

Available applied behavior analysis research indicates that token reinforcement has been the predominant procedure used to alter academic skills of behaviorally disordered students. Token reinforcement procedures have been applied within individual tutorial sessions, small group situations, total classrooms, and large-scale resource programs.

Much of our understanding about the relationship of behavioral principles to cognitive and academic performance comes from the work of Staats, who developed a research-based theory of learning which addresses the acquisition, mastery, and remediation of academic skills (Staats, 1968, 1971, 1973; Staats, Brewer, & Gross, 1970). In much of this research, token reinforcers were used to motivate student performance across many teaching sessions. In an early applied study, Staats and Butterfield (1965) taught reading to a 14-year-old behaviorally disordered delinquent youth using a programmed reading curriculum adapted for use with token reinforcers. The tutorial reading program, in which tokens were delivered contingent on appropriate oral reading, silent reading, reading comprehension, and vocabulary, was in effect over a 4.5-month period for approximately one hour per day. The authors reported substantial improvement in the student's performance: he learned and retained many new words, his reading achievement level increased almost 2.5 years, he passed all of his school courses for the first time, and his school misbehaviors were eliminated. Extensions of this pioneering effort have included training paraprofessionals to conduct a similar reading tutorial program. For instance, Staats, Minke, Goodwin, and Landeen (1967) trained volunteers to administer the token program to behaviorally disordered junior high school students with reading disorders. Educationally significant reading gains were recorded for participating students. Thomas, Neilsen, Kuypers, and Becker (1969) also utilized the procedures developed by Staats to teach reading to a six-year-old behaviorally disordered student. Increases in reading accuracy and rate, and decreases in disruptive behavior were associated with implementation of the program.

Token reinforcement procedures for academic improvement have also been applied to groups of pupils. For example, Rickard, Clements, and Willis (1970) used token reinforcers to improve the arithmetic performance of five behaviorally disordered children attending a therapeutic summer camp. Students could earn tokens for completing a predetermined number of frames in a programmed arithmetic text, and additional tokens were available for satisfactory performance on in-program tests. Compared to a no-token baseline period, arithmetic productivity increased substantially when token reinforcement contingencies were applied. Additional evidence of effectiveness was suggested by pupil gains in arithmetic proficiency on a standardized achievement test. In a related study with emotionally disturbed campers (Rickard, Melvin, Creel, & Creel, 1973), it was found that placing the token contingency upon improvement (exceeding the median number of frames completed on three prior days) produced better results than placing the contingency upon actual frames completed.

Token reinforcement was adapted for use in resource room services to elementary-age children with behavior disorders by Quay, Glavin, Annesley, and Werry (1972). Their large-scale research project featured token reinforcement to encourage appropriate academic behaviors such as starting, continuing work on, and completing academic tasks assigned to students working in the resource classroom. Daily resource sessions lasted 60 minutes; students had to work during the first three 15-minute segments of the session, thus accumulating tokens. During the final quarter of the session, a student could either exchange tokens for rewards, or continue working to earn additional tokens. The majority of participating students attended one resource session daily for reading instruction, although a few students attended an additional daily arithmetic session or the arithmetic session only. This resource room procedure was in effect for virtually the entire school year in three separate schools. Dependent variables included an attention-to-task measure that was repeatedly recorded for the experimental pupils both in the resource room and in their regular classrooms, and for behaviorally disordered control pupils who did not take part in the experimental resource room program; there was also pre- and postexperiment achievement testing with a standardized instrument.

Results of this study show that on the attention-to-task variable, experimental pupils were much improved while functioning in their special resource room as compared both to their own performance in the regular classes and to the control pupils' performance in regular classes. More importantly, the reading and arithmetic achievement of the experimental pupils exceeded that of the control pupils to a degree that was both statistically significant and educationally important (experimental pupils showed about a 1-year improvement in both reading and arithmetic, gains exceeding average gains shown by their schools as a whole). This report indicated the efficacy of a token-based resource room for the behaviorally disordered, as implemented on a large scale in an applied educational setting. The experimental design used by Quay et al. (1972) did not permit an analysis of the token procedures alone, but only the entire experimental resource room of which token reinforcement was obviously a crucial component.

Token programs have also been applied to the teaching of more complex academic skills. For example, Brigham, Graubard, and Stans (1972) used token reinforcement to modify compositional writing skills of 13 students in a special adjustment class. These pupils received tokens for appropriate social behavior during a baseline period, whereas during treatment they could maximize their tokens by producing compositions that were more "creative" (contained more words, more difficult words, and more new words). The token contingencies clearly increased the number of words in the pupils' compositions, although its effects upon the number of different words and new words were equivocal. Furthermore, the students' compositions improved substantially in overall quality: trained judges who rated the compositions on specific compositional features found those written during the token reinforcement intervention superior to those written during baseline.

Another complex skill trained through token reinforcement procedures is knowledge of current events. Working with juvenile delinquents, Tyler and Brown (1968) found that tokens awarded contingent upon accurate responses to questions based on the previous night's televised newscast produced greater response accuracy than noncontingent tokens. In a similar study, Phillips, Phillips, Fixsen, and Wolf (1971) compared the effects of token reward, token cost, and combined token reward and cost procedures on the accuracy of delinquents' responses to questions developed from recent newscasts. The combined reward and cost procedure was best for increasing the number of youths who watched the evening news and for maximizing their accuracy on daily current events tests.

The use of token reinforcement procedures with the behaviorally disordered does not invariably produce desired academic improvements. This is shown by a report on a token reinforcement program in a classroom for institutionalized disturbed boys (Cotler, Applegate, King, & Kristal, 1972). Consultation was given to the classroom teacher regarding how to set up a management system in which social, consumable, and token reinforcers were to be contingent upon a pupil's showing appropriate study behavior, completing arithmetic problems, and working the problems accurately. Although the experimenters were satisfied with the power of the program to produce improved study behavior, improvements in quantity and quality of work output were inconsistent, and indeed tended to deteriorate during some treatment phases. The authors cited several factors that might have accounted for their mixed success.

On balance, however, the available evidence indicates that token reinforcement programs can be powerful and flexible educative tools for teachers of behaviorally disordered pupils. Thus, the literature on token reinforcement for improving academic functioning of the behaviorally disordered is generally in harmony with similar research available on retarded pupils (e.g., Birnbrauer, Wolf, Kidder, & Tague, 1965), underachievers (e.g., Wolf, Giles, & Hall, 1968), the culturally disadvantaged (e.g., Clark, Lachowicz, & Wolf, 1968), and nonhandicapped pupils in regular classrooms (e.g., McLaughlin, 1975).

**Reciprocity of disturbance and academic performance**

Classroom applications of behavioral principles have largely been directed toward reducing disruption or increasing ontask behavior, and a variety of procedures have been shown to be effective in promoting task-oriented pupil behavior. However, research has also shown that such behavioral improvements do not necessarily lead to beneficial changes in academic functioning (e.g., Ferritor, Buckholdt, Hamblin, & Smith, 1972). On the other hand, a number of recent studies with nondisturbed pupils have shown that behavioral procedures intended to strengthen academic functioning also promote improvements in classroom conduct (e.g., Ayllon & Roberts, 1974; Kirby & Shields, 1972). Because behaviorally disordered pupils frequently evidence serious problems in both classroom conduct and academic achievement (Kauffman, 1977; Ross, 1974), studies of this population that address the interrelationship of these two behavior patterns are of particular interest.

Hundert, Bucher, and Henderson (1976) studied both appropriate behavior and academic performance in five boys during arithmetic period in a psychiatric hospital school classroom. The effects of reinforcement for appropriate behavior were contrasted to those of reinforcement for academic performance. Compared to a no-reinforcement baseline, the appropriate-behavior contingency increased appropriate behavior but had a negligible effect on arithmetic accuracy; the performance-accuracy contingency substantially increased both appropriate behavior and correctness. Similarly, Haubrich and Shores (1976) contrasted student use of study cubicles to reinforcement contingent on correct reading comprehension performance, with respect to the effect of each intervention upon attention-to-task and level of correctness on reading comprehension. Compared to baseline conditions, both the cubicle and the academic-performance contingency conditions increased attending (although reinforcement was more effective than the cubicle); only the performance-accuracy contingency, however, increased reading comprehension.

This type of research was substantially extended by Marholin and his associates (Marholin & Steinman, 1977; Marholin, Steinman, McInnis, & Heads, 1975); they compared an ontask contingency to an academic-performance contingency for their effects upon the conduct and academic functioning of pupils in a classroom for the behaviorally disordered, both while the teacher was present and when she left the children on their own in the classroom. Not unexpectedly, the teacher's absence led to less ontask behavior and more disruption; however, the students' inappropriate behavior was at a substantially lower level when they were being reinforced for academic performance. The Marholin studies suggest that procedures in which a behaviorally disordered pupil is reinforced for competent academic functioning, rather than for desirable classroom conduct, not only are likely to "kill two birds with one stone" (increase appropriate behavior as well as academic performance), but may also aid the pupil to become more independent of teacher surveillance.

Studies with behaviorally disordered (Hundert et al., 1976; Marholin & Steinman, 1977; Marholin et al., 1975) and nondisturbed (e.g., Ayllon & Roberts, 1974; Kirby & Shields, 1972) pupils suggest that a positive relationship between academic performance and classroom deportment may be obtained when the reinforcement contingency is placed upon academic performance but not when placed on deportment. It also appears that the focus on improved academic functioning can improve the conduct of behaviorally disordered pupils in the absence of the teacher; if so, this type of research into maintaining behavioral improvement needs to be pursued.

**Self-control**

The issue of pupil self-control has been addressed from a broad range of viewpoints (e.g., Fagen, Long, & Stevens, 1975; Polsgrove, 1977), including the behavioral model (e.g., Mahoney, 1974; Thoresen & Mahoney, 1974). Problems in defining and experimentally demonstrating self-control have been extensively discussed elsewhere (e.g., Bandura, 1971). In applied behavior analysis, self-control is generally dealt with through demonstrations that by engaging in certain behaviors a pupil can improve his own functioning in other behaviors. Various self-management procedures have been shown to affect favorably pupil conduct and/or academics (e.g., Glynn & Thomas, 1974). There are relatively few studies of behaviorally disordered pupils' self-management of academic responding, however.

In three separate studies, Lovitt and Curtiss (1968) investigated the effects of self-verbalization on various aspects of the arithmetic performance of a behaviorally disordered student. Initially, the student was requested merely to write the answer to each of the arithmetic problems. During treatment, the student was required to verbalize the problem aloud prior to writing the answer. In a follow-up baseline phase, the student was told to answer without any self-verbalization. Arithmetic performance improved when the self-verbalization treatment was introduced, and it continued to improve after the self-verbalization requirement was withdrawn. In a similar investigation, Grimm, Bijou, and Parsons (1973) reported a study in which two behaviorally disordered students were taught a self-verbalization problem-solving strategy to successfully complete number concept tasks. At first, intermittent reinforcement consisting of teacher attention was found to be maintaining the pupils' accuracy at about 50 percent correct. In the next phase, a one-to-one tutor–pupil arrangement with continuous reinforcement for correct responses, it was found that accuracy rates did not change. For the problem-solving strategy, those responses necessary to complete the tasks were identified and trained. Training consisted of requiring the students to verbalize the response chain while receiving social reinforcers for attending and token reinforcers for correct completion. Once a high degree of accuracy was obtained, the students were no longer required to make excessive use of the problem-solving technique. Fading of the problem-solving technique was not accompanied by a loss of accuracy. However, the research design used did not allow an analysis of the various teaching components.

In another series of investigations, Lovitt and Curtiss (1969) sought to determine the differential effects of teacher-imposed and student-imposed contingencies on a student in a self-contained behavioral disorders classroom. The dependent measure was rate of academic response, representing the student's performance in all daily scheduled academic areas. Results indicated that self-imposed contingencies led to higher rates of academic responding, even when the teacher-imposed contingencies were identical to those of the pupil.

The opportunity to engage in self-management has also been examined in terms of its reinforcing potential. In a series of self-management studies with learning and behaviorally disordered pupils (Lovitt, 1973), one project (Experiment II) was intended to compare the effects of pupil versus teacher scheduling on the reading accuracy of a behaviorally disordered pupil. Following a baseline period in which the teacher determined all activities, student scheduling of activities was contingently applied in a treatment phase: if the student did not exceed a predetermined level of errors in phonics instruction, he was allowed to schedule the order of the remaining five class activities. Student scheduling led to an acceleration in the rate of correct phonetic responses and a lower rate of incorrect responses. This study is not so much an investigation of self-control as an indication that student self-scheduling of daily activities may be preferred over teacher scheduling, and as such can be used to reinforce less preferred activities such as working on reading skills (cf. Homme, de Baca, Devine, Steinhorst, & Rickert, 1963).

One issue in self-management appears to be the accuracy of student self-recording. Informal observation, as well as some research evidence (e.g., Kaufman & O'Leary, 1972), indicates that errors, usually in a direction that puts oneself in a more favorable light, can often be found in pupil self-management. Thus, Hundert and Batstone (1978) investigated methods to ensure accuracy of behaviorally disordered children's self-reporting of academic success. Self-ratings of four students from a special class in a psychiatric hospital were studied under three sequentially introduced experimental conditions: (1) baseline, (2) reinforced self-recording, and (3) surveillance. Reinforced self-recording consisted of providing token reinforcers contingent on the number of correct arithmetic responses as recorded by a student. In the surveillance phase, students were additionally required to submit their workbooks to the teacher, and were told that tokens would be lost for inaccuracies. Arithmetic accuracy data showed that exaggerated reports of accuracy increased during the self-recording phase but decreased during the surveillance condition. More importantly, accuracy of academic responses increased during the surveillance phase.

Applied behavior analysis of self-control is not well developed at present. There is only a small body of literature on the effects of self-control procedures upon children's academic responding, and very few studies with behaviorally disordered pupils, despite widespread assertions that one main need of the behaviorally disordered is to develop self-control. Clearly, this area is in need of research attention.

**Summary**

In Table 2, behavioral interventions for improving academic functioning of behaviorally disordered pupils, as reviewed in this section, are depicted according to the chief intervention utilized and the variety of academic behavior modified. Even a cursory scanning of Table 2 reveals the areas in which research attention has been concentrated and those that have been neglected. As previously mentioned, the most frequently researched procedure has been some variety of token reinforcement. In fact, many studies categorized as featuring some other procedure actually utilized token reinforcement in addition to the more salient teaching strategy (e.g., Grimm et al., 1973). Thus, studies with the behaviorally disordered extend the general body of literature on token reinforcement for academic competence and further establish token reinforcement as a useful technique for academic remediation. Further research needs to build on this foundation in several ways.

First, token reinforcement subsumes numerous procedural variations that need to be examined more closely in the context of academic remediation: for example, comparisons of token earning versus cost versus combined procedures, various amounts of delay between token acquisition and exchange for backup resources, and contrasts of individual versus group performance requirements. Second, the record of success established for token reinforcement indicates that this technique may be used as a standard against which to evaluate other academic improvement procedures; that is, the comparative effects upon student academic performance of a standard token reinforcement procedure and of a new or unestablished strategy can be determined through some appropriate single-case experimental technique (for instance, one in which the token reinforcement condition serves as a baseline). Another area in need of research is the educational significance of specific behavior changes produced by token techniques. Although token reinforcement clearly can produce substantial changes in academic target responses, it still needs to be shown that the magnitude of an obtained improvement is sufficient to move the student's academic functioning to within the normal range, or at least represents distinct progress in that direction. This type of evaluation of teaching procedures, referred to as

## TABLE 2
## APPLIED BEHAVIOR ANALYSIS STUDIES WITH PUPILS WITH BEHAVIOR DISORDERS INDEXED BY
## INTERVENTION AND TARGET BEHAVIOR

| Intervention | Reading | Arithmetic | Spelling | Standardized achievement test | Complex academic skill | Academic performance |
|---|---|---|---|---|---|---|
| Social activity or consumable reinforcement | 6 | 11 | 44 | | | 24 |
| Token reinforcement | 17, 39, 40, 41 | 11, 17, 26, 33 | | 10, 15, 18, 32 | 4 | 9, 24, 34 |
| Reinforcement of academic responses to modify disruptive behavior | 14 | 16, 23 | | | | 25 |
| Self-control | 19 | 11, 17, 19, 20 | | | | 19, 21 |

*Note.* Numbers correspond to studies listed in Table 1.

"social validation," will be addressed in a later section of this chapter.

Available research does not support differential attention as an academic behavior modification technique for behaviorally disordered students, primarily because there is so little research in this area. The use of a free-time contingency to motivate work completion and accuracy has received some support. Self-control procedures have not been sufficiently investigated as yet, although available reports are promising—especially those in which the student is taught to engage in antecedent behaviors of a problem-solving or mnemonic nature prior to performance of the target response (e.g., Lovitt & Curtiss, 1968). Applied behavior analysis research with normal pupils and those identified as experiencing educational handicap other than behavior disorder suggests several additional academic instruction techniques of potential usefulness with the behaviorally disordered, including systematic antecedent control, contingency contracting, and overcorrection (e.g., Foxx & Jones, 1978; Haring, Lovitt, Eaton, & Hansen, 1978; Tharp & Wetzel, 1969). The insufficiency of research on any teaching procedure for academic behavior, aside from token reinforcement, must be redressed if behaviorally disordered pupils are to benefit from their "potential."

Most of the academic intervention procedures have been directed toward basic reading and computational skills. Handwriting, spelling, and oral communications are other varieties of basic educational skills in which behaviorally disordered pupils may show incompetence, and behavioral applications for improvement in these skills are needed. Attention must also be turned toward skill-building techniques for other school subjects, and effective procedures in this area are likely to be more complex than those used with the basic skills. Moreover, it is widely believed that behaviorally disordered pupils can benefit from participation in sex education, substance-abuse education, individual or group counseling procedures, classroom or school governance, physical education programs, and assorted other experiences; insofar as appropriate participation by a pupil in these activities can be empirically measured through direct observation or other techniques, behavioral interventions in these areas may be beneficial and should be experimentally examined.

## EDUCATING ADOLESCENTS

Early reports of behavioral interventions for adolescents typically involved juvenile delinquents, and a notable body of research has accumulated in this area (for reviews, see e.g., Braukmann & Fixsen, 1975;

Burchard & Harig, 1976; Davidson & Seidman, 1974). Some of these studies are directed to improving the educational performance of delinquents; more recently, behavioral approaches to educating behaviorally disordered adolescents other than delinquents have been reported, although the total number of relevant reports is still small. The principal behavioral treatments may be classified as social reinforcement, token reinforcement, group-oriented contingencies, home and community programs, self-control, instructional packages, and training youths to be behavior modifiers.

**Social reinforcement**

The effects of differential adult attention upon children's behavior is the most extensively studied behavioral intervention (Hersen & Barlow, 1976). This research has been predominantly concerned with elementary-age children, and very few studies with behaviorally disordered adolescent pupils are available. In one of these, the disruptive talkouts of a 13-year-old behaviorally disordered boy in a self-contained junior high school class were dramatically reduced by differential praise for low rates of talking out (Hall, et al., 1971). However, Broden, Hall, Dunlap, and Clark (1970) reported only partial success with a differential attention procedure. In an attempt to improve the classroom study behavior of a 13-year-old student in a self-contained behavioral disorders class, the authors found that while differential attention increased study behavior, frequent outbursts of disruptive behavior persisted. Only when a token reinforcement system was combined with differential teacher attention did the pupil's disruptiveness subside to an acceptable level. Thus it appears that differential attention can be effective with behaviorally disordered adolescent pupils, but the addition of other intervention procedures may be necessary. Parenthetically, considering the large number of reports of the effectiveness of differential teacher attention for improving the behavior of younger pupils, the scarcity of such applications to behaviorally disordered adolescent pupils suggests that the intervention may have been tried some number of times, found wanting, and not reported.

**Token reinforcement**

Token reinforcement has been used extensively with behaviorally disordered adolescents and predelinquent and delinquent youths to alter a wide variety of classroom-related behaviors including ontask behavior, studying, assignment completion, reading and arithmetic skills, academic proficiency, and verbal skills (see Kazdin, 1977, for an extensive review and evaluation of token programs). In an early investigation, Meichenbaum, Bowers, and Ross (1968) modified the classroom deportment of 10 delinquent girls. When a student exhibited task-appropriate behavior she was given feedback via a note from a classroom observer; and the notes were exchangeable for money at a later time. The authors found that appropriate classroom deportment increased when these experimental conditions were introduced.

Several programs have used token reinforcement to increase the quantity of academic work completed. Tyler (1967) provided tokens to a 16-year-old institutionalized delinquent for increased "effort" shown in the classroom, as determined by daily and weekly teacher evaluations. The tokens could be exchanged for special privileges within the institution. Results showed a clear increase in academic material completed and a slight increase in the student's semester grade average. Harris, Finfrock, Giles, Hart, and Tsosie (1975) contrasted social praise to token reinforcement procedures for modifying completion of assignments by five delinquent youths in a residential center. In the token program, students could earn points for completing all class assignments; points were withdrawn for incomplete assignments. This token program substantially increased the number of assignments completed and improved semester grade averages as well. Phillips (1968) reported a program that sought to increase the completion of academic assignments of three delinquents living in a community home. Four different contingencies were contrasted: (1) money for completed assignments, (2) weekly curfew extensions, (3) daily curfew extensions, and (4) points for completed assignments. Points were redeemable for privileges and amenities available in the family-style living situation. The point contingency condition was found to be superior to the other conditions, producing nearly total homework completion for all students.

Although the completion of academic work is important, the acquisition of academic skills and proficiencies is an even more critical goal for students. Token programs have been applied toward this goal with behaviorally disordered adolescents. In a report by Bednar, Zelhart, Greathouse, and Weinberg (1970), two groups of 16 delinquent pupils were exposed to a Staats and Butterfield (1965) type reading program. One group received tokens (money) for accurate reading, the other group did not. Both groups showed improvement during the reading program but the token group evidenced significantly superior improvement in word recognition and reading comprehension on a standardized achievement test. Additionally, teacher ratings of student persistence, attention, opinion of school, cooperation, and sociability favored the token group.

Other token programs for improving the academic performance of behaviorally disordered adolescents (reviewed previously) include those described by Brigham et al. (1972), Phillips et al. (1971), Staats and Butterfield (1965), Staats et al. (1967), and Tyler and Brown (1968).

Some of the most valuable token economy studies are those that have described and evaluated token reinforcement procedures to improve a variety of educationally critical behaviors within special classrooms for behaviorally disordered adolescent pupils. For example, Kaufman and O'Leary (1972) used token reinforcement procedures to encourage appropriate conduct and productive effort in remedial reading classes for adolescent pupils in psychiatric hospital classrooms. Their program markedly reduced disruptive behavior and increased reading skills in these pupils. Furthermore, Kaufman and O'Leary (1972) contrasted reward versus cost token procedures, that is, one in which pupils earned tokens for appropriate behavior versus one in which pupils started with tokens but lost them for inappropriate behavior. This careful evaluative study revealed that (1) there were no notable differential effects of the two procedures upon pupil behaviors, (2) there were no harmful side effects of the token punishment procedure (response cost), and (3) when responsibility for performance evaluation and token allocation was given over to the pupils themselves, inappropriate behavior remained at low levels.

In another classroom-scale study, Heaton, Safer, Allen, Spinnato, and Prumo (1976) utilized a quasi-experimental design to examine the efficacy of a junior high special classroom for pupils with extended records of discipline problems. Identified pupils at one school were assigned to a token reinforcement classroom, whereas comparison students at two other schools remained in regular classrooms. Students in the token classroom received praise and tokens contingent on starting, continuing, and completing academic work, and on appropriate social behavior; other procedures such as contingency contracting and "individualized instruction" were also in evidence in this token classroom. The students exchanged points for afternoon access to a game room, early school dismissal, or other attractive rewards; also, their parents were encouraged to establish home-based contingency programs. End of the year comparisons on conduct and academic variables favored the experimental groups. Token classroom students were less likely to be absent from school, terminate school enrollment, be sent to the principal's office, or be suspended; they were also superior to the controls in reading achievement, although not in spelling and arithmetic achievement.

CASE-II was a behaviorally based intervention into juvenile delinquency located at the federal National Training School for Boys (Cohen & Filipczak, 1971). In CASE-II, virtually all activities of participant youths were regulated through point and other contingency systems, with educational activities as the major focus. Youths took part in individualized programs geared for improvement in academic and other skills intended to improve their chances for proper adjustment following release. Self-instructional materials and programs were widely used for teaching academics; they allowed the youths to be free to pace their own participation and mastery of educational goals. Points earned through demonstrations of mastery of educational skills and through performance of noneducational behaviors were used by the boys to purchase desired items, special privileges, amenities of life at CASE-II (e.g., a private room rather than dormitory sleeping arrangements, noninstitutional clothing, etc.), extra visitation or furlough rights, money, and so on. Outcome evaluation data showed that CASE-II youths achieved between 1 and 2 years growth in academics (prorated for a year; average stay in CASE-II was 7 months) and gained, on the average, over 10 points on IQ test scores. They also showed lower recidivism rates than other national training school youths.

Behaviorally disordered adolescents have occasionally conducted token reinforcement educative programs for their peers. Bailey, Timbers, Phillips, and Wolf (1971) had delinquent youths conduct speech therapy for peers with articulation disorders. In these sessions, the peer therapists modeled correct pronunciations, provided approval for correct pronunciation by their clients, corrected articulation errors, and determined point earnings for their peer clients. Not only did this intervention produce decreases in articulation errors, the improvement generalized to untreated words and sentences and to standard tests of articulation.

In summary, educational programs based on token reinforcement have been used to improve academic skills, conduct problems, and other behaviors relevant to the normalization of behaviorally disordered adolescents. These programs have been implemented in junior and senior high school tutorial and classroom settings and in correctional facilities for delinquent youths.

## Group-oriented contingencies

In a group-oriented contingency, the consequences for an entire group of individuals are determined by the performance of a particular member of the group (dependent group contingency) or by the performance of the group as a whole (interdependent group contingency). For extensive discussions of group-oriented contingencies, see Litow and Pumroy (1975) and McLaughlin (1974).

McCarty, Griffin, Apolloni, and Shores (1977) applied group-oriented contingencies to improve arithmetic computational skills of behaviorally disordered adolescents in a residential setting. Two types of interdependent group-oriented contingencies were examined: "cumulative" and "mixed." In the cumulative condition, four students earned monetary reinforcers for each problem worked correctly by each member; in the mixed condition, an additional requirement was that in order for any student to receive his earnings, each of the four had to solve at least three problems correctly. Both contingencies produced clear improvements in the student's arithmetic performance.

Group-oriented contingencies have also been used in conjunction with the more common individual contingencies. For instance, Graubard (1969) studied various intervention procedures for modifying academic and social behavior of eight behaviorally disordered adolescents who were under court-ordered residential therapy. The school day for these boys included periods in which structured reading and arithmetic lessons were presented, as well as other educational subjects and activities. Appropriate conduct and task-oriented behavior were encouraged through teacher praise and exhortation and additionally, during various treatment phases, by an interdependent group-oriented contingency or the interdependent contingency plus individual contingencies for each pupil. The group contingency involved points dispensed to the group if all pupils were behaving appropriately when a "bonus bell" rang; the bonus bell rang at variable time intervals that were not predictable by the pupils (similar to "good behavior games", e.g., Wolf, Hanley, King, Lachowicz, & Giles, 1970). Group reinforcers were only given if every student in the group achieved a minimum number of points. In the group-plus-individual contingency condition, each student could also achieve individually selected rewards based solely on his own appropriate behavior. The group contingency produced more appropriate and less inappropriate student behavior than the no-contingency condition; even greater behavioral gains were achieved in the group-plus-individual contingencies condition. The research design used did not permit a direct comparison of the two treatments, however.

Group-oriented contingencies can be practical and economical teaching procedures for classrooms or other groups of pupils. Most investigations of group contingencies have involved younger pupils (see, e.g., Litow & Pumroy, 1975); research needs to be extended to behaviorally disordered adolescent pupils.

**Home- and community-based interventions**

Intervention programs based on applied behavior analysis principles can be found in which appropriate school functioning of behaviorally disordered adolescents is encouraged through contingencies that are managed by individuals in the pupil's home or community environment. For example, parents, surrogate parents, or other individuals may deliver token reinforcement and provide other consequences based on behavior occurring at school. Bailey, Wolf, and Phillips (1970) worked with five predelinquent youths residing at a community group-home treatment setting and attending local schools. Each boy was required to carry a daily report card with him to school, and his teacher marked it according to whether or not he studied and obeyed classroom rules. Upon return home, points required to purchase privileges and other rewards were awarded by the group-home managers if the report card indicated that the student had behaved appropriately at school; otherwise home privileges were lost. This procedure improved the boys' conduct in school; furthermore, the pupils' behavioral improvements were maintained even when the feedback and reinforcement system was changed from a daily to an intermittent basis.

Similarly, Schumaker, Hovell, and Sherman (1977) helped the parents of three behaviorally disordered junior high school students implement a home-based token reinforcement program for school performance. A school counselor taught the parents the basic rules of contingency management and assisted in the negotiation of home contingencies. Students were required to take a daily report card to each teacher (six per student) for marking of a daily grade; parental praise and home privileges were contingent on school conduct and classwork as indicated by the daily grades. This program increased the percentage of rules followed, the amount of schoolwork completed, and the semester grade averages of each of the students. In a subsequent experiment, these authors found that the success of the program was detrimentally affected by deletion of the home privilege backup reinforcers, and that, at least in the initial stages of the program, parental praise yielded only limited success.

Parents may not always be the most suitable candidates for the implementation of contingency management programs; other family or community persons of importance to the student may also serve in this capacity. For example, MacDonald, Gallimore, and MacDonald (1970) described a project to improve the school attendance of six chronic truants enrolled in a special education motivation class. An attendance counselor contacted significant individuals who might be able and willing to make readily available incentives contingent upon improved school attendance by the students. The counselor assisted these "mediators" to negotiate a school attendance "deal" with the student, in which the contingent relationship between school attendance and reinforcers was made explicit. Results of this study indicated noteworthy increases in school attendance for the students involved upon implementation of this program. The MacDonald et al. (1970) use of significant community individuals as mediators was based on the classic report of a large-scale social casework project for behaviorally disordered children and youth that utilized behavioral principles—the Behavior Research Project (Tharp & Wetzel, 1969).

The home and community studies suggest that educationally important behavior of behaviorally disordered adolescents can be developed through programs in which contingencies are implemented by persons found in the student's home or community. One might speculate that this type of intervention program could have benefits beyond the educational behaviors targeted for change, because mediators trained to implement specific contingencies may come to adopt contingency management as a general strategy for dealing with behaviorally disordered pupils in diverse situations. This potentially important treatment direction is clearly in need of further research.

### Self-control

Interest in behavioral approaches to promoting self-control has, in a few cases, extended to the investigation of such processes in behaviorally disordered adolescents. Santogrossi, O'Leary, Romanczyk, and Kaufman (1973) taught nine adolescent male pupils enrolled in a remedial class in a psychiatric hospital to evaluate their own behavior during class sessions. As a result, the pupils' self-evaluations correlated very closely with teacher evaluations, but the procedure did not reduce disruptive behavior. However, upon implementation of a conventional token reinforcement program in this classroom, disruptive behavior was dramatically decreased. In a second self-control study, Seymour and Stokes (1976) taught four delinquent girls in a vocational education situation to self-record their work-related behavior and the statements they made to staff members that called attention to the work that they were doing ("cues"). A therapist provided tokens to the girls contingent upon their accurate self-recording. Compared to the baseline condition, in which tokens were provided directly for work-related behaviors, the self-recording procedure increased work behavior and work completed. Furthermore, the self-recording increased the number of cues made by the girls to the staff and increased staff praise of the girls' work. These desirable student and staff behaviors were generally maintained at the increased rate when the token reinforcers were eliminated in a final phase of the study.

The shortage of research in this area precludes general conclusions, but it does appear that self-management procedures in the absence of reinforcement contingencies are unlikely to be successful (e.g., Fixsen, Phillips, & Wolf, 1972; Santogrossi et al., 1973); they can be strengthened with the addition of a token reinforcement component (which can eventually be removed) (Seymour & Stokes, 1976). Given that the importance of self-control among children and adolescents is widely accepted, further investigation of self-control procedures with behaviorally disordered adolescents is clearly required.

### Instructional packages

Instructional packages are composite treatment programs that feature several distinguishable teaching components. For example, "reinforced modeling" is a package that may include many treatment components, such as specific instructions with rationale, instructor demonstration, coperformance of instructor and client, client performance with feedback, corrections, and reinforcement, videotaped self-evaluation, and practice in the natural environment (Bandura, 1976). Designed to teach a specific skill, an instructional package is used without particular concern for identifying which of its various components lead to behavioral change (Kazdin & Wilson, 1978). Among the available instructional packages are ones to teach creative writing (Brigham, Graubard, & Stans, 1972), handwriting (Brigham, Finfrock, Breunig, & Busell, 1972), spelling (Lovitt, et al., 1969), and other academic and vocationally related skills. Fortunately, there are a few studies in which instructional packages for behaviorally disordered adolescents have been evaluated.

For example, Clark, Boyd, and Macrae (1975) trained six pupils in a special education class for delinquent youths to provide the common autobiographical information needed to complete job applications. The instructional package featured the teacher demonstrating the correct responses and leaving a permanent example for observation, student practice of correct responses with and without the presence of the example, immediate correction of errors, and token reinforcement for correct performance. This procedure successfully taught nine critical autobiographical items (e.g., name, birthdate, address, information about references). The students learned the items and how to use the information correctly in completing job applications. Similarly, the conversational skills of delinquent girls were modified through a modeling-based instructional package (Minkin et al., 1976). The four subjects were taught to ask conversationally appropriate questions and provide positive verbal feedback to adults through a training package composed of verbal instructions with a rationale, modeling of the desired conversational skills, directed practice with verbal feedback, and reinforcement for desired performance. Results showed that the conversational skills of these girls was substantially improved by the treatment, and furthermore, that these skills reached levels superior to those of normal girls of the same age.

Instructional packages for behaviorally disordered adolescents appear to be promising enough to encourage additional applied research, particularly because they may be superior to reinforcement for the remediation of some behavior disorders. How instruction packages may best be combined with reinforcement or other educative procedures, how best to sequence components of a complex behavior that is to be learned, and what verbal or other memory-enhancing strategies can facilitate acquisition and ensure maintenance of complex skills are some of the issues that need to be addressed by applied behavior analysis research into educative procedures for behaviorally disordered adolescents.

## Changing the change agent

In most educational procedures the change target is the behavior of a student. In a behavioral approach, teachers, parents, and even peers are therefore trained to restructure environmental contingencies that will induce and encourage more desirable behavior on the part of the student. At times, such training may be unfeasible or impossible due to the unavailability of trainers, time and expense factors, resistance to trying new teaching procedures, or other reasons. Alternatively, deviant students may be trained to modify the behavior of teachers and peers in ways that might subsequently improve the behavior of the deviant pupils themselves.

For example, Rosenberg and Graubard (1975) trained seven behaviorally disordered pupils in a self-contained classroom to modify the behavior of regular class teachers (two per student) with whom they were mainstreamed. Through individual and group verbal instruction in behavioral principles, repeated practice of these principles, simulation and role playing, and videotaped critiques, the students were trained to reinforce favorable and ignore negative behaviors on the part of their mainstream teachers. For appropriate teacher behavior, the students would praise and express pleasure (e.g., "Gee, it makes me feel good and work so much better when you praise me"). They would also nonverbally reinforce their teachers (sit up straight, make eye contact) contingent upon specified appropriate teaching practices. Furthermore, they were taught to break eye contact or otherwise ignore undesirable teacher behavior, such as provocations. The authors reported that this training produced therapeutic significant increases in positive teacher–student contacts and decreases in negative ones. In a second experiment, the emotionally handicapped pupils were similarly taught to use behavioral principles to improve the behavior of their normal classmates. While the Rosenberg and Graubard (1975) report indicated that the favorable changes in teacher and peer behavior were not maintained once the behaviorally disordered pupils ceased their reinforcement procedures, other reports (e.g., Polirstok & Greer, 1977) indicate that such changes in teacher behavior can be durable. The previously described study by Seymour and Stokes (1976) also provided evidence that staff members improved in their treatment of behaviorally disordered pupils as a function of cueing procedures undertaken by the pupils.

### Summary

Table 3 presents reports of behavioral interventions for adolescent behaviorally disordered students according to treatment techniques and target performance. The uneven distribution of available investigations indicates some of the needed directions for research. Token reinforcement is the most frequently reported procedure, and available research fairly clearly demonstrates that token programs are generally effective in improving various behaviors relevant to the education of behaviorally disordered adolescents. Token reinforcement procedures are actually more prevalent than indicated in Table 3 because treatment procedures classified under other headings frequently included token contingencies as an integral feature.

Research on token procedures for educating behaviorally disordered adolescents can probably now move beyond demonstrations that these procedures can work to the careful examination of other issues. For example, the various possible components of these token programs (e.g., instructions, feedback, manner of token delivery, response cost features, and other components) need to be analyzed for the purpose of streamlining teaching procedures. Additionally, behavior changes brought about in a token program need to be studied with regard to their durability as the program is removed: various techniques to facilitate

# TABLE 3
## APPLIED BEHAVIOR ANALYSIS STUDIES ON ADOLESCENT PUPILS INDEXED BY INTERVENTION AND EDUCATIONAL TARGET BEHAVIOR

| Intervention | Attendance | Classroom deportment | Completed academic assignments | Academic skills and proficiency | Standardized achievement tests G.P.A.* | Oral communication skills | Statements of others |
|---|---|---|---|---|---|---|---|
| Nontoken reinforcement | | 5, 9, 12 | | 24 | | | |
| Token reinforcement | | 3, 5, 9, 18, 15, 25, 27, 36, 38, 39, 42 | 9, 18, 29, 38 | 3, 7, 9, 25, 30, 39, 40, 43 | 3, 8, 15, 18, 39, 40 | 2, 28, 38 | 38 |
| Group-oriented contingencies | | 10 | | 10, 26 | | | |
| Home- and community-based instruction | 22 | 1, 37 | 13, 37 | | 13, 37 | | |
| Self-control | | 18, 36, 38 | 38 | | | | 38 |
| Instructional packages | | | | 7 | | 28 | |
| Students as change agents | | 31 | | | | | 31, 35 |

Note. Numbers correspond to studies listed in Table 1.
*G.P.A. is student's grade point average.

maintenance (e.g., Stokes & Baer, 1977) have to be studied with behaviorally disordered adolescents in educational settings. Earlier it was pointed out that token programs have been used successfully to improve basic academic skills; the need for research that extends such procedures to more complex skills and other school subjects is particularly crucial to behaviorally disordered adolescents, because, of course, these pupils are expected to achieve in a wide range of advanced informational, problem-solving, and performance proficiencies. For example, vocational–career education for educationally handicapped adolescents (Brolin & Brolin, 1979; Cegelka, 1979) is an area in which the usefulness of token reinforcement programs needs to be experimentally examined. Other research considerations in the remedial use of token economies have been discussed by Kazdin (1977).

Although differential teacher attention has proven to be very powerful with younger pupils, beneficial effects of this technique have not been apparent with behaviorally disordered adolescents. It is possible that the reinforcing value of attention from adults for such individuals is superceded by that from peers, or that many disturbed adolescents associate adult attention more closely with punishment than with reinforcement. At any rate, available studies indicate that the conditions under which differential attention will reliably reinforce desirable educational behaviors of behaviorally disordered adolescents remain unknown; this is an unfortunate situation because differential attention can be implemented so readily and inexpensively. Research is needed to determine how differential attention can be used successfully either alone or as a supplement to other treatments; it may, for instance, be useful in maintaining behavioral gains originally brought about through other treatments.

The findings on group-oriented contingencies are suggestive enough to encourage additional research along several lines. First, it is of interest to compare group versus individual versus combined contingencies. Furthermore, several different types of group-oriented contingencies have been developed (e.g., Litow & Pumroy, 1975); the relative effectiveness, for various educational goals, of dependent, independent, and interdependent group-oriented contingencies ought to be determined. Group-oriented motivational techniques with behaviorally disordered adolescents need to be researched with regard to their potential detrimental effects. For example, O'Leary and Drabman (1971) noted that some students may be unable to perform the behaviors required, and some may be more reinforced by undermining the procedure or preventing the group's achieving criterion than by the rewards available; also, one might suspect that threats and other pressures on an individual student may pose a particular problem with behaviorally disordered adolescents.

The scarcity of experimental evaluations of self-control allows only limited discussion. It appears that among disturbed adolescents, self-management procedures are unlikely to be successful alone; at least in the initiation of a self-control program, some strong behavioral teaching procedure such as token reinforcement seems to be required. It may be that self-management can aid in maintaining behavioral changes as other teacher-managed techniques are phased out (Kaufman & O'Leary, 1972).

The few studies of instructional packages to teach complex responses are promising. Further research must examine the contribution of various components to the overall effectiveness of a package; for instance, the necessity of a token reinforcement component in such packages is of interest. Clearly, however, research on instructional packages for specific skills related to adjustment and survival should be continued and extended to a wide assortment of adaptive behavior patterns needed by behaviorally disordered adolescents.

## IMPORTANT RESEARCH DIRECTIONS

Appraisal of the status of behavioral research on behaviorally disordered pupils as reviewed above depends to some extent upon the criteria one uses. Because scientific research on educative procedures arising from nonbehavioral models is almost totally absent, the body of educative techniques associated with applied behavior analysis appears quite strong by default. Some of the major gaps in existing research and needed directions have been indicated in the preceding reviews, and numerous others could also have been suggested. Thus, while the major research goal for proponents of the various nonbehavioral models of intervention continues to be that of supplying some credible demonstrations that their preferred techniques are capable of producing specifiable improvements in the functioning of behaviorally disordered pupils, this task has been accomplished to a considerable extent for the behavioral model. Further applied behavior analysis research can be directed toward developing more complete technologies for educating behaviorally disordered pupils through investigations that build on and extend available findings.

The single-case experimental methodology, characteristic of applied behavior analysis (e.g., Hersen & Barlow, 1976; Kazdin, 1975), is responsible in large measure for the progress that has been made and is well suited to serve in the further development of needed educational technologies. In the following sections, suggestions are made as to how this methodology might be applied in order to redress some of the shortcomings of available research and to advance efforts to build technologies for educating behaviorally disordered pupils.

### Systematic replication

Perhaps the most obvious conclusion of the preceding reviews is that the fundamental research need is simply an increase in the amount of applied behavior analysis with behaviorally disordered pupils. A logical direction for further research is suggested by the fact that numerous behavioral techniques have been shown to be effective for problems of relevance to the behaviorally disordered, but have not been directly examined in the context of education of these pupils. To cite only a few of the illustrations of this point, Bornstein and Quevillon (1976) found an instructional package for a pupil's self-control to be notably successful in improving the classroom behavior of impulsive preschoolers; Lovitt (1975, 1976) demonstrated the beneficial effects of remedial teaching strategies featuring careful control of antecedent stimulus events upon a variety of basic educational skills of pupils with learning disabilities; and Bornstein, Bellack, and Hersen (1977) examined the effectiveness of an instructional package for improving deficient assertiveness and social skills among regular classroom pupils. Encouraging as the results of these and many other behavioral interventions are, it is risky to assume that they may be directly applied in educational situations for behaviorally disordered pupils. Such intervention procedures are, however, starting points for potentially valuable systematic replication efforts.

Systematic replication is the repetition of an experiment that has demonstrated the effectiveness of a particular technique, but with variation of one or more important aspects, such as subject, setting, intervention agent, response characteristic, or the like (Hersen & Barlow, 1976; Sidman, 1960). In systematic replication with behaviorally disordered pupils, a selected educative technique would be examined through a collection of applied behavior analysis studies in order to determine whether or not the technique produces essentially similar behavior changes each time it is applied. If so, subsequent systematic replication may take place in which settings, change agents, responses, or other educationally important aspects of the original teaching situation are varied. On the other hand, if the original systematic replication series yielded inconsistent results, subsequent experimentation must examine possible reasons for the failure to replicate.

Systematic replication obviously calls for careful and laborious effort sustained over significant periods of time. However, in areas where systematic replication has taken place, important advances in the technology for helping people change have become available (Hersen & Barlow, 1976). The lack of systematic research on educational interventions for the behaviorally disordered is largely at the root of the present nearly chaotic situation with regard to programs for these pupils: too frequently the best that can be done is to recommend teaching procedures that have been demonstrated successful somewhere, as implemented by some sort of change agent, with some type of normal or handicapped pupil.

## Comparisons among behavioral procedures

Assuming that a greater quantity of applied behavior analysis research with behaviorally disordered pupils becomes available, it will be necessary to evaluate the relative effectiveness of different techniques that are known to be capable of producing desirable improvements in behavior. Such comparisons may be performed through group experimental research, but prerequisite conditions for such research (e.g., a sufficient number of subjects, random assignment to treatment conditions, and so on) will only infrequently be available in educational settings. Single-case methodologies permit educational experimentation in situations where group research is unfeasible. One of the welcome developments in applied behavior analysis is the growing number of studies that have compared two or more behavioral interventions to determine their relative effectiveness in improving a particular target behavior.

Applied behavior analysis research designs that can compare educational interventions include the reversal design and the simultaneous treatment design. In comparisons using the reversal design, for example, phases characterized by intervention $X$ can be alternated with phases characterized by intervention $Y$: particularly if the investigation is replicated several times, with alternation of which treatment is applied first, this design can indicate which of the two educational procedures produces more desirable behavior change (e.g., larger effects, more rapid change, etc.). Walker, Hops, and Fiegenbaum (1976, Experiment I) utilized a reversal design to compare various treatment procedures for behavior and learning problems in a special classroom for acting-out pupils at an elementary school. Their results permitted selection of the most effective intervention for management of this class.

Intervention comparisons can also be accomplished through the simultaneous treatment design (Kazdin & Hartmann, 1978). This research strategy permits rapid determination of the relative strengths of two or more concurrently implemented techniques. Browning and Stover (1971) utilized this design to identify the most effective of three alternative techniques intended to reduce the "grandiose bragging" of a young inpatient at a residential psychiatric facility. The design features, advantages, limitations, interpretations, and other aspects of the simultaneous treatment design are discussed by Kazdin and Hartmann (1978). Clearly, educational programs for behaviorally disordered pupils will benefit appreciably from expanded efforts to compare available teaching procedures along similar lines.

### Generalization and maintenance

Assuming that there is sufficient clear evidence that a given educational intervention for behaviorally disordered pupils is effective in producing desired behavior changes, research attention must be directed toward generalization and maintenance questions. Single-case experimental methodologies are again useful in this context. In a review of applied behavior analysis generalization literature, Stokes and Baer (1977) suggested that for practical purposes an intervention shows generalized effects "when no extratraining manipulations are needed for extra changes; or . . . when some extra manipulations are necessary, but their cost or extent is clearly less than that of the direct intervention" (p. 350).

Only limited research on the generalized effects of educational treatment for behaviorally disordered pupils is available. For example, Drabman, Spitalnik, and O'Leary (1973) found evidence of some generalization over time and situation for a procedure in which behaviorally disordered pupils were taught to rate their own conduct in order to earn token points in a special classroom. Walker, Hops, and Johnson (1975), working with behaviorally disordered children whose adjustment problems had been substantially reduced within a special class setting, found that the improved levels of behavior could be generalized to regular classroom settings to which the pupils were mainstreamed; the improvements were maintained for months within the regular classrooms by training the regular classroom teachers to use simple forms of behavior modification (special class behavior modification procedures were quite extensive). Clearly, much additional applied behavior analysis research needs to be directed toward questions of the generalization and maintenance of improvements in the educational functioning of behaviorally disordered pupils.

## Social validation

Applied behavior analysis research has traditionally been concerned with producing behavior changes of magnitudes sufficient to have practical (and usually immediate) value. Interventions that produce small effects have been assigned little applied value, even if such effects are statistically significant. In addition to this "experimental" criterion for judging the importance of an intervention, another criterion, *social validation,* has recently received increased attention. Social validation is the determination of the extent to which obtained changes in behavior actually bring the pupils' behavior into line with prevailing standards or expectations for adequate functioning. Kazdin (1977) has suggested two general strategies for social validation of an intervention: social comparison and subjective evaluation. In the social comparison approach, direct assessment of target behavior is carried out not only for the behaviorally disordered pupil but also for another individual or individuals to whom the identified pupil can be appropriately compared. For example, Walker and Hops (1976) collected data on the appropriate classroom behavior of disruptive pupils and their classmates. These data showed that the behavioral intervention procedures substantially improved the educational functioning of identified pupils; furthermore, the behavior of the target pupils, markedly different from that of their peers at referral, was brought to within "normal" levels following intervention. Other studies utilizing normative peer data to socially validate intervention procedures offer further information on the implementation and usefulness of the social comparison procedure (e.g., Patterson, 1974; Patterson, Cobb, & Ray, 1973; Patterson, Shaw, & Ebner, 1969; Walker & Hops, 1973; Walker et al., 1975; Walker, Mattson, & Buckley, 1971).

In the subjective evaluation approach to social validation, consumer satisfaction with obtained behavior changes is gauged by having individuals who normally interact with the treated pupil (e.g., peers, teachers, other school personnel, or parents), or who are especially qualified for some other reason (e.g., special expertise), judge qualitative aspects of the target pupil's functioning. For instance, in the previously described Brigham, Graubard, & Stans (1972) study of composition-writing skills, there was direct measurement of objective components of writing (number of words, different words, and new words). In addition, the compositions were submitted to judges (five college students unaware of the experiment) who scored each composition according to quality in particular dimensions such as mechanical aspects, vocabulary, development of ideas, and so on. In this study, although the intervention procedure consistently produced improvement on only one of the objective dependent variables (number of words used), the judges' subjective ratings of composition quality clearly indicated that the subjects' compositions produced during treatment were better than those written during baseline. Other important applications of the subjective evaluation strategy for socially validating intervention efforts have arisen from the work at Achievement Place, in Lawrence, Kansas, a community group home for predelinquent youths (see, e.g., Phillips, Fixsen, Phillips, & Wolf, 1979). Subjective evaluation procedures were used to verify the importance of results arising from behavior modification projects for improving the quality of the youths' conversation skills (Maloney, et al., 1976), interactions with law enforcement personnel (Werner, Minkin, Minkin, Fixsen, Phillips, et al., 1975), and communication with parents (Willner, et al., 1977).

Social validation procedures can help indicate the degree to which a behaviorally disordered pupil's functioning is discrepant from that of comparison pupils, suggest objective criteria for reducing or terminating interventions, and estimate the degree to which behavioral improvement approaches the level needed for adequate adjustment or competence. For these reasons, future applied behavior analysis research efforts will be obliged to consider social validation criteria. In particular, social validation has rarely been utilized in applied research on the academic functioning of behaviorally disordered pupils and on behavioral programs for adolescents with behavior disorders.

**Other issues**

Applied behavior analysis research efforts designed to improve special education for behaviorally disordered pupils must address several other important questions. They will be only briefly suggested here, because each presupposes an increased quantity of appropriate research along some of the lines suggested above. First, teaching procedures frequently consist of several basic components. Experimental demonstrations that a teaching procedure is effective leave unanswered the question of whether some component may be omitted without loss of effectiveness; particularly if a component is expensive, time consuming, or distasteful to implement, it may be important to engage in component analyses in order to streamline the teaching package (see e.g., Harris & Sherman, 1973).

Notwithstanding the intrinsic appeal of pleas for eclectic approaches to providing special education, it is conceivable that treatments based on different educative models are differentially effective for certain behavioral disorders, or even that one approach is generally more effective than the others. Through previously mentioned strategies for making comparisons among behavioral procedures, behavioral and non-behavioral treatments for the same behavior disorder can be directly compared. Based in part on such comparisons, recent critical reviews of behavior modification and psychotropic drugs for hyperactive pupils (Kauffman & Hallahan, 1979; Kazdin & Wilson, 1978) have tentatively concluded that behavioral educative procedures are superior to drugs, particularly with regard to academic and cognitive functioning.

For purposes of the proceding reviews, applied behavior analysis studies were selected if the subjects were clearly identified as "behaviorally disordered" (including "delinquent"). It may be that identification for special educational purposes is the only common feature of this population, or that the behaviorally disordered group actually consists of several subpopulations (see, e.g., Quay, 1977; Spivack & Swift, 1973). In any case, the vast majority of the adolescent studies reviewed in this paper were concerned with disruptive or acting-out forms of behavior disorders. While additional research along these lines is clearly indicated, attention must also be turned toward interventions for behavior disorders that chiefly impede personal development (e.g., lack of assertiveness and other social skills). In regard to the academic skills research reviewed, although it is clear that behaviorally disordered pupils typically show poor educational achievement (Oliver, 1974; Roberts & Baird, 1972; Silberberg & Silberberg, 1971), whether and how their academic difficulties differ from those of learning disabled or underachieving pupils is not known. Research that addresses these issues is likely to be of major significance to the practice of special education.

## CONCLUSION

In a relatively brief span of time the behavioral model has developed to the point where it has much to offer special educators. Various behavioral interventions have been shown to be effective for improving a broad range of behaviors, especially the performance disabilities of the various types of handicapped children. The reviews of behavioral procedures for improving the academic functioning of behaviorally disordered pupils and for educating behaviorally disordered adolescents reveal both progress made and directions to pursue. Further development of teaching technologies in these areas will require applied research that follows up on the information gained from past efforts. While available research clearly indicates that the use of behavioral principles in educating behaviorally disordered pupils is coming of age, there can be no question that continued progress will demand intensive, continuing effort and a commitment to applied research in educational settings.

# References

Agras, W. S. *Behavior modification: Principles and clinical applications* (2nd ed.). Boston: Little, Brown, 1978.

Axelrod, S. *Behavior modification for the classroom teacher*. New York: McGraw-Hill, 1977.

Ayllon, T., & Roberts, M. D. Eliminating discipline problems by strengthening academic performance. *Journal of Applied Behavior Analysis*, 1974, *7*, 71–76.

Baer, D. M., Wolf, M. M., & Risley, R. R. Some current dimensions of applied behavior analysis. *Journal of Applied Behavior Analysis*, 1968, *1*, 91–97.

Bailey, J. S., Timbers, G. D., Phillips, E. L., & Wolf, M. M. Modification of articulation errors of pre-delinquents by their peers. *Journal of Applied Behavior Analysis*, 1971, *4*, 265–281.

Bailey, J. S., Wolf, M. M., & Phillips, E. L. Home-based reinforcement and the modification of pre-delinquent classroom behavior. *Journal of Applied Behavior Analysis*, 1970, *3*, 223–233.

Bandura, A. Vicarious- and self-reinforcement processes. In R. Glaser (Ed.), *The nature of reinforcement*. New York: Academic Press, 1971.

Bandura, A. Effecting change through participant modeling. In J. D. Krumboltz & C. E. Thoresen (Eds.), *Counseling methods*. New York: Holt, Rinehart, & Winston, 1976.

Becker, W. C. Applications of behavior principles in typical classrooms. In C. Thoresen (Ed.), *Behavior modification in education. Seventy-second yearbook of the National Society for the Study of Education* (Part I). Chicago: University of Chicago Press, 1973.

Bednar, R. L., Zelhart, P. F., Greathouse, L., & Weinberg, S. Operant conditioning principles in the treatment of learning and behavior problems with delinquent boys. *Journal of Counseling Psychology*, 1970, *17*, 492–497.

Birnbrauer, J. S., Wolf, M. M., Kidder, J. D., & Tague, C. E. Classroom behavior of retarded pupils with token reinforcement. *Journal of Experimental Child Psychology*, 1965, *2*, 219–235.

Bornstein, M. R., Bellack, A. S., & Hersen, M. Social-skills training for unassertive children: A multiple-baseline analysis. *Journal of Applied Behavior Analysis*, 1977, *10*, 183–196.

Bornstein, P. H., & Quevillon, R. P. The effects of self-instructional package on overactive preschool boys. *Journal of Applied Behavior Analysis*, 1976, *9*, 179–188.

Braukmann, C. J., & Fixsen, D. L. Behavior modification with delinquents. In M. Hersen, R. M. Eisler, & P. M. Miller (Eds.), *Progress in behavior modification* (Vol. 1). New York: Academic Press, 1975.

Brigham, T. A., Finfrock, S. R., Breuning, M. K., & Bushell, D. The use of programmed materials in the analysis of academic contingencies. *Journal of Applied Behavior Analysis*, 1972, *5*, 177–182.

Brigham, T. A., Graubard, P. S., & Stans, A. Analysis of the effects of sequential reinforcement contingencies on aspects of composition. *Journal of Applied Behavior Analysis*, 1972, *5*, 421–429.

Broden, M., Hall, R. V., Dunlap, A., & Clark, R. Effects of teacher attention and a token reinforcement in a junior high school special education class. *Exceptional Children*, 1970, *36*, 341–349.

Brolin, J. C., & Brolin, D. E. Vocational education for special students. In D. Cullinan & M. H. Epstein (Eds.), *Special education for adolescents: Issues and perspectives*. Columbus, Ohio: Merrill, 1979.

Browning, R. M., & Stover, D. O. *Behavior modification in child treatment: An experimental and clinical approach*. Chicago: Aldine-Atherton, 1971.

Burchard, J. D., & Harig, P. T. Behavior modification and juvenile delinquency. In. H.

Leitenberg (Ed.), *Handbook of behavior modification and behavior therapy.* Englewood Cliffs, N.J.: Prentice-Hall, 1976.

Cegelka, P. T. Career education. In D. Cullinan & M. H. Epstein (Eds.), *Special education for adolescents: Issues and perspectives.* Columbus, Ohio: Merrill, 1979.

Chan, A., Chiu, A., & Mueller, D. J. An integrated approach to the modification of classroom failure and disruption: A case study. *Journal of School Psychology,* 1970, *8,* 114–121.

Clark, H. B., Boyd, S. B., & Macrae, J. W. A classroom program teaching disadvantaged youths to write biographic information. *Journal of Applied Behavior Analysis,* 1975, *8,* 67–75.

Clark, M., Lachowicz, J., & Wolf, M. M. A pilot basic education program for school dropouts incorporating a token reinforcement system. *Behavior Research and Therapy,* 1968, *8,* 183–188.

Cohen, H. L., & Filipczak, J. A. Programming educational behavior for institutionalized adolescents. In H. C. Rickard (Ed.), *Behavioral intervention in human problems.* New York: Pergamon Press, 1971.

Cotler, S. B., Applegate, G., King, L. W., & Kristal, S. Establishing a token economy program in a state hospital classroom. A lesson in training student and teacher. *Behavior Therapy,* 1972, *3,* 209–222.

Cullinan, D., Epstein, M. H., & Kauffman, J. M. The behavioral model and children's behavior disorders: Foundations and evaluations. In R. McDowell, F. Wood, & G. Adamson (Eds.), *The Emotionally Disturbed Child.* Boston: Little, Brown, in press.

Davidson, W. S., II, & Seidman, E. Studies of behavior modification and juvenile delinquency: A review, methodological critique, and social perspective. *Psychological Bulletin,* 1974, *81,* 998–1011.

Drabman, R., Spitalnik, R., & O'Leary, K. D. Teaching self-control to disruptive children. *Journal of Abnormal Psychology,* 1973, *82,* 10–16.

Evans, G. W., & Oswalt, G. L. Acceleration of academic progress through the manipulation of peer influence. *Behavior Research and Therapy,* 1968, *6,* 189–196.

Fagen, S. A., Long, N. J., & Stevens, D. J. *Teaching children self-control.* Columbus, Ohio: Merrill, 1975.

Ferritor, D. E., Buckholdt, D., Hamblin, R. L., & Smith, L. The noneffects of contingent reinforcement for attending behavior on work accomplished. *Journal of Applied Behavior Analysis,* 1972, *5,* 7–18.

Fink, A. H., Glass, R. M., & Guskin, S. L. An analysis of teacher education programs in behavior disorders. *Exceptional Children,* 1975, *42,* 47.

Fixsen, D. L., Phillips, E. L., & Wolf, M. M. Achievement Place: The reliability of self-reporting and peer-reporting and their effects on behavior. *Journal of Applied Behavior Analysis,* 1972, *5,* 19–30.

Foxx, R. M., & Jones, J. R. A remediation program for increasing the spelling achievement of elementary and junior high school students. *Behavior Modification,* 1978, *2,* 211–230.

Gardner, W. I. *Learning and behavior characteristics of exceptional children and youths.* Boston: Allyn & Bacon, 1977.

Glynn, E. L., & Thomas, J. D. Effect of cueing on self-control of classroom behavior. *Journal of Applied Behavior Analysis,* 1974, *7,* 299–306.

Graubard, P. S. Utilizing the group in teaching disturbed delinquents to learn. *Exceptional Children,* 1969, *36,* 267–272.

Grimm, J. A., Bijou, S. W., & Parsons, J. A. A problem solving model for teaching remedial arithmetic to handicapped young children. *Journal of Abnormal Child Psychology,* 1973, *1,* 26–39.

Hall, R. V., Fox, R., Willard, D., Goldsmith, L., Emerson, M., Owen, M., Davis, F., &

Porcia, E. The teacher as observer and experimenter in the modification of disputing and talking-out behaviors. *Journal of Applied Behavior Analysis*, 1971, *4*, 141–149.

Haring, N. G. (Ed.). *Behavior of exceptional children* (2nd ed.). Columbus, Ohio: Merrill, 1978.

Haring, N. G., Lovitt, T. C., Eaton, M. D., & Hansen, C. L. *The fourth R: Research in the classroom*. Columbus, Ohio: Merrill, 1978.

Harris, V. W., Finfrock, S. R., Giles, D. K., Hart, B. M., & Tsosie, P. C. The effects of performance contingencies on the assignment completion behavior of severely delinquent youths. In E. Ramp & G. Semb (Eds.), *Behavior analysis: Areas of research and application*. Englewood Cliffs, N.J.: Prentice-Hall, 1975.

Harris, V. W., & Sherman, J. A. Use and analysis of the "good behavior game" to reduce disruptive classroom behavior. *Journal of Applied Behavior Analysis*, 1973, *6*, 405–417.

Haubrich, P. A., & Shores, R. Attending behavior and academic performance of emotionally disturbed children. *Exceptional Children*, 1976, *42*, 337–338.

Heaton, R. C., Safer, D. J., Allen, R. P., Spinnato, N. C., & Prumo, F. M. A motivational environment for behaviorally deviant junior high school students. *Journal of Abnormal Child Psychology*, 1976, *4*, 263–275.

Hersen, M., & Barlow, D. *Single-case experimental design*. New York: Pergamon Press, 1976.

Hewett, F. M. *The emotionally disturbed child in the classroom*. Boston: Allyn & Bacon, 1968.

Homme, L. E., de Baca, P. C., Devine, J. V., Steinhorst, R., & Rickert, E. J. Use of the Premack principle in controlling the behavior of nursery school children. *Journal of the Experimental Analysis of Behavior*, 1963, *6*, 544.

Hundert, J., & Batstone, D. A practical procedure to maintain pupils' accurate self-rating in a classroom token program. *Behavior Modification*, 1978, *2*, 93–111.

Hundert, J., Bucher, B., & Henderson, M. Increasing appropriate classroom behavior and academic performance by reinforcing correct work alone. *Psychology in the Schools*, 1976, *13*, 195–200.

Kauffman, J. M. *Characteristics of children's behavior disorders*. Columbus, Ohio: Merrill, 1977.

Kauffman, J. M., & Hallahan, D. P. Learning disability and hyperactivity (with comments on minimal brain dysfunction). In B. B. Lahey & A. E. Kazdin (Eds.), *Advances in clinical child psychology* (Vol. 2). New York: Plenum Press, 1979.

Kaufman, K. F., & O'Leary, K. D. Reward, cost, and self-evaluation procedures for disruptive adolescents in a psychiatric hospital school. *Journal of Applied Behavior Analysis*, 1972, *5*, 293–309.

Kazdin, A. E. *Behavior modification in applied settings*. Homewood, Ill.: Dorsey, 1975.

Kazdin, A. E. Assessing the clinical or applied significance of behavior change through social validation. *Behavior Modification*, 1977, *1*, 427–452.

Kazdin, A. E. *History of behavior modification: Experimental foundations of contemporary research*. Baltimore: University Park Press, 1978.

Kazdin, A. E., & Hartmann, D. P. The simultaneous-treatment design. *Behavior Therapy*, 1978, *9*, 912–922.

Kazdin, A. E., & Wilson, G. T. *Evaluation of behavior therapy: Issues, evidence, and research strategies*. Cambridge, Mass.: Ballinger, 1978.

Kirby, F. D., & Shields, F. Modification of arithmetic response rate and attending behavior in a seventh-grade student. *Journal of Applied Behavior Analysis*, 1972, *5*, 79–84.

Krumboltz, J. D., & Thoresen, C. E. (Eds.). *Counseling methods*. New York: Holt, Rinehart, & Winston, 1976.

Litow, L., & Pumroy, D. K. A brief review of classroom group-oriented contingencies. *Journal of Applied Behavior Analysis*, 1975, *8*, 341–347.

Lovitt, T. C. Self-management projects with children with behavioral disabilities. *Journal of Learning Disabilities*, 1973, *6*, 15–28.

Lovitt, T. C. Applied behavior analysis and learning disabilities. Part II: Specific research recommendations and suggestions for practitioners. *Journal of Learning Disabilities*, 1975, *8*, 504–518.

Lovitt, T. C. Applied behavior analysis techniques and curriculum research: Implications for instruction. In N. G. Haring & R. L. Schiefelbusch (Eds.), *Teaching special children*. New York: McGraw-Hill, 1976.

Lovitt, T. C., & Curtiss, K. A. Effects of manipulating an antecedent event on mathematics response rate. *Journal of Applied Behavior Analysis*, 1968, *1*, 329–333.

Lovitt, T. C., & Curtiss, K. A. Academic response rate as a function of teacher- and self-imposed contingencies. *Journal of Applied Behavior Analysis*, 1969, *2*, 49–53.

Lovitt, T. C., Guppy, T. E., & Blattner, J. E. The use of free-time contingency with fourth graders to increase spelling accuracy. *Behavior Research and Therapy*, 1969, *7*, 151–156.

MacDonald, W. S., Gallimore, R., & MacDonald, G. Contingency counseling by school personnel: An economical model of intervention. *Journal of Applied Behavior Analysis*, 1970, *3*, 175–182.

Mahoney, M. J. *Cognition and behavior modification*. Cambridge, Mass.: Ballinger, 1974.

Maloney, D. M., Harper, T. M., Braukmann, C. J., Fixsen, D. L., Phillips, E. L., & Wolf, M. M. Teaching conversation-related skills to predelinquent girls. *Journal of Applied Behavior Analysis*, 1976, *9*, 371.

Marholin, D., McInnis, E. T., & Heads, T. B. Effect of two free-time reinforcement procedures on academic performance in a class of behavior problem children. *Journal of Educational Psychology*, 1974, *66*, 872–879.

Marholin, D., & Steinman, W. M. Stimulus control in the classroom as a function of the behavior reinforced. *Journal of Applied Behavior Analysis*, 1977, *10*, 465–578.

Marholin, D., Steinman, W. M., McInnis, E. T., & Heads, T. B. The effect of a teacher's presence on the classroom behavior of conduct-problem children. *Journal of Abnormal Child Psychology*, 1975, *3*, 11–25.

McCarty, T., Griffin, S., Apolloni, T., & Shores, R. E. Increased peer teaching with group-oriented contingencies for arithmetic performance in behavior-disordered adolescents. *Journal of Applied Behavior Analysis*, 1977, *10*, 313.

McLaughlin, T. F. A review of applications of group-contingency procedures used in behavior modification in the regular classroom: Some recommendations for school personnel. *Psychological Reports*, 1974, *35*, 1299–1303.

McLaughlin, T. F. The applicability of token reinforcement systems in public school systems. *Psychology in the Schools*, 1975, *12*, 84–89.

Meichenbaum, D. H., Bowers, K. S., & Ross, R. R. Modification of classroom behavior of institutionalized female adolescent offenders. *Behavior Research and Therapy*, 1968, *6*, 343–353.

Minkin, N., Braukmann, C. J., Minkin, B. L., Timbers, G. D., Timbers, B. J., Fixsen, D. L., Phillips, E. L., & Wolf, M. M. The social validation and training of conversational skills. *Journal of Applied Behavior Analysis*, 1976, *9*, 127–139.

O'Leary, K. D., & Drabman, R. Token reinforcement programs in the classroom: A review. *Psychological Bulletin*, 1971, *75*, 379–398.

Oliver, L. I. *Behavior patterns in school of youth 12–17 years*. (National Health Survey, Series 11, No. 139, U.S. Department of Health, Education and Welfare). Washington, D.C.: U.S. Government Printing Office, 1974.

O'Neil, S. M., McLaughlin, B. N., & Knapp, M. B. *Behavioral approaches to children with developmental delays*. St. Louis: Mosby, 1977.

Patterson, G. R. An application of conditioning techniques to the control of a hyperactive child. In L. P. Ullman & L. Krasner (Eds.), *Case studies in behavior modification.* New York: Holt, Rinehart, & Winston, 1965.

Patterson, G. R. Interventions for boys with conduct problems: Multiple settings, treatments, and criteria. *Journal of Consulting and Clinical Psychology,* 1974, *42,* 471–481.

Patterson, G. R., Cobb, J. A., & Ray, R. S. A social engineering technology for retraining the families of aggressive boys. In H. E. Adams & I. P. Unikel (Eds.), *Issues and trends in behavioral therapy.* Springfield, Ill.: Thomas, 1973.

Patterson, G. R., Shaw, D. A., & Ebner, M. J. Teachers, peers, and parents as agents of change in the classroom. In F. A. M. Benson (Ed.), *Modifying deviant social behaviors in various classroom settings.* Eugene, Ore.: University of Oregon, 1969.

Phillips, E. L. Achievement Place: Token reinforcement procedures in a home-style rehabilitation setting for pre-delinquent boys. *Journal of Applied Behavior Analysis,* 1968, *1,* 213–223.

Phillips, E. L., Fixsen, D. L., Phillips, E. A., & Wolf, M. M. The teaching family model: A comprehensive approach to residential treatment of youth. In D. Cullinan & M. H. Epstein (Eds.), *Special education for adolescents.* Columbus, Ohio: Merrill, 1979.

Phillips, E. L., Phillips, E. A., Fixsen, D. L., & Wolf, M. M. Achievement Place: Modification of the behaviors of pre-delinquent boys within a token economy. *Journal of Applied Behavior Analysis,* 1971, *4,* 45–59.

Polirstok, S. R., & Greer, R. D. Remediation of mutually aversive interactions between a problem student and four teachers by training the student in reinforcement techniques. *Journal of Applied Behavior Analysis,* 1977, *10,* 707–716.

Polsgrove, L. Self control: An overview of concepts and methods for child training. *Proceedings of a conference at the Advanced Institute for Trainers of Teachers for Seriously Emotionally Disturbed Children,* 1977, pp. 29–55.

Quay, H. C. Patterns of aggression, withdrawal, and immaturity. In H. C. Quay & J. S. Werry (Eds.), *Psychopathological disorders of childhood.* New York: Wiley, 1972.

Quay, H. C. Measuring dimensions of deviant behavior: The behavior problem checklist. *Journal of Abnormal Child Psychology,* 1977, *5,* 277–287.

Quay, H. C., Glavin, J. P., Annesley, F. R., & Werry, J. S. The modification of problem behavior and academic achievement in a resource room. *Journal of School Psychology,* 1972, *10,* 187–197.

Quay, H. C., Werry, J. S., McQueen, M. M., & Sprague, R. L. Remediation of the conduct problem child in the special class setting. *Exceptional Children,* 1966, *32,* 509–515.

Rickard, H. C., Clements, C. B., & Willis, J. W. Effects of contingent and noncontingent token reinforcement upon classroom performance. *Psychological Reports,* 1970, *27,* 903–908.

Rickard, H. C., Melvin, K. B., Creel, J., & Creel, L. The effects of bonus tokens upon productivity in a remedial classroom for behaviorally disturbed children. *Behavior Therapy,* 1973, *4,* 378–385.

Roberts, J., & Baird, J. T. *Behavior patterns of children in school* (DHEW Publication No. [HSM] 72-1042). Washington, D.C.: U.S. Government Printing Office, 1972.

Rose, T. L., Epstein, M. H., Cullinan, D., & Lloyd, J. Educational programming for behaviorally disordered adolescents. In G. Brown, R. McDowell, & J. Smith (Eds.), *Educating children with behavior disorders.* Columbus, Ohio: Merrill, in press.

Rosenberg, H. E., & Graubard, P. Peer usage of behavior modification. *Focus on Exceptional Children,* 1975, *7,* 1–10.

Ross, A. O. *Psychological disorders of children: A behavioral approach to theory, research, and therapy.* New York: McGraw-Hill, 1974.

Santogrossi, D. A., O'Leary, K. D., Romanczyk, R. G., & Kaufman, K. F. Self evaluation by adolescents in a psychiatric hospital school token program. *Journal of Applied Behavior Analysis,* 1973, *6,* 277–287.

Schumaker, J. B., Hovell, M. F., & Sherman, J. A. An analysis of daily report cards and parent managed privileges in the improvement of adolescents' classroom performance. *Journal of Applied Behavior Analysis*, 1977, *10*, 449–464.

Seymour, F. W., & Stokes, T. F. Self-recording in training girls to increase work and evoke staff praise in an institution for offenders. *Journal of Applied Behavior Analysis*, 1976, *9*, 41–54.

Sidman, M. *Tactics of scientific research: Evaluating experimental data in psychology.* New York: Basic Books, 1960.

Silberberg, N. E., & Silberberg, M. C. School achievement and delinquency. *Review of Educational Research*, 1971, *41*, 17–33.

Spivack, G., & Swift, M. The classroom behavior of children: A critical review of teacher-administered rating scales. *Journal of Special Education*, 1973, *7*, 55–91.

Staats, A. W. *Learning, language, and cognition.* New York: Holt, Rinehart, & Winston, 1968.

Staats, A. W. *Child learning, intelligence, and personality.* New York: Harper & Row, 1971.

Staats, A. W. Behavior analysis and token reinforcement in educational behavior modification and curriculum research. In C. E. Thoresen (Ed.), *Behavior modification in education: 72nd yearbook of the National Society for the Study of Education.* Chicago: University of Chicago Press, 1973.

Staats, A. W., Brewer, B. A., & Gross, M. C. Learning and cognitive development: Representative samples, cumulative-hierarchical learning, and experimental-longitudinal methods. *Monographs of the Society for Research in Child Development*, 1970, *35* (8, Whole No. 141).

Staats, A. W., & Butterfield, W. H. Treatment of nonreading in a culturally deprived juvenile delinquent: An application of reinforcement principles. *Child Development*, 1965, *36*, 925–942.

Staats, A. W., Minke, K. A., Goodwin, W., & Landeen, J. Cognitive behavior modification: "Motivated learning" reading treatment with subprofessional therapy technicians. *Behavior Research and Therapy*, 1967, *5*, 283–299.

Stokes, T. F., & Baer, D. M. An implicit technology of generalization. *Journal of Applied Behavior Analysis*, 1977, *10*, 349–367.

Swift, M. S., & Spivack, G. Clarifying the relationship between academic success and overt classroom behavior. *Exceptional Children*, 1969, *36*, 99–104.

Swift, M. S., & Spivack, G. Academic success and classroom behavior in secondary schools. *Exceptional Children*, 1973, *39*, 392–399.

Tharp, R. G., & Wetzel, R. J. *Behavior modification in the natural environment.* New York: Academic Press, 1969.

Thomas, D. A., Nielsen, L. J., Kuypers, D. S., & Becker, W. C. Social reinforcement and remedial instruction in the elimination of a classroom behavior problem. *Journal of Special Education*, 1969, *2*, 291–305.

Thoresen, C. E., & Mahoney, M. J. *Behavioral self-control.* New York: Holt, Rinehart, & Winston, 1974.

Tyler, V. O. Application of operant token reinforcement to academic performance of an institutionalized delinquent. *Psychological Reports*, 1967, *21*, 249–260.

Tyler, V. O., & Brown, G. D. Token reinforcement of academic performance with institutionalized delinquent boys. *Journal of Educational Psychology*, 1968, *59*, 164–168.

Walker, H. M., & Hops, H. The use of group and individual reinforcement contingencies in the modification of social withdrawal. In L. A. Hamerlynck, L. C. Handy, & E. J. Mash (Eds.), *Behavior change: Methodology, concepts, and practice.* Champaign, Ill.: Research Press, 1973.

Walker, H. M., & Hops, H. Use of normative peer data as a standard for evaluating classroom treatment effects. *Journal of Applied Behavior Analysis,* 1976, *9,* 159–168.

Walker, H. M., Hops, H., & Feigenbaum, E. Deviant classroom behavior as a function of combinations of social and token reinforcement and cost contingency. *Behavior Therapy,* 1976, *7,* 76–88.

Walker, H. M., Hops, H., & Johnson, S. M. Generalization and maintenance of classroom treatment effects. *Behavior Therapy,* 1975, *6,* 188–200.

Walker, H. M., Mattson, R. H., & Buckley, N. K. The functional analysis of behavior within an experimental class setting. In W. C. Becker (Ed.), *An empirical basis for change in education.* Chicago: Science Research Associates, 1971, 236–263.

Werner, J. S., Minkin, N., Minkin, B. L., Fixsen, D. L., Phillips, E. L., & Wolf, M. M. "Intervention package": An analysis to prepare juvenile delinquents for encounters with police officers. *Criminal Justice and Behavior,* 1975, *2,* 55–83.

Williams, R. B., Jr., & Gentry, W. D. (Eds.). *Behavioral approaches to medical treatment.* Cambridge, Mass.: Ballinger, 1977.

Willner, A. G., Braukmann, C. J., Kirigin, K. A., Fixsen, D. L., Phillips, E. L., & Wolf, M. M. The training and validation of youth-preferred social behaviors of child-care personnel. *Journal of Applied Behavior Analysis,* 1977, *10,* 219–230.

Wolf, M. M., Giles, D. K., & Hall, R. V. Experiments with token reinforcement in a remedial classroom. *Behavior Research and Therapy,* 1968, *6,* 51–64.

Wolf, M. M., Hanley, E. L., King, L. A., Lachowicz, J., & Giles, D. K. The timer-game: A variable interval contingency for the management of out-of-seat behavior. *Exceptional Children,* 1970, *37,* 113–117.

Zimmerman, E. H., & Zimmerman, J. The alteration of behavior in a special classroom situation. *Journal of the Experimental Analysis of Behavior,* 1962, *5,* 59–60.

# REVIEW OF EDUCATIONAL–TREATMENT PROCEDURES FOR AUTISTIC CHILDREN

Andrew L. Egel
*University of Maryland, College Park*

Robert L. Koegel
*University of California, Santa Barbara*

Laura Schreibman
*Claremont Men's College*

Autism is a severe form of mental disorder which greatly affects the lives of the children, their parents, and their community. When people refer to autism they are typically describing children who display a majority of the following symptoms: (1) a lack of appropriate speech (the children are usually nonverbal or echolalic, i.e., they parrot phrases spoken to them, but are unable to use them meaningfully in other contexts); (2) a lack of appropriate social behavior (the children either appear to be oblivious to other people's presence or relate to people in a bizarre manner); (3) apparent sensory deficit (the children are often incorrectly suspected of being blind or deaf); (4) a lack of appropriate play (the children usually ignore toys or interact inappropriately with them, for example, they may throw or mouth a toy truck); (5) inappropriate and out of context emotional behavior (the children may display

Preparation of this manuscript was supported by U.S. Public Health Service Grants MH 28231 and MH 28210 from the National Institute of Mental Health and by Office of Education Research Grant G007802084 and Model Demonstration Grant G0078001720 from the Bureau of Education for the Handicapped. An earlier draft of this manuscript was submitted by the senior author to the Department of Education, University of California, Santa Barbara, in partial fulfillment of the requirements for the Ph.D. degree.

The authors wish to thank Amy Miller, Julie Williams, Glen Dunlap and Drs. John Cotton, Ray Hosford, and John Wilson for their helpful comments during the completion of this manuscript.

Address all editorial correspondence to Andrew L. Egel, Department of Special Education, College Park, Md. 20742.

extreme tantrums, hysterical laughter, or, on the other hand, a virtual absence of emotional response); (6) high rates of stereotyped, repetitive behaviors, referred to as self-stimulation (e.g., flapping fingers or rhythmically rocking for hours without pause); and (7) isolated areas of high-level functioning ("splinter skills," especially in the areas of music, number configurations, and manipulation of mechanical instruments) in the context of otherwise low-level intellectual functioning (Rimland, 1978). Another frequently cited characteristic is their normal physical appearance. As children, they present no associated physical deformities (although years of untreated autistic responding may eventually lead to physical abnormalities in posture, teeth, etc.) and, indeed, they are usually portrayed as cute and physically attractive.

These types of behaviors have in the past resulted in the exclusion of autistic children from the public schools. Recently, however, there has been a proliferation of educational and treatment programs for autistic children. These programs have varied considerably in both their conceptualizations of the etiology of autism and their treatment methodologies. There are currently three major orientations with extensive treatment programs: (1) the psychoanalytic approach; (2) approaches based on sensory-deficit models; and (3) the behavior modification approach. Since this literature review focuses on the most current descriptions of replicable educational procedures and evaluations based upon empirical data, more space has been devoted to the last two areas, especially behavior modification (which shares these emphases). However, for the sake of comprehensiveness, literature in all three areas is reviewed and discussed.

## PSYCHOANALYTIC APPROACH

### Theoretical perspective

According to traditional psychoanalytic theories, all infants experience frustration in one form or another. This frustration can lead to a "liminal" or "subliminal" withdrawal by the child. Bettelheim (1967) suggested that mothers with no psychological pathologies react to the infant's withdrawal with "mothering acts" such as feeding, rocking, cuddling, or stroking. However, mothers with psychological pathologies react to the child's withdrawal with extreme negative feelings coupled with rejection and/or counterwithdrawal. The child responds to the mother's hostility with inward rage, a feeling of powerlessness in a threatening environment, and complete withdrawal. In other words, while the initial withdrawal is not necessarily caused by the mother, her extreme reaction to her child compounds the withdrawal, setting in motion what Bettelheim referred to as "chronic autistic disease." Others (e.g., Mahler, 1952; Rank, 1955; Weiland & Rudnick, 1961) have suggested that it is not the mother's psychopathology that is responsible for the child's withdrawal, but rather it is the child's misperception of the mother's behavior that causes the withdrawal. *Autistic withdrawal* is the child's means of adapting to a threatening reality represented by the mother (Bettelheim, 1967; Rank & MacNaughton, 1950; Ruttenberg, 1971). As the child withdraws, all libidinal energy is used for protection, resulting in the arrest of ego development (Weiland & Rudnick, 1961). The child avoids any direct interaction with the environment in order to prevent events from coming to awareness (because experiencing them would be too painful). Overt behaviors such as self-stimulation, echolalia, insistence on sameness, etc. illustrate the child's attempts to maintain a homeostatic psychic environment (Ruttenberg, 1971).

**Educational–treatment procedures**

The most comprehensively described psychoanalytic school models are probably those based on Bettelheim's (e.g., 1967) and Ruttenberg's (1971) writings. Both attempt to establish an environment in which the child no longer needs to rely on his (theoretically) defensive autistic behaviors to survive. Instead, the procedures are described as allowing the child to develop a strong concept of his self and world without the pressures and frustrations that were originally present in the home environment that maintained the need for complete withdrawal. The psychoanalytic approach has deliberately deemphasized the defining of specific procedures. Instead, the children are encouraged through a variety of means to engage in any behavior through which they choose to express their growing autonomy (Bettelheim, 1967). For example, rather than attempt to toilet train a child, a therapist might encourage the child to demonstrate his autonomy by frequent and random elimination, since (according to traditional psychoanalytic theory) normal children develop autonomy during the anal stage (Blum, 1966). No effort is made to toilet train the child since this would only serve to increase the child's frustration. Other examples include encouraging the child to play in his own way with materials such as crayons, puzzles, and/or paper, to engage in aggressive or passive behavior, and to eat in any manner (e.g., with hands or with silverware; Bettelheim, 1967). The therapist responds to the child's attempts at autonomy with love, acceptance, and understanding. As the child regains a sense of selfness, other procedures such as tactile and kinesthetic stimulation can be used to further encourage growth and to help the child recognize the presence of nonthreatening others. It is through the reemergence of the self and a growing sense of autonomy that cognitive areas such as language develop. Autistic behaviors decrease because the child no longer needs to defend himself from reality.

Since others (e.g., Hartman, Kris, & Lowenstein, 1946; Rank & MacNaughton, 1950) have noted that normal emotional, perceptual, and cognitive growth depends on the establishment of an object relationship with another human being, approaches based on these and Ruttenberg's (1971) model have attempted to provide an environment which allows for complete gratification through contact with consistent and positive mother substitutes. The teachers develop this relationship by engaging the child in as much tactile, vocal, and kinesthetic stimulation as the child will tolerate. Other procedures involve imitating the child's behavior and vocalizations. Following the child's initial acceptance of the mother substitutes, various self-help and cognitive skill-building programs are introduced. The teacher's level of expectation is always based on the child's overall emotional, functional, and developmental level, since expectations not commensurate with these levels could result in frustration and further withdrawal.

**Evaluation**

The psychoanalytic approach has been advocated because it emphasizes an understanding and treatment of the total syndrome of autism and because its theoretical perspective is comprehensive and well developed. In addition, Bettelheim (1968) has offered his case descriptions and subjectively reported a high success rate as evidence of the benefits that can be gained from a psychoanalytically based treatment program. However, others have criticized both the theoretical perspective and effectiveness of the psychoanalytic approach (e.g., Rimland, 1964; Rutter, 1971; Schopler & Reichler, 1971a, b; Weiland, 1971; Wing, 1968). First, there is no empirically validated evidence that autistic children have in fact been exposed to the extreme negative conditions that psychoanalysts feel cause autistic withdrawal (Rutter, 1971). Second, there is no empirical evidence of greater pathology in parents of autistic children. In fact, investigations have revealed that the personalities of the parents of autistic children fall well within the "normal" range (e.g., DeMyer, et al., 1972; McAdoo & DeMyer, 1978; Pitfield & Oppenheim,

1964; Schopler & Loftin, 1969). Others have suggested that any parent abnormalities that are found most likely result from rather than cause the child's pathology (e.g., Rimland, 1964; Rutter, 1968; Schopler & Reichler, 1971b). While one cannot fail to be impressed with Bettelheim's subjective reports of high (up to 80 percent) success rates, the generality of his claim of significant improvements has been questioned in light of his employment of selection criteria in admitting children to the program and in the absence of empirical verification (Greenfeld, 1972; Merritt, 1968; Shapiro, 1978).

In the absence of specific treatment descriptions, it is obviously difficult to make systematic evaluations of psychoanalytic techniques. However, investigations have been conducted to compare the relative gains made by children in a psychoanalytically oriented treatment program with the gains made by children not receiving any treatment (Kanner & Eisenberg, 1955; Levitt, 1957, 1963). These studies found that the autistic children in the psychotherapy group did not make greater gains than those who received no treatment. Furthermore, Bartak and Rutter (1973) and Rutter and Bartak (1973) designed a series of studies to compare systematically the effectiveness of an analytically-oriented program with two other programs that emphasized a more structured and educational approach. While possible changes in internal dynamics were not (and could not at this time be) evaluated, data were obtained with respect to educational objectives. It was found that children in the psychoanalytic group made significantly *less* progress in areas such as speech, reading skills, and arithmetic skills and engaged in significantly *more* deviant behavior (e.g., self-stimulation).

## SENSORY-DEFICIT APPROACH

### Theoretical perspective

Many theories of autism focus on hypothesized deficits in sensory integration. For example, Ornitz and Ritvo (1968) have discussed the dysfunction in terms of a "perceptual" or "sensorimotor inconstancy." They postulate that an (underlying) failure of homeostatic regulation in the vestibular system results in an inability to modulate sensory input and motor output. Without control over incoming sensory stimulation, the child experiences random underloading and overloading of the central nervous system. The disturbances of motility and perception that are characteristic of autistic children (Ornitz & Ritvo, 1976) clearly exemplify the behavioral excitation and inhibition that would result from this type of dysfunction. Motor excitation is characterized by self-stimulatory behaviors such as hand-flapping, rocking, whirling, and toe-walking. In contrast, motor inhibition is characterized by posturing and prolonged immobility. Perceptual disturbances suggesting excitation are manifested in heightened awareness and overreactivity to sensory stimuli. Thus the child may attend to fine visual and tactile detail and may respond to barely audible sounds. Overreactivity may be manifested as extreme fear reactions to new or intense sounds, extreme distaste for specific foods, and agitation from excessive proprioceptive and vestibular stimulation. The underreactivity to loud or sudden noises, painful stimulation, and human contact are examples of inhibited sensory input in autistic children (Ornitz, 1971). Thus, the behavior of the autistic child suggests that sensory input is either inadequately "dampened" (i.e., overreactive) or excessively "dampened" (i.e., underreactive; Ornitz & Ritvo, 1968). Other disturbances, such as those in relating and language, are viewed as secondary to the underlying sensorimotor dysfunction.

Ornitz and Ritvo (1976) have relied on studies of rapid eye movement (REM) sleep and the oculor motor response (nystagmus) to support their model of sensory dysfunction. These studies have demonstrated the following: (1) an abnormal inhibition of the autistic child's oculor motor response to vestibular stimulation (e.g., Ornitz, Brown, Mason, & Putnam, 1974); and (2) an immature organization of REM bursts in response to vestibular stimulation during REM sleep (e.g., Ornitz, Forsythe, & de la Pena, 1973). Thus, clinical observations and indirect neurophysiological evidence point to a disturbance in the vestibular system.

Other investigators have based their theories of sensory dysfunction on a developmental model of receptor preferences (e.g., Goldfarb, 1956; Schopler, 1965; Stroh & Buick, 1964). Perceptual development is characterized as an orderly progression from preference and dependence on proximal receptors (such as tactile, kinesthetic, and gustatory) early in life, to the dominance of the distal sensory modalities (visual and auditory) in later life. Stroh and Buick (1964) and Schopler (1965) suggested that the failure to progress from proximal to distal receptor usage is the basic deficit in autism. Since both vision and audition are so intimately involved in communication and other cognitive skills, the question of receptor preferences has important implications. Clinical observations of autistic children seem to provide support for the dominance of near receptor functions. Ritvo and Provence (1953) reported that autistic children tend to explore their surroundings by mouthing or touching new objects. Goldfarb (1961) noted similar findings with schizophrenic children. He pointed out that the schizophrenic children in his program demonstrated a preference for near receptors such as touch, taste, and smell rather than visual or auditory modalities.

Early experimental investigations also supported the near-receptor preference model. Hermelin and O'Connor (1964) compared the responses of autistic and retarded children to light, sound, and tactile stimuli. Their results demonstrated that the autistic children responded more frequently than the retarded children to the tactile (near receptor) stimuli. In another investigation designed to compare the time spent in visual versus tactile exploration, Schopler (1966) found that schizophrenic children spent less time with visual stimuli than either retarded or normal children. In addition, the data for the normal children showed a tendency for increased visual preferences with increased age, thus supporting the notion of a transition from near-receptor to far-receptor modalities with age.

Schopler and Reichler (1971b) have attempted to account for some of the behavioral characteristics of autistic children by a receptor-deficit formulation. For example, the failure to learn appropriate social behavior and the apparent sensory deficit often reported are seen as resulting from the inability to organize and coordinate sensory information. Self-stimulatory behavior is seen as being due to a failure to reach a mental or visual representation of the sensorimotor coordination. The child is thought to be arrested at the point of meaningless repetitive behavior (Schopler, 1966).

DesLauriers and Carlson (1969) have related the developmental arrest and learning problems characteristic of autistic children to an impairment in the processing of the affective components of sensory experiences. Drawing from Routtenberg's (1968) model of arousal, they suggest that sensory experiences are mainly processed through two systems. System I, the reticular formation, is predominantly concerned with attending to sensory stimulation. In other words, System I must be active for the production and selection of the appropriate response to the sensory input. System II, the midbrain limbic system, processes the affective, pleasurable, or painful qualities of sensory stimulation. Under normal conditions the two systems are in a constant state of arousal. They are arranged in such a manner that each suppresses the activity of the other. This reciprocal suppression allows for the systems to be in a dynamic equilibrium. For example, with the presentation of a new or novel stimulus, System I is activated; a response is emitted, and the occurrence of a reward or punishment stimulates System II. Activation of System II inhibits the activity of System I. Thus, while System I is necessary for alerting the organism to attend to the stimuli and emit responses, it is System II which is aroused during the actual learning process. DesLauriers and Carlson proposed that the behavioral manifestations of autism (e.g., self-stimulation, language delay, and lack of appropriate social behavior) result from an imbalance in the two systems, such that System I dominates or inhibits System II. Thus, the child, while capable of attending and responding to novel stimuli, is unable to establish any associations between response and reward contingencies.

Clinical observations of autistic children also lend support to this model. Autistic children are often described as being aloof, detached, and emotionally unresponsive to events occurring around them. In addition, the stereotypic responses characteristic of autistic children are seen as the result of behavioral responses for which no affective feedback is processed.

Other investigators (e.g., Ayres, 1972; Ayres and Heskett, 1972; Ball, 1971; Frostig, 1966; Kephart, 1960) have also written extensively on the relationship between sensory-integrative deficits and learning disorders such as autism. While their theories and those reviewed above may emphasize different aspects of sensory functioning, they all postulate that underlying sensory-integrative dysfunction is responsible for the abnormal behaviors characteristic of autistic children.

**Educational–treatment procedures**

Numerous educational–treatment procedures for autistic children have evolved from sensory-deficit models. Schopler and Reichler (1971a, 1971b) developed a program in which near-receptor modalities are emphasized in order to facilitate cortical control and integration of perceptual information. Specific interventions have been developed to encourage growth in the three areas in which the child is thought to be especially deficient: (1) human relatedness; (2) perceptual–motor organization; and (3) cognitive functioning.

The absence of age-appropriate relatedness is viewed as characteristic of autistic children. The development of relatedness is especially important, since other areas such as imitation and language are dependent on responsiveness. Initially, the therapist attempts to include himself in all of the child's activity. The child is not allowed to move about the room or engage in any activity without the mediation of the therapist. Withdrawal and self-stimulatory behaviors are immediately stopped and redirected into some activity that includes the adult. Stimulation is provided by the adult through the near-receptor modalities, since sensory input through these channels is processed without confusion. The stimulation may include cuddling, lifting, bouncing, stroking, or swinging the child. As the child responds more favorably to this type of interaction, the therapist begins to impose more demands. For example, the therapist may require that some action or task be completed before meeting the child's request.

Although the deficits in perceptual–motor integration are related to the child's lack of social behavior, the teaching procedures used to promote it are different. The focus in perceptual-motor training is the continuous exercise of perceptual-motor tasks to yield improvement in the child's awareness and coordinated use of his body. For example, basic perceptual exercises are developed to facilitate eye–hand coordination (e.g., assisting the child in using both hands to clap, stacking blocks, or puzzle building), balance (e.g., using balance beams), and perceptual discriminations (e.g., using a graded series of cups or puzzles). During therapy there is a gradual attempt to develop the coordinated use of near- and far-receptor modalities. This enables the child to develop a constancy of perception and awareness.

As the child's overall organization of perceptual information increases, the emphasis turns to the cognitive impairments. The primary concern in this area is the development of receptive and expressive means of communication. This might involve teaching the child to recognize and name objects in his environment, to discriminate colors, forms, and sizes, expressive and receptive use of action verbs, number concepts, etc. Development of some concepts may be facilitated by incorporating the sensory modalities. For example, a therapist may begin teaching a child the concept of up and down by lifting him up and down and saying the appropriate word. Others working within a sensory-deficit framework have employed behavior modification techniques (e.g., Hingtgen & Churchill, 1971).

An important component of Schopler and Reichler's program is the inclusion of the parents in every aspect of treatment (Schopler, 1974; Schopler & Reichler, 1971b). The basic developmental philosophy of the program is explained and the parents are taught how to incorporate the techniques discussed above into their everyday interactions. In this way, the child receives treatment throughout most of the day. These authors suggest that the use of parents as cotherapists should facilitate the acquisition, maintenance, and generalization of the skills taught to the child.

Frostig (1966) has also developed a program for autistic children based on the assumption that perceptual deficiencies are the primary cause of the child's behavioral, social, and cognitive retardation. She and her colleagues have proposed an educational treatment program designed to remediate the child's deficits by emphasizing perceptual and sensory experiences. During the initial phase of Frostig's (1966) treatment program, the therapist attempts to establish a relationship with the child by engaging him in physical activities. This phase is similar to Schopler and Reichler's development of relatedness, and relies on many of the same treatment procedures. Physical contact is promoted through cuddling, rocking, stroking, swinging, or lifting the child. Withdrawal, self-stimulatory behavior, or self-injurious behavior is immediately stopped and the activity is redirected in an appropriate manner that includes the therapist. As the child begins to accept and seek out the relationship, the therapist attempts to increase the child's awareness of himself. Frostig suggested that techniques such as giving tactile stimulation, directly imitating the child's actions and feelings, showing the child his reflection in a mirror to encourage self-recognition, and encouraging simple perceptual–motor tasks will enable the child to develop a sense of bodily awareness.

As the child's awareness increases, the efforts to promote perceptual development are intensified. This phase of the treatment is considered the most crucial since the growth of language, cognitive processes, and motor functions are all dependent on perceptual development (Frostig, 1975). The therapist exposes the child to the sight, sound, smell, and taste of all the objects in his environment. Physical activities of all kinds (e.g., climbing, jumping, swinging, balancing, and running) are also encouraged. The intention is to decrease perceptual confusion, thus increasing the child's ability to utilize all of his senses in understanding the environment.

The treatment program designed by DesLauriers and Carlson (1969) emphasizes the importance of exposing the child to pleasurable and gratifying sensory experiences. They suggested that the stimulation necessary to bring about a meaningful affective response from the child may best be provided within play situations. The kinesthetic and tactile stimulation, together with the "excitement, novelty, and fun," provided by a play situation can create a level of arousal intense enough to overcome the high thresholds of affective receptivity created by the inhibition of System II by System I. DesLauriers and Carlson noted that within the play situation the therapist must begin by serving as the center of the child's activities. The child is not allowed to be isolated or engage in behaviors such as self-stimulation. Instead, the therapist uses kinesthetic and tactile stimulation to ensure that the child is cognizant of the therapist's presence. All activities must take place in a highly intense affective climate. This is achieved by emphasizing the "fun" quality of the therapist–child interactions. The child's acceptance of the relationship that emerges out of these interactions is considered to be the first attempt at communication. The therapist attempts to increase communication by intensifying both the affective climate and the sensory stimulation possibilities of the play situation. No special efforts are made, however, to teach the child any specific skills or concepts (DesLauriers, 1978). Instead, it is believed that the child will start learning as exposure to a variety of human experiences in an environment of affective and sensory stimulation is increased. Once the affective barrier is overcome and the child begins to learn, it is possible to use ordinary teaching methods to develop new skills.

**Evaluation**

At the present time there are extensive data to suggest that autistic children differ from normal children in their responses to incoming stimuli (e.g., Hingtgen & Bryson, 1972). Thus, it is not surprising that there has been a proliferation of theories and treatment programs based on models of underlying sensory dysfunction. However, the exact nature of the autistic child's sensory deficits have not been clearly demonstrated. Ornitz and his colleagues' conclusion that a dysfunction in the vestibular system is the primary basis for autism has been questioned in light of the fact that their studies have lacked the control groups necessary to determine whether or not the findings are specific to autism; also, few of their results have been replicated (Yule, 1978). Ornitz and Ritvo (1968) have suggested that faulty modulation of sensory input and motor output could result in random processing or random responding to identical stimulus input. However, research by Alpern (1967) has demonstrated that autistic children are very reliable in their performances on psychological tests, in that they tend to pass or fail the same items each time the test is presented. According to Ornitz and Ritvo's theory, the autistic child's response pattern should be random, since the test items would not be perceived as identical upon re-presentation. Similar problems with this aspect of the theory have been noted in light of the research on stimulus overselectivity (e.g., Lovaas, Schreibman, Koegel, & Rehm, 1971). Rather than responding randomly to stimulus presentations (as would be expected from Ornitz and Ritvo's model), the autistic children in the latter research tended to repeatedly respond primarily on the basis of one aspect of the stimulus presentation (e.g., visual or auditory). In summary then, while there is some support for the notion that the vestibular system is involved in the development of autism, there is a need for considerably more research in this area.

Empirical research has also been equivocal regarding the view that autism results primarily from a failure to progress from near- to far-receptor usage. Schopler's (1966) study did not find a difference between normal, retarded, and schizophrenic children in their preference for tactile stimulation. In addition, he did not find that the normal children decreased in their preference for near-receptor stimulation with age. Hermelin and O'Connor (1965) also failed to find evidence of receptor preference. They presented a light paired with either a tone or a verbal command ("come here") to autistics, Down's Syndrome retardates, and non-Down's Syndrome retardates. All responses, regardless of modality of presentation, were rewarded. While both groups of retarded children demonstrated light dominance, the results demonstrated that the autistic children responded primarily on the basis of position cues, and thus did not respond differentially to the modality of presentation or the type of auditory stimulus. Lovaas et al. (1971) found that while normal children would respond to all components of a stimulus complex consisting of auditory, visual, and tactile cues, autistic children responded on the basis of either the visual or auditory stimuli. None of them responded to the tactile stimulus.

The empirical evidence does not adequately support the notion of near-receptor modality preferences in autistic children. However, Schopler and Reichler (1971b) have noted that autistic children do benefit from their treatment procedures. Without a systematic evaluation, however, it is difficult to attribute improvements to an emphasis on the near-receptor modalities per se.

DesLauriers and Carlson's suggestion that autism results from a dysfunction of the reticular formation associated with abnormal arousal levels has also been questioned (Rutter, 1978). Empirical evidence on the arousal levels of autistic children is inconclusive. Some studies have pointed to chronically high levels of arousal (Hutt, Hutt, Lee, & Ounsted, 1965), and others to chronically low levels of arousal (Rimland, 1964), while still others have postulated alternating periods of under- or over-arousal (Ornitz & Ritvo, 1968). DesLauriers and Carlson have not presented any neurological studies to substantiate their claim of a specific dysfunction. Until such data are presented (with the appropriate controls as suggested by Yule, 1978), DesLauriers and Carlson's hypothesis cannot be considered "proven."

While DesLauriers and Carlson (1969) and DesLauriers (1978) have presented case studies illustrating the effectiveness of their procedures, the lack of a systematic evaluation of the treatment methods makes it difficult to determine the important variables. Without some empirical verification that it is the high affective content of the play sessions that is responsible for improvements, the critical elements in the effectiveness of "theraplay" remain in question.

Several educators and researchers have questioned the fundamental assumption underlying Frostig's program, i.e., that the development of perceptual or sensorimotor abilities is essential to functioning in more advanced areas (e.g., Goodman & Hammill, 1973; Mann, 1970, 1971). Although much of the critical research has not been focused directly on autism, it has attempted to establish whether or not Frostig's program of perceptual–motor training in general facilitates improvements in other areas. In a review of the research pertaining to Frostig's perceptual training program, Hammill, Goodman, and Wiederholt (1974) noted that 13 of the 14 studies reviewed failed to find significant gains in the reading achievement scores of children who had received the training. In addition, Mann and Goodman (1976) noted that a majority of studies examining the effectiveness of Frostig's program on the development of perceptual motor skills per se reported no significant differences between trained and nontrained subjects.

From the above review, and on the basis of our knowledge of autism and neurological functions, it may be premature to implicate a specific sensory-integrative system (Yule, 1978). The effectiveness of treatment methods based on the assumptions of a specific sensory deficit has not yet been empirically demonstrated. While improvements have been reported, it is difficult to establish that they are a function of a specific type of improved sensory processing.

## BEHAVIOR MODIFICATION

### Theoretical perspective

The behavioral model differs considerably from the others reviewed in this chapter. The psychogenic and sensory-deficit approaches viewed autism as a specific syndrome resulting from an underlying disturbance. In contrast, rather than postulating a specific etiology (with the exception of Ferster, 1961), behavior modification has sought to promote specific treatment changes in behavior that can be observed and measured directly. A basic assumption of the behavioral model is that, independent of original cause, behaviors (both normal and deviant) are strengthened or weakened as a result of their interaction with the positive (rewarding) and negative (punishing) consequences provided by the environment.

121

Within this model, behaviorists have suggested that child development consists primarily of the acquisition of behaviors and stimulus functions (Lovaas & Koegel, 1973; Lovaas & Newsom, 1976; Lovaas, Schreibman, & Koegel, 1974). From a behavioral perspective, one would attempt to increase deficient behaviors by reinforcing their occurrence and reduce behavioral excesses either by systematically removing the reinforcers that may be maintaining the behaviors, or by systematically applying aversive stimuli each time the behaviors occur. Similarly, one might attempt to treat autistic children by manipulating antecedents and consequences of the behavior to make aspects of the environment more "meaningful."

Ferster and DeMyer (1962) provided the first demonstration of how the behavior of autistic children could be controlled by an explicit set of environmental contingencies. They found that they could teach autistic children simple behaviors such as lever pulling or matching to sample when these behaviors were required for the child to receive a desired reward (candy). The importance of this study lies not in what was taught, but in the empirical demonstration that systematic manipulation of environmental contingencies could result in the acquisition of new behaviors. Later studies (e.g., Wolf, Risley & Mees, 1964; Wolf, Risley, Johnston, Harris, & Allen, 1967) confirmed and extended the findings of Ferster and DeMyer. These studies all used principles from learning theory to demonstrate that the behavior of autistic children was lawful; that is, by arranging an explicit system of contingent rewards and punishments the behavior of autistic children could be modified.

### Educational–treatment procedures

Rather than attempting to devise a treatment procedure designed to correct an underlying deficiency, behavior modification primarily has sought to develop procedures for changing individual behaviors based on an analysis of the variables that might influence them. As such, it should be clear that the relevant literature cuts across many traditional diagnostic categories. If two children exhibit the same behavior, regardless of whether or not they have different global diagnoses (autism, mental retardation, aphasia, etc.), they are likely to have been included in the research. An important aspect of a behavioral treatment program is its emphasis on the objective measurement of all phases of the program (Kozloff, 1974). Continual measurement of a behavior allows a therapist to assess whether or not the treatment is having any impact on the child's behavior.

A first step in developing a behavioral treatment program is to identify and operationally define those behaviors that the therapist desires to change. Making an operational definition involves describing the target behavior in a manner that would allow reliable measurement by independent observers (Schreibman & Koegel, in press). An operational definition of a behavior enables the therapist to discriminate precisely the correctness of a response and to determine the direction of treatment. Once the target behaviors have been operationally defined, the therapist should determine what variables influence the behaviors. This involves a detailed examination of both the events that precede the behavior *(antecedents)* and those that follow it *(consequences)*. Isolating the influencing variables enables the therapist to manipulate them in order to facilitate the acquisition of appropriate behaviors and stimulus functions. For example, the type of instruction presented *(antecedent event)* may influence whether or not the child responds correctly. Schreibman & Koegel (in press) suggest that instructions that are long and complicated may contain a number of irrelevant stimuli that make it difficult for a child to discriminate the intent of the instruction. The consequences that follow a behavior are particularly important in determining whether or not the behavior will recur. A positive consequence *(reinforcer)* should follow a target behavior that a therapist desires to increase, while a negative consequence *(punisher)* should follow a target behavior that is to be reduced. Whether or not a consequence is a *functional* reinforcer or punisher is determined solely by its effect on a behavior. For example, if a particular consequence (e.g., candy or music) increases a behavior it is a functional reinforcer. If, on the other hand, the consequence decreases behavior, it is a functional punisher. The manner in which the therapist delivers a consequence is as important as ensuring that it is functional. Schreibman & Koegel (in press) have noted four basic rules for applying consequences: (1) the consequence must be delivered immediately after the response; (2) the consequence delivery must be consistent; (3) the consequence must be delivered so that it is unambiguous; and (4) the consequence should be discriminable from all other aspects of the therapist–child interaction.

*Eliminating behavioral excesses*

Prior to teaching new skills, the therapist must reduce or eliminate any behaviors that significantly interfere with the acquisition of adaptive behaviors. Interfering behaviors can usually be classified into three groups: (1) disruptive behaviors such as tantrums and aggression; (2) self-stimulatory behaviors; and (3) stimulus overselectivity.

*Disruptive behavior.* One of the most salient problems that a

123

therapist must deal with is the disruptive behavior of autistic children. The most salient of these are severe tantrums and self-destructive behavior. Since tantrums are characteristic of many autistic children, research within the behavioral model has led to the development of effective techniques for eliminating tantrumous behavior. *Extinction* is an effective and frequently used procedure for reducing undesirable behavior. Typically, in an extinction procedure a therapist withholds a reinforcer contingent on a particular behavior. For example, if a child's tantrums are maintained by the reinforcer of teacher attention, ceasing to provide that attention eliminates the tantrums. While extinction is an effective procedure, research has demonstrated several possible drawbacks to its use. First, there is usually a gradual reduction in the strength of the behavior, rather than a sharp, dramatic drop (cf. Lovaas & Simmons, 1969). Second, there is usually an initial (temporary) increase in the strength of the behavior; that is, once the attention maintaining a child's tantrum is no longer present, the intensity of the tantrum may increase as the child attempts to "recover" the lost attention.

*Punishment* has also been shown to be an effective treatment procedure for eliminating tantrums and aggressive behavior (Lichstein & Schreibman, 1976; Lovaas & Simmons, 1969; Tate & Baroff, 1966). A review of the literature indicates that a wide variety of effective punishment techniques are available. Many times a mild verbal "No" has been sufficient to reduce the undesirable behavior, while in other cases physical punishment in the form of a quick slap on the hand or even contingent electric shock has been necessary. However, therapists may find the use of physical punishment too extreme for a particular behavior, or such severe punishment may be inappropriate in certain situations. As a result, a variety of other, less severe punishment procedures have also been developed to control disruptive behavior (cf. Lichstein & Schreibman, 1976).

One relatively mild, yet effective, procedure for dealing with outbursts is *time-out,* defined by White, Nielsen, and Johnson (1972) as an "arrangement in which the occurrence of a response is followed by a period of time in which a variety of reinforcers are no longer available." In a classroom situation, this may involve placing the child in a small, bare room for a specific time following the undesirable behavior, or it may merely involve the therapist looking away from the child (if the reinforcers are primarily social). Time-out has been used extensively for eliminating behavior across a wide variety of children and in varying situations. One of the earliest empirical demonstrations of its effectiveness was conducted by Wolf et al. (1964), who demonstrated that tantrums and self-destructive behavior in an autistic child could be reduced effectively by placing him alone in a room each time the behavior occurred. Similar to the procedures related above, the authors suggested that it is desirable to positively reinforce incompatible nondeviant behavior in combination with time-out.

While time-out has been shown to be an extremely effective punishment technique for reducing undesirable behavior, there are several important parameters to consider when implementing the procedure. One consideration is the optimum duration that a child should be placed in time-out. The literature shows that time-out intervals of 2 minutes (Bostow & Bailey, 1969) to 3 hours (Burchard & Tyler, 1965) have been used successfully. White et al. (1972) pointed out that a majority of investigators reported successful results using time-out durations in the range of 5–20 minutes. It can be inferred from the above studies that there is no consensus on an "optimum" duration for time-out. Duration appears to be dependent on the child and the particular behavior that is to be reduced. An effective time-out duration for one child may be completely ineffective for another.

Recent research has pointed out that this is also true of the time-out procedure in general. Solnick, Rincover, and Peterson (1977) suggested that there is no "standard" time-out procedure that will effectively reduce problem behavior. In a recent study designed to examine possible punishing as well as *reinforcing* effects of time-out, Solnick et al. found that when time-out was employed to suppress tantrumous behavior, it had the opposite effect; that is, time-out resulted in a substantial increase in the frequency of tantrums. Upon further analysis, it was shown that the time-out period was used by the child to engage in self-stimulatory behavior. In other words, the increase in tantrumous behavior appeared to be a function of increased sensory reinforcement resulting from the opportunity to engage in self-stimulation. These results suggest that teachers using time-out should ensure that the child is not engaging in preferred behaviors during the time-out period.

A related finding from the Solnick et al. (1977) study suggested that the effectiveness of a time-out procedure may also be influenced by the nature of the "time-in" setting. The authors found that when the time-in setting was not highly reinforcing ("impoverished"), time-out was ineffective in reducing the frequency of spitting and self-injurious behavior. In a situation such as this, time-out may serve as a negative reinforcer in that the child's behavior removes him from an undesirable situation (e.g., an unsuccessful environment). However, when the time-in environment was highly reinforcing ("enriched") the same time-out procedure was effective in reducing the undesirable behaviors (Carr, Newsom, & Binkoff, 1976; Solnick et al., 1977).

Additional techniques for reducing tantrums and other undesirable behaviors have been developed and may be employed when time-out is inappropriate. Plummer, Baer, and LeBlanc (1977) found that in situations where time-out had the effect of negatively reinforcing inappropriate behavior, the use of paced instructions (instructions regardless of the child's behavior) was another effective alternative to time-out. One final point to note about time-out is that, in some cases, time-out may be costly in terms of available teaching time, since it requires the child to be removed from the teaching environment each time the inappropriate behavior occurs. Clark, Rowbury, Baer, and Baer (1973) suggested that the use of an intermittent schedule of time-out would reduce inappropriate behavior while allowing for more teaching time. Their results indicated that time-out used as a consequence for every third or fourth occurrence of an inappropriate act was nearly as effective as a schedule in which time-out was applied for every occurrence of the disruptive behavior.

Foxx and Azrin (1972) reported on a method referred to as *restitution* or *overcorrection* for eliminating physically disruptive acts. The restitution procedure proposed by Foxx and Azrin has two objectives: (1) to overcorrect the environmental effects of an inappropriate act, and (2) to require the disruptor to practice thoroughly overly correct forms of appropriate behavior. The first objective is achieved through the use of restitutional overcorrection. This procedure requires the disruptive individual to return the disturbed situation to a greatly improved state, thus providing an instructive situation in which the individual is required to assume personal responsibility for the disruptive act. For example, a child who smeared paint on a floor might be required to clean up the mess and then vacuum and wax the area. The second objective is achieved through positive practice overcorrection. Using this procedure, the child who smeared the paint on the floor, rather than on an appropriate sheet of paper, might be required to paint appropriately on the paper several times. When no environmental disruption occurs, the restitutional overcorrection is not applicable and only the positive practice is used. The effectiveness of overcorrection as a procedure for eliminating aggressive disruptive behavior was clearly demonstrated by Foxx and Azrin (1972). They employed an overcorrection procedure to reduce aggressive behavior (e.g., physical assault, property damage, tantrums, and biting). The results show that whereas time-out and social disapproval had both been ineffective in eliminating the above behaviors, overcorrection reduced the disruptive behaviors to a near zero level within 1–2 weeks. Overcorrection thus appears to be a viable means for reducing acts of aggression. The procedure (as described by its proponents) may lessen some of the negative aspects of other punishment procedures, it may educate the individual in appropriate behavior, and it may involve relatively little staff training (Foxx & Azrin, 1972). Additional research, however, appears necessary in order to substantiate these latter points. Axelrod, Brantner, and Meddock (1978) reviewed overcorrection research and noted that potential side effects have yet to be carefully examined, the need for maintaining topographical similarity between the response and its consequence is unclear, and many parameters of maximally efficient administration of overcorrection (such as duration of the consequence) are still unknown.

*Self-stimulatory behavior.* One type of disruptive behavior which deserves special attention is self-stimulatory behavior. Self-stimulatory behavior is the persistent stereotyped, repetitive behavior that is considered to be one of the most defining characteristics of autistic children. It is also one of the most formidable obstacles for educating these children. Lovaas, Litrownik, and Mann (1971) observed that responding to previously functional auditory cues was disrupted when a child engaged in self-stimulatory behavior, yet recovered when self-stimulation was absent. They suggested that when a child is engaged in self-stimulation, he may not be able to attend to more relevant stimuli. With this issue in mind, Koegel and Covert (1972) attempted to teach a simple discrimination task to three autistic children with high levels of self-stimulatory behavior. Their results clearly established that self-stimulatory behavior can interfere with the acquisition of a new stimulus discrimination. They found that although they continued responding, none of the children learned the discrimination while engaging in self-stimulation. However, when self-stimulation was suppressed, the children acquired the discrimination. This apparent inverse relationship between self-stimulation and the acquisition of new, appropriate behaviors has been demonstrated repeatedly. Risley (1968) and Foxx and Azrin (1973a) found that various prosocial and attentional behaviors increased when self-stimulation was suppressed, while others have pointed to increases in behaviors such as appropriate play (Epstein, Doke, Sajwaj, Sorrell, & Rimmer, 1974; Koegel, Firestone, Kramme, & Dunlap, 1974).

Therapeutic procedures utilized in attempts to suppress self-stimulation have varied, as have the results. One procedure involved reinforcing responses incompatible with self-stimulation. For example, Mul-

127

hern and Baumeister (1969) reinforced two retarded children for sitting still to reduce their self-stimulatory rocking behavior. They found that this procedure reduced the rocking behavior by about one-third. Other (e.g., Dietz & Repp, 1973; Herendeen, Jeffrey, & Graham, 1974) have also employed reinforcement to substantially reduce self-stimulatory behavior. Despite the demonstrated effectiveness of reinforcing incompatible behavior to reduce self-stimulation, it has not been successful in completely suppressing self-stimulatory behavior. Furthermore, others using this procedure (e.g., Foxx & Azrin, 1973a) have not obtained decreases in self-stimulatory behavior of the magnitude previously reported.

A second procedure that has been used effectively to reduce and eliminate self-stimulatory behavior employs physical punishment. The punishment has taken the form of contingent electric shock (Lovaas, Schaeffer, & Simmons, 1965; Risley, 1968) and contingent slaps on the thigh or hand (Bucher & Lovaas, 1968; Foxx & Azrin, 1973a; Koegel & Covert, 1972; Koegel et al., 1974). Each of these studies has demonstrated that contingent physical punishment is a highly effective method for suppressing self-stimulation. However, as noted above, such severe punishment procedures can have many problems, and time-out probably will increase the behavior. As a result, other investigators have developed alternative punishment techniques that also are effective in suppressing self-stimulatory behavior. Robinson, Hughes, Wilson, Lahey, and Haynes (1974) found that the use of response-contingent water squirts was effective in reducing self-stimulatory behavior. The authors noted the relative ease with which this procedure was applied. Furthermore, it required very little time (1–3 seconds) to deliver the punishment and therefore did not require the teacher to leave one child in order to deliver punishment to another. Despite these benefits, the complete and enduring elimination of self-stimulatory behavior was not achieved. In addition, the authors indicated that the reduced levels of self-stimulation did not generalize beyond the classroom environment.

Another mild punishment procedure that has been shown to be extremely effective in suppressing self-stimulation is overcorrection (Foxx & Azrin, 1973a). Foxx and Azrin (1973a) compared several techniques used to suppress self-stimulation (including punishment by a slap and reinforcement for not engaging in self-stimulation) with positive practice overcorrection. Their results showed that the only procedure that eliminated self-stimulatory behavior in the experimental session and during the entire school day was the positive practice overcorrection procedure. For example, a child who mouthed objects was required to repeatedly use mouth wash. The treatment was effective across several types of self-stimulatory behaviors, including head-weaving, object-mouthing, hand-clapping, and hand-mouthing. Furthermore, the results suggested that a verbal reprimand in conjunction with an occasional application of the overcorrection procedure was sufficient to maintain reduced levels of self-stimulation. Other investigators (e.g., Azrin, Kaplan, & Foxx, 1973; Epstein et al., 1974; Herendeen et al., 1974) have confirmed and extended the above findings. Thus overcorrection appears to be a viable method for substantially reducing self-stimulatory behaviors. While positive practice overcorrection offers an effective alternative to intense physical punishment and reinforcement of incompatible responses, its practicality in applied settings may be limited due to the demand on therapist time and energy. The technique demands (in some settings) more attention to a particular individual than a therapist may be able to afford.

Despite some successes with the above procedures in reducing self-stimulatory behavior, the "generalized, durable elimination of self-stimulatory behaviors" has not been achieved (Rincover & Koegel, 1977a). Recently, investigators have suggested that the difficulty in eliminating self-stimulation may be a function of its internal reinforcing properties; that is, self-stimulation may be viewed as operant behavior maintained by its sensory consequences (Rincover, Newsom, Lovaas, & Koegel, 1977). For example, a behavior such as finger-flapping may be maintained by the resulting proprioceptive feedback. The conceptualization of self-stimulatory behavior as behavior maintained by the auditory, proprioceptive, or visual consequences has led to the development of a new procedure for eliminating self-stimulation. The procedure of *sensory extinction* is based on the notion that self-stimulatory behavior should extinguish when the reinforcing (sensory) consequences are removed. Rincover (1978a) has demonstrated the effectiveness of sensory extinction for eliminating self-stimulation. He found that it reliably extinguished when specific sensory consequences were removed and increased when those consequences were permitted. Since the sensory reinforcers maintaining the self-stimulation were distinct across children, different sensory extinction procedures were required for different self-stimulatory behaviors. For example, for one child a blindfold was used to eliminate the visual feedback produced by twirling objects, while for another child a carpeted area was used to mask the auditory feedback produced by plate spinning. The above finding was consistently replicated across children. The results of this procedure have far-ranging clinical implications. Rincover (1978a) suggested that the procedure requires very little staff training or child surveillance, has an immediate effect, and should require relatively little effort to program the generalization and maintenance of treatment gains.

While additional research is needed to establish more concretely the parameters involved in the durable elimination of self-stimulation, the systematic analysis of the controlling variables thus far known has provided therapists with procedures for increasing the effectiveness of the learning environment.

*Stimulus overselectivity.* Characteristic of many autistic children is a tendency to respond to only a very restricted portion of their environment. Researchers investigating the learning abilities of autistic children have become increasingly concerned about this problem, which has been referred to as stimulus overselectivity (Lovaas, Schreibman, Koegel, & Rehm, 1971). Specifically, it appears that when autistic children are presented with a learning situation that requires responding to multiple cues within a complex stimulus, their behavior comes under the control of a very limited portion of those cues.

In the first experimental demonstration of this problem, Lovaas et al. (1971) trained normal, retarded, and autistic children to make a response in the presence of a complex stimulus consisting of visual, auditory, and tactile cues. When the components of the stimulus complex were then presented individually, the authors found that the normal children responded equally to all three of the component cues; the autistic children, however, responded primarily to one of the component cues. In other words, each of the separate cues became equal in controlling the behavior of the normal children, but, in marked contrast, the autistic child responded only in the presence of the auditory component (three children) or the visual component (two children). Additionally, the authors found that the autistic children could be taught to respond to the nonfunctional cues when these cues were presented alone. Thus, the study suggested that the deficit was not a function of a specific sensory impairment, but was a problem in responding to a component cue in the context of other cues. Since the original demonstrations by Lovaas et al., this finding has been replicated in a two-cue situation (Lovaas & Schreibman, 1971), with all visual cues (Koegel & Wilhelm 1973), and with auditory cues (Reynolds, Newsom, & Lovaas, 1974). A comprehensive review of these and other studies related to stimulus overselectivity has been provided by Schreibman and Koegel (in press).

The implications of these findings become apparent when one examines the number of situations that are encountered that require the ability to respond on the basis of multiple cues. Overselectivity has been discussed as a variable influencing language acquisition (Lovaas et al., 1971; Reynolds, Newsom, & Lovaas, 1974), social behavior (Schreibman & Lovaas, 1973), observational learning (Varni, Lovaas, Koegel, & Everett, 1979), prompting (Koegel & Rincover, 1976; Rincover, 1978b; Schreibman, 1975), and generalization (Rincover & Koegel, 1975).

The severity of the overselectivity problem has led to research investigating treatment techniques for eliminating it. In one study, Schover and Newsom (1976) attempted to teach autistic children to respond to multiple cues by overtraining an already learned discrimination. Their results indicated that through overtraining they were able to increase the number of cues that the children responded to. Schreibman, Koegel, and Craig (1977), further investigating the overtraining procedure, found that overtraining per se (just exposure) did not increase the number of cues to which the child responded. Instead, they found that prolonged interspersing of unreinforced probe trials with component cues among reinforced trials with the stimulus complex eliminated overselectivity (in 13 of 16 autistic children who were initially overselective).

Koegel and Schreibman (1977) carried this line of research one step further. They taught four autistic and four normal children a conditional discrimination requiring a response to multiple cross-modal (auditory and visual) cues. Their results showed that the autistic children learned the discriminations, although they did not learn them with ease, nor did they learn them in the same manner as normal children. The autistic children persistently tended to respond at a higher level to one of the component cues and only after many (typically hundreds of) trials did they learn to respond on the basis of both cues. This was, however, optimistic in that they did learn to respond to multiple cues. Furthermore, in one case, when an autistic child was taught a series of successive conditional discriminations, the child eventually learned a generalized set to respond to new conditional discriminations on the basis of both component cues. The results of these studies suggest that the selective responding characteristic of many autistic children is a problem that is modifiable through the manipulation of environmental events.

*Acquisition of new behaviors and stimulus functions*

The previous investigations have described a behavioral approach for reducing or eliminating behaviors that significantly interfere with the learning process. The manipulation of antecedent and consequence variables is also crucial for teaching new behaviors and stimulus functions. In a behavioral treatment program the antecedent variables usually manipulated are the instructions ($S^D$) and prompt stimuli. As previously suggested, the manner in which an instruction is given can influence whether or not a child learns a particular response. The therapist must ensure that the child is attending to the instruction and that the instruction serves as an easily discriminable cue for a particular response (Schreibman & Koegel, in press). To achieve this, the therapist may initially be required to reinforce attending behaviors such as eye contact, or sitting in a chair. Once attending behaviors are established the therapist can enhance the discriminability of the instruction by making it short and specific to the desired response.

The establishment of a stimulus as discriminative for a response ($S^D$) is one aspect of the acquisition of stimulus functions. In this case the child learns to make a certain response when presented with a specific $S^D$, and not to make the response when the $S^D$ is absent. Carr, Schreibman, and Lovaas (1975) demonstrated how a particular antecedent event influenced immediate echolalia. They found that the children tended to echo only those questions and commands which had not previously been established as discriminative for a specific response. For example, a child might respond appropriately to the question, "What's your name?" but would echo a nonsense phrase such as "Min dar snick." They suggested that those stimuli which were not discriminative for a response were meaningless for the children; the children tended to respond appropriately only for those stimuli that were meaningful.

Often, the desired behavior is not evoked by the $S^D$ alone. When this occurs, it may be necessary to manually guide or prompt the response. *Prompts* are extra cues that help the child to respond correctly (Koegel & Rincover, 1976). For example, if the $S^D$ "Touch red" does not evoke a response from the child, the therapist can manually guide the child's hand to the red stimulus while presenting the $S^D$. Prompting can be an extremely useful technique to establish a response. However, it must be gradually removed so that the control of the response is shifted from the prompt stimuli to the $S^D$. Returning to the previous example, rather than guiding the child through the entire response, the therapist might only move the child's hand half-way. Less and less guidance would be used until the prompt was completely eliminated.

While the removal of a prompt may seem to be a relatively simple procedure, many studies have shown that autistic children have a particularly difficult time shifting from the prompt stimuli to the training stimuli (e.g., Koegel & Rincover, 1976; Schreibman, 1975). The results of these studies are not surprising in light of what is known about stimulus overselectivity. Since most prompting procedures require the child to respond to multiple cues (prompt and training stimuli), the overselectivity would influence the child to respond on the basis of a limited number of the cues present. Schreibman (1975) and Rincover

(1978b) have attempted to remediate this problem by developing special treatment procedures for prompting and prompt fading.

Schreibman (1975) developed a method for allowing the autistic child to learn with prompts even if he was overselective. She used prompts that were contained within the training stimulus (within-stimulus prompt). This procedure does not require the child to respond to multiple cues since the prompt is not extra to the training stimulus but is part of it. In comparing the within-stimulus prompt with extra-stimulus prompts, Schreibman found that the children learned the discrimination only when the within-stimulus prompt was employed. The within-stimulus prompting procedure can be illustrated by the following example. In teaching a child to recognize the difference between a $p$ and a $b$ a teacher might emphasize (through exaggeration) the orientation of the stems of the letters. The orientation of the stems is considered the relevant component of the discrimination since the other components of the letters are redundant. The exaggerated component is then gradually faded until the child is discriminating between the appropriate-sized letters. Since the prompt is contained within the final stimulus, it requires the child to respond only on the basis of this stimulus and not other additional cues.

Rincover (1978b) has extended Schreibman's work by examining four treatment procedures designed to facilitate prompt fading. The most effective technique was a within-stimulus distinctive-feature fading procedure. In this procedure, a child is pretrained to respond to a feature of one stimulus which is not a part of the other stimulus (i.e., a distinctive feature). For example, in an $E$ versus $F$ discrimination, the bottom line of the $E$ is the distinctive feature which would be emphasized. During pretraining this feature is exaggerated and presented alone. Subsequently, the stimuli are presented with the pretrained feature superimposed on the correct choice. At that point, the exaggerated feature is gradually faded until the stimulus takes its normal form. This procedure, a special form of within-stimulus prompting, appears to be the most effective prompting procedure known for autistic children at this time.

There are two other procedures that a behavior therapist can use to facilitate learning when the target response is not already in the child's repertoire. These are especially helpful when attempting to teach a complex response. For example, a complex response can be redefined so that the child initially need only approximate it to be rewarded. Thus in a *shaping* procedure, a therapist initially rewards the closest approximation to the appropriate response in the child's repertoire. Gradually, the therapist requires the child to respond with closer and closer approximations until the complex response is made. In this procedure, the child is only rewarded for a response that is at least as good as those preceeding it. The effectiveness of shaping as a treatment procedure was empirically demonstrated in the language programs of Hewett (1965) and Lovaas (1969). In these programs, the children were initially rewarded for all vocalizations. Then, the children were rewarded only if any vocalization occurred within a specific time limit following the therapist's vocalization. In the third step, only responses that actually matched the therapist's vocalization were rewarded. Thus, the therapist shaped a specific vocalization by reinforcing successive approximations to the desired response.

Complex behaviors can also be broken into a series of smaller component parts. Each component is taught individually until the child performs the complex response. While each component is taught individually, each step is dependent on the child having learned the previous step. This procedure is referred to as *chaining* since each individual response can be viewed as links in a chain. For example, before a child can tie his shoes successfully, he must learn several preliminary responses (e.g., crossing the laces). Beginning with the simplest step, the therapist rewards the child for each successive step completed until the shoes are tied. Chaining is also a useful technique for teaching speech. The therapist might start by teaching the child simple words and gradually require the child to respond with phrases of increasing length.

While the antecedent variables are important to the development of new behaviors and stimulus functions, perhaps the most important variables to be considered are consequences. The appropriate use of consequences (as previously discussed) can enable a therapist to teach a wide range of behaviors. The importance of using functional rewards is highlighted by the autistic child's characteristic lack of motivation.

Many researchers view the characteristic lack of motivation in autism as related to the potency or desirability of available reinforcers (e.g., Ferster, 1961; Lovaas & Newsom, 1976). Most educators of autistic children rely on primary (e.g., food) and/or social (e.g., praise) reinforcers. A number of investigators (e.g., Ferster, 1961; Lovaas & Newsom, 1976; Lovaas, Schaeffer, & Simmons, 1965) have noted the difficulty involved in establishing meaningful social rewards for many autistic children. As a result of these difficulties most teachers must depend on primary rewards such as food to motivate and maintain the children's behavior. However, reliance on primary rewards can create serious problems. Lovaas and Newsom (1976) pointed out that these rewards may become artificial for older children since they exist only in limited settings such as treatment environments. Second, they suggested that reliance on food rewards results in limited generalization since other environments in which the child interacts may not prescribe primary

134

rewards. An additional problem that can arise is that the children may become satiated and as a result refuse to continue working. These issues can represent severe difficulties for an educator attempting to teach and motivate autistic children.

Some investigators have attempted to help solve these difficulties by developing procedures for establishing functional secondary rewards and by investigating alternative forms of reinforcement. The acquisition of secondary reinforcers is seen as very important to overall development since events such as praise, hugs, smiles, approval, etc. appear to support so much behavior. The autistic child's typical unresponsiveness to social stimuli has already been noted. However, two studies have succeeded in establishing social stimuli as reinforcers for autistic children. Lovaas, Schaeffer, and Simmons (1965) attempted to build social behavior using a negative reinforcement paradigm. They set up a situation in which an appropriate response to a therapist's verbal command ("come here") was required to terminate an aversive stimulus. Their results demonstrated that schizophrenic children could be taught to respond to social stimuli. In the second study, Lovaas, Freitag, Kinder, Rubenstein, Schaeffer, and Simmons (1966) found that three steps were considered important in establishing social stimuli as reinforcing. First, they found it necessary to establish the social reward ("good") as a discriminative stimulus. This required the child to attend to the social stimulus for reinforcement. Second, it was found that an intermittent schedule of reinforcement during training produced a more durable secondary reward. Finally, the authors noted that responding for the social reward was facilitated when self-stimulatory behavior was suppressed.

In an investigation designed to assess globally autistic children's motivation (independent of the type of reinforcer) Koegel and Egel (1979) examined the influence of correct task completion upon motivation to respond to instructional activities. Due to their severe learning handicaps, autistic children may experience very low levels of reinforcement for their attempts to respond to learning tasks. The results demonstrated that when the children worked at tasks where they were typically incorrect their overall attempts to respond to those tasks generally decreased. However, educational procedures designed to maximize correct responding (and receipt of reinforcers) served to increase the children's motivation (overall attempts to respond) on those tasks.

Attempts are also being made to develop new reinforcers. As suggested previously (in the section on Self-stimulatory behavior), one can conceptualize self-stimulation as behavior being maintained by the sensory feedback it produces. This form of sensory stimulation may be

135

inferred to be highly reinforcing since autistic children characteristically spend hours engaged in self-stimulatory behavior (Lovaas et al., 1971; Rimland, 1964). Rincover et al. (1977) designed a study to investigate the reinforcing properties of sensory stimulation for autistic children. They initially determined the preferred sensory stimuli for each child and then attempted to motivate the children to respond using the sensory stimuli as reinforcement. More specifically, brief presentations of the child's preferred sensory event (e.g., low-frequency strobe light, popular music) were presented contingent on correct responses. Their results conclusively demonstrated that sensory stimulation used as reinforcement produced high levels of responding that were relatively durable over time. The authors noted that while the use of primary reinforcers such as food tended to result in problems of satiation and lack of generalization, the autistic children in this study never became satiated in the general area of their preferred sensory stimulation (e.g., music). Furthermore, when the children did become satiated on a specific sensory event (e.g., a particular song), a minor change in the sensory event led to a recovery of the high rate of responding.

These findings are very encouraging in light of their therapeutic implications. Rincover and Koegel (1977a) have pointed out that treatment gains could be enhanced if sensory reinforcers were used in therapy. This is especially true since (1) these types of reinforcers are relatively easy to identify and provide, and (2) their use may facilitate the generalization of treatment gains from the classroom to other situations since sensory reinforcers are not necessarily limited to a particular setting.

Appropriate behavioral repertories and stimulus functions can therefore be seen as resulting from the manipulation of antecedent and consequence variables. A convenient procedure for ordering these elements of the learning process to maximize control and efficiency is the *discrete trial format* (for a comprehensive discussion of the discrete trial format, see Schreibman & Koegel, in press). Briefly, a discrete trial consists of four basic components: (1) a stimulus or instruction; (2) the child's response; (3) the therapist's consequence; and (4) the intertrial interval. As previously noted, a prompt may be used if the instruction alone does not evoke a response. These are referred to as *discrete* trials because a distinct intertrial interval is included between one trial's consequence and the next trial's instruction.

The essence of a behavioral treatment program has been presented in this section. It can be seen as involving primarily three steps: (1) operational definition of the target behaviors the therapist desires to change; (2) analysis of the variables (antecedent and consequence) which
136

influence the target behaviors; and (3) systematic manipulation of those variables to obtain the desired change in the target behaviors.

**Evaluation**

The behavioral treatment model has been used successfully in teaching autistic children a wide variety of adaptive behaviors from self-care skills (e.g., Foxx & Azrin, 1973b; Marshall, 1966; Plummer et al., 1977) to reading (e.g., Hewett, 1964; Rosenbaum & Breiling, 1976). Behaviorists have also been successful in reducing or eliminating those behaviors considered most deviant (e.g., Lovaas & Simmons, 1969; Rincover, 1978a,b). However, some aspects of the behavioral model have been criticized (e.g., Hemsley, Howlin, Berger, Hersov, Holbrook, et al., 1978). A major criticism has been the failure of treatment gains to generalize from the clinic to other environments (e.g., home). This was clearly shown in a study by Lovaas, Koegel, Simmons, and Long (1973). They found that, despite dramatic gains made by autistic children during treatment, those children who were institutionalized following therapy regressed significantly. Other investigators have also noted the failure of treatment to generalize to other situations without special intervention in the extratherapy environment (e.g., Baer, Wolf, & Risley, 1968; Birnbrauer, 1968; Kale, Kaye, Whelan, & Hopkins, 1968; Kazdin & Bootzin, 1972; Stokes & Baer, 1977; Stokes, Baer & Jackson, 1974; Wahler, 1969; Walker & Buckley, 1972). Consequently, behavioral researchers have attempted to (1) understand the variables that might influence generalization and (2) develop procedures for promoting generalization. One variable that may limit the extent to which a behavior learned in a classroom generalizes to other environments is the number of relevant stimuli that control the behavior. Rincover and Koegel (1975) demonstrated that the failure of four autistic children to generalize a response learned in one setting to another was due to the acquisition of stimulus control by irrelevant stimuli that were not present in the extratherapy environment. In order to bring about the generalization of treatment gains to extratherapy settings, it was necessary to introduce into the extratherapy setting the stimuli that came to control responding in the treatment environment. The authors pointed out that a therapist working with autistic children must be sure that new behaviors are learned on the basis of relevant stimuli intended to achieve control.

It is interesting, however, to note that the above results did not hold true for all of the children in the study. Six children showed some transfer of treatment gains across settings without special intervention. These children apparently learned to respond to a stimulus that was

137

functional in both the therapy and extratherapy settings. Rincover and Koegel suggested that in cases where the children do initially transfer (which may be more common than is noticeably apparent), it may be beneficial to emphasize methodologies for maintaining treatment gains in other settings rather than for producing transfer. Koegel and Rincover (1977) designed a study to assess possible differences between variables affecting the transfer and the maintenance of treatment gains across settings. Initially, the authors continuously recorded responding to a particular instruction (e.g., "Touch your nose") in both a therapy and extratherapy setting. The results showed that while one child's responding failed to generalize to the extratherapy environment, the responding of two other children did generalize. However, further testing demonstrated that responding in the extratherapy setting was not maintained. Koegel and Rincover suggested that the lack of response maintenance in the extratherapy setting may be a result of the child forming a discrimination between an environment in which contingent rewards are given and one in which few contingent rewards are provided.

In order to reduce the discriminability of the reinforcement schedules, Koegel and Rincover manipulated two variables: (1) the schedule of reinforcement in the treatment setting, and (2) the presence of noncontingent reinforcement in the extratherapy environment. The results showed that extratherapy responding extinguished within a very short number of trials when a continuous reinforcement schedule was employed in the treatment. As the schedule of reinforcement in the therapy was gradually thinned (from continuous reinforcement to reinforcement for every fifth response), responding in the extratherapy environment was maintained over longer and longer periods of time. The presentations of noncontingent reinforcement in the extratherapy setting had a similar effect on the durability of responding. Furthermore, the results showed that a thin schedule of reinforcement in the treatment environment in conjunction with the periodic use of noncontingent reinforcement in the extratherapy setting produced the greatest response maintenance.

Other procedures for promoting generalization of treatment gains have been reported throughout the behavioral literature (for an extensive review see Stokes and Baer, 1977). Several procedures can be adapted quite easily for use in a classroom situation. Investigations have shown that multiple therapists can be employed to facilitate generalization from the original teacher to others in the child's environment. Stokes, Baer, and Jackson (1974) found that a greeting response taught to four retarded children by one experimenter did not generalize to other staff members.

However, high levels of generalization and maintenance of the response were noted after a second experimenter taught and maintained the response in conjunction with the first experimenter. Lovaas and Simmons (1969) also found it necessary to use multiple therapists to ensure generalized suppression of self-destructive behavior. Additional research has also shown that generalization is enhanced if instruction takes place in a number of settings beyond the original environment (e.g., Griffiths & Craighead, 1972; Lovaas & Simmons, 1969). Thus the research has pointed out that in order to program generalization it may be necessary to continue the training with other people in a variety of settings.

A convenient method that incorporates both of these approaches is available to the educator of autistic children: training parents in the use of behavioral techniques (Kozloff, 1973; Wing, 1972). Lovaas et al. (1973) and Schreibman and Koegel (1975) have found that treatment gains were maintained only for those children who went from treatment to homes in which the parents had received training in behavioral techniques. This is not surprising in light of the research cited above. Trained parents satisfy the need for multiple therapists discussed by Stokes et al. (1974). In addition, parents are likely to work with the child in a vast number of settings (e.g., grocery store, restaurants, etc.) outside of the classroom. Furthermore, parent training clearly provides an area for maintaining treatment gains outside of a treatment setting. Obviously, the impact of parent training on the education of autistic children is potentially tremendous.

Investigations have also been conducted to determine if generalization of treatment gains could be programmed from within the clinic. Most of these investigations have focused on the type of reinforcers used and the nature of the treatment setting. The problems encountered in using primary (food) rewards with autistic children have already been discussed: their use leads to rapid satiation and a lack of generalization due to the limited environments in which they are available. Thus, it is conceivable that generalization would be enhanced if reinforcers that were also present in the "natural" environment were used (Stokes & Baer, 1977). The research conducted by Rincover et al. (1977) suggested that the use of sensory reinforcement may facilitate generalization of treatment gains since sensory reinforcers may be considered natural or universal in that they occur frequently in settings other than the treatment environment.

Rincover et al. (1977) have also suggested that the use of sensory reinforcers in the treatment or classroom environment could significantly enhance the children's motivation to participate in learning tasks. The relationship between high levels of motivation within the treatment setting and the generalization of treatment gains was demonstrated by Turner (1978), who found that children who showed high levels of motivation (as measured by level of interest) in a language remediation program were more likely to generalize the use of target structures to a nonremediated environment.

Investigations also have been conducted to determine the parameters of *response generalization*. This term refers to the changes that occur in nonreinforced behaviors (which are generally similar to the target behaviors) as a result of the reinforcement contingencies applied to target behaviors (Kazdin & Bootzin, 1972). The most extensive research has been in the area of generalized imitation. Baer and Sherman (1964) found that repeated social reinforcement for three imitative responses led to imitation of a fourth response for which the children were never reinforced. Manipulation of the contingencies demonstrated that it was the reinforcement of the initial imitative responses that maintained the fourth imitation. The authors suggested that the children had learned that behavioral similarity was discriminative for reinforcement. Therefore, they suggested that similarity should take on reinforcing as well as discriminative functions. This phenomenon has been especially important in teaching speech to autistic children. Lovaas, Berberich, Perloff, and Schaeffer (1966) found that as imitative speech training progressed it became easier to evoke new, nonreinforced imitative vocalizations. Others have demonstrated that this type of generalization also occurs in the teaching of generative grammars (Baer & Guess, 1971; Guess, 1969; Guess, Sailor, Rutherford, & Baer, 1968; Schumaker & Sherman, 1970).

The procedures reviewed above exemplify a behavioral approach to a specific problem area. In this case, the research emphasis of the behavioral model has provided the beginnings of a technology for programming stimulus and response generalization.

A second criticism of the behavioral model is that the treatment relies heavily on a one-to-one therapist—child ratio (e.g., Callias, 1978). However, research has been completed that demonstrates that autistic children can learn in group situations (Hamblin, Buckholdt, Ferritor, Kozloff, & Blackwell, 1971). Koegel and Rincover (1974) and Rincover and Koegel (1977b) developed a behavioral technology for teaching autistic children in group situations. In the first study, they demonstrated that gradually increasing the group size with a concurrent thinning of the reward schedule resulted in consistent performance and acquisition of new behaviors in groups of up to eight children and only one teacher. The second study introduced a procedure for increasing the amount of independent work within the group. Essentially, the authors taught the children step by step to produce an increasing number of written responses. Once this was accomplished, the therapist was able to circulate among the various children distributing instructions and rewards individually. These results have important implications for integrating the autistic child into classes of more highly functioning (e.g., normal) children.

The emphasis on developing empirical methods for integrating or mainstreaming autistic children into the public school system (cf. Dunlap, Koegel, & Egel, 1979) is an important difference between the behavioral model and the psychoanalytic and sensory deficit approaches. In the psychoanalytic model, the development of educational procedures is secondary to the creation of a strong emotional bond between therapist and child and the development of the child's autonomous self. Although some of the sensory-deficit proponents have recognized the need to develop group instruction procedures (e.g., Frostig, 1966), there has been very little emphasis on the development of specific procedures for teaching autistic children in a group.

Finally, behaviorists have been criticized for their reliance on primary (food) reinforcers to develop appropriate behaviors. The problems associated with relying on primary rewards have already been discussed. However, recent research has sought to identify other types of functional rewards (Devany and Rincover, 1978; Rincover et al., 1977; Rincover, Cook, Peoples, & Packard, 1979). In addition, Rincover and Koegel (1977a) have suggested that combining the techniques developed by Lovaas et al. (1965, 1966) for conditioning social stimuli and those developed for producing generalization and maintenance (Stokes & Baer, 1977) could lead to the generalized use of social reinforcement for the acquisition, generalization, and maintenance of behavior.

The strength of the behavioral model lies in its research-based treatment methodology. Unlike the psychoanalytic and sensory-deficit treatment approaches, which rely mainly on subjective impressions, the results of behavioral treatment programs can be directly measured. Compared to the other approaches, this emphasis has resulted in a number of advantages. First, it has led to an empirically based understanding of many of the variables that influence the behavior of autistic children. Second, the procedures have been clearly and operationally defined so that replication of the treatment procedures and the results are possible. Third, the procedures have been empirically demonstrated to be effective. Finally, the proponents of the behavioral model have succeeded in teaching autistic children a wide range of adaptive skills.

141

## SUMMARY

The three major approaches to educating autistic children have been reviewed and discussed in terms of their underlying theoretical orientations and their treatment procedures. The psychoanalytic understanding of autism focuses on an abnormal mother–child relationship. The essential aspect of the treatment is the creation of a warm and loving environment in which the child would not feel threatened. In this environment autistic behaviors would decrease because the child would no longer be required to defend himself. Although the theory is highly developed and many practitioners are enthusiastic about the effects of treatment, there is a lack of empirical evidence to support the theory or the effectiveness of the treatment procedures.

The sensory-deficit model emphasizes an underlying problem of sensory integration. Treatment procedures range from an emphasis on near-receptor processing to providing an environment with high affective stimulation. While the procedures emphasize different aspects of sensory development, they are all based on the assumption of an underlying sensory integrative deficit. However, there does not appear to be enough evidence to support any specific theory of sensory dysfunction or the effectiveness of individual treatment variables within those treatment programs derived from the numerous theories.

The behavioral model differs from the others in that it does not postulate a specific etiology. Instead, this approach seeks to promote subsequent changes in behavior by manipulating specific environmental events. The behavioral treatment program primarily involves three steps: (1) the operational definition of target behaviors; (2) the analysis of the variables that influence the behaviors; and (3) the manipulation of those variables to obtain the desired changes. While the behavioral model has met with some criticism, its research-based treatment methodology offers a number of advantages; in particular, it can be used to relate specific treatment results to concrete treatment interventions, thus providing numerous easily replicable, empirically validated intervention procedures.

Overall, based on the literature to date, one must conclude that steady, cumulative progress is being made in both the understanding and treatment of autism. The elimination of both many individual autistic behaviors and the diagnosis of autism itself appears to be possible for many autistic children at this time. This possibility, coupled with the fact that continual progress is evident in almost all of the remaining "difficult" areas leads to a generally optimistic attitude in most lines of research.

# References

Alpern, G. D. Measurement of "untestable" autistic children. *Journal of Abnormal Psychology*, 1967, *72*, 478–486.

Ayres, A. J. *Sensory integration and learning disorders*. Los Angeles: Western Psychological Services, 1972.

Ayres, A. J. & Heskett, W. M. Sensory integrative dysfunction in a young schizophrenic girl. *Journal of Autism and Childhood Schizophrenia*, 1972, *2*, 174–181.

Axelrod, S., Brantner, J. P., & Meddock, T. D. Overcorrection: A review and critical analysis. *The Journal of Special Education*, 1978, *12*, 367–391.

Azrin, N. H., Kaplan, S. J., & Foxx, R. M. Autism reversal: Eliminating stereotyped self-stimulation of retarded individuals. *American Journal of Mental Deficiency*, 1973, *18*, 241–248.

Baer, D. M., & Guess, D. Receptive training of adjective inflections in mental retardates. *Journal of Applied Behavior Analysis*, 1971, *4*, 129–139.

Baer, D. M., & Sherman, J. Reinforcement control of generalized imitation in young children. *Journal of Experimental Child Psychology*, 1964, *1*, 37–39.

Baer, D. M., Wolf, M. M., & Risley, T. Some current dimensions of applied behavior analysis. *Journal of Applied Behavior Analysis*, 1968, *1*, 91–97.

Ball, T. S. *Itard, Seguin and Kephart. Sensory education—A learning theory interpretation*. Columbus, Ohio: Merrill, 1971.

Bartak, L., & Rutter, M. Special educational treatment of autistic children: A comparative study. I. Design of study and characteristics of units. *Journal of Child Psychology and Psychiatry*, 1973, *14*, 151–179.

Bettelheim, B. *The empty fortress*. New York: Free Press, 1967.

Bettelheim, B. Reply to G. C. Merritt's review of "The Empty Fortress." *American Journal of Orthopsychiatry*, 1968, *38*, 930–933.

Birnbrauer, J. S. Generalization of punishment effects: A case study. *Journal of Applied Behavior Analysis*, 1968, *1*, 201–211.

Blum, G. *Psychodynamics: The science of unconscious mental forces*. Belmont, California: Brooks/Cole, 1966.

Bostow, D. E., & Bailey, J. Modification of severe disruptive behavior using brief timeout and reinforcement procedures. *Journal of Applied Behavior Analysis*, 1969, *2*, 31–37.

Bucher, B., & Lovaas, O. I. Use of aversive stimulation in behavior modification. In M. R. Jones (Ed.), *Miami Symposium of the Prediction of Behavior, 1967: Aversive stimulation*. Coral Gables, Fla.: University of Miami Press, 1968.

Burchard, J. D., & Tyler, V. O., Jr. The modification of delinquent behavior through operant conditioning. *Behaviour Research and Therapy*, 1965, *2*, 245–250.

Callias, M. Educational aims and methods. In M. Rutter & E. Schopler (Eds.), *Autism: A reappraisal of concepts and treatment*. New York: Plenum Press, 1978.

Carr, E. G., Newsom, C. D., & Binkoff, J. A. Stimulus control of self-destructive behavior in a psychotic child. *Journal of Abnormal Child Psychology*, 1976, *3*, 331–351.

Carr, E. G., Schreibman, L., & Lovaas, O. I. Control of echolalic speech in psychotic children. *Journal of Abnormal Child Psychology*, 1975, *3*, 331–351.

Clark, H. B., Rowbury, T., Baer, A. M., & Baer, D. M. Timeout as a punishing stimulus in continuous and intermittent schedules. *Journal of Applied Behavior Analysis*, 1973, *6*, 443–455.

DeMyer, M., Pontues, W., Norton, J., Barton, S., Allen, J., & Steele, R. Parental practices and innate activity in autistic and brain-damaged infants. *Journal of Autism and Childhood Schizophrenia*, 1972, *2*, 49–66.

DesLauriers, A. M. Play, symbols, and the development of language. In M. Rutter & E. Schopler (Eds.), *Autism: A reappraisal of concepts and treatment*. New York: Plenum Press, 1978.

DesLauriers, A. M., & Carlson, C. F. *Your child is asleep: Early infantile autism.* Homewood, Ill.: Dorsey Press, 1969.

Devany, J. & Rincover, A. *Experimental analysis of ethical issues: I. Using self-stimulation as a reinforcer in the treatment of developmentally delayed children.* Paper presented at the 12th annual meeting of the Association for Advancement of Behavior Therapy, Chicago, November 1978.

Dietz, S. M., & Repp, A. L. Decreasing classroom misbehavior through the use of DRL schedules of reinforcement. *Journal of Applied Behavior Analysis,* 1973, *6,* 457–463.

Dunlap, G., Koegel, R. L., & Egel, A. L. Autistic children in school. *Exceptional Children,* 1979, *45,* 552–558.

Epstein, L. H., Doke, L. A., Sajwaj, T. E., Sorrell, S., & Rimmer, B. Generality and side effects of overcorrection. *Journal of Applied Behavior Analysis,* 1974, *7,* 385–390.

Ferster, C. B. Positive reinforcement and behavioral deficits of autistic children. *Child Development,* 1961, *32,* 437–456.

Ferster, C. B., & DeMyer, M. A method for the experimental analysis of the behavior of autistic children. *American Journal of Orthopsychiatry,* 1962, *32,* 89–98.

Foxx, R. M. & Azrin, N. H. Restitution: A method of eliminating aggressive–disruptive behavior of retarded and brain damaged patients. *Behaviour Research and Therapy,* 1972, *10,* 15–27.

Foxx, R. M. & Azrin, N. The elimination of autistic self-stimulatory behavior by overcorrection. *Journal of Applied Behavior Analysis,* 1973a, *6,* 1–14.

Foxx, R. M., & Azrin, N. *Toilet training the retarded.* Champaign, Ill.: Research Press, 1973b.

Frostig, M. *Special education and training methods with autistic children: Educational therapy versus conditioning.* Unpublished manuscript, 1966. (Available from the Marianne Frostig Center of Educational Therapy, Los Angeles, California).

Frostig, M. *The training of perceptual and integrative functions.* Paper presented at the International Conference for the Joint Council for the Education of Handicapped Children, Canterbury, England, 1975.

Goldfarb, W. Receptor preferences in schizophrenic children. *Archives of Neurology and Psychiatry,* 1956, *76,* 643–652.

Goldfarb, W. *Childhood schizophrenia.* Cambridge: Harvard University Press, 1961.

Goodman, L., & Hammill, D. The effectiveness of Kephart-Getman activities in developing perceptual–motor and cognitive skills. *Focus on Exceptional Children,* 1973, *4,* 1–9.

Greenfeld, J. *A child called Noah: A family journey.* New York: Holt, Rinehart, & Winston, 1972.

Griffiths, H. & Craighead, W. E. Generalization in operant speech therapy for misarticulation. *Journal of Speech and Hearing Disorders,* 1972, *37,* 457–468.

Guess, D. A functional analysis of receptive language and productive speech: Acquisition of the plural morpheme. *Journal of Applied Behavior Analysis,* 1969, *2,* 55–64.

Guess, D., Sailor, W., Rutherford, G., & Baer, D. An experimental analysis of linguistic development: The productive use of the plural morpheme. *Journal of Applied Behavior Analysis,* 1968, *1,* 292–307.

Hamblin, R. L., Buckholdt, D., Ferritor, D., Kozloff, M., & Blackwell, L. *The humanization processes: A social behavioral analysis of children's problems.* New York: Wiley, 1971.

Hammill, D., Goodman, L., & Wiederholt, J. L. Visual–motor processes: Can we train them? *Reading Teacher,* 1974, *27,* 469–478.

Hartman, H., Kris, E., & Lowenstein, R. Comments on the formation of the psychic structure. *Psychoanalytic Study of the Child,* 1946, *2,* 11–38.

Hemsley, R., Howlin, P., Berger, M., Hersov, L., Holbrook, D., Rutter, M., & Yule, W. Treating autistic children in a family context. In M. Rutter & E. Schopler (Eds.), *Autism: A reappraisal of concepts and treatment.* New York: Plenum Press, 1978.

Herendeen, D. L., Jeffery, D. B., & Graham, M. C. *Reduction of self-stimulation in institutionalized children: Overcorrection and reinforcement of non-responding*. Paper presented at the 8th annual meeting of the Association for Advancement of Behavior Therapy, Chicago, November 1974.

Hermelin, B., & O'Connor, N. Effects of sensory input and sensory dominance on severely disturbed autistic children and on subnormal controls. *British Journal of Psychology,* 1964, *55,* 201–206.

Hermelin, B., & O'Connor, N. Visual imperception in psychotic children. *British Journal of Psychology,* 1965, *56,* 455–460.

Hewett, F. M. Teaching reading to an autistic boy through operant conditioning. *American Journal of Orthopsychiatry,* 1964, *34,* 613–618.

Hewett, F. M. Teaching speech to autistic children through operant conditioning. *American Journal of Orthopsychiatry,* 1965, *35,* 927–936.

Hingtgen, J. N., & Bryson, C. Q. Research developments in the study of early childhood psychoses: Infantile autism, childhood schizophrenia, and related disorders. *Schizophrenia Bulletin,* 1972, *5,* 8–54.

Hingtgen, J. N., & Churchill, D. W. Differential effects of behavior modification in four mute autistic children. In D. W. Churchill, G. D. Alpern, & M. K. DeMyer (Eds.), *Infantile autism*. Springfield, Ill.: Thomas, 1971.

Hutt, S. J., Hutt, C., Lee, D., & Ounsted, C. A behavioural and electroencephalographic study of autistic children. *Journal of Psychiatric Research,* 1965, *3,* 181–197.

Kale, R. J., Kaye, J. H., Whelan, P. A., & Hopkins, B. L. The effects of reinforcement on the modification, maintenance, and generalization of social responses of mental patients. *Journal of Applied Behavior Analysis,* 1968, *1,* 307–314.

Kanner, L., & Eisenberg, L. Note on the follow-up studies of autistic children. In P. H. Hoch & J. Bubin (Eds.), *Psychopathology of Childhood*. New York: Grune & Stratton, 1955.

Kazdin, A. E., & Bootzin, R. R. The token economy: An evaluative review. *Journal of Applied Behavior Analysis,* 1972, *5,* 343–372.

Kephart, N. C. The slow learner in the classroom. Columbus, Ohio: Merrill, 1960.

Koegel, R. L., & Covert, A. The relationship of self-stimulation to learning in autistic children. *Journal of Applied Behavior Analysis,* 1972, *5,* 381–387.

Koegel, R. L., & Egel, A. L. Motivating autistic children. *Journal of Abnormal Psychology,* 1979, *88,* 418–426.

Koegel, R. L., Firestone, P. B., Kramme, K. W., & Dunlap, G. Increasing spontaneous play by suppressing self-stimulation in autistic children. *Journal of Applied Behavior Analysis,* 1974, *7,* 521–528.

Koegel, R. L., & Rincover, A. Treatment of psychotic children in a classroom environment: I. Learning in a large group. *Journal of Applied Behavior Analysis,* 1974, *7,* 45–59.

Koegel, R. L., & Rincover, A. Some detrimental effects of using extra stimuli to guide learning in normal and autistic children. *Journal of Abnormal Child Psychology,* 1976, *4,* 59–71.

Koegel, R. L., & Rincover, A. Research on the difference between generalization and maintenance in extra-therapy responding. *Journal of Applied Behavior Analysis,* 1977, *10,* 1–12.

Koegel, R. L., & Schreibman, L. Teaching autistic children to respond to simultaneous multiple cues. *Journal of Experimental Child Psychology,* 1977, *24,* 299–311.

Koegel, R. L., & Wilhelm, H. Selective responding to the components of multiple visual cues by autistic children. *Journal of Experimental Child Psychology,* 1973, *15,* 442–453.

Kozloff, M., *Reaching the autistic child: A parent training program*. Champaign, Ill.: Research Press, 1973.

Kozloff, M., *Educating children with learning and behavioral problems*. New York: Wiley, 1974.

Levitt, E. E. The results of psychotherapy with children: An evaluation. *Journal of Consulting Psychology*, 1957, *21*, 189–196.

Levitt, E. E. Psychotherapy with children: A further evaluation. *Behaviour Research and Therapy*, 1963, *1*, 45–51.

Lichstein, K. L., & Schreibman, L. Employing electric shock with autistic children: A review of the side effects. *Journal of Autism and Childhood Schizophrenia*, 1976, *6*, 163–174.

Lovaas, O. I. *Behavior modification: Teaching language to psychotic children* (Instructional film). New York: Appleton-Century-Crofts, 1969.

Lovaas, O. I., Berberich, J. P., Perloff, B. F., & Schaeffer, B. Acquisition of imitative speech in schizophrenic children. *Science*, 1966, *151*, 705–707.

Lovaas, O. I., Freitag, G., Kinder, M. I., Rubenstein, B. D., Schaeffer, B., & Simmons, J. Q. Establishment of social reinforcers in two schizophrenic children on the basis of food. *Journal of Experimental Child Psychology*, 1966, *4*, 109–125.

Lovaas, O. I., & Koegel, R. L. Behavior therapy with autistic children. Offprint from the Seventy-second Yearbook of the National Society for the Study of Education. Behavior Modification, 1973. Chicago: The University of Chicago Press, 1973.

Lovaas, O. I., Koegel, R. L., Simmons, J. Q., & Long, J. S. Some generalization and follow-up measures on autistic children in behavior therapy. *Journal of Applied Behavior Analysis*, 1973, *6*, 131–166.

Lovaas, O. I., Litrownik, A., & Mann, R. Response latencies to auditory stimuli in autistic children engaged in self-stimulatory behavior. *Behaviour Research and Therapy*, 1971, *9*, 39–49.

Lovaas, O. I., & Newsom, C. D. Behavior modification with psychotic children. In H. Leitenberg (Ed.), *Handbook of behavior modification and behavior therapy*. Englewood Cliffs, N.J.: Prentice Hall, 1976.

Lovaas, O. I., Schaeffer, B., & Simmons, J. Q. Building social behavior in autistic children by use of electric shock. *Journal of Experimental Research and Personality*, 1965, *1*, 99–109.

Lovaas, O. I., and Schreibman, L. Stimulus overselectivity of autistic children in a two stimulus situation. *Behaviour Research and Therapy*, 1971, *9*, 305–310.

Lovaas, O. I., Schreibman, L., & Koegel, R. L. A behavior modification approach to the treatment of autistic children. *Journal of Autism and Childhood Schizophrenia*, 1974, *4*, 111–129.

Lovaas, O. I., Schreibman, L., Koegel, R. L., & Rehm, R. Selective responding by autistic children to multiple sensory input. *Journal of Abnormal Psychology*, 1971, *77*, 211–222.

Lovaas, O. I., & Simmons, J. Q. Manipulation of self-destruction in three retarded children. *Journal of Applied Behavior Analysis*, 1969, *2*, 143–157.

Mahler, M. S. On child psychosis and schizophrenia. Autistic and symbiotic infantile psychoses. *Psychoanalytic Study of the Child*, 1952, *7*, 286–305.

Mann, L. Perceptual training: Misdirections and redirections. *American Journal of Orthopsychiatry*, 1970, *40*, 30–38.

Mann, L. Perceptual training revisited: The training of nothing at all. *Rehabilitation Literature*, 1971, *32*, 322–327.

Mann, L., & Goodman, L. Perceptual training: A critical retrospect. In E. Schopler & R. Reichler (Eds.), *Psychopathology and child development: Research and treatment*. New York: Plenum Press, 1976.

Marshall, G. R. Toilet training of an autistic eight year old through operant conditioning therapy: A case report. *Behaviour Research and Therapy*, 1966, *4*, 242–245.

McAdoo, G. W., & DeMyer, M. K. Personality characteristics of parents. In M. Rutter

& E. Schopler (Eds.), *Autism: A reappraisal of concepts and treatment*. New York: Plenum Press, 1978.

Merritt, G. C. Review of "The Empty Fortress" by B. Bettelheim. *American Journal of Orthopsychiatry*, 1968, *38*, 926–930.

Mulhern, T., & Baumeister, A. A. An experimental attempt to reduce stereotypy by reinforcement procedures. *American Journal of Mental Deficiency*, 1969, *74*, 69–74.

Ornitz, E. M. Childhood autism: A disorder of sensorimotor integration. In M. Rutter (Ed.), *Infantile autism: Concepts, characteristics and treatment*. London: Churchill Livingstone, 1971.

Ornitz, E. M., Brown, M. B., Mason, A., & Putnam, N. H. The effect of visual input on vestibular nystagmus in autistic children. *Archives of General Psychiatry*, 1974, *31*, 369–375.

Ornitz, E. M., Forsythe, A. B., & de la Pena, A. The effects of vestibular and auditory stimulation on the REMs of REM sleep in autistic children. *Archives of General Psychiatry*, 1973, *29*, 786–791.

Ornitz, E. M., & Ritvo, E. R. Perceptual inconstancy in early infantile autism. *Archives of General Psychiatry*, 1968, *18*, 76–98.

Ornitz, E. M., & Ritvo, E. R. The syndrome of autism: A critical review. *American Journal of Psychiatry*, 1976, *133*, 609–621.

Pitfield, M., & Oppenheim, A. N. Child rearing attitudes of mothers of psychotic children. *Journal of Child Psychology and Psychiatry and Allied Disciplines*, 1964, *5*, 51–57.

Plummer, S., Baer, D. M. & LeBlanc, J. M. Functional considerations in the use of procedural timeout and an effective alternative. *Journal of Applied Behavior Analysis*, 1977, *10*, 689–706.

Rank, B. Intensive study and treatment of preschool children who show marked personality deviations, or "atypical development," and their parents. In G. Caplan (Ed.), *Emotional problems of early childhood*. New York: Basic Books, 1955.

Rank, B., & MacNaughton, D. A clinical contribution to early ego development. *Psychoanalytic Study of the Child*, 1950, *5*, 53–65.

Reynolds, B. S., Newsom, C. D., & Lovaas, O. I. Auditory overselectivity in autistic children. *Journal of Abnormal Child Psychology*, 1974, *2*, 253–263.

Rimland, B. *Infantile autism*. New York: Appleton-Century-Crofts, 1964.

Rimland, B. Inside the mind of an autistic savant. *Psychology Today*, 1978, *12*, 68–80.

Rincover, A. Sensory extinction: A procedure for eliminating self-stimulatory behavior in developmentally disabled children. *Journal of Abnormal Child Psychology*, 1978a, *6*, 299–310.

Rincover, A. Variables affecting stimulus-fading and discriminative responding in psychotic children. *Journal of Abnormal Psychology*, 1978b, *87*, 541–553.

Rincover, A., Cook, R., Peoples, A., & Packard, D. Using sensory extinction and sensory reinforcement principles for programming response generalization. *Journal of Applied Behavior Analysis*, 1979, *12*, 221–233.

Rincover, A., & Koegel, R. L. Setting generality and stimulus control in autistic children. *Journal of Applied Behavior Analysis*, 1975, *8*, 235–246.

Rincover, A., & Koegel, R. L. Research on the education of autistic children: Recent advances and future directions. In B. B. Lahey & A. E. Kazdin (Eds.), *Advances in clinical child psychology* (Vol. 1). New York: Plenum Press, 1977a.

Rincover, A., & Koegel, R. L. Classroom treatment of autistic children: II. Individualized instruction in a group. *Journal of Abnormal Child Psychology*, 1977b, *5*, 113–126.

Rincover, A., Newsom, C. D., Lovaas, O. I., & Koegel, R. L. Some motivational properties of sensory stimulation in psychotic children. *Journal of Experimental Child Psychology*, 1977, *24*, 312–323.

Risley, T. R. The effects and side effects of punishing the autistic behaviors of a deviant child. *Journal of Applied Behavior Analysis*, 1968, *1*, 21–34.

Ritvo, S., & Provence, S. Form perception and imitation in some autistic children: Diagnostic findings and their contextual interpretation. *Psychoanalytic Study of the Child*, 1953, *8*, 115–161.

Robinson, E., Hughes, H., Wilson, D., Lahey, B. B., & Haynes, S. *Modification of stereotyped behaviors of "autistic" children through response-contingent water squirts*. Paper presented at the 8th annual meeting of the Association for Advancement of Behavior Therapy, Chicago, November 1974.

Rosenbaum, M. S., & Breiling, J. The development of functional control of reading comprehension behavior. *Journal of Applied Behavior Analysis*, 1976, *9*, 323–334.

Routtenberg, A. The two arousal hypotheses: Reticular formation and limbic system. *Psychological Review*, 1968, *75*, 52–61.

Ruttenberg, B. A psychoanalytic understanding of infantile autism and its treatment. In D. W. Churchill, G. D. Alpern, & M. K. DeMyer (Eds.), *Infantile autism*. Springfield, Ill.: Thomas, 1971.

Rutter, M. Concepts of autism: A review of research. *Journal of Child Psychology and Psychiatry*, 1968, *9*, 1–25.

Rutter, M. The description and classification of infantile autism. In D. W. Churchill, G. D. Alpern, & M. K. Demyer (Eds.), *Infantile autism*. Springfield, Ill.: Thomas, 1971.

Rutter, M. Etiology and treatment: Cause and cure. In M. Rutter & E. Schopler (Eds.), *Autism: A reappraisal of concepts and treatment*. New York: Plenum Press, 1978.

Rutter, M., & Bartak, L. Special educational treatment of autistic children: A comparative study. II. Follow-up findings and implications for services. *Journal of Child Psychology and Psychiatry*, 1973, *14*, 241–270.

Schopler, E. Early infantile autism and receptor processes. *Archives of General Psychiatry*, 1965, *13*, 327–335.

Schopler, E. Visual versus tactile receptor preference in normal and schizophrenic children. *Journal of Abnormal Psychology*, 1966, *71*, 108–114.

Schopler, E. Changes in direction with psychotic children. In A. Davis (Ed.), *Child personality and psychopathology: Current topics* (Vol. 1). New York: Wiley, 1974.

Schopler, E., & Loftin, J. Thinking disorder in parents of young psychotic children. *Journal of Abnormal Psychology*, 1969, *14*, 281–287.

Schopler, E., & Reichler, R. J. Psychobiological referents for the treatment of autism. In D. W. Churchill, G. D. Alpern, & M. K. DeMyer (Eds.), *Infantile autism*. Springfield, Ill.: Thomas, 1971a.

Schopler, E., & Reichler, R. J. Developmental therapy by parents with their own autistic child. In M. Rutter (Ed.), *Infantile autism: Concepts, characteristics and treatment*. London: Churchill Livingstone, 1971b.

Schover, L. R., & Newsom, C. D. Overselectivity, developmental level and overtraining in autistic and normal children. *Journal of Abnormal Child Psychology*, 1976, *4*, 289–298.

Schreibman, L. Effects of within-stimulus and extra-stimulus prompting on discrimination learning in autistic children. *Journal of Applied Behavior Analysis*, 1975, *8*, 91–112.

Schreibman, L., & Koegel, R. L. Autism: A defeatable horror. *Psychology Today*, 1975, *8*, 61–67.

Schreibman, L., & Koegel, R. L. A guideline for planning behavior modification programs for autistic children. In S. M. Turner, K. S. Calhoun, & M. E. Adams (Eds.), *Handbook of clinical behavior therapy*. New York: Wiley, in press.

Schreibman, L., Koegel, R. L., & Craig, M. S. Reducing stimulus overselectivity in autistic children. *Journal of Abnormal Child Psychology*, 1977, *5*, 425–436.

Schreibman, L., & Lovaas, O. I. Overselective response to social stimuli by autistic children. *Journal of Abnormal Child Psychology*, 1973, *1*, 152–168.

Schumaker, J., & Sherman, J. A. Training generative verb usage by imitation and reinforcement procedures. *Journal of Applied Behavior Analysis, 1970, 3,* 273–287.

Shapiro, T. Therapy with autistic children. In M. Rutter & E. Schopler (Eds.), *Autism: A reappraisal of concepts and treatment.* New York: Plenum Press, 1978.

Solnick, J. V., Rincover, A., & Peterson, C. R. Determinants of the reinforcing and punishing effects of time-out. *Journal of Applied Behavior Analysis, 1977, 10,* 415–428.

Stokes, T. F., & Baer, D. M. An implicit technology of generalization. *Journal of Applied Behavior Analysis, 1977, 10,* 349–368.

Stokes, T. F., Baer, D. M., & Jackson, R. L. Programming the generalization of greeting responses in four retarded children. *Journal of Applied Behavior Analysis, 1974, 7,* 599–610.

Stroh, G., & Buick, D. Perceptual development and childhood psychoses. *British Journal of Medical Psychology, 1964, 37,* 291–299.

Tate, B. G., & Baroff, G. S. Aversive control of self-injurious behavior in a psychotic boy. *Behaviour Research and Therapy, 1966, 4,* 281–287.

Turner, B. L. *The effects of choice of stimulus materials on interest in the remediation process and the generalized use of language training.* Unpublished master's thesis, University of California, Santa Barbara, 1978.

Varni, J., Lovaas, O. I., Koegel, R. L., & Everett, N. L. An analysis of observational learning in autistic and normal children. *Journal of Abnormal Child Psychology, 1979, 7,* 31–43.

Wahler, R. G. Setting generality: Some specific and general effects of child behavior therapy. *Journal of Applied Behavior Analysis, 1969, 2,* 239–246.

Walker, H. M., & Buckley, N. K. Programming generalization of treatment effects across time and across settings. *Journal of Applied Behavior Analysis, 1972, 5,* 209–224.

Weiland, H. I. Discussion of treatment approaches. In D. W. Churchill, G. D. Alpern, & M. K. DeMyer (Eds.), *Infantile autism.* Springfield, Ill.: Thomas, 1971.

Weiland, H. I., & Rudnik, R. Considerations of the development and treatment of autistic childhood psychosis. *Psychoanalytic Study of the Child, 1961, 16,* 549–563.

White, G. D., Nielsen, G., & Johnson, S. M. Time-out duration and the suppression of deviant behavior in children. *Journal of Applied Behavior Analysis, 1972, 5,* 111–120.

Wing, J. Review of "The Empty Fortress" by B. Bettelheim. *British Journal of Psychology, 1968, 114,* 788–791.

Wing, L. *Autistic children; A guide for parents.* New York: Brunner/Mazel, 1972.

Wolf, M. M., Risley, T., Johnston, M., Harris, F., & Allen, E. Application of operant conditioning procedures to the behavior problems of an autistic child: A follow-up and extension. *Behaviour Research and Therapy, 1967, 5,* 103–111.

Wolf, M. M., Risley, T., & Mees, H. Application of operant conditioning procedures to the behaviour problems of an autistic child. *Behaviour Research and Therapy, 1964, 1,* 305–312.

Yule, W. Research methodology: What are the "correct controls"? In M, Rutter & E. Schopler (Eds.), *Autism: A reappraisal of concepts and treatment.* New York: Plenum Press, 1978.

# CHANGING PERSPECTIVES IN THE EDUCATION OF THE GIFTED

Barbara G. Ford
*Northern Illinois University*

Reva C. Jenkins
*University of Kansas*

The education of the gifted child in the United States has received a great deal of attention in the past ten years, primarily because of the inclusion of this group of children in the category of exceptional children. The recognition that these children have special needs that necessitate a differentiated approach in curriculum is growing. A similar surge of interest in gifted children was seen in the late 1950s as a direct result of the launching of the Sputnik space satellite; but attitudes toward the gifted as a special population have historically been far from consistent.

## HISTORICAL ATTITUDES TOWARD THE GIFTED CHILD

Definitions of and attitudes toward the gifted have varied as widely through the years as attitudes toward any other exceptional population. Feelings have ranged from total awe of the talented individual to total condemnation of the gifted person as a potential maniac or a dangerous genius on the verge of insanity. Because of the precociousness and advanced development of many of these gifted individuals, they have often been viewed as alien, abnormal, and suspect. Many of the most talented individuals in history have only been appreciated posthumously. In general, one might say that public attitudes have been most favorable toward those gifted individuals whose talents fit in most comfortably with the value systems and needs of their societies. In contrast, those individuals who dared to challenge accepted mores or presumed to improve upon the established perspectives were persecuted, ignored, or ridiculed.

In order to rationalize the position of those more gifted than ourselves in our midst, it has been widely accepted that nature balances out extreme abilities with weaknesses or character flaws of some kind: thus, the publication of such books as *The Men of Genius* (Lombroso, 1891), and *The Insanity of Genius* (Nisbet, 1891) encouraged popular support of the theory that a disproportionately large number of gifted people throughout history have been mentally unstable. As Tannenbaum said in *Education of the Gifted* (National Educational Association, 1950, p. 25), "Psychoanalysts have gone so far as to characterize history as a summation of the sublimated neuroses of the great men of all times."

Fortunately for gifted children, several studies undertaken over the past 80 years have refuted many of these prejudices. The study with probably the greatest impact on attitudes toward gifted people was one initiated by Louis Terman in the early 1900s; the first report of this study appeared in Volume I of *Genetic Studies of Genius* in 1925. In this study, over 1500 children in California with IQ's of 140 and above on the Stanford-Binet were studied with regard to intellectual, social, and recreational interests, school achievement, health and physical history, and personality and character traits. Through the accumulation of extensive data on each child and periodic follow-up throughout the lives of this population, Terman was able to controvert many of the commonly held attitudes about the eccentricity of gifted people. Indeed, the Terman research showed the gifted child to be even better adjusted throughout life than the average person, to be a person who capitalizes on his or her potential rather than "burning out early," as was typically expected, and to be physically at least on a par with if not superior to average children.

In the case of the most highly gifted children (IQ's of 180 and above), other researchers, such as Hollingworth (1942), showed that although these children might be more inclined to be emotionally unstable because of the vast difference between their abilities and those of the general population, special programs can have a great deal to do with whether or not these children adjust well socially. Cox (1926) followed up on Terman's research with Volume II of *Genetic Studies of Genius* entitled *The Early Mental Traits of 300 Geniuses,* which was a retrospective study of the characteristics of most of the prominent contributors to the knowledge of the Western World. This work, along with the continuing research of Terman and the increasing interest in psychological testing throughout the 1930s and 1940s, continued to chip away at negative attitudes concerning gifted individuals.

The year 1947 was very important in the history of the gifted education movement. The American Association for Gifted Children was established at that time, and the book, *The Gifted Child Grows Up* (Terman & Oden, 1947) appeared to spark increased interest among educators regarding the nature and needs of gifted students. The Educational Policies Commission of the National Education Association (NEA) published a monograph entitled *Education of the Gifted* (NEA, 1950) which further articulated the special educational needs of gifted children. When *The Gifted Child* (Witty, 1951) was published for the American Association for Gifted Children, the movement was on its way.

In 1953 the National Association for Gifted Children was formed in an effort to provide a forum for both teachers and parents of gifted children. This organization has published *The Gifted Child Quarterly* since that time, the most long-standing journal devoted to the education and social needs of gifted children in the United States. Other publications followed (e.g., Hall, 1956; Passow, 1955; Witty, 1952). Then in 1957 the launching of Sputnik startled most Americans into the realization that we had not been encouraging our most able students to the degree necessary for international competition.

Both public and private finds were now poured into special programs to develop excellence, especially in the fields of science and mathematics. For several years following Sputnik, academically gifted students were pushed and prodded through the educational system with the expectation that they would utilize their talents to help us compete with the Russians in the space race. Unfortunately as the United States regained its status in the stratosphere, the interest in the development of intellectual talent began to drop off. The aerospace industry became overcrowded with too many engineers and scientists, and many programs for the gifted were dropped in favor of other financial priorities in the school districts. Luckily, with the formation of the Association for the Gifted, a division of the Council for Exceptional Children, pressure was brought to bear at the federal level which led to a nationwide study of educational provisions for the gifted (Marland, 1972) and the establishment of the Office of the Gifted and Talented within the U.S. Office of Education.

Because of that report and the legislation that directed it (Elementary and Secondary Education Act of 1972, PL #91-230, Section 806), a broadened definition of gifted and talented children was established. Up until that time gifted children had generally been thought of as chiefly intellectually or academically gifted; although musicians, artists, dancers, and inventors were looked upon as highly talented contributors to society, they might not have been included in a commonly accepted definition of giftedness. The definition established by an advisory panel to the Commissioner of Education in 1970–1971, and quoted by Marland (1972) described the gifted child as follows:

> Gifted and talented children are those identified by professionally qualified persons who by virtue of outstanding abilities are capable of high performance. These children require differentiated educational programs and/or services beyond those normally provided by the regular school program in order to realize their contribution to self and society. Children capable of high performance include those with demonstrated achievement and/or potential ability in any of the following areas, singularly or in combination:
> 1. General intellectual ability
> 2. Specific academic aptitude
> 3. Creative or productive thinking
> 4. Leadership ability
> 5. Visual and performing arts
> 6. Psychomotor ability
> It can be assumed that utilization of these criteria for identification of the gifted and talented will encompass a minimum of three to five per cent of the school population. (p. 2)

Although there has been a running debate among experts in this field as to the validity of the inclusion of all of these areas of talent it can be assumed that at this time a definition of gifted children must include a variety of talent areas; the most obvious area is still intellectual giftedness, although officially defined areas such as creative thinking must also be considered fundamental categories of giftedness. A review of the most recent federal legislation at the conclusion of this chapter will address this issue.

One of the most positive changes that can be seen in the attitude toward gifted children over the past 70 years is the increasing delight in and support of gifted children by their parents. Whereas parents used to dread having a child who was much out of the ordinary (although highly talented), most parents today are very happy to have a talented child, even though high abilities may involve some social problems or exceptional needs for special training and education (O'Neill, 1978). Although giftedness is a mixed blessing, more and more parents are happy to have gifted children in their families and are eager to help provide any stimulation or encouragement necessary for the full development of their children's abilities (Elkind, 1979). This attitude represents a substantial change in public opinion and cannot help but benefit everyone as the talents of more of these children are discovered and encouraged.

One of the most pressing questions now facing educators of the gifted and talented is that of identification (Cunningham, Thompson, Alston, & Wakefield, 1978; Roeper, 1977; Treffinger, Renzulli, & Feldhusen, 1971). In light of the broadened definition of giftedness and the increased sophistication of instrumentation for the assessment of abilities, approaches to the identification of this population have been clarified and at the same time become more complicated. Therefore, a discussion of the most practical and widely accepted approaches to identification follows.

## IDENTIFICATION OF THE GIFTED AND TALENTED

Approaches to identification of the gifted student have been as varied as the definition itself. Since most early definitions were based on performance, identification consisted mainly of an assessment, through observation, of an individual's productivity. If the products were not those valued by the society at the time, the person would probably not be categorized as gifted. Another drawback to identification based solely on performance is the fact that gifted people could not be identified until they had made major contributions to some field of endeavor. This means that it would be very difficult to identify a child as gifted unless that child was particularly precocious, as in the case of a prodigy such as Mozart who was composing and performing concerts at a very early age. Indeed, if a society waits until a person has achieved great things to label that person gifted, many gifted individuals will only be identified very late in life or even after death. There is also the possibility that much talent will go undeveloped because potential will not be sought among children or adolescents (Terman, 1925).

The narrow definition of giftedness in terms of only intellectual ability also tended to leave many of the most gifted individuals out of the identification process. For instance, such brilliant thinkers as Albert Einstein, Charles Darwin, and Thomas Edison might have been missed by an identification procedure in which only an IQ test was administered. These people, known for their highly creative or original thinking, may not have tested well on a conventional standardized intelligence test; based on their behavior, they were even thought to have learning problems by the adults who observed them at the time!

In view of the broadened definition of giftedness and the efforts to identify gifted children at an early age so as best to meet their educational needs and develop their abilities, multiple criteria for identification are now utilized in most programs. As early as 1958 researchers such as Getzels and Jackson noted the necessity for using a broad range of criteria in the process of identifying gifted children. Other writers supporting this viewpoint included Jarecky (1959) and Witty (1965).

Among the different measures or approaches most commonly used in a screening process are standardized intelligence tests, standardized achievement tests, recommendation by teachers or other school personnel such as guidance counselors or administrators, auditions or performances under controlled conditions, peer nomination, self-nomination, parent nomination, creativity tests, interest inventories, and personality tests (Barbe & Renzulli, 1975; Gallagher, 1966, 1974).

Of course, certain of these approaches are more effective and economical in terms of time and money than others. Specific instruments within categories (such as "intelligence tests") may also be more accurate than similar instruments within the same category. If anything, research has shown that despite the acknowledged flaws of standardized testing, such testing is still far more accurate than personal judgment in identifying most talented students in a school setting. An important study by Pegnato and Birch (1959) showed that teachers' judgment was only 45 percent effective in identifying gifted children in their own classrooms. Results indicated that teachers not only named children as gifted who were not, but also missed a substantial proportion of the students who were legitimately gifted. In a review of the literature dealing with the role of teacher judgment in the identification process, Gallagher (1966) noted that "most authorities would agree that teachers' opinions definitely need supplementing with more objective rating methods" (p. 12).

The authors believe that guided teacher judgment, aided by a checklist of behaviors that have been corroborated by research as characteristic of gifted individuals, can be more objective than the Pegnato and Birch study indicated. Therefore, we believe that teacher judgment should be a part of the identification process, guided by instruments, such as *Scales for Rating the Behavioral Characteristics of Superior Students* (Renzulli, Hartman, Callahan, Smith, 1976), which have been found to correlate highly with the results of standardized instruments.

Standardized tests, whether of intelligence or achievement, have also been criticized as being indicators only of what a child already knows and what his/her culture values rather than tests of potential ability. Children from backgrounds with different values may perform very poorly on such tests, while children from the dominant culture who have accumulated good test-taking skills may score very high (Torrance, 1969, 1972). It has been suggested by one theorist (Renzulli, 1976) that we refine our definition of gifted children to distinguish between those who are merely good "lesson learners" and those who show a greater potential for productivity and creativity. In Renzulli's definition, a good test taker might also be a good lesson learner but may never produce or add to any body of knowledge, and in retrospect would not be considered a gifted individual. Although this approach makes sense, it is probably still wise to include the good test takers in the definition of gifted people, or at least those with potential; thus they would not be kept out of a program and would at least be given the opportunity to develop that potential. Whether the gift was brought to fruition would certainly lie in the individual's own motivation and desire to achieve.

Several writers (Connecticut State Department of Education, 1974, Gowan, 1967b, Gowan & Torrance, 1971). have described similar screening processes by which most gifted children in a school district might be identified. The first step in this process is selection of the area or areas of giftedness which the identifiers will attempt to evaluate. The choice of instruments will vary greatly depending on the talent areas selected to be assessed. The next step is to look at standardized test information on all possible candidates for selection. Group test information might be examined first, and then certain children could be retested individually to obtain more accurate scores or descriptions of abilities. After this information has been compiled, teacher judgment is taken into consideration. Achievement scores and grades are then looked at, and in most cases a meeting of staff would be advised, during which time teachers, administrators, guidance counselors, and possibly even parents could provide input as to the suitability of certain students for that program. It is assumed that the pool of children who are considered for the program would be larger than the ultimate number chosen; therefore, based on the standardized test information, recommendations, and input from the staffing, potential candidates should be ranked as to their probable suitability for inclusion in the program. Then, starting from the top down, the available places in the program can be filled. All the students selected for the program may not be agreed upon by all members of the decision-making committee, but, as Gowan (1967b) has noted, this should not be a source of concern. A few students one might not consider suitable for a program may still profit from it: "If the program doesn't do anything for any one of these children they can always be taken out with a minimum of educational damage. If it does do something for them, the guidance committee has the satisfaction of knowing either that: 1) it has made a good guess, or 2) that it has acquired an important friend" (Gowan, 1967b; p. 2)

After identifying students for special programming, many districts have difficulty deciding which curriculum design would be most appropriate for their students. Aside from the content of the program (which may, as in the case of mathematics, dictate the most appropriate curricular approach), (Stanley, George, & Solano, 1977), several distinct approaches to curriculum modification for the gifted have been researched and developed in recent years. A discussion of the various theories may give some indication of the variety of current programming in gifted education.

## PROGRAM APPROACHES

### Acceleration: moving students through the curriculum faster

Acceleration is an approach to educational provisions for gifted students that has been both supported strongly and criticized severely at different times in the past. It is presently experiencing a resurgence of support based on the positive outcome of an extensive study, The Study of Mathematically Precocious Youth (SMPY), that has been carried out at The Johns Hopkins University since 1971 (see below). Earlier researchers such as Pressey (1949), Worcester (1956), Hobson (1963), and Friedenberg (1966) showed that acceleration is beneficial for most students who participate in it, despite emotional prejudice to the contrary on the part of educators. Most of Terman and Oden's (1947) group of gifted students graduated from high school at least one year early, and based on that research Terman advocated moderate amounts of acceleration for gifted students. Other programs, such as the accelerated college program at the University of Chicago during the 1930s and college and university acceleration programs supported by the Fund for the Advancement of Education (1953, 1957), demonstrated that students entering college early tended to adjust well and come through the college experience in a highly successful manner.

Based on this type of support from the literature and previous research projects, Stanley and his associates at The Johns Hopkins University initiated the SMPY project and have carried it through to the present time. Groups of children in the seventh grade who were identified as gifted on standardized mathematics exams such as the Scholastic Aptitude Test were given the opportunity to move through mathematics courses at both the high school and college level at an accelerated rate, thereby graduating from high school early and entering college with advanced placement. In the first full-length report about SMPY's initial work (Stanley, Keating, & Fox, 1974), a detailed description of the program showed that not only were these students identified early, but systematic efforts were made to describe their abilities further and to develop their potential to the fullest extent. This systematic support and development has led to great success with these students; SMPY's follow-up of the students who have completed the accelerated program and gone on to various colleges and universities shows that these students adjust very well and indeed are very happy to have been given the opportunity to be accelerated through the regular high school curriculum.

Since acceleration involves only a difference in speed rather than a qualitatively different curriculum, it has been criticized by proponents of enrichment as merely administrative juggling. However, the research of Stanley and others has shown that acceleration can be a viable alternative to programming for gifted students and requires at least as much, if not more, flexibility on the part of school personnel for its implementation as the best of enrichment programs. As Stanley (1977, p. 89) has noted, the effects of the SMPY program are very obvious:

> . . . It is almost preposterous to suggest that if SMPY had not found a certain youth when he was an over-age sixth grader and helped him in many ways to move ahead educationally fast and well he would, nevertheless, have been graduated from a major university at barely seventeen years of age. The youngest recipient of a bachelor's degree in 1971 at Johns Hopkins was 19 years 10 months old (Eisenberg, 1977). Two years later, under SMPY's influence, the youngest was 17 years 7 months old, and three months later he had completed a master's degree also. Now seventeen-year-old graduates are frequent. Similar strong observations could be made about SMPY's programs, such as the effects of the fast math classes (Fox, 1974b; George & Denham, 1976; Stanley, 1976b).

If the SMPY project and efforts to replicate it in other states continue to prove successful, these data will offer new support for acceleration as an alternative in programming for the intellectually gifted.

### Taylor's model for multiple talent teaching

C. W. Taylor's (1971) conception of ability is a direct descendent of the factor analytic approach employed in exploration of the nature of intelligence. He notes the influence of the pioneering work of the Thurstones and most notably of Guilford in shaping the notion that intelligence encompasses more than simply intellectual ability (i.e., "academic talent"). Taylor claims that typical intelligence tests tap no more than eight of the 120 "specific and separate high level talents" (Taylor, 1971, p. 9) delineated in the Guilford Structure of the Intellect model. Thus, Taylor concludes that intelligence tests miss 11/12ths of the important intellectual talents now measurable.

Of greatest importance in Taylor's (1971) conception of giftedness is his assertion that by expanding education's focus from cultivation of the academic talents to include the five additional talents described in his model (i.e., creating, planning, forecasting, communicating, and decision making), virtually every child would be gifted in some talent area.

Applications of Taylor's Multiple Talents model have been made primarily in the areas of enrichment. Taylor (1978) has identified nine types of enrichment: knowledge; experiential; environmental and situational; depth-of-involvement; research participation (exploration); non-intellectual (affective); talent; and combinations (of the above). He asserts that these types of enrichment would be of potential benefit to all students (i.e., not only the gifted and talented) by enriching their future careers and lives. Taylor also claims that talent-focused enrichment is comprehensive enough to include all other forms of enrichment. However, unlike the effects of implementing the other varieties, Taylor (1978) states that as teachers focus on talents, the following by-products emerge: there is greater student involvement, thus more of the student's potential human characteristics surface and classes become more humanized; and then more individualizing occurs, thus more individuality and humanity become manifested in each classroom, and so on.

### Williams' model for cognitive–affective behaviors

A rather extensive elaboration and application of the Multiple Talents approach is reflected in the work of F. E. Williams (1970). His Guilfordian model for implementing cognitive–affective behaviors in the classroom allows the educator to manipulate the learning environment through combinations of aspects of the following three dimensions: the curriculum, teacher behavior, and pupil behaviors. Williams rationale focuses on the need for the educational process to combine affective and cognitive functioning in order to enhance effective human development and the emergence of the fully functioning, creative individual. His major work includes 387 lesson ideas designed to facilitate this process.

### Treffinger's model: self-directed learning

D. J. Treffinger's (1978) work in this area focuses on the predisposition of the gifted student to express independence in thought and judgment. He points out, however, that parents and educators often (incorrectly) assume that this *potential* is synonymous with the *skills* essential for the realization of the capacity for self-direction. He further asserts that self-directed learning is not simply the removal of all standards and boundaries from learning situations (or "doing whatever you want to do, whenever you want to do it"). Instead, Treffinger defines self-directedness as responsible autonomy and cites five general goals for self-directed learning (Treffinger, 1978, p. 15):

1. Learning to function more effectively in one's total environment (classroom, school, home, and community) with peers, teachers, parents, and other adults;

2. Learning to make choices and decisions based on self-knowledge of needs and interests;

3. Learning to assume responsibility for choices and decisions by completing all activities at a satisfactory level of achievement and in an acceptable time frame;

4. Learning to define problems and to determine a course of action for their solution;

5. Learning to evaluate one's own work and be able to answer the question, "How well can I do what I want to do?"

He claims that these goals can be most effectively reached through the support and deliberate assistance of the home and school in order to promote the development of necessary skills.

Treffinger sets forth 11 guidelines for parents and teachers to help chart the way to achieving the self-directed learning goals described earlier (Treffinger, 1978, pp. 15–19):

1. Admonitions are inadequate.
2. Don't assume.
3. Don't smother self-directedness by doing for them things they can do (or can learn to do) for themselves.
4. Adults must have or develop an attitude of openness and support for self-directed learning.
5. Learn to defer judgment.
6. Emphasize the continuity of problems and challenges.
7. Provide systematic training in problem-solving and the skills of independent research and inquiry.
8. Treat difficult situations at home or school as opportunities to use creative problem-solving techniques, not merely as problems requiring the unilateral wisdom of an adult.
9. Be alert to audiences that are appropriate for sharing children's efforts, or for opportunities to create such audiences.
10. Help students learn how to direct their own learning gradually—don't expect it to happen all at once.
11. CREATE! Be a model of self-directed learning in your own life.

(pp. 15–19)

Treffinger and his associates have developed general guidelines for producing individualized instructional units, with a planning matrix (SCATS) based on an adaptation of Bloom's (1972) work. The SCATS allows teachers to evaluate their teaching styles along several dimensions according to the degree of self-directed learning the style engenders. He delineates five teaching styles: command, task, peer-partner, pupil–teacher contracts, and self-directed style. Thus the questionnaire might be employed in categorizing one's teaching style as well as in monitoring progress toward promoting self-directed learning in one's classroom.

## Renzulli's enrichment triad model

J. S. Renzulli's (1977) conception of giftedness is based on three assumptions: (1) giftedness is a multidimensional construct; (2) previous attempts to define giftedness operationally have not resulted in an adequate foundation for appropriate, defensible programming; and (3) the gifted individual possesses the unique capacity to act as the creative producer (rather than as the consumer) of knowledge in any sphere of human activity. His formulation and subsequent definition is based on a review of research that focuses on identifying those characteristics which distinguish eminent creative/productive individuals. Thus giftedness is an interaction of three clusters of characteristics which are then brought to bear on an area of human endeavor.

Renzulli summarizes his major conclusions and generalizations emanating from the research review in the following definition (Renzulli, 1978, p. 261):

> Giftedness consists of an interaction among three basic clusters of human traits — these clusters being above average general abilities, high levels of task commitment, and high levels of creativity. Gifted and talented children are those possessing or capable of developing this composite set of traits and applying them to any potentially valuable area of human performance. Children who manifest or are capable of developing an interaction among the three clusters require a wide variety of educational opportunities and services that are not ordinarily provided through regular instructional programs.

He goes on to defend the operational nature of this definition by asserting that it meets three important criteria:

> First, it is derived from the best available research studies dealing with characteristics of gifted and talented individuals. Second, it provides guidance for the selection and/or development of instruments and procedures that can be used to design defensible identification systems. And finally, the definition provides direction for programming practices that will capitalize upon the characteristics that bring gifted youngsters to our attention as learners with special needs.

Renzulli has devised a model designed to enhance the development of giftedness as delineated above. The model also represents an attempt to respond to two concerns relative to the indefensibility of many self-styled "differentiated" programs for gifted and talented students (Renzulli, 1977, p. 1):

> 1. What is (or should be) different about the types of learning experiences that are advocated for gifted students?
> 2. Isn't what you are doing for the gifted also good for nearly all youngsters?

The model incorporates three types of activities. The first two, General Exploratory Activities and Group Training Activities, are designated appropriate for all children, while the third type, Individual and Small Group Investigations of Real Problems, is considered suitable only for the gifted. Renzulli asserts that articulation between the types of activities is crucial to implementing the model. "Feed-in" to the model from the regular curriculum and the environment in general is of almost equal importance.

Thumbnail sketches of the three elements of the Enrichment Triad Model are as follows: Type I activities are designed to bring the learner in contact with a wide variety of fields of endeavor. The purpose of these activities is to help the learner identify a topic or area of study in which he or she might have a sincere interest. Type II enrichment consists of methods, materials, and techniques that are mainly concerned with the development of thinking and feeling processes. The open-ended nature of these activities permits a wide range of responses and provides a bridge into Type III for the learner and the teacher. In Type III enrichment, the learner thinks, feels, and acts as the adult creative producer; i.e., the student engages in activities in which he or she becomes an actual investigator of a real world problem or topic, using appropriate methods of inquiry. Further distinguishing characteristics of Type III enrichment are that the student communicates the results of the investigation to an authentic audience, that there is a tangible product emanating from the experience, and that the teacher acts primarily as a facilitator in identifying the problem providing methodological assistance, and securing an authentic audience.

### Torrance: creative and future problem solving

When "creative problem-solving" techniques are mentioned in writings for educators of the gifted, E.P. Torrance is invariably cited. As a pioneer in the testing (Torrance Tests of Creative Thinking [Torrance, 1974]) and systematic development (Myers & Torrance, 1964, 1966) of creative thinking and problem solving, Torrance has convinced innumerable educators of the validity of such techniques. The latest application of the Torrance approach to creative problem solving has been the Future Problem-Solving Bowl, a competition that offers gifted students the opportunity to brainstorm and evaluate solutions to significant problems of the future. As noted in his discussion of this program (Torrance & Reynolds, 1978), a positive vision of the future is important to the fullest utilization of present talent, and gifted children are generally more deeply concerned about the future than children of more average abilities.

The Future Problem-Solving Program was initiated in 1974 and has since involved over 300 schools and 10,000 students in 26 states during the 1977–1978 academic year alone. Procedures during the 1977–1978 school year were as follows:

In September 1977, copies of the *Handbook for Training Teams in Future Problem Solving* were mailed to participating teachers, who were also asked to administer a pretest for purposes of program evaluation. Practice problems to be solved by participating teams were sent at intervals over the next several months. Student teams were asked to obtain and analyze information, define the problems, brainstorm alternative solutions, develop and apply appropriate criteria to evaluate alternatives, decide on best solutions, and plan for implementation. On the basis of performance on these problems, teams for the annual Bowl competition at the University of Georgia were selected. At the Bowl, awards were given for team problem solving, scenario writing, and solution selling (Torrance & Torrance, 1978).

Although gifted students may have more natural ability in the problem-solving process, according to Torrance (1978) they apparently need practice in problem solving and may even initially lag behind their less able peers in this area because the gifted are so seldom challenged to really use their abilities. Therefore, the results of the Future Problem-Solving Program have been positive for two reasons: the problem-solving abilities of the gifted students involved were shown by pre- and posttests to be improved by practice, and the students generally responded enthusiastically to the program.

Certainly more research needs to be done to determine how to better refine the problem-solving skills of these students. As Torrance and Reynolds (1978) noted, those gifted students who described themselves on several instruments as being "right-hemisphere" thinkers were better problem solvers than those who described themselves as being "left-hemisphere" thinkers; this is only one aspect of this problem that could warrant further investigation. In light of the burgeoning interest in futuristics and the need to solve world problems of monumental proportions, the work in training gifted students to solve problems has just begun. The University of Georgia program under Torrance and his associates will probably have a lasting impact on the field of gifted education.

### Trends in research

Research in gifted education has been topically diverse, with investigators carrying out myriad "one-shot" studies. However, certain problems have demanded greater research attention—among them the problems of the gifted who are culturally different, the problems of gifted girls, and self-concept and attitude issues. These issues continue to attract research interest as their complexity defies easy resolution.

The culturally different gifted population (sometimes referred to as the disadvantaged gifted in the literature) has been the subject of special conferences, topical journal issues, and research over the past ten years. Most investigative interest has been centered on the discovery of adequate identification procedures for this group (Gallagher, 1974; Torrance, 1964, 1969). Instruments such as the Alpha Biographical Inventory (Taylor & Ellison, 1968) have been developed for use with these students, and existing tests such as the Torrance Tests of Creative Thinking have been analyzed as to their bias against or in favor of disadvantaged groups (Torrance, 1971). (No significant bias was found in the Torrance Tests of Creative Thinking.) A nine-page "Selected Bibliography on Culturally Different Gifted" (Bruch, 1978) highlights some of the better studies done on this issue. Tentative agreement has been reached on the necessity for specially adapted identification procedures and programs, but as Khatena, (1978), the 1978–1979 President of the National Association for Gifted Children, pointed out, giftedness is still a special feature of a minority *within* any minority group; the number of culturally different gifted children to be found will still tend to be small.

Gifted women and girls are receiving a larger share of research interest as a result of the women's movement. Longitudinal and descriptive studies have shown gifted women to be underachievers in relation to their potential (Groth, 1969; Helson, 1971; Terman & Oden, 1959) and in need of special guidance to ensure the utilization of that potential (Almquist & Angrist, 1971; Shakeshaft & Palmieri, 1978). The more creative a woman is, the less likely she is to assume a traditionally passive female sex role (Morse & Bruch, 1978); less creative women do not consciously realize that passivity may restrict their self-development (Bruch & Morse, 1978). Creative women appear to be more complex, indeed *prefer* complexity (Helson, 1967); but a lack of correlation between complexity and the quantity of creative output suggests that qualities inhibiting creativity performance are yet to be identified (Bruch & Morse, 1978) As Blubergs (1978) notes, "more studies have been done on the personality characteristics of gifted females than on any other aspect of their psychological make-up or lives" (p. 539). Apparently, the assumption is made that generalities about gifted women's personalities will lead to more appropriate programming or guidance; whether this result will follow remains to be seen.

Attitudinal surveys and studies have found the concerns of the gifted to be as wide ranging as those of any group, yet a sense of identity

(Gilmore, 1974), confidence (Bachtold, 1978), and general social adjustment (Cohn, 1978) have been found to be characteristic of the group as a whole. A great majority of gifted students are happy to take part in special programming (Ford, 1978) and prefer to receive tangible rewards or recognition (grades) for their academic efforts (Johnson & Yarborough, 1978). An entire issue of the *Gifted Child Quarterly* (Summer, 1977) was recently devoted to the issue of *Guidance for the Gifted,* techniques of counseling at a special laboratory at the University of Wisconsin were described (Colangelo & Pfleger, 1977; Zaffrann & Colangelo, 1977) and directions such counseling will take in the future were anticipated (Perrone & Pulvino, 1977). This recognition of the special needs of gifted students in regard to guidance, career counseling, etc., is a positive indication that educators are acknowledging that these students may indeed need special help and will not always "make it on their own."

Bearing in mind the diversity of approaches to research and programing for gifted students, it is important to note the present and future probabilities of support for such programs by the U.S. Office of Education. Because of the expanding federal awareness and support for such programs, the education of gifted and talented students has made phenomenal strides in the 1970s. A look at the most recent federal legislation benefiting these students effectively summarizes the trends in the education of the gifted, and may give the reader an idea of the future of the movement.

## FEDERAL LEGISLATION

A social critic once compared America to a rocking chair, always in motion but going nowhere.
Abraham J. Tannenbaum (1972, p. 14)

The Marland Commission's (1972) *Report to the Congress* on the state of education for the gifted and talented illustrates all too clearly that concern for providing special educational opportunities for the gifted and talented has been subject to the everchanging tides of national interest. An effect of the *Report* was to make apparent the need for a sustained, concerted national effort to heighten awareness of these students' unique needs and to assure that their education would not be perceived as the "icing on the curriculum cake" (Tannenbaum, 1972). The remainder of this section traces federal involvement in promoting programs for this segment of our population. Highlights of each year are presented, ending with the projected programming for the years 1978-1979.

As a result of the findings of the Marland Commission study, the U.S. Commissioner of Education established an advocate office within the Office of Education, the Office of Gifted and Talented (OGT). This office was to maintain program responsibility for education for the gifted and talented within the Office of Education in the Bureau for the Education of the Handicapped. Although the OGT possessed no specific funds, the commissioner directed salary and expense funds for two professionals and support staff. The commissioner also directed certain parts of authorizations which contained discretionary funds to the education of the gifted and talented.

One last significant development emanating from the 1972 study was the assignment of a staff member in each of the 10 designated regional offices of education as a gifted and talented education advocate. From 1972 through 1977, these individuals served as resource persons to both state and local educational agencies in their regions.

The first legislation for the gifted and talented was passed in 1974 as part of the Elementary and Secondary Education Act Amendments (PL 93-380, Section 404). The Special Projects Act contained within it a proration of 6.25 percent of its total funds as available for the gifted and talented. In fiscal year 1976, the Act's first year of operation, 2.56 million dollars was allocated to the program for the gifted and talented.

Program regulations, published in May 1976, permitted support to

state education agencies, and local education agencies for programs and projects in gifted and talented education; to institutions of higher education and other appropriate public and private agencies, including state education agencies and local education agencies for leadership personnel training; and to both public and private, including non-profit agencies for the operation of model projects in provision of services to the gifted and talented.

Programs and projects supported in fiscal year 1976 under this authority were designated to 25 State Departments of Education, 18 local education agencies, 2 institutions of higher education (and 1 local education agency for leadership training), and 6 public and private nonprofit agencies for operation of model projects. One contract award for development of information products was made to a nonprofit agency. The State Educational Agencies that were supported in fiscal year 1976 are listed in Table 1. In that year 68 percent of the available funds were expended to support the 25 states. The majority of the projects funded were designed to support activites that would increase the capacity of the states and other administrative systems to initiate, operate, and extend educational opportunities at the pre school, elementary, and secondary levels for gifted and talented students. (Sisk, 1978).

In fiscal year 1977 the OGT budget was again $2.56 million.

### TABLE 1
### STATE EDUCATIONAL AGENCIES THAT WERE
### SUPPORTED BY THE SPECIAL PROJECTS ACT IN
### FISCAL YEAR 1976

| | |
|---|---|
| Alabama | New Jersey (Multistate Consortium: |
| California | Connecticut,Rhode Island, |
| Colorado | NewHampshire, and |
| Florida | Vermont) |
| Georgia | New York |
| Hawaii | North Carolina |
| Idaho | North Dakota |
| Iowa | Pennsylvania |
| Kentucky | South Carolina |
| Maine | South Dakota |
| Maryland | Texas |
| Massachusetts | Wisconsin (Multistate Consortium: |
| Mississippi | Illinois, Michigan, Ohio, Indiana, |
| Missouri | and Minnesota) |
| Nebraska | Wyoming |

Programs and projects supported in that year were designated to 31 State Departments of Education, 17 local education agencies, 2 institutions of higher education, 1 national private association (and 1 local education agency for leadership training), and 5 public and private nonprofit agencies for operation of model projects. One contract was awarded to an institution of higher education for information services.

A wide variety of local projects were funded in 1977 to provide alternative models for local education agencies in the planning stages of developing programs for the gifted and talented while simultaneously serving the needs of these children (Sisk, 1978).

In fiscal year 1978, OGT announced that 37 State Education Agency grants were awarded, totaling $1,419,732. Of these, 36 were for new projects and 1 was for continuation funding. Fourteen local education agency grants were funded, totaling $240,742. Five demonstration continuing model projects were funded for $200,000, and $487,267 was awarded to four institutions of higher education for continuing grants.

As of 1978 there were 40 full-time consultants to work with the gifted and talented. This represents a sharp increase compared to the 10 state consultants reported in 1972 by the Maryland Commission. Other developments included 24 states possessing appropriate legislation (including permissive and mandatory), as compared to 21 states reporting such legislation in 1972. Forty-three states reported that they were utilizing Title IV funds for the gifted and talented; the monies ranged from $950,000 (Pennsylvania) to $8500 (Maine). Many of the Title IV projects featured inservice training to upgrade teacher competencies in working with gifted students. Nine states (Alabama, California, Georgia, Kansas, Mississippi, New Mexico, North Carolina, North Dakota, West Virginia) reported that they have certification for teachers of the gifted. The National Leadership Training Institute (LTI, funded by OGT and first directed by the Council for Exceptional Children in 1972, and then from 1973 to the present time by a local education agency in Ventura, California) has emphasized in its training the importance of comprehensive state planning. As of 1977, 32 states with whom the LTI had worked had developed comprehensive state plans for the gifted and talented which have been adopted by their state boards of education.

On Octber 15, 1978, the Gifted and Talented Children's Act of 1978 became law (PL 95-561, Title IX, Part A). Due primarily to the efforts of Senators Jacob Javits (R-NY) and Robert Stafford (R-VT) and Representative Carl Purcell (R-MI), the new Act made some important changes from the previous legislation. The major features of the Act include the following provisions (Association for the Gifted, October 1978, p. 1):

1. Gifted/talented funds would come under Title IX-a.
2. The term "gifted and talented" has been redefined.
3. Appropriation for FY 1978 is $3,780,000.
4. Authorization of FY 1979 is $25,000,000 with an increase in authorization of $5,000,000 each year until FY 1983 when the authorization reaches $50,000,000.
5. 25% of the total appropriation would remain under commissioner's discretionary funds.
6. 75% of the total appropriation would go to states if they make application. Of the state funds, 90% would go to local educational agencies and the remaining 10% would go for state administrative costs.
7. If the appropriation level reaches $15,000,000, the program would revert to a state formula award with each state receiving an amount of money based on total school age population. No state would receive less than $50,000.

The Congress hereby finds and declares that:

(1) the Nation's greatest resource for solving critical national problems in areas of national concern is its gifted and talented children,

(2) unless the special abilities of gifted and talented children are developed during their elementary and secondary school years, their special potentials for assisting the Nation may be lost, and

(3) gifted and talented children from economically disadvantaged families and areas often are not afforded the opportunity to fulfill their special and valuable potentials due to indequate or inappropriate educational services. (Sec. 901 (b))

Purpose:

It is the purpose of this part to provide financial assistance to State and local educational agencies, institutions of higher education, and other public and private agencies and organizations, to assist such agencies, institutions and organizations to plan, develop, operate, and improve programs designed to meet the special educational needs of gifted and talented children. (Sec. 901 (c))

Definition:

For the purposes of this part, the term "gifted and talented children" means children and, whenever applicable, youth, who are identified at the preschool, elementary, or secondary level as possessing demonstrated or potential abilities that give evidence of high performance capability in areas such as intellectual, creative, specific academic, or leadership ability, or in the performing and visual arts, and who by reason thereof, require service or activities not ordinarily provided by the school. (Sec. 902)

This legislation represents a goal that the council for Exceptional Children has worked very long and hard to obtain. Dorothy Sisk, Director of the OGT, reminds educators that the battles are never ending: "The crucial point needing stress at this time is that every individual must assume responsibility and be concerned about gifted and talented if the United States is to continue the encouraging pace of development for programs for gifted and talented that has been realized in the last decade." (Sisk, 1978).

# References

Almquist, E. M., & Angrist, S. S. Role model influences on college women's career aspirations. *Merill-Palmer Quarterly,* 1971, *17,* 263–279.

Association for the Gifted. *TAG Upate* July 1978, *1.*

Bachtold, L. M. Reflections of gifted learners. *Gifted Child Quarterly,* 1978, *22,* 116–124.

Barbe, W. B., & Renzulli, J. S. *Psychology and education of the gifted* (2nd ed.). New York: Irvington, 1975.

Bloom, B. S. (Ed.). *Taxonomy of educational objectives, handbook 1, cognitive domain.* New York: David McKay Company, 1972.

Blubergs, M. Personal studies of gifted females: An overview and commentary. *Gifted Child Quarterly,* 1978, *22,* 539–547.

Bruch, C B. Selected bibliography on culturally different gifted. *Gifted Child Quarterly,* 1978, *22,* 385–393.

Bruch, C. B. & Morse, J. A. Initial study of creative (productive) given under the Bruch-Morse model. *Gifted Child Quarterly,* 1978, *22,* 526–535.

Chambers, J A. Relating personality and biographical factors to scientific creativity. *Psychological Monographs,* 1964, *78* (7, Whole No. 584).

Cohn, S. J. Myth no. 2: Educational acceleration leads to the social maladjustment of intellectually talented youths. *Gifted Child Quarterly,* 1978, *22,* 125–127.

Colangelo, N., & Pfleger, L. R. A model counseling laboratory for the gifted at Wisconsin. *Gifted Child Quarterly,* 1977, *21,* 321–325.

Connecticut State Department of Education. *Identification of the gifted* (Report of a task force on identification). Hartford, 1974.

Cox, C. M. *The genetic studies of genius* (Vol. 2): *The early mental traits of three hundred geniuses.* Stanford, Calif.: Stanford University Press, 1926.

Cunningham, C. H., Thompson, B., Alston, H. L., & Wakefield, J. A. Use of S.O.I. abilities for prediction. *Gifted Child Quarterly,* 1978, *22,* 506–512.

Eisenberg, A. R. *Academic acceleration and the relationships between age and grade point average.* Baltimore: Study of Mathematically Precocious Youth, Department of Psychology, The Johns Hopkins University, 1977.

Elkind, D. Growing up faster. *Psychology Today,* February 1979, 28–45.

Ford, B. G. Student attitudes toward special programming and identification. *Gifted Child Quarterly,* 1978, *22,* 489–497.

Fox, L. H. A mathematics program for fostering precocious achievement. In J. C. Stanley, D. P. Keating, & L. H. Fox (Eds.), *Mathematical talent: Discovery, description and development.* Baltimore: The Johns Hopkins University Press, 1974, pp. 101–125.

Friedenberg, E. Z. The gifted student and his enemies. In E. Z. Friedenberg (Ed.), *The dignity of youth and other atavisms.* Boston: Beacon Press, 1966, pp 119–135.

Fund for the Advancement of Education of the Ford Foundation. *Bridging the gap between school and college.* New York: Research Division of the Fund, 1953.

Fund for the Advancement of Education of the Ford Foundation. *They went to college early.* New York: Research Division of the Fund, 1957.

Gallagher, J. J. *Research summary on gifted child education.* Springfield, Ill.: Superintendent of Public Instruction, State of Illinois, 1966.

Gallagher, J. J. (Ed.). *Talent delayed . . . talent denied: The culturally different child.* Reston, Va.: Foundation for Exceptional Children, 1974.

George, W. C. & Denham, S. A. Curriculum experimentation for the mathematically talented. In N. D. Keating (Ed.), *Intellectual talent: Research and development.* Baltimore: The Johns Hopkins University Press, 1976, p. 103–131.

Getzels, J. W., & Jackson, P. W. The meaning of "giftedness"—An examination of an expanding concept *Phi Delta Kappan,* 1958, *40,* 75–77.

Getzels, J., & Jackson, P. *Creativity and intelligence.* New York: Wiley, 1962.

171

Gilmore, J. V. *The productive personality,* San Francisco: Albion, 1974.

Gowan, J. C. Identifying gifted students for a program. *Accent on Talent,* 1967b, *2*(2), 1.

Gowan, J. C., & Torrance, E. P. *Educating the ablest.* Itaasca, Ill.: Peacock, 1971.

Groth, N. J. *Vocational development for gifted girls: A comparison of Maslovian needs of gifted males and females between the ages of ten and seven years.* Paper presented before the American Personnel and Guidance Association, 1969.

Hall, P. *Gifted children: The Cleveland story.* World, 1956.

Helson, R. Personality characteristics and developmental history of creative college women. *Genetic Psychology Monographs,* 1967, *76,* 72–76.

Helson, R. Women mathematicians and the creative personality. *Journal of Consulting and Clinical Psychology* 1971, *36,* 210–219.

Hobson, J. R. High school performance of underaged pupils initially admitted to kindergarten on the basis of physical and psychological examinations. *Educational and Psychological Measurement.* 1963, *33,* 159–170.

Hollingworth, L. M. *Children above 180 IQ, Stanford-Binet.* New York: World Book, 1942.

Jarecky, R. K. Identification of the socially gifted. *Exceptional Children,* 1959, *25,* 415–419.

Johnson, R. A, & Yarborough, B. H. The effects of marks on the development of academically talented elementary pupils. *Gifted Child Quarterly,* 1978, *22,* 498–505.

Khatena, J. President's message. *Gifted Child Quarterly,* 1978, *22,* 265–266.

Lombroso, C. *The men of genius.* London: Scott, 1891.

Marland, S. P. *Education of the gifted and talented: Report to the Congress of the United States by the U.S. Commissioner of Education and background papers submitted to the U.S. Office of Education.* Washington D.C.: U.S. Government Printing Office, 1972.

Morse, J. A., & Bruch, C. B. A comparison of sex roles of creative–productive versus non-productive women. *Gifted Child Quarterly,* 1978, *22,* 520–525.

Myers, R. E., & Torrance, E. P. *Invitations to thinking and doing.* Boston: Ginn, 1964.

Myers, R. E., & Torrance, E. P. *For those who wonder.* Boston: Ginn, 1966.

National Educational Association, Educational Policies Commission, *Education of the gifted.* Washington, D.C.: 1950.

Nisbet, J. F. *The insanity of genius.* London: Kegan Paul, Trench, Trubner, 1891.

O'Neill, K. K. Parent involvement: A key to the education of gifted children. *Gifted Child Quarterly,* 1978, *22,* 235–242.

Passow, A. H. *Planning for talented youth: Considerations for public schools.* New York: Bureau of Publications, Teachers' College, Columbia University, 1955.

Pegnato, C. C., & Birch, J. W. Locating gifted children in junior high school. *Exceptional Children,* 1959, *25,* 300–304.

Perrone, P. A., & Pulvino, C. J. New direction in the guidance of the gifted and talented. *Gifted Child Quarterly,* 1977, *21,* 326–335.

Pressey, S. L. Educational acceleration: Appraisals and basic problems. *Bureau of Educational Research Monographs* (No. 31). Columbus: The Ohio State University, 1949.

Renzulli, J. S. *The enrichment triad model: A guide for developing defensible programs for the gifted and talented.* Mansfield Center, Conn.: Creative Learning Press, 1977.

Renzulli, J. S. What makes giftedness? Reexamining a definition. *Phi Delta Kappan,* 1978, *60,* pp. 180–184; 261.

Renzulli, J. S., Hartman, B., Callahan, C., & Smith, L. *Scales for rating behavioral characteristics of superior students.* Weathersfield, Conn.: Creative Learning Press, 1976.

Roeper, A. The young gifted child. *Gifted Child Quarterly,* 1977, *21,* 388–396.

Shakeshaft, C., & Palmieri, P. A. A divine discontent: Perspectives on gifted women. *Gifted Child Quarterly,* 1978, *22,* 468–477.

Sisk, D. A. Education of the gifted and talented: A national perspective. *World Council for Gifted and Talented Children News Letter,* October 1978.

Stanley, J. C. Special fast math classes taught by college professors to fourth through twelfth graders. In D. P. Keating (Ed.), *Intellectual talent: Research and development.* Baltimore: The Johns Hopkins University Press, 1976, pp. 132–159.

Stanley, J. C., George, W. C., & Solano, C. H. *The gifted and creative: A fifty year perspective.* Baltimore: The Johns Hopkins University Press, 1977.

Stanley, J. C., Keating, D. P., & Fox, L. H. (Ed.). *Mathematical talent: Discovery, description and development.* Baltimore: The Johns Hopkins University Press, 1974.

Tannenbaum, A. J. A forward & backward glance at the gifted. *The National Elementary Principal,* February, 5, 1972, *51,* 14–23.

Taylor, C. W. Multi-talent potential. In *Project Implode, igniting creative potential.* Salt Lake City: Project Implode, Bella Vista–IBRIC, 1971, pp. 6–14.

Taylor, C. W. (Ed.). *Teaching for talents and gifts, 1978 status: Developing implementing multiple talent teaching.* Salt Lake City: Utah State Board of Education 1978.

Taylor, C. W., & Ellison, R. L. *Alpha biographical inventory.* Salt Lake City: Institute for Behavioral Research in Creativity, 1968.

Terman, L. M. *Mental and physical traits of a thousand gifted children, genetic studies of genius* (Vol I). Stanford, Calif.: Stanford University Press, 1925.

Terman, L. M., & Oden, M. H. *The gifted child grows up, genetic studies of genius* (Vol. IV). Stanford, Calif.: Stanford University Press, 1947.

Terman, L. M., & Oden, M. H. *The gifted group at mid-life.* Stanford, Calif.: Stanford University Press, 1959.

Torrance, E. P. Identifying the creatively gifted among economically and culturally disadvantaged children. *Gifted Child Quarterly,* 1964, *8,* 171–176.

Torrance, E. P. *Issues in the identification and encouragement of gifted disadvantaged children.* Paper presented to participants in Operation Talent Search, Morehead State University, Morehead, Ky., January 17, 1969.

Torrance, E. P. Are the Torrance Tests of Creative Thinking biased against or in favor of disadvantaged groups? *Gifted Child Quarterly,* 1971, *15,* 75–80.

Torrance, E. P. Training teachers and leaders to recognize and acknowledge creative behavior among disadvantaged children. *Gifted Child Quarterly,* 1972, *16,* 3–10.

Torrance, E. P. *Torrance tests of creative thinking.* Lexington, Mass.: Personnel Press, Ginn, 1974.

Torrance, E. P. Giftedness involving future problems, *The Journal of Creative Behavior.* 1978, *12*(2), 75–86.

Torrance, E. P., & Reynolds, C. R. Images of the future gifted adolescents: Effects of alienation and specialized cerebral functioning. *The Gifted Child Quarterly,* 1978, *22*(1), 40–54.

Torrance, E. P., & Torrance, J. P. Future problem solving: National interscholastic competition and curriculum project. *The Journal of Creative Behavior,* 1978, *12*(2), 87 689.

Treffinger, D. J. Guidelines for encouraging independence and self-direction among gifted students. *Journal of Creative Behavior,* 1978, *12,* 14–20.

Treffinger, D. J., Renzulli, J. S, & Feldhusen, J. F. Problems in the assessment of creative thinking. *Journal of Creative Behavior,* 1971, *5,* 104–112.

Williams, F. E. *Classroom ideas for encouraging thinking and feeling.* Buffalo, N.Y.: Disseminators of Knowledge (DOK), 1970.

Witty, P. (Ed.). *The Gifted child.* Boston: Heath, 1951.

Witty, P. *Helping the gifted child*. Chicago Science Research Associates, 1952.

Witty, P. A decade of progress in the study of the gifted and creative pupil. In W. B. Barbe (Ed.), *Psychology and education for the gifted*. New York: Appleton-Century-Crofts, 1965, pp. 35–39.

Worcester, D. A. *The education of childen of above-average mentality*. Lincoln, Neb.: University of Nebraska Press, 1956.

Zeffrann, R. T., & Colangelo, N. Counseling with gifted and talented students. *Gifted Child Quarterly*, 1977, *21*, 305–321.

# BIOFEEDBACK APPLICATIONS WITH HANDICAPPED CHILDREN AND YOUTH

Sebastian Striefel

*Utah State University*

Richard Baer

*University of Arkansas*

Recent years have seen a rapidly expanding technology for dealing with problems of the handicapped. This chapter will focus on one aspect of that technology, biofeedback. For the purposes of this paper, biofeedback will be defined as "the use of instrumentation to mirror psychophysiological processes of which the individual is not normally aware and which may be brought under voluntary control" (Fuller, 1978, p. 39). Historically, what an individual felt or thought about his own or another person's behavior could not be defined accurately in terms of measurements of physical change (Brown, 1974). Biofeedback instrumentation now allows for verification that certain physiological states exist internally and provides information as to how these physiological states are affected by thoughts and feelings. Biofeedback uses physiological recording equipment to detect signs of inner physiological activity and feeds this information back to the individual. Such feedback allows the individual to modify his physiology. Many biofeedback devices have long been used in medicine for diagnostic purposes; they now are being used for treatment purposes. In the past, if an individual was unsure about an internal physiological state, he would go to a doctor, have various tests conducted, and then have the doctor interpret for him what the test results meant, for example, a blood pressure of 125/90. Now an individual

The authors would like to thank Richard Sanok and Dr. Glen Latham for their helpful comments in reviewing this manuscript, Janet Mecham for secretarial services, and Peggy Hauser for collecting information articles.

can have the added component of feedback, which can allow him to modify his own physiology in a desired direction.

The details of biofeedback training and experimentation are rather complicated and require specialized knowledge from several disciplines such as medicine, psychology, electroencephalography (EEG), physiology, and electronics (Downs, 1974). Stoyva (1976) has stated that a critical first step in biofeedback is the modification of the physiological response of concern, such as muscle activity in muscle reeducation or brain wave activity in epilepsy. Control is achieved by providing the individual with immediate information about his biological condition. This information allows the individual to try different strategies for modifying his biological system. After control has been achieved, one tries to identify the experiential concomitants of the physiological modifications so that the changes can be produced and maintained without the continued need for exposure to the biofeedback machine. Retention of the learned skill depends on motivation, reinforcement, and the extent of overlearning obtained (Fuller, 1978). It also depends on the degree to which the biofeedback trainer has successfully programmed for physiological generalization to occur to the rest of the individual's environment and to stress-producing situations. In biofeedback, responsibility for establishing and maintaining change is largely returned to the individual.

Some of the instruments used for biofeedback training include, (1) thermometers for providing skin temperature feedback, (2) electromyographs (EMG) for providing muscle activity feedback, (3) electroencephalographs for providing brain wave amplitude and frequency feedback, (4) stethoscopes for heart rate feedback, (5) automated blood pressure cuffs for blood pressure feedback, (6) pneumographs for providing respiration feedback, and (7) electrodermographs for providing skin resistance or skin potential change feedback. The latest equipment is geared for clinical use; it is flexible, versatile, sensitive to change, and rejects artifacts. To be useful, biofeedback must produce changes that are large, durable, safe, and generalize to situations outside the training environment (Schwartz, 1973).

This review covers biofeedback applications with children and youth classified as handicapped, In PL 93-516 the U.S. Congress defined a handicapped individual as "any person who a) has a physical or mental impairment which substantially limits one or more of such person's major life activities, b) has a record of such an impairment, or c) is regarded as having such an impairment" (*Federal Register,* 1977). The studies cited here include those biofeedback applications that have been shown to be effective with handicapped individuals under age 21 or that have been effective with an older handicapped population and have promise for this younger age group. In the first group of studies reviewed, biofeedback has been applied in an effort to directly control or eliminate a handicapping condition, e.g., epilepsy, hyperactivity, and muscle reeducation. This chapter will be concerned with the state of the art of these biofeedback applications. The second group of biofeedback studies have dealt with problems common to normal and handicapped individuals alike, e.g., headaches and pain. Most published biofeedback studies fall into this category. This review will not deal with most of those applications since they are adequately covered in reviews by Fuller (1978), Katkin, Fitzgerald, and Shapiro (1978), and Shapiro and Surwit (1976), but will include some of the problem areas that are common among the handicapped, e.g., stuttering.

## BIOFEEDBACK APPLICATIONS TO SPECIFIC HANDICAPS

### Epilepsy

Epilepsy is an intermittent disorder of the central nervous system that is associated with a sudden discharge of cerebral neurons; it is usually self-limited (Aird & Woodbury, 1974). It may include a loss of consciousness, convulsive movements, and/or a disturbance of movement, sensation, or behavior (Arangio, 1974; Sutherland, Tait, & Eadie, 1974). Biofeedback approaches have been developed for epilepsy because the drugs used to control its manifestations are not without side effects nor are they effective with all individuals. Biofeedback approaches to epilepsy have focused on attempts to modify the characteristics of the EEG results obtained from epileptics (Shapiro & Surwit, 1976) and are based on earlier experimental efforts by Sterman (1973).

Sterman (1973) trained cats to increase a subdominate 12–14-Hz (cycles per second) rhythm appearing over the sensorimotor cortex; this training is called sensorimotor rhythm (SMR) conditioning. Once so trained, the cats were very resistant to drug-induced seizures. These findings led directly to attempts to deal with epilepsy in human patients. In one study a 23-year-old female with major motor seizures was conditioned to increase her production of SMR and concurrently her seizure frequency decreased from 1.92 per month to .66 per month (Sterman & Friar, 1972). Sterman, MacDonald, and Stone (1974) replicated the SMR training procedure with four epileptic and four nonepileptic subjects. Training occurred for 3 sessions per week for 6 months to 2 years, and again the production of SMR increased and seizure frequen-

177

cy decreased. Questions raised concerning Sterman's results included the following (Shapiro & Surwit, 1976): (1) Is the SMR a meaningful EEG rhythm in man or only in cats? (2) Could the results be accounted for by other variables such as placebo effects or relaxation? (3) Do the results of the studies support a neuronal reorganization hypothesis as suggested by Sterman?

Several attempts to replicate Sterman's results followed. Finley, Smith, and Etherton (1975) provided 11–13-Hz SMR training to a 13-year-old male who experienced 75 falling down seizures for every 10 hours of wakefulness. After training, SMR had increased from 10 to 70 percent of the time during each session and seizures had decreased from 8 per hour to less than 1 per .75 hour, as noted in a 1-year follow-up (Finley, 1976). Lubar and Bahler (1976) reported improvement in the seizure frequencies of eight epileptic patients ranging in age from 10 to 27 years using similar procedures. Seifert and Lubar (1975) reported seizure reductions in five of six epileptics given SMR biofeedback training.

Kaplan (1975) engaged in some efforts to train a dominant frequency in the 6–12-Hz range (SMR is a subdominant frequency). She attributed improvements to success in learning to relax rather than to learning a specific EEG rhythm.

Although many questions have been raised concerning the adequacy of the designs used in the aforementioned studies, and different opinions exist as to what accounted for the reductions in seizure activity, it is apparent that seizure activity did decrease as a function of some variables (controlled or uncontrolled) associated with the procedures used. The advantages of biofeedback approaches in the management of epileptics seem to be in controlling seizures in those individuals for whom medications are not effective (25 percent of the epileptic population), and in replacing medications with self-control procedures (Lubar & Bahler, 1976). The results to date seem to warrant continued efforts to learn more about controlling epilepsy through biofeedback. For more information the reader is referred to a review by Rudrud and Striefel (1978).

## Hyperactivity

The term *hyperactivity* has been used to describe child behavior that is manifested by excessive motor activity, brief attention span, distractibility, impulsivity, and irritability (Laufer & Denhoff, 1957; Wender, 1972). These behaviors interfere with the child's adjustment to the environment and often preclude normal achievement in a school setting. The most prevalent treatment for hyperactivity has been the use of drugs; however, drugs have many potential problems (Connors & Eisenberg, 1963; Douglas, 1975; Levy, 1966; Stroufe, 1975), including various side effects.

Several biofeedback approaches have been utilized in attempting to deal with hyperactivity. Braud, Lupin, and Braud (1975), in an uncontrolled study with a 6½-year-old boy, used EMG biofeedback to reduce the number of seconds of tension in the frontalis muscle. Both teachers and parents reported that the subject was calmer and improved over a three-month period when he practiced his biofeedback technique. Haight, Irvine, and Jampolsky (1976), in a study with an experimental and control group, also used EMG biofeedback for decrements in frontalis muscle tension. Behavior rating scales were collected before and after seven weeks of training. The results indicated decreases in hyperactivity for all subjects in both the experimental and in the control group but no EMG changes occurred in either group. Striefel (1978) conducted EMG frontalis biofeedback training with eight boys using a single-subject, multiple-baseline design. After two to five months of daily training, all subjects showed decrements in their frontalis EMG of 50 percent or more; however, there were few changes in the number of hyperactive behaviors recorded by observers in the classroom. In one subject there was a decrease in gross movements, such as "out of seat", but not in overall level of hyperactive behavior. One subject reduced his overall level of hyperactive behaviors by 50 percent; however, this was correlated with a change in teaching techniques in the classroom. The other six subjects showed no changes in overall hyperactive behavior levels.

Taken together, the results of studies using EMG biofeedback with hyperactive children are contradictory. Since there were differences in procedures, further research will be necessary before conclusive statements can be made.

Other types of biofeedback modes have also been used in attempts to control hyperactivity. Lubar and Shouse (1976), using a single-subject reversal design, exposed a male hyperactive subject to SMR conditioning, a drug-only condition, and a combination of a drug plus SMR. Chin EMG levels increased as a function of SMR conditioning, and the SMR plus drug condition was most effective. Eight of 13 behaviors observed in the classroom changed substantially in the desired direction. Reliability data were good. Nall (1973) studied three groups—an alpha training group, a placebo group, and a control group—and found that there were no changes in hyperactivity. Simpson and Nelson (1974) conducted a study using a control group and an experimental group that received biofeedback training on controlling their breathing rates. After 3.5 months of training there were no differences between groups on behavior rating scales completed by teachers nor on scores of four Attention and Vigilance tests or on five subtests of the WISC. Respiratory measures and hyperactive behaviors were not different between the two groups. Moreland (1977) used a procedure in which a four-year-old male was seated in a chair, movement of which would terminate videotaped cartoons being observed on television. After eight weeks of baseline and biofeedback training, hyperactivity, in this situation, was significantly reduced. No measurements were made of behavior changes in other locations.

To date, several biofeedback studies have reported success in decreasing hyperactivity, but all of these studies lacked control groups or control procedures or were conducted with only one subject. In all studies having more than one subject and having appropriate control procedures, no significant change in hyperactive behavior was found. It is difficult to account for these differences in results since different procedures, definitions of hyperactivity, and equipment were used. Clearly, biofeedback is in need of more research before its utility in dealing with hyperactivity can be determined. Striefel's (1978) review of biofeedback applications to hyperactivity is recommended to readers interested in further inquiry into this area.

**Muscle reeducation**

Recently, there has been increasing interest in applying biofeedback procedures to individuals experiencing motor problems due to cerebral palsy and other types of neurological diseases or trauma. Research in this area has generally focused on the ability of EMG feedback procedures to increase an individual's control of motor responses. Although the *Cumulated Abridged Index Medicus* and other sources listed a good number of studies in this area, few have included children as subjects, and those that have, have focused primarily on the problems of children with cerebral palsy.

Skrotzky, Gallenstein, and Osternig (1978) have investigated the efficacy of EMG feedback procedures for increasing the active range of motion (ROM) in the ankle of spastic diplegic cerebral palsied patients. In this study four subjects aged 11–29 years received 20 sessions of EMG feedback training over a period of 10 days. During each session both auditory and visual EMG feedback was provided from the ankle muscles as the subject engaged in a series of flexing exercises. In each subject, one randomly selected ankle was trained during the first 10 sessions. Results of the study showed that after 10 sessions active ROM had increased in the first trained ankle for all four subjects. The range of improvement was from 20 to 500 percent. Similarly, after the 20th session the second trained ankle of each subject had also increased in active ROM. The range of improvement here was from 33 to 450 percent.

Active ROM for each subject in this study was tested again at four- and nine-week follow-up sessions. At these times it was noted that the only two subjects who maintained the gains made during feedback training were originally classified as exhibiting moderate cerebral palsy, while the two who failed to maintain gains were classified as moderately severe. The authors note that, in general, overlearning appears to be a necessary condition for the maintenance of gains achieved through muscle reeducation techniques and suggest that this may account for the differential results obtained with moderate and moderately severe subjects. Perhaps with additional EMG feedback training the moderately severe subjects might have maintained the gains they made.

In an interesting series of studies, Finley and his colleagues have shown EMG feedback training from the frontalis muscle to be effective in improving the speech and motor functioning of cerebral palsied patients. Six athetoid patients aged 14–31 served as subjects in the first study (Finley, Niman, Standley, & Ender, 1976). One case was classified as mild, three as moderate, and two as severe. Following a series of speech and motor tests each subject was exposed to 12 sessions of auditory and visual EMG feedback from the frontalis muscle of the forehead. Results of the study showed that frontalis EMG levels decreased significantly for all subjects as a result of training, that speech functioning improved for four of the six subjects, and that motor functioning improved for all subjects. The authors note that the two subjects who showed no improvement in speech functioning were the two classified as severe and that neither had speech either before or after training. They also note that, in general, the degree of improvement in speech and motor functioning appeared to be negatively related to the degree of impairment, i.e., the less the impairment the greater the degree of improvement.

Finley, Niman, Standley, and Wansley (1977) systematically replicated their previous study with a group of spastic cerebral palsied children aged six to ten years. Procedures in this study were identical to those in the previous one with the following exceptions. While engaged in feedback sessions the children were reinforced with candy, a toy, or a token after every minute during which they met a criterion for lowering frontalis EMG levels. The initial 12 training sessions were followed by six weeks of no training and four weeks of retraining (6–8 sessions). Results of the study showed that mean EMG levels declined during the first training period, increased during no training, and decreased again during retraining. All children showed improvement in motor function following the first training period, and three of the four showed improvement in speech functioning. During the no training period three of the four subjects showed significant deterioration in speech and motor functioning. Finally, all but one child made further gains during the retraining period. The authors note that the one child who failed to show gains during retraining had moved from the area. This made it necessary to attempt retraining in his home with portable equipment and without the benefit of the candy, toy, and token reinforcement system. This finding suggests that the incorporation of reinforcement procedures with biofeedback procedures may be critical in determining children's responses to treatment.

A few attempts have been made to teach cerebral palsy patients to hold their heads upright. Harris, Spelman, and Hymer (1974) used a helmet which provided the wearer with feedback about the direction and degree of tilt of the head from vertical. A movie projector could also be turned on or off depending on the degree of tilt. Nine children received daily 30-minute sessions and all improved in head stability. Duration increased from a few seconds to as much as five minutes in some cases. In addition, extraneous movements decreased and some generalization occurred to teaching and therapy situations where the helmet was not used. Wooldridge and Russell (1976/1977), using a similar device with 12 cerebral palsied children, also reported improved head control, although it varied across subjects. Substantial generalization of improvement was found for some of these children outside the treatment session.

The importance of neuromuscular reeducation for the rehabilitation of stroke patients is attested to by the number of published studies of EMG biofeedback. Marinacci and Horande (1960) used EMG feedback and increased the function of the muscles in the left arm by 20 percent in a one-hour training session with a hemiplegic. Andrews (1964) monitored various muscles of the upper extremity in 20 hemiplegic patients who had experienced strokes 1–14 years previously. Seventeen subjects were able to produce controlled muscle contractions within five minutes of receiving feedback training. Johnson and Garton (1973) used EMG training with ten hemiplegic patients with paralyzed anterior tibialis muscles. Nine of the subjects wore a leg brace for ambulation at the onset of the study. After training for 2, 8, and 16 weeks, respectively, three subjects could walk without a brace. The remaining subjects still required the brace but were reported to have made significant functional improvements as measured by gross foot dorsiflexion.

Jacobs and Felton (1969) reduced spasticity in neck-injured subjects using EMG feedback to the degree that neuromuscular activity in the trapezius muscles was indistinguishable between normal and neck-injured subjects. Brudny, Korein, Levidow, Grynbaum, Leiberman, et al. (1974) used visual and auditory EMG feedback training with 2 quadriparesis, 13 hemiparesis, 13 torticollis, 5 dystonia, and 3 facial spasm patients. All patients had previously been unresponsive to chemotherapy, surgery, and psychotherapy. After 24–36 sessions of training, 32 patients had gained symptomatic relief and several had increased voluntary movements. Appropriate controls which would allow for better evaluation of feedback procedures were called for by the authors in future research efforts in this area.

Wannstedt and Herman (1978) provided 30 ambulatory patients with hemiparesis with auditory feedback of weight bearing on the involved leg in order to achieve symmetrical standing. These patients placed only 20–40 percent of their body weight on the hemiparetic limb at the onset of the study in comparison to 43–57 percent of body weight on each limb by normal subjects. Seventy-seven percent of the subjects achieved symmetrical standing during only one session of training, and 16 of the 20 patients who continued to receive training achieved the goal of symmetrical standing without feedback by the end of the study.

Additional verification and simplification of biofeedback procedures in dealing with motor involvement problems may provide for a variety of improvements in the skills of individuals classified as handicapped. In some cases it might result in enough improvements to remove the classification of "being handicapped" from an individual.

### Learning disabilities

Hunter, Russell, Russell, and Zimmerman (1976) have compared the effects of biofeedback training in handwarming on normal and LD children. Based on previous research the authors speculated that LD children would learn to warm their hands just as well as normal children and that the self-control learned during the biofeedback task might have positive effects on learning in general. In this study a group of 30 LD children were matched with regard to age, grade, race, sex, teacher estimates of IQ level, and socioeconomic status with a group of 30 normal children. Half the subjects in each group were assigned to an experimental group and the other half to a control group. Treatment for the experimental group consisted of five 15-minute sessions during which they were given visual feedback as they attempted to increase their hand temperature. The same procedure was employed with the control subjects except that feedback was provided from yoked controls. All subjects were pre- and posttested on a variety of psychometric measures.

The results showed that children in the experimental group were significantly better at increasing their hand temperature within sessions than the control group. Furthermore, LD children were significantly better at the task within sessions than normal children. Across sessions the experimental group showed significantly greater handwarming than the control group but there was no difference on this variable between LD and normal children. It was noted that younger children (second graders) were significantly better at increasing their hand temperature within sessions than older children (third and fourth graders). Finally, only one of the psychometric measures was correlated with physiological performance. Increases on the Auditory–Visual Integration test were significantly correlated ($-.36$) with the subjects' ability to increase hand temperature within sessions. In summary, only one difference between normal and LD children was noted. LD children were better able to increase their hand temperature within sessions. The results suggest that when irrelevant stimuli are reduced, and reinforcement is immediate and consistent, LD children may learn at least as well as normals. These findings, if substantiated in future research, may have relevant implications for teaching LD children other skills.

Guralnick and Mott (1976) used respiration feedback to teach an 11-year-old LD child to control his breathing patterns. The study was undertaken because the child's inability to hold his breath or to control his inhalations and exhalations interfered with speech productions. The results show that the LD child could learn to control his respiration; but the study must be regarded as tentative since it provided no data concerning the effects of learning to control respiration on the child's speech production.

Murphy, Darwin, and Murphy (1977) present evidence that EEG biofeedback procedures may have more of an effect on performance variables for LD children than the handwarming procedure tested by Hunter et al. (1976). These researchers provided three groups of LD subjects with EEG alpha feedback training, EEG beta feedback training, or no training. The authors report that results of the study indicated that the alpha-trained group significantly decreased in projective anxiety and giving up of interpersonal control, and increased in expressed interpersonal warmth and arithmetic achievement. These researchers also report on an LD boy who, after 35 sessions of varied EEG training, showed a significant increase in performance IQ and academic performance.

Although results are promising, replications are needed to substantiate the usefulness of biofeedback in dealing with LD. Future research might investigate how changes in other physiological parameters of LD children are related to variables such as academic performance, peer interaction, and attention.

### Asthma

Two biofeedback procedures have been demonstrated to be effective in improving asthma. The first involves EMG feedback related to bronchial constriction and dilation. Davis, Saunders, Creer, and Chai (1973) assigned 24 asthmatic children to one of two experimental groups or to a control group. Following eight days of baseline, during which daily measures of peak expiratory flow rate (PEFR) were taken for all subjects, one group received five 30-minute sessions of modified Jacobsonian relaxation training. A second group received five 30-minute sessions of combined modified Jacobsonian relaxation training and EMG feedback training from the frontalis muscle. The third group served as a no treatment control. Posttreatment daily measures of PEFR were collected for eight days.

The results revealed a significant difference in the PEFR of the three groups following treatment. The responses of the two experimental groups were superior to the response of the control group, and the response of the combined relaxation–feedback group was superior to that of the relaxation only group. These findings, however, were only true for children who had been previously classified as nonsevere asthmatics not receiving steroid treatment. No significant difference between groups was found for children previously classified as severe asthmatics (receiving steroid treatment). Moreover, it was noted that treatment effects for the nonsevere group were not maintained over the posttreatment baseline period. Finally, the authors report that there was no correlation between EMG levels and either positive or negative PEFR changes. Thus, it is difficult to attribute improvement in PEFR response to the treatment procedures. The authors suggest that some other variable may have been operating to produce the changes.

More recently, Kotses, Glaus, Crawford, Edwards, and Scherr (1976) have tested the effects of frontalis EMG feedback alone on children's asthmatic responses. These researchers divided 36 asthmatic children into three groups. One group received frontalis EMG feedback, a second yoked control group received false feedback, and the third group served as a no treatment control. The results of the study indicated that the true feedback group had reliably lower EMG levels at the end of treatment and that only this group showed improved PEFR.

Khan and his colleagues (Khan, 1977; Khan, Staerk, & Bonk, 1973), in a series of experiments, have shown biofeedback training of forced expiratory volume (FEV) to be effective in improving asthmatic responses in children. The research design employed in both studies was essentially the same. All subjects were first asked to inhale saline solution after being told it contained the substance they were allergic to. On the basis of this test a group of reactors and nonreactors were identified. Next, half the reactors and half the nonreactors were assigned to an experimental group, while the other children were assigned to a control group. Training for the experimental group was carried out in two phases. During the first phase the children were trained to increase their FEV via feedback. Successful attempts to increase FEV were followed with presentation of a light and praise from the experimenter. The training procedure during the second phase was the same as during phase one, except that at the beginning of each session bronchoconstriction was induced. A variety of procedures for inducing bronchoconstriction were employed, including recall of previous asthma attacks, inhalation of saline vapors, audiotapes of wheezing, voluntary hyperventilation, exercise, and, as a last resort, medication.

The subjects in the first study (Khan et al., 1973) were followed for a period of 8–10 months. Results indicated that during this time the experimental group had significantly less use of medication, fewer emergency room visits, and fewer asthma attacks. The subjects in the second study (Khan, 1977) were followed for 1 year. The results of this study showed that experimental reactors and nonreactors and control reactors manifested significant improvement in the number of asthma attacks occurring over the course of the follow-up period. There was no significant difference in number of asthma attacks between the two reactor groups; however, the experimental nonreactors had significantly fewer attacks than the control nonreactors. Furthermore, although the two reactor groups did not differ with respect to duration of attacks, the experimental nonreactors had significantly shorter attacks than the control nonreactors. Finally, no differences in use of medication or number of emergency room visits were noted among the groups.

Although the results obtained in biofeedback applications to asthma cannot all be attributed to the variables manipulated, the picture to date is promising. Future research might well establish biofeedback as a viable intervention technique for asthma.

**Facial expressions in the blind**

Webb (1977) reported on a procedure to teach facial expressions to blind subjects. A normal child learns to interpret the meaning of facial expressions and then to produce them himself. A blind child is not provided with necessary information to develop appropriate facial patterning. While most expressions involve several muscles in one way or another, Webb decided to deal only with surface muscles in order to avoid the use of intramuscular electrodes that would cause subject discomfort. Facial expressions of normal individuals were filmed and shown to judges who placed descriptors on them. Each expression was presented three times and those with high disagreements were eliminated. The expressions chosen for training were happiness, surprise, and anger. Webb inspected the films to determine which muscles were visibly contracted to establish criteria for training.

Five blind subjects were selected to participate in pretraining, training, and posttraining phases. In pretraining, each subject was told to express happiness, anger, and surprise and these expressions were put on film. The subjects were then trained while receiving auditory feedback (different for each muscle) from the specific muscles to produce the three different facial expressions. During posttraining, expressions were again filmed. A panel of four judges rated pre- and posttraining expressions. The majority of errors occurred in pretraining expressions; thus, the results indicate that the facial expressions of the blind subjects improved considerably as a result of myoelectric feedback training. These procedures have implications for the blind but need replication with proper controls, more subjects, more expressions, and extended data concerning generalization of expressions to the normal environment.

## BIOFEEDBACK APPLICATIONS TO PROBLEMS ASSOCIATED WITH VARIOUS HANDICAPS

**Elimination of subvocalizations**

Several studies have demonstrated that biofeedback procedures are useful in decreasing subvocalizations (talking to oneself while reading), a response, it has been hypothesized, that may interfere with reading ability. Following earlier pilot work (Hardyck, Petrinovich, & Ellsworth, 1966), Hardyck and Petrinovich (1969) demonstrated that EMG feedback from the vocal musculature was effective in decreasing subvocalizations in college and high school students who were slow readers. In the first of this series of experiments college students were divided into an experimental and a control group. After the resting and reading EMG levels of the vocal musculature were determined for all subjects, the experimental subjects were given three sessions of biofeedback training. Training consisted of presenting the subjects with a tone each time their EMG level exceeded its resting level as they read light fictional material. Control subjects had their EMG levels recorded while reading during their first three sessions and then were exposed to three sessions of the training procedure. Results showed that the experimental subjects eliminated subvocalizations within one hour, while control subjects showed no change during the first three sessions. Similarly, control subjects eliminated subvocalizations within one hour once training was begun.

In the second of this series of experiments, Hardyck and Petrinovich used the same EMG feedback procedure with a group of high school students in grades 7–12. The results were similar to those obtained for the college students except that it took longer for the procedure to be effective (1–3 sessions) and it was not effective for the younger children, i.e., the seventh graders. Older children of above average and average intelligence, like college students, tended to learn the experimental task within a few minutes and showed no tendency to revert to subvocalizing at a one-month follow-up session. Children of below average intelligence were noted to take longer to learn and did not maintain gains during follow-up.

No immediate increase in reading speed following treatment was observed for either high school or college subjects. However, college students reported less fatigue when reading for periods of one to three hours—perhaps, the authors suggest, because of more relaxed breathing patterns allowed by the elimination of subvocalizations. Finally, the authors report that at a six-month follow-up session, a small sample of high school students seemed to derive more benefit from their reading instruction and had increased their reading speed considerably.

Recently, Parsky and Papsdorf (1976) have reported results that tend to confirm the findings of Hardyck and Petrinovich (1969). In this study 24 students were divided into an experimental and a control group. The experimental group received eight 30-minute sessions of EMG biofeedback training to reduce subvocalizations over a period of 12 weeks. Half the subjects in the experimental and control groups received regular classroom reading instruction during the course of the study, while the other half received individualized reading instruction. The results of the study showed significant reductions in mean EMG level during silent reading for subjects who had received biofeedback training.

No differences were found among the four groups in vocabulary or reading comprehension, although all showed improvement over the course of the study. Procedures such as these might have benefit for students who have been classified as LD and who have difficulty in reading. Conclusive research is not yet available.

## Stuttering

*Stuttering* can be defined as any unusual prolongation, hesitation, or repetition of a syllable (Hanna, Wilfling, & McNeill, 1975). Stuttering is accompanied by a spasm of the laryngeal muscles; thus EMG spikes from the throat differentiate periods of stuttering from periods of normal speech (Hanna et al., 1975). EMG biofeedback has been used to reduce laryngeal muscle tension, and thus stuttering, in several studies. Although none of these studies have employed young children as subjects, two have included adolescents. In the earliest of these studies, Hanna et al. (1975) treated a 19-year-old male with a ten-year history of stuttering which had been intractable to more conventional forms of therapy. The subject was trained in two sessions separated by a six-day interval. During each session the subject was provided with auditory EMG feedback from his throat muscles as he responded verbally to cards from the Thematic Aperception Test (TAT). Session I was divided into four periods. During Periods 1 and 3 the subject responded to TAT cards with feedback on; during Periods 2 and 4 he responded without feeback. Session II was also divided into four periods. The subject received feedback during Periods 1 and 4, no feedback during Period 2, and false feedback from a yoked control during Period 3.

Stuttering was reduced to less than 50 percent of baseline levels during both feedback periods in both sessions. During no feedback periods, stuttering was higher than during feedback periods but lower than baseline, indicating some generalization of the effects of the feedback training. Finally, the level of stuttering during the false feedback period of Session II was higher than when feedback was provided but lower than when no feedback was provided. The authors suggest that during the false feedback period the tone heard by the subject may have served as a discriminative stimulus for relaxation of the throat muscles which, in turn, decreased the rate of stuttering. Finally, it was noted that the rate of stuttering in this subject was associated with the level of EMG activity in his throat muscles: high levels of EMG activity were associated with high levels of stuttering and low EMG levels were associated with low levels of stuttering. This finding suggests a high probability that the decrease in stuttering in this subject was a function of the lowered levels of EMG activity achieved in his throat muscles via the feedback procedure.

Lanyon (1977), following an earlier pilot study (Lanyon, Barrington, & Newman, 1976), has demonstrated the efficacy of biofeedback training to lower the EMG levels of the masseter muscles of the face as a treatment for stuttering. Nineteen adolescent and adult stutterers served as subjects for this series of experiments. Initially, all were trained via visual feedback to lower the EMG levels of their masseter muscles to 4–5 microvolts (amplitude) quickly and reliably. Once this was accomplished, subjects were trained on a variety of graded speaking tasks ranging from reading a one-syllable word to making a spontaneous four-word statement. Two types of feedback training were employed— direct and indirect. During direct feedback training the subject relaxed, watching the feedback meter until his masseter EMG level met a specified criteria; then he engaged in the appropriate speaking task. Indirect feedback training was similar but the subject could not see the feedback meter. The experimenter monitored the meter and said "no" if the subject tried to speak before meeting the relaxation criteria and "go ahead" if he had not spoken within 4 seconds of meeting the relaxation criteria. Each task was trained until the subject did not stutter on approximately 90–95 percent of his responses. Once the subjects had met this criterion they were tested on the task just accomplished. Testing consisted of having the subject engage in the newly learned task during alternating periods of feedback on and feedback off. The results showed that both the direct and indirect feedback training procedures dramatically decreased stuttering.

Biofeedback seems to be a viable method for dealing with stuttering; however, replication and comparison studies with other treatment techniques should be conducted to confirm that it is both effective and economical.


## Vocal intensity

Brody, Nelson, and Brody (1975) reported using visual feedback of vocal amplitude to increase normal vocal intensity in two mildly retarded adults. One subject generalized this change in speech to spontaneous conversational settings, but it decreased over a five-month period. A voice-operated relay was used to turn on a light when vocal intensity was 65 decibels or greater. However, since the study lacked proper control procedures, the results are, at best, suggestive.

## Functional colitis

*Functional colitis* is a condition of chronic diarrhea for which no organic cause can be identified. Its symptoms include intermittent irregularity of bowel habits with frequent diarrhetic bowel movements (5–15 or more per day) usually accompanied by abdominal cramps. In severe cases it can virtually keep an individual homebound. Furman (1973 provided direct auditory feedback of intestinal motility to five patients in an effort to develop voluntary control of intestinal contractions. To do so he used an electronic stethoscope to amplify the sounds of intestinal motility to provide auditory feedback. Within five training sessions all five subjects had achieved at least partial or intermittent control. The frequency and intensity of episodes spontaneously decreased. The higher the degree of control achieved in increasing and decreasing motility, the greater was the symptom relief. No follow-up study was conducted.

## Self-injurious behavior

Schroeder, Peterson, Solomon, and Artley (1977) reported that EMG feedback collected from the trapezius muscle resulted in a greater decrement in amplitude and a longer duration of low-amplitude muscle activity than did restraint alone in two severely retarded chronic head bangers. The usefulness of EMG in preventing self-injurious behavior was not determined; however, both subjects exhibited idiosyncratic EMG patterns just prior to the occurrence of self-injurious behavior.

## Bruxism

*Bruxism,* defined as the grinding or clenching of teeth during sleep, is considered to occur in 78 percent or more of the U.S. population (Kardachi & Clarke, 1977). Bruxism can result in unaesthetic wearing of the teeth, loss of the alveolar bone which supports the teeth, and facial pain. EMG signals from the masseter and temporalis muscles were amplified and an oscillator was used to provide auditory tone feedback that varied in frequency with the intensity of muscle activity. Eight of nine subjects were successful in reducing the duration of bruxism activity while sleeping (Kardachi & Clarke, 1971). The auditory signal did not awaken any of the subjects. There was no reduction in the duration of bruxism on control days, suggesting that there was no generalization to occasions when feedback was not provided.

## Counseling

Kater and Spires (1975) report on a rather unique application of biofeedback procedures in a counseling situation with a grade school boy. The subject had been seen by the school counselor for several months and was still having difficulty expressing his thoughts and feelings to the counselor. He had originally been referred because he was highly inhibited both in his school work and ability to relate to others. Use of a temperature-training feedback device which taught the boy to increase his hand temperature appeared to facilitate his relaxation and expression of feelings. Unfortunately, it is difficult to draw any conclusions on the basis of these results. Additional studies are needed to verify or disprove the value of hand warming in counseling.

## AREAS OF CONCERN

The studies reviewed in this chapter indicate that biofeedback has been used with a variety of handicaps and other conditions that are common among individuals classified as handicapped. In many cases the results suggest positive benefits for those individuals involved in biofeedback training. Many problems remain, however, that must be resolved before biofeedback can be added to the standard list of generally used special education techniques. The major areas of concern include the following: (1) a lack of controlled studies, (2) a lack of information on the relationship of various physiological parameters, (3) the effectiveness and economy of biofeedback, (4) ethical issues, (5) motivation, (6) a lack of information on the generalization of positive results, and (7) a lack of trained personnel.

In 1976 Shapiro and Surwit stated that there was "not one" properly controlled study on the effectiveness of biofeedback in dealing with a particular physiological problem. At present, one would still be hard pressed to identify an ideal study. That ideal study would need a precise definition of the disorder being treated, proper control procedures (including random subject selection), physiological data on several parameters, reliability of behavioral data collected, long-term follow-up, and precise specification of the procedures used. Carefully controlled studies, of course, are essential before biofeedback can be readily accepted as a treatment of choice.

To date, the majority of biofeedback applications have focused on controlling individual functions in isolation. In the future, the measurement and control of multivariate patterns of physiological responding should be possible (Schwartz, 1976). It is possible that some of the conflicting results obtained in the past might be accounted for by unmeasured variables that are correlated in different ways in different individuals with the physiological parameter being treated (e.g., producing a generalized relaxation of the skeletal system in one subject and generalized relaxation of the autonomic system in another subject might result in conflicting results when only specific EEG rhythms are recorded). Measurements of patterns of responding might shed light on such relationships, and thus help identify the critical variables.

Another area of concern is the economy of biofeedback. Shapiro and Surwit (1976) have raised questions about the time and effort required of both the trainee and the trainer to achieve effective results with biofeedback. Will a patient engage in biofeedback training if his problems can be dealt with effectively via medication? Generally speaking, it is human nature to proceed on the path of least resistance and to do what is easiest. It might well be that biofeedback's most promising use will be with problems for which medications are not available (e.g., muscle reeducation) or the medications have serious side effects, or with problems that have been resistant to known medications (e.g., 25 percent of epilepsy cases). It is also possible that additional work in biofeedback could result in some fairly efficient training procedures that would enhance its acceptance as a treatment of choice. Additional research is needed that compares biofeedback with medication, relaxation training, and other commonly used treatments.

It is anticipated that results demonstrating effectiveness and efficiency will accumulate simultaneously over the next several years. To date, the majority of biofeedback procedures have been implemented in the clinic or research laboratory. Few published reports exist on classroom applications of biofeedback, particularly with the handicapped, although Mulholland (1973) called for such intervention several years ago. Much work needs to be done in the collection of data on economical methods of implementing proven biofeedback procedures in the classroom, assuming that it is feasible to do so. It will be necessary to establish programs to train teachers in biofeedback procedures or to find positions and funding in schools for persons who already possess expertise in biofeedback. The widespread implementation of biofeedback procedures in classrooms for the handicapped seems to be some years away at best.

Fuller (1978) has pointed out the ethical concerns that are particularly relevant to biofeedback: (1) we should use caution in terms of the claims made for biofeedback; (2) there is a need for informed consent and awareness of experimental applications; (3) medical disorders should be accepted for treatment only if standard treatments have been applied, and then only in conjunction with medical consultation; and (4) the practitioner should have appropriate specialized training in biofeedback.

Shapiro and Surwit (1976) have pointed out the problems related to subject motivation. It is not sufficient to assume that feedback alone will result in behavioral change. For some individuals, feedback may well not serve as a functional reinforcer. This is very likely to be the case when dealing with individuals classified as mentally retarded and with children in general (e.g., Finley et al., 1977). In some cases the relationship between the problem faced by the handicapped individual and the biofeedback training approach and goals may be incomprehensible to the trainee. In such cases the trainer must implement the procedures used in behavior modification in which functional reinforcers are identified and implemented.

The secondary gains accruing to an individual as a function of maintaining his/her physiological disorder (e.g., a child with asthma may keep his/her mother from engaging in social functions by having asthmatic attacks) can also pose motivational problems (Shapiro & Surwit, 1976). In such cases the individual must be taught appropriate alternatives for dealing with his environment—alternatives that preclude the need to maintain the physiological disorder.

A third motivational concern raised by Shapiro and Surwit (1976) is related to strongly entrenched behaviors that are in conflict with the treatment goals. They used the example of an individual being treated for hypertension who gambled at the race track on weekends even though it raised his blood pressure. In working with the handicapped, an example might be the individual who has seizures that are triggered by flashing lights and who undergoes biofeedback training but refuses to give up going to discos where flashing lights are an integral part of the environment.

Another critical issue concerns the generalization of results obtained in the training situation to the rest of the individual's environment, particularly to those stress-inducing situations that trigger problem behaviors for the trainee (e.g., the classroom for the hyperactive child). In some cases, such as muscle reeducation, the natural contingencies in the environment may well take over and ensure that generalization to other environments occurs. For example, an individual trained to hold his head up may well continue to do so after training whenever someone speaks to him or whenever the television is on in front of him. In other cases the trainer may need to spend considerable time and effort in programming to ensure generalization. Shapiro and Surwit (1976) have indicated several methods of initiating such generalization. One is to turn the biofeedback off for longer and longer periods in the training setting (after the subject has mastered the task) while requiring the trained response. They also suggest desensitization procedures in which subjects are exposed to stress-producing events (e.g., visualizing a situation which previously produced stress) and are required to maintain the trained response.

## CONCLUSION

This chapter has been a review of the state of the art of biofeedback applications to the problems of handicapped children and youth. Biofeedback, as a mode of treatment, is still relatively new. Thus, it suffers from many of the problems encountered by any new approach, including (1) a lack of properly controlled studies, (2) a lack of data on both effectiveness and efficiency, (3) a lack of trained personnel, and (4) an era of fadism marked by overapplication to areas in clinical settings before appropriate data are available. It appears to be relatively certain that biofeedback is here to stay, since its potential usefulness is just beginning to be demonstrated. To date, success has been reported in the following areas: treating epilepsy, hyperactivity, and asthma; training facial expressions and muscle reeducation; increasing vocal intensity and the expression of feelings; and eliminating stuttering, functional colitis, self-injurious behavior, and bruxism.

Whereas widespread applications in the special education classroom are still somewhat in the future, the implications for the handicapped are too apparent to be overlooked. Biofeedback is one of the few approaches that has shown promise for dealing with problems heretofore untreatable, such as certain cases of muscle reeducation and seizure control in which medications are ineffective or have severe side effects. The problems related to properly controlled studies, trainee motivation, and generalization of results to environments other than the training setting can all be dealt with on an empirical basis. Each of these problems has been dealt with, to some degree, in other areas of treatment and can similarly be overcome through field tests in the biofeedback area. Biofeedback is an area that also offers an opportunity for dealing with precise human behaviors previously untreatable because of measurement problems. It offers a new vista for dealing with problems of the handicapped. Continued research and clinical application must be encouraged.

# References

Aird, R. B., & Woodbury, D. M. *The management of epilepsy.* Springfield, Ill.: Thomas, 1974.

Andrews, J. M. Neuromuscular reeducation of hemiplegia with the aid of electromyography. *Archives of Physical Medicine and Rehabilitation.* 1964, *45,* 530–532.

Arangio, A. J. *Behind the stigma of epilepsy.* Washington, D.C.: Epilepsy Foundation of America, 1974.

Braud, L., Lupin, M., & Braud, W. The case of electromyographic biofeedback in the control of hyperactivity. *Journal of Learning Disabilities,* 1975, *8,* 21–26.

Brody, D. M., Nelson, B. A., & Brody, J. F. The use of visual feedback in establishing normal vocal intensity in two mildly retarded adults. *Journal of Speech and Hearing Disorders,* 1975, *40,* 502–507.

Brown, B. B. *New mind, new body.* New York: Harper & Row, 1974.

Brudny, M. D., Korein, J., Levidow, L., Grynbaum, B. B., Leiberman, A., & Friedman, L. Sensory feedback therapy as a modality of treatment on central nervous system disorders of voluntary movement. *Neurology,* 1974, *24,* 925–932.

Conners, C. K., & Eisenberg, L. The effects of methylphenidate on symptomatology and learning in disturbed children. *American Journal of Psychiatry,* 1963, *120,* 458–464.

*Cumulated Abridged Index Medicus,* 1979, *10,* Bethesda, Maryland: Department of Health, Education and Welfare.

Davis, M. H., Saunders, D. R., Creer, T. L., & Chai, H. Relaxation training facilitated by biofeedback apparatus as a supplemental treatment in bronchial asthma. *Journal of Psychosomatic Research,* 1973, *17,* 121–128.

Douglas, A. Are drugs enough?—To treat or to train the hyperactive child. *International Journal of Mental Health,* 1975, *4,* 199–212.

Downs, H. Foreward. In B. Brown, *New mind, new body.* New York: Harper & Row, 1974.

*Federal Register,* May 4, 1977, *42* (86), 22676. Washington, D.C.: Department of Health, Education and Welfare.

Finley, W. W. Effects of sham feedback following successful SMR training in an epileptic: Follow-up study. *Biofeedback and Self-Regulation,* 1976, *1,* 227–235.

Finley, W. W., Niman, C., Standley, J., & Ender, P. Frontal EMG–biofeedback training of athetoid cerebral palsy patients. *Journal of Biofeedback and Self-Regulation,* 1976, *1,* 169–182.

Finley, W. W., Niman, C., Standley, J., & Wansley, R. Electrophysiological behavior modification of frontal EMG in cerebral palsied children. *Journal of Biofeedback and Self-Regulation,* 1977, *2,* 59–79.

Finley, W. W., Smith, H. A., & Etherton, M. D. Reduction of seizures and normalization of the EEG in a severe epileptic following sensorimotor biofeedback training: Preliminary study. *Biological Psychology,* 1975, *2,* 189–203.

Fuller, G. D. Current status of biofeedback in clinical practice. *American Psychologist,* 1978, *33,* 39–48.

Furman, S. Intestinal biofeedback in functional diarrhea: A preliminary report. *Journal of Behavior Therapy and Experimental Psychiatry,* 1973, *4,* 317–321.

Guralnick, M. J., & Mott, D. E. Biofeedback training with a learning disabled child. *Perceptual and Motor Skills,* 1976, *42*(1), 27–30.

Haight, M. J., Irvine, A. B. & Jampolsky, G. G. *The response of hyperkinesis to EMG biofeedback.* Paper presented at the Biofeedback Research Society, Colorado Springs, Colorado, March 1976.

Hanna, R., Wilfling, F., & McNeill, B. A biofeedback treatment for stuttering. *Journal of Speech and Hearing Disorders,* 1975, *40,* 270–273.

Hardyck, C. D., & Petrinovich, L. F. Treatment of subvocal speech during reading. *Journal of Reading*, 1969, *12*, 361–422.

Hardyck, C. D., Petrinovich, L. F., & Ellsworth, D. W. Feedback of speech muscle activity during silent reading: Rapid extinction. *Science*, 1966, *15*, 1467–1468.

Harris, F. A., Spelman, F. A., & Hymer, J. W. Electronic sensory aids as treatment for cerebral palsied children. *Physical Therapy*, 1974, *54*, 354–365.

Hunter, S. H., Russell, H. L., Russell, E. D., & Zimmerman, R. L. Control of fingertip temperature increases via biofeedback in learning disabled and normal children. *Perceptual and Motor Skills*, 1976, *43*, 743–755.

Jacobs, A., & Felton, G. S. Visual feedback of myoelectric output to facilitate muscle relaxation in normal persons and patients with neck injuries. *Archives of Physical Medicine and Rehabilitation*, 1969, *30*, 34–39.

Johnson, H. E., & Garton, W. H. Muscle reeducation in hemiplegia by use of electromyographic device. *Archives of Physical Medicine and Rehabilitation*, 1973, *54*, 320–323.

Kaplan, B. J. Biofeedback in epileptics: Equivocal relationship of reinforced EEG frequency to seizure reduction. *Epilepsia*, 1975, *16*, 427–489.

Kardachi, B. J., & Clarke, N. G. The use of biofeedback to control bruxism. *Journal of Periodontology*, 1977, *48*, 639–642.

Kater, D., & Spires, J. Biofeedback: The beat goes on. *The School Counselor*, 1975, *23*, 16–21.

Katkin, E. S., Fitzgerald, C. R., & Shapiro, D. Clinical applications of biofeedback: Current status and future prospects. In H. L. Pick, H. W. Leibowitz, J. E. Singer, A. Steinschneider, & H. W. Stevenson (Eds.), *Psychology: From research to practice*. New York: Plenum Press, 1978.

Khan, A. U. Effectiveness of biofeedback and counter-conditioning in the treatment of bronchial asthma. *Journal of Psychosomatic Research*, 1977, *21*, 97–104.

Khan, A. U., Staerk, M., & Bonk, C. Role of counter-conditioning in the treatment of asthma. *Journal of Psychosomatic Research*, 1973, *17*, 389–392.

Kotses, H., Glaus, K. D., Crawford, P. L., Edwards, J. E., & Scherr, M. S. The effect of operant conditioning of the frontalis muscle on peak expiratory flow in asthmatic children. *Biofeedback and Self-Regulation*, 1976, 332. (Abstract)

Lanyon, R. I. Effect of biofeedback-based relaxation on stuttering during reading and spontaneous speech. *Journal of Consulting and Clinical Psychology*, 1977, *45*, 860–866.

Lanyon, R. I., Barrington, C. C., & Newman, A. C. Modification of stuttering through EMG biofeedback: A preliminary study. *Behavior Therapy*, 1976, *7*, 96–103.

Laufer, M. W., & Denhoff E. Hyperkinetic behavior syndrome in children. *Journal of Pediatrics*, 1957, *50*, 463–474.

Levy, S. The hyperkinetic child: A forgotten entity, its diagnosis and treatment. *International Journal of Neuropsychiatry*, 1966, *2*, 330–336.

Lubar, J. F., & Bahler, W. W. Behavioral management of epileptic seizures following EEG biofeedback training of the sensorimotor rhythm. *Biofeedback and Self-Regulation*, 1976, *1*, 77–104.

Lubar, J. F., & Shouse, M. N. EEG and behavioral changes in a hyperactive child concurrent with training of the sensorimotor rhythm (SMR): A preliminary report. *Biofeedback and Self-Regulation*, 1976, *1*, 293–306.

Marinacci, A. A., & Horande, M. Electromyogram in neuromuscular reeducation. *Bulletin of the Los Angeles Neurological Society*, 1960, *25*, 57–71.

Moreland, K. L. Stimulus control of hyperactivity. *Perceptual and Motor Skills*, 1977, *45*, 916.

Mulholland, T. B. It's time to try hardware in the classroom. *Psychology Today*, 1973, *7*, 103–104.

Murphy, P. J., Darwin, J., & Murphy, D. A. EEG feedback training for cerebral dysfunction; A research program with learning disabled adolescents. *Biofeedback and Self-Regulation*, 1977, *2*, 288. (Abstract)

Nall, A. Alpha training and the hyperkinetic child—Is is effective? *Academic Therapy*, 1973, *9*(1), 5–19.

Parsky, L., & Papsdorf, J. D. EMG biofeedback supposives of subvocalization in reading disabled grade VI students. *Biofeedback and Self-Regulation*, 1976, 330. (Abstract)

Rudrud, E., & Striefel, S. *Behavioral approaches to the treatment of epilepsy: A critical review.* Unpublished manuscript, Utah State University, 1978.

Schroeder, S. R., Peterson, C. R., Solomon, L. J., & Artley, J. J. EMG feedback and the contingent restraint of self-injurious behavior among the severely retarded; Two case illustrations. *Behavior Therapy*, 1977, *8*, 738–741.

Schwartz, G. E. Biofeedback as therapy, some theoretical and practical issues. *American Psychologist*, 1973, *28*, 666–673.

Schwartz, G. E. Self regulation of response patterning implications for psychophysiological research and therapy. *Biofeedback and Self-Regulation*, 1976, *1*, 7–30.

Seifert, A. R., & Lubar, J. F. Reduction of epileptic seizures through EEG biofeedback training. *Biological Psychology*, 1975, *3*, 157–184.

Shapiro, D., & Surwit, R. S. Learned control of physiological function and disease. In H. Leitenberg (Ed.), *Handbook of behavior modification and behavior therapy.* Englewood Cliffs, N.J.: Prentice-Hall, 1976.

Simpson, D. D., & Nelson, A. E. Attention training through breathing control to modify hyperactivity. *Journal of Learning Disabilities*, 1974, *7*, 274–283.

Skrotzky, K., Gallenstein, J. S., & Osternig, L. R. Effects of electromyographic feedback training on motor control in spastic cerebral palsy. *Physical Therapy*, 1978, *58*, 547–552.

Sterman, M. B. Neurophysiologic and clinical studies of sensorimotor EEG biofeedback training: Some effects on epilepsy. *Seminars in psychiatry*, 1973, *5*, 507–525.

Sterman, M. B., & Friar, L. Suppression of seizures in an epileptic following sensorimotor EEG feedback training. *Electroencephalography and Clinical Neurophysiology*, 1972, *33*, 89–95.

Sterman, M. B., MacDonald, L. R., & Stone, R. K. Biofeedback training of the sensorimotor EEG rhythm in man: Effects on epilepsy. *Epilepsia*, 1974, *15*, 395–416.

Stoyva, J. Self-regulation: A context for biofeedback. *Biofeedback and Self-Regulation*, 1976, *1*, 1–6.

Striefel, S. *A critical review of biofeedback applications to hyperactivity.* Paper presented at Hyperactivity Workshop, Reno, Nev., 1978.

Stroufe, L. A. Drug treatment of children with behavior problems. In F. D. Horowitz, M. Hetherington, S. Scarr-Salapatek, & G. Siegel (Eds.), *Review of child development research* (Vol. 4). Chicago: University of Chicago Press, 1975.

Sutherland, J. M., Tait, H., & Eadie, M. J. *The epilepsies, modern diagnosis and treatment.* London: Churchill Livingstone, 1974.

Wannstedt, A. T., & Herman, R. M. Use of augmented sensory feedback to achieve symmetrical standing. *Physical Therapy*, 1978, *58*, 553–559.

Webb, C. The use of myoelectric feedback in teaching facial expressions to the blind. *Biofeedback and Self-Regulation*, 1977, *2*, 147–160.

Wender, P. H. The minimal brain dysfunction syndrome in children. *Journal of Nervous and Mental Disease*, 1972, *155*, 55–71.

Wooldridge, C. P., & Russell, G. Head position training with the cerebral palsied child: An application of biofeedback techniques. *Biofeedback and Self-Control*, 1976/1977 Annual, pp. 527–534.

# TECHNOLOGY IN SPECIAL EDUCATION

A. Edward Blackhurst
*University of Kentucky, Lexington*

Alan M. Hofmeister
*Utah State University, Logan*

To many special educators, "technology" is equated with equipment and hardware such as audio-visual equipment, teaching machines, and computers. As the Commission on Instructional Technology (1970) pointed out in its report to the President and Congress, such a conceptualization is inadequate. While it is true that things such as television, films, projectors, and computers are considered components, technology is much broader than the use of items of hardware and software. As the Commission reported:

> Instructional technology is a systematic way of designing, carrying out, and evaluating the total process of learning and teaching in terms of specific objectives, based on research in human learning and communication, and employing a combination of human and nonhuman resources to bring about more effective instruction. (p. 19)

At approximately the same time that the Commission released its findings, Haring reviewed the application of instructional technology to special education curriculum design and concluded (Haring, 1970, p. 25):

> In the natural setting, educational technology is being applied in two ways: (1) through automated and non-automated media for display and measurement as part of the task of instruction, and (2) as a set of procedures which systematizes instruction.

Both the Commission on Instructional Technology and Haring were reflecting distinctions developed earlier by Banathy (1968), Dale (1967), Gagne (1968), Heinich (1968), and Silverman (1968).

---

Both authors are Past-Presidents of the Association for Special Education Technology.

199

In 1977, after an extensive study, the American Association for Educational Communications and Technology (AECT) adopted and published a comprehensive definition of educational technology. Space limitations preclude the reproduction of this 16-part definition; however, the introductory sentence states (AECT, 1977, p. 1):

> Educational technology is a complex, integrated process involving people, procedures, ideas, devices, and organizations for analyzing problems and devising, implementing, evaluating, and managing solutions to those problems involved in all aspects of human learning.

The AECT report goes to some length to differentiate between educational technology and instructional technology. However, it is common practice to use these terms interchangeably. Consequently, the terms will be used synonymously in this review.

Technology has been applied to many major problems in special education, with highly significant results. A summary of some of these major technological developments is presented in Table 1.

Regardless of whether or not technological applications have involved the use of machines, a common element has been the emphasis on systematic and integrated approaches to education. Nevertheless, considerable variations can be noted in the application of many of these systematic approaches. The particular field of research in human learning that a researcher chooses to stress is usually a major source of such variation. Haring (1970), for example, reported a strong preference for learning principles based on the experimental analysis of behavior (Sidman, 1960). In contrast, Scandura (1966) stated that some of the principles of learning theory were only of secondary importance in "real-life learning," and the entering competencies a child has may be more important than such principles as reinforcement.

Such differences in emphasis are still evident in special education today and may be associated with differing special education populations. Persons working with profoundly retarded children, where responsiveness to any environmental stimuli may be low, often stress principles of reinforcement. Those working with mildly handicapped persons, where curriculum content is more complex and pupil responsiveness to environmental stimuli is higher, may stress principles such as concept analysis (Becker, Engelmann, & Thomas, 1975). However, while areas of inquiry and approaches to instruction may vary, the common element in technological orientations is that the problems of learning and education are approached in a systematic fashion, regardless of whether media hardware and equipment are involved in the implementation.

In the following review of the application of technology to special education, it will be seen that two approaches, one stressing media applications and one stressing systems technology, are in evidence. The differences between the approaches are growing less distinct, as illustrated by the fact that persons working with media are tending to stress systems procedures to guide their product development processes (Thiagarajan, Semmel, & Semmel, 1974).

## MEDIA TECHNOLOGY

Educational media are those nonhuman resources "born of the communications revolution which can be used for instructional purposes alongside the teacher, textbook, and blackboard" (AECT, 1977, p. 171). These generally represent devices (hardware) with accompanying materials (software) that are used to transmit messages (content). Some devices, however, are used primarily to facilitate communication or physcial functioning and do not require special software for their utilization, as will be illustrated later.

Because of space limitations and the relatively large potential body of information that could be covered in this section, the authors have elected to limit discussion to either relatively recent developments in the media field or to those devices that have specific applications to the handicapped. Several references will be made to secondary sources that provide composite reviews in several different areas, e.g., Lance's (1973) review of media technology and its implications for the handicapped. This document, the most complete review of media technology up to its date of publication, should be reviewed by anyone interested in this particular topic.

### Computer technology

Computers are used with the handicapped for the same purposes they are used with the nonhandicapped, namely, computer-assisted instruction (CAI), computer-managed instruction (CMI), and information storage and management. Cartwright and Hall (1974) discussed many of these uses in a previous review. CAI has been shown to be effective with various handicapped populations (Fletcher & Beard, 1973; Goldenburg, 1977) and with their teachers (Cartwright, 1977). The increasing record-keeping and program-monitoring requirements of the Education for All Handicapped Children Act of 1975 (PL 94-142) have also given rise to the increased use of computers for general record-keeping purposes, such as the storing and updating of Individualized Education Programs

# TABLE 1
## SOME MAJOR MILESTONES IN TECHNOLOGY THAT HAVE AFFECTED SPECIAL EDUCATION

| | |
|---|---|
| 1808 | The precursor of braille is developed as a series of raised dots for sending military messages at night. |
| 1834 | The braille code, using six dots, is published by Louis Braille. |
| 1874 | The audiophone bone conduction amplifier is invented. |
| 1892 | The Braille typewriter is developed. |
| 1900 | The first electrical amplifying device for the hearing impaired is invented. |
| 1913 | Printed letters are translated to musical tones for blind readers using the Optophone prototype. |
| 1914 | The Tadoma method is developed for teaching deaf-blind children; the simplex hearing tube, which uses a funnel to catch sound, is invented. |
| 1916 | The Intelligence Quotient is introduced with the publication of the Stanford-Binet Scale of Intelligence. |
| 1920 | A human emotional response is conditioned by Watson in an experimental setting. |
| 1926 | Pressey develops a teaching machine that uses programmed instruction; a phonograph audiometer is developed to identify hearing impairments. |
| 1928 | Radios are distributed to blind citizens by the American Foundation for the Blind; seeing eye dogs are also introduced to the United States. |
| 1930 | A standard report form is developed for eye examinations. |
| 1934 | The printing visagraph is developed to enlarge printed pages and put them into raised form; the Gault Teletactor amplifies speech vibrations so that the deaf can receive them tactually; Talking Books for the blind are produced on long-playing records. |
| 1935 | The Waldman Air Conduction Audiometer is developed to detect hearing impairments. |
| 1938 | Pitch is translated into a visual image by the Coyne Voice Pitch Indicator. |
| 1947 | The Perkins Brailler is developed; printing of large-type books is initiated by The American Printing House for the Blind. |
| 1949 | Speech is transformed to visual patterns by the cathode ray translator. |
| 1952 | Blind students use the Stenomask to dictate lecture notes while listening. |
| 1953 | The megascope is invented to project and magnify printed material. |
| 1954 | B. F. Skinner publishes "The Science of Learning and the Art of Teaching." |
| 1960 | Lumsdaine & Glaser publish *Teaching Machines and Programmed Learning*. |

1962    Mager publishes "Preparing Objectives for Programmed Instruction."

1965    Mobility in the blind is facilitated through the invention of the Kay binaural sensor; studies are performed using token economies.

1966    The laser cane is developed for use by the blind.

1967    The National Society for the Study of Education 66th Yearbook is devoted to programed instruction.

1968    A device is invented for compressing speech to more than 320 words per minute without distortion.

1971    The Optacon enables the blind to convert ink print to tactile impressions of letters.

1972    A braille writer of pocket size is developed; Kay Spectacles, which enable the blind to determine the precise location of obstacles, are developed as mobility aids.

1974    A braille calculator is developed; reading material can be magnified 25 times and displayed on a TV screen using the Visualtek Miniviewer; the electronic blackboard is developed to transmit writing over telephone lines for display on TV screens.

1975    A talking calculator is developed to provide audio output; speech synthesizers help persons with impaired speech to make spoken sentences; spectograms of speech can be frozen on a TV monitor using the speech spectograph display; Cybercom permits the severely handicapped to communicate via electric typewriter and message board operated by speech or a pneumatic switch; speed of recorded speech can be regulated using the Variable Speed Control Disc; individual educational programs are mandated for the handicapped in PL 94-142.

1976    The Kurzweil Reader translates printed material into synthesized speech for visually impaired persons; the partially seeing can enlarge ordinary printed material using the Optiscope illuminated enlarger; auditory stimulation can be provided to some deaf persons using cochlear implants; brain waves can be recorded during normal activity by an electroencephalograph vest.

1977    The development of artificial limbs is facilitated by the use of computer technology; a reduction of muscle spasms for some cerebral palsied and epileptic persons can be accomplished through the implanting of electrodes in the brain.

1978    Paperless braille is invented to store printed materials on magnetic recording tape.

*Note.* Much of the material in this table was abstracted from the work of Nazzaro (1977).

(IEPs) (Lehrer & Daiker, 1978; Marshall & Johnson, 1978). It should be noted that use of the computer to manage special educational records creates special problems, particularly in regard to the issue of privacy of records. Grayson (1978) noted that because the computer can store and analyze information on a scale unthinkable by manual processing, the privacy of the individual is now threatened on an unprecedented scale.

Computers have, for many years, assisted in the diagnosis and testing of special populations through the remote scoring of tests and through direct on-line interactions at terminals (MacLeod & Overhew, 1977; Suppes, Fletcher, Aonatti, Lorton, & Searle, 1973).

The use of computers as aids in the diagnosis and remediation of speech problems has been evaluated with some evidence of success. For example in diagnosis and remediation efforts, the computer can analyze a client's speech and then provide a visual display of it. This has been found to assist the hearing impaired person to assess the quality of his or her speech (Boothroyd, Archambault, Adams, & Storm, 1978; Nickerson, Kalikaw, & Stevens, 1976).

The increase in the application of computers to special education has been closely linked to the development of microprocessor technology. The introduction of microprocessors has significantly decreased the costs and increased the capacity, reliability, and portability of computers and has extended their usefulness to the handicapped (Bodner, Hoelen, & Zogley, 1978; Foulds & Gaddis, 1975; Nelson & Cassalter, 1977). For example, small, personal computers developed for the home computer market have been applied to the instructional and communicative needs of the physically handicapped (Scully, 1978). Additional examples of such computer applications will be provided in later sections.

**Telecommunication systems**

The potential use of telecommunication systems for delivering educational services to exceptional children and those who work with them is great. However, this potential remains largely untapped; only a few projects have been conducted to explore the feasibility of their applications.

Graf (1974, p. 588) defined telecommunications as "all types of systems in which electric or electromagnetic signals are used to transmit information between or among points." The logic behind the electronic transfer of information was summarized by Wolff (1976 p. A 6–2):

1. Information is the raw material of instruction and learning.
2. The user should dictate the form, time, and place of needed information.

3. It is cheaper to move information to the user than to move the user to the information.
4. It is cheaper to move information electronically than any other way.
5. Most information can be stored, updated, and retrieved electronically.
6. All electronically stored information can be electronically distributed to large numbers of remote users.
7. Electronically stored and/or transmitted information can be given to the user in any electronically-related form such as cathode ray tube image, full audio-visual, computer printout, or facsimile.

Although assumptions 3 and 4 are probably not valid unless appropriate hardware is in place and certain economies of scale are met, the above propositions are well taken—particularly in light of the ever-increasing demands on individuals' time and current concerns over energy consumption necessitated by personal travel. With the advent of the video disc, video graphics, and fiber optic technologies that will be described in greater detail in the next section, they will probably have even greater validity in the future.

Blackhurst (1978) has described the various telecommunication systems that are currently available. He has also illustrated some ways that these might be used for educational purposes. These ways will be summarized in the remainder of this section.

The most readily available telecommunication system is, of course, the nation's telephone system. This can be used for transmitting lectures, conducting interviews, audio teleconferencing, transmitting data, and many other applications. Telephone systems have been very useful in providing instruction to homebound students (Carr, 1964). The telephone was first used for this purpose in 1940 (Hill, 1956). In a recent review, Parker (1977) concluded that classroom instruction conducted via telephone is at least as effective as face-to-face instruction.

In the area of special education, Hershey (1977) found that inservice training related to the education of the gifted conducted via telephone produced significantly higher performance than instruction that was provided in face-to-face or contrast group instruction. Tawney (1977a) demonstrated that telephones could also be used to link various interface and instructional devices located in the homes of severely handicapped infants to a central computer control station. CAI programs such as the PLATO system have also been transmitted over telephone lines (Ballard & Eastwood, 1974).

Computer conferencing (Infomedia Corporation, 1978) is a relatively new system that can be used via telephone lines. This system has been available since 1977, and enables anyone who has a computer terminal connected to a time-shared computer network to participate.

Users store messages in the computer for all persons who are participants. At any convenient time, by entering a code number, a user can query the system to determine whether there are any messages. If so, a response can be entered into the system to be retrieved at the initiator's convenience. This "electronic mail system" will have significant implications for remote conferencing and information exchange.

Open-circuit audio and video broadcast systems are most closely associated with either commercial or educational (public) radio and television. For the most part, these are single-channel systems that are expensive to operate and require special licensing. Obviously, if programing is to proceed over commercial channels it must have broad audience appeal. Educational programing for children, however, is frequently transmitted during school hours by educational television stations. These stations also broadcast inservice and credit courses for adults; however, these courses are becoming more infrequent and/or are broadcast at times that are inconvenient because educational stations are becoming more and more involved with the broadcasting of cultural programing and programing for children. Perhaps the greatest potential of mass media for serving the handicapped will be its role in educating the general public in matters related to the handicapped, such as was demonstrated by the nation-wide broadcast of the program, *Including Me*, in 1978 (Capital Cities Communications, 1978). This program provided an overview of different exceptionalities and showed how persons with different disabilities could be integrated into everyday activities. The considerable potential for mass media to affect the attitudes of children toward the handicapped has not been overlooked. Considerable emphasis has been placed upon incorporation of content related to the handicapped in children's programs such as *Mister Roger's Neighborhood* (Sharapan, 1973), *Sesame Street*, and *Zoom*. As Donaldson and Martinson's (1977) research also demonstrated, video and audio programing can also effectively influence the attitudes of adults toward the handicapped.

Community antenna television (CATV), which is now often referred to as cable TV, enables the provision of many television channels (normally 26 channels in most major market systems) to the ultimate user—whether it be the individual, school, or community center. The technology also permits, in many cases, interaction by the subscriber; that is, users may transmit "upstream" back to the studio (Baldwin, Greenberg, Block, Eulenberg, & Muth, 1978). This facilitates interactive audio, video, and computer utilization.

Instructional systems such as Time-Shared Interactive Computer Controlled Instructional Television (TICCIT) can be adapted for use with cable technology, as was demonstrated in the New York project that provided instruction to homebound physically handicapped students (Tawney, 1977b). When used with other distribution systems, such as communication satellites, CATV holds great promise for the delivery of educational services (Parker & Riccomini, 1975).

Instructional Television Fixed Service (ITFS) is a special band of television channels reserved for the exclusive use of educational institutions. It was first established by the Federal Communications Commission in 1963 to respond to the needs of instructional television for multichannel transmission capability at costs considerably lower than conventional VHF or UHF television. ITFS operates at frequencies higher than those used by open broadcast stations. For this reason, special antennas and converters must be installed on each building which is to receive ITFS signals. This equipment converts the transmission to signals that can then be received by ordinary television receivers. Once established, ITFS is economical to use for regional applications; it permits flexibility, repetition, and interaction; and it reserves a place in the telecommunications spectrum for the exclusive use of the licensed operator (Blackhurst, 1978). Green and Lazarus (1977) have demonstrated how ITFS can be used to assist regular class teachers with mainstreaming problems.

Communication satellite systems can receive and transmit the signals of any electronic medium (Polcyn, 1973). They have the advantage that they are insensitive to distance, can reach areas that may be blocked by terrain such as mountains, and are useful in remote and sparsely populated areas that may be outside the range of other radio and television stations. A major barrier to the expanded use of satellites is the high cost of earth terminals and the limited availability of satellites and satellite time.

Two National Aeronautics and Space Administration (NASA) operated, high-powered experimental satellites have been used in a variety of educational experiments (Bystrom, 1974; Federation of Rocky Mountain States, 1975; Morgan, Singh, Rothenberg, & Robinson, 1975; NASA, 1974; Pal, 1976; Schwartz, 1976). The largest of these was in Appalachia, where inservice education, including courses related to the gifted and early childhood education of the handicapped, were broadcast to persons in an eight-state area (Bramble & Ausness, 1976). The great potential of communication satellites for educational purposes has received further elaboration by participants in a conference sponsored by the National Institute of Education (1977).

The Council for Exceptional Children (1978) also demonstrated the use of satellites to relay portions of the First World Congress on Special Education from Scotland to the United States. In another application, a portable satellite earth terminal was used to demonstrate how satellites could be used to facilitate live, audio-visual teleconferencing among special education teachers who were separated by approximately 2500 miles (Blackhurst, Williams, Churchill, Allen, & Siegel, 1980).

Future applications of telecommunications will most likely utilize hybrid systems that combine several technologies such as telephone, radio, ITFS, CATV, and/or satellites. Nilles, Carlson, Gray, and Hanneman (1976) concluded that telecommunications is a viable alternative to moving people. Their studies supported this conclusion on the basis of energy saving, attitude of participants, convenience, and student performance. However, they also concluded that the general public does not fully comprehend either the potential or the operation of such telecommunication developments.

**Interface devices**

In 1960, the implications of teaching machines for educating the handicapped were described by Stolurow (1960). Shortly thereafter, Glaser and his colleagues introduced the concept of the student–subject matter interface to the educational community (Glaser, Ramage, & Lipson, 1964). According to these individuals, an interface is any device that is used by students to facilitate their interaction with subject matter. More recently, such devices have also been referred to as man–machine communication systems (Kafafian, 1970) or communication end-instruments (Skinner, 1977).

Some of the implications of the interface concept for special education were illustrated by Blackhurst (1965), who speculated about various types of electromechanical devices that could be constructed to aid exceptional persons in their interaction with subject matter and with other individuals. It is interesting to note that many of the devices that were described in his article for potential future development are now a reality. In fact, technological advances have led to the development of interfaces that have gone beyond those that were being proposed approximately 15 years ago. Several of these will be highlighted in this section.

A major thrust of computer-related applications has been communication facilitation. Other technical aids also exist to support communication. Such aids range from the use of regular typewriters with mildly learning disabled pupils (Cothran & Mason, 1978) to complex and expensive closed-circuit television systems to magnify print for the visually handicapped (Genesky, Peterson, Clewett, & Yoshimura, 1978; Inde, 1978). Two of the best sources describing communication aids are the *Nonvocal Communication Resource Book* (Vanderheiden, 1978) and *Sensory Aids For The Blind And Visually Impaired* (American Foundation for the Blind, 1978).

The present-day communication boards with associated microprocessor technology (McDonald & Schultz, 1973; McNaughton, 1976; Von Bruns-Connolly & Shane, 1978) had origins in the diode–transistor systems of the mid-1960's. These early systems allowed the handicapped person, through a single paddle switch, to cause a light to scan behind an alpha-numeric display. When the desired character was reached, it could be held or typed on a teletypewriter (Roy & Charbonneau, 1974).

Nelson and Cassalter (1977) reported on the use of a microcomputer linked to two pupils with communication boards, a teacher, and a voice synthesizer. The communication boards utilized Bliss symbols, representing speech sounds. The synthesizer stored the name of each symbol in a memory as it was selected. On command, the whole sentence or phrase could be spoken by the synthesizer. Such systems are particularly relevant for persons with severe speech impairments.

A major benefit of such electronic communication aids lies in their ability to facilitate language development and language interaction. In some cases, dramatic improvements in language have resulted through their use, particularly in severely and multiply handicapped pupils whose potential had been grossly underestimated (Elder & Bergman, 1978; Kucherawy & Kucherawy, 1978). Along these lines Shane, Reynolds, and Geary (1977) have voiced a cautionary note with regard to the recent emphasis on nonvocal communication approaches for the severely handicapped, e.g., Bliss symbols. They recommend that an individual's verbal capability should first be explored carefully to determine potential for speech. They also note that it is possible to be severely handicapped, to appear nonvocal, and yet still have the potential to communicate verbally.

Microprocessor-based aids for the visually handicapped have been widely heralded (Sinclair & Sanderson, 1978). A hand-held, battery-operated calculator that speaks the name of each key as it is pressed is comparatively inexpensive and widely available (Brugler, 1978). The Opticon, which allows the blind person to read ordinary print through a conversion of the visual images to a tactile image and braille computer printing terminals, has received considerable acceptance (Joquiss, 1978; Ryan & Bedi, 1978). Since computers can now print in braille, information storage for the blind may be greatly facilitated. Compact and less expensive data cassettes can now serve to store information for them, as opposed to the space-consuming braille volumes of the past.

One of the most interesting interface devices, which has significant implications for the blind, is the Kurzweil reading machine. This computer-based device converts ordinary print materials, such as books, magazines, and typewritten correspondence, directly into spoken English at the rate of 150 words per minute. The user can also direct the machine to repeat or skip passages, spell out difficult words letter by letter, mark passages for future reference, and express the capitalization and punctuation in a sentence (Kurzweil, 1978).

A prototype braille information processor has also been developed for use by the visually impaired (Telesensory Systems, Inc., 1978). This electronic, "paperless" braille system is portable and enables the user to read braille on a 20-cell electronic tactile display rather than on paper. Thus, information for the blind may be stored on cassettes rather than on bulky braille paper. The user can also enter information into the cassette using a keyboard. A microcomputer then enables the user seeking information to automatically retrieve it from the cassette. Since the device is also an audio recorder, both braille and verbal messages can be stored. An optional visual display enables seeing persons to monitor and enter information into the system.

Galton (1977) reported on several other devices to aid the visually impaired. A cane has been developed that contains three laser beams that send out beams of light which result in auditory and tactile feedbacks if there are obstacles directly in front of the walker, a drop-off, or low-hanging obstacles in the person's path. Two other systems in prototype form also hold considerable promise for the blind. One uses a tiny, battery-powered camera worn in the frame of a pair of glasses that transmits visual images to an elastic garment that fits over the abdomen of the wearer. The wearer can receive vibrations from the more than 1000 electrodes in the garment that correspond to the visual images registered by the camera. Another such device transmits electrical impulses directly to electrodes implanted in the visual cortex of the brain. Initial tests of this system appear to be promising. Also available are devices to enable persons with retinitis pigmentosa to see at night.

A number of interface devices have been developed by Kafafian (1970). These include modified keyboards for electric typewriters that enable persons to use their feet, fists, or mouth to operate the typewriter. One interface uses a single control stick for this purpose, while another has split the typewriter keyboard into two 7-key devices, each of which could be strapped to an arm of a wheelchair; Kafafian has also developed a briefcase-size unit to be used for transmitting a visual display of the manual alphabet over the telephone so as to enable deaf individuals to communicate via this medium.

Devices that can be used to compress the rate of speech have been found to be effective with visually impaired children and those with severe reading problems (Short, 1972). These devices discard small fragments of the recorded speech and close up the gaps so that there are no distortions in pitch or quality, as one might find when speeding up a 33 1/3 rpm record to 45 or 78 rpm (Foulke, 1966).

A potentially significant interface for deaf persons is closed captioning. Norwood (1976) reported on research that showed that about 10 percent of ordinary television viewers find captions to be distracting. Consequently, a system has been developed that permits stations to caption television programs and broadcast them in such a way that the captions will not appear on the television screen unless a special decoding device is attached to the television set. The television watching of the deaf can thus be enhanced without infringing upon the television pleasures of the hearing. Efforts are now underway to encourage television stations to purchase the necessary captioning and encoding equipment. Decoding equipment will be available through commercial department stores.

In 1968, Sullivan, Frieden, and Cordery published a manual (now somewhat dated) that described numerous ways that the telephone can be modified for use by persons with a wide variety of physical disabilities. These modifications include the use of hands-free equipment, microswitches, amplifiers, card dialers, and other dialing and holding aids. Using these, persons who are disabled or restricted in their ability to travel could participate in educational programs or communicate with others through technological interfaces with the telephone system.

Several other interface devices are described in the proceedings of a conference on systems devices for the disabled (Foulds & Lund, 1976). These include aids for travel, eating, communication, and numerous other prosthetic and orthotic appliances.

Sixty-one different communications end-instruments are described in a report prepared by Skinner (1977). This useful document provides a narrative description of each device, a picture, and a check sheet that classifies each device along a variety of dimensions.

Recent hardware developments in communication aids have created problems in dissemination and instructional applications. Vanderheiden and Luster (1976) have suggested that priority be given to the following:

1. The generation and dissemination of cumulative information on the aids that already exist.
2. The development of projects to exemplify appropriate field uses of communication hardware.
3. The implementation of field evaluation for existing communication aids.
4. The refinement of existing aids rather than the development of new ones.

As the state of the art in microprocessing and electrical engineering continues to improve, it is anticipated that the handicapped will be major beneficiaries through the development of interfaces that will compensate for their disabilities. Several current developments appear to have particular potential for the field of education. It will be interesting to observe the progress that will be made in these areas during the coming years.

One such emerging technology is video discs. Video disc systems represent a dramatic change in storage and flexibility over present video systems. For example, a single disc costing less that $10 could record and store the *Encyclopedia Britannica* using only 4 percent of its available capacity; and 54,000 individual slides, each capable of being accessed randomly, could be stored on one side of a video disc. If the disc is used for storing motion pictures, one side of the disc can store 30 minutes of video programming. The disc's visual images can also be stored in combination with more than one audio track. For example, film (still or motion) sequences with two language tracks, one in English and one in Spanish, may be stored and accessed randomly. National marketing for such video disc systems was projected for late 1978 in the United States (Braun, 1978; Wood & Stephens, 1977). While marketing has been somewhat delayed, it appears that it will soon be a commonplace reality.

Braun (1978) reported that few educators are aware of the existence of video discs and that fewer still have given any thought to how they might use systems to improve the learning environments of their students. Among the few researchers who are investigating the use of video discs in education are Thorkildsen, Williams, and Bickel (1978). They are exploring the use of video disc technology with moderately retarded pupils.

Video graphics is another area of great potential. In the past, instructional programmers working with CAI who wished to use complex visual images had to have the computer connected to some prerecorded visual image system, such as a slide projector (Cogen, 1969). Such visual image systems resulted in considerably increased cost and decreased reliability of the total system. Now, through microprocessor technology, visual images can be stored and generaged in the computer (Free, 1978). Although video graphics (sometimes called computer graphics) do not have the audio advantages of video disc systems, they nevertheless have considerable potential for educational applications with the handicapped, particularly with the hearing impaired and deaf populations.

Another development that will probably revolutionize telecommunications and related distribution systems is fiber optics (Whittaker, 1976). Coupled with laser technology, such distribution systems will vastly increase the number of audio messages or television channels that can be transmitted, and also improve their quality. For example, it would theoretically be feasible to transmit the entire contents of the 30-volume *Encyclopedia Britannica* in .10 second. A conventional pair of copper wires can handle up to 24 simultaneous phone calls, while 2 optical fibers can accommodate the equivalent of 33,000 such calls (Powell, 1977). If these distribution systems are eventually installed, the implications for the transmission of information through telecommunications, as discussed earlier, would be considerable.

## SYSTEMS TECHNOLOGY

Gallagher (1970) has defined a system as a combination of elements functioning in relationship to each other. He has pointed out that we do not really have an educational system, according to this definition. We have an educational tradition that stresses autonomous units and self-contained operations rather than interactive, mutually responsive elements. In recent years, however, the field of special education has developed a number of subsystems that have the potential for being integrated into a larger educational system. Several of these will be discussed in this section.

### Instructional programs

The implementation of PL 94-142 has, in one bold move, placed systems technology on center stage. The major operational component of PL 94-142 is the IEP (Abeson & Zettel, 1977). While there is a variety of uses of the term "program" in education, the definition of "program" in 94-142 is conceptually similiar to the systems technology concept of a program. This concept was stabilized in the late 1960's when the field of programmed learning shifted from its earlier emphasis on format

(Hofmeister, 1971). This switch has been described by Green (1967, p. 79) as follows:

> In looking into the future, it seems clear that the day of the classic self-instructional program, as it has come to be recognized in the past decade, is almost over. We have passed through the dark ages of controversy over such matters as whether a branching program is superior to a linear program; whether an overt response is necessary to the learning process; whether it is more or less desirable to incorporate small steps into a program, and whether people are pigeons.

Corey (1967), in clarifying the then new definition of an instructional program, listed the following elements: determination of objectives; analysis of instructional objectives; relevant population characteristics, e.g., entering behavior; evidence of success of instruction; and construction of the instructional environment. These elements are all present in the definition of an IEP, namely: statement of annual goals (for determination of objectives); short-term instructional objectives (for analysis of instructional objectives); present levels of educational functioning (for relevant population characteristics); provision for program monitoring and review (for evidence of success of instruction); and statement of services to be provided (for constructing the instructional environment).

The fact that a given procedure (e.g., use of IEPs) is consistent with systems technology does not necessarily make that procedure effective. There is, for example, considerable conflict in research findings related to the use of behavioral objectives (Crutcher & Hofmeister, 1975). Stolovitch (1978), in discussing the value of behavioral objectives, stated: "The special education technologist has a particular mission to assist in discovering what ways, if any, instructional objectives contribute to improved learning for the handicapped" (p. 36).

The major justification for the use of IEPs appears to be ethical and legal, and a substantial program-specific research base does not exist. In researching the impact of IEP procedures on math achievement with the mildly handicapped, Boehmer and Hofmeister (1979) were able to show gains in favor of IEP users versus nonusers. The range of research possibilities in this area has been somewhat reduced because the use of control groups of handicapped pupils would now be a violation of federal law.

A major contribution of the implementation of systems technology in classroom procedures will be the potential for blending research and practice (Lovitt, 1978). Instead of confining research procedures and projects to the researcher, the techniques advocated by Lovitt stress the involvement of the classroom teacher in the search for data to validate and modify classroom practices.

**Instructional packages**

The Commission on Instructional Technology (1970) noted that technology does not have to move people, it transmits the impact of people. One of the vehicles used in instructional technology to transmit impact is the instructional package. In reporting on the development and validation of a mediated package for training parents of preschool mentally retarded children, Hofmeister and Latham (1972) recommended further study of the use of mediated training packages as a practical method of treatment well within the resources of many agencies.

A *learning package* has been defined as a systemized way of delivering content and processes to a learner (Kapfner & Kapfner, 1972). The term *package* implies a self-contained and portable system. Most packages can, in fact, be sent through the mail. A package may consist of printed materials alone; however, many include slides, cassette tapes, videotapes, and films (Stowitschek & Hofmeister, 1975). Blackhurst and Wright (1978) illustrated how systematic computer approaches could facilitate planning for the development of instructional packages. A special education package must not only provide portability and systemized development and delivery of content and process, it must also be validated for a given population of handicapped persons. Only after validation with a specific target population should the term "packaged program" be applied in the strict instructional technology usage.

The approach to packaging that is having the most extensive impact in special education is one that stresses the use of relatively low-cost printed materials that give precise and practical instructions for teaching specific skills to given populations of handicapped learners. Such packages are considerably more generalizable when they are validated for use by paraprofessionals and parents (Thiagarajan, 1975). Examples of such packages include the *Training for Independence Series* (1977) and the *Project MORE Series* (1976).

**Competency-based teacher education**

One of the most significant forces that has affected special education personnel preparation during the 1970s is competency-based teacher education (CBTE). Blackhurst (1977) described a model for developing CBTE programs in special education and listed characteristics of such programs as follows:

1. Competencies that are required for any professional preparation program are publicly stated.

2. Objectives for the various educational experiences are stated in behavioral terms.
3. Criteria for evaluating when objectives have been met and competencies attained are specified and made available to students.
4. Alternative learning activities and multiple entry points are available to individualize the instructional program for students.
5. Where possible, time for completing instructional activities is variable, while achievement is held constant.
6. Instructors and students both share accountability for performance.

The parallels between these conceptualizations and those related to instructional programs for children (see above) should be obvious. Similarly, CBTE programs make considerable use of instructional packages in their delivery of the instructional program.

Implicit in competency-based approaches to teacher education is the obvious notion that students must have the opportunity to demonstrate the competencies that they have developed. Consequently, most CBTE programs have rather extensive field components.

Considerable efforts have been expended to identify and specify competencies for various special education professions, including teachers of the educable mentally retarded (Rotberg, 1968), special education curriculum consultants (Altman & Meyen, 1974), teachers of the secondary-level educable mentally retarded (Brolin & Thomas, 1972), special education supervisors (Harris & King, 1974), directors of special education (Anderson & Schipper, 1974), directors of special education resource centers (Blackhurst, Wright, & Ingram, 1974), clinical teachers (Schwartz & Oseroff, 1975), special education professors (Ingram & Blackhurst, 1975), teachers of children with learning and behavior disorders (Blackhurst, McLoughlin, & Price, 1977), teachers of the gifted (Altman, Faherty, & Patterson, 1978), teachers of the severely handicapped (Fredericks, Anderson, Baldwin, Grove, Moore, et al., 1977), teachers of the learning disabled (Newcomer, Magee, Wilson, & Brown, 1978), and elementary teachers involved in mainstreaming (Redden & Blackhurst, 1978).

Although these competency lists have some apparent validity, it should be emphasized that most have not been validated from the standpoint of whether they in fact make a difference. As Shores, Cegelka, and Nelson (1973) noted, this is one of the major tasks facing instructional designers who are involved with CBTE.

Once competencies and objectives have been developed, instruction can be delivered in a variety of media and formats. In addition to instructional packages (mentioned in the previous section), an array of alternatives has been used. Among these are CAI (Cartwright & Cartwright, 1973), gaming (Semmel & Baum, 1973), videotapes (Currie, 1976), microteaching (Shea & Whiteside, 1974), automated teacher-feedback systems (Semmel, 1972), adjunct autoinstruction (Renne & Blackhurst, 1977), alternative mediated formats (Donaldson & Martinson, 1977), modules (Blackhurst, Cross, Nelson, & Tawney, 1973; Wixson, 1975), multiplier effect models (Meyen, 1969), change agent models (Anderson, Hodson, & Jones, 1975), and contingency management systems (Tawney, 1972).

As Blatt (1976) has demonstrated, not all special education professors are supportive of CBTE. Nevertheless, more and more states are moving toward competency-based teacher certification and federal funding for training grants is contingent upon proposals that reflect competency-based programming. In addition to the references mentioned in this section, the interested reader is referred to the comprehensive treatments of CBTE in special education by Creamer and Gilmore (1974), Blackhurst (1977), Semmel, Semmel, and Morrissey (1976), and the special issues of certain journals that are completely devoted to the topic. These include:

*Behavioral Disorders,* 1976, *1* (2).
*Teacher Education and Special Education,* 1978, *1* (2).
*Journal of Teacher Education,* 1978, *29* (2).

### Technical assistance systems

Since 1966, various technical assistance services have been available to special education teachers, administrators, and project personnel. Largely supported by federal funds, these services have ranged from the loan of instructional materials to computer-based information storage and retrieval. Originally, these services were provided by Special Education Instructional Materials Centers (SEIMCs). A special issue of *Exceptional Children* [1968, *35* (3)] provides a good overview of the original SEIMC Network.

Shortly after the SEIMCs were established, Regional Media Centers for the Deaf and an Instructional Materials Reference Center for the Visually Handicapped were added to the Network. A National Center on Educational Media and Materials for the Handicapped (NCEMMH) was also added (LaVor, Forsythe, Wexler, Duncan, & Milenson, 1969). Lance (1973) has written an overview of all of these projects and their services.

In 1974, the federal program that supported these various projects was reconceptualized. The program developed Area Learning Resource Centers (ALRCs), which provided technical assistance on media and materials, Regional Resource Centers (RRCs), which provided aid in diagnostic and prescriptive programming, and several special offices dealing with materials development and distribution. Coordination was provided by the NCEMMH and the Coordinating Office for Regional Resource Centers (CORRC) (Blackhurst, 1974).

Another federal program shift occurred in 1977, and the special offices, ALRCs, and CORRC were eliminated. The RRCs were relocated and took on the responsibility of providing technical assistance to the states in a variety of services related to the implementation of PL 94-142. These services included information storage and retrieval of professional literature (CEC, 1978a) and the availability of instructional materials on a national basis (Risner, 1978). Other technical assistance services have been available to support the efforts of early childhood special education projects, developmental disabilities projects, gifted and talented projects, leadership training projects, and others (Reynolds, 1974).

Although the various federally funded projects have provided many valuable services to the field, the potential for the development of a national special education network that could provide services on a coordinated basis was never fully realized. This is due, in large part, to the number of switches in program emphasis that have been made as well as an absence of a well-defined federal policy related to the development and operation of such services that was acceptable to top-level administrators. One of the long-term benefits that accrued from these projects is the existence of approximately 800 local centers providing technical assistance of various types to special educators located in different size geographical regions within the various states. These centers were primarily developed as a result of the efforts of the regional SEIMCs. Several information storage and retrieval systems are also now available as a result of developments in the original SEIMC network (Lance, 1977). The technology of technical assistance is now being continued and refined by such agencies as the Technical Assistance Development System (Clifford & Trohanis, 1976.)

Perhaps one of the most significant outgrowths of these federal technical assistance programs has been the development of a cadre of professionals who have acquired interest and competence in applying technology to the field of special education. In fact, as a result of the impetus primarily from persons who were involved with these earlier projects, a new professional organization was developed. The Association for Special Education Technology (ASET) was organized as a national affiliate of the AECT (Cotzin, 1973). The major goals of this association are as follows:

1. To facilitate improvements and adaptations of materials for special education.
2. To stimulate development of new technologies for special education.
3. To identify and publicize unique instructional needs of special education.
4. To foster cooperation among special education and instructional technology interest groups.
5. To encourage the development and production of effective special education materials.
6. To promote improved federal legislation for technology in special education.
7. To assist in the placement of instructional technologists in special education.

In 1978, the first issue of the *Journal of Special Education Technology* was published by this organization to serve as the major vehicle for disseminating professional literature relevant to these stated purposes.

## BARRIERS

Lance (1977) stated that the field of instructional technology has made more progress in the development of systematic approaches to instruction than in the use of nonhuman resources to improve education. He concluded that the gap between technological invention and adoption is due to several factors: (1) educators are conservative and view technology as too risky; (2) technology is perceived as a threat to jobs and personal interactions with children; (3) costs are too high; and (4) the vehicles for bridging the gap between the development of technology and its implementation are yet to be fully developed.

In addition to these, the following barriers to the implementation and greater use of technology were identified by some 75 experts who attended a national conference on technology in special education (Blackhurst, et al., 1979):

1. User needs for which the applications of technology have the greatest relevance have not been adequately defined.
2. There are insufficient data which compare the effectiveness of

programs delivered via machine and face-to-face programming.
3. Initial start-up and hardware costs are usually high.
4. Systems using telecommunications are most cost-effective when economies of scale have been realized.
5. There is a paucity of information concerning cost-effectiveness.
6. Good software is expensive and time consuming to develop.
7. There is a shortage of personnel who have the experience or education to provide quality programming.
8. Many decision makers and potential users have negative attitudes toward technology.
9. Equipment manufacturers are frequently not interested in working with educators because of perceived lack of profitability in educational enterprises.
10. Local authority is threatened when others develop curriculum content and control the delivery system.
11. Political and geographical boundaries frequently militate against the development of large-scale cooperative efforts.
12. Insufficient channels are available for most telecommunication systems. Regulation and licensing of these systems also impede the development of additional ones.

It should be noted that these barriers represent opinions and are not necessarily valid or based on empirically verified data. However, they do represent the thinking of many professionals who have been involved in educational technology. If there is validity to any of these perceived barriers, then it is obvious that they will need to be overcome if broader applications of technology in special education are to be realized.

## CONCLUSION

Even in light of the aforementioned barriers, this review has prompted the authors to conclude that technology has played a valuable role in the education and habilitation of exceptional people and has the potential for playing an even greater role in these respects in the future. Gough (1968) has suggested that technology can and does contribute to the solution of many problems associated with deficiencies and limitations in educational services for the handicapped.

More recently, Lance (1977) predicted an even greater utilization of technology in order (1) to facilitate the integration of handicapped children into the least restrictive environment, (2) to help meet the needs of the severely handicapped, (3) to compensate for physical and sensory impairments, (4) to manage the development and implementation of IEPs, and (5) to respond to pressures to improve the educational system.

One additional concluding point should be emphasized: The great majority of the sources cited in this review represent descriptive articles. In general, there has been a paucity of research that has specifically attempted to assess the effectiveness of different technologies or their employment as alternatives to other approaches. Many of the conclusions that have been drawn concerning the application of technology to the education of the handicapped have been based upon logic more than empirical data. Future efforts should be devoted to the development of empirical studies that can be used as the basis for decision making relative to the development and use of the technological alternatives in special education.

# References

Abeson, A., & Zettel, J. The end of the quiet revolution. The Education of All Handicapped Children Act of 1975. *Exceptional Children,* 1977, *44,* 114–128.

Altman, R., Faherty, A., & Patterson, J. D. *CITE: Gifted competency identification for teacher education.* Jefferson City, Mo.: Department of Elemenatry and Secondary Education, 1978.

Altman, R., & Meyen, E. L. Some observations on competency based instruction. *Exceptional Children,* 1974, *40,* 260–65.

American Foundation for the Blind, *Sensory aids for the blind and visually impaired.* New York: 1978.

Anderson, D. R., Hodson, G. D., & Jones, W. G. *Instructional programming for the handicapped student.* Springfield, Ill.: Thomas, 1975.

Anderson, E. B., & Schipper, W. V. *Functions/tasks of state directors of special education.* Washington, D.C.: National Association of State Directors of Special Education, 1974.

Association for Educational Communications and Technology, *Educational technology: Definition and glossary of terms.* Washington, D.C.: 1977.

Baldwin, T. F., Greenberg, B. S., Block, M. P., Eulenberg, J. B., & Muth, T. A. *Michigan State University—Rockford two-way cable project.* (NSF Grant APR75-14286). East Lansing, Mich.: Michigan State University, Department of Telecommunication, 1978.

Ballard, R. & Eastwood, L. F. *Telecommunications media for the delivery of educational programming.* St Louis: Washington University Center for Development Technology, 1974.

Banathy, B. H. *Instructional systems.* Palo Alto, Calif.: Fearon, 1968.

Becker, W., Engelmann, S., & Thomas, D. *Teaching II: Cognitive learning and instruction.* Chicago: Scientific Research Associates, 1975.

Blackhurst, A. E. Technology in special education—some implications. *Exceptional Children,* 1965, *31,* 449–456.

Blackhurst, A. E. The learning resource center program—Blueprint for the future. *Teaching Exceptional Children,* 1974, *6,* 216–217.

Blackhurst, A. E. Competency-based special education personnel preparation. In R. D. Kneedler & S. G. Tarver (Eds.), *Changing perspectives in special education.* Columbus, Ohio: Merrill, 1977.

Blackhurst, A. E. Using telecommunication systems for delivering inservice training. *Viewpoints in Teaching and Learning,* 1978, *54,* 27–40.

Blackhurst, A. E., Cross, D. P., Nelson, C. M., & Tawney, J. W. Approximating noncategorical teacher education. *Exceptional Children,* 1973, *39,* 284–88.

Blackhurst, A. E., McLoughlin, J. A., & Price, L. M. Issues in the development of programs to prepare teachers of children with learning and behavior disorders. *Behavioral Disorders,* 1977, *2,* 157–168.

Blackhurst, A. E., Williams, N. D., Churchill, E. O., Allen, M. A., & Siegel, A. J. *Utilization of communication satellites in the education of the handicapped* (Final report, Project No. G007604403). Washington, D.C.: Bureau of Education for the Handicapped, U. S. Office of Education, 1980.

Blackhurst, A. E., & Wright, W. S. Computer facilitated planning for the development of special education instructional products. *Journal of Special Education Technology,* 1978, *1,* 37–45.

Blackhurst, A. E., Wright, W. S., & Ingram, C. F. *Competency specification for directors of special education resource centers* (Project OEG-0-72-4305 (603)). Washington, D. C.: Bureau of Education for the Handicapped, U. S. Office of Education, 1974.

Blatt, B. On competencies and incompetencies, instruction and destruction, individualization and depersonalization: Reflections on the now movement. *Behavioral Disorders,* 1976, *1,* 89–96.

Bodner, M. S., Hoelen, G. M., Zogley, W. J. Further developments on an interactive language for the severely handicapped. In J. C. Warren (Ed.), *The Third West Coast Computer Faire Conference Proceedings*. Palo Alto, Calif.: Computer Faire, 1978, pp. 45–47.

Boehmer, D., & Hofmeister, A. The effect of a monitoring system on the math achievement of the educable mentally retarded. *Journal of Special Education Technology*, 1979, *2:1*, 13–17.

Boothroyd, A., Archambault, P., Adams, R. E., & Storm, R. D. Use of computer-based systems of speech training aids for deaf persons. In *Readings in deaf education*. Guilford, Conn.: Special Learning Corporation, 1978.

Bramble, W. J., & Ausness, C. Appalachia's on the beam. *American Education*, 1976, *12*, 21–24.

Braun, L. *Microcomputers and video disc systems: Magic lamps for educators?* Stony Brook, N. Y.: State University of New York at Stony Brook, National Center for Curriculum Development, 1978.

Brolin, D., & Thomas, B. *Preparing teachers of secondary level educable mentally retarded: A new model* [Project OEG-0-4814 (603)]. Washington, D.C.: U. S. Office of Education, 1972.

Brugler, J. S. Microcomputer-based sensory aids for the handicapped. In J. C. Warren (Ed.), *The Second West Coast Computer Faire Conference Proceedings*. Palo Alto, Calif.: Computer Faire, 1978, pp. 70–72.

Bystrom, J. W. *The application for international interactive service support communications*. Paper presented at the Royal Society of London meeting on the Introduction of Satellites into Educational Systems, 1974.

Carr, D. B. Teleteaching—A new approach to teaching elementary and secondary home-bound pupils. *Exceptional Children*, 1964, *31*, 118–126.

Capital Cities Communications, *Including me* (60-minute video tape). Washington, D.C.: 1978.

Cartwright, G. P. The current and future role of educational technology. In R. D. Kneedler & S. G. Tarver (Eds.), *Changing perspectives in special education*. Columbus, Ohio: Merrill, 1977, pp. 84–102.

Cartwright, G. P., & Cartwright, C. A. Early identification of handicapped children: A CAI course. *Journal of Teacher Education*, 1973, *24*, 128–134.

Cartwright, G. P., & Hall, K. A. A review of computer uses in special education. In L. Mann & D. Sabatino (Eds.), *The second review of special education*. Philadelphia: JSE Press, 1974, pp. 307–350.

Clifford, R., & Trohanis, P. (Ed.). *Technical assistance in special education agencies*. Chapel Hill, N. C.: Frank Porter Graham Child Development Center, University of North Carolina, 1976.

Cogen, V. The computer's role in education and use with the exceptional child. *Mental Retardation*, 1969, *7*, 38–41.

Commission on Instructional Technology. *To improve learning: A report to the President and the Congress of the United States*. Washington, D. C.: U. S. Government Printing Office, 1970.

Corey, S. M. The nature of instruction. In P. C. Lange (Ed.), *Programmed instruction: The sixty-sixth yearbook of the National Society for the Study of Education* (Part II). Chicago: University of Chicago Press, 1967.

Cothran, A., & Mason, G. The typewriter: Time-tested tool for teaching reading and writing. *The Elementary School Journal*, 1978, *78*, 171–173.

Cotzin, A. G. The association for special education technology, *Audiovisual Instruction*, 1973, *18*, 26.

Council for Exceptional Children. *CEC overview*. Reston, Va.: Author, 1978a.

Council for Exceptional Children. *Update*, Vol. 10, No. 1, Reston, Va.: 1978b.

223

Creamer, J. J., & Gilmore, J. T. (Eds.). *Design for competence based education in special education*. Syracuse: Division of Special Education and Rehabilitation, Syracuse University, 1974.

Crutcher, C. E., & Hofmeister, A. M. Effective use of objectives and monitoring. *Teaching Exceptional Children*, 1975, *7*, 78–79.

Currie, R. *Facilitating educational achievement through telecommunication*. West Lafayette, Ind.: Purdue University, 1976.

Dale, E. Historical setting of programmed instruction. In P. C. Lange (Ed.), *Programmed instruction: The sixty-sixth yearbook of the National Society for the Study of Education* (Part II). Chicago: University of Chicago Press, 1967.

Donaldson, J., & Martinson, M. C. Modifying attitudes toward physically disabled persons. *Exceptional Children*, 1977, *43*, 337–341.

Elder, P. S., & Bergman, J. S. Visual symbol communication instruction with nonverbal, multiply-handicapped individuals. *Mental Retardation*, 1978, *16*, 107–112.

Federation of Rocky Mountain States. *Satellite technology demonstration* (final report). Denver: 1975.

Fletcher, J. D., & Beard, M. H. *Computer-assisted instruction in language arts for hearing-impaired students*. Stanford, Calif.: Stanford University, Institute for Mathematical Studies in Social Sciences, 1973.

Foulds, R. A., & Gaddis, E. The practical application of an electronic communication device in the special needs classroom. In E. Kwatmy & R. Zuckerman (Eds.), *Devices and systems for the disabled*. Philadelphia: Temple University, 1975.

Foulds, R. A., Lund, B. L. (Eds.). *1976 Conference on Systems and Devices for the Disabled*. Boston: Tufts University Biomedical Engineering Center, 1976.

Foulke, E. Comparison of comprehension of two forms of compressed speech. *Exceptional Children*, 1966, *33*, 169–173.

Fredericks, H. D., Anderson, R. B., Baldwin, V. L., Grove, D., Moore, W. G., Moore, M., & Beaird, J. H. *The identification of competencies of teachers of the severely handicapped* (Project No. OEG-0-H-2775). Washington, D.C.: Bureau of Education for the Handicapped, U. S. Office of Education, 1977.

Free, J. Video graphics—pictorial displays: You draw with your home computer. *Popular Science*, 1978, *213*, 108–111.

Gagne, R. M. Educational technology as technique. *Educational Technology*, 1968, *8*, 5–14.

Gallagher, J. J. *The search for the educational system that doesn't exist* (ERIC Document No. ED 047-442). Paper presented at Council for Exceptional Children meeting, San Antonio, Tex., December 1970.

Galton, L. New devices to help the blind and near-blind. *Parade, Lexington Herald-Leader*, April 17, 1977, pp. 18–21.

Genesky, S. M., Peterson, H. E., Clewett, R. W., & Yoshimura, R. I. A second-generation interactive classroom television system for the partially sighted. *Journal of Visual Impairment and Blindness*, 1978, *72*, 41–45.

Glaser, R., Ramage, W. W., & Lipson, J. I. (Eds.). *The interface between student and subject matter*. Pittsburgh: The University of Pittsburgh Learning Research and Development Center, 1964.

Goldenburg, P. *Special technology for special children: Computers as prostheses to serve communication and autonomy in the education of handicapped children*. Presented at the Annual Meeting of the American Educational Research Association, New York, 1977. (ERIC Document EC 100 864, ED 140 526)

Gough, J. A. Educational media and the handicapped child. *Exceptional Children*, 1968, *34*, 561–564.

Graf, R. F. (Ed.). *Dictionary of electronics*. Fort Worth, Tex.: Radio Shack, 1974.

Grayson, L. P. Education, technology, and individual privacy. *Educational Communication and Technology*, 1978, *26*, 195–206.

Green, D., & Lazarus, B. Project interchange—California teachers conference via satellite. *Educational/Instructional Television*, 1977, *9*, 1–3.

Green, E. J. The process of instructional programming. In P. C. Lange (Ed.), *Programmed instruction: Sixty-sixth yearbook of the National Society for the Study of Education* (Part II). Chicago: University of Chicago Press, 1967.

Haring, N. G. The new curriculum design in special education. *Educational Technology*, 1970, *10*, 24–31.

Harris, B. M., & King, J. D. *Professional supervisory competencies: Competency specifications for instructional leadership personnel in special edecation*. Austin: University of Texas Special Education Supervisory Training Project, 1974.

Heinich, R. Educational technology as technology. *Educational Technology*, 1968, *8*, 1–4.

Hershey, M. Telephone instruction: An alternative educational delivery system for teacher in-service. *The Gifted Child Quarterly*, 1977, *21*, 213–217.

Hill, A. S. Teaching shut-ins by telephone. *Exceptional Children*, 1956, *22*, 299–304.

Hofmeister, A. Programmed instruction revisited: Implications for educating the retarded. *Education and Training of the Mentally Retarded*, 1971, *6*, 172–176.

Hofmeister, A., & Latham, G. Development and validation of a mediated package for training parents of preschool mentally retarded children. *Improving Human Performance Quarterly*, 1972, *1*, 3–7.

Inde, K. Low-vision training in Sweden, *Journal of Visual Impairment and Blindness*, 1978, *72*, 307–310.

Infomedia Corporation, *PLANET News*. Palo Alto, Calif.: May 1978.

Ingram, C. F., & Blackhurst, A. E. Teaching and advising competencies of special education professors. *Exceptional Children*, 1975, *42*, 85–93.

Joquiss, R. S. Microprocessors in aids for the blind. In J. C. Warren (Ed.), *The second West Coast Computer Faire Conference proceedings*. Palo Alto, Calif.: Computer Faire, 1978, pp. 44–45.

Kafafian, H. *Study of man–machine communications systems for the handicapped*. Washington, D.C.: Cybernetics Research Institute, 1970.

Kapfner, P. G., & Kapfner, M. B. Introduction to learning packages. *Educational Technology*, 1972, *12*, 9–11.

Kucherawy, D. A., & Kucherawy, J. M. An electrical communication system for a nonverbal, profoundly retarded, spastic quadriplegic. *Education and Training of the Mentally Retarded*, 1978, *13*, 342–344.

Kurzweil, R. *The Kurzweil report—Technology for the handicapped*. Cambridge, Mass.: Kurzweil Computer Products, 1978.

Lance, W. D. *Instructional media and the handicapped*. Stanford, Calif.: ERIC Clearinghouse on Media and Technology, Stanford University, 1973.

Lance, W. D. Technology and media for exceptional learners: Looking ahead. *Exceptional Children*, 1977, *44*, 92–97.

LaVor, M., Forsythe J., Wexler S., Duncan, J., & Milenson, R. National Center on Educational Media and Materials for the Handicapped, Public Law 91-61. *Exceptional Children*, 1969, *36*, 211–214.

Lehrer, B. E., Daiker, J. F. Computer based information management for professionals serving handicapped learners. *Exceptional Children*, 1978, *44*, 578–585.

Lovitt, J. Blending research and practice. *Journal of Special Education Technology*, 1978, *1*, 5–11.

MacLeod, I., & Overhew, D. Computer aided assessment and development of basic skills. *The Exceptional Child*, 1977, *24*, 18–35.

Marshall, G. R., & Johnson, P. *Following the programs and services for the develop-*

*mentally disabled: The direct use of systems technology* (Quarterly report). Boulder, Colo.: IPP Systems, 1978.

McDonald, E. T., & Schultz, A. R. Communication boards for cerebral-palsied children. *Journal of Speech and Hearing Disorders,* 1973, *38,* 73–88.

McNaughton, S. Bliss-symbols: An alternative symbol system for the nonvocal, prereading, child. In G. C. Vanderheiden & K. Grilley (Eds.), *Non-vocal communication techniques and aids for the severely handicapped.* Baltimore: University Park Press, 1976, pp. 85–104.

Meyen, E. L. *Demonstration of dissemination practices on special class instruction for the mentally retarded: Utilizing master teachers as inservice educators* (Project OEG-3-7-02883-0499). Washington, D.C.: Bureau of Education for the Handicapped, U. S. Office of Education, 1969.

Morgan, R. P., Singh, J. P., Rothenberg, D., & Robinson, B. E. *Large-scale educational telecommunications systems for the U. S.: An analysis of educational needs and technological opportunities.* St Louis: Washington University Center for Development Technology, 1975.

National Aeronautics and Space Administration. *NASA News.* Washington, D.C.: May 21, 1974.

National Institute of Education. *Background papers for conference on educational application of satellites.* Washington, D.C., 1977.

Nazzaro, J. N. *Exceptional time tables: Historic events affecting the handicapped and gifted.* Reston, Va.: Council for Exceptional Children, 1977.

Nelson, P. J., & Cassalter, J. G. The potential of microcomputers for the physically handicapped. In J. C. Warren (Ed.), *The first West Coast Computer Faire Conference proceedings.* Palo Alto, Calif.: Computer Faire, 1977.

Newcomer, P., Magee, P., Wilson, J., & Brown, L. Competencies for teachers of learning disabled children and youth. In *Code of ethics and competencies for teachers of learning disabled children and youth.* Reston, Va.: Council for Exceptional Children, Division for Children with Learning Disabilities, 1978.

Nickerson, R. S., Kalikaw, D. N. & Stevens, K. N. Computer-aided speech training for the deaf. *Journal of Speech and Hearing Disorders,* 1976, *41,* 120–132.

Nilles, J. M., Carlson, F. R., Gray, P., & Hanneman, G. J. *The telecommunications–transportation tradeoff.* New York: Wiley, 1976.

Norwood, M. J. Captioned films for the deaf. *Exceptional Children,* 1976, *43,* 164–166.

Pal, Y. SITE is happening. *Space,* 1976, *2,* 1–20.

Parker, L. A. Teleconferencing as an educational medium: A ten year perspective from the University of Wisconsin–Extension. In M. Monson, L. Parker, & B. Riccomini (Eds.), *A design for interactive audio.* Madison, Wis.: University of Wisconsin–Extension, 1977.

Parker, L. A., & Riccomini, B. *A report on university applications of satellite/cable technology.* Madison, Wis.: University of Wisconsin–Extension, 1975.

Polcyn, K. A. *An educator's guide to communication satellite technology.* Washington, D. C.: Andromeda, 1973.

Powell, J. Fiber optics: At the threshold of a communications revolution. *Science Digest,* 1977, *8,* 28–35.

*Project MORE Series.* North Brook, Ill. Hubbard, 1976.

Redden, M. R., & Blackhurst, A. E. Mainstreaming competency specification for elementary teachers. *Exceptional Children,* 1978, *44,* 615–617.

Renne, D. J., & Blackhurst, A. E. The effect of adjunct autoinstruction in an introductory special education course. *Exceptional Children,* 1977, *43,* 224–225.

Reynolds, M. C. (Ed.). *National technical assistance systems in special education.*

Minneapolis: University of Minnesota, Leadership Training Institute/Special Education, 1974.

Risner, M. T. A brief overview of NIMIS I/II: Implications for future dissemination. *Journal of Special Education Technology*, 1978, *1*(2), 35–37.

Rotberg, J. M. Teacher education: Defining the tasks of teachers of the educable mentally retarded. *Education and Training of the Mentally Retarded*, 1968, *3*, 146–149.

Roy, O. Z., & Charbonneau, J. R. A communications system for the handicapped (COHHANDI). In K. Copeland (Ed.), *Aids for the handicapped*. London: Sector, 1974, pp. 89–98.

Ryan, S. G., & Bedi, D. N. Toward computer literacy for visually impaired students. *Journal of Visual Impairment and Blindness*, 1978, *72*, 302–306.

Scandura, J. M. Teaching—technology or theory. *American Educational Research Journal*, 1966, *3*, 139–146.

Schwartz, L., & Oseroff, A. *The clinical teacher for special education*. Tallahassee: Florida State University, 1975.

Schwartz, M. R. In the Northwest, it's WAMI. *American Education*, 1976, *12*, 21–24.

Scully, T. Microcomputer communication for the handicapped. In J. C. Warren (Ed.), *The second West Coast Computer Faire Conference proceedings*. Palo Alto, Calif.: Computer Faire, 1978, pp. 32–42.

Semmel, M. I. Toward the development of a computer-assisted teacher training system (CATTS). *International Review of Education*, 1972, *18*, 561–568.

Semmel, M. I., & Baum, R. B. Increasing teachers' understanding through anticipation games. *Viewpoints*, 1973, *49*, 59–69.

Semmel, M. I., Semmel, D. S., & Morrissey, P. A. *Competency-based teacher education in special education: A review of research and training programs*. Bloomington, Ind.: Indiana University Center for Innovation in Teaching the Handicapped, 1976.

Shane, H. C., Reynolds, A. T., & Geary, D. The elicitation of latent oral communicative potential in a severely handicapped adult: Procedures and implications. *AAESPH Review*, 1977, *2*, 201–208.

Sharapan, H. B. Mister Roger's neighborhood: A resource for exceptional children. *Audiovisual Instruction*, 1973, *18*, 18–20.

Shea, T. M., & Whiteside, W. R. *Special education microteaching*. Edwardsville, Ill.: Southern Illinois University, 1974.

Shores, R., Cegelka, P., & Nelson, C. M. A review of research on teacher competencies. *Exceptional Children*, 1973, *40*, 192–197.

Short, S. H. Rate controlled speech. *Audiovisual Instruction*, 1972, *17*, 45–46.

Sidman, M. *Tactics of scientific research*. New York: Basic Books, 1960.

Silverman, R. E. Two kinds of technology. *Educational Technology*, 1968, *8*, 1–10.

Sinclair, F. L., & Sanderson, J. Talking calculator survey. *Journal of Visual Impairment and Blindness*, 1978, *72*, 151–152.

Skinner, F. *Telecommunications for vocational rehabilitation* (Vol. 3): *End-instrument survey* (Grant 22-P-5790513) Washington, D.C.: Rehabilitation Services Administration Office of Human Development, Department of Health, Education and Welfare, 1977.

Stolovitch, H. D. An objective look at objectives. *ASET Report*, 1978, *2*, 35–36.

Stolurow, L. M. Teaching machines and special education. *Educational and Psychological Measurement*, 1960, *20*, 429–448.

Stowitschek, J. J., & Hofmeister, A. M. Parent training packages. *Children Today*, 1975, *4*, 28–35.

Sullivan, R. A., Frieden, F. H., & Cordery, J. *Telephone services for the handicapped*. New York: Institute of Rehabilitation Medicine, New York University Medical Center, 1968.

Suppes, P., Fletcher, J. D., Aonatti, M., Lorton, P. V., & Searle, B. W. *Evaluation of computer assisted instruction in elementary mathematics for hearing-impaired students* (Tech. Rep. 200). Stanford, Calif.: Stanford University, Institute for Mathematical Studies in the Social Sciences, 1973.

Tawney, J. W. *Practice what you preach: A project to develop a contingency-managed "methods" course, and to measure the effects of this course by in-field evaluation.* Lexington, Ky.: University of Kentucky, 1972.

Tawney, J. W. *Telecommunications for the severely handicapped* (Final report No. OEC-0-74-7539). Washington, D.C.: Bureau of Education for the Handicapped, U. S. Office of Education, 1977a.

Tawney, J. W. Educating severely handicapped children and their parents through telecommunications. In N. G. Haring & L. J. Brown (Eds.), *Teaching the severely handicapped* (Vol. 2). New York: Grune & Stratton, 1977b.

Telesensory Systems. *TSI Newsletter,* No. 19. Palo Alto, Calif.: 1978.

Thiagarajan, S. *The history and futureology of programmed tutoring for paraprofessionals.* Paper presented at the Management and Training of Paraprofessional Personnel Workshop, Utah State University, Logan, 1975.

Thiagarajan, S., Semmel, D. S., & Semmel M. I. *Instructional development for training teachers of exceptional children: A sourcebook.* Reston, Va.: Council for Exceptional Children, 1974.

Thorkildsen, R., Williams, J. B., & Bickel, W. K. *Implications of video disc microprocessor instructional systems for special education.* Logan, Utah: Utah State University, Exceptional Child Center, 1978.

*Training for independence series.* Niles, Ill.: Developmental Learning Materials, 1977.

Vanderheiden, G. C. *Non-vocal communication resource book.* Baltimore: University Park Press, 1978.

Vanderheiden, G. C., & Luster, M. J. *Communication techniques and aids to assist in the education of non-vocal severely physically handicapped children: A state of the art review.* Madison, Wis.: University of Wisconsin, Trace Research and Development Center for the Severely Communicatively Handicapped, 1976.

Von Bruns-Connolly, S., & Shane, H. C. Communication boards: Help for the child unable to talk. *The Exceptional Parent,* 1978, *8,* 19–22.

Wittaker, R. Will fiber optics start another revolution? *Broadcast Engineering,* December 1976, pp. 22–26.

Wixson, S. E. Student's reactions to competency based special education courses. *Exceptional Children,* 1975, *41,* 437.

Wolff, E. A. (Ed.). *Public service communications satellite user requirements workshop.* Greenbelt, Md.: Goddard Space Flight Center, 1976.

Wood, R. K., & Stephens, K. G. An educators guide to video disc technology. *Phi Delta Kappan,* 1977, *58,* 466–467.

# NONDISCRIMINATORY ASSESSMENT: PERSPECTIVES IN PSYCHOLOGY AND SPECIAL EDUCATION

Thomas R. Kratochwill
*University of Arizona*

Sandra Alper
*University of Missouri, Columbia*

Anthony A. Cancelli
*University of Arizona*

During the past few years psychological and educational assessment have advanced considerably. There has been a proliferation of new tests and assessment procedures as well as a multitude of reports on norming, reliability, validity, standardization, and other psychometric characteristics of traditional and new tests. With this has come a growing literature on the pros and cons of traditional testing and assessment options (e.g., Cronbach, 1975), especially with regard to those assessment practices that are believed discriminatory against certain individuals and groups. The concept of nondiscriminatory assessment has been a central theme in recent federal legislative and judicial actions which have provided guidelines for the evaluation and placement of children and youth being considered for special education services. In this chapter we describe some directions psychologists and educators have taken in trying to understand and apply nondiscriminatory assessment techniques and procedures with children and youth. We review the utility and potential of these procedures and address issues concerning the integra-

The authors express sincere appreciation to Daniel J. Reschly for his comments on an earlier draft of the chapter, Marian F. Kratochwill for her editorial work on the chapter, and Judy Landrum and Trish Vandiver for typing various drafts.

229

tion of nondiscriminatory strategies in psychological and educational practice.

Many past discussions of nondiscriminatory assessment have revolved around two major issues, namely, assessment of minorities and traditional testing such as measures of intelligence or IQ. These two influences appear to have prevented the advancement of the concept of nondiscriminatory assessment as far as it can be extended. Thus, while various discussions of nondiscriminatory assessment have made an impact on assessment practices and procedures, the resulting applications have been useful but limited in effect. On the one hand, there has been an adherence to a test-based or psychometric model of assessment. Against the impressive methodological and conceptual advances made, much has remained the same over time—there has been a continued reliance on certain evaluation devices such as intelligence tests (e.g., the Wechsler scales, Wechsler, 1955, 1974), perceptual motor tests (e.g., the Bender Visual Motor Gestalt Test, Bender, 1938; the Developmental Test of Visual Perception, Beery & Buktenica, 1967), and personality tests (e.g., the Rorschach Ink Blot Test, Rorschach, 1942; the Thematic Aperception Test, Murray, 1943). On the other hand, nondiscriminatory assessment has primarily focused on the assessment of minorities or culturally different children and youths, particularly on the issues of whether or not certain testing practices are biased or unfair when used with Black, Latino, or Native American individuals (cf. Reschly, 1979).

Significant advances in nondiscriminatory assessment may require a break with these two conventional concepts that pervade the current literature. As an alternative, Reschly (1979) proposed that assessment procedures should be evaluated on dimensions of discrimination within the context of how they influence individuals, regardless of race or cultural background. Thus, when assessment results in effective interventions or services (in either regular or special education), it has met the spirit of being nondiscriminatory. When certain assessment practices result in decisions that militate against effective intervention or services, one must entertain the possibility that discriminatory practices are occurring.

A final introductory note is in order. When faced with the task of writing a review of nondiscriminatory assessment we were immediately confronted with incredible diversity and basic disagreements over assessment in general and nondiscriminatory assessment in particular. In our preparation for this chapter we were faced with literally thousands of references, most of which should be included in any comprehensive presentation of the issues. Nevertheless, space limitations and the nature of the topic preclude a comprehensive review of all the issues in depth. Indeed, there are already books (e.g., Oakland, 1977; Samuda, 1975) and chapters (e.g., Reschly, 1979) as well as numerous major articles devoted to various facets of nondiscriminatory assessment. In some areas, this made our task easier; in others it complicated our efforts due to the diversity of viewpoints represented. Rather than focusing on a limited portion of the literature to review in depth, our goal is to present a broad overview of the major issues that have developed and need to be embraced. Our intent is to outline some parameters of nondiscriminatory assessment as currently viewed, and as how they might be represented in the future. Therefore, we have sampled from a wide and diverse range of publications rather than limiting the review to major themes presented in special education.

## CURRENT SCOPE OF NONDISCRIMINATORY TESTING/ASSESSMENT

Since conventional standardized tests are the central aspects of the traditional assessment process, they have been the primary focal point of criticism, and many writers have focused conceptual and methodological efforts toward revising conventional tests and testing procedures. Thus, many efforts, though not all, to address nondiscriminatory assessment have been focused on a psychometric test model. This is reflected in the pluralistic assessment procedures developed by Mercer and Lewis (1978) as well as those in PL 94-142 (see *Federal Register,* 1977, pp. 42496–42497). Generally, definitions of nondiscriminatory assessment have also adhered to this model.

In recent years a number of other options have been considered in the development of nondiscriminatory assessment measures (Alley & Foster, 1978; Flaugher, 1978; Oakland & Matuszek, 1977; Reschly, 1979; Sattler, 1974). Each of these is examined within the context of the methodological and conceptual issues raised.

### Moratorium on conventional tests

One of the most radical alternatives proposed to eliminate discriminatory assessment has been a plea for a moratorium on certain standardized tests (Cleary, Humphreys, Kendrick, & Wesman, 1975). For example, the Association of Black Psychologists maintained that current standardized tests should not be used with black children (Williams, 1970, p. 5):

The Association of Black Psychologists fully supports those parents who have

231

chosen to defend their rights by refusing to allow their children and themselves to be subjected to achievement, intelligence, aptitude and performance tests which have been made and are being used to—A. Label black people as uneducable. B. Place black children in "special" classes and schools. C. Perpetuate inferior education in blacks. D. Assign black children to educational tracts [sic]. E. Deny black students higher educational opportunities. F. Destroy positive growth and development of black people.

One argument against traditional testing is that such tests may violate the ethnic minority child's civil and constitutional rights under the provisions of the Fourteenth Amendment for equal protection under the law (Williams, 1971). Also embedded within this general issue is the assumption that traditional testing may lead to low expectancy, thus producing a self-fulfilling prophecy of low performance for minority children (cf. Sattler, 1974). These issues, while linked, need to be analyzed separately.

With regard to the moratorium issue, several objections have been raised. First, given the elimination of traditional standardized tests, examiners may turn to subjective appraisals of clients, examiners may gather data unsystematically, and assessment may occur without benefit of regional or national norms (cf. Messick & Anderson, 1974). Presumably, such consequences could increase discriminatory practices against minority groups (Alley & Foster, 1978). As Sattler (1970) pointed out, decisions "would be based less on evidence and more on prejudice and caprice" (p. 186). Some minimal data tend to suggest that elimination of IQ tests could possibly result in greater rather than less overrepresentation of minorities in special classes (e.g., Zucker & Prieto, 1977). Another issue raised is that a proposed moratorium on tests is based on "emotional reactions" that tend to impede rational thinking (Kennedy, 1978). Presumably, social inequities would not be corrected by throwing out tests. A third response was provided in a footnote in the American Psychological Association (APA) *Standards for Educational and Psychological Tests* (Davis 1974) which makes three points. First, it is argued that a moratorium on testing overemphasizes the inappropriateness of the tests themselves as opposed to the misuse of the tests. Second, it is pointed out that stopping the use of tests would only lead to decisions being made with less dependable measures. Third, it is suggested that tests are useful in finding talent and potential for performance not otherwise identified; a moratorium on testing would deny this benefit.

### Concerns over special class placement

Testing may lead to special class placement as well as labeling. Major questions have been raised over the efficiency of special classes as well as the stigma and low expectancy that are presumed to be associated with them (Meyers, Sundstrom, & Yoshida, 1974; Reschly, 1979). With regard to the efficiency of special classes, both Johnson (1962) and Dunn (1968) raised concerns about the rationale for placement of children in classes for the mentally retarded. In a brief review of this literature, Meyers et al. (1974) noted that while some studies have demonstrated the failure of special class placement (e.g., Guskin & Spicker, 1968; Kirk, 1964; MacMillan, 1971), methodological problems in research in that area tend to make the evidence equivocal. The authors note that the most controlled studies tend to support the efficacy of the special class placement.

The issue of stigma and expectancy is even more difficult to analyze. Reschly (1979) noted that although the evidence confirms the assertion that labels do create expectancies, the outcome of these studies may be an artifact of the methodology used. For example, in studies where college students or teachers are provided only the label and/or no or only brief exposure to the labeled child, a relatively large expectancy effect is reported (Ysseldyke & Foster, 1978). However, in studies employing the same basic methodology but a more lengthy exposure to the labeled child, the expectancy effect either does not occur or diminishes over time (e.g., Reschly & Lamprecht, in press; Yoshida & Meyers, 1975). Thus, research bearing on this issue is unclear and the fact that few studies have been conducted in natural settings raises doubts about the external validity of such research.

In regard to the "self-fulfilling prophecy" phenomenon, research is also inconclusive. Rosenthal and Jacobson's (1968) work has been criticized on methodological grounds (cf. Elashoff & Snow, 1971; Humphreys & Stubbs, 1977; MacMillan, Jones, & Aloia, 1974; Snow, 1969; Thorndike, 1968), and at least some studies have failed to reflect the expectancy effect (e.g., Claiborn, 1969; Fleming & Anttonen, 1971; Ginsburg, 1970; Gozali & Meyen, 1970).

Another issue relates to the "prelabeling" experiences of children classified as retarded in schools (Meyers et al., 1974; Reschly, 1979). It may be erroneous to assume that formal labeling (for example, by a school psychologist) through use of an IQ test is the most important step in the classification process. Consideration must also be given to two general variables (Meyers et al., 1974). First, the prelabeled history of the child may be based on chronic failure and differential treatment by the teacher—meaning the child may not have been a success in the regular classroom. Second, postlabeling may depend on the teacher's behavior. The particular actions taken by the teacher may inhibit or facilitate the child's adjustment. Research sorting out some of these issues is sorely needed. An analysis of the numbers of majority and

233

minority students referred versus the number actually placed could be useful, but few studies exist.

Two final issues of concern are the findings that (1) many people probably misinterpret the meaning of mild retardation (Oakland, 1977), and (2) people so labeled find the label quite aversive (cf. Edgerton, 1967; Jones, 1972; MacMillan et al., 1974). Since it is probably impossible to completely eliminate classification, as this may result in the failure to receive services (Hobbs, 1975), it may be necessary to revise existing classification schemes and minimize the risks through appropriate assessment and services (Reschly, 1979). It does seem that "the basic question is not whether to classify, but how to classify" (Achenbach, 1974, p. 543). Recent developments in behavioral classification schemes hold some promise (e.g., Adams, Doster, & Calhoun, 1977; Bandura, 1968; Ferster, 1965; Quay, 1972). Unfortunately, it appears that it will be many years before a truly behavioral classification system will be worked out. The collection of extensive data that relate specifically to treatment seems to be a promising alternative at present.

**Language parameters**

Language is one parameter that has been examined in cross-cultural testing; it was considered an assessment issue as early as 1910, when large numbers of immigrants came into the United States. To make tests less discriminatory, tests or test directions have been translated into the "primary" or "dominant" language of the client. Some tests (e.g., WISC, Wechsler 1949; Illinois Test of Psycholinquistic Abilities, Kirk, McCarthy, & Kirk, 1971) have been translated into another language such as Spanish, but the number of translated tests is relatively small. The tactic of translating tests into the presumed primary language of the client is one criterion for nondiscriminatory assessment in PL 94-142.

This option, which may be in the spirit of nondiscriminatory assessment, has also been criticized on methodological and conceptual grounds. Several dimensions of criticism can be identified. First, this approach assumes that the clinician must first determine the primary or dominant language of the client. Unfortunately, the lack of adequate language assessment instruments has hindered assessment efforts as well as the implementation of special language programs and identification of eligible students. Major problems have been (1) the determination of what language skills and linguistic structures to describe and (2) the identification of adequate tools or instruments to measure language (cf. Silverman, Boa, & Russell, 1976). In an effort to address the national policy of the Bilingual Education Act of 1974, Silverman et al. (1976) published *Oral Language Tests for Bilingual Students,* wherein devices purporting to measure various facets of language were evaluated on dimensions of validity, examinee appropriateness, technical excellence, and administrative usability. The evaluation took place on commercially available tests, tests under development or undergoing field testing, and tests used for experimental purposes.

The results of this evaluation were not very promising; of the 24 tests, very few could be used for languages other than Spanish, e.g., MAT-SEA-CAL Oral Proficiency Tests, 1976. Unfortunately, at the time of the review, this instrument was at the field test stage and was not available for mass distribution. Another general problem was that the tests had a restricted age–grade range. Thus, clinicians are faced with a situation in which tests used to assess language dominance suffer from psychometric and/or appropriateness limitations.

A second and related issue concerns the concept of bilingualism (Sattler, 1974). Due to a form of bilingualism in which children use, for example, English in school and Spanish outside school (home and community), they may fail to develop a sufficient mastery of either language. In a number of studies Spanish has been used, either in test directions only or in the complete test, to administer standardized intelligence tests to Spanish-speaking children (e.g., Chandler & Plakos, 1969; Galvan, 1967; Holland, 1960; Keston & Jimenez, 1954). In a review of these studies, Sattler (1974) noted that such procedures are not only fraught with hazards, but "translation of a test makes it a hybrid belonging to neither culture" (p. 39). Moreover, while it is presumed that assessment should be conducted in the primary language of the child, whether or not bilingualism represents a problem depends upon the way in which the two languages were acquired (Anastasi & Cordova, 1953). As Sattler (1974) noted, "The child who learns one language at home and another at school may be limited in his mastery of both languages, whereas the child who learns to express himself in at least one language in all types of situations will have minimal handicaps, if any" (p. 35).

A third issue is that while one might be able to deal with the bilingual situation (debatable, as suggested here), the problem is exacerbated in polylingual cases. Consider the situation in which a Mexican-American child speaks English in school, Spanish at home, and an American Indian dialect in the community. This polylingualism not only complicates the language issue, but may create another problem, namely, speech difficulties (Sattler, 1974). Presumably, the patterns of speech inculcated by the use of one language (e.g., Spanish), can interfere with the correct speaking of another (e.g., English) (Beberfall, 1958; Chavez, 1956; Perales, 1965). Thus, children may never become proficient in speaking either language (Holland, 1960) and testing in either may result in discriminatory practices. Furthermore, as in the case of Spanish-speaking groups, children may borrow from a limited English vocabulary to complete expressions begun in Spanish, they may give English words Spanish pronunciations and meanings, and they may have difficulties in pronunciation and enunciation (Perales, 1965).

Fifth, even if English is the primary language, there is considerable variation among cultural groups in terms of complex language idioms, colloquialisms, words and phrases with multiple meanings, and words and phrases of similar but not identical meanings within a language (Garcia, 1976). Even if the so-called primary language is English, testing procedures may not equate for differing cultural or subcultural information, learning strategies, and value systems (Alley & Foster, 1978). However, research on dialectal variations (standard English or black dialect) in which the Stanford-Binet Form L–M (Quay, 1971) or the Wechsler Preschool and Primary Scale of Intelligence (WPPSI) (Crown, 1970) were administered has shown that these variations failed to influence significantly the IQs obtained by black children. Oakland and Matuszek (1977) noted that language biases may be encountered in assessing black children who manifest elements of nonstandard dialects. For example, some tests use language styles that are significantly different from those manifested by blacks (or other minorities), in which language patterns also are ordered, rule governed, and effectively expressive (Bartell, Grill, & Bryen, 1973; Gay & Abrahams, 1973).

In conclusion, while language translation may appear to be a promising alternative for obtaining a nondiscriminatory measure, a critical appraisal suggests that this tactic is fraught with methodological and conceptual problems.

## Minority group examiners

One tactic that has been suggested in the spirit of meeting nondiscriminatory assessment criteria is to use a minority group examiner. Specifically, the examiner's race has been hypothesized to be an important factor in affecting the minority child's test performance through (1) the possibility that the child's perception of the testing situation leads to inappropriate behaviors which are judged by the tester to reflect low ability, and (2) the possibility that final scores are biased by the examiner's expectancies for performance by minority children resulting from pretest referral information and unfamiliarity with the examinees' cultural background and dialect (Meyers et al., 1974, p. 22). Presumably, this tactic relates mostly to person-to-person forms of assessment (e.g., individual IQ testing) rather than other methods that do not involve a direct interpersonal relationship (e.g., group achievement testing in the classroom). Garcia (1972) made the following recommendation: "Be skeptical about utilization of standard diagnostic instruments when used to identify the learning behaviors and capabilities of bilinguals. Instead, utilize bilingual clinicians to assist in the identification process" (p. 3).

Other writers have noted that racial differences may affect the examiner–examinee relationship (e.g., Anastasi, 1958; Anastasi & Foley, 1949; Garth, 1922; Hilgard, 1957; Klineberg, 1935; 1944; Pettigrew, 1964; Pressey & Teter, 1919; Riessman, 1962; Strong, 1913). Flaugher (1978) noted that sex and ethnic differences can create an "atmosphere bias," and this possibility definitely belongs in the list of aspects of test bias. In fact, he argues that the very act of testing itself may be unfair to some individuals because the situation inhibits normal performance. Presumably, nondiscriminatory assessment could be reduced if the examiner possessed a language, value system, cultural information, and learning strategies similar to those of the client.

While appealing, the proposed solution of using minority group examiners also has problems. The first problem is a practical one. Minority group children represent a heterogeneous population, so it becomes difficult to know what group or groups of children should be so classified (Sattler, 1974). For example, Valentine (1971) found 14 different Afro-American subgroups in one urban community and each had more or less distinct cultures. Sattler (1974) noted that the label "minority group children" is typically used to designate people whose values, customs, patterns of thought, language, and interests are different from the dominant culture in which they live (Liddle, 1967). This conceptualization includes such groups as blacks, Mexicans, Indians, Puerto Ricans, and subculture whites (Appalachians, foreign born, unskilled laborers, etc.). Thus, it frequently would be impossible to use this alternative. Even if this alternative were employed, differential treatment of one person toward another may reflect social class differences to a greater extent than racial or ethnic differences. Moreover, the examiner and child may end up employing a conventional "discriminatory test," a situation that may be frustrating to both individuals (Alley & Foster, 1978).

Research in this area has not been helpful in clarifying the various issues. A review of the literature tends to indicate that the examiner's influence on test performance is a very complex issue that has been subjected to insufficient and inadequately designed research (e.g., Flaugher, 1978; Katz, 1970; Meyers et al., 1974; Reschly, 1979; Samuel, 1977; Sattler, 1970, 1973, 1974). In a review of this area, Epps (1974) noted that there is little known about how the sex of the examiner affects the performance of children or how the examiner's sex interacts with the examinee's sex in multiracial or monosocial settings. Research is limited because either investigations have involved only male examiners or data for both sexes have not been analyzed or reported separately.

Epps (1974) was able to identify some trends from his review of this area. Data from various studies indicated that the age of the examinee mediates the race-of-examiner effect. Furthermore, the negative impact of testers of a different race on black and on white children is strongest in the early years; in later years the negative impact tends to decrease and the difference can have a facilitating effect (cf. Katz, Atchison, Epps, & Roberts, 1972). In testing situations where no whites are present, the belief that they are competing with whites rather than with other blacks has an effect on a black student's performance (Epps, Katz, Perry, & Runyon, 1971). Presumably, with black testers, the implied comparison enhances performance. There is also some evidence to suggest that the nature of the effect of implied white comparison is mediated by the subject's perception of the probability that (s)he will be successful in the testing situation (Katz et al., 1972). Thus, when probability of success is relatively high (black norms), white testers have a facilitating effect; when the probability of success is relatively low (white norms), black testers have a facilitating effect. Other studies support this finding (e.g., Savage & Bowers, 1972; Watson, 1972), but Epps (1974) notes that this area needs further clarification. Moreover, the relation between the task itself and the race-of-examiner and race-of-comparison effects needs to be clarified.

Unfortunately, many authors disagree about the effects of examiners. Baughman (1971) reports results of a study (Baughman & Dahlstrom, 1968) that suggest that both race of administrator and type of IQ test may influence scores of black children. Crown (1970) studied the effect of race of examiner on white and black kindergarten children on the WPPSI. She found that regardless of race, subjects tested by black examiners received higher verbal scores than those tested by white examiners, but performance scores remained similar.

Sattler (1974) noted that the examiner's race does not usually affect the performance of black or white subjects on individual or group-administered intelligence tests. Although one study reported a significant race-of-examiner variable (Forrester & Klaus, 1964) and two studies found that the examiner's race played a significant role which some groups but not with others (Abramson, 1969; Canady, 1936, as analyzed by Sattler, 1966), the small number of studies in this area and the small number of examiners used in many studies confounds individual differences and race differences among examiners (Sattler, 1974). Meyers et al. (1974) noted that race of the examiner per se may not necessarily lead to deviant response patterns by the minority child. Negative responses may be evoked only when certain modes of interactions are initiated (e.g., outright expression of disappointment). As these authors note, personal examining style and the milieu created by the white examiner may be more related to testing behavior than examiner race per se (e.g., Bucky & Banta, 1972; Yando, Zigler, & Gates, 1971).

### Modifications in test procedures

Departures from standard procedures have also been examined as a possible way to reduce discrimination in testing. In some respects, this type of procedure represents an "atmosphere" change, but on a different dimension. It is assumed that if a client does not perform as well as possible during individual testing, the results will be an inaccurate reflection of classroom performance (Reschly, 1979). Only some representative examples of work in this area are discussed here (see Sattler, 1974, for some other dimensions).

Some research has been directed at explicating motivational and situational parameters which presumably allow testing situations to yield a valid assessment of a child's cognitive abilities. For example, research evaluating the use of familiar examiners (Thomas, Hertzig, Dryman, & Fernandez, 1971), positive pretest interactions between examiner and child (Jacobson, Berger, Bergman, Milham, & Greeson, 1971), and testing location (Seitz, Abelson, Levine, & Zigler, 1975) has suggested that a motivational explanation for the poor performance of economically disadvantaged minority children is plausible. Research has demonstrated that disadvantaged children dislike evaluation (Labov, 1970; Zigler, Ableson, & Seitz, 1973) and the testing milieu (Bee, Streissguth, Van Egevan, Leckie, & Nyman, 1970; Johnson, 1974; Labov, 1970). Both direct (Sacks, 1952; Zigler et al., 1973) and vicarious (Piersel, Brody, & Kratochwill, 1977) models exposed to an examinee prior to a test administration have facilitated performance. Indeed, Piersel et al. (1977) found that a pretest vicarious situation in which minority group children viewed a seven-minute videotape of a white examiner testing a minority child under positive conditions (e.g., praise) resulted in only 14.3 percent of the WISC-Revised (WISC-R) scores being 1 SD below the mean, whereas 42.8 percent and 52.4 percent of the scores were 1 SD below the mean under standard and feedback conditions, respectively. Thus, the test may have discriminated against many children based on demonstrated motivational factors.

Research has also shown that minority preschool children (both black and white) obtain higher scores on the Stanford-Binet (Form L–M) when a test administration procedure allows a maximum number of successes early in the testing experience than under standard procedures (Zigler & Butterfield, 1968). Ali and Costello (1971) found that randomizing the difficulty level of the items on the Peabody Picture Vocabulary Test (PPVT), along with other procedural changes, led to higher scores than did a standard procedure in a group of black preschool children.

Studies designed to identify motivational variables that may increase test performance have employed a wide variety of subjects, tests, and incentives. Some investigators (e.g., Ayllon & Kelly, 1972; Bergan, McManis, & Melchert, 1971; Edlund, 1972; Hurlock, 1925) have reported that when responses were reinforced, test performance was higher than previously (and/or the performance of control subjects under standard conditions). Results are not always in favor of reinforcement. Benton (1936), Maller and Zubin (1932), and Tiber and Kennedy (1964) observed no significant difference in performance between subjects tested under standard conditions and those tested under reinforcement conditions. Clingman and Fowler (1976) investigated the effects of candy reinforcement on IQ test scores in first and second graders. There were no differences among three conditions (candy given contingent on correct responses, candy given noncontingently, or no candy given) on test–retest administrations of the Stanford-Binet (Form L–M).

More recently, Smeets and Striefel (1975) compared deaf children's scores on the Raven Progressive Matrices (Raven, 1938) when tested under (1) end-of-session reinforcement, (2) noncontingent reinforcement, (3) delayed reinforcement, and (4) immediate contingent reinforcement. While the mean posttest score of subjects tested under the immediate-reinforcement condition was significantly higher than that of any other group, no significant differences were observed among the mean posttest scores of the three other groups.

Clingman and Fowler (1976) compared the effects of contingent candy reward, noncontingent candy reward, and no candy on the IQ scores (PPVT, Forms A and B) of children whose initial scores placed them in three different IQ levels. Results showed that candy given contingent upon each correct response increased IQ scores for the initially low-scoring subjects, but had no effect on the scores of middle- and high-scoring subjects.

In minority group investigations, some findings have shown that reinforcement (e.g., praise or candy) did not affect black children's Stanford-Binet scores (Quay, 1971; Tiber & Kennedy, 1964) and that feedback and reward led to significantly higher WISC Verbal Scale scores of lower class white children, but not of lower class black or middle class white children (Sweet, 1969). Roth and McManis (1972) tested retarded adults with organic brain damage on the Block Design Subtests of the Wechsler Adult Intelligence Scale (WAIS) and found that when every correct response was reinforced the responses were less accurate than when no reinforcement was given.

Generally, studies have not indicated what reinforcement procedure constitutes an optimal motivational condition. Variations among studies also make trends difficult to identify. Many studies have focused on the effects of certain types of reinforcers, such as praise (Bergan et al., 1971; Hurlock, 1925; Roth & McManis, 1972; Tiber & Kennedy, 1964) and candy (Edlund, 1972; Tiber & Kennedy, 1964) on test performance. While in some studies subjects received reinforcement immediately after every correct response (e.g., Bergan et al., 1971; Edlund, 1972; Roth & McManis, 1972), in other studies subjects received reinforcement after every subtest or when the test was completed (Ayllon & Kelly, 1972; Hurlock, 1925; Tiber & Kennedy, 1964). In other investigations subjects were promised reinforcement if they performed better (Benton, 1936; Maller & Zubin, 1932).

Problems in this area are not likely to be solved with the type of pervasive between-group research strategy used to investigate reinforcer effectiveness (Kratochwill & Severson, 1977). There may be no best reinforcer for a random group of children (Parton & Ross, 1965), but this does not preclude the possibility of finding an effective individual reinforcer. After reviewing approximately 60 studies in the reinforcement literature, Schultz and Sherman (1976) were unable to draw any practical conclusions, but did concur with Bisett and Rieber's (1966) observation: effective reinforcers should be individually determined rather than depending on a priori judgments. In addition to reinforcement hierarchy approaches (Forness, 1973), the functional analysis paradigm could provide an empirical determination of reinforcing events (Bijou & Grimm, 1975; Bijou & Peterson, 1971; Lovitt, 1975).

Several issues remain problematic in this literature. First, mixed results and failures to replicate make this literature difficult to interpret.

Second, Conner and Weiss (1974) noted that it is unwarranted to assume that an increase in correct responses is necessarily paralleled by an increase in "cognitive ability." Presumably, if the effects of reinforcement in a test-taking situation are limited to a motivational function, and if all populations from which samples are drawn demonstrate the same increase in motivation, then administration of reinforcement will shift the distribution of scores upward, resulting in each subject's relative position remaining the same (Conner & Weiss, 1974). However, Clingman and Fowler (1976) noted that if future research substantiates the notion that only select populations benefit from reinforcement in pretests, then the use of reinforcement would not increase the motivational level of all subjects (in contrast to Conner and Weiss's position), but would selectively enhance the performance of children for whom correct responding is not maintained by other than external reinforcement. Clarification of this in future research would elucidate the importance of these variables in nondiscriminatory assessment.

A third concern is related to the actual practice of deviating from standard procedures. Deviation from standard procedures changes the meaning of the scores (Cronbach, 1960) and may invalidate test norms (Braue & Masling, 1959; Sattler, 1974; Strother, 1945). Some test manuals encourage examiners to give approval for effort, rather than success (Dunn, 1965; Terman & Merrill, 1960); however, this procedure provides approval for incorrect as well as correct responses and, while possibly increasing the total number of responses, may not affect the number of correct responses (Clingman & Fowler, 1976).

### Culture-fair/culture-specific testing

One conventional proposal for meeting the spirit of nondiscriminatory assessment is the creation of "culture-fair" tests. Presumably, such tests were originally developed to minimize language, reading skill, speed, and other factors that may be culture specific and in order to minimize cultural differences affecting test content and test-taking behaviors (Oakland & Matuszek, 1977). Examples of culture-fair tests include the Leiter International Performance Scale, Cattell's Cuture-Fair Intelligence Tests, and Raven's Progressive Matrices (see Samuda, 1975, for other examples).

So-called culture-fair tests do not fare well as nondiscriminatory measures. There is some concensus that no test can be regarded as culture-fair (Anastasi, 1961; Sattler, 1974; Vernon, 1965). Sattler (1974) noted that " . . . *no test can be culture-fair if the culture is not fair*" (p. 34). Attempts to develop nonverbal tests that are culture-fair have also met with problems. Language is but one dimension on which tests could be discriminatory. Social skills, test-taking behaviors, and other factors may be more important dimensions on which to focus. Even if language is a primary concern, nonverbal tests are also not culture-fair because they depend on cognitive behaviors that are related to language systems (Cohen, 1969; Sattler, 1974). Furthermore, at least for black children, nonverbal tests (or sections of tests) have been found to be as difficult as or more difficult than verbal tests (see Sattler, 1974, for a review). A major point is that tests, intelligence and otherwise, cannot be created so that differential exposure to learning has no influence on performance. Thus, since many conventional tests are designed to predict the individual's ability to learn skills in the general or dominant culture, tests that tap other skills will not typically yield meaningful correlations to that dominant culture.

The intent to progress through the "general culture" can also be challenged. It is possibly this concern that has led to the development of culture-specific assessment. In this movement, assessment devices are designed for each of the major subcultural groups in U.S. society (cf. Laosa, 1977a). One example is the Black Intelligence Test of Cultural Homogeneity (BITCH) for adolescents and adults. This is a vocabulary test that includes 100 multiple-choice items that deal exclusively with black culture (Williams, 1972). Another example is the Enchilada Test (Ordiz & Ball, 1972), which has 31 multiple-choice items that deal with experiences that are common to Mexican-American barrio children. These culture-specific measures are used for a specific group and are not designed to predict performance in the dominant culture. They have clearly demonstrated the problems that an individual from the dominant culture would have on a test designed for a specific minority group.

Issues of culture fairness have been linked to different models of test fairness in general. This issue is discussed next.

### Statistical analysis of outcome

One method of assessing the discriminatory function of tests is to be less concerned with the biased nature of each of the items making up the test and concentrate more on the utility of the test in predicting outcomes. From this perspective, divesting a test's content of all shades of cultural bias is of less importance than establishing the test's fairness in predicting success for both minority and nonminority group members. Two reasons for movement in this direction are noted: First, many users of norm-referenced standardized tests, such as the WISC-R, perceive the major utility of such a test in providing information necessary for

243

predicting future performance on some established criteria such as academic achievement. Since this is seen as the primary importance of these tests, fairness in predicting equally well for all children is seen as an essential ingredient for establishing a test's psychometric validity. Second, after witnessing the futility of removing the cultural bias from test items, as attempted in the culture-fair movement, some individuals have turned to other criteria to determine test bias, such as those embodied in the statistical analysis of outcomes.

Two principal concerns have been addressed in the statistical determination of test bias. The first deals with variation in the validity coefficients of regression equations for tests separately derived for minority and nonminority group members. The second deals with the relation between minority and nonminority group means for both the criterion and predictor variables used (Anastasi, 1976).

The former concern, called *slope bias,* occurs when the regression lines used to predict a criterion score from a test score have different slopes for minority and nonminority groups. When this occurs, predictions of future performance based on regression equations established with scores from only one of the groups may result in bias toward the other group. Research investigating slope bias has been criticized for being methodologically inadequate (Anastasi, 1976). Those studies of most relevance to the present discussion have dealt with the academic performance of samples of Black and Anglo-American college students as predicted from performance on the College Board Scholastic Aptitude Test (Cleary, 1968; Kendrick & Thomas, 1970; Stanley & Porter, 1967). In general, these studies have indicated little variation in either single-group or differential validity for the Black and Anglo samples.

Three studies dealing with the prediction of academic achievement of minority and nonminority school-age children based on school-related abilities tests showed similar results (Bergan & Parra, 1979; Mitchell, 1967; Reschly & Sabers, 1979). Mitchell (1967) compared the validities of two readiness tests against the achievement of Black and Anglo children at the end of their first school year. The validities of the two tests were not significantly different for the two ethnic groups. Bergan and Parra (1979) predicted the performance on a letter-learning task for samples of Anglo and bilingual Mexican-American children from performance on the WPPSI administered under different language conditions. In this study a nonsignificant interaction between scores on the learning task and performance on the WPPSI for the different treatment groups provided no support for slope bias. In the Reschly and Sabers (1978) study, differences in the slopes of regression equations derived from scores on the Metropolitan Achievement Test and WISC-R for samples of Anglo, Black, Chicano, and Native American Papago children from a variety of grade levels (1–9) provided unclear results. It was reported that the directions of differences in slopes, when found, were about equally divided, with Anglo slopes being higher for some comparisons but lower for others.

As indicated above, research in this area is inconclusive. Reviews of this literature have drawn three different conclusions: that ethnic differences in validity are real (Katzell & Dyer, 1977); that differential validity can be regarded as a methodological artifact (Boehm, 1977); and that more research is needed (Bartlett, Bobko, & Pine, 1977). This confusing state of affairs has prompted Flaugher (1978) to conclude that since single-group and differential validity have been so elusive and difficult to detect, maybe they are not "very potent phenomena" in relation to other forms of test bias, to which we should turn our attention.

The second concern in determining the bias of a test in predicting outcome measures is commonly referred to as *intercept bias*. Intercept bias occurs when the regression lines established for minority and nonminority samples cross the *y*-intercept at different points. Intercept bias can be present in the absence of slope bias. Research evidence of intercept bias has been somewhat limited. Tentative conclusions have indicated that intercept bias in a variety of ability tests has resulted in the overprediction of minority performance in several criteria measures, including college and law school grades (Cleary, 1968; Temp, 1971). In the Reschly and Saber (1978) study mentioned above, an analysis of the regression equations suggested the presence of intercept bias. Using a common regression line for the groups examined, the authors reported that in nearly all cases non-Anglo performance was overpredicted and Anglo performance underpredicted.

As evidenced above, research bearing on bias in the outcome of tests commonly used in schools to substantiate important decisions concerning placement is at best inconclusive. Although some consistent findings indicating that the presence of intercept bias results in overprediction of non-Anglo performance have been reported, the quantity of research is limited. If either slope or intercept bias exists in the prediction of future academic performance from tests such as the WISC-R, any decision influenced by the results of the test may be biased unless this factor is taken into account. Since most validity studies tend to include predominantly nonminority children, the potential for inaccurate predictions for minority group children based on such studies is increased.

In recent years, several models of fairness in selection have been

245

proposed that are designed to adjust for bias resulting from tests predicting differently for minority and nonminority groups. Three of the more popular models (Cleary, 1968; Darlington, 1971; Thorndike, 1971), will be briefly discussed. For a thorough analysis of each of the models, the reader is referred to Petersen and Novick (1976).

Cleary's (1968) model argues for the use of the best possible prediction equation for minority and nonminority groups. If tests are shown to predict differently for different groups, Cleary proposes the use of different cutoff points for each group as an adjustment so that the same criterion score can be predicted.

In the model proposed by Thorndike (1971), the fair use of tests in any selection process should be governed not by the test's ability to predict a desirable criterion score but by a quota for selection established by determining the percentages of each group demonstrated to be successful on the criterion variable. Thorndike argues that this eliminates the inherent bias in the selected ratios of members of different groups in the Cleary model when different cutoff scores are used with different regression lines. Thorndike's objection to the Cleary model is demonstrated in the following example. Suppose two regression lines, one for blacks and one for whites, are used to predict performance on a criterion variable. Next, suppose the black regression line is below the white regression line and that performance on both the predictor and criterion variable is lower for blacks. Given a less than perfect correlation between the predictor and criterion, and a cutoff at the white mean on the criterion variable, a smaller percentage of blacks would be selected if the black regression line were used for selection of blacks than would be the case if the percentage of blacks were determined by use of performance on the criterion variable directly. This comes about as a result of blacks having to score higher in comparison to the black mean on the criterion than whites do in comparison to the white mean in order to be selected.

A third popular model, proposed by Darlington (1971), argues that choices such as those made in the placement of children in special education classes cannot be made on purely psychometric grounds. Instead, he proposes that selection criteria be adjusted to include consideration of the importance of such decisions and to provide minority group members with an advantage in the selection process.

As Flaugher (1978) has pointed out, the development of these and other models of selection can be viewed as the evolution of mathematical expressions of different value systems and there can be no single standard for selection fairness. In this context, the conclusion can be reached that there is no really fair model of selection, " . . . only systems that are more or less popular with decision makers" (Flaugher, 1978, p. 676).

**Renorming conventional tests**

Another procedure that has been advocated to overcome the limitations of traditional tests is to renorm the already existing tests (e.g., Alley & Foster, 1978; Mercer, 1971, 1973a, 1973b; Oakland & Matuszek, 1977; Sattler, 1974). It should be noted that many tests that are commonly used across all ethnic groups suffer from inadequate norms (Salvia & Ysseldyke, 1978). Given that the specific test's norms are not appropriate for certain cultural groups, specific norms could be developed. This would permit better comparisons of one minority child's performance to the performance of other children of the same minority group. Presumably, national norms could be used if certain cultural groups are included in the normative sample, and/or local norms could be developed. In this case, an individual's test scores would then be interpreted with reference both to standard norms and to specific sociocultural group norms.

Mercer's (1971, 1973b) work in the development of pluralistic norms for the interpretation of test scores is one example of this approach. Culture-specific measures such as BITCH (Williams, 1974) and learning-potential assessment (cf. Budoff, 1972) can be represented under the rubric of pluralistic assessment (Mercer & Ysseldyke, 1977). The pluralistic model encompasses a variety of approaches that may make testing procedures more responsive to cultural pluralism and less bound to Anglo-American culture. Pluralistic approaches presumably broaden the cultural base of testing procedures and attempt to control for the cultural component of the test. Mercer (1973b, p. 260) describes a pluralistic evaluation procedure:

> We have examined the possibility of taking sociocultural differences into account by using a pluralistic clinical perspective to interpret the meaning of any set of clinical scores. Such a diagnosis would have three characteristics not presently a part of clinical evaluations. It would use the traditional criteria of the lowest 3 percent to define subnormality. It would use two dimensions, IQ and adaptive behavior, to evaluate mental retardation, and both measures would have to be failed before making an evaluation of clinical retardation. It would use pluralistic norms to interpret the meaning of a specific IQ or adaptive behavior score. Such norms would evaluate the individual's performance in relation to others from similar sociocultural backgrounds.

In the pluralistic approach, each child is located in the distribution of scores for his or her group and the score is interpreted within that distribution. Multiple regressions are used to predict the average score for persons from a variety of sociocultural backgrounds in order to develop multiple normative frameworks. In this procedure the sociocultural characteristics of the child's family are entered into a multiple-regression equation, each characteristic is multiplied by its weight, and the equation is solved to provide the average test score predicted for a person of the child's background. When the child's score is compared with the predicted score, his or her evaluation on dimensions of normal or abnormal depends upon the score location in a distribution of scores predicted for other children from similar sociocultural settings (Mercer & Ysseldyke, 1977). Multiple norms using this regression analysis for estimating learning potential of Black, Chicano/Latino, and Anglo-American clients on the basis of sociocultural characteristics have been developed for the WISC-R (Mercer & Lewis, 1978). However, Mercer's pluralistic norms are based upon samples of children from California only.

The pluralistic approach to assessment and the renorming alternative both have a number of limitations. A general problem, alluded to earlier in the chapter, relates to cultural and linguistic diversity. Given the great degree of variation within and between various cultural groups, it would be difficult to develop norms for each specific group. Presumably, local norms could be generated; but even then the norming standards would have to be revised continually to reflect changing local population dimensions over time.

Using Thorndike's (1974) position, Alley and Foster (1978) noted that pluralistic normative data have several limitations, including relevancy, reliability, and bias. In describing criterion variability which has been unaccounted for by a test, Thorndike (1974) noted that relevance is only partially controlled on tests of either prediction or criterion. Thus, most tests measure only a part of the school curriculum and it is not easy to determine whether the unmeasured aspects of school performance will help or inhibit a minority child. Similarly, no test accounts for 100 percent of the variance in actual school achievement. Thus, "It becomes impossible to be sure what adjustment in critical score, if any, is appropriate for minority group members" (Thorndike, 1974, p. 45).

Unreliability of measures is another problem. Alley and Foster (1978) note that although Thorndike provides a rationale and statistical procedure to obtain an estimation of the true criterion difference, based on means, standard deviations, and a reliability coefficient, of both the majority and minority culture to provide statistical fairness, one must still decide if this "statistical fairness" provides a "socially fair" test.

A final point made by Thorndike (1974, p. 44) is that "if the criterion measure is itself biased in an unknown direction or degree, no rational procedure can be set up for the "fair" use of the test." The point here is that different cultural groups may value different criterion measures and a test of conventional academic achievement or potential may still be discriminatory.

A third major issue that militates against normative data is related to the maintenance of the status quo (Alley, 1976; Alley & Foster, 1978). Presumably, the tactic of using conventional tests but establishing new norms implies that minority children will still do worse than majority culture children—a "procedure which solidifies the status quo of minority children" (Alley & Foster, 1978, p. 5).

A final criticism relates specifically to Mercer's (1973b) work on mental retardation. Goodman (1977) criticized Mercer's work on mental retardation because it is based on "diagnosticism"—the assumption that retardation is an entity of biological origin and unfavorable sequelae, rather than a set of behaviors emerging from a diversity of causes. It is argued that pluralistic assessment and normative standards are irrelevant to instruction. Goodman (1977, p. 204) notes:

> In conceding the possible use of different tests or cutoff points for different subgroups, it should be stressed that the results would not be considered an assessment of aptitude, as Mercer holds, but merely an improved means of matching curriculum to current function. Pluralistic assessment is valid only in so far as it better predicts a child's achievement in a pluralistic curriculum, not as a measure of underlying potential. As long as a system retains universal goals for all its students, pluralistic standards remain inappropriate.

## PROPOSED NONDISCRIMINATORY ASSESSMENT OPTIONS

As limitations of traditional testing practices become more salient and widespread, alternatives to conventional procedures have emerged. Of course, many of these alternative procedures developed independently of traditional procedures and therefore have their own history. In this section some assessment techniques that embrace different conceptual and/or methodological dimensions in assessment are briefly described.

### Piagetian assessment procedures

There has been a noticeable lack of reliance on standardized intelligence tests in the development of Piaget's theory (Brainerd, 1978). Thus, the theory has made virtually no use of findings generated by such tests; Piaget and others affiliated with the theory rely on clinical methods instead. Nevertheless, some new assessment models are based on the work of Piaget (Laosa, 1977a). For example, Struthers and DeAvila (1967) developed the Cartoon Conservation Scales, which is a test for children that can be administered on a group basis. The test seems to be appropriate as a measure of cognitive development with regard to certain aspects of the Piagetian conservation concept. This approach in nondiscriminatory assessment may be valuable in that there appears to be a similarity in cognitive development of children from diverse cultural backgrounds when assessed on certain Piagetian tasks (DeAvila & Harassy, 1975).

A number of Piagetian assessment procedures have been reviewed by Johnson (1976). However, many of these tap specific skills (e.g., conservation of number, Swanson, 1976a); and represent "experimental" or "research" instruments at this time. Thus, their usefulness in nondiscriminatory assessment remains unknown. However, within the context of a broadened scope of assessment, these devices may be useful in the assessment of specific skills (Johnson, 1976).

### Learning-potential assessment

Generally, the learning-potential approach views assessment as an examination of learning and strategies which facilitate acquisition of new information or skills (Kratochwill, 1977). The rationale behind learning-potential assessment bears similarities to Piaget's work on intellectual development (Haywood, Filler, Shifuran, & Chatelant, 1974); that is, within the Piagetian paradigm, intelligence is viewed as a process rather than a static entity unmodifiable by experience.

Work in the learning-potential area has been affiliated with Haywood in Nashville, Tennessee; Budoff in Cambridge, Massachusetts; and Feuerstein in Jerusalem. These investigators and their associates have adapted test-based models for assessment of and intervention with the mentally retarded (see Haywood et al., 1974, and Kratochwill, 1977, for overviews). Haywood et al. (1974) noted that verbal abstraction abilities can be improved during the assessment of mentally retarded people from different cultural environments. For example, some research indicates that mentally retarded clients are able to perform better on Wechsler's Similarities subtest when examples of each concept are provided (Gordon & Haywood, 1969). These results replicate with retarded children and adults from culturally different environments (Haywood & Switzky, 1974).

The learning-potential work of Budoff and his associates has used a test–train–retest assessment paradigm on such instruments as Kohs' Block Design Test (Budoff, 1967), the Wechsler Performance Scale (Budoff, 1969), Raven's Progressive Matrices (Budoff & Hutton, 1972), and a modification of Feuerstein's (1968) early Learning Potential Assessment Device (Budoff, 1969). These tasks are sensitive to modification via instruction or coaching and typically assessment can yield three types of performers. *High scorers* gain little from coaching. Those who initially score low and demonstrate performance gains following instruction are labeled *gainers*. *Nongainers* initially score low but do not show gains following training (Budoff, Meskin, & Harrison, 1971). A major implication of Budoff's work has been that,

A large proportion of IQ-defined retardates, who come from low income homes and have no history of brain injury, show marked ability to solve these tasks when they are presented in the learning potential assessment format. The data indicate that the more able students by this criterion are educationally, not mentally, retarded, and the ability they demonstrate prior to or following tuition is not specific to the particular learning potential task. (Budoff, 1972, p. 203)

A final area of work within the learning-potential paradigm is represented in the work of Feuerstein and his associates (Feuerstein, 1968; 1970; Feuerstein & Rand, 1978). Like the test–train–retest paradigm of Budoff and his associates, Feuerstein's strategy is designed to promote the best possible learning and motivational conditions for the child. The Learning Potential Assessment Device is designed to assess what an individual can learn rather than the traditional inventory of what one has learned and current problem-solving ability (Feuerstein & Rand, 1978). An Instructional Enrichment program has been developed to facilitate "learning to learn." This program uses abstract, content-free, organizational, spatial, temporal, and perceptual exercises.

The work in learning-potential assessment appears to be promising for the field of nondiscriminatory assessment (Alley & Foster, 1978; Laosa, 1977a; Mercer & Ysseldyke, 1977). Indeed, Mercer and Ysseldyke (1977) include the learning-potential assessment paradigm as part of the pluralistic assessment "model." There is some evidence to support the learning-potential strategy. For example, Budoff and Hutton (1972) found that if they provided only 1 hour of structured experiences in problem solving to children who initially scored low on Raven's Progressive Matrices, 50 percent of these low-performance children scored at the 50th percentile (or above) on a posttest administered after training. These gainers represented minority groups. Similar results have been found with "learning disabled children" (Platt, 1976). Sewell and Severson (1974) also found that Raven's Progressive Matrices (see Budoff & Friedman, 1964) usefully differentiated low socio-economic status (SES) Black children who could profit from learning experiences. Nevertheless, there are unanswered questions related to how learning-potential assessment can yield prescriptive information for classroom instruction, especially in content areas (math, reading, etc.), and how the training can be generalized (Kratochwill, 1977).

## Diagnostic–clinical teaching

Diagnostic–clinical teaching (Kratochwill, 1977; Lerner, 1976) bears similarity to learning-potential strategies. These strategies differ from "diagnostic–prescriptive teaching" (Salvia & Ysseldyke, 1978; Ysseldyke, 1973; Ysseldyke & Salvia, 1974), which has been affiliated with test-based aptitude–treatment interaction paradigms (Cronbach & Snow, 1976; Levin, 1977). Diagnostic–clinical teaching actually embraces a number of different strategies that are not, at present, guided by any particular theoretical area. Typically, it involves the actual teaching of curriculum-related material under conditions that maximize learning (e.g., stimulus materials, mediational strategies, reinforcement, feedback). Thus, its relevance in the nondiscriminatory assessment area is that it focuses on (1) tasks that nearly all children experience in the school curriculum and (2) direct intervention for successful curriculum mastery. For example, Meyers and Hammill (1969, 1973) recommended teaching words to children under conditions that maximize learning and suggested that learning disabled children should be evaluated on learning tasks that have been normed.

Likewise, Hutton and Niles (1974) proposed trial teaching as a supplement to traditional testing. Severson (1971, 1973) suggested a process learning assessment strategy based on teaching academic content under different conditions. In research employing four to eight words to be learned, predictive validity relations have ranged from .30 to .73 with achievement test criteria (Kratochwill & Severson, 1977; Sewell & Severson, 1974).

While these procedures represent a promising area of nondiscriminatory assessment, a paucity of research and a limited range of content remain limitations on their usefulness (Kratochwill, 1977).

## Child development observation

In a similar tradition to learning-potential assessment and diagnostic–clinical teaching is the "child development observation" (CDO) procedure, designed by Ozer and his associates (Ozer, 1966, 1968, 1978, 1980; Ozer & Dworkin, 1974; Ozer & Richardson, 1974). A major objective of CDO is to simulate the process of learning by using protocols that sample skills and conditions under which a given child's learning problems may be solved. Different teaching strategies are also enacted to see how the child learns best.

The CDO procedure may be useful in nondiscriminatory assessment in that it does not conform to traditional testing paradigms, no score is derived in relation to a group norm, decisions do not promote diagnostic labeling, and relating assessment data to classroom functioning is intrinsic to evaluation (Ozer & Richardson, 1974). However, there are no data on the reliability and validity of the procedure, verbal skills are heavily emphasized in certain areas of assessment, and the CDO does not systematically sample from classroom tasks (Kratochwill, 1977).

## Clinical neuropsychological assessment

The field of neuropsychology is concerned with delineating brain–behavior relationships. Neuropsychology includes a number of different, sometimes only remotely related, disciplines of which clinical neuropsychology is but one. Clinical neuropsychology focuses on developing knowledge about human brain–behavior relationships, or delineating the psychological correlates of brain lesions (Davison, 1974; Reitan, 1966). Intellectual, sensorimotor, and personality deficits are measured and related to brain lesions or to brain damage in the broader sense of physiological impairment. The work in this area is rooted in academic psychology, behavioral neurology, and particularly psychometric psychology.

Clinical neuropsychology depends upon standardized behavioral observations with an emphasis on normative psychological assessment devices. Within this context, behavior is defined operationally and, usually, quantified along continuous distributions (Davison, 1974). Clinical neuropsychologists are typically not merely concerned with distinguishing brain damage from other conditions; rather, they are interested in refining descriptions of clinical conditions, including inferences relative to the location and extent of brain damage, as well as probable medical and psychological conditions accounting for the abnormal behavior.

A considerable amount of information has been obtained during the past decade about the behavioral characteristics of brain-damaged persons as a result of neuropsychological study in the areas of mental retardation, learning disabilities, behavioral disabilities, and convulsive disorders (Reitan & Davison, 1974). In addition, studies have been conducted on individuals with confirmed cerebral lesions wether or not these individuals manifest learning or behavioral problems (Reitan, 1974). Finally, neuropsychological studies of normal children have been undertaken (e.g., Kimura, 1967).

Further research in neuropsychological assessment techniques could lead to some interesting applications relative to identification, classification, and intervention strategies. The concept of brain dysfunction as a primary factor in learning disabilities, for example, has received increasing attention over the past 20 years. By characterizing all children having learning disabilities as having minimal brain dysfunction, many professionals seem to have attributed learning disabilities to neurogenic factors. However, much of the research relevant to this hypothesized relationship is hampered by the problem that learning disabled children do not constitute a homogeneous group (e.g., Hallahan & Kauffman, 1978).

Typically, the term "learning disabled" has been used to refer to children who show a discrepancy between current level of school performance and measures of academic potential that is not due to mental retardation, cultural, sensory, or educational inadequacies, or serious behavioral disturbances (Bateman & Schiefelbusch, 1969). This type of general definition lacks sufficient objective criteria, so that children who have specific disabilities in reading, spelling, or arithmetic, or multiple deficits are all categorized as learning disabled children. Moreover, such children often have been referred to by the term "minimal brain dysfunction." The lack of precision with which educators have used the terms minimal brain dysfunction and learning disability may account in part for the inconsistencies found in identification and placement practices.

Recent studies in neuropsychological assessment techniques, such as one conducted by Ahn (1977), offer the promise for the development of a multiple discriminate function utilizing relevant information for the more precise classification of large groups of learning disabled children. Ahn (1977) found significant patterns of difference between three different groups of presumably learning disabled children (i.e., verbal underachievers, arithmetic underachievers, and mixed underachievers) and normal children in quantitative electrophysiological measures (i.e., EEG-evoked potentials).

Results such as these lend plausibility to the contention that neuropsychological assessment techniques may prove useful for the more accurate identification and classification of children possessing different specific learning disabilities. At the very least, further research in this area should increase educators' and psychologists' knowledge of the many different types of problems referred to under the general label of learning disabilities.

Davison (1974) has discussed the potential utility of clinical neuropsychological assessment techniques relative to intervention. Of particular import here is the fact that the same behavioral deficits may be due to various causal factors and, therefore, require different interventions. A reading problem, for example, may be due to a structural abnormality of the brain or to an abnormal learning history. Traditional assessment devices which emphasize previously acquired products do not reveal any functional links between impairment and response to be investigated in order to determine *why* a person functions as (s)he does. Inappropriate responses or failure to respond may be interpreted as lack of ability when, in fact, the primary problem may be failure to comprehend directions (DuBose, Langley, & Stagg, 1977). Thus, for remedial purposes, the etiology of a particular deficit may take on importance. The basis of failure may be more significant in terms of prescribing appropriate intervention strategies than the failure itself. Traditional methods of psychodiagnostic assessment typically are not able to differentiate among the many possible etiological factors that may be involved in impaired performance.

One cannot accurately predict the outcomes of further investigation into this area as yet. Increasing our understanding of brain–behavior relationships will require extensive study of the behavior of humans with brain damage of varying location, extent, etiology, etc. It may be that the product will be merely some interesting descriptive statistics. Undoubtedly, however, increased knowledge of brain–behavior correlates holds potent implications for nondiscriminatory assessment techniques as well as decisions based on assessment data. Much additional work needs to be done with children to make these procedures more applicable to the area of nondiscriminatory assessment.

### Criterion-referenced assessment

Criterion-referenced assessment, which has gained wide popularity in recent years, has been touted by many as implicitly nondiscriminatory. There is some support for this claim. Unlike norm-referenced assessment, which depends upon comparison of children in the assessment of abilities and skill level achievement, criterion-referenced tests measure the extent to which a child has mastered an absolute preestablished standard of performance. Thus, treating each child as an individual rather than comparing him/her to others of different backgrounds and experiences may be viewed as nonbiased and nondiscriminatory (Mercer & Ysseldyke, 1977).

Another reason for the claim that criterion-referenced tests are nondiscriminatory is that within this system no concern is given to differences between ability and achievement. Criterion-referenced tests are theoretically derived from precisely defined behavioral objectives and are designed to sample behaviors of immediate and relevant concern, such as math and reading skills in school settings. Since the behaviors sampled during assessment are so closely linked to those behaviors of immediate concern, there is less chance that nonessential and possibly discriminatory factors such as variation in cultural background will interfere with the measurement.

While proponents of criterion-referenced assessment claim it is a nondiscriminatory assessment procedure, discrimination with respect to the choice of those tasks established as important in the educational process can still discriminate against minority populations and reflect the value system of the majority group. However, the argument still holds that the test is essentially devoid of bias and it is the use and choice of tests that can result in discriminatory practice.

Since criterion-referenced assessment has often been discussed as a nondiscriminatory strategy for the assessment of minority as well as nonminority group children, a brief discussion of some of the advances in criterion-referenced assessment within the past few years will follow, along with suggestions for how criterion-referenced tests may be incorporated into an evaluation scheme for the selection of children for special education classes.

Since the term criterion-referenced measurement was first used by Glaser and Klaus (1962), much attention has been given to continued clarification as to what the term means as well as a delineation of the issues that need to be addressed in the improvement of the measure (Hambleton, Swaminathan, Algina, & Coulson, 1978). As first conceived in the behavioral literature, criterion-referenced tests were precise measures of highly specific discrete behavior capabilities and generally included behaviors purported to be hierarchically sequenced as arrived at through task analysis procedures such as those reported by Gagné (1962) and Resnick, Wang, and Kaplan (1973). In more recent years, items included in criterion-referenced measures have more often been considered as representative of domains or clusters of highly related behaviors rather than specific capabilities. Thus, instead of conceptualizing a behavioral objective as capable of being measured by only one highly specific behavior, objectives are viewed as representative of a class or domain of behaviors. Under optimal circumstances each domain represents a single class of responses, so that success in one item implies success on all items. As a consequence of this conceptualization the term "domain-referenced tests" has become popularized. It is generally understood today that whether one prefers the use of criterion-referenced (Hambleton et al., 1978) or domain-referenced (Subkoviak & Baker, 1977) measurement, the concept of "domain" is implied. Since domains, as conceptualized, are composed of clusters of items and only a sample of items are drawn from each domain for testing purposes, a whole new area of traditional concerns over test developments procedures and the psychometric properties of criterion-referenced tests has evolved. Much work has been accomplished in recent years to advance the psychometric credibility of these tests, as demonstrated in reviews of developments in this area by Hambleton et al. (1978) and Subkoviak and Baker (1977).

Another approach that improves the measurement capabilities of criterion/domain-referenced tests is based on the empirical validation of homogeneous item domains (Bergan, 1978; Bergan, Cancelli & Luiten, 1978; Cancelli, 1978; Dayton & Macready, 1976; Macready & Merwin, 1973). This approach has, through the use of advances made in work with latent structure analysis, advanced the design of criterion/domain-referenced tests by focusing attention on empirically validating sets of homogeneous item domains. While most test theorists to date have acknowledged the desirability of constructing domains based on homogeneous sets of items so that success on one item implies success on all items, until recently, empirical procedures for the establishment of homogeneous item domains have not been available. Such an approach holds much promise for assessment in educational settings since it closely links assessment with education planning (Cancelli, 1978).

Along with breakthroughs in the area of empirically validating homogeneous item domains from which criterion/domain-referenced tests can be constructed, empirical procedures for the hierarchical ordering of these domains have also become available (Bergan, in press). With the advent of procedures for empirically validating both the scope and sequence of domains of homogeneous items, a new form of criterion/domain-referenced assessment, referred to as "path-referenced assessment" (Bergan, 1978), has been proposed. This assessment procedure is designed to provide information about the learner which will allow for both the pinpointing of skill deficits or domain deficiencies and the identification of the "path" or sequence of curriculum instruction that will lead most efficaciously to mastery of the terminal objective desired.

As described above, much advancement in the area of criterion/domain-referenced assessment has been made to date and the future for continued work in this area looks promising. However, while arguments for the nondiscriminatory nature of criterion/domain-referenced assessment can be convincing, the employment of these types of tests in an evaluation scheme useful in the placement of children in special education classes is still considered limited by many professionals. Since decisions concerning placement are to a large extent based on concerns for degree of deviation from the norm and criterion/domain-referenced tests fail to provide a normative standard for comparing children, it has often been argued that such measures, while appropriate for teacher use in the classroom, are inappropriate as a testing activity per se (Holmeister, 1975). As Ebel (1970) has charged:

> Criterion-referenced measures of educational achievement, when valid ones can be obtained, tell us in meaningful terms what a man knows or can do. They do not tell us how good or how poor his knowledge or ability may be. Excellence or deficiency are necessarily relative concepts. They cannot be defined in absolute terms. (p. 36)

Two methods that can help make criterion/domain-referenced tests more useful in special education placement decisions can be briefly mentioned here. The first method makes use of a process of social validation as an alternative to psychometrically established norms (Kazdin, 1977; Wolf, 1978). Social validation consists of two procedures. First, the client's behavior is compared to that of a peer (or peers) who is considered normal or nondeviant. Second, subjective evaluations of the client's performance are solicited from people (e.g., teachers and parents) in the natural environment. The use of such a procedure assumes that the behavior selected for change is of social importance (e.g., acquiring reading skills).

Another method of making criterion-referenced measures more relevant to the selection process is to provide norms for the test. Since the essence of the nondiscriminatory measures lies in its conceptual nature and design rather than in the fact that it has no norms, this strategy has much appeal. However, the legitimacy of having a test that is both norm referenced and criterion referenced has been questioned by several writers in recent years (Subkoviak & Baker, 1977). In brief, concern has been raised over the fact that the items on a criterion-referenced test are randomly selected from each domain during test construction, while test theory governing the selection of items for norm-referenced devices indicates that in order to best discriminate between better and poorer achievers, items that are passed by half a sample of the population are best. While it has been argued that the random sampling of items is the best strategy for most accurately representing an individual's mastery of the domains tested, such procedures do not result in tests best capable of comparing people. While such arguments suggest the need for caution in norm-referenced interpretations of criterion-referenced tests, they do not entirely deny their usefulness in decision making about special education placement.

## Observational assessment

Observational assessment strategies have been most commonly affiliated with behavior therapy approaches (see earlier discussion), but they are certainly not limited to this orientation. Observational approaches share a diverse background, and subsumed under the rubric of this measurement strategy are a large number of rating scales, checklists, and direct observational codes (Boehm & Weinberg, 1977; Cartwright & Cartwright, 1974; Flanders, 1966; Hunter, 1977; Johnson & Bolstad, 1973; Jones, Reid, & Patterson, 1974; Kent & Foster, 1977; Lipinski & Nelson, 1974; Lynch, 1977; Medley & Metzel, 1963; Rosenshine & Furst, 1973; Sackett, 1978a, 1978b; Sitko, Fink, & Gillespie, 1977; Weick, 1968; Weinberg & Wood, 1975; Wright, 1960). In this section we are primarily discussing those codes that meet the criteria for direct observational devices as advanced by Jones et al. (1974). Jones et al. noted that the characteristics of a naturalistic observational system include "recording of behavioral events in their natural settings at the time they occur, not retrospectively; the use of trained impartial observer-coders; and descriptions of behaviors which require little if any reference by observers to code the events (p. 46). Observational assessment strategies are being recommended as part of more comprehensive evaluations to reduce discriminatory assessment practices (Mercer & Ysseldyke, 1977; Tucker, 1977), and an increase in the use of this assessment strategy is likely. Presumably, a major advantage of observational methods in nondiscriminatory assessment is that they focus directly on the target behavior of interest in the setting in which a problem has been identified, thereby having the potential to relate directly to an intervention, and they reduce the inference in assessment of the academic or social problem.

The wealth of information available and the complexity of the topic make a detailed discussion of this assessment option impossible here. Clearly, observational assessment represents a promising alternative in meeting the spirit of nondiscriminatory assessment. To contribute to this goal many issues need to be addressed. First, it is important to distinguish between observational procedures and actual observational instruments. Many clinicians use and have used some type of observational procedures in everyday practice (e.g., observing the child in the classroom, or requesting a teacher to record data on some academic problem). Thus, this type of assessment is relatively common and will remain so in the future. On the other hand, there are relatively few observational instruments for direct observation of behavior in the natural environment. Note here that we are excluding the relatively large number of rating scales and checklists in common use as they do not meet the Jones et al. (1974) definition. Moreover, many of the available instruments are quite limited in scope, i.e., they focus on a relatively specific range of behaviors or problems.

Like other assessment devices, observational procedures and instruments must adhere to established psychometric guidelines. Unfortunately, for many instruments, work to establish their credibility is just beginning. One of the major concerns is with the reliability of the observational system. Reliability refers to both the reliability of the instrument per se, and their use by observers to establish interobserver agreement. Many factors can influence the reliability of measurement (Kent & Foster, 1977), such as the formula used to calculate interobserver agreement, the complexity of the coding system, the knowledge that reliability is being assessed, biased observers, cheating, consensual observer drift, and instrument decay.

Another problem with many of the observational procedures and instruments is the lack of validity data. Unfortunately, the concept of validity has been largely ignored in observational assessment, possibly due to the presumed face validity of behavioral definitions which may obscure other validity considerations (Johnson & Bolstad, 1973; Jones et al., 1974; Kent & Foster, 1977). The generality of observational data across different settings is a third problem (Ciminero & Draburan, 1977). Some research suggests that behavior of children or parents in one setting may not be comparable to their behavior in other settings (Forehand & Atkeson, in press). Thus, assessment of the problem in multiple settings, or where the problem occurs with highest frequency, may be necessary.

This cost of observational assessment will also typically be a problem. Cost considerations will be salient where large numbers of observer-codes are used, and where a problem occurs across many different situations. Observational assessment also yields a large amount of data, so a high cost will be associated with transforming and communicating these data.

Finally, the absence of normative data on observational assessment may be a limitation when comprehensive behavior-coding systems are used for special class decision making. Although the use of norms may not be necessary in all cases, some type of comparative data will typically be necessary to establish deviance in a particular setting (Nelson & Bowles, 1975). Local norms as well as social validation of the problem could be employed in such cases (see earlier discussion of social validation in criterion-referenced assessment).

The use of observational assessment strategies and the development of observational instruments is a promising area in assessment in general and nondiscriminatory assessment in particular. Like other assessment procedures described in this section, much remains to be done to make this approach more credible. Nevertheless, at this time it represents a powerful assessment alternative for use both prior to treatment and to assess the effects of a treatment program.

## LEGISLATIVE AND JUDICIAL INFLUENCES

This section briefly outlines some of the key federal legislative and judicial actions influencing the assessment of minority children in the schools and attempts to presage the use of standardized aptitude and achievement tests based on court decisions to date. An excellent and comprehensive review of the legislative and judicial influences on minority assessment practices in the schools is provided by Oakland and Laosa (1977).

### Legislation

Since state governments claim legal control over education under the Tenth Amendment to the Constitution of the United States, the federal government has historically made its impact on education and assessment practices indirectly through control of federal assistance. The Fifth and Fourteenth Amendments to the Constitution, the Civil Rights Act of 1964, the Educational Amendments of 1972, the Rehabilitation Act of 1973, and the Education of All Handicapped Children Act of 1975 (PL 94-142) have all had either a direct or indirect impact on minority assessment.

The Fifth and Fourteenth Amendments both guarantee "due process," and the Fourteenth Amendment also guarantees "equal protection under the law." The "due process" provision of the Amendments requires that all laws be fairly applied, while the "equal protection" clause of the Fourteenth Amendment abolishes discriminatory practices for unjustifiable reasons such as race or ethnic background. Rights granted under the Fifth and Fourteenth Amendments, however, did not have a direct impact on assessment practices in the schools until judicial interpretations established them as applicable.

In 1964, the Civil Rights Act passed by Congress contained direct antidiscrimination provisions guarding against discrimination based on race, color, or national origin. All schools receiving federal monies were in jeopardy of losing their funding if they did not comply with the law. As a result of this law and several court actions to be discussed below, guidelines for nondiscriminatory assessment were either directly written into subsequent legislation, such as PL 94-142, or offered as regulations or memoranda from governmental agencies for already existing laws. The most comprehensive set of federal guidelines to data, entitled *Elimination of Discrimination in the Assignment of Children to Special Education Classes for the Mentally Retarded*, was prepared by the U.S. Department of Health, Education and Welfare Office of Civil Rights (OCR) in 1972. Reflecting recommendations provided to OCR by psychologists, sociologists, and educators, this memorandum requires that minority children be assessed for placement in classes for the mentally retarded only after a careful review of academic aptitude and achievement test results, medical and socioeconomic background data, a teacher's report, and adaptive behavior data. Other factors to be considered should include the child's incentive–motivational and learning style, language skills and preferences, interpersonal skills, and nonacademic behavioral patterns.

### Judicial decisions

Courts have been reluctant to interfere with assessment practices in the schools as they have traditionally perceived assessment as school business within the purview of state and local school boards. The courts have had a standing policy that they have no legal rights to interfere with how the schools go about the business of education. However, in recent years the courts have demonstrated a willingness to judge school cases in which the constitutional rights of an individual have allegedly been violated.

These were the circumstances when, in 1954, the U.S. Supreme Court decided in favor of the plaintiffs in *Brown* v. *Board of Education* and ruled against the doctrine of "separate but equal." Since that decision, lawsuits have become commonplace among those who wish to change education in the United States. Several offended groups since that time have alleged discrimination by the schools as a function of assessment practices and have used legal channels in an attempt to bring about change. Usually charging a violation of rights guaranteed by the Fifth and Fourteenth Amendments of the Constitution and the 1964 Civil Rights Act, plaintiffs have challenged educational decisions on a variety of issues pertinent to minority assessment.

Two early cases indirectly involved with assessment were *PARC— Pennsylvania Association for Retarded Children* v. *Commonwealth of Pennsylvania* (1971) and *Mills* v. *Board of Education of the District of Columbia* (1972). Both cases were primarily concerned with the right of a district to exclude children from school as uneducable. While neither case directly examined tests given to children, it was understood from these cases that tests cannot be used to deny children a free public education. In a Louisiana case, *Lebanks* v. *Spears* (1973), a similar ruling with respect to exclusion from school was handed down. However, in addition to this primary ruling, the court also ruled that placement in classes for the mentally retarded cannot be made without evidence indicating an IQ of below 70 obtained from an individually administered intelligence test and subnormal adaptive behavior with evidence that neither measurement was inappropriately influenced by the sociocultural background of the child. *Lau* v. *Nichols* (1974) is another case that was not primarily concerned with testing in which discriminatory testing practices were addressed in the ruling by the court. In this case the plaintiffs were Chinese-American students who charged failure on the school's part to provide special language instruction to all Chinese-speaking students. In the court's ruling, which found in favor of the plaintiffs, safeguards were ordered to be established by a task force to ensure proper use of assessment techniques with bilingual or non-English-speaking students. The task force's findings were later released through the OCR in August 1975 (Oakland & Laosa, 1977).

One of the most popular cases involving assessment practices in the schools was *Diana* v. *California State Board of Education* (1970). In this case, which was ultimately settled out of court, nine Mexican-American public school students brought suit against the school board for alleged discriminatory practices in the placement of children in classes for the mentally retarded. The plaintiffs argued that children who were originally placed in classes for the educable mentally retarded (EMR) on the basis of IQ scores derived from administration of the Stanford-Binet and WISC were found to score on an average of 15 points higher when retested by a bilingual examiner. This evidence was offered in support of charges that testing practices were discriminatory in that they inappropriately placed too heavy an emphasis on verbal facility with the English language and resulted in disproportionate percentages of Hispanic children in EMR classes. In an out-of-court settlement of the case, it was agreed that future testing of non-Anglo-American children being considered for placement in EMR classes would be conducted in both English and the child's primary language. Furthermore, tests or sections of tests that would not be dependent on vocabulary, general information, and other unfair verbal questions would be required. It was further agreed that Mexican-American and Chinese-American children already placed in EMR classes would be reevaluated in accordance with the new testing guidelines. Psychologists in the state were also to develop norms for an IQ test based on a Mexican-American sample. Finally, any school district still with a disproportionate percentage of Hispanics in EMR classes had to submit an explanation for the disparity. Similar arrangements were also made out of court in the settlement of *Guadalupe* v. *Tempe Elementary School District* (1971), a class action suit brought in behalf of Mexican-American and Yaqui Indian children in Arizona.

While *Diana* brought national attention to the problem of linguistic bias in IQ testing, another famous case, *Larry P.* v. *Riles* (1972), focused attention on the cultural bias of tests against black children. As in *Diana*, evidence was provided showing that when the black children who were the plaintiffs in the case were retested, all scored significantly above the IQ cutoff point of 75 on the individual intelligence tests that were used to place them in EMR classes. The retesting was conducted by black psychologists who made special attempts to establish rapport and maintain motivation during testing to reduce the effect of the cultural background of the plaintiffs. Credit was also given for nonstandardized answers that showed an intellectual approach to problems within the context of the children's unique background. As in *Diana*, evidence bearing on the disproportionately high number of black children in EMR classes was offered. Although evidence was provided by the schools that they had used a number of procedures to determine placement as mandated by the state after *Diana*, the court ruled that too much emphasis was placed on IQ test scores in making placement decisions with consequent racial imbalance in the composition of EMR classes. The court further responded by requesting a moratorium on the use of the Stanford-Binet and WISC-R in the placement of minority group children in special education programs for the educable mentally handicapped and learning disabled. Subsequent action taken by the California State Board of Education broadened the request by the court to include all children considered for placement in these classes. This action has resulted in increased use of alternative strategies for intellectual assessment and a reduction in the number of placements made (Oakland & Laosa, 1977).

An overall analysis of court rulings to date involving school assessment practices suggests that arguments alleging a denial of equal educational opportunity have not been consistently effective in bringing about change. Such charges have resulted in courts analyzing the facts of the case in terms traditionally utilized in "equal protection clause" violations. Consequently, in order to prove a denial of equal protection, evidence that the state has invidiously discriminated against a class of people must be presented (Tractenberg & Jacoby, 1977). In cases arguing an overrepresentation of minority group members in special education classes, one need only show that schools have a rational basis for such placements to justify their actions. If the procedures governing placement are rational, then courts have been reluctant to interfere, since such decisions are perceived by the court as a function of the school administration. More success in bringing about change has been forthcoming when arguments against testing and placement practices show that they lead to the formation of a "suspect classification." A suspect classification can be understood as the consequence of any selection or decision-making process used for one purpose which results in the formation of a class or grouping of people as a by-product of the process. Race and ethnic background have been clearly identified by the U.S. Supreme Court as suspect classifications, with poverty and sex being other possible candidates (Tractenberg & Jacoby, 1977). If the formation of a suspect classification leads to differential treatment, then a compelling need for such classification must be provided. Such compelling needs have not been satisfactorily demonstrated; the result is that sole reliance on tests for placement have been limited or barred (Tractenberg & Jacoby, 1977).

Recent court rulings in the area of minority employment are pertinent to the present discussion and suggest one type of evidence courts will use to establish a compelling need for forming a suspect classification. Rulings in the cases of *Griggs et al.* v. *Duke Power Company* (1971) and the subsequent *U.S.* v. *Georgia Power Company* (1973) imply that if selection decisions can be made utilizing assessment devices high in both content and predictive validity, a strong case can be made for the fairness of a decision-making process which leads to disproportionate representation in selection. In *Griggs et al.* v. *Duke Power Company,* the Supreme Court rejected intelligence testing as a valid criterion for determining employment since it led to discriminatory practices in hiring. The decision was based on the fact that the criterion had not been demonstrated to be a reasonable measure of job performance. Criteria used for employment, including standardized test findings, must be shown to be valid and not serving to maintain previously established discriminatory practice.

In a subsequent case (*U.S.* v. *Georgia Power Company*), guidelines for the use of tests which may lead to the formation of a suspect classification were more specifically detailed. Concurrent validation techniques were rejected by the court in favor of predictive validation techniques that are established after a period of time during which information obtained from the tests is not used to determine placement but rather is utilized to gain sufficient evidence regarding the test's predictive validity. Such a ruling may have important implications for future cases alleging discrimination in special education placement.

It would seem that one way to claim that a test does not discriminate unfairly against a class of people, even though its use results in differential treatment, would be to provide evidence in several areas. One important area would involve the demonstration that the test predicts equally well for all. This evidence cannot be provided if the predictive utility of the instrument is established while the test is already being used for placement. If such were the case then the performance measurement would be prejudicially influenced by the differential treatment (different class placements) provided the children. Such a methodology would have the potential for maintaining discriminatory practices as they now exist.

To make adequate use of an instrument that predicts differentially for various groups, different norms would have to be established accordingly or adjustments would have to be made in the selection process using the test information. A multitude of problems in the latter procedure were discussed in the section on the Statistical Analysis of Outcomes. This issue, as well as others involved in judging the psychometric integrity of tests for both minority and nonminority populations, is extremely complex, and as Anastasi (1976) has warned, "the statistically unsophisticated must step warily" (p. 197). Because of these complexities the courts have often been at a disadvantage in weighing the technical aspects of such cases. Judicial officials often utilize guidelines established by governmental agencies and professional organizations as authoritative sources in answering technical psychometric questions. In an analysis of recent court decisions, Lerner (1978) has identified a trend toward judicial reliance on the *Standards for Educational and Psychological Tests* (APA, 1974) as the authoritative source in such matters. Lerner argued for future revisions of the *Standards* to maintain scientific fidelity and to allow the court to make comparative decisions regarding preference for evaluative schemes.

## INFLUENCE OF PROFESSIONAL ASSOCIATIONS

Professional organizations have had an impact on the area of human assessment in various ways. Professional groups offer training programs, make public statements, publish guidelines, and are sometimes involved in certification and licensing individuals who offer these services (Oakland & Laosa, 1977). In this section, we review some of the professional groups that have set forth standards for assessment practice. It should be noted that although a number of professional groups have considered issues relevant to nondiscriminatory assessment, only a few have provided any formal guidelines. The professional organizations that have provided standards for assessment and practice are listed in Table 1.

**TABLE 1**
**PROFESSIONAL ORGANIZATIONS THAT HAVE PROVIDED STANDARDS/**
**GUIDELINES FOR ASSESSMENT/PRACTICE**

American Educational Research Association (AERA)

American Personnel and Guidance Association (APGA)

American Psychological Association (APA)

Association of Black Psychologists (ABP)

Association for Advancement of Behavior Therapy (AABT)

National Association for the Advancement of Colored People (NAACP)

National Association of School Psychologists (NASP)

National Council of Measurement in Education (NCME)

National Education Association (NEA)

Society for the Study of Social Issues[a] (SSSA)

[a]The SSSA is Division 9 of the American Psychological Association.

### Groups representing minorities

Representing blacks, the National Association for the Advancement of Colored People (NAACP) held a conference on minority testing in 1976. Its report (Gallagher, 1976) pointed to uses and misuses of tests, psychometric issues, public policy, and a code to help ensure the fair use of tests. The Association of Psychologists for La Raza (APLR), an organization for Chicano psychologists, does not have an official position on minority assessment. However, in 1972–1973 the president of the association responded to the APA report on "Educational Use of Tests with Disadvantaged Students" (Cleary et al., 1975). Although the report stressed fair assessment practices, Bernal (1975) pointed to various oversights in the report—such as the omission of many key criticisms of testing and test development with minority group children and recommendations for improving test development with minorities—and noted that the report shifted the blame for testing to practitioners.

As noted earlier, in 1968 the Association of Black Psychologists (ABP) proposed a moratorium on the use of psychological tests in schools with children from disadvantaged backgrounds. A year later, the ABP prepared a position statement in which parents received support for refusing to allow their children and themselves to be subjected to achievement, intelligence, aptitude, and performance tests that discriminate against blacks. More recently, Jackson (1975) labeled the APA report (Cleary et al., 1975) "blatantly racist." He noted that a moratorium is no longer enough; what is needed is government intervention and sanctions against testing practices.

## National Education Association (NEA)

The NEA membership approved a resolution to establish a moratorium on standardized tests during a Human Relations Conference in 1972 (Bosma, 1973). Later in the year, the NEA policy-making Representative Assembly passed three resolutions (Oakland & Laosa, 1977, pp. 22–23): (1) to encourage the elimination of group-standardized intelligence, aptitude, and achievement tests until completion of a critical appraisal, review, and revision of current testing programs; (2) to direct the NEA to call immediately a national moratorium on standardized testing and set up a task force on standardized testing to research the topic and make its findings available to the 1975 Representative Assembly for further action; and (3) to request the NEA task force on testing to report its findings and proposals at the 1973 Representative Assembly. Again in 1973 the NEA task force called for a national moratorium on standardized testing until 1975. The NEA Representative Assembly also reviewed the moratorium resolution on testing, noting that tests should not be used in a way that will deny students full access to equal educational opportunity.

## American Personnel and Guidance Association (APGA)

During the 1970 annual convention of APGA the Senate adopted a resolution which expressed concern over minority group testing. Subsequently, the Association for Measurement and Evaluation in Guidance (AMEG, a division of APGA) prepared a position statement on the use of tests, and with the assistance of AMEG, APGA, and the National Council of Measurement in Education (NCME), a paper was adopted as an official position of these organizations (AMEG, 1972). The document indicates that "professional associations, including the measurement societies, do not have the authority to control intentional discrimination against particular groups, though individual members acting in accordance with their own consciences may being to bear such powers as their positions afford them" (p. 386). It states that issues relating to test misuse should go through the court system, boards of education, civil service commissions, and other public groups.

**National Association of School Psychologists (NASP)**

NASP represents practicing and academic school psychologists in the United States and some foreign countries. Since school psychologists are actively involved in assessment in applied settings, the NASP delegate assembly has adopted a number of resolutions (e.g., Resolutions 3, 6, and 8) that have bearing on nondiscriminatory assessment practices (NASP, 1978). Resolution 3 indicates that school psychologists should protect children, especially those in minority groups, from abuses through the malpractice of school psychology. Improvement of instruments is one suggestion for accomplishing this.

Resolution 6 militates against the position that blacks and other minority groups manifest an inferiority in intellectual functioning based on inherited genetic characteristics. The NASP has taken the position that there is inadequate scientific support for genetic differences in intelligence among people and that further research is needed.

Resolution 8, recognizes

> . . . that individuals of different socio-cultural backgrounds differ in their readiness to succeed in school; that professional members of minority groups have indicated that it is a disservice to minority individuals to suggest that they need not do well on tests or achieve a basic education; and that objective measures are less biased than subjective judgments in assigning children to special programs in schools. (p. 104)

Some specific suggestions for standards relating to professional involvement, assessment standards, standards for parent and/or student involvement, standards for educational programming and follow-through, and training standards follow these resolutions (NASP, 1978, pp. 105–107).

**Association for Advancement of Behavior Therapy (AABT)**

In May 1977, the Board of Directors of the AABT adopted a statement on "Ethical Issues for Human Services." Although the "issues" do not mention nondiscriminatory assessment specifically, they are formulated so as to be relevant across as many settings and populations as possible. Interestingly, the statements are conceptualized within the domain of treatment rather than assessment per se. Eight questions are asked and each is accompanied by more specific questions elucidating the concept. The major questions are as follows:

1. Have the goals of treatment been adequately considered?

2. Has the choice of treatment methods been adequately considered?

3. Is the client's participation voluntary?

4. When another person or an agency is empowered to arrange for therapy, have the interests of the subordinate client been sufficiently considered?

5. Has the adequacy of treatment been evaluated?

6. Has the confidentiality of the treatment relationship been protected?

7. Does the therapist refer the clients to other therapists when necessary?

8. Is the therapist qualified to provide treatment?

## The American Psychological Association (APA), American Educational Research Association (AERA), and the National Council on Measurement in Education (NCME)

As a major organization representing psychologists, the APA has been actively involved in providing standards for psychological practice. An early effort to address issues relating to assessment of minority children occurred within the Society for the Study of Social Issues (SSSI), Division 9 of the APA. The SSSI published a monograph in which testing of minority groups was discussed within the context of selection, use, interpretation, and sensitivity to whether tests differentiate reliably, the predictive validity, and are adequately interpreted with minority group children (Deutsch, Fishman, Kogan, North, & Whiteman, 1964).

Two more recent sets of standards were developed which have direct relevance for the assessment of individuals. *Ethical Standards of Psychologists* (APA, 1972) and *Standards for Educational and Psychological Tests* (APA, 1974) both contain guidelines on how tests are to be used and developed. The *Standards* were first developed in 1954 (at that time they were called *Technical Recommendations for Psychological Tests and Diagnostic Techniques*) and were endorsed by the AERA and the NCME. Thereafter, the three organizations worked together to publish the 1966 *Standards for Educational and Psychological Tests and Manuals,* followed by the 1974 *Standards.*

While the *Ethical Standards of Psychologists* contains material relating to the psychologist's responsibilities, competence, and moral and legal standards, and issues regarding confidentiality, test security, test interpretations, and test publications, the *Standards for Educational and Psychological Tests* expands the *Ethical Standards* by providing more detailed and specific guidelines for test developers and users. These guidelines apply to any assessment procedure, device, or aid—i.e., to any systematic basis for drawing inferences about people (p. 2). Standardized tests are considered a special case of an assessment procedure. It has become quite apparent that many assessment procedures and devices used in psychology and education do not conform to the *Standards*.

Although the *Standards* do not specifically deal with the concept of nondiscriminatory assessment, it is assumed that adherence to the *Standards* will result in assessment that is less discriminatory than if the guidelines were not followed. Nevertheless, a footnote in the *Standards* did indicate a position against the proposed moratorium (see earlier discussion).

A final document, prepared at the request of the APA's Board of Scientific Affairs, was entitled "Educational Uses of Tests with Disadvantaged Students" (Cleary et al., 1975). This document (referred to in a previous section) (1) presented a comprehensive definition of abilities with special reference to general intelligence, (2) summarized some common classes of test misuse and misinterpretation, (3) reviewed the kinds of statistical information needed to use a test effectively, and (4) discussed existing alternatives to ability tests and reviewed new types of tests and new information needed to make more effective evaluations of students in schools. Although the report draws heavily on the *Standards for Educational and Psychological Tests*, emphasizes test evaluation on the basis of validity (content, construct, and criterion related) to determine fairness, and emphasizes the correct use of test, it was severely criticized (Bernal, 1975; Jackson, 1975). Some of these criticisms were presented in previous sections.

### Relationship between the Supreme Court and professional organizations

Despite several early efforts on the part of professional organizations, significant change in psychological and educational assessment practices with minority children in schools did not occur until impetus was provided by legislative and judicial action (e.g., PL 94-142). Another issue that has recently emerged relates to the actual use of the *Standards for Educational and Psychological Tests* in legal issues. The question is: "When a legal challenge to test use arises, what set of standards will the Supreme Court of the United States rely upon in deciding whether that particular test use in that particular situation is acceptable in technical, psychometric terms?" (Lerner, 1978, p. 915). Although no definitive answer to the question is apparent, as previously noted, Lerner (1978) indicates that the Court appears to be moving away from reliance upon and deference to federal agency guidelines and toward reliance upon professional standards as reflected in the *Standards*. Various excerpts quoted in her article suggest that the Court is indeed moving in this direction.

## SOME FUTURE PERSPECTIVES

Our review closes on a note similar to the one expressed in the introduction. It has been suggested that many features of assessment have remained very much the same. This is most dramatically illustrated in the literature on nondiscriminatory assessment, wherein, with some notable exceptions, issues have focused on quite conventional testing practices. Several areas of concern and potential options for improving traditional assessment practices have been detailed in the preceding pages. Our review suggests that while these concerns and options have generated much research and scholarly analysis in recent years, much still needs to be done. While there appears to be support in calling for a moratorium on testing, the spinoff effects of such an option are considered by many to have the potential to result in more discriminatory practices than currently exist with testing. A concern for the usefulness of special education placement has also been frequently raised. A review of the literature indicates that research efforts bearing on questions concerning the effectiveness of special education, the expectancy effect, the self-fulfilling prophecy phenomenon, and the effects of pre- and postlabeling on providing appropriate intervention have been inconclusive. Resulting discussions calling for a revision in existing classification schemes, possibly through behavioral classification, however, seem to hold promise for the future.

Concerns over the effects of language bias in assessment have generally met with research endeavors fraught with methodological problems. Questions concerning possible important differences between "primary" and "dominant" language and an adequate definition of bilingualism have for the most part remained unanswered. Consequent strategies designed to account for possible discrimination in assessment as a function of language also have problems. A lack of conceptually and psychometrically valid language assessment instruments has hampered efforts. Similar problems concerning the validity of translating present instruments into various languages have also not been adequately investigated.

There has also been concern that the race of the examiner can result in discriminatory assessment. Research designed to answer these questions has far to go in elucidating the issues here. The resultant option of using same race examiners has obvious practical problems and the cost of effecting such a strategy seems at present to outweigh the yet unknown benefits.

Movement toward the development of tests that are fair to the various subcultures in the United States has also met with little success. While such efforts have served to stimulate discussion concerning the various assumptions underlying intelligence testing, little else has been accomplished. One of the more popular movements to date has involved the purging of traditional psychometric devices of their discriminatory elements through renorming. Most notable in the effort has been the work of Mercer. However, the acceptance of such an approach necessitates acceptance of the assumption that retardation, as traditionally understood, is an entity of presumed biological origin. This is based on "diagnosticism," which adheres to the proposition that pure cases of deficit originate in biology; this position can be disputed by instances in which retardation is considered a by-product of social circumstances (Goodman, 1977). Such an approach promotes a poor prognosis and fails to identify instructional tactics for such children. Thus, this renorming approach attempts to remove the cultural bias from conventional tests so that a measure of native intelligence can be obtained.

Research endeavors aimed at addressing two additional concerns and proposed options, namely the modification of test procedures and the statistical analysis of outcomes, have provided some refinement of the initial questions posed. With respect to the former, concerns for cultural differences in motivational and situational factors have resulted in much research. Research examining situational variability, for example, has demonstrated that the performance of minority children can be enhanced through modifying factors such as the use of familiar examiners. Such findings have pointed the way for future investigations to determine if the enhancement of performance through whatever means serves to invalidate the predictive utility of commonly used psychometric instrumentation. With respect to the statistical analysis of outcomes, while still somewhat sparse, research has pointed to the existence of intercept bias, resulting in the overprediction of non-Anglo performance. Continued work in this area, combined with the refinement of selection models of fairness, appears to hold promise for the future.

As an alternative to traditional testing, several models of assessment have been reviewed. While all the procedures discussed appear to be potentially valuable as alternatives or supplements to traditional methods, the recent advances in criterion-referenced and observational assessment strategies appear to have evolved to a point where they can now be considered as quite useful as nondiscriminatory assessment strategies. The eventual use of these strategies as commonly employed procedures for collecting data relevant to special education decision making appears to rest in the hands of practitioners.

As our review has pointed out, assessment practices can be discriminatory in many different ways. Discriminatory practices can be traced to the theoretical orientation and training of the clinician—which translates into his/her practice, the scope of the assessment process, the specific assessment devices and techniques used, the purpose for which assessment is undertaken, the psychometric credibility of the devices and procedures, and the ethical and legal factors which surround the assessment process. However, the primary issue is the nature of the assessment process. The conceptualization of assessment as nondiscriminatory when it leads to effective interventions and services seems to be a productive approach for future work in the field.

# References

Abramson, T. The influence of examiner race on first-grade and kindergarten subjects' Peabody Picture Vocabulary Test scores. *Journal of Educational Measurement,* 1969, *6,* 241–246.

Achenbach, T. M. *Developmental psychopathology.* New York: Ronald Press, 1974.

Adams, H. E., Doster, J. A., & Calhoun, K. S. A psychologically based system of response classification. In A. R. Ciminero, K. S. Calhoun, & H. E. Adams (Eds.), *Handbook of behavioral assessment.* New York: Wiley–Interscience, 1977.

Ahn, H. *Electroencephalographic evoked potential comparisons of normal children and children with different modes of underachievement.* Unpublished doctoral dissertation, University of Iowa, 1977.

Ali, F., & Costello, J. Modification of the Peabody Picture Vocabulary Test. *Developmental Psychology,* 1971, *5,* 86–91.

Alley, G., & Foster, C. Nondiscriminatory testing of minority and exceptional children. *Focus on Exceptional Children,* 1978, *9,* 1–14.

Alley, M. R. *Methods of assessing the performances of exceptional children who represent minority groups.* Paper presented at Regional Problems of Exceptional Children Meeting, Regional MSEO and GAC, Kansas City, Mo., June 1976.

American Psychological Association, *Ethical standards of psychologists.* Washington, D.C., 1972.

American Psychological Association, American Educational Research Association, & National Council on Measurement in Education. *Standards for educational and psychological tests.* Washington, D.C.: American Psychological Association, 1974.

Anastasi, A. *Differential psychology* (3rd ed.). New York: Macmillan, 1958.

Anastasi, A. Psychological tests: Uses and abuses. *Teachers College Record,* 1961, *62,* 38–393.

Anastasi, A. *Psychological testing.* (4th ed.). New York: Macmillan, 1976.

Anastasi, A., & Cordova, F. A. Some effects of bilingualism upon the intelligence test performance of Puerto Rican children in New York City. *Journal of Educational Psychology,* 1953, *44,* 1–19.

Anastasi, A., & Foley, J. P., Jr. *Differential psychology* (2nd ed.). New York: Macmillan, 1949.

Association for Measurement and Evaluation in Guidance, American Personnel and Guidance Association, & National Council for Measurement in Education. The responsible use of tests: A position paper of AMEG, APGA, and NCME. *Measurement and Evaluation in Guidance,* 1972, *5,* 385–388.

Ayllon, T., & Kelly, K. Effects of reinforcement on standardized test performance. *Journal of Applied Behavior Analysis,* 1972, *5,* 477–484.

Bandura, A. A social learning interpretation of psychological dysfunctions. In P. Lowdon & D. Rosenhan (Eds.), *Foundations of abnormal psychology.* New York: Holt, Rinehart, & Winston, 1968.

Bartell, N., Grill, J., & Bryen, D. Language characteristics of black children: Implications for assessment. *Journal of School Psychology,* 1973, *11,* 351–364.

Bartlett, C. J., Bobko, P., & Pine, S. M. Single-group validity: Fallacy of the facts? *Journal of Applied Psychology,* 1977, *62,* 155–157.

Bateman, B. D., & Schiefelbusch, R. L. Educational identification, assessment, and evaluation procedures. In *Minimal brain dysfunction in children* (Phase II). N & SDCP Monograph, U.S. Department of Health, Education, and Welfare, 1969.

Baughman, E. E. *Black Americans: A psychological analysis.* New York: Academic Press, 1971.

Baughman, E. E., & Dahlstrom, W. G. *Negro and white children: A psychological study in the rural south.* New York: Academic Press, 1968.

Beberfall, L. Some linguistic problems of the Spanish-speaking people of Texas. *Modern Language Journal,* 1958, *42,* 87–90.

Bee, H. L., Streissguth, A. P., Van Egeven, L. F., Leckie, M. S., & Nyman, B. A. Deficits and value judgments: A comment on Sroufe's critique. *Developmental Psychology,* 1970, *2,* 146–149.

Beery, K. E., & Buktenica, N. *Developmental Test of Visual–Motor Integration.* Chicago: Follett, 1967.

Bender, L. *A visual motor Gestalt test and its clinical use.* New York: American Orthopsychiatric Association 1938, Research Monograph No. 3.

Benton, A. L. Influence of incentives upon intelligence test scores of school children. *Journal of Genetic Psychology,* 1936, *49,* 494–497.

Bergan, A., McManis, D. L., & Melchert, P. A. Effects of social and token reinforcement on WISC block design performance. *Perceptual Motor Skills,* 1971, *32,* 871–880.

Bergan, J., Cancelli, A. & Luiten, J. *Mastery assessment with latent class and quasi-independence models representing homogeneous item domains.* Journal of Educational Statistics, in press.

Bergan, J. R. Behavioral assessment: Path-referenced assessment. In J. R. Bergan (Chair), *Behavioral approaches to psychoeducational assessment.* Symposium presented at the meeting of the American Psychological Association, Toronto, Canada, August, 1978.

Bergan, J. R. The structural analysis of behavior: An alternative to the learning hierarchy model. *Review of Educational Research,* in press.

Bergan, J. R., & Parra, E. Variations in IQ-testing and instruction and the letter learning and achievement of Anglo and bilingual Mexican-American children. *Journal of Educational Psychology,* 1979, *71,* 819–826.

Bernal, E. A response to "Educational uses of tests with disadvantaged subjects." *American Psychologist,* 1975, *30,* 93–95.

Bijou, S. W., & Grimm, J. A. Behavioral diagnosis and assessment in teaching young handicapped children. In T. Thompson & W. S. Dockens, III (Eds.), *Applications of behavior modification.* New York: Academic Press, 1975.

Bijou, S. W., & Peterson, R. F. Psychological assessment in children: A functional analysis. In R. McReynolds (Ed.), *Advances in psychological assessment* (Vol. 2). Palo Alto, Calif.: Science and Behavior Books, 1971.

Bisett, B. M., & Rieber, M. The effects of age and incentive value on discrimination learning. *Journal of Experimental Child Psychology,* 1966, *3,* 199–206.

Boehm, S., & Weinberg, R. A. *The classroom observer: A guide for developing observation skills.* New York: Teachers College Press, 1977.

Boehm, V. R. Differential prediction: A methodological artifact? *Journal of Applied Psychology,* 1977, *62,* 146–154.

Bosma, B. The NEA testing moratorium. *Journal of School Psychology,* 1973, *11,* 304–306.

Brainerd, C. J. *Piaget's theory of intelligence.* Englewood Cliffs, N.J.: Prentice-Hall, 1978.

Braue, B. B., & Masling, J. M. Intelligence tests used with special groups of children. *Journal of Exceptional Children,* 1959, *26,* 42–45.

*Brown* v. *Board of Education of Topeka.* 347 U.S. (1954).

Bucky, S., & Banta, T. Racial factors in test performance. *Developmental Psychology,* 1972, *6,* 7–13.

Budoff, M. Learning potential among institutionalized young adult retardates. *American Journal of Mental Deficiency,* 1967, *72,* 404–411.

Budoff, M. Learning potential: A supplementary procedure for assessing the ability to reason. *Seminars in Psychiatry,* 1969, *1,* 278–290.

Budoff, M. Providing special education without special classes. *Journal of School Psychology,* 1972, *10,* 199–205.

Budoff, M., & Friedman, M. "Learning potential" as an assessment approach to the adolescent mentally retarded. *Journal of Consulting Psychology,* 1964, *28,* 433–439.

Budoff, M., & Hutton, L. The development of a learning potential measure based on Raven's Progressive Matrices. *Studies in Learning Potential*, 1972, *1*, 18.

Budoff, M., Meskin, J., & Harrison, R. Educational test of the learning-potential hypothesis. *American Journal of Mental Deficiency*, 1971, *76*, 159–169.

Canady, H. R. The effect of "rapport" on the IQ: A new approach to the problem of racial psychology. *Journal of Negro Education*, 1936, *5*, 209–219.

Cancelli, A. Behavioral assessment: Structure on domains in psychoeducational assessment. In J. R. Bergan (Chair), *Behavioral approaches to psychoeducational assessment*. Symposium presented at the meeting of the American Psychological Association, Toronto, Canada, August 1978.

Cartwright, C., & Cartwright, G. P. *Developing observation skills*. New York: McGraw-Hill, 1974.

Chandler, J. T., & Plakos, J. Spanish-speaking pupils classified as educable mentally retarded. *Integrated Education*, 1969, *1*, 8–33.

Chavez, S. J. Preserve their language heritage. *Childhood Education*, 1956, *33*, 165–185.

Ciminero, D. R., & Draburan, R. S. Current developments in the behavioral assessment of children. In B. B. Lahey & A. E. Kazdin (Eds.), *Advances in child clinical psychology* (Vol. 1). New York: Plenum Press, 1977.

Claiborn, W. L. Expectancy effects in the classroom: A failure to replicate. *Journal of Educational Psychology*, 1969, *60*, 377–383.

Cleary, T. A. Test bias: Prediction of grades of Negro and white students in integrated colleges. *Journal of Educational Measurement*, 1968, *5*, 115–124.

Cleary, T. A., Humphreys, L., Kendrick, A., & Wesman, A. Educational uses of tests with disadvantaged students. *American Psychologist*, 1975, *30*, 15–41.

Clingman, J., & Fowler, R. L. The effects of primary reward on the IQ performance of grade-school children as a function of initial IQ level. *Journal of Applied Behavior Analysis*, 1976, *9*, 19–23.

Cohen, R. A. Conceptual styles, culture conflict and nonverbal tests of intelligence. *American Anthropologist*, 1969, *71*, 828–856.

Conner, J. J., & Weiss, F. L. A brief discussion of the efficacy of raising standardized test scores by contingent reinforcement. *Journal of Applied Behavior Analysis*, 1974, *7*, 351–352.

Cronbach, L. J. *Essentials of psychological testing* (2nd ed.). New York: Harper, 1960.

Cronbach, L. J. Beyond the two disciplines of scientific psychology. *American Psychologist*, 1975, *30*, 116–127.

Cronbach, L. J., & Snow, R. E. *Aptitudes and instructional methods: A handbook for research on interactions*. New York: Irvington/Naiburg, 1976.

Crown, P. J. *The effects of race of examiner and standard vs. dialect administration of the Wechsler Preschool and Primary Scale of Intelligence on the performance of Negro and white children*. (Doctoral dissertation, Florida State University.) Ann Arbor, Mich.: University Microfilms, 1970, No. 71-18, 356.

Darlington, R. Another look at "culture fairness." *Journal of Educational Measurement*, 1971, *8*, 71–82.

Davis, F. *Standards for educational and psychological tests*. Washington, D.C.: American Psychological Association, 1974.

Davison, L. A. Introduction to clinical neuropsychology. In Reitan, R. M., & Davison, L. A. (Eds.), *Clinical neuropsychology: Current status and applications*. Washington, D.C.: Winston, 1974.

Dayton, C. M., & Macready, G. B. A probabilistic model for validation of behavioral hierarchies. *Psychometrika*, 1976, *41*, 189–204.

DeAvila, E. A., & Harassy, B. E. Piagetian alternatives to IQ: Mexican American study. In N. Hobbs (Ed.), *Issues in the classification of exceptional children*. San Francisco: Jossey-Bass, 1975.

Deutsch, M., Fishman, J. A., Kogan, L., North, R., & Whiteman, M. Guidelines for testing minority group children. *Journal of Social Issues,* 1964, *20*(2), 129–145.

*Diana* v. *California State Board of Education.* No. C-70 37 RFP, District Court of Northern California (February 1970).

DuBose, R. F., Langley, M. B., & Stagg, V. Assessing severly handicapped children. *Focus on Exceptional Children,* 1977, *9,* 1–13.

Dunn, L. M. *Peabody Picture Vocabulary Test.* Circle Pines, Minn.: American Guidance Service, 1965.

Dunn, L. Special education for the mildly retarded: Is much of it justifiable? *Exceptional Children,* 1968, *35,* 5–22.

Ebel, R. L. Some limitations of criterion-referenced measurement. In *Testing in turmoil: A conference on problems and issues in educational measurement.* Greenwich, Conn.: Educational Records Bureau, 1970.

Edgerton, R. B. *The cloak of competence: Stigma in the lives of the mentally retarded.* Berkeley: University of California Press, 1967.

Edlund, C. V. The effect on the test behavior of children, as reflected in the IQ scores when reinforced after each correct response. *Journal of Applied Behavior Analysis,* 1972, *5,* 317–319.

Elashoff, J. D., & Snow, R. E. *Pygmalion reconsidered: A case study in statistical inference: Reconsideration of the Rosenthal-Jacobson data on teacher expectancy.* Worthington, Ohio: Jones, 1971.

Epps, E. G. Situational effects in testing. In L. P. Miller (Ed.), *The testing of black students.* Englewood Cliffs, N.J.: Prentice-Hall, 1974.

Epps, E. G., Katz, I., Perry, A., & Runyon, E. Effects of race of comparison referent and motives on Negro cognitive performance. *Journal of Educational Psychology,* 1971, *62*(3), 201–208.

*Federal Register,* August 23, 1977, 42474-42518. *Education of handicapped children. Regulations implementing Education for All Handicapped Children Act of 1975.*

Ferster, C. B. Classification of behavior pathology. In L. Krasner & L. P. Ullmann (Eds.), *Research in behavior modification.* New York: Holt, Rinehart, & Winston, 1965.

Feuerstein, R. Learning potential assessment device. In B. W. Richards (Ed.), *Proceedings of the first congress of the International Association for the Scientific Study of Mental Deficiency.* Reigate, Surrey, England: Jackson, 1968.

Feuerstein, R. A dynamic approach to the causation, prevention, and alleviation of retarded performance. In H. C. Haywood (Ed.), *Social–cultural aspects of mental retardation.* New York: Appleton-Century-Crofts, 1970.

Feuerstein, R., & Rand, R. *The dynamic assessment of retarded performers: The learning potential assessment device, theory, instruments, and techniques.* Baltimore: University Park Press, 1978.

Flanders, N. A. *Interaction analysis in the classroom: A manual for observers* (Rev. ed.), Ann Arbor, Mich.: University of Michigan, 1966.

Flaugher, R. L. The many definitions of test bias. *American Psychologist,* 1978, *33,* 671–679.

Fleming, E. S., & Anttonen, R. G. Teacher expectancy or My Fair Lady. *American Educational Research Journal,* 1971, *8,* 241–252.

Forehand, R., & Atkenson, B. M. Generality of treatment effects with parents as therapists: A review of assessment and implementation procedures. *Behavior Therapy,* in press.

Forness, S. E. The reinforcement hierarchy. *Psychology in the Schools,* 1973, *10,* 168–177.

Forrester, B. J., & Klaus, R. A. The effect of race of the examiner on intelligence test scores of Negro kindergarten children. *Peabody Papers in Human Development,* 1964, *2,* 1–7.

Gagné, R. M. The acquisition of knowledge. *Psychological Review,* 1962, *69,* 355–365.

Gallagher, B. G. (Ed.). *NAACP report on minority testing.* National Association for the Advancement of Colored People, May 1976.

Galvan, R. R. *Bilingualism as it relates to intelligence test scores and school achievement among culturally deprived Spanish-American children.* (Doctoral dissertation, East Texas State University), Ann Arbor, Mich.: University Microfilms, 1967, No. 68-1131.

Garcia, J. IQ: The conspiracy. *Psychology Today,* 1972, *40.*

Garcia, R. L. *Unique characteristics of exceptional bilingual students.* Paper presented at the regional meeting of MSOE and MPC, Kansas City, Mo., June 9, 1976.

Garth, T. R. The problem of racial psychology. *Journal of Abnormal and Social Psychology,* 1922, *17,* 215–219.

Gay, G., & Abrahams, R. Does the pot melt, boil, or brew? Black children and white assessment procedures. *Journal of School Psychology,* 1973, *11,* 330–340.

Ginsburg, R. E. *An examination of the relationship between teacher expectancies and students' performance on a test of intellectual functioning.* (Doctoral dissertation, University of Utah). Ann Arbor, Mich.: University Microfilms, 1970, No. 71-922.

Glaser, R., & Klaus, A. J. Proficiency measurement: Assessing human performance. In R. M. Gagne (Ed.), *Psychological principles in system development.* New York: Holt, Rinehart, & Winston, 1962.

Goodman, J. F. The diagnostic fallacy: A critique of Jane Mercer's concept of mental retardation. *Journal of School Psychology,* 1977, *15,* 197–206.

Gordon, J. E., & Haywood, H. C. Input deficits in cultural familial retardation. Effects of stimulus enrichment. *American Journal of Mental Deficiency,* 1969, *73,* 604–610.

Gozali, J., & Meyen, E. L. The influence of the teacher expectancy phenomenon on the academic performances of educable mentally retarded pupils in special classes. *Journal of Special Education,* 1970, *4,* 417–424.

*Griggs et al.* v. *Duke Power Company.* 401 U.S. 424 (1971).

*Guadalupe* v. *Tempe School District.* (F. August 1971, U.S. District Court of Arizona).

Guskin, S. L., & Spicker, H. H. Educational research in mental retardation. In N. R. Ellis (Ed.), *International review of research in mental retardation* (Vol. 3). New York: Academic Press, 1968.

Hallahan, D. P., & Kauffman, J. M. *Exceptional children.* Englewood Cliffs, N.J.: Prentice-Hall, 1978.

Hambleton, R. K., Swaminathan, H., Algina, J., & Coulson, D. B. Criterion-referenced testing and measurement: A review of technical issues and development. *Review of Educational Research,* 1978, *48,* 1–48.

Haywood, H. C., Filler, J. W., Shifuran, M. A., & Chatelant, G. Behavioral assessment in mental retardation. In P. McReynolds (Ed.), *Advances in Psychological Assessment III.* San Francisco: Jossey-Bass, 1974.

Haywood, H. C., & Switzky, H. N. Children's verbal abstracting: Effects of enriched input, age, and IQ. *American Journal of Mental Deficiency,* 1974, *78,* 556–565.

Hilgard, E. R. *Introduction to psychology* (2nd ed.). New York: Harcourt, Brace, 1957.

Hobbs, N. *The futures of children.* San Francisco: Jossey-Bass, 1975.

Hofmeister, A. Integrating criterion-referenced testing and instruction. In W. Hively & M. Reynolds (Eds.), *Domain-referenced testing in special education.* Minneapolis: Leadership Training Institute/Special Education, University of Minnesota, 1975.

Holland, W. R. Language barrier as an education problem of Spanish-speaking children. *Exceptional Children,* 1960, *27,* 42–50.

Humphreys, L., & Stubbs, J. A longitudinal analysis of teacher expectation, student expectation, and student achievement. *Journal of Educational Measurement,* 1977, *14,* 261–270.

Hunter, C. P. Classroom observation instruments and teacher inservice training by school psychologists. *School Psychology Monograph,* 1977, *3*(2), 45–88.

Hurlock, E. B. An evaluation of certain incentives used in school-work. *Journal of Educational Psychology,* 1925, *16,* 145–159.

Hutson, B. A., & Niles, J. A. Trial teaching: The missing link. *Psychology in the Schools,* 1974, *11,* 188–191.

279

Jackson, G. On the report of the Ad Hoc Committee on Educational Uses of Tests with Disadvantaged Students, *American Psychologist,* 1975, *30,* 88–92.

Jacobson, L. I., Berger, S. E., Bergman, R. L., Milham, J., & Greeson, L. E. Effects of age, sex, systematic conceptual learning, acquisition of learning sets, and programmed social interaction on the intellectual and conceptual development of preschool children from poverty backgrounds. *Child Development,* 1971, *42,* 1399–1415.

Johnson, D. L. The influences of social class and race on language test performance and spontaneous speech of preschool children. *Child Development,* 1974, *45,* 517–521.

Johnson, O. G. Special education for the mentally handicapped: A paradox. *Exceptional Children,* 1962, *19,* 62–69.

Johnson, O. G. (Ed.). *Tests and measurements in child development: Handbook II.* San Francisco: Jossey-Bass, 1976.

Johnson, S. M., & Bolstad, O. D. Methodological issues in naturalistic observation: Some problems and solutions for field research. In L. A. Hamerlynck, L. C. Handy, & E. J. Mash (Eds.), *Behavior change: Methodology, concepts, and practice.* Champaign, Ill.: Research Press, 1973.

Jones, R. Labels and stigma in special education. *Exceptional Children,* 1972, *38,* 553–564.

Jones, R. R., Reid, J. B., & Patterson, M. R. Naturalistic observations in clinical assessment. In P. McReynolds (Ed.), *Advances in psychological assessment* (Vol. 3). San Francisco: Jossey-Bass, 1974.

Katz, I. Experimental studies of Negro-white relationships. In L. Berkowitz (Ed.), *Advances in experimental social psychology* (Vol. 5). New York: Academic Press, 1970.

Katz, I., Atchison, C. O., Epps, E. G., & Roberts, S. O. Race of evaluator, race of norm, and expectancy as determinants of black performance. *Journal of Experimental Social Psychology,* 1972, *8,* 1–15.

Katzell, R. A., & Dyer, F. J. Differential validity revived. *Journal of Applied Psychology,* 1977, *62,* 137–145.

Kazdin, A. E. Assessing the clinical or applied significance of behavior change through social validation. *Behavior Modification,* 1977, *1,* 427–452.

Kendrick, S. A., & Thomas, C. L. Transition from school to college. *Review of Educational Research,* 1970, *40,* 151–179.

Kennedy, D. A. Rationality, emotionality, and testing. *Journal of School Psychology,* 1978, *11,* 16–24.

Kent, R. N., & Foster, S. L. Direct observational procedures: Methodological issues in naturalistic settings. In A. R. Ciminero, K. S. Calhoun, & H. E. Adams (Eds.), *Handbook of behavioral assessment.* New York: Wiley, 1977.

Keston, M. J., & Jimenez, C. A study of the performance on English and Spanish editions of the Stanford-Binet Intelligence Test by Spanish American children. *Journal of Genetic Psychology,* 1954, *85,* 263–269.

Kimura, D. Functional asymmetry of the human brain in dichotic listening. *Cortex,* 1967, *3,* 153–178.

Kirk, S. A. Research in education. In H. A. Stevens & R. Heber (Eds.), *Mental retardation: A review of research.* Chicago: University of Chicago Press, 1964.

Kirk, S., McCarthy, J., & Kirk, W. *Illinois Test of Psycholinguistic Abilities.* Urbana, Ill.: University of Illinois Press, 1971.

Klineberg, O. *Race differences.* New York: Harper, 1935.

Klineberg, O. Tests of Negro intelligence. In O. Klineberg (Ed.), *Characteristics of the American Negro.* New York: Harper, 1944.

Kratochwill, T. R. The movement of psychological extras into ability assessment. *Journal of Special Education,* 1977, *11,* 299–311.

Kratochwill, T. R., & Severson, R. A. Process assessment: An examination of reinforcer effectiveness and predictive validity. *Journal of School Psychology,* 1977, *15,* 293–300.

Labov, W. The logic of nonstandard English. In F. Williams (Ed.), *Language and poverty.* Chicago: Markham, 1970.

Laosa, L. M. Nonbiased assessment of children's abilities: Historical antecedents and current issues. In T. Oakland (Ed.), *Psychological and educational assessment of minority children.* New York: Brunner/Mazel, 1977a.

Laosa, L. M. Socialization, education, and continuity: The importance of the sociocultural context. *Young Children,* 1977b.

*Larry P. v. Riles.* 343 F. Suppl. 1306 (1972).

*Lau v. Nichols.* 414 U.S. pp. 563–572 (January 21, 1974).

*Lebanks v. Spears,* 60 F.R.D. 135 (E.D. La. 1973).

Lerner, B. The Supreme Court and the APA, AERA, NCME test standards: Past references and future possibilities. *American Psychologist,* 1978, *33,* 915–919.

Lerner, J. W. *Children with learning disabilities: Theories, diagnosis, teaching strategies* (2nd ed.). Boston: Houghton Mifflin, 1976.

Levin, J. R. *Learner differences: Diagnosis and prescription.* Hinsdale, Ill.: Dryden Press, 1977.

Liddle, M. P. The school psychologist's role with the culturally handicapped. In J. F. Magary (Ed.), *School psychological services in theory and practice.* Englewood Cliffs, N.J.: Prentice-Hall, 1967.

Lipinski, D. P., & Nelson, R. O. Problems in the use of naturalistic observation as a means of behavioral assessment. *Behavior Therapy,* 1974, *5,* 341–351.

Lovitt, T. C. Applied behavior analysis and learning disabilities—Part I: Characteristics of ABA, general recommendations, and methodological limitations. *Journal of Learning Disabilities,* 1975, *8,* 432–443.

Lynch, W. W. Guidelines to the use of classroom observation instruments by school psychologists. *School Psychology Monograph,* 1977, *3*(1), 1–22.

MacMillan, D. L. Special education for the mildly retarded: Servant or savant? *Focus on Exceptional Children,* 1971, *2,* 1–11.

MacMillan, D., Jones, R., & Aloia, G. The mentally retarded label: A theoretical analysis and review of research. *American Journal of Mental Deficiency,* 1974, *79,* 241–261.

Macready, G. B., & Merwin, J. C. Homogeneity within item forms in domain-referenced testing. *Educational and Psychological Measurement,* 1973, *33,* 351–361.

Maller, J. B., & Zubin, J. The effects of motivation upon intelligence test scores. *Journal of Genetic Psychology,* 1932, *41,* 136–151.

*MAT-SEA-CAL Oral Proficiency Tests.* Seattle: Seattle Public Schools, 815 Fourth Ave. N., Seattle, Wash. 98109.

Medley, D. M., & Metzel, H. E. Measuring classroom behavior by systematic observation. In N. L. Gage (Ed.), *Handbook of research on teaching.* Chicago: Rand MacNally, 1963.

Mercer, J. R. Sociocultural factors in labeling mental retardates. *Peabody Journal of Education,* 1971, *48,* 188–203.

Mercer, J. R. Implications of current assessment procedures for Mexican American children. *Journal of the Association of Mexican American Educators,* 1973a, *1,* 25–33.

Mercer, J. R. *Labeling the mentally retarded.* Berkeley, Calif.: University of California Press, 1973b.

Mercer, J., & Lewis, J. *Technical manual: SOMPA: System of Multicultural Assessment.* New York: Psychological Corporation, 1978.

Mercer, J. R., & Ysseldyke, J. Designing diagnostic–intervention programs. In T. Oakland (Ed.), *Psychological and educational assessment of minority children.* New York: Brunner-Mazel, 1977.

Messick, S., & Anderson, S. Educational testing, individual development and social responsibility. In R. W. Tyler & R. M. Wolf (Eds.), *Crucial issues in testing.* Berkeley: McCutchan, 1974.

Meyers, C., Sundstrom, P., & Yoshida, R. The school psychologist and assessment in special education: A report of the Ad Hoc Committee of APA Division 16. *Monographs of Division 16 of the American Psychological Association*, 1974, *2*(1), 3–57.

Meyers, P., & Hammill, D. *Methods for learning disorders*. New York: Wiley, 1969.

Meyers, P., & Hammill, D. Deprivation or learning disability: Another dilemma for special education. *Journal of Special Education*, 1973, *7*, 409–411.

*Mills v. Board of Education of the District of Columbia*. 348 F. Suppl. 866 (DDC), 1972.

Mitchell, B. C. Predictive validity of the Metropolitan Readiness Tests and the Murphy-Durrell Reading Readiness Analysis for white and Negro pupils. *Educational and Psychological Measurement*, 1967, *27*, 1047–1054.

Murray, H. A. *Thematic Apperception Test*. Cambridge, Mass.: Harvard University Press, 1943.

*National Association of School Psychologists Principles for Professional Ethics*. National Association of School Psychologists, P.O. Box 55, Southfield, Mich. 48037, 1978.

Nelson, R. O., & Bowles, P. E. The best of two worlds—Observation with norms. *Journal of School Psychology*, 1975, *13*, 3–9.

Oakland, T. (Ed.). *Psychological and educational assessment of minority children*. New York: Brunner-Mazel, 1977.

Oakland, T., & Laosa, L. M. Professional, legislative and judicial influences on psycho-educational assessment practices on schools. In T. Oakland (Ed.), *Psychological and educational assessment of minority children*. New York: Brunner-Mazel, 1977.

Oakland, T., & Matuszek, P. Using tests in nondiscriminatory assessment. In T. Oakland (Ed.), *Psychological and educational assessment of minority children*. New York: Brunner-Mazel, 1977.

Ordiz, C. C., & Ball, M. *The Enchilada Test*. Institute for Personal Effectiveness in Children, 1972.

Ozer, M. N. *Solving learning and behavior problems of children*. San Francisco: Jossey-Bass, 1980.

Ozer, M. N. The use of operant conditioning in the evaluation of children with learning problems. *Clinical Proceedings, Children's Hospital of Washington, D.C.*, 1966, *22*, 235.

Ozer, M. N. The neurological evaluation of school-age children. *Journal of Learning Disabilities*, 1968, *1*, 84.

Ozer, M. N. Involving the teacher in the child evaluation process. *Journal of Learning Disabilities*, 1978, *11*, 422–426.

Ozer, M. N., & Dworkin, N. D. The assessment of children with learning problems: An inservice teacher training program. *Journal of Learning Disabilities*, 1974, *7*, 15–20.

Ozer, M. N., & Richardson, H. B. The diagnostic evaluation of children with learning problems: A "process" approach. *Journal of Learning Disabilities*, 1974, *7*, 30–34.

*PARC—Pennsylvania Association for Retarded Children* v. *Commonwealth of Pennsylvania*. 344 F. Suppl. 1257 (E.D. Pa. 1971).

Parton, D. A., & Ross, A. O. Social reinforcement of children's motor behavior. A review. *Psychological Bulletin*, 1965, *64*, 65–73.

Perales, A. M. The audio-lingual approach and the Spanish-speaking student. *Hispania*, 1965, *48*, 99–102.

Petersen, N. S., & Novick, M. R. An evaluation of some models for culture-fair selection. *Journal of Educational Measurement*, 1976, *13*, 3–29.

Pettigrew, T. F. *A profile of the Negro American*. Princeton, N.J.: Van Nostrand, 1964.

Piersel, W. C., Brody, G. H., Kratochwill, T. R. A further examination of motivational influences on disadvantaged children's intelligence test performance. *Child Development*, 1977, *48*, 1142–1145.

Platt, J. S. *The effect of the modified Raven's Progressive Matrices learning potential coaching procedure on Raven's posttest scores and their correlation value with productive variables of learning disabilities.* Unpublished doctoral dissertation, University of Kansas, 1976.

Pressey, S. L., & Teter, M. F. A comparison of colored and white children by means of a group scale of intelligence. *Journal of Applied Psychology,* 1919, *3,* 277–282.

Quay, H. C. Patterns of aggression, withdrawal, and immaturity. In H. C. Quay & J. S. Werry (Eds.), *Psychopathological disorders of childhood.* New York: Wiley, 1972.

Quay, L. Language, dialect, reinforcement, and the intelligence test performance of Negro children. *Child Development,* 1971, *42,* 5–15.

Raven, J. C. *Progressive matrices.* England: H. K. Lewis, 1938. (U.S. distributor: Psychological Corporation)

Reitan, R. M. A research program on the psychological effects of brain lesions in human beings. In N. R. Ellis (Ed.), *International review of research in mental retardation* (Vol. 1). New York: Academic Press, 1966.

Reitan, R. M. Psychological effects of cerebral lesions in children of early school age. In R. M. Reitan & L. A. Davison (Eds.), *Clinical neuropsychology: Current status and applications.* Washington, D.C.: Winston, 1974.

Reitan, R. M., & Davison, L. A. (Eds.). *Clinical neuropsychology: Current status and applications.* Washington, D.C.: Winston, 1974.

Reschly, D. J. Nonbiased assessment. In G. Phye & D. J. Reschly (Eds.), *School psychology: Perspectives and issues.* New York: Academic Press, 1979.

Reschly, D. J., & Lamprecht, M. Expectancy effects of labels: Fact or artifact? *Exceptional Children,* in press.

Reschly, D. J., & Sabers, D. *An examination of test bias for black, Chicano, and Native American Papago children.* Unpublished manuscript, Iowa State University, 1978.

Resnick, L. B., Wang, M. C., & Kaplan, J. Task analysis in curriculum design: A hierarchically sequenced introductory mathematics curriculum. *Journal of Applied Behavior Analysis,* 1973, *6,* 679–710.

Riessman, F. *The culturally deprived child.* New York: Harper, 1962.

Rorschach, H. [*Psychodiagnostics: A diagnostic test based on perception*] (P. Lenkau & B. Kronenberg, trans.). Berne: Hans-Huber, 1942. (First German edition, 1921; U.S. distributor, Grune & Stratton.)

Rosenshine, B., & Furst, N. The use of direct observation to study teaching. In R. Travers (Ed.), *Second handbook of research on teaching.* Chicago: Rand McNally, 1973.

Rosenthal, R., & Jacobsen, L. *Pygmalion in the classroom: Teacher expectations and pupils' intellectual development.* New York: Holt, 1968.

Roth, G., & McManis, D. L. Social reinforcement effects on block design performance of organic and nonorganic retarded adults. *American Journal of Mental Deficiency,* 1972, *77,* 181–189.

Sackett, G. P. (Ed.). *Observing behavior* (Vol. 1): *Theory and applications in mental retardation.* Baltimore: University Park Press, 1978a.

Sackett, G. P. (Ed.). *Observing behavior* (Vol. 2): *Data collection and analysis methods.* Baltimore: University Park Press, 1978b.

Sacks, E. L. Intelligence scores as a function of experimentally established social relationships between child and examiner. *Journal of Abnormal and Social Psychology,* 1952, *47,* 354–358.

Salvia, J., & Ysseldyke, J. E. *Assessment in special and remedial education.* Boston: Houghton Mifflin, 1978.

Samuda, R. J. *Psychological testing of American minorities: Issues and consequences.* New York: Dodd, Mead, 1975.

Samuel, W. Observed IQ as a function of test atmosphere, tester expectation, and race of tester: A replication for female subjects. *Journal of Educational Psychology,* 1977, *69,* 593–604.

Sattler, J. M. Statistical reanalysis of Candady's "The effect of 'rapport' on the IQ: A new approach to the problem of racial psychology." *Psychological Reports*, 1966, *19*, 1203–1206.

Sattler, J. M. Racial "experimenter effects" in experimentation, testing, interviewing, and psycho-therapy. *Psychological Bulletin*, 1970, *73*, 137–160.

Sattler, J. M. Intelligence testing of ethnic minority groups and culturally disadvantaged children. In L. Mann & D. A. Sabatino (Eds.), *The first review of special education* (Vol. 2). Philadelphia: JSE Press, 1973.

Sattler, J. M. *Assessment of children's intelligence.* Philadelphia: Saunders, 1974.

Savage, J. E., Jr., & Bowers, N. D. *Tester's influence on children's intellectual performance.* Washington, D.C.: U.S. Office of Education, 1972. (ERIC microfiche No. 064 329).

Schultz, C. B., & Sherman, R. H. Social class, development, and differences in reinforcer effectiveness. *Review of Educational Research*, 1976, *46*, 25–29.

Seitz, V., Abelson, W. D., Levine, E., & Zigler, E. Effects of place of testing on the Peabody Picture Vocabulary Test scores of disadvantaged Headstart and non-Headstart children. *Child Development*, 1975, *46*, 481–486.

Severson, R. A. The case for the classroom management consultant. *Experimental Publications System*, 1971, *11*. (Ms. No. 397-36)

Severson, R. A. Behavior therapy with learning disabled children. In M. B. Rosenberg (Ed.), *Educational Therapy* (Vol. 3). Seattle: Straub, 1973.

Sewell, T. E., & Severson, R. A. Learning potential and intelligence as cognitive predictors of achievement in first grade children. *Journal of Educational Psychology*, 1974, *66*, 948–965.

Silverman, R. J., Boa, J. K., & Russell, R. H. *Oral language tests for bilingual students. An evaluation of language dominance and proficiency instruments* (No. 300-75-0329). U.S. Department of Health, Education and Welfare, Office of Education, 1976.

Sitko, M. C., Fink, A. H., & Gillespie, P. H. Utilizing systematic observation for decision making in school psychology. *School Psychology Monograph*, 1977, *3*(1), 23–44.

Smeets, P. M., & Striefel, S. The effects of different reinforcement conditions on the test performance of multihandicapped deaf children. *Journal of Applied Behavioral Research*, 1975, *8*, 83–89.

Snow, R. E. Review of R. Rosenthal and L. Jacobson "Pygmalion in the classroom." *Contemporary Psychology*, 1969, *14*, 197–199.

Stanley, J. C., & Porter, A. C. Correlation of Scholastic Aptitude Test scores with college grades for Negroes versus whites. *Journal of Educational Measurement*, 1967, *4*, 199–218.

Strong, A. C. Three hundred fifty white and colored children measured by the Binet-Simon Measuring Scale of Intelligence: A comparative study. *Pedogogical Seminary*, 1913, *20*, 485–515.

Strother, C. R. Evaluating intelligence of children handicapped by cerebral palsy. *Crippled Child*, 1945, *23*, 82–83.

Struthers, J., & DeAvila, E. A. *Development of a group measure to assess the extent of prelogical and precausal thinking in primary school age children.* Paper presented at the Annual Convention of the National Science Teachers' Association, Detroit, 1967.

Subkoviak, M. J., & Baker, F. B. Test theory. In L. S. Shulman (Ed.), *Review of research in education.* Itasca, Ill.: Peacock, 1977.

Swanson, J. E. *Learning potential as a predictor of behavioral changes in learning disabled elementary students.* Unpublished master's thesis, University of Kansas, 1976.

Swanson, R. A. Conceptual behavior battery: Conservation of numbers. In O. G. Johnson (Ed.), *Tests and measurements in child development: Handbook II.* San Francisco: Jossey-Bass, 1976a.

Swanson, R. A. Conceptual behavior battery: Numerical operations. In O. G. Johnson (Ed.), *Tests and measurements in child development: Handbook II.* San Francisco: Jossey-Bass, 1976b.

Swanson, R. A. Conceptual behavior battery: Seriation A and B. In O. G. Johnson (Eds.), *Tests and measurements in child development: Handbook II*. San Francisco: Jossey-Bass, 1976c.

Sweet, R. C. *Variations in the intelligence test performance of lower-class children as a function of feedback or monetary reinforcement*. (Doctoral dissertation, University of Wisconsin). Ann Arbor, Mich.: University Microfilms, 1969, No. 70-3721.

Temp, G. Test bias: Validity of the SAT for blacks and whites in thirteen integrated institutions. *Journal of Educational Measurement*, 1971, *8*, 245–251.

Terman, L. M., & Merrill, M. A. *Manual for the third revision, Stanford-Binet Intelligence Scale*. Boston: Houghton Mifflin, 1960.

Thomas, A., Hertzig, M. E., Dryman, I., & Fernandez, P. Examiner effects in IQ testing of Puerto Rican working class children. *American Journal of Orthopsychiatry*, 1971, *41*, 809–821.

Thorndike, R. L. Review of R. Rosenthal and L. Jacobson, "Pygmalion in the classroom." *American Educational Research Journal*, 1968, *5*, 708–711.

Thorndike, R. L. Educational measurement for the seventies. In R. L. Thorndike (Ed.), *Educational measurement* (2nd ed.). Washington, D.C.: American Council on Education, 1971.

Thorndike, R. L. Concepts of culture-fairness. In R. W. Tyler & R. M. Wolf, *Crucial issues in testing*. Berkeley: McCutchan, 1974.

Tiber, N., & Kennedy, W. A. The effects of incentives on intelligence test performances of different social groups. *Journal of Consulting Psychology*, 1964, *28*, 187.

Tractenberg, P. L., & Jacoby, E. Pupil testing: A legal view. *Kappan*, 1977, *59*, 249–254.

Tucker, J. Operationalizing the diagnostic–intervention process. In T. Oakland (Ed.), *Psychological and educational assessment of minority children*. New York: Brunner-Mazel, 1977.

U.S. Department of Health, Education and Welfare, Office of Civil Rights. *Elimination of discrimination in the assignment of children to special education classes for the mentally retarded*. Mimeo to state and local education agencies, November 28, 1972.

*U.S.* v. *Georgia Power Company*, 474 F2d 906 (1973).

Valentine, C. A. Deficit difference and bicultural models of Afro-American behavior. *Harvard Educational Review*, 1971, *41*, 137–157.

Vernon, P. E. Ability factors and environmental influences. *American Psychologist*, 1965, *20*, 723–733.

Watson, P. IQ: The racial gap. *Psychology Today*, 1972, *6*(4), pp. 48–50; 97–99.

Wechsler, D. *Manual for the Wechsler Intelligence Scale for Children*. New York: Psychological Corporation, 1949.

Wechsler, D. *Manual for the Wechsler Adult Intelligence Scale*. New York: Psychological Corporation, 1955.

Wechsler, D. *Manual for the Wechsler Intelligence Scale for Children—Revised*. New York: Psychological Corporation, 1974.

Weick, K. E. Systematic observational methods. In G. Lindzey & E. Dronson (Eds.), *The handbook of social psychology* (Vol. 2). Don Mills, Ontario: Addison-Wesley, 1968.

Weinberg, R., & Wood, R. *Observation of pupils and teachers in mainstream and special education settings: Alternative strategies*. Minneapolis: Leadership Training Institute/Special Education, University of Minnesota, 1975.

Williams, R. Danger: Testing and dehumanizing black children. *Clinical Child Psychology Newsletter*, 1970, *9*(1), 5–6.

Williams, R. Danger: Testing and dehumanizing black children. *The School Psychologist*, 1971, *25*, 11–13.

Williams, R. *The BITCH-100: A culture specific test*. Paper presented at the 80th Annual Convention of the American Psychological Association, Honolulu, September 1972.

Williams. R. The problem of the match and mismatch in testing black children. In L. Miller

(Ed.), *The testing of black students: A symposium.* Englewood Cliffs, N.J.: Prentice-Hall, 1974.

Wolf, M. M. Social validity: The case for subjective measurement or how applied behavior analysis is finding its heart. *Journal of Applied Behavior Analysis,* 1978, *11,* 203–214.

Wright, H. F. Observational child study. In P. H. Hussen (Ed.), *Handbook of research methods in child development.* New York: Wiley, 1960.

Yando, R., Zigler, E., & Gates, M. The influence of Negro and white teachers rated as effective or noneffective on the performance of Negro and white lower-class children. *Developmental Psychology,* 1971, *5,* 290–299.

Yoshida, R., & Meyers, E. Effects of labeling as educable mentally retarded on teachers; Expectancies for change in students' performance. *Journal of Educational Psychology,* 1975, *67,* 521–527.

Ysseldyke, J. E. Diagnostic prescriptive teaching: The search for aptitude–treatment interactions. In L. Mann & D. A. Sabatino (Eds.), *The First Review of Special Education* (Vol. 1). Philadelphia: JSE Press, 1973.

Ysseldyke, J., & Foster, G. Bias in teachers' observations of emotionally disturbed and learning disabled children. *Exceptional Children,* 1978, *44,* 613–615.

Ysseldyke, J. E., & Salvia, J. Diagnostic–prescriptive teaching: Two models. *Exceptional Children,* 1974, *41,* 181–186.

Zigler, E., Abelson, W. D., & Seitz, V. Motivational factors in the performance of economically disadvantaged children on the Peabody Picture Vocabulary Test. *Child Development,* 1973, *44,* 294–303.

Zigler, E., & Butterfield, E. C. Motivational aspects of changes in IQ test performance of culturally deprived nursery school children. *Child Development,* 1968, *39,* 1–14.

Zucker, S., & Prieto, A. Ethnicity and teacher bias in educational decisions. *Instructional Psychology,* 1977, *4,* 2–5.

# LABELS AND EXPECTANCIES FOR HANDICAPPED CHILDREN AND YOUTH

Robert Algozzine
Cecil D. Mercer
*University of Florida*

The field of special education exists because some children seem to require more intensive educational programming than that traditionally available in regular classrooms. To become eligible for this special treatment, exceptional children must be identified and then placed into special classes. As a result of this initial assessment, a label is often assigned to the child to indicate his/her categorical variety of handicap. For the most part, the label has become the basis for classification, and classification is seen as necessary for allocation of treatment.

## CLASSIFICATION IN SPECIAL EDUCATION

Historically, when children thought to be abnormal (i.e., classified differently) were excluded from public schools, the pragmatic need for a sophisticated classification system was not apparent; however, when public schools began to provide services to special children the need for more precise classification systems increased. Early treatment programs for special children originated during the 18th and 19th centuries (Schmid, 1979). Starting with these initial programs, the need for labeling and classifying children has intensified.

Numerous labels have been assigned to exceptional children. For example, Cruickshank (1972) notes that approximately 40 labels have

R. Algozzine is indebted to John Salvia for planting the "labeling controversy" seed and fostering the growth of that seed and the author's efforts toward resolving the controversy during his career. The professional assistance of Karen Algozzine, Leila R. Cantara, Don Goldberg, and Sandra Johnson in preparation of this chapter is also acknowledged, as is the personal loss to Greg Aloia which prevented his participation in the project.

been used to describe the exceptional category now referred to as specific learning disabilities. Exhaustive lists of labels also exist for other categories of exceptionalities (Smith & Neisworth, 1975). Currently, the Education for All Handicapped Children Act of 1975 (PL 94-142) uses nine separate categories of handicapped children; however, Haring (1978) notes that some special educators are promoting a two-category system— the mildly handicapped and the severely handicapped.

The practice of labeling and classifying individuals has become a major social issue. The magnitude of the problem is apparent. For example, in the summer of 1972, Elliot Richardson, then the Secretary of the Department of Health, Education and Welfare, commissioned a systematic examination of current policies in an attempt to develop recommendations for improving the classification system. Dr. Nicholas Hobbs of Vanderbilt University headed the major review and organized the efforts of over 30 work groups studying various aspects of the labeling process. The findings of this investigation are presented in a summary report, *The Futures of Children* (Hobbs, 1975) and a two-volume source book, *Issues in the Classification of Children* (Hobbs, 1976).

Many attempts to investigate labeling have been confounded by confusing it with other separate but related issues (e.g., placement, test bias). The labeling issue in special education is relatively straightforward (i.e., what happens when a categorical label is assigned to a child?). The effects of this process may be examined from two perspectives: (1) the impact of the label on the perceptions and behavior of the child himself, and (2) the impact of the label on the perceptions and behavior of others who interact with the child; the two are closely related. In essence, the labeling issue focuses on the question, "Does the label influence or generate perceptions and behaviors which do more harm than good for the child?"

Since the activity of classifying and labeling is to some extent an arbitrary convenience, these effects are important. As Szasz (1970) points out, "Today, particularly in the affluent West, all of the difficulties and problems of living are considered psychiatric diseases, and everyone (but the diagnosticians) is considered mentally ill" (p. 4); the activity is omnipresent, the consequences are therefore important. From this standpoint, there is nothing inherently good or bad about labeling—it is simply a behavior we engage in to bring order to our lives. As with any other behavior, it gains value by the effect it has on our lives.

In our discussion of the labeling issue, the focus will be on those effects which occur after the assignment of the label. It is recognized that the issue itself includes several other factors. For example, assignment of labels is possible because a set of categories exists which has been arbitrarily selected from the domain of categories which is available. Similarly, the categories have been developed and exist primarily due to a consental agreement among "professionals;" this in no way implies that the categories are qualitatively valuable or pragmatically valid. Finally, identification procedures must exist, prior to the assignment of a label, to link the basic assumptions to final outcomes. With these considerations qualified, positive and negative aspects of labeling will be discussed.

**Positive aspects of labeling**

The primary objective that ultimately permeates the rationale for labeling exceptional children is that the label will directly or indirectly facilitate treatment. Labeling and consequent treatment are more conspicuous in some instances than in others. For example, the label "hearing impaired" more often implies specific treatments than the label "learning disabled." The use of labeling to improve communications among researchers, establish prevalence estimates, determine etiologies, design prevention programs, place in special education, and obtain funds are examples of indirect and direct uses of labeling to provide or improve treatment efforts.

Gallagher (1976) discusses three positive uses of labeling: (1) it can lead to differentiated treatment; (2) it facilitates the search for etiology and prevention of various disorders; and (3) it serves to increase public awareness and secure more funding for research, training, and service delivery. The perspective presented here is that a primary advantage is realized when children receive increasingly beneficial treatment as a function of being labeled.

**Negative aspects of labeling**

The problems of labeling may be viewed along two major fronts. First, to the extent that a label fails directly or indirectly to lead to differentiated treatment for an individual child, it fails to serve a useful function. Second, labeling may actually be harmful to the child. When a child's perceptions and behaviors, as well as those of others, are altered by labeling in a manner which results in restricting the social, emotional, and/or academic growth of the child, labels are harmful.

The specific harmful aspects of labeling include the following:

1.   Labels may causes individuals to develop negative feelings about themselves and to act differently than nonlabeled peers.

2.   Labels may be stigmatizing, causing others to view the labeled individual in a negative manner and to openly express those views.

3.   Labels may serve as expectancy-generating stimuli that affect interpersonal relationships.

The first and second harmful aspects of labeling have been discussed in detail elsewhere (Goffman, 1963; Jones, 1977); it is the expectancy-generating quality of labels that is the focus of this chapter. As Gallagher (1976) pointed out, labels are likely to be around for some time; the activity of classifying and categorizing is a fundamental to human survival. It is only through systematic analysis of this labeling activity as applied to children and the expectancies that it produces that meaningful, productive efforts may be realized from it.

## EXPECTANCIES IN SPECIAL EDUCATION

One's expectations (or expectancies in general) may be defined as the predicted probability of the occurrence of a future event. Exceptional children may have expectations that specific events will occur in their environments, or that general conditions which occurred previously will continue to prevail. Parents and teachers may also have specific and generalized expectancies for their own behavior as well as that of the children with whom they interact. It has been demonstrated that these probabilities of future events (i.e., expectancies) are influential in personal and interpersonal performance.

### Personal performance and expectancies

One of the earliest attempts to explain some of the relationships between expectancies and performances was made by Rotter (1954). Building on the work of Hull, Thorndike, and others, Rotter postulated that behavior was a function of the expectancy that that behavior would lead to reinforcement and the perceived value of the reinforcing event (Kazden, 1978; Mercer & Snell, 1977; Rotter, 1975). Within this context, expectancies are thought of as general or specific. Generalized expectancies are based on previous experience in similar situations and are viewed as more global in nature than specific expectancies, which relate primarily to particular situations. Rotter's model has received considerable support (Cromwell, 1963; Mercer & Snell, 1977).

An alternative explanation for the causes of behavior has been suggested by Weiner's (1974) attribution theory. An *attribution* can be thought of as the "inference an observer makes about the causes of behavior—either his own or another person's" (Bar-Tal, 1978, p. 259), or what one expects to happen based on what one thinks should happen. Weiner, Frieze, Kukla, Reed, Rest, et al. (1971) analyzed achievement-related behavior as a fuction of an individual's perceived causes for success and failure. In discussing this "attributional model of achieve-ment-related behavior," Bar-Tal (1978) presented four primary factors which have been used as causal ascriptions for behavior: luck, ability, effort, and task difficulty. A similar discussion has been presented elsewhere (Falbo, 1975; Frieze, 1973; Jones, 1977; Weiner, Heckhausen, Meyer, & Cook, 1972).

Within Weiner's framework, ability and effort are considered as internal, or under the individual's control, while luck and task difficulty are seen as external, or not under the individual's control. The extent to which an individual perceives events to be the result of his/her own actions or beyond his or her own control has also been referred to as *locus of control* (Lefcourt, 1972; Mercer & Snell, 1977; Rotter, 1966).

Locus of control, then, differentiates causal ascriptions for behavior along one dimension. A second dimension that is seen as differentiating the causal elements within Weiner's model is their stability over time. Luck and effort are considered unstable, while ability and task difficulty are thought to be stable factors. A variety of studies have provided empirical support for the relationships posited by Weiner and his associates (Jones, 1977).

It should be evident that the models proposed by Rotter and Weiner are related. Success or failure attributed to a stable dimension (i.e., ability or task difficulty) within Weiner's model would be likely to result in expectations of similar future performance, while performance attributed to unstable causes (i.e., luck or effort) would be likely to result in altered expectations for future performance (Bar-Tal, 1978). Success or failure at a task may influence attributions as well as expectancies. Success and failure may be seen as the source of attributions and expectancies which may be viewed as the source of success or failure (performance). Performance can be seen as the basis for performance; however, it is important to note that this seemingly oversimplified relationship is mediated by expectancies and attributions.

### Performance predictions and expectancies

Similarly, within this context, the causal ascriptions for a disability (or handicap) may have considerable impact on the decisions made about individuals who possess that disability. For example, if a handicap is seen as stable and internal, particular types of performances may come to be expected from individuals who possess that disability. Similarly, the individual's treatability may be seen as more or less predictable dependent upon the attributions and expectations generated by the handicap. The nature of intervention efforts for an individual whose disability was thought to be internal but changeable (unstable) would be likely to be different.

Some research to support these relationships has been completed. For example, Palmer (1977) found that teachers' attributions for successful or unsuccessful student performances were directly related to their instructional prescriptions. In a study by Severance and Gasstrom (1977), the attributes of ability, effort, and task difficulty, as well as expectations for future performance, were perceived differently for children labeled as "mentally retarded" than for those not similarly labeled. In another investigation, Lavelle (1977) found that parents of normal achievers attributed their children's success to ability and failure to luck or lack of effort. The results were somewhat different for handicapped children. Parents of retarded children attributed success to luck and failure to lack of ability. In light of Weiner's model, it would appear that the parents of the normal children studied by Lavelle had high expectancies for their children's success and low expectancies for their failure. Similarly, it seems the retarded children's parents had low expectancies for their children's success and high expectancies for their failure. Lavelle also found that parents of "educationally handicapped" children attributed both success and failure to an unstable factor (i.e., effort). This suggests that their expectations varied as a function of their child's success or failure and the way in which they viewed it; equally, the results seem to support a rather unstable nature for educational handicaps as opposed to retardation and/or normalcy.

Some studies of the nature of personal performance expectancies held by exceptional children have also been completed. Children identified as mentally retarded have been shown to have high expectancies for failure relative to normal children. This characteristic was thought to result in a failure-avoidance motivational system rather than a success-striving motivational system (Cromwell, 1963); however, Mercer and Snell (1977) suggested that that may not be the case and indicated that several variables interact to produce any effects. Retarded children exhibit a tendency *not to do;* therefore, their opportunities for success are minimized. They do tend to respond favorably to success as opposed to failure experiences; however, they have come to expect success much less than failure. Keogh, Cahill, and MacMillan (1972) found that educationally handicapped boys attributed task interruption to their own lack of ability. A variety of other studies have investigated the effects of success or failure on the performance of exceptional children (Mercer & Snell, 1977).

### Interpersonal performances and expectancies

In addition to the explanations of the relationship between expectancies and personal performances which have been discussed, interpersonal predictions of the probabilities of the future behavior of others have also been studied. In summarizing the literature related to the influence of interpersonal expectancies on student performances, Brophy and Good (1974) stated that "the idea that teacher expectations can function as self-fulfilling prophesies appears to be an established fact rather than a mere hypothesis" (p. 77). Similarly, they have noted that the observation (or expectation) that a child is a low achiever may result in different teacher–pupil interactions than the observation (or expectation) that a child is a high achiever. This phenomenon, coupled with possible attributions which suggest that the achievement is stable or unstable, may result in biased interactions and subsequently different performances for some children.

A variety of factors have been shown to influence teachers' predictions of the future performance (i.e., expectations) of their children; actual interactions with those children as well as their classroom achievements have also been shown to be differentially affected by teachers' expectancies (Baker & Crist, 1971; Brophy & Good, 1974; Dusek, 1975). Within this context, the biasing factors may be thought of as naturally occurring or experimentally induced. Organismic characteristics upon which individuals may be sorted and which result in differential predictions of future performances have been shown to have powerfully biasing effects. In fact, such naturally occurring factors as appearance (Algozzine, 1975; Berscheid & Walster, 1974; Ross & Salvia, 1975; Salvia, Sheare, & Algozzine, 1975), race (Coates, 1972; Datta, Schaefer, & Davis, 1968; Rubovitz & Maehr, 1973), sex (Carter, 1952; Jackson & Lahaderne, 1967; Lippett & Gold, 1959; Meyer & Thompson, 1956; Palardy, 1969), behavior (Algozzine, 1977; Algozzine, Mercer, & Countermine, 1977; Curran, 1977), and achievement level of older siblings (Seaver, 1973) have been shown to affect differentially the formation and transmission of classroom teachers' expectations.

Experimentally induced expectations differ from naturally occurring ones in that the former are manipulated by the researcher in an attempt to bring about differential outcomes for different levels of the expectancy biaser. The now classic Oak School experiment (Rosenthal & Jacobsen, 1968) stimulated a tremendous number of other experimental attempts to produce differential teacher–pupil interactions (both expected and actual ones). While this study has met with considerable criticism (Elashoff & Snow, 1971; Jensen, 1969; Snow, 1969; Thorndike, 1968), a number of investigators have shown that teachers hold differential expectations and/or perform differently with children for whom they hold high or low expectations (Beez, 1970; Brophy & Good, 1974; Dusek, 1975; Medinnus & Unruh, 1971; Meichenbaum, Bowers, & Ross, 1969; Rothbart, Dalfen, & Barrett, 1971; Rubovitz & Maehr, 1971).

The mechanism through which interpersonal expectancies seem to operate has been discussed by many researchers (Berger, Cohen, & Zelditch, 1966; Brophy & Good, 1974; Entwistle & Webster, 1972; Finn, 1972; Foster, 1976; Jones, 1977; McGuire, 1966; Schain, 1972; Sutherland, 1976). In general, models for explaining teacher expectancy effects suggest that an individual must attend to, understand, and retain the stimulus generating the expectancy prior to responding in harmony with it. Within this context, expectancy-generating stimuli may be thought of as cues that help in organizing one's knowledge, personel perceptions, and behavior. They serve as distinguishing features to which individuals assign various other characteristics, qualities, and/or behavioral attributes in an attempt to establish, alter, or verify a personal belief system. Many authors have discussed this general topic from a variety of theoretical perspectives (Heider, 1958; Jones, 1977; Kelly, 1955).

When stimuli present themselves (or are presented) to target individuals who may react to them, the interpersonal expectancy model is set into operation. If teachers, parents, and/or other caretakers have attended to, comprehended, and retained the stimulus, it may serve to establish, alter, or verify a belief or preconceived bias within them. This first level of transmission (i.e., to the target subject) is clearly essential for any additional effects to be observed.

After the initial phase has occurred, the next involves transmission to an individual on whom the now existent bias shall have its effect. Of course, this child or subject must attend to, comprehend, and retain the transmitted bias for it to establish, alter, or verify any expectancy effects which may result in differential performances by that subject. It must be stressed that effects at this level are clearly a function of establishments, alterations, and verifications in other individuals. To observe only outcomes (i.e., effects) may lead to spurious conclusions unless each previous stage of transmission has been shown to be operational with regard to the stimuli being investigated.

Research regarding many expectancy-generating stimuli has been conducted relative to various levels of transmission and effects. For example, teachers have been shown to rate identical case studies differently depending upon the type of picture (i.e., a previously rated attractive or unattractive child) attached (Ross & Salvia, 1975). In addition to establishing biases in teachers, attractiveness has been shown to be a differentiating factor in the self-concept and peer acceptance scores of children (Salvia, Sheare, & Algozzine, 1975); equally, classroom interactions and school performance records of attractive and unattractive peers have been found to be different (Adams & Cohen, 1974; Algozzine, 1976b; Salvia, Algozzine, & Sheare, 1977). Similar findings relative to other biasing factors are readily available (Brophy & Good, 1974; Dusek, 1975; Jones, 1977).

It is evident that personal and interpersonal expectancies are important factors in the lives of children. An individual's performance in a given situation or at a selected task would be likely to be influenced by the expectancies he/she holds relative to that performance as well as the predicted probabilities for performance held by others. Of importance to the field of special education is the extent to which labels operate as stimuli that generate expectancies.

## LABELS IN SPECIAL EDUCATION

In discussing a labeling approach to understanding deviance, Jones (1977, p. 90) suggested that two key factors are important:

1. The idea that particular types or categories of people are expected by others to display certain additional characteristics and/or to be consistently deviant.
2. Once we have discovered that another is a certain type, we react to them in ways that push them into secondary and/or career deviance, thereby confirming our initial expectations.

It seems then that labels serve as convenient reference points upon which to make predictions as to the future behaviors of labeled individuals, as well as representing key words with which a variety of other characteristics may be associated. It is when these implied stereotypical characteristics and/or expectations are negative that labels become a problem. Few people would mind being called a "genius" unless that meant they would always be expected to say and do brilliant things and to only associate with other people thought to be in the same category. Similarly, it is not the special education label per se that is problemmatic, but the fact that the label serves as an expectancy-generating stimulus which has less than favorable associated qualities.

In a theoretical analysis and review of research regarding the mentally retarded label, MacMillan, Jones, and Aloia (1974) suggested that the labeling phenomenon is highly complex; they discussed a variety of factors which they felt contributed to the effects of being labeled (i.e., multiple labels, formal versus informal labeling, acceptance or denial of validity of labels, prelabeling experiences, and others). These factors are clearly related to those offered by Brophy and Good (1974) in their discussion of the reasons expectancy effects appear in some studies and not in others.

**Analysis of labeling literature**

Differential effects have been demonstrated in studies which have manipulated various special education labels; selected investigations are presented in Table 1. It should be noted that no attempt has been made to present an exhaustive tabular summary of the labeling literature. Those studies that are included in Table 1 were reported concurrently with or subsequent to the MacMillan, Jones, and Aloia (1974) review; an attempt was also made to select at least one investigation which related to each stage of expectancy transmission previously discussed. When possible, effects with various types of target groups (i.e., parents and teachers) have been included.

In light of the results presented in Table 1 and those investigations reviewed but not included in that table, it is reasonable to conclude that labels serve as expectancy-generating stimuli. Within the context of biasing factors which result in differential expectancy effects (Brophy & Good, 1974), labels seem to represent powerfully biasing stimuli. When extreme categorical groups were compared, differential effects were observed (Foster, Ysseldyke, & Reese, 1975; Holroyd & McArthur, 1976; Sutherland & Algozzine, 1979); however, when more similar groups were compared, the results were more equivocal (Algozzine, Mercer, & Countermine, 1977; Algozzine & Sutherland, 1977; Foster & Ysseldyke, 1976; Mooney & Algozzine, 1978). It must be noted that the notion of "extreme groups" is clearly a relative one; that is, the disability groups represented in the Foster and Ysseldyke study were seen as different from the normal group and, similarly, the disability groups in the Algozzine and Sutherland study may be viewed as "extremes" although not in comparison to a normal group.

## Establishing a research perspective

The expectancy-generating effects of labels have been demonstrated to a similar degree in experimental and naturally occurring situations of short and long duration. Moreover, the expectations of a variety of different individuals have been shown to be influenced by labels. It is important, however, to note that the studies selected were representative of a hierarchical analysis approach to interpersonal expectancies. All studies that investigated initial transmission to a target subject demonstrated differential effects. Only one investigation (Dembo, Yoshida, Reilly, Reilly, 1978) was included which assumed that this initial level of transmission had occurred. No differential effects were observed, but it is difficult to assess the importance of this result. If no effects were transmitted to the target group (i.e., the special education teachers of the children studied), then one would not expect any to be present in a study of transmissions at a higher level (i.e., to the children). No studies have shown that special education teachers negatively react to special education labels; if anything, this group of professionals is more tolerant and less susceptible to negative biasing. There is no way of knowing the actual reasons for the Dembo et al. outcome since no analysis of initial expectancy transmission was conducted.

MacMillan, Jones, and Aloia (1974) reviewed many similar studies (some demonstrated effects and others did not) and concluded that "regardless of the dependent measure employed [self-concept, acceptance, lowered achievement, postschool adjustment], the evidence does not support the conclusion that there is a detrimental labeling effect" (p. 252). The dependent measures suggested are clearly those one might analyze in subsequent stages of expectancy transmissions. From the perspective presented here, it appears that one should not study the effects of expectancy-generating stimuli (i.e., labels) without considering a *sequential* analysis of these effects. If the initial target is uneffected by the label or expectancy-generating stimulus, it is unlikely that differential performances will occur in other individuals with whom the target subject might interact.

While many studies have demonstrated that target subjects can be influenced by labels, few have examined the extent to which effects are transmitted to labeled individuals. Two are noteworthy. Farina, Thaw, Felner, and Hust (1976) utilized "normal," "mentally retarded" (due to "congenital defect since birth"), and "mentally ill" confederates as subjects for electric shocks administered by undergraduate students (i.e., initial targets). An analysis of results indicated that the "mentally

297

**TABLE 1**

**SELECTED INVESTIGATIONS WITHIN INTERPERSONAL EXPECTANCY MODEL**

| Investigators | Label(s) being studied[a] | Method of investigation | Target individual(s) | Results |
|---|---|---|---|---|
| Gottlieb, 1974 | MR vs. N, competent vs. incompetent | Videotaped presentation, experimental comparison | Transmission to classmates | Fourth-grade children were more influenced by degree of competence than by labels |
| Foster et al., 1975 | ED vs. N | Hypothetical and videotaped presentations, experimental comparisons | Transmission to undergraduate students | ED child rated more negatively in both presentations |
| Holroyd & McArthur, 1976 | Autism, Down's syndrome, and outpatient clinical | Naturalistic comparison | Transmission to affected children's mothers | Some differences between mothers of autistic and MR children, relative severity of problem, and family integration; between mothers of autistic children and others relative to general problems; and between mothers of subnormal children and others relative to general retardation and social dependency |

| Study | Labels Compared | Method | Transmission | Findings |
|---|---|---|---|---|
| Foster & Ysseldyke, 1976 | LD vs. ED vs. MR vs. N | Hypothetical and videotaped presentations, experimental comparison | Transmission to teachers | More negative expectancies held for MR than for LD or ED; however, all special education categories viewed less favorably than N |
| Copeland & Weissbrod, 1976 | MR vs. non-MR | Stories in which labeled or nonlabeled child engaged in various sex-typed behaviors | Transmission to teachers of N and MR children as well as caretakers of MR children | Stories were rated as typical when nonretarded children were portrayed in sex-appropriate, desirable behavior and when MR children were portrayed in undesirable behavior regardless of sex appropriateness |
| Moores & Grant, 1976 | MR | Completion of questionnaires regarding expectations | Transmission to nurses caring for hospitalized MR adults | Differences in staff expectations were noted |
| Gottlieb & Siperstein, 1976 | MR vs. four similar labels which differed in severity and age portrayed | Experimental comparison of subjects assigned to one of five label conditions | Transmission to undergraduate students studying mental retardation | Nondescript MR person rated between mildly MR and severely MR ones in terms of favorability of respondents' attitudes |

(continued)

**TABLE 1** *(continued)*

| Investigators | Label(s) being studied[a] | Method of investigation | Target individual(s) | Results |
|---|---|---|---|---|
| Farina et al., 1976 | N vs. MR vs. mentally ill | Labeled confederates, experimental comparison | Transmission to undergraduate students; transmission to labeled subject | Shocks to subject thought to be organically MR were shorter and of less intensity than those to N or mentally ill (nonorganic) subjects |
| Algozzine et al., 1977 | LD vs. ED | Hypothesized child was portrayed with label appropriate or inappropriate behaviors | Transmission to undergraduate teachers-in-training | Characteristic behaviors were viewed differently when thought to be exhibited by an LD or ED child |
| Algozzine & Sutherland, 1977 | LD vs. ED | Hypothetical child exhibiting aggressive behavior was rated in four case studies, experimental comparison | Transmission to undergraduate teachers-in-training | Child was viewed more favorably when thought to be LD than when thought to be ED |
| Seitz & Geske, 1977 | MR vs. non-MR | Videotaped presentations | Transmission to mothers of N | Mothers rated MR differently whether or not the label |

| Author/Year | Comparison | Manipulation | Subjects | Results |
|---|---|---|---|---|
| | | of mother–child interactions were presented in labeled and nonlabeled conditions | children and graduate students | was present; graduate students did not respond similarly; some altruistic response tendencies were noted relative to MR-labeled child |
| Siperstein & Gottlieb, 1977 | Down's syndrome vs. children with N appearance in competent or less competent portrayal | Audiotaped presentations of spelling performance depicted for MR or non-MR child | Transmission to fourth and fifth graders | Competent, nonstigmatized children were rated higher than noncompetent, stigmatized children; some respondent sex and popularity differences were indicated |
| Severance & Gasstrom, 1977 | MR vs. non-MR | Description of 10-year-old boy or girl was manipulated to portray success or failure at a puzzle; MR label was sometimes present | Transmission to undergraduate students | Ability, effort, and task difficulty were perceived differently for labeled as compared to unlabeled target children |

(continued)

**TABLE 1** *(continued)*

| Investigators | Label(s) being studied[a] | Method of investigation | Target individual(s) | Results |
|---|---|---|---|---|
| Mooney & Algozzine, 1978 | LD vs. ED | Characteristic behaviors of LD and ED children were rated | Transmission to vocational teachers | Behaviors of LD children were seen as less disturbing and bothersome than behaviors of ED children |
| Siperstein & Gottlieb, 1978 | Severe vs. mildly MR | Completion of questionnaires regarding school and community integration | Transmission to parents, teachers, and others likely to be interested in mainstreaming | Attitudes expressed toward community and school integration were more positive for mildly MR individuals |
| Dembo et al., 1978 | EMR vs. EH | Naturalistic study in which teacher–pupil classroom interactions were analyzed for EMR and EH children in special class | Transmission to EH children by their teachers | No differentially interaction patterns were evident in different types of special classrooms |
| Sutherland & Algozzine, 1979 | LD vs. N | Experimental study in which undergraduate | Transmission to undergraduate student and to | Performance of normal fourth-grade children was differentially affected by |

students
taught
children
labeled as LD
or N

labeled or
nonlabeled child for
production of effect

label assigned to them
prior to interaction with
undergraduate "teacher"

[a]ED, emotionally disabled; EH, emotionally handicapped; EMR, educable mentally retarded; LD, learning disabled; MR, mentally retarded; N, normal.

retarded" confederate received shorter shocks of less intensity than the other subjects; however, it must be noted that the "mentally retarded" label also was accompanied by other referent material (i.e., congenital defect since birth) which might have caused the observed effects. Surtherland and Algozzine (1979) provided the only study in which the total proposed interpersonal expectancy model was investigated. Normal fourth-grade children (i.e., labeled subjects) were randomly assigned to be either "learning disabled" or "normal." Undergraduate students (i.e., initial targets) were asked to teach these children to complete a complex visual–motor task. The actual performance of the children was monitored and served as the dependent measure (i.e., interaction product) for the research. Under these conditions, girls labeled and treated as learning disabled performed significantly lower than girls represented and treated as normal; boys were not similarly affected. The extent to which these results are generalizable to other labels and behaviors remains to be shown. However, the study nicely represents the relationships previously discussed: what did you expect?

It seems then that special education labels may generate differential expectations within interpersonal relationships. That exceptional children exhibit different personal expectancy levels and/or attributional responses to success and failure has also been shown (Cromwell, 1963; Harway, 1962; Hayes & Prinz, 1976; Horai & Guarnaccia, 1975; Gruen, Ottinger, & Ollendick, 1975; MacMillan, 1975; Mercer & Snell, 1977; Robbins & Harway, 1977; Shuster & Gruen, 1971). Although evidence exists suggesting that labeling is *not* a negative process (McMillan et al., 1974), it seems from the analyses presented here that negative effects may result from labels as expectancy-generating stimuli. In fact, less than favorable outcomes have been demonstrated at various stages of expectancy transmission.

This is not to say that all studies reviewed demonstrated negative effects from labeling; however, those with contrary results can easily be explained within the suggested framework for interpreting expectancy studies. For example, Yoshida and Meyers (1975) investigated the effects of the label "mentally retarded" on teachers' expectancies for a child's future performance. No differences were indicated as a function of label or type of teacher; however, teachers' predictions did differ as a function of the number of performance trials they observed. The teachers were told they "were participating in a teacher judgment experiment" and asked them to rate "probable future performance of the child on the concept formation task" (p. 524). Unfortunately, this aspect of the study serves to confound the results obtained relative to the effects of labels in that the child's performance was manipulated to reflect improvement over trials. The teachers attended to this aspect of the experiment and it may or may not have influenced their attention to the label assigned to the child. Badad (1977) presented results which were interpreted as "Pygmalion in reverse;" his high-expectancy group actually was poorest on the dependent measure. It is important to note that no measure of the extent to which the participating teachers "bought" the expectancy inducement was included; in fact, Badad conducted the research with a group of EMR children whose teachers were told they would bloom or not bloom after the teachers had been working with them for the entire year. This presentation and that of others (Brophy & Good, 1974; Jones, 1977) would suggest that that attempted manipulation was doomed to failure.

In MacMillan's (1971) critical analysis of Dunn's (1968) reliance on the "Pygmalion" data to support the notion of self-fulfilling prophecies in special education, he commented that, if one could extrapolate so easily from the Rosenthal and Jacobsen (1968) work, "the problem could be solved immediately by simply labeling the children under consideration 'gifted' and thereby increase the teachers' expectancy for them to succeed" (p. 6). The obvious oversimplification indicated by MacMillan is clearly not within the domain of acceptable standards for an expectancy to be considered powerful. Foremost, the expectancy-generating stimulus must be attended to, comprehended, and retained (that is, it must be believable) before it can exert any further differential effects which can be investigated.

## SUMMARY AND IMPLICATIONS

Labels serve many purposes. They permit the grouping of a variety of different characteristics, qualities, and/or concepts so that we may better deal with them. Labels also have been shown to be expectancy-generating stimuli in interpersonal relationships. Expectancies are important as mediators for the attributions assigned to personal successes and failures as well as for the assignment of interpersonal attributions. Not only do they help us to decide what to expect, they assist in our interpretations of why certain outcomes occur or do not occur. In fact, none of this is necessarily harmful, deleterious, or bad. The problem arises when label-based groupings serve little positive advantage, expectancies generated by labels are qualitatively and/or quantitatively negatively biased, or attributions assigned to a labeled child's performance are different from those assigned to the success or failure of a nonlabeled youngster. It seems that these negative results of labels (as expectancy-generating stimuli) are prevalent within the current labeling literature.

The more practical-minded readers have probably begun to ask one of the following questions, or ones similar to them:

1. Can we reverse these seemingly negative effects?
2. Can negative effects of labels be eliminated?

Obviously, the answers to both of these questions is "Yes, but not in a simplistic manner" such as that described by MacMillan (1971). We cannot simply go around telling people that children are not what we told them they were before or what they thought they actually were. It does seem that we can change the perspective of many people by providing them with additional experiences and information of a positive nature. For example, the attitudes of a group of undergraduate teachers in training toward the behavior of disturbed children have been shown to improve from an intensive practicum experience with disturbed children (Herr, Algozzine, & Eaves, 1976). Peterson (1975) conducted a study in which ratings of mentally retarded peers were somewhat improved by increased contacts among the children. Similarly, improved attitudes toward mental retardation have been shown to result from carefully structured institutional tours (Cleland & Chambers, 1959; Kimbrell & Luckey, 1964; LeUnes, Christensen, & Wilkerson, 1975).

An alternative means of alleviating the effects of labeling may be developed from the observation that not all target subjects respond similarly to an expectancy-generating stimulus. Algozzine (1976a) has shown that regular and special class teachers were differentially affected by behaviors characteristic of emotionally handicapped children. Foster, Algozzine, and Ysseldyke (in press) have shown that teachers and less experienced teachers in training demonstrated different susceptibility to stereotypical bias with regard to the special education label of "emotionally disturbed." If different degrees of bias susceptibility can become predictable, an important avenue will have been opened through which the negative aspects of expectancy-generating stimuli may be brought under some control.

Another, perhaps more interesting approach has developed from studies which have shown that the effects of labels plus associated behaviors (or expanded descriptions) may be different than those of the labels, behaviors, or descriptions alone. Gottlieb (1974) found that the expressed attitudes of fourth-grade children were more influenced by the level of competence of the labeled child than by the label assigned to the child. Strichart and Gottlieb (1975) observed that imitation behavior in a nonretarded child increased in relation to the competence of the retarded model. Gottlieb and Siperstein (1976) suggested that differences in attitudes may be observed as a function of the nature of the "attitude referent" presented; labels were viewed differently than labels plus descriptions. Within this context, subjects thought to be retarded due to "congenital defect since birth" were treated more favorably than "mentally ill" (no etiology) or normal subjects in the study by Farina et al. (1976), and mental illness thought to be medically based was viewed quite differently from mental illness presumed to have a social-learning basis (Farina, Fisher, Getter, & Fisher, 1978).

While it may be unproductive to try to replace an already established label (expectancy, bias), it would appear to be quite productive to attempt to alter or embellish that label; that is, one may not be able to supplant the existing attitudes and/or expectations that a teacher holds for a child with Down's syndrome by suggesting that that child really is "gifted," but one may be able to alter the existing feelings by suggesting *additional* positive qualitites that the child possesses. Young and Algozzine (1980) altered the peer and social acceptance ratings of a fourth-grade youngster by telling his classmates that in addition to those things they had already seen and/or knew about the child, he possessed several positive features (i.e., he was good at sports and told very funny stories). No other attempts to alter expectancies, attitudes, and/or effects of labeling by supplying additional information have been identified. This is clearly an area in which productive research could greatly alleviate the seemingly negative aspects of labels as expectancy-generating stimuli.

Regardless of the perspective one takes toward the labeling issue, it remains an area of concern within special education. As mentioned earlier, the project concerning "issues in the classification of children" directed by Hobbs (1975, 1976) was a major investigation. In fact, the validity and impact of many of the recommendations included in the summary report (Hobbs, 1975) have been substantiated by their inclusion in PL 94-142. For example, the following recommendations of the Hobbs report are included in that law:

1. Parents should have an effective voice in the design, conduct, and evaluation of special programs.

2. Procedural safeguards should be established to ensure due process in classifying and placing handicapped children.

3. Handicapped children should be educated in as near to normal settings as possible.

4. Public schools should be given an advocacy role and responsibility for the handicapped from birth to maturity.

The current status of the labeling literature does not permit decisions based on definitive research; thus, expert judgment must continue to delineate best practices. It is of utmost importance that these practices aim at creating conditions that facilitate the delivery of beneficial services (i.e., treatments) and mitigate the negative effects of labeling. It is apparent that the results from research incorporating all components of the labeling paradigm are needed to guide decisions concerning the long-term effects of labeling children.

# References

Adams, G., & Cohen A. Children's physical and interpersonal characteristics that effect student–teacher interactions. *The Journal of Experimental Education,* 1974, *43,* 1–5.

Algozzine, B. The disturbing child: What you see is what you get? *The Alberta Journal of Education Research,* 1976a, *22,* 330–333.

Algozzine, B. What teachers perceive—Children receive? *Communication Quarterly,* 1976b, *24,* 41–47.

Algozzine, B. The emotionally disturbed child: Disturbed or disturbing? *Journal of Abnormal Child Psychology,* 1977, *5,* 205–211.

Algozzine, B., Mercer, C. D., & Countermine, T. The effects of labels and behavior on teacher expectations. *Exceptional Children,* 1977, *44,* 131–132.

Algozzine, B., & Sutherland, J. The "learning disabilities" label: An experimental analysis. *Contemporary Educational Psychology,* 1977, *2,* 292–297.

Algozzine, R. F. *Attractiveness as a biasing factor in teacher–pupil interactions.* Unpublished doctoral dissertation, The Pennsylvania State University, 1975.

Badad, E. Y. Pygmalion in reverse. *Journal of Special Education,* 1977, *11,* 81–90.

Baker, J. P., & Crist, J. L. Teachers expectancies: A review of the literature. In J. D. Elashoff & R. E. Snow (Eds.), *Pygmalion reconsidered.* Worthington, Ohio: Jones, 1971.

Bar-Tal, D. Attributional analysis of achievement-related behavior. *Review of Educational Research,* 1978, *48,* 259–271.

Beez, W. V. *Influence of biased psychological reports on "teacher" behavior and pupil performance.* Unpublished doctoral dissertation, Indiana University, 1970.

Berger, J., Cohen, B., & Zelditch, M. Status characteristics and expectations status: A process model. In J. Berger, M. Zelditch, & B. Anderson (Eds.), *Sociological theories in progress* (Vol. 1). Boston: Houghton Mifflin, 1966.

Berscheid, E., & Walster, E. Physical attractiveness. In L. Berkowitz (Ed.), *Advances in experimental social psychology* (Vol. 7). New York: Academic Press, 1974.

Brophy, J. E., & Good, T. L. *Teacher–student relationships: Causes and consequences.* New York: Holt, Rinehart, & Winston, 1974.

Carter, R. How invalid are marks assigned by teachers? *Journal of Educational Psychology,* 1952, *43,* 213–228.

Cleland, C., & Chambers, W. Experimental modification of attitudes as a function of an institutional tour. *American Journal of Mental Deficiency,* 1959, *64,* 124–130.

Coates, B. White adult behavior toward black and white children. *Child Development,* 1972, *43,* 143–154.

Copeland, A. P., & Weissbord, C. S. Differences in attitudes toward sex-typed behavior of nonretarded and retarded children. *American Journal of Mental Deficiency,* 1976, *81,* 280–288.

Cromwell, R. L. A social learning approach to mental retardation. In N. R. Ellis (Ed.), *Handbook of mental deficiency.* New York: McGraw-Hill, 1963.

Cruickshank, W. M. Some issues facing the field of learning disabilities. *Journal of Learning Disabilities,* 1972, *5,* 380–388.

Curran, T. *Mainstreaming attitudes as a function of behavioral expectations.* Unpublished doctoral dissertation, The Pennsylvania State University, 1977.

Datta, L., Schaefer, E., & Davis, M. Sex and scholastic aptitude as variables in teachers' ratings of the adjustment and classroom behavior of Negro and other seventh-grade students. *Journal of Educational Psychology,* 1968, *59,* 94–101.

Dembo, M. H., Yoshida, R. K., Reilly, T., & Reilly, V. Teacher–student interaction in special education classrooms. *Exceptional Children,* 1978, *45*(3), 212–213.

Dunn, L. Special education for the mildly retarded—Is much of it justifiable? *Exceptional Children,* 1968, *34,* 5–22.

Dusek, J. Do teachers bias children's learning? *Review of Educational Research,* 1975, *45,* 661–684.

Elashoff, J. D., & Snow, R. E. (Eds.). *Pygmalion reconsidered.* Worthington, Ohio: Jones, 1971.

Entwistle, D., & Webster, M. Raising children's performance expectations. *Social Science Research,* 1972, *1,* 147–158.

Falbo, T. The achievement attributions of kindergarteners. *Developmental Psychology,* 1975, *11,* 529–530.

Farina, A., Fisher, J. D., Getter, H., & Fischer, E. H. Some consequences of changing people's views regarding the nature of mental illness. *Journal of Abnormal Psychology,* 1978, *87,* 272–279.

Farina, A., Thaw, J., Felner, R. D., & Hust, B. E. Some interpersonal consequences of being mentally ill or mentally retarded. *American Journal of Mental Deficiency,* 1976, *80,* 414–422.

Finn, J. Expectations and the educational environment. *Review of Educational Research,* 1972, *42,* 387–410.

Foster, G. G. *Expectancy and halo effects as a result of artifically induced teacher bias.* Unpublished doctoral dissertation, The Pennsylvania State University, 1976.

Foster, G. G., Algozzine, B., & Ysseldyke, J. Classroom teacher and teacher in training susceptibility to stereotypical bias. *The Personnel and Guidance Journal* (in press).

Foster, G. G., & Ysseldyke, J. Expectancy and halo effects as a result of artificially induced bias. *Contemporary Educational Psychology,* 1976, *1,* 37–45.

Foster, G. G., Ysseldyke, J., & Reese, J. I wouldn't have seen it, if I hadn't believed it. *Exceptional Children,* 1975, *41,* 469–473.

Frieze, I. *Studies of information processing and the attributional process.* Unpublished doctoral dissertation, University of California, Los Angeles, 1973.

Gallagher, J. J. The sacred and profane uses of labeling. *Mental Retardation,* 1976, *14,* 3–7.

Goffman, E. *Stigma: Notes on the management of a spoiled identity.* Englewood Cliffs, N.J.: Prentice-Hall, 1963.

Gottlieb, J. Attitudes toward retarded children: Effects of labeling and academic performance. *American Journal of Mental Deficiency,* 1974, *79,* 268–273.

Gottlieb, J., & Siperstein, G. N. Attitudes toward mentally retarded persons: Effects of attitude referent specificity. *American Journal of Mental Deficiency,* 1976, *80,* 376–381.

Gruen, G. E., Ottinger, D. R., & Ollendick, T. H. Probability learning in retarded children with differing histories of success and failure in school. *American Journal of Mental Deficiency,* 1975, *79,* 417–423.

Haring, N. G. (Ed.). *Behavior of exceptional children* (2nd ed.). Columbus, Ohio: Merrill, 1978.

Harway, V. T. Self-evaluation and goal-setting behavior in handicapped children. In E. P. Trapp & P. Himmelstein (Eds.), *Readings on exceptional children.* New York: Appleton-Century-Crofts, 1962.

Hayes, C. S., & Prinz, R. J. Affective reactions of retarded and nonretarded children to success and failure. *American Journal of Mental Deficiency,* 1976, *81,* 100–102.

Heider, F. *The psychology of interpersonal relations.* New York: Wiley, 1958.

Herr, D., Algozzine, B., & Eaves, R. Amelioration of biases held by teacher trainees toward disturbingness of behavior. *Journal of Educational Research,* 1976, *69,* 261–264.

Hobbs, N. *The futures of children.* San Francisco: Jossey-Bass, 1975.

Hobbs, N. *Issues in the classification of children* (Vols. 1 & 2). San Francisco: Jossey-Bass, 1976.

Holroyd, J., & McArthur, D. Mental retardation and stress on the parents: A contrast between Down's syndrome and childhood autism. *American Journal of Mental Deficiency,* 1976, *80,* 431–436.

Horai, J., & Guarnaccia, V. J. Performance and attributions to ability, effort, task, and luck of retarded adults after success or failure feedback. *American Journal of Mental Deficiency,* 1975, *79,* 690–694.

Jackson, P., & Lahaderne, H. Inequalities of teacher–pupil contacts. *Psychology in the Schools,* 1967, *4,* 204–211.

Jensen, A. How much can we boost IQ and scholastic achievement? *Harvard Educational Review,* 1969, *39,* 1–123.

Jones, R. A. *Self-fulfilling prophecies.* Hillsdale, N.J.: Lawrence Erlbaum Associates, 1977.

Kazden, A. E. *History of behavior modification.* Baltimore: University Park Press, 1978.

Kelly, G. A. *The psychology of personal constructs.* New York: Norton, 1955.

Keogh, B. K. Cahill, C. W., & MacMillan, D. L. Perception of interruption by educationally handicapped children. *American Journal of Mental Deficiency,* 1972, *77,* 107–108.

Kimbrell, D., & Luckey, R. Attitude change resulting from open house guided tours in a state school for mental retardates. *American Journal of Mental Deficiency.* 1964, *69,* 21–22.

Lavelle, N. *Parents' expectations and causal attributions concerning their children's performance on school related tasks.* Unpublished doctoral dissertation, University of California, Los Angeles, 1977.

Lefcourt, H. M. Recent developments in the study of locus of control. In B. A. Maher (Ed.), *Progress in experimental personality research* (Vol. 6). New York: Academic Press, 1972.

LeUnes, A., Christensen, L., & Wilkerson, D. Institutional tour effects on attitudes related to mental retardation. *American Journal of Mental Deficiency,* 1975, *79,* 732–735.

Lippett, R., & Gold, M. Classroom social structure as a mental health problem. *Journal of Social Issues,* 1959, *15,* 40–49.

MacMillan, D. L. Special education for the mildly retarded: Servant or savant? *Focus on Exceptional Children,* 1971, *2,* 1–11.

MacMillan, D. L. Effect of experimental success and failure on the situational expectancy of EMR and nonretarded children. *American Journal of Mental Deficiency,* 1975, *80,* 90–95.

MacMillan, D. L., Jones, R. L., & Aloia, G. F. The mentally retarded label: A theoretical analysis and review of research. *American Journal of Mental Deficiency,* 1974, *79,* 241–261.

McGuire, W. Personality and susceptibility to social influence. In E. G. Borgatta & W. W. Albert (Eds.), *Handbook of personality theory and research.* New York: Appleton-Century-Crofts, 1966.

Medinnus, G., & Unruh, R. *Teacher expectations and verbal communication.* Paper presented at the annual meeting of the Western Psychological Association, 1971.

Meichenbaum, D., Bowers, H., & Ross, R. A behavioral analysis of teacher expectancy effect. *Journal of Personality and Social Psychology,* 1969, *13,* 306–316.

Mercer, C. D., & Snell, M. E. *Learning theory research in mental retardation.* Columbus, Ohio: Merrill, 1977.

Meyer, W., & Thompson, G. Sex differences in the distribution of teacher approval and disapproval among sixth grade children. *Journal of Educational Psychology,* 1956, *47,* 385–396.

Mooney, C., & Algozzine, B. A. comparison of the disturbingness of LD and ED behaviors. *Journal of Abnormal Child Psychology,* 1978, *6,* 401–406.

Moores, B., & Grant, G. W. B. Nurses' expectations for accomplishment of mentally retarded patients. *American Journal of Mental Deficiency,* 1976, *80,* 644–649.

311

Palardy, J. What teachers believe—What children achieve. *Elementary School Journal,* 1969, *69,* 370–374.

Palmer, D. *An attributional investigation of teachers' instructional prescriptions for normal, educationally handicapped and educable mentally retarded pupils.* Unpublished doctoral dissertation, University of California, Los Angeles, 1977.

Peterson, G. F. Factors related to the attitudes of nonretarded children toward their EMR peers. *American Journal of Mental Deficiency,* 1975, *79,* 412–416.

Robbins, R. L, & Harway, N. I. Goal setting and reactions to success and failure in children with learning disabilities. *Journal of Learning Disabilities,* 1977, *10,* 356–362.

Rosenthal, R., & Jacobsen, L. *Pygmalion in the classroom: Teacher expectation and pupils' intellectual development.* New York: Holt, Rinehart, & Winston, 1968.

Ross, M. B., & Salvia, J. Attractiveness as a biasing factor in teacher judgments. *American Journal of Mental Deficiency,* 1975, *80,* 96–98.

Rothbart, M., Dalfen, S., & Barrett, R. Effects of teachers' expectancy on student–teacher interaction. *Journal of Educational Psychology,* 1971, *62,* 49–54.

Rotter, J. B. *Social learning and clinical psychology.* Englewood Cliffs, N.J.: Prentice-Hall, 1954.

Rotter, J. B. Generalized expectancies for internal versus external control of reinforcement. *Psychological Monographs,* 1966, *80*(1, Whole No. 609).

Rotter, J. B. Some problems and misconceptions related to the construct of internal versus external control of reinforcement. *Journal of Consulting and Clinical Psychology,* 1975, *43,* 56–67.

Rubovits, P., & Maehr, M. Pygmalion analyzed: Toward an explanation of the Rosenthal-Jacobsen findings. *Journal of Personality and Social Psychology,* 1971, *19,* 197–203.

Rubovits, P., & Maehr, M. Pygmalion black and white. *Journal of Personality and Social Psychology,* 1973, *25,* 210–218.

Salvia, J., Algozzine, B., & Sheare, J. Attractiveness and school achievement. *Journal of School Psychology,* 1977, *15,* 60–67.

Salvia, J., Sheare, J., & Algozzine, B. Facial attractiveness and personal social development. *Journal of Abnormal Child Psychology,* 1975, *3,* 171–178.

Schain, S. *Learning of low ability children and tutor behavior as a function of the self-fulfilling prophecy.* Unpublished doctoral dissertation, University of Illinois, 1972.

Schmid, R. E. Historical perspectives of learning disabilities. In C. D. Mercer (Ed.), *Children and adolescents with learning disabilities.* Columbus, Ohio: Merrill, 1979.

Seaver, W. B. Effects of naturally induced teacher expectancies. *Journal of Personality and Social Psychology,* 1973, *28,* 333–342.

Seitz, S., & Geske, D. Mothers' and graduate trainees' judgements of children: Some effects of labeling. *American Journal of Mental Deficiency,* 1977, *81,* 362–370.

Severance, L. J., & Gasstrom, L. L. Effects of the label ''mentally retarded'' on causal explanations for success and failure outcomes. *American Journal of Mental Deficiency,* 1977, *81,* 547–555.

Shuster, S. O., & Gruen, G. E. Success and failure as determinants of the performance prediction of mentally retarded and nonretarded children. *American Journal of Mental Deficiency,* 1971, *76,* 190–196.

Siperstein, G. N., & Gottlieb, J. Physical stigma and academic performance as factors affecting children's first impressions of handicapped peers. *American Journal of Mental Deficiency,* 1977, *81,* 455-462.

Siperstein, G. N., & Gottlieb, J. Parents' and teachers' attitudes toward mildly and severely retarded children. *Mental Retardation,* 1978, *16,* 321–322.

Smith, R. M., & Neisworth, J. T. The exceptional child: A functional approach. New York: McGraw-Hill, 1975.

Snow, R. Unfinished pygmalion. *Contemporary Psychology,* 1969, *14,* 197–199.

Strichart, S. S., & Gottlieb, J. Imitation of retarded children by their nonretarded peers. *American Journal of Mental Deficiency*, 1975, *79*, 506–512.

Sutherland, J. H. *The learning disabilities label as a biasing factor in the complex visual–motor integration performance of normal fourth grade children.* Unpublished doctoral dissertation, The Pennsylvania State University, 1976.

Sutherland, J. H., & Algozzine, B. The learning disabilities label as a biasing factor in the visual–motor performance of normal children. *Journal of Learning Disabilities*, 1979, *12*, 8–14.

Szasz, T. *Ideology and insanity.* Garden City, N.Y.: Doubleday-Anchor, 1970.

Thorndike, R. Review of Pygmalion in the classroom. *American Educational Research Journal*, 1968, *5*, 708–711.

Weiner, B. *Achievement motivation and attribution theory.* Morristown, N.J.: General Learning Press, 1974.

Weiner, B., Frieze, I., Kukla, A., Reed, L., Rest, S., & Rosenbaum, R. M. *Perceiving the causes of success and failure.* New York: General Learning Press, 1971.

Weiner, B., Heckhausen, H., Meyer, W., & Cook, R. Causal ascriptions and achievement behavior: The conceptual analysis of effort. *Journal of Personality and Social Psychology*, 1972, *21*, 239–248.

Yoshida, R. K., & Meyers, C. E. Effects of labeling as educable mentally retarded on teachers' expectancies for change in a student's performance. *Journal of Educational Psychology*, 1975, *67*, 521–527.

Young, S., & Algozzine, B. Social acceptability as a function of labels and assigned attributes. *American Journal of Mental Deficiency*, 1980, *84*, p.589–595.

# IMPLICATIONS OF MAINSTREAMING: A CHALLENGE FOR SPECIAL EDUCATION

Marty Abramson

*Texas A&M University*

Mainstreaming appears to be a topic involving simplistic analyses, but proves instead to be a particularly complex issue that is resistant to elementary investigation. The philosophical, economic, theoretical, and humanistic issues relating to mainstreaming are particularly deceptive. While most individuals have extolled the virtues of the mainstreaming principle, indications are that mainstreaming as a practice may have major problems. Is it possible that special educators have so convinced themselves that mainstreaming will be a success that evidence to the contrary receives little attention? Has such an abundance of emotional, economic, and administrative resources been committed to the principle of mainstreaming that the possible failure of the resultant practice may go unrealized? In essence, has special education become the unwitting victim of its own superselling techniques?

Special educators may be in a position of having promised far more than they can deliver. In referring to a similar major educational change, compensatory education, Winschel (1970, p. 5) noted the following:

> The problem, then, is that we have promised too much and in the promising have floundered upon the rising expectations of our clients. . . . Perhaps the problem lies in our having failed with many to do the ordinary with any extraordinary skill—and we have sought to hide our ommissions behind labels.

The goals of compensatory education programs were similar to the goals that special educators are advocating today. With the notion of mainstreaming has come a reaffirmation of the need for active parent involvement, adequately trained regular education teachers, and modified curricula intended to promote social interaction and academic improvement. With so little that is new, how can special educators promise for the future what they have been unable to deliver in the past? The answer to this question lies in the tendency of special educators to adopt the most current *Zeitgeist,* regardless of past events.

Unlike the scientists, who first gather data and analyze information about a situation and only then apply what they have learned to a problem (Bakan, 1977), special educators eschew this process. Implementation often precedes experimentation in educational practice, thereby making the foundation of educational development haphazard and subject to trial-and-error procedures. The integration of exceptional children into general education, commonly referred to as mainstreaming, is one example of this tendency.

## DEFINITION OF MAINSTREAMING

In its most elementary form, "mainstreaming means moving handicapped children from their segregated status in special education classes and integrating them with 'normal' children in regular classrooms" (Brenton, 1974, p. 23). More precise definitions are available (see, for example, Kaufman, Gottlieb, Agard, & Kukic, 1975), but all have one common property. This common property is the establishment of an educational environment that is as near normal as possible. Therefore, for any given handicapped child, mainstreaming could refer to a placement that ranges from a regular class with no help, to placement in a special class on a full-time or part-time basis.

Whether a particular child's placement represents a mainstreamed environment is very much dependent upon the severity of the handicap itself and the ability of the child to adapt and thrive in the regular classroom. Therefore, for many handicapped children, full-time maintenance in the regular classroom may be considered mainstreaming, while for other children, placement in a self-contained class could similarly be viewed as mainstreaming. The key element in mainstreaming, as was pointed out earlier, is the provision of an education in the most normal or advantageous setting possible. Thus, if a special class proves to be most advantageous for a handicapped child, then that is the most appropriate setting. Conversely, if the special class cannot be demonstrated to be beneficial, the child is served in the regular classroom. There are many gradations between these two extremes.

The intent of this chapter is to examine several of the issues dealing with the mainstreaming movement. Mainstreaming is discussed as a general process that is not unique to any single handicapping condition nor degree of severity. Thus, the conclusions drawn are broad and are not intended to reflect findings with any specific population. The focus of the present discussion is global, centering on historical, social, economic, and political factors that will influence future decisions in special education.

A caveat should first be noted: The notion of mainstreaming is fairly new, and therefore it is not surprising that our knowledge regarding its usefulness or nonusefulness is only in the embryonic stage. As with any controversial issue, different studies have reported dissimilar results, thereby making interpretation a virtually impossible task.

The studies cited reflect the author's viewpoint. It is a perspective that has seldom been expressed, but of late is finding increasing support among those working in educational settings and in society at large. Nonetheless, definitive answers to many of the questions involving mainstreaming will only come about through continued investigation.

## BRIEF HISTORY OF SPECIAL EDUCATION IN THE UNITED STATES

During various periods of American history, schools have taken on a number of different functions. For the colonial settlers, schools served as caretakers for children whose parents were struggling to survive, and as guardians of their religious faith. To better serve these functions, Massachusetts (in 1642) became the first state to pass a compulsory education law, requiring that all children attend school (Looft, 1973). Although the concept of compulsory education was to be overlooked in the future educational developments, it was returned to as it influenced education in the 20th century; first in regard to racial groups and later with exceptional individuals.

Following the American Revolution at the end of the 18th century, education was reconceived as a political necessity to ensure the safety and liberty of the public. As Thomas Jefferson noted, the public's welfare (primarily the white citizenry) took precedence over an individual's achievement and fulfillment: "Every government degenerates when trusted to the rulers of the people alone. The people themselves therefore are its only safe depositories. And to render even them safe, their minds must be improved to a certain degree. . . . The influence over government must be shared among all the people" (1972, pp. 148–149).

A few years later, the function of schools again changed. Education based on social class or race gave way to the concept of good education for all (Butts, 1975–1976). Schools were assigned the responsibility of making certain that all attending left equally educated; not only that they be provided equal educational opportunity, but also equal educational results. As a practical matter, this latter goal was never achieved.

Following the Civil War and during the early 20th century, education again changed based on the demands of society. As the industrial revolution progressed, the emphasis of the schools shifted to provide training for employment purposes (Coleman, 1968). Skilled labor was essential to ensure the economy's growth (Gintis, 1972).

Apart from the economic needs associated with education, the 20th century saw the perpetration of a great social myth (Greer, 1972)—education as the equalizer of all men. It was education that was to take the illiterate, poor, and destitute immigrants and form them into the great middle-class working force. The schools were never very successful in raising the overall standards of the lower class (Greer, 1972). Still, educators were not very reluctant when society turned to the schools to bring about this social change. Most believed that the schools could make up for inequalities that existed previously. Regrettably, this outcome was never realized.

The American public school system has also failed to provide equal education for handicapped children (Abeson & Zettel, 1977; Goldberg & Lippman, 1974). Nevertheless, society has again turned to special and regular educators to effect a major change. In view of the fact that the public schools have never been able to serve their expressed function of equalizer or provider of equal opportunities (Looft, 1973), it is only speculative whether they can accomplish this task with children who have handicaps.

Historically, mainstreaming was a predictable event in the ever-increasing march toward expanded services for minority group children. Instead of providing solely for the education of handicapped children, mainstreaming was a means of compensating for past inequities and ensuring that, in the future, greater than equal opportunity (in the form of expanded services, increased time in educational settings, etc.) would be available.

## EVOLUTION OF MAINSTREAMING

With this overview of education complete, it becomes more apparent how the mainstreaming movement came about. Just as education adopted the American value of every individual having the opportunity to achieve his or her greatest ambitions, special education adopted a similar value system, though somewhat later. Principally, mainstreaming was initiated to provide handicapped children with the greatest opportunity to achieve personal fulfillment and success to the maximum of their ability.

However, recent historical developments within special education are the result of more than just the adoption of idealistic American beliefs. They are also the result of a mixture of political, social, economic, and administrative factors. In fact, changes in special education have come about only with the insistent prodding of parents, consumer groups, and legislative mandates (Keogh & Levitt, 1976; Weintraub, 1972).

As was noted earlier, schools have always been looked to as solvers of the nation's social ills. When it was found, for example, that the disadvantaged were lacking the necessary knowledge and skills to be successful, schools were charged to carry out the legislative mandate of equal education, and then later, compensatory education. These types of programs spanned the preschool, elementary, and secondary school years and came to be known as Head Start, Title I, and Upward Bound.

In a similar fashion, schools have been directed to follow through on many social action programs. It should therefore come as no surprise that the schools were asked to solve the problem of integrating the handicapped into the mainstream of society. What was surprising was that the schools were asked to accomplish this integration task in the face of their reported inability to successfully accomplish a similar task with minority group children involved in regular education (Payne, Mercer, Payne & Davison, 1973; Smith & Bissell, 1970; Westinghouse Learning Corporation/Ohio University, 1969). In spite of this seeming inability on the part of the schools to initiate social change, both judicial decisions and legislative mandates directed the schools to institute major educational and social changes for handicapped children.

It is apparent that schools have never been effective as agents of social change. For each problem identified by society, schools created new palliatives to be disseminated to those in need. Evolving from the courts and assorted governmental bodies, mainstreaming is the latest remedy, whose dissemination is directed toward handicapped children.

**Judicial decisions**

Court decisions preceded legislative directives and prompted the schools to provide for the needs of those children with handicaps. Through a series of court cases, the overriding principle of appropriate, equal, and free education was sustained for all persons, including the handicapped. Mainstreaming was one means by which an education could be made available to those who were handicapped and, at the same time, comply with the requirements of the court decisions.

The impact of the courts on handicapped individuals can be traced to the landmark decision of the U.S. Supreme Court in *Brown* v. *Board of Education of Topeka* (1954). Although the specific intent of this decision was to ensure integrated and equal educational facilities for various racial groups, it was also influential in making available a free

319

public education to all. Thus, the notion of free and appropriate education, the cornerstone of mainstreaming, had its contemporary origin in the civil rights movement of the 1950's and 1960's.

Support for integrated education was also to be found in court decisions which struck down the prevalent practice of ability stratification, commonly known as the tracking system (Chapin, 1978). The courts, in the cases of *Hobson* v. *Hansen* (1967) and *Smuck* v. *Hobson* (1969), found that the lower tracks typically were discriminatory in their failure to include those groups of children in the overall educational system. For the first time, the courts had affirmed that classification of individuals for unequal educational purposes was not justifiable, particularly on the basis of race, ethnic background, and the like. Later, this basic notion of segregation as an indefensible practice was employed by the advocates of handicapped children and the proponents of integrated educational classes.

The most notable reaffirmation of the principle of integrated education was the consent agreement resulting from the *PARC—Pennsylvania Association for Retarded Children* v. *Commonwealth of Pennsylvania* (1972). The court declared that the needs of handicapped children could best be met by providing educational programs that paralleled those provided for nonhandicapped children. In asserting this basic principle, the courts extended legal precedents which had been established in civil rights cases to the needs of the handicapped.

A short time later, the case of *Mills* v. *Board of Education of the District of Columbia* (1972) provided for two additional elements. First it determined that the constitutional rights of handicapped children must be safeguarded by declaring that a due process procedure must be employed in the educational placement of these individuals (Chapin, 1978). Second, and perhaps more importantly, it rejected school districts' claims that a free and suitable education could not be provided due to insufficient funds. Thus, one of the most frequently cited arguments against extending appropriate educational opportunity to exceptional children was struck down. Regardless of the cost, equal access to educational programs was to be provided.

Thus, the mass movement toward mainstreaming resulted in part from the precedents that have been established in a limited number of court cases. Findings such as those in the cases of *PARC* and *Mills* made it clear that special education fell far short of providing for the needs of handicapped children. It is likely that this determination of the courts, favoring more normalized educational programming, contributed to the legislative mandates providing for education in the "least restrictive environment"—a term that was analagous with mainstreaming.

**Legislative mandates**

Abeson (1972) noted that by 1972 approximately 70 percent of the states had enacted legislation requiring public education for all handicapped children. Much of this activity on the part of state legislatures was in direct response to earlier judicial decisions portending the necessity of such legislation. Later and more complete legislation initiated by the states was intended, at least in part, to ensure that federal assistance would continue to be provided.

An early legislative act established policy not only for educational settings, but also for virtually any situation in which one might find a handicapped person. PL 93-112, the Vocational Rehabilitation Act of 1973, provided that no discrimination of handicapped persons, child or adult, would be acceptable. Specifically, Section 504 of the Act noted that "no otherwise qualified handicapped individual in the United States . . . shall, solely by reason of his handicap, be excluded from the participation in, be denied the benefits of, or be subjected to discrimination under any program or activity receiving Federal financial assistance."

In 1974, Congress enacted the Education Amendments (PL 93-380), which specified that states were to make educational opportunities available to handicapped children. This stance was reaffirmed and extended with the establishment of the Education for All Handicapped Children Act (PL 94-142), which became law on November 29, 1975. In some sense PL 94-142 further refined and elucidated the intent of section 504, particularly as it pertained to educational concerns. The passage of the law received the support of parents as well as many other concerned individuals "who refused to let an idea whose time had come be allowed to walk rather than run" (Melcher, 1976, p. 129). The prudence of these interest groups in "forcing" legislation will be discussed in a later section. Suffice it to say, those who exhibited enthusiasm for the legislation were not basing their zeal on existing educational programs that had demonstrated great changes for exceptional children.

The focus of PL 94-142 was not directly on mainstreaming, although it did provide for the education of handicapped children in the least restrictive environment. Moreover, the legislation supported the litigation that had dealt with the right to education and guaranteed children with handicaps that the education they received would be free and appropriate. In essence, it was a promise that the civil rights of handicapped children would no longer be violated. Provisions were also made for administrative elements and financial support to state and local education agencies. A thorough review of this crucial law is beyond the scope of this chapter; there are several excellent sources that explicate the law and its intended meaning for educational policy (Ballard & Zettel, 1977, 1978a, 1978b; Corrigan, 1978).

Regrettably, the enabling legislation exceeded the immediate capabilities of the educators who were to implement the legislation. In fact, it outstripped the state of the art and was inconsistent with much of the research available at the time. As a result, educational agencies were confused, special educators were apprehensive, and regular educators were unsure of their role in carrying out the various laws. Many of these uncertainties still remain.

In summary, many of the tenets originally posited in the courts were contained within the federal legislation. While the legislation did not deal specifically with the concept of mainstreaming, it did declare that a free and appropriate education in the least restrictive environment was the right of all handicapped children. For many state and local school systems, "free and appropriate" was interpreted to mean the inclusion of these children in the mainstream of education whenever possible. Mainstreaming became the watchword for the principle that had been established in the courts and governing bodies of this country.

## Normalization as a predecessor of mainstreaming

There was one further historical trend that contributed to the evolution of mainstreaming. This was the normalization principle. In a very real sense, it was the commitment of the helping professions to normalize conditions for institutionalized persons that paved the way for exceptional children to be mainstreamed. While the belief in ". . . existence as close to the normal as possible" (Nirje, 1969, p. 181) originated in the Scandinavian countries, a similar concept found acceptance in this country. A short time after the principle of normalization was adopted for institutional and community settings, mainstreaming was advocated for special education. Mainstreaming in education came to be analagous to normalization in institutional and community environments.

As applied to educational settings, normalization suggested classroom placement as close to the regular classroom as possible, interaction with nonhandicapped peers, and frequent reevaluation based on the child's needs (MacMillan, 1977). Little attention was focused on whether normalization had been successful in previous settings. A philosophical principle had been adopted, modified slightly to suit educators, and then translated into practice. While normalization was accepted as a goal to be strived for (Throne, 1975), there were indications that it was never readily achievable. It may be that mainstreaming was also built upon a principle whose practice was ineffective.

It is apparent that the principle of mainstreaming evolved as a response to many historical, social, and legal pressures. It represented society's faith in the schools to prepare all children equally, regardless of their backgrounds or deficits, to be solvers of the nations ills, and to bring about social and educational reform. However, the principle was never distinguished from the practice (MacMillan, Jones, & Meyers, 1976).

A number of writers noted the lack of differentiation between mainstreaming as a principle and mainstreaming as a practice (Keogh & Levitt, 1976; MacMillan et al., 1976). In the rush to mainstream children, there was growing concern that enough attention had not been given to the implementation of the principle (Martin, 1974). Some even went so far as to suggest that mainstreaming would ". . . fall beneath the weight of its own publicity unless the principle (was) separated from attempts to implement the principle" (MacMillan et al., 1976, p. 4).

### Research on the practice of mainstreaming

Since mainstreaming as a principle has been widely advanced and disseminated, it might be expected that the practices related to the principle have been the subject of careful and thorough examination. As Corman and Gottlieb (1978) indicate, this has not been the case: "Today, approximately 8 years after the initial movement toward mainstreaming, a body of research exists. . . . The extent of this research has been small, however, when one considers that, by 1974, 37 states had passed laws mandating some form of mainstreaming" (p. 252).

While interest in the principle of mainstreaming has increased (Corman & Gottlieb, 1978; Meisgeier, 1976), there has been comparatively little concern for determining the effectiveness of mainstreaming (Gickling & Theobald, 1975; MacMillan & Semmel, 1977), particularly in relation to various alternatives. It may be that the principle of mainstreaming is not easily amenable to empirical verification in spite of the fact that it is possible to identify several of the underlying assumptions relating to the principle. These assumptions include the beliefs that mainstreaming can reduce stigmata and increase the social acceptability of mainstreamed handicapped children, obtain the support of regular education personnel, and increase the academic performance of mainstreamed children. A selective review of the research literature in each of these areas follows.

### Reduction of social stigmata

Until recent times, those involved in special education programs have held that placement in special classes is superior to regular class placement. It was assumed that the special class would provide a less frustrating environment and more opportunities for success, and reduce the social rejection frequently encountered by children with handicaps. Many investigations have supported the belief that handicapped children are often not accepted or liked by their normal peers (e.g., Baldwin, 1958; Johnson, 1950; Johnson & Kirk, 1950; Parish, Ohlsen, & Parish, 1978).

Despite these investigations, one of the basic goals underlying the mainstreaming movement was the reduction of stigmata associated with exceptional individuals by their normal peers (Christoplos & Renz, 1969) and their increased social acceptability. Overall, this result has not occurred. Investigations of social acceptability have highlighted the fact that exceptional children who are placed in integrated classrooms are less accepted by normal peers (Bryan, 1976; Goodman, Gottlieb, & Harrison, 1972; Gottlieb & Budoff, 1973; Iano, Ayers, Hellers, Mc-Gettigan, & Walker, 1974). Moreover, social acceptability and attitude change do not seem to result solely from increased exposure to exceptional individuals (Cleland & Chambers, 1959; Lilly, 1971; Rucker & Vincenzo, 1970).

Several studies have attempted to improve the social acceptability of exceptional populations by placing handicapped and nonhandicapped children in close proximity to each other and having them work toward some superordinate goal. The findings are mixed. Some investigators have found that social acceptance can be improved (Chennault, 1967; McDaniel; 1970), although the gains are not maintained over several weeks (Lilly, 1971; Rucker & Vincenzo, 1970). Most research does not support the belief that regular classroom integration will improve the social status of children with handicaps.

It is evident that social acceptance does not come about solely by integration of handicapped and nonhandicapped children (Gottlieb, Semmel, & Veldman, 1978). Improvement in social acceptance requires a structured, intensive approach to cooperative interaction that is a part of the integral operations of the normal class day (Ispa & Matz, 1978). Additionally, it requires that peers view the handicapped child as capable of performing the same tasks as any other member of the class (Ballard, Corman, Gottlieb, & Kaufman, 1977). The ability to perform the same tasks as the members of a normal peer group contradicts the fact that many of these children are handicapped. Thus, the attainment of social acceptance may be an impossibility if that acceptance is dependent upon "being normal."

A rather interesting approach to this problem of social acceptance has been taken by Kitano, Stiehl, and Cole (1978), who suggest that handicapped children are developmentally delayed in their ability to take the perspective of others, and thus, exhibit inappropriate social behavior. Supporting evidence for this inability to role-take comes from Bruininks (1978), who found that handicapped populations were inaccurate in assessing their own level of social acceptance within a group. Even in mainstreamed settings, handicapped children evaluated themselves positively (Parish & Copeland, 1978) and evidenced increased self-esteem (Strang, Smith & Rogers, 1978), although much of our evidence indicates that they are less socially acceptable to peers (Gottlieb, 1975). This inability to perceive or be affected by the feelings of others may be due to inadequate feedback and would help to explain why handicapped children exhibit atypical behaviors. If this is indeed true, increasing social acceptance may be a matter of training role-taking abilities in handicapped populations. This is certainly a technique that merits further investigation.

The lack of social acceptability encountered by exceptional individuals suggests that somehow they are dissatisfied with their current status. While there is some evidence to support this belief (Gozali, 1972), it is possible that the ineptness of the individuals would have been recognized regardless of their placement in special classes. Mainstreaming was advocated as a means of removing children with handicaps from a deprecating and unfavorable environment (Sabatino, 1972). However, for a discipline that emphasizes the need for individualization and ensuring the rights of the child, we have paid little attention to the fact that many children in special classes prefer to remain in special education programs (Flynn, 1974; McKinnon, 1970; Warner, Thrapp, & Walsh, 1973).

## Educators in the practice of mainstreaming

The success or failure of mainstreaming will certainly be dependent upon the abilities of both the special education and regular education teacher. Perhaps even more importantly, success will be very much dependent upon the attitudes of these teachers toward handicapped children and each other (Mitchell, 1976). In addition, a number of other teacher variables could influence the mainstreaming outcome.

In the past, many special education teachers specialized by selecting a population and severity level to work with. As a result, many teachers elected to teach those children who represented the upper level of the disability spectrum. With many of the mildly handicapped returning to the regular classroom for all or most of the day, special education teachers will increasingly be asked to serve a more severely involved population. Thus, the ability to "specialize" will become limited, and teachers may be forced to work with handicapped students they know little about. The effect of this reorientation on special education teachers is unknown.

Since mainstreaming will involve the transition from special classes to regular classes, regular education teachers will need to assume responsibility for ensuring a smooth passage. With minimal training, regular educators will be expected to adapt their curricula to virtually any type of handicapped child (Turnbull & Schulz, 1979). These curricular changes, however, will not necessarily be accompanied by a reduction in the number of students in the classroom, additional support services, or additional funding. The attitudes of regular education teachers toward mainstreaming will be reflected in their willingness to cooperate and bargain about various aspects of programs (Bateman, 1979). However, it is not likely that these changes will endear regular education teachers to mainstreaming programs, and thus cooperation may be minimal.

There is also some evidence to indicate that regular education teachers feel impotent in the decision-making processes involved in special education placement and programming. In a recent study, Yoshida, Fenton, Maxwell, and Kaufman (1978) found that, as compared to other personnel, regular classroom teachers consistently rated themselves lower in variables related to participation and overall satisfaction in the planning team process. These results indicate that teachers do not see themselves as having sufficient input into decisions that are being made about handicapped children placed in their classrooms. In view of the pivotal role regular teachers will play in the implementation of mainstreaming, more attention needs to be paid to actively involving teachers in the mainstreaming process and ensuring that they are satisfied with their roles.

**Attitudes of teachers toward handicapped children**

Emotional and attitudinal factors enter not only into the teaching process, but also the learning process. Little is known about the importance of attitudes, ways to change prevailing attitudes, or the effects of differential attitudes on instruction. Only recently have we begun to focus on finding out how regular educators perceive children with handicaps. The results of these studies are not very encouraging and suggest that teacher attitudes and instructional practices in regard to handicapped children are unfavorable (e.g., Palmer, 1979; Parish & Copeland, 1978; Parish & Dyck, 1979).

Although there is some evidence indicating that regular education teachers are favorably inclined toward integrating handicapped children (Guerin & Szatlocky, 1974), the vast majority of studies have demonstrated no such favoritism. Regular classroom teachers have consistently indicated their lack of support for the integration of exceptional children in the regular classroom (Gickling & Theobald, 1975; MacMillan, Meyers, & Yoshida, 1978; Moore & Fine, 1978; Shotel, Iano, & McGettigan, 1972; Vacc & Kirst, 1977).

It has been suggested that it is the lack of knowledge and experience that accounts for the fears and prejudices exhibited by many regular educators (Kraft, 1973; Payne & Murray, 1974). However, the evidence is to the contrary and indicates that, following an experience in an integrated setting, the percentage of teachers who initially favor integrated programs declines (Shotel et al., 1972). Moreover, regular and special education teachers have expressed the opinion that self-contained special classrooms are more effective for the mildly handicapped (Gickling & Theobald, 1975).

There is some evidence to indicate that many of the attitudes seen in regular classroom teachers may be formed before the actual teaching process begins. In a recent study by Parish, Eads, Reece, and Piscitello (1977), undergraduate students, many of whom were in non-special education fields, negatively evaluated characteristics of handicapped children after completing an introductory course in special education. The course reviewed the various exceptionalities and corrected the students' misconceptions. Compared to prospective special education teachers, prospective regular classroom teachers selected significantly more negative adjectives to describe handicapped children. It appears that training and experience do not change teachers' perceptions of handicapped children (Panda & Bartel, 1972), nor improve their attitudes toward integrated classrooms (Gickling & Theobald, 1975).

Ultimately, the success of mainstreaming will be largely dependent upon regular educators (MacMillan et al., 1976). Whether the support from teachers will be readily available will not be known for some time. Although the major teacher organizations have expressed their support for the mainstreaming concept, this support has not been unqualified (see Reynolds & Birch, 1977, for a discussion). Nevertheless, mainstreaming practices are predicated on the belief that teachers will be helpful participants and that support networks will be in place. We may be wrong on both counts.

### Academic performance

Apart from the concerns involving peer acceptance and the possible reluctance of regular educators to participate in the mainstreaming endeavor, questions have also arisen about the effects of mainstreaming on academic performance. Those who believe that mainstreaming can have only a beneficial effect on handicapped children point to the presence of appropriate role models in the regular classrooms. It is assumed that the availability of regular children will also allow for tutorial help to be provided for those children with handicaps who might be in need of such help. Not only would this improve academic functioning, but as a result of social interaction, peer acceptance and understanding would evolve. As was noted earlier, however, peer acceptance does not result from social contact.

Those who suggest that mainstreaming will be detrimental to academic achievement emphasize the fact that handicapped children will be in classrooms containing larger numbers of children. This could mean less individualized instruction and an increasingly competitive atmosphere, resulting in more instances of failure than success.

In many respects, the arguments that favor and oppose mainstreaming have parallels to similar arguments dating back to the special education movement of the early 1940's. Then, as today, educators were moving toward integrated classrooms as a response to the detrimental effects labeling had on those who were placed in self-contained special education programs (Martin, 1940). The 1960's saw a return to categorical special education programs, largely at the insistence of parent groups and as a result of their lobbying efforts (Cegelka & Tyler, 1970). Federal monies were available to school districts that utilized organizational structures employing segregated special education classrooms. With the advent of mainstreaming, a return to the integration of the 1940's seems likely.

What evidence exists to indicate that one organizational structure is better than another in promoting academic performance? Currently, there are very little data to lend support to either integrated or segregated classrooms. This is particulary true of mainstreaming as it is defined today—as the least restrictive environment the child can be placed in to benefit maximally from educational opportunities. The diversity of programs under the rubric of mainstreaming makes a determination of effectiveness extremely difficult. Studies of integrated programs have shown results ranging from success (e.g., Haring & Krug, 1975; Walker, 1972) to failure (e.g., Keogh & Levitt, 1976). By far, most studies indicate that there are essentially no differences in academic performance between the handicapped child placed in a regular classroom and a similar child placed in a special education classroom (Budoff & Gottlieb, 1976; Ritter, 1978; Vacc, 1972).

While the results of such studies may seem encouraging, in at least one study, regular classroom children in an integrated setting, following completion of the first year, were academically below their normal peers who did not have handicapped children in the classroom (Bradfield, Brown, Kaplan, Rickert, & Stannard, 1973). It may be that too much time was spent improving the academic performance of the handicapped children, to the detriment of the regular children. If this finding is borne out in future studies, moral and ethical questions will need to be raised and resolved.

In the final analysis, the necessary data for decision making are lacking. Most of the efficacy studies have been plagued with methodological difficulties yielding inconclusive results. An entire philosophy of mainstreaming as an efficacious practice has been based on 40 years of inconclusive studies. Although illogical, this reflects the tendency of special education to adopt the prevalent philosophy of the time and to put that philosophy into practice.

## ECONOMIC CONSIDERATIONS

A final area that will affect mainstreaming is economics. The influence of economics on educational practice is frequently overlooked. While it is accurate that money alone cannot provide education, it is inconceivable that education could occur without it.

There are a number of factors that threaten to change the course of future educational financing. One of these factors is the 1971 court decision in *Serrano* v. *Priest* (1971). In declaring that John Serrano's complaint against the State of California's public school financing pattern was warranted, the court noted that disparities in local property tax levies resulted in educational inequities. School districts with a low level of taxable property could not generate the income of more affluent school districts. Thus, affluent school districts could provide higher quality education than districts with an inadequate tax base.

The Serrano decision was a further extension of the belief in equal rights. The court held that it was not enough to provide a suitable education for all children if some school districts could offer a better education than others. While the decision took place in California, it could just as easily have occurred in other states that depend heavily on local property taxes to fund education.

For special education the meaning was clear. In those poor school districts that had a large number of handicapped children, equal numbers of dollars would have to be spent as were available to wealthy districts. For the first time, state education agencies were required to come up with new school financing formulas intended to equalize expenditures of money for all children in all school districts. While the Serrano decision did not strike down the use of property taxes, it did help to eliminate the inequities that were perpetrated by their use at the time.

Currently, there is a growing nation-wide opposition to the increased financing of education. This opposition has taken the form of a taxpayer revolt against property taxes. While a taxpayer revolt was inevitable, the fact that the attack was directed in part toward education was unexpected. However, it could have been predicted by examining the forces that were operating. Raising the costs of education were judicial decisions and legislation that made higher taxes unavoidable as schools sought to comply with a variety of state and federal directives. Attempting to maintain or reduce educational expenditures were taxpayers seeking relief from burdensome taxes. A collision between these two forces was unavoidable.

The passage of Proposition 13 in California provides some insight into how taxpayers view education. It is fair to say that they were angry to learn that educational spending had increased 83 percent between 1970 and 1976 (Baratz & Moskowitz, 1978). In addition, a number of polls indicated that reductions in educational services were preferred to decreases in fire, police, or similar public services. California is not an isolated case. Other states are currently considering legislation to limit spending and to cut or hold the line on taxes.

**Special education and the taxpayer revolt**

It is the higher cost of educating the handicapped child that is frequently cited as the reason that equal educational opportunity has not been provided (Thomas, 1973). In certain circumstances costs do increase as the result of additional personnel, unique facilities, and transportation requirements (Rossmiller, Hale, & Frohreich, 1970). It is possible that property taxes will increase in response to the need for the least restrictive environment and a free appropriate education for all handicapped children. At the very least, special education administrators will find themselves competing for a limited amount of money and facing a school board that is reluctant to raise taxes.

PL 94-142 requires that states assume much of the financial responsibility for compliance. The federal government will contribute to the cost of a free appropriate education for handicapped children, but only to a certain degree. This amount is based on the national average per pupil expenditure (NAPPE), which is the amount needed to educate a nonhandicapped student. The NAPPE is multiplied by a predetermined percentage (1978, 5 percent; 1979, 10 percent; 1980, 20 percent; 1981, 30 percent; and 1982, 40 percent) times the number of handicapped children being served in each state (Ballard & Zettel, 1978a). The monies are allotted to the state education agencies, which must then pass on at least 75 percent of the total allotment. Therefore, the money that a local school district receives could be as little as 7.5, 15, 22.5, and 30 percent of the national average per pupil expenditure. Local districts are to bear the typical costs of educating handicapped children, while federal monies are intended to assume the excess costs. The percentages cited represent authorized levels of funding. The actual percentage of money provided to the states is dependent on how much money Congress appropriates to fund the program each year.

It has been estimated that it costs two to four times more to educate a handicapped child than a regular education child (Cober, Hayes, Mulvilhill, & Reynolds, 1978). The 40 percent that the government is expected to contribute will force schools to either raise property taxes or look for financial support elsewhere. Thus, as a result of legislation designed to benefit children with handicaps, the public schools will be faced with a need to be in compliance with federal legislation and, at the same time, to control expenditures.

The specific financial implications of the legislation remain uncertain, but they will depend upon state counts of handicapped children, the expansion of services to those ages 3–21, the regulations allowing for a redefinition of those children characterized as learning disabled, and the amount of money appropriated by Congress. With the schools serving at least two populations they have not traditionally served before (children ages 3–5 and 18–21), it is nearly certain that school revenues will have to be increased.

PL 94-142 was enacted before taxpayers became as sensitive to how their dollars were spent. Although well meaning, the legislation did not provide sufficient funds for implementing the requirements (Marver, 1976). It did not take into account that education as a whole receives most of its revenue from local sources (48 percent) rather than state (44 percent) or federal (8 percent) sources (Gallup, 1978). In order to receive any federal aid, local and state education agencies will be compelled to comply with the legislation. Given the present mood of the taxpayer, it is unlikely that state or local education agencies will be able to supplement the available local funds (Wilken & Porter, 1977) or that additional federal dollars will become available (Stafford, 1974).

Monies allocated to programs are affected by the state of the general economy, as well as by national and state priorities (Simches, 1975). As inflation increases and the general outcry from the population at large for relief from excessive taxation grows louder, various agencies will be pressed to establish priorities for the utilization of resources. It is apparent that social welfare and educational programs are often delegated to the lower end of such priority ladders. Questions concerning the commitment of resources to those in need of special education services will become frequent as funds become scarce. This scenario will not be limited to federally initiated programs. Given the domino effect of public school financing, the impact will also be felt at the state and local levels.

While the principle of mainstreaming costs nothing, the general practice of mainstreaming, with all of its programmatic implications and related services, could be an expensive venture. It has been estimated that provision of full service to all handicapped children will eventually involve the doubling or tripling of present resources, or, to put it another way, spending twice as much on handicapped children as regular children (Wilken & Porter, 1977). However, without improved information on finances and services, it will be some time before it will be known how mainstreaming compares to previous programs that emphasized less integration, fewer services, and limited clientele. While no one can say with certainty that mainstreaming will be costly, indications are that practices related to the mainstreaming principle, broadly defined, will mean increased costs and additional funding.

One final point needs to be made concerning economics and handicapped populations. Special education as a formalized and systematic process is a great experiment. The vast amounts of money that have been expended on those with special needs can best be viewed as "seed money." It is hoped that money spent today will have a long-lasting effect and result in future savings. Through the teaching of skills necessary for independent functioning and economic self-sufficiency, society hopes that the exceptional individual will assume responsibility for his own needs upon leaving the formal educational environment. We live in a technological society where the ultimate personal, institutional, and governmental criterion of success is often measured in monetary terms. In the final analysis, it will be the ability of handicapped adults to reduce their economic dependency on society that will determine the future direction of mainstreaming.

Society does not continue to invest in projects that falter—regardless of the humanitarian interest served. Special educators would do well to investigate all facets of the mainstreaming practice to ensure that failure does not occur. In view of what has happened to similar educational endeavors (e.g., compensatory education, desegregation, etc.), mainstreaming must be a success or we jeopardize much that we have gained in providing for the education of handicapped children.

Farber (1968) has suggested that society does little more than pay lip-service to major educational or social problems, while ignoring their causes. This allows us ". . . to foster the illusion that something is being done (we are making progress) when, in fact, nothing or, at best, very little is being accomplished (the status quo is being maintained)" (Farber & Lewis, 1972, p. 92). In light of the low level of economic support mentioned earlier, and the inadequate planning that has gone into implementing mainstreaming, perhaps society is once again attempting to maintain the status quo. Special educators need to examine whether a true societal commitment to the practice of mainstreaming exists, or only the illusion of such a commitment.

## SUMMARY

Mainstreaming originated from the interaction of three forces—historical changes within education and society, judicial decisions, and state and federal legislative mandates. As a principle, mainstreaming was not based on any empirical evidence that suggested that integrated programs for handicapped children would be beneficial, but on humanistic zeal and the desires of parents and special educators. In fact, much of the available information at the time indicated that integrated programs were of little value.

Recently, there has been an accumulation of information relating to the practice of mainstreaming. We have learned, for example, that nonhandicapped children often do not view their handicapped classmates in a favorable light. In addition, the placement of handicapped and nonhandicapped children in the same classroom, as would be suggested by a mainstreaming model, does not ensure increased social acceptance or reduced stigmatization. Thus, one of the purported benefits of main-streaming has little evidentiary support at this time.

An increasing emphasis has been placed on the importance of the regular teacher's attitudes toward handicapped children in the classroom. A number of studies have indicated that regular classroom teachers perceive handicapped children to be socially and academically inferior to regular children. However, it is these very teachers who will be required to accept handicapped children into their classrooms. The effects of these negative attitudes on the practice of mainstreaming are unknown, but it is certain that they will be influential in the success or failure of any integration program.

Studies that have investigated the academic performance of hand-icapped children in regular classrooms are more difficult to interpret.

Although a few investigators have found improvement in academic areas, the bulk of the research indicates no differences between achievement in integrated classrooms and that in self-contained special education classrooms. The comparable performance across diverse settings may at first seem reassuring. However, there is some evidence to indicate that it is the regular classroom child who becomes academically impoverished when handicapped children are placed in the classroom. Whether this is an artifact of a single study remains to be seen, but it is likely that schools will not be anxious to accept handicapped children into regular classrooms if their education is at the expense of the other children.

In the final analysis, education is an economic institution. Schools, like banks or factories, must show a profit or a product. The profit must be in direct relationship to the time and money invested to produce the product. With ever-increasing economic pressures being exerted on taxpayers, special educators will be pressed to show that their educational output is cost efficient. If 18 years of education and training (ages 3–21) cannot develop a self-sufficient and independently functioning person, it is unlikely that special education, as we know it today, will persevere. At this time, there is some question as to whether the necessary skills and technology to ensure positive results are present in our schools.

## CONCLUSIONS

Some years ago, Stephen Vincent Benet remarked, "We don't know where we're going, but we're on our way." Had he been talking about special education, he could not have been more prophetic. Special educators have attempted to accomplish a series of lofty goals for handicapped children. The dedication to the task at hand is evident, but only time will tell if the fortuitous moment was present to create a sound and viable alternative to segregated special classes.

In their struggle to obtain the very best for handicapped children, special educators have been governed by the principle of *more,* that is, "that *much* is good, but *more* is better" (Looft, 1973, p. 28). More money, more promises, more personnel, more cooperation, more accepting attitudes, etc., are all part of the *more* syndrome special education is creating. Admittedly, new programs and innovations require more, but now it is time that we operate on the principle of *enough.* If we do not, school boards and taxpayers will assume this function.

The question that arises is "What can we do now?" As a practical matter, it would be disconcerting to retreat from an accepted, and believed in, principle. On the other hand, forging ahead, when evidence suggests that the principle loses merit when it is transformed into practice, would be foolhardy. What is needed is a compromise solution.

The answer is twofold. First, those involved in special education must reduce the publicity accorded mainstreaming. As publicity increases, promises and expectations of the general public also increase. Media programs have extolled the virtues of comparable education for exceptional and normal children, with the eventual goal of getting the handicapped child into the mainstream of American life. Evidence is mounting that many exceptional children will not achieve acceptance by their normal peers. How will they enter the mainstream?

For the exceptional child an educational start equal to that received by normal children will not ensure an equal finish. The expectation of parents, teachers, legislators, and the general public may have been raised too high. Special educators must moderate their position and admit that they do not know whether mainstreaming will be an effective practice.

Second, more experimental research and small-scale demonstration projects are needed to evaluate the effects of mainstreaming of handicapped children (Jones, Gottlieb, Guskin, & Yoshida, 1978; Mac Millan & Semmel, 1977). The federal law does not require that any child be mainstreamed. The only requirement is that children be placed in the least restrictive environment. We might do well to limit the number of students involved in these programs, at least at the outset.

To date, there is little support for mainstreaming as a means of improving the social acceptability or academic performance of exceptional children. With the continued investigation of various means of implementing the mainstreaming principle, and a determination of the resultant effects, the move toward integrated placement will progress more slowly, but more confidently.

In the final analysis, mainstreaming will be judged by its ability to take the handicapped person from childhood to adulthood and achieve some measure of self-sufficiency and independence. If it fails due to a lack of preparedness on the part of those involved, special education may be set back. Prudence and knowledge should govern our use of mainstreaming with handicapped children.

# References

Abeson, A. Movement and momentum: Government and the education of handicapped children. *Exceptional Children,* 1972, *39,* 63–66.

Abeson, A., & Zettel, J. The end of the quiet revolution: The Education for All Handicapped Children Act of 1975. *Exceptional Children,* 1977, *44,* 115–128.

Bakan, D. Political factors in the development of American psychology. *Annals of the New York Academy of Science,* 1977, *291,* 222–232.

Baldwin, W. K. The educable mentally retarded child in the regular grades. *Exceptional Children,* 1958, *25,* 106–108.

Ballard, M., Corman, L., Gottlieb, J., & Kaufman, M. J. Improving the social status of mainstreamed retarded children. *Journal of Educational Psychology,* 1977, *69,* 605–611.

Ballard, J., & Zettel, J. Public Law 94-142 and Section 504: What they say about rights and protections. *Exceptional Children,* 1977, *44,* 177–184.

Ballard, J., & Zettel, J. Fiscal arrangements of Public Law 94-142. *Exceptional Children,* 1978a, *44,* 333–337.

Ballard, J., & Zettel, J. The managerial aspects of Public Law 94-142. *Exceptional Children,* 1978b, *44,* 457–462.

Baratz, J. C., & Moskowitz, J. H. Proposition 13: How and why it happened. *Phi Delta Kappan,* 1978, *60,* 9–11.

Bateman, B. An interview with Barbara Bateman, *Academic Therapy,* 1979, *14,* 353–358.

Bradfield, R. H., Brown, J., Kaplan, P., Rickert, E., & Stannard, R. The special child in the regular classroom. *Exceptional Children,* 1973, *39,* 384–390.

Brenton, M. Mainstreaming the handicapped. *Today's Education,* 1974, *63,* 20–24.

*Brown v. Board of Education of Topeka* 347 U. S. 483, 74s. ct. 1138, 41L Ed. 256, (1954).

Bruininks, V. L. Actual and perceived peer status of learning-disabled students in mainstream programs. *Journal of Special Education,* 1978, *12,* 51–58.

Bryan, T. H. Peer popularity of learning disabled children: A replication. *Journal of Learning Disabilities,* 1976, *9,* 49–53.

Budoff, M., & Gottlieb, J. Special class mainstreamed: A study of an aptitude (learning potential) X treatment interaction. *American Journal of Mental Deficiency,* 1976, *81,* 1–11.

Butts, R. F. The search for purpose in American education. *The College Board Review,* 1975–1976, No. 98, 2–19.

Cegelka, W. J., & Tyler, J. L. The efficacy of special class placement of the mentally retarded in proper perspective. *Training School Bulletin,* 1970, *65,* 33–68.

Chapin, R. C. The legal rights of children with handicapping conditions and the process of mainstreaming. *Peabody Journal of Education,* 1978, *56,* 18–23.

Chennault, M. Improving the social acceptance of unpopular educable mentally retarded pupils in special classes. *American Journal of Mental Deficiency,* 1967, *72,* 455–458.

Christoplos, R., & Renz, P. A critical examination of special education programs. *Journal of Special Education,* 1969, *8,* 321–329.

Cleland, C. C., & Chambers, I. L. The effect of institutional tours on attitudes of high school seniors. *American Journal of Mental Deficiency,* 1959, *64,* 124–130.

Cober, J. G., Hayes, R. B., Mulvilhill, P. J., & Reynolds, R. N. Pennsylvania programs for the handicapped get good marks for quality, cost, and effectiveness. *Phi Delta Kappan,* 1978, *38,* 7–22.

Coleman, J. The concepts of equality of educational opportunity, *Harvard Educational Review,* 1968, *38,* 7–22.

Corman, L., & Gottlieb, J. Mainstreaming mentally retarded children; A review of research. In N. R. Ellis (Ed.), *International review of research in mental retardation* (Vol. 13). New York: Academic Press, 1978.

Corrigan, D. C. Public Law 94-142: A matter of human rights; A call for change in schools and colleges of education. In J. K. Grosenick & M. C. Reynolds (Eds.), *Teacher education: Renegotiating roles for mainstreaming.* Reston, Va.: Council for Exceptional Children, 1978.

Farber, B. *Mental retardation: Its social context and social consequences.* Boston: Houghton Mifflin, 1968.

Farber, B., & Lewis, M. Compensatory education and social justice. *Peabody Journal of Education,* 1972, *49,* 85–96.

Flynn, T. M. Regular-class adjustment of EMR students attending a part-time special education program. *Journal of Special Education,* 1974, *8,* 167–173.

Gallup, G. J. The 10th annual Gallup poll of the public's attitudes toward the public schools. *Phi Delta Kappan,* 1978, *60,* 33–45.

Gickling, E. E., & Theobald, J. T. Mainstreaming: Affect or effect. *Journal of Special Education,* 1975, *9,* 317–328.

Gintis, H. Toward a political economy of education. A radical critique of Ivan Illich's "Deschooling Society." *Harvard Educational Review,* 1972, *42,* 70–96.

Goldberg, I. G., & Lippman, L. Plato had a word for it. *Exceptional Children,* 1974, *40,* 325–334.

Goodman, H., Gottlieb, J., & Harrison, R. H. Social acceptance of EMRs integrated into a nongraded elementary school. *American Journal of Mental Deficiency,* 1972, *76,* 412–417.

Gottlieb, J. Public, peer, and professional attitudes toward mentally retarded persons. In M. J. Begab & S. A. Richardson (Eds.), *The mentally retarded and society: A social science perspective.* Baltimore: University Park Press, 1975.

Gottlieb, J., & Budoff, M. Social acceptability of retarded children in nongraded schools differing in architecture. *American Journal of Mental Deficiency,* 1973, *78,* 15–19.

Gottlieb, J., Semmel. M. I., & Veldman, D. J. Correlates of social status among mainstreamed mentally retarded children. *Journal of Educational Psychology,* 1978, *70,* 396–405.

Gozali, J. Perception of the EMR special class by former students. *Mental Retardation,* 1972, *10,* 34–35.

Greer, C. *The great school legend.* New York: Basic Books, 1972.

Guerin, G. R., & Szatlocky, K. Integration programs for the mentally retarded. *Exceptional Children,* 1974, *41,* 173–177.

Haring, N. G., & Krug, D. A. Placement in regular programs: Procedures and results. *Exceptional Children,* 1975, *41,* 413–417.

*Hobson* v. *Hansen.* 269 F Supp. 401 (DDC, 1967).

Iano, R. P., Ayers, D., Heller, H. B., McGettigan, J. F., & Walker, V. S. Sociometric status of retarded children in an integrative program. *Exceptional Children,* 1974, *40,* 267–271.

Ispa, J. & Matz, R. P. Integrating handicapped preschool children within a cognitively oriented program. In M. J. Guralnick (Ed.), *Early intervention and integration of handicapped and nonhandicapped children.* Baltimore: University Park Press, 1978.

Jefferson, T. Speech given in Philadelphia, November 12, 1794. *Notes on the State of Virginia* (2nd American ed.). New York: Norton, 1972.

Johnson, G. O. A study of the social position of mentally handicapped children in the regular grades. *American Journal of Mental Deficiency,* 1950, *55,* 60–89.

Johnson, G. O., & Kirk, S. A. Are mentally-handicapped children segregated in the regular grades? *Journal of Exceptional Children,* 1950, *17,* pp. 65–68; 87–88.

Jones, R. L., Gottlieb, J., Guskin, S., & Yoshida, R. K. Evaluating mainstreaming programs: Models, caveats, considerations and guidelines. *Exceptional Children,* 1978, *44,* 588–601.

Kaufman, M. J., Gottlieb, J., Agard, J. A., & Kukic, M. B. Mainstreaming: Toward an explication of the construct. In E. L. Meyen, G. A. Vergason, & R. J. Whelan (Eds.), *Alternatives for teaching exceptional children.* Denver: Love, 1975, pp. 35–54.

Keogh, B. K., & Levitt, M. L. Special education in the mainstream: A confrontation of limitations. *Focus on Exceptional Children,* 1976, *8,* 1–11.

Kitano, M. K., Stiehl, J., & Cole, J. T. Role taking: Implications for special education. *Journal of Special Education,* 1978, *12,* 59–74.

Kraft, A. Down with (most) special education classes. *Academic Therapy,* 1973, *8,* 207–216.

Lilly, M. S. Improving social acceptance of low sociometric status, low achieving students. *Exceptional Children,* 1971, *37,* 341–348.

Looft, W. R. Conceptions of human nature, educational practice and individual development. *Human Development,* 1973, *16,* 21–32.

MacMillan, D. L. *Mental retardation in school and society.* Boston: Little, Brown, 1977.

MacMillan, D. L., Jones, R. L., & Meyers, C. E. Mainstreaming the mildly retarded: Some questions, cautions, and guidelines. *Mental Retardation,* 1976, *14,* 3–10.

MacMillan, D. L., Meyers, C. E., & Yoshida, R. K. Regular class teachers' perceptions of transition programs for EMR students and their impact on the students. *Psychology in the Schools,* 1978, *15,* 99–103.

MacMillan, D. L., & Semmel, M. I. Evaluations of mainstreaming programs. In E. L. Meyen, G. A. Vergason, & R. J. Whelan (Eds.), *Instructional planning for exceptional children.* Denver: Love, 1979, 446–470.

Martin, E. W. Some thoughts on mainstreaming. *Exceptional Children,* 1974, *41,* 150–153.

Martin, L. C. Shall we segregate our handicapped? *Journal of Exceptional Children,* 1940, *6,* 223–237.

Marver, J. D. The cost of special education in nonpublic schools. *Journal of Learning Disabilities,* 1976, *9,* 43–52.

McDaniel, C. O. Participation in extracurricular activities, social acceptance, and social rejection among educable mentally retarded students. *Education and Training of the Mentally Retarded.* 1970, *5,* 4–14.

McKinnon, A. J. Parent and pupil perceptions of special classes for emotionally disturbed children. *Exceptional Children,* 1970, *37,* 302–303.

Meisgeier, C. A review of critical issues underlying mainstreaming. In L. Mann & D. A. Sabatino (Eds.), *The third review of special education.* New York: Grune & Stratton, 1976.

Melcher, J. W. Law, litigation, and handicapped children. A helping relationship: Federal programs for special children. *Exceptional Children,* 1976, *43,* 126–130.

*Mills v. Board of Education of the District of Columbia,* 348F. Supp. 866 (DDC, 1972).

Mitchell, M. M. Teacher attitudes. *High School Journal,* 1976, *59,* 302–311.

Moore, J., & Fine, M. J. Regular and special class teachers' perceptions of normal and exceptional children and their attitudes toward mainstreaming. *Psychology in the Schools,* 1978, *15,* 253–259.

Nirje, B. The normalization principle and its human management implications. In R. B. Kugel & W. Wolfensberger (Eds.), *Changing patterns in residential services for the mentally retarded.* Washington, D. C.: President's Committee on Mental Retardation, 1969.

Palmer, D. Regular classroom teachers' attributions and instructional prescriptions for handicapped and nonhandicapped pupils. *Journal of Special Education,* 1979, *13,* 325–337.

Panda, K. C., & Bartel, N. R. Teacher perception of exceptional children. *Journal of Special Education,* 1972, *6,* 261–266.

*PARC—Pennsylvania Association for Retarded Children v. Commonwealth of Pennsylvania,* 343 F. Supp. 279, (E. D. Pa., 1972).

Parish, T. S., & Copeland, R. F. Teachers' and students' attitudes in mainstreamed classrooms. *Psychological Reports,* 1978, *43,* 54.

Parish, T. S., & Dyck, N. Stereotypes of normal and handicapped children: A stumbling block for mainstreaming. Paper presented at the meeting of the American Educational Research Association, San Francisco, California, April 1979.

Parish, T. S., Eads, G. M., Reece, N. H., & Piscitello, M. A. Assessment and attempted modification of future teachers' attitudes toward handicapped children. *Perceptual and Motor Skills*, 1977, *44*, 540–542.

Parish, T. S., Ohlsen, R. L., & Parish, J. G. A look at mainstreaming in light of children's attitudes toward the handicapped. *Perceptual and Motor Skills*, 1978, *46*, 1019–1021.

Payne, J. S., Mercer, C. D., Payne, R. A., & Davison, R. G. *Head start: A tragicomedy with epilogue*. New York: Behavioral Publications, 1973.

Payne, R., & Murray. C. Principal's attitudes toward the integration of the handicapped. *Exceptional Children*, 1974, *41*, 123–125.

Public Law 93–112, *Vocational Rehabilitation Act of 1973*, Section 504, July 26, 1973.

Public Law 93–380, *Education Amendments of 1974*, August 21, 1974.

Public Law 94–142, *Education for All Handicapped Children Act*, November 29, 1975.

Reynolds, M. C., & Birch, J. W. *Teaching exceptional children in all America's schools: A first course for teachers and principals*. Reston, Va.: Council for Exceptional Children, 1977.

Ritter, D. R. Surviving in the regular classroom; A follow-up of mainstreamed children with learning disabilities. *Journal of School Psychology*, 1978, *16*, 253–256.

Rossmiller, R., Hale, J., & Frohreich, L. *Educational programs for exceptional children: Resource configurations and costs*. University of Wisconsin, 1970.

Rucker, C. N., & Vincenzo, F. M. Maintaining social acceptance gains made by mentally retarded children. *Exceptional Children*, 1970, *36*, 679–680.

Sabatino, D. A. Resource rooms: The renaissance in special education. *Journal of Special Education*, 1972, *6*, 335–347.

*Serrano v. Priest*. 5 Cal, 3rd 584; 96 Cal. Rptr. 601; 487 P. 2d 1241, (1971).

Shotel, J. R., Iano, R. P., & McGettigan, J. F. Teacher attitudes associated with the integration of handicapped children. *Exceptional Children*, 1972, *38*, 677–683.

Simches, R. Economic inflation: Hazard for the handicapped. *Exceptional Children*, 1975, *41*, 229–242.

Smith, M. S., & Bissell, J. S. Report analysis: The impact of Head Start. *Harvard Educational Review*, 1970, *40*, 51–104.

*Smuck v. Hobson*. 408 F 2d 175, (D. C. Cir., 1969).

Stafford, R. T. The handicapped: Challenge and decision. *Exceptional Children*, 1974, *40*, 485–488.

Strang, L., Smith, M. D., & Rogers, C. M. Social comparisons, multiple reference groups, and the self-concepts of academically handicapped children before and after mainstreaming. *Journal of Educational Psychology*, 1978, *70*, 487–497.

Thomas, M. A. Finance: Without which there is no special education. *Exceptional Children*, 1973, *39*, 475–480.

Throne, J. M. Normalization through the normalization principle: Right ends, wrong means. *Mental Retardation*, 1975, *13*, 23–25.

Turnbull, A. P., & Schultz, J. B. *Mainstreaming handicapped students: A guide for the classroom teacher*. Boston: Allyn & Bacon, 1979.

Vacc, N. A. Long term effects of special class intervention for emotionally disturbed children. *Exceptional Children*, 1972, *39*, 15–22.

Vacc, N., & Kirst, N. Emotionally disturbed children and regular class teachers. *The Elementary School Journal*, 1977, *77*, 309–317.

Walker, V. The efficacy of the resource room for educating mentally retarded children. Unpublished doctoral dissertation, Temple University, 1972.

Warner, F., Thrapp, R., & Walsh, S. Attitudes of children toward their special class placement. *Exceptional Children*, 1973, *40*, 37–38.

Weintraub, F. J. Recent influences and law regarding the identification and educational placement of children. *Focus on Exceptional Children,* 1972, *4*(2), 1–11.

Westinghouse Learning Corporation/Ohio University. *The impact of Head Start: An evaluation of the effects of Head Start on children's cognitive and affective development.* Volumes I and II. Washington, D. C.: Office of Economic Opportunity, June 12, 1969.

Wilken, W. H., & Porter, D. O. *State aid for special education: Who benefits.* Washington, D. C.: National Institute of Education (NIE-G-74-0021), December 1, 1977.

Winschel, J. F. In the dark . . . reflections on compensatory education 1960–1970. In J. Hellmuth (Ed.), *Disadvantaged child—compensatory education: A national debate* (Vol. 3). New York: Brunner/Mazel, 1970.

Yoshida, R. K., Fenton, K. S., Maxwell, J. P., & Kaufman, M. J. Group decision making in the planning team process: Myth or reality? *Journal of School Psychology,* 1978, *16,* 237–244.

# CAREER AND VOCATIONAL EDUCATION FOR THE HANDICAPPED: A HISTORICAL PERSPECTIVE

Sidney R. Miller
*Southern Illinois University, Carbondale*

Norma J. Ewing
*Southern Illinois University, Carbondale*

L. Allen Phelps
*University of Illinois*

## PRETRANSITIONAL TRENDS

Twentieth century Western society provides many of its citizens many more career opportunities (U. S. Department of Labor, 1978) than societies existing prior to the advent of the differentiated occupational structure. This differentiation of opportunity has created for contemporary society and it's handicapped individuals significantly more complex career opportunities than existed over 2000 years ago. Historically, the handicapped have consistently been a societal perturbation. During the periods of the ancient Roman and Greek civilizations, few handicapped individuals were thought to be able to perform a useful function. They were thus generally neglected and reduced to beggary. Other, less handicapped young men were trained and employed as bearers for the armies, or oarmen for ships, or were given other tasks requiring minimal skills. The young women were provided jobs as house servants, laundry maids, or women of pleasure. At the heights of both the Roman and Greek civilizations the plight of the handicapped in seeking and holding jobs were critical concerns of the socially conscious political and military leaders.

Around the 15th and 16th centuries, some European nations began to look upon their identified handicapped populations with minimal tolerance and initiated remedial efforts in response to the needs of some mildly handicapped. The transition is evidenced by the willingness of the

341

royal courts of France and Italy to support limited amounts of habilitation and rehabilitation of the deaf and blind.

In medieval times and up to the Renaissance, education for the majority of the Europeans was not formalized. Vocational preparation was likely to be handled by the church, proficient craftsmen, or parents. Under each of these three vocational preparation "models," mildly disabled individuals able to contribute to the family's economic resources were not usually perceived as handicapped. The measure of a "civilized" society then was not its literacy level. In most cases, individuals with minimal skills were provided training which could lead to vocational and economic independence. Just before and during the Renaissance, as the mercantile classes began to emerge, labor guilds began to assume the role of the church and that of individual craftsmen in the preparation of youth to perform useful jobs. Many of the individuals trained by the various guilds, churches, and craftsmen were handicapped but were not labeled as such if their basic motor skills and physical appearance did not result in significant deviance from the physical and social norms of the times.

## TRANSITIONAL PERIOD

In the 18th century, during the early stages of the European industrial age, the philosopher Jean Jacques Rousseau advocated individualized education—training that would enable man to live a productive and useful life. Implementing many of Rousseau's individualized education ideas, European education Phillip von Fellenberg, in the 17th century, provided the poor and handicapped with academic and vocational training. Unfortunately, von Fellenberg's training of the students reflected their social class more than their cognitive and physical competencies. Indeed, this focus on an individual's socioeconomic standing rather than cognitive and physical status persisted through the 18th and 19th centuries, i.e., until contemporary concepts of intellectual measurement based on the works of the French psychologist Alfred Binet emerged.

Edward Sequin, also concerned with education of the poor during the mid-19th century, contributed greatly to the training of the "feeble-minded" so that they could adequately function in society. While he initially began serving the severely handicapped in institutions, his later efforts focused on training that would enable the individual to perform tasks in the community which they had been previously denied. In 1848, Dr. Harvey B. Wilbur opened a private school in Massachusetts where he emphasized Sequin's policies of sensory stimulation, encouragement of curiosity, socialization, and habit formation. In addition, he stressed the use of concrete objects and the need for practical utility in the education of the severely handicapped. During the late 19th century, Dr. Maria Montessori also used many of Sequin's methods to train the retarded to perform useful and self-sustaining tasks—work which she carried on into the 20th century.

In 1850 the Perkins School for the Blind, borrowing heavily from European efforts to serve the handicapped, began the first workshop for the handicapped in the United States. The workshop—which provided employment for the blind—was begun as a supplement to vocational education. Perkins' workshop was one of the first successful efforts in the United States to establish equal educational and work opportunities for the handicapped (Nelson, 1971). Other centers for the blind in Pennsylvania and New York attempted to create such workshops in the 1860s and 1870s, but the financial burden associated with their paying the handicapped forced their closing. Toward the end of the 19th century, the financial bases of workshops were strengthened and their numbers began to increase, reaching from the Atlantic to the Pacific Ocean.

With the evangelistic efforts of Jane Addams and William James, attitudes in the United States began to change early in the 20th century, and handicapped youth began to receive services through public agencies that were designed to promote self-sufficiency and vocational competency. This change resulted, however, more from laws mandating compulsory schooling in society in general than from a universal commitment to help the handicapped. A review of the literature during this period demonstrated little concern for adolescent students with a handicapping condition. Evans (1971) noted that not until midway through the 20th century did the concept of vocational education move from long-term training of a few competent, highly motivated students for highly specialized jobs, to short- and long-term preparation that was dependent on student and community needs and goals.

## 20TH CENTURY AWAKENING

The independent efforts of a few educators provided marginal impetus for the vocational preparation of the handicapped in the United States during the first two decades of the 20th century, but this service was not provided through traditional educational units. Doll (1967) noted an early program outlined by Anderson in 1971 that involved a specialized curriculum for the mentally handicapped which included three different instructional levels—kindergarten, departmental, and trade—geared to different degrees of retardation. The kindergarten level stressed self-care skills and sensory, speech, motor, and physical training. At the departmental level, shop and industrial work, home economics, music, and practical academics were emphasized. The trade level was designed to prepare students for unskilled trades such as janitorial, domestic, and factory work. It is Wallin (1917) to whom credit should be given as one of the first to involve the community in the vocational habilitation/rehabilitation of the handicapped. Wallin distinguished between two types of programs for two different handicapped populations—the severely and the trainable handicapped. He advocated separate vocational schools, custodial care in the public schools, habilitation and rehabilitation facilities near major cities, and outpatient, follow-up, and evaluation services. Unfortunately, both his and Anderson's efforts were directed toward institutionalized adult populations rather than handicapped people functioning in the community.

In the second decade of the 20th century, industrial schools began to emerge, offering specialized training for adults in various craft and skilled labor areas. It was then, in early 1917, that Congress passed the Smith-Hughes Act, providing for the vocational rehabilitation and employment of persons who had been disabled during World War I. This law was the first of a parade of federal laws which slowly and profoundly reshaped services for the handicapped. It should be noted that the Smith-Hughes Act arose from economic necessity rather than a national call to serve the handicapped. At the time of its passage, the United States had become deeply involved in World War I. Unless its wounded had received rehabilitative treatment, they would become social and economic burdens on the nation. It should also be noted that the Smith-Hughes Act established the first federally supported vocational education in the secondary schools, creating funds for programs of agricultural education, home economics, and trade and industrial education.

The following year, the Vocational Rehabilitation Act of 1918 was enacted. This law provided additional financial support to discharged veterans suffering from war-related handicaps and ensured that their training would be cost free. Within the Rehabilitation Act, Congress also took special note of the blind, inquiring into the cost of translating books into braille and producing such books for the visually handicapped.

Cegelka (1974) observed that efforts in the 1920s to provide services for the handicapped were short lived because of the economic depression that extended from the mid-1920s on. During the 1930s, the federal government initiated programs to reduce the high number of unemployed youths. While none of these programs were specifically directed at the handicapped, some of the mildly handicapped benefited from such New Deal programs as the Civilian Conservation Corps. This and other programs provided employment to the unemployed and handicapped through the initiation of civic building projects. Specific educational efforts to serve the handicapped were curtailed during the depression years of the 1930s and remained curtailed until both the depression moderated and World War II ended in the mid 1940s.

The vocational movement had both its staunch supporters and ardent opponents in the early 20th century. The traditional school was criticized for its failure to provide vocational direction to youth, for its inattention to the needs of the working-class student, and for its overemphasis on the moral and cultural aspects of life instead of the practical (Thompson, 1973). One of the most prominent supporters of vocational education during this period was John Dewey. Dewey had always maintained a strong interest in alleviating social problems, expecially those of the underprivileged. He viewed the vocational and industrial training movement as incorporating many of the components—active learner participation, a relevant and practical curriculum, and instruction in social efficiency and continuous adjustment—of an effective, progressive educational system (Meyer, 1949).

Educators in the liberal arts during the 1920s, 1930s, and 1940s feared that vocational training would break down the standards of the dominant liberal arts–oriented college preparatory curriculum. They attacked the movement as being anti-intellectual, a threat to the traditional method of teaching from the classics, and, in general, not a legitimate form of education. Industrial management and labor were also divided on the question of vocational education. Industrial management supported the movement, anticipating that an increased manpower pool resulting from such training was a way of combating the increasing power of labor unions. Labor, on the other hand, feared that vocational education would eventually glut the trained manpower market and thus become a pawn in management's scheme to undermine the unions (Cremin, 1961).

In 1938 the passage of the Wagner-O'Day Act added momentum to the commitment of the federal government to the rights of handicapped persons. Among its provisions, it made it mandatory that various agencies purchase predesignated commodities from workshops for the blind. The federal government's commitment was further expanded in the 1939 Social Security Amendment, which provided for $3.5 million for annual grants to the states for vocational rehabilitation.

The provisions of the Wagner Act, like the preceding congressional laws, continued to focus primarily on sensory-impaired adults, who had the support of vocal advocacy groups. It was not until the enactment of the 1943 Vocational Rehabilitation Amendments that state rehabilitation agencies were ordained to provide services to the mentally handicapped. The Barden-LaFollette Amendments to the 1943 legislation specifically provided services and vocational rehabilitation counseling for the more severely mentally handicapped and broadened considerably the concept of rehabilitation for all persons (Dybwad, 1961). However, 10 years after the passage of the 1943 Rehabilitation Act, a National Association for Retarded Children subcommittee on sheltered workshops, headed by J. Clifford MacDonald, was able to identify only 10 sheltered workshops for the retarded in the United States. In an effort to stimulate the expansion of the concept of providing special work settings for the handicapped which are free of social and production stress factors found in traditional work environments, MacDonald organized additional workshop settings and published a guide to other agencies. Largely as a result of this effort, the 1954 Vocational Rehabilitation Amendments included a short-term provision for the expansion of state vocational programs for the handicapped; 39 workshops, backed by a miniscule $40,000 of federal funds, were approved. The amendments did, however, include an extension and improvement provision designed to keep the workshops in operating order. The law also provided federal funds for research activities; and, in 1955 the first research effort in a sheltered workshop was approved by the Office of Vocational Rehabilitation. Then, as now, research on basic issues of adolescent development and vocational education for the handicapped, while not completely neglected, was sparse, spasmodic, frequently superficial, and given a low priority among government and school leaders.

One effort in vocational preparation for the handicapped which emerged in the 1950s through the public education system was the work–study program. It became a leading strategy in preparing the handicapped for the world of work (Brolin, 1976; Clark, 1976; Hull, 1976; Malouf & Halpern, 1976). One of the earliest programs was housed at Southern Illinois University (Kolstoe, 1975). The program was a three-phase approach, beginning with a controlled work experience in school, moving to a permanent job placement and experience, and eventually leading to employment. This model was eventually validated in the Lansing, Michigan, public schools, which endorsed in practice the concept that mentally retarded youths must receive training in specialized environments, but that sheltered job experiences must also acquaint and prepare these youth to function in the outside world of work.

## THE KENNEDY INFLUENCE

It was not until the 1962 report of the President's Panel on Mental Retardation, which advocated vocational training and related services for every retarded youth, that clear national priorities emerged. The report stipulated that the vocational services include funding for instruction in appropriate vocational areas; cooperative work-study-experience programs; on-the-job training programs; and vocational guidance. The report also listed two major obstacles to vocational training of the handicapped: (1) failure of the various institutions and agencies serving the handicapped students to work together for their benefit; and (2) fewer job openings available to the handicapped (Cohen, 1964). The position stated by the report reflected the new direction outlined by President John F. Kennedy's 1962 State of the Union Address in which he stated, "to help those less fortunate of all, I am recommending a new program of public welfare, stressing service instead of support, rehabilitation instead of relief, and training . . . instead of prolonged dependence."

Portions of the Vocational Education Act of 1963 implemented recommendations of the 1962 Presidental Panel on Vocational Education. The act included provisions for: the development of new areas in vocational education and expansion of existing programs for handicapped and disadvantaged persons; part-time work for students in need of funds to continue full-time vocational training; and the extension of vocational education to populations who had been neglected by previous programs. The neglected populations include those who were underemployed in the existing labor market, minorities, school dropouts, and individuals with educational handicaps. This committment was enlarged in 1964 by the passage of the Economic Opportunities Act, which sought to remedy the lack of appropriate training for the educationally handicapped and disadvantaged who left public education without the requisite skills to find employment (Peters, 1971). The legislation reflected the perceptions of President Lyndon B. Johnson. In his 1964 State of the Union message, he stated that the nation's efforts should be directed toward ensuring all individuals an opportunity to be healthy, productive members of society, free to pursue their individual hopes and aspirations.

Despite the call to meet individual needs, the vocational community maintained a business as usual attitude during most of the 1960s. A major hindrance faced by the vocational community in fostering special programs was the public schools' excessive focus on traditional academic skills. A survey of vocational programs indicated that only two programs sought to develop the appropriate social and vocational skills in individuals with average or below average intelligence (Miller & Sabatino, 1975). Goldstein (1969) believed that vocational education had placed too much emphasis on academic instruction and too little on the development of socio-occupational competence. The legislation of the 1960s, however, provided a much needed moral impetus for improved vocational education programming for the handicapped, despite the fact that fiscal incentives to initiate such programs were sparse.

While the 1963 Vocational Education Act (PL 88-210) and the 1964 presidential message to the nation specified the urgent need for improved programs and services for the handicapped, there was only minimal effort on the part of states to respond to the provisions in the Act and the sentiments of Congress. One major factor that began to grease the wheels of change in the states was the Social Security Act, which allowed the use of social security monies to educate children and youth. The 1968 amendments to the Vocational Education Act reiterated the priority of vocational education for the handicapped, and designated 10 percent of each state's basic grant to be used exclusively for vocational programs for the handicapped.

Many states have failed to respond to federal legislation and regulations. There is agreement in the literature that while the 1963 Vocational Education Act and the 1968 amendments made vocational education for the handicapped a priority in principle, there has generally been limited access for the handicapped to adequate vocational training within the various states (Evans & Clark, 1976; Mann, Goodman, & Weiderholt, 1978; Olympus Research Corporation, 1974; Phelps, 1977; Weisenstein, 1976).

## EARLY SERVICE DELIVERY MODELS

Work–study, sheltered workshops, and special classes programs were the primary models for vocational training for the handicapped during the 1950s and 1960s, and they maintained their popularity well into the 1970s. These programs became the prototypes for the 1970s largely because what little research does exist tends to support these models. Phelp's (1956) found that 68 percent of the students in special programs designed to promote job-related self-reliance were employed and an additional 11 percent were listed in categories of housewives, armed services, and unemployed. Porter and Milazzo (1958) reported that 75 percent of those in special education classes were eventually employed, compared to 17 percent of the nonspecial class group. Dinger (1961) reported an 83 percent success rate for work–study participants. In

Phelp's (1956) and Dinger's (1961) studies, positive findings were inflated by a liberal inclusion of activities in the employment category (e.g., student or housewife). Chaffin, Spellman, Regan, and Davidson (1971) drew more cautious conclusions after two follow-up studies revealed that cooperative work–study programs achieved limited success. The findings showed that former work–study students were earning more than a comparison group of non-work–study students. While 83 percent of the work–study students were employed, 75 percent of the non-work–study students were employed. Results in other reports have not supported work–study programs. According to Anttonen's (1974) follow-up studies of graduates from a work–study program in Oregon, 50–75 percent of the graduates sampled 2 years after leaving the program were unemployed.

Research was also conducted during this period to examine the community and occupational adjustment of handicapped individuals. The major pieces of research included those by Craighead and Mercatoris (1973), Halpern (1973), Halpern, Raffeld, and Littman (1972), Jackson (1973), Kokaska (1968), Shalock and Harper (1978), Strickland and Arrell (1967), and Tobias (1970). In general, these studies found that former educable mentally retarded students made relatively positive employment adjustments after completing programs that provided them with increased occupational preparation. Research also revealed a critical need for personal, social, and daily living skills among such students. Several studies revealed that such skills are often significant determinants of vocational success and community adjustment (Burger, Collins, & Doherty, 1970; Kolstoe, 1965; Sali & Amir, 1971; Shalock & Harper, 1978) and that those retarded youth who adjusted best following schooling were individuals with more skills and socially appropriate behaviors. Results of such vocational adjustment research, as well as contemporary employment and educational data, led to the enactment of several major legislative initiatives, many of which were focused on improving career development opportunities for handicapped individuals.

## LEGISLATION OF THE 1970S

The limited impact of the legislation of the 1960s on the handicapped became evident in the early 1970s. Martin (1972) noted that only 21 percent of the handicapped youth leaving school would be fully employed or going on to college. Another 40 percent would be underemployed, and 26 percent would be unemployed. The other 13 percent would probably be dependent on family or others. Hudson (1971), foreshad-

349

owing Martin's position, reported that success of the handicapped in leaving a controlled public setting and being integrated into society was dependent on their job training and subsequent employment. Miller (1978) and Sabatino (1974) held that this training depends on a properly integrated academic and vocational curriculum. However, a review of 40 vocational programs revealed only 5 that focused on the academic and vocational aspects of learning and minimized the psychotherapeutic aspects of learning. Among the same 40 programs, only 3 models delineated responsibilities for educators in vocational settings. This report underscored the need for the handicapped to receive more appropriate training in order to improve their competitive stance in the job market.

The General Accounting Office (1976) and the House of Representatives Subcommittee on Elementary, Secondary, and Vocational Education (Tindall, 1977), and the House Subcommittee on Select Education (1979) reported that in the 1970s several states either underused or failed to use the 10 percent of federal vocational education funds as specified in the 1968 Vocational Education Act Amendments. There was evidence that the ratio of handicapped students in vocational education programs had actually declined relative to the total enrollment in vocational education during the late 1960s and early 1970s when compared with enrollment ratios of the early 1960s.

Weisenstein (1976) observed that in spite of legislative directives the handicapped were being underserved in vocational programs, statewide vocational programs were rare, special or separate vocational programs were most common, and there was a shortage of trained personnel to manage vocational programs for the handicapped. The Olympus Research Corporation (1974) report concluded that provisions of the 1968 amendments were not being implemented carefully: goals were not being clearly defined, needs of the handicapped individuals were not being identified, and priorities for the vocational education of the handicapped were not being established. It is difficult to reach any data-based decision on state efforts since information provided by the states to the Office of Education has been incomplete and unreliable. Even though federal funds were available for program development, most states and local school districts appeared unprepared to design and implement the numerous alternatives needed to provide adequately for the education of the secondary-age handicapped youth.

In the early and mid-1970s, additional federal legislation generated a new impetus for improved vocational opportunities for the handicapped. This new legislation demonstrated the federal government's commitment to end exclusion and discrimination against handicapped persons. Societal barriers which had continued to limit the participation of the handicapped in vocational education were dealt a critical blow by passage of four pieces of legislation and accompanying sets of regulations which relate in whole, or in part, to the vocational education of the handicapped. Section 504 of the Rehabilitation Act of 1973 (PL 93-112), the 1973 Comprehensive Employment and Training Act (PL 93-203), the Education for All Handicapped Children Act of 1975 (PL 94-142), and the Vocational Education Amendments of 1976 (PL 94-482) each provided increased fiscal considerations, which, as expected, stimulated vocational preparation of the handicapped. Section 504 of the Rehabilitation Act of 1973 prohibited discrimination on the basis of handicap in any private or public program receiving federal assistance. Section 503, a companion set of regulations, required businesses having more than $50,000 per year in federal contracts to initiate an affirmative action plan to recruit, train, and promote qualified handicapped persons.

PL 94-142 mandated the involvement of all segments of public education, including vocational education in serving the handicapped. The Act established the right of the handicapped between the ages of 3 and 21 to a free and appropriate education; this mandate includes the right to an appropriate vocational education. The action of the Congress and the Bureau of Education for the Handicapped legally and economically compelled all the state departments of education to place greater emphasis on programs for the secondary-age handicapped youth. Despite all the previous legislation, there had been no clear legal requirements to serve the adolescent, and, as a result, school districts throughout the nation placed the majority of monies and personnel into serving the primary school-age child, with a significantly lesser effort in the middle and high schools. A result of this school and state policy was that many handicapped youth dropped out of school prior to graduation (Malouf & Halpern, 1976). The 1973 Comprehensive Employment and Training Act made provisions for providing training to the handicapped student who leaves school. The intent of the Act was to assist those individuals who are either unemployed, underemployed, and/or disadvantaged.

The Vocational Education Amendments of 1976 (PL 94-482) further strengthened the funding base and program planning for implementation of vocational programs for the handicapped at the federal, state, and local level. The Act was designed to interface with PL 94-142. According to Hull (1976), the implementation of PL 94-142 and PL 94-482 necessitates a high level of cooperation and collaboration between vocational and special education personnel at many levels to provide appropriate vocational services for the handicapped. Poor societal attitudes, discriminatory practices, and low expectations of the handicapped have been affected by these three demanding pieces of legislation.

## NEW LOOK AT EDUCATIONAL MEANS AND GOALS

In 1976 the American Association of Colleges for Teacher Education surveyed 630 of their 839 member institutions to determine the extent to which career education was prevalent in teacher education programs. It was noted that in 1975–1976, 112 schools of education were conducting career education activities or programs for specialists that would work with mentally handicapped children; 69 schools of education had initiated career education programs for personnel working with the physically handicapped (McLaughlin, 1976). In a recent national survey of teacher education programs, Brock (1977) received responses from 113 universities and colleges. Only 25 schools (22 percent) reported existing programs which trained vocational/special education personnel. State teacher certification officials were also surveyed. Eight states now require special education preparation (courses) for teacher certification in all fields. Brock notes that the trend to rethink and modify existing programs is likely to continue, but cautions that critical decisions concerning the number and types of modifications must be made.

Another aspect of the discussion of personnel preparation and appropriate services to handicapped students during the 1970s was whether the states should provide certification that ranges from kindergarten to the 12th grade, or whether the certification and training patterns should reflect the cognitive, physical, and psychosocial differences between preadolescence and adolescence. Gilmore and Argyros (1978) report that only 9 of the 50 states after certificates of special education at either the elementary or secondary level; the remaining states provide certification for grades K–12. The issue of types of certification became critical since most school-related special education personnel believe that most teachers with K–12 certification are not prepared to assist the adolescent. Many believe the solution is the separation of the current K–12 certification into elementary and secondary licensure.

Despite passage of the legislation designed to promote education of the handicapped during the 1970s, there continued to be considerable disenchantment with the quality, quantity, and direction of vocational programs serving handicapped learners. Appropriate vocational programs for the handicapped had not developed rapidly or consistently.

Numerous barriers to the delivery of vocational services to the handicapped had been identified. Several problems have slowed the development of vocational programming for the handicapped: lack of trained personnel, inadequate and incomplete needs assessment, limited interagency communication, few direct teacher certification initiatives, and little differentiated vocational curricula for the handicapped.

Reports in the 1970s also indicated that few handicapped individuals were receiving appropriate vocational education in public schools (General Accounting Office, 1976; Phelps, 1977). Evans and Clark (1976) reported that a large number of persons in the age group 15–21 years received no vocational education or were enrolled in regular vocational programs taught by teachers unprepared to identify and meet the handicapped student's needs. Razeghi and Halloran (1978) reported that only 1.7 percent of the total fiscal year 1976 enrollment in vocational programs was identified as handicapped, while as many as 10–12 percent of the school age population are assumed to be handicapped. Of the handicapped enrolled in vocational classes, 70 percent were placed in separate classes (Olympus Research Corporation, 1974). Mann et al. (1978) concluded that only a small minority of handicapped students have profited from appropriate vocational programs. Clark (1976) stated that in spite of the cumulative years of experience, there has been little operational change in philosophy, program options, assessment procedures, types of work placement, or program results compared to that reported in the literature 8–10 years ago. The literature strongly supports the position that there is a need for further expansion of education programs that provide adequate vocational preparation for the handicapped.

The literature during the late 1970s further reflected increased interest in altering the old operational philosophy so that vocational preparation for the handicapped could be instituted in the public schools. A growing number of articles, books, and conference and workshop reports were published relating to the topic. Among the publications emerging during the mid- and late 1970s were articles and books (Brolin, 1974; D'Alonzo & Miller, 1977; Miller, 1978; Phelps, 1977; Phelps & Lutz, 1977; Sabatino & Mauser, 1978) addressing the issue of developing vocational and career education programs for the handicapped. These publications sought to clarify procedures and methodology dealing with the following:

1. Identification of handicapped youth.
2. Assessment of adolescent cognitive and performance levels and potential.

353

3. Programming for youth reflecting a career–vocational orientation.
4. Procedures for providing instruction.
5. Procedures for behavior management.
6. Support agencies such as the Department of Labor, United Way, and industrial and retail firms.
7. Strategies for coordination of in-school resources, such as counselor involvement and effective communication between vocational and special educators.

The Olympus (1974) report noted that, in many instances, the handicapped student has encountered problems in competing with the nonhandicapped student in regular vocational classes, and consequently their opportunities to obtain vocational training have been restricted. The severely handicapped, as a result, have been trained in separate sheltered workshops, while less severely handicapped have received services through separate programs or institutions. Significant barriers to successfully mainstreaming the handicapped in regular vocational classes have been attitudinal barriers, lack of personnel preparation, and the availability of few satisfactory curriculum delivery models.

In 1976 the U.S. Office of Career Education released the results of a survey on career education in the nation's schools. The American Institute for Research (AIR) (1976) conducted the survey, one portion of which interfaces with the Olympus (1974) report. Like Olympus, AIR evaluated the available materials. In the AIR survey, 3000 commercial and noncommercial instructional materials were assessed. Materials appropriate for use with both physically and mentally handicapped were very limited in number. Less than 10 percent of the 797 commercial materials reviewed were deemed appropriate for these groups by independent raters. The percentage of noncommercial instructional material appropriate for the physically and mentally handicapped was found to be slightly higher. Students with special problems are ignored by makers of commercial and noncommercial materials addressing career and vocational programs (McLaughlin, 1976). Two years later, Miller, Benson, Demus, and Weaver (1978) found commercial publishers demonstrating increased interest in developing materials for secondary-age handicapped youth. Nevertheless, analysis of the materials still demonstrated a continuing inadequacy in the number, variety, and appropriateness of the materials being produced.

During the 1970s the career education concept began to emerge and held some attraction for both the special educator and vocational educator working with handicapped youth (Miller, 1978). The attraction of the special educator to career education was seen in the changing perception of the educational community as articulated by Hoyt (1977):

1. The belief that a general education was the most effective means for preparing for work was altered due to increased technological growth. With the increasing unemployability during the late 1960s of individuals who had general education backgrounds, it became evident that general education must complement a set of specific marketable vocational skills. Students should exit secondary school programs prepared to enter the workforce or continue their education.

2. As a result of increased geographical and occupational mobility, most individuals found it increasingly necessary to continually reassess their career skills and upgrade periodically.

3. As a result of rapid technological growth and specialization, it became increasingly critical that an emphasis be placed on helping school teachers cope with and manage career changes.

4. The strategies for schooling had moved to the view that the world of paid employment must become part of the student's classroom.

5. It was no longer assumed that the more years of schooling one had accumulated, the more successful one would become. It was recognized that the amount and kind of education required as preparation for work varies from occupation to occupation, and from individual to individual.

6. In response to the civil rights movement, the belief that the best educational and occupational opportunities should be reserved for white, able-bodied males no longer predominated. It was now believed that the full range of opportunities should be made available, to the maximum extent possible, to handicapped persons, females, and minorities, as well as to all others in society.

AIR (1976), under the directorship of Dr. Donald H. McLaughlin, examined programs and practices in 900 nationally representative local school districts. The data from the study suggested that 49 percent of the nation's students were in school districts reporting special efforts at the secondary level to broaden the career opportunities of physically handicapped youth. They further concluded that secondary programs serving approximately 70 percent of the nation's students had initiated special career education efforts for the mentally retarded; and 39 percent of the programs had provisions for gifted youth. At the secondary level there was low percentage of districts with a formal policy statement on career education and/or special education services for the mildly to severely handicapped adolescents.

It was also concluded by the AIR study that there were fewer special career education efforts for the physically handicapped, mentally handicapped, and gifted populations, at the elementary level, but the few districts that did have such activities tended to be districts that had adopted formal career education policies. Career education programming on behalf of special populations in general tended to be greater in districts with extensive career education implementation. The AIR report concluded that "career education is generally making a contribution to the equalization of career opportunities for all young people in America, but a great deal has yet to be done."

The principal rationale for treating career development as a major priority in the education of the handicapped was economic in nature. An analysis of 1970 census data conducted by the President's Committee on Employment of the Handicapped (1975) revealed that only 42 percent of the handicapped were employed, compared with 59 percent of the total population. In addition, handicapped persons tended to have lower earnings. Fourteen percent fewer handicapped than nonhandicapped men had earnings of about $7000 a year. These differences may be related, at least in part, to barriers associated with education. The census data also revealed that 14 percent more handicapped than nonhandicapped people never got beyond the eighth grade in their formal schooling, thus further supporting the findings of Malouf and Halpern (1976) that many handicapped youths drop out of school because of inadequate and inappropriate services.

## CAREER EDUCATION

Since the early 1970s, career education has been given numerous and diverse definitions. The most frequently cited definitions were those provided by the U.S. Office of Education—which is the agency given credit for introducing the concept (Bailey and Stadt, 1973, p. 268). The Career Education Incentive Act of 1977 (PL 95-207), provides the most recent and most widely accepted definition:

> Career education . . . means the totality of experiences, which are designed to be free of bias and stereotyping (including bias or stereotyping on account of race, sex, economic status or handicap), through which one learns about, and prepares to engage in, work as a part of his or her way of living, and through which he or she relates work values to other life roles and choices.

One of the major purposes of the Career Education Incentive Act of 1977 was to "increase the emphasis placed on career awareness, exploration, decision making, and planning, and . . . to promote equal opportunity in making career choices through the elimination of bias and stereotyping, including bias and stereotyping on account of race, sex, age, economic status, and handicap."

In its initial development there was a tendency to equate the term "career education" as being synonymous with "vocational education." Evans (1975) prepared a widely cited paper assessing the similarities and contrasts between the two concepts. Evans noted that vocational education represents a body of substantive knowledge designed to provide students with specific vocational skills necessary for entry into the occupational society. Career education's main thrust, on the other hand, was toward providing students with the skills and attitudes necessary for coping with change in the occupational society, including basic skills, decision-making, job-seeking, and job-holding skills, and good work habits and a meaningful set of work values.

In general, career education is viewed as a developmental concept. The phases of career education through which individuals progress is regarded as commensurate with vocational maturation. This made the concept particularly attractive to special educators (Miller, 1978). The growth stages in career education were described by Hoyt, Evans, Mackin, and Mangum (1974):

1. Awareness of primary work roles played by persons in society.

2. Exploration of work roles that an individual might consider as important, possible, and probable for himself or herself.

3. Vocational decision making (which can go from a highly tentative to a very specific form).

4. Establishment (including preparing for and actually assuming a primary work role).

5. Maintenance (all of the ways in which one gains—or fails to gain—personal meaningfulness and satisfaction from the primary work role he or she has assumed).

In 1979, the Council for Exceptional Children sponsored for the first time a conference on Career Education for Exceptional Individuals. It was the intent of the conference to facilitate the development of programs and services for children and youth. What the conference highlighted, however, was the lack of data concerning the field of career and vocational education for the handicapped. This deficiency was alluded to by Brolin (1974) and Miller (1978), and it is demonstrated through a review of the literature that numerous processes and components of programs for secondary youth have either been inadequately researched or not addressed through systematic evaluation. Brolin and

D'Alonzo (1979) articulated six issues in the area of career education for the handicapped:

1. Recognizing that the differences between career and vocation for the handicapped needs to be addressed and delineated.

2. Articulating the role of career education in the school curriculum and the community to achieve its stated aims of educating the whole person.

3. Ensuring that appropriate services are provided to handicapped students integrated into the regular educational environment.

4. Using mainstreaming as a vehicle in carrying out the goals of career education.

5. Developing and evaluating systematic program delivery processes and course options.

6. Implementing personnel preparation at the inservice and preservice levels.

Looking at the issue from an individual rather than a programmatic perspective, Hoyt (1977) identified some career-oriented competencies essential for the handicapped and nonhandicapped individual to possess if he/she is to become a productive self-sustaining member of the community. The individuals should be

1. Equipped with good work habits.

2. Equipped with a personally meaningful set of work values that foster in them a desire to work.

3. Equipped with career decision-making skills, job-hunting skills, and job-getting skills.

4. Equipped with a degree of self-understanding and understanding of educational–vocational opportunities sufficient for making sound career decisions.

5. Aware of means available to them for continuing and recurrent education.

6. Either placed or actively seeking placement in a paid occupation, in further education, or in a vocation consistent with their current career decisions.

7. Actively seeking to find meaning and meaningfulness through work in productive uses of leisure time.

8. Aware of means available to themselves for changing career options and of social and personal constraints impinging on career alternatives.

Concurrent with the problems of developing viable secondary

career education programs for handicapped youth in the 20th century has been the rapid change in the occupational structure of society. Many of the problems associated with developing appropriate secondary level programs are attributable to the changing nature of work and employment. In response to these changes, the U.S. Office of Education issued a position statement regarding the need for comprehensive education for handicapped persons in September 1978 (*Federal Register*). The position adopted was one of ensuring that "an appropriate and comprehensive . . . education is available and accessible to every handicapped person." The *Federal Register* notes that comprehensive education is the responsibility of all segments of the educational system, not just vocational or special education. Comprehensive vocational education must include the following: (1) cooperative relationships between the educational and employment sectors to facilitate the transition from school to work; (2) programs and services to develop basic skills and career decision-making skills, as well as occupational competencies; (3) appropriate sequential instruction; (4) the elimination of attitudinal and environmental barriers; and (5) efforts to assist employers in meeting their affirmative and action goals for employment of the handicapped. This comprehensive view suggests that numerous components, in addition to skill training, are critical. Phelps (1978) suggests a similar thrust in providing full vocational education opportunities for handicapped populations. The full opportunity to benefit from vocational education is contingent upon meaningful prevocational and career exploration experiences, appropriate career guidance, opportunities to participate in vocational student organizations, and appropriate postschool placement and follow-up services.

Several authors have urged the necessity of interagency efforts and professional collaboration as the key strategy for ensuring that the programming and services delivered to each student are indeed comprehensive and integrated. The comprehensive thrust involves coordination of and effective communication among a number of agencies.

## CONCLUSIONS AND RECOMMENDATIONS

The coming decade will be critical in determining the type and level of services which will be provided handicapped adolescents in the 21st century. To ensure that services for youth reach an appropriate level, those servicing the adolescent need to address several issues. Brolin and D'Alonzo (1979) cite six major issues relating to the present state of the art of programs for secondary-age handicapped youth. During the 1970s and into the 1980s a major debate rages regarding the optimum curriculum mix, the principal question being, "Should the training received be primarily job centered or life centered?" The career education movement suggested that a variety of life-functioning roles are critical, including occupational, family, citizen, consumer, and avocational. While conceding that a multifaceted curriculum is essential for handicapped learners, others (Phelps, 1978; Tindall, 1977) argued for expanding specific vocational education opportunities because of previously limited preparation of this population in job entry skills.

Brolin and D'Alonzo (1979) also posed the question of whether career and vocational education should be a separate program or be designed to be interwoven with other educational processes of the schools. As the career and vocational education movement gained in popularity, it was treated in extremely diverse ways at the implementation level. Some schools elected to add career education courses, while others have placed a major emphasis on infusing the concepts of career and vocational education via inservice staff development. To some extent the problem has been compounded by the mainstreaming movement. In addition to examining curriculum relevance to the world of work, regular class teachers have been required to teach students they haven't been prepared to instruct (in either regular classes or special environments). The nature of infusion, integration, and systematic change for programs and personnel serving adolescent handicapped learners has become increasingly complex and deserves extensive research attention.

Closely related to the mainstreaming movement is the issue of instructional responsibility. At the secondary level special educators have been hesitant to suggest mainstream placement for handicapped students for several reasons. Clark (1975) argues that the departmentalized curriculum at the secondary level inhibits communication among the teaching staff and is often inflexible. Such barriers may preclude the effective implementation of the shared instruction responsibility concept reflected in the Individualized Education Program requirement of PL 94-142.

There are several issues related directly to program improvement that are crucial for the development and improvement of vocational opportunities for handicapped learners. While PL 94-142 and other federal legislation implied the need for accountability, there have been relatively little literature and only limited resources for conducting program evaluations. In part, this is due to initial large-scale efforts to establish programs in the late 1960s. The resultant lack of aggregate evaluation data makes efforts to determine the efficacy of various programming models extremely limited. In their 1974 national assessment of vocational programs for the handicapped, the Olympus Research Corporation noted a serious poverty of evaluative effort and information at both the state and local level. From an extensive analysis of 25 states and 92 local programs, it was clear that outcome and student follow-up reports were neither required by state education agencies nor done by local districts. The only records maintained, other than fiscal records, were those compiled upon the initiative of individual local directors.

Another critical concern for the future is efficacy data. With recent major legislative initiatives drastically influencing the design and delivery of vocational programming one might surmise that large-scale research efforts are underway to monitor developments and improve efforts in the profession. It appears almost paradoxical to the authors that no major empirical or longitudinal research efforts are underway to test the efficacy of various forms of vocational programming for different disabled persons. The need clearly exists for research that can document recent efforts and improve upon the grossly limited knowledge base regarding vocational programming for the handicapped.

As noted earlier, perhaps the largest problem is that of reeducating the vocational and career educators that are confronted daily with larger numbers of handicapped learners in their classes. In a 1977 survey of 113 teacher education programs, Brock found that only 25 schools (22.5 percent) reported existing programs to train vocational–special education personnel. The General Accounting Office (1974) reviewed the inservice training received by vocational educators and found that over 80 percent of those surveyed had received no information and training regarding the teaching of handicapped students. While inservice and preservice training programs have been in existence for several years, many of them have not realized large enrollments until recently (1977–1978), and the impact of such efforts will take time. For example, to provide substantive inservice education to the 350,000 vocational educators (teachers, administrators, and counselors) will require substantial time and resources. Efforts to provide these forms of training should be planned to maximize impact through the training of trainers, peer interaction and teaching, dissemination networks, and infusing efforts into existing professional development structures, such as state and national professional conferences. An excellent review of teacher training programs in the area of vocational education for the handicapped was prepared by Griffin, Clelland, Pynn, Smith, Adamson, et al. (1978). Efforts to establish and improve teacher training programs designed for the diverse audiences involved in vocational programming are much needed. Counselors, administrators, teachers, aides, and work experience coordinators from vocational education, special education, and vocational rehabilitation, as well as parents and employers, continue to need appropriate forms of preservice and inservice training. The training must focus not only on the delivery of services, but also on effective strategies for community-based collaboration and cooperation among and within these groups.

The needs, demands, and challenges of the future are cogently summarized in a recent position statement released by the U.S. Office of Education that appeared in the *Federal Register* (September 26, 1978). The statement takes the position that "an appropriate comprehensive vocational education will be available and accessible to every handicapped person." Several key components are described as constituting comprehensive vocational education: (1) cooperative relationships between the educational and employment sectors to facilitate the transition from school to work; (2) programs and services to develop basic skills and career decision-making skills; (3) appropriate sequential career development instruction; (4) elimination of attitudinal and environmental barriers; and (5) assistance to employers in meeting their affirmative action goals for employment of the handicapped.

In the foreseeable future, it appears that the major focus will be placed upon improving the quality and quantity of vocational education and employment opportunities for handicapped persons. The 1960s and 1970s can be characterized as the decades of human rights advocacy. Now that mandates for access and equality of opportunity are clearly established, efforts must be channeled toward evaluating, strengthening, and improving the programs and services provided. To achieve this end, a number of specific efforts are needed to accomplish the following: (1) expand our knowledge of the efficacy of current and innovative programs; (2) broaden the awareness and knowledge of educators, parents, and employers regarding the education and employment of handicapped individuals; (3) improve efforts to evaluate programs and disseminate evaluative information; and (4) expand efforts to develop, test, and install appropriate curricula and programs.

# References

American Institute for Research in the Behavioral Sciences, Report No. SR—205-76. Trends Career Guidance, 1976.

Anttonen, J. E. Integrated programs for the mildly handicapped. *Academic Therapy,* 1974, *9,* 235–240.

Bailey, J. L., & Stadt, R. W. *Career education: New approaches to human development.* Bloomington, Ill.: McKnight, 1973.

Brock, R. J. Preparing vocational and special education personnel to work with special needs students: State of the art, 1977. Menomonie: University of Wisconsin-Stout, 1977.

Brolin, D. E. *Programming retarded in career education* (Working Paper No. 1). Unpublished manuscript, University of Missouri-Columbia, September 1974.

Brolin, D. E. *Vocational preparation of retarded citizens.* Columbus, Ohio: Merrill, 1976.

Brolin, D. E., & D'Alonzo, B. J. Critical issues in career education for the handicapped students. *Exceptional Children,* 1979, *45*(4), 246–253.

Brolin, D., Durand, R., Kroner, K., & Muller, P. Post-school adjustment of educable retarded students. *Education and Training of the Mentally Retarded,* 1975, *10*(3), 144–149.

Burger, K., Collins, H., & Doherty, D. Self-concept of EMR and Non-retarded adolescents. *American Journal of Mental Deficiencies,* 1970, *75,* 285–289.

Cegelka, W. J. A review of the development of work–study programs for the mentally retarded. In L. Daniels (Ed.), *Vocational rehabilitation of the mentally retarded.* Springfield, Ill.: Thomas, 1974.

Chaffin, J., Spellman, C., Regan, E., & Davidson, R. Two follow-up studies for former educable mentally retarded students from the Kansas Work Study Project. *Exceptional Children,* 1971, *37,* 28–31.

Clark, G. M. The state of the art in secondary programs for the handicapped. *Thresholds in Secondary Education,* 1976, *2,* 10–11.

Clark, G. M. Mainstreaming for the secondary educable mentally retarded: Is it defensible? *Focus on Exceptional Children,* 1975, *7*(2), 1–6.

Craighead, W. E., & Mercatoris, M. Mentally retarded residents as paraprofessionals: A review. *American Journal of Mental Deficiency,* 1973, *78,* 339–347.

Cremin, L. A. *The transformation of the school.* New York: Knopf, 1961.

D'Alonzo, B. J., & Miller, S. R. A management model for learning disabled adolescents. *Teaching Exceptional Children,* 1977, *9,* 58–60.

Dinger, J. C. Post-school adjustment of former educable retarded pupils. *Exceptional Children,* 1961, *66,* 353–360.

Doll, E. E. Trends and problems in the education of the mentally retarded: 1800–1940. *American Journal of Mental Deficiency,* 1967, *72,* 175–183.

Dybwad, G. Rehabilitation for the adult retardate. *American Journal of Public Health,* 1961, *51,* 998–1004.

Evans, R. N. *Foundations of vocational education.* Columbus, Ohio: Merrill, 1971.

Evans, R. N. Career education and vocational education: Similarities and contrasts. *Monographs on Career Education.* Washington, D.C.: U.S. Office of Education, 1975.

Evans, R. N., & Clark, C. N. Vocational education for the special needs student: Competencies and models for personnel preparation (Final report, Special Project No. PCE-A6-021) of the Illinois State Board of Education, Division of Adult, Vocational and Technical Education. Urbana, Ill.: University of Illinois, 1976.

*Federal Register,* Nondiscrimination on the basis of handicap, May 4, 1977, *42*(86). Washington, D.C.: Department of Health, Education and Welfare.

*Federal Register,* PL 94-142, September 25, 1978, *42*(163). Washington, D.C.: Department of Health, Education and Welfare, Office of Education.

General Accounting Office. What is the role of federal assistance for vocational education? Washington, D.C.: Comptroller General of the United States, December 1974.

General Accounting Office. *Training educators for the handicapped: A need to redirect federal programs.* Washington, D.C.: Comptroller General of the United States, September 1976.

Gilmore, J. F., & Argyros, N. S. *Special education certification: A state of the art survey.* Research Fund of the Board of Regents of the University of the State of New York, the State Education Department, Office for the Education of Children with Handicapping Conditions, by the United States Office of Education for the Handicapped, Division of Personnel Preparation, Grant G007602968, Project No. 451AH60852, 1978.

Goldstein, H. Construction of a social leaning curriculum. *Focus on Exceptional Children,* 1969, *1,* 1–10.

Griffin, G., Clelland, R., Pynn, M. E. B., Smith, J., Adamson, G., & LaCasse, R. J. *A consumer's guide to personnel preparation programs: The training of professionals in vocational education for the handicapped.* Arlington, Va.: University of New Mexico Dissemination Project, 1978.

Halpern, A. S. General unemployment and vocational opportunities for EMR individuals. *American Journal of Mental Deficiency,* 1973, *78,* 123–127.

Halpern, A., Raffeld, R., & Littman, I. *Longitudinal evaluation of work–study programs for the educable mentally retarded in Oregon: Progress Report* (Working Paper No. 62). Unpublished manuscript, University of Oregon-Eugene, August 1972.

House of Representatives Committee on Education and Labor. *General issues in elementary and secondary education.* Ninety-Fifth Congress, First Session on H. R. 15, 1977.

Hoyt, K. B. *A primer for career education.* Washington, D.C.: U.S. Government Printing Office, 1977.

Hoyt, K. B., Evans, R. N., Mackin, E., & Mangum, G. L. *Career education: What it is and how to do it.* Salt Lake City: Olympus Publishing Company, 1974.

Hudson, J. B. *An evaluation of training provided in correctional institutions under the Manpower Development and Training Act, Section 251* (Vol. 1): *Perspectives on office rehabilitation: Final report.* Springfield, Va: National Technical Information Service, 1971.

Hull, M. E. *The effects of selected variables on the formation of vocational concepts by educable mentally retarded students.* Unpublished doctoral dissertation, Texas A & M University, 1976.

Jackson, R. N. Prognostic significance of performance. Verbal ability patterns in predicting employment adjustment of EMR adolescents. *American Journal of Mental Deficiency,* 1973, 78, 331–333.

Kokaska, C. J. The occupational status of the educable mentally retarded: A review of follow-up studies. *Journal of Special Education,* 1968, *2,* 369–377.

Kolstoe, O. P. An examination of some characteristics which discriminate between employed and non-employed mentally retarded males. *American Journal of Mental Deficiency,* 1975, *66,* 472–482.

Kolstoe, O. P. *Language in employability* (In proceedings of the Institute on the communication processes of the mentally retarded as they relate to social and vocational adjustment). University of Connecticut, Storrs, Vocational Rehabilitation Administration (DHEWO, Washington, D. C., 1965.

Malouf, D., & Halpern, A. Review of secondary level special education. *Thresholds in Secondary Education,* 1976, *2*(6), XXX.

Mann, L., Goodman, L., Weiderholt, J. *Teaching the learning disabled adolescent.* Boston: Houghton Mifflin, 1978.

Martin, E. W. Individualism and behaviorism as future trends in educating handicapped children. *Exceptional Children,* 1972, *38,* 517–525.

McLaughlin, D. H. *Career education in the public schools 1974–75: A national survey.* Palo Alto, Calif.: American Institutes for Research, 1976.

Meyer, A. E. *The development of education in the twentieth century* (2nd ed.). New York: Prentice-Hall, 1949.

Miller, S. R. Career and vocational education: The necessity for a planned future. In Sabatino, D. A. & Mauser, A. J. (Ed.), *Intervention strategies for specialized secondary education.* Boston, Mass.: Allyn & Bacon, 1978.

Miller, S. R. *Secondary assessment and programming.* Unpublished manuscript.

Miller, S. R., Benson, C. A., Demus, W., & Weaver, J. *Secondary special education materials taxonomy.* Evanston, Ill.: Illinois Regional Resource Center at Northern Illinois University and Evanston Township High School District 202, 1978.

Miller, S. R., & Sabatino, D. A. Handbook on Vocational Education in Correctional Settings. Illinois Department of Corrections, Springfield, Illinois, 1975.

Nelson, H. *Workshops for the handicapped in the United States.* Springfield, Ill.: Thomas, 1971.

Olympus Research Corporation. *An assessment of vocational programs for the handicapped under Part B of the 1968 Amendments to the Vocational Education Act.* Salt Lake City: Olympus Research Corporation, 1974.

Peters, H. J. *Vocational guidance and career development: Select readings.* New York: Macmillan, 1971.

Phelps, A. The expanding federal commitments to vocational education and employment of handicapped individuals. *Education and Training of the Mentally Retarded,* 1977, *12,* 186–192.

Phelps, A. Providing full vocational education opportunity for special populations. *UCLA Educator,* 1978, *20,* 13–18.

Phelps, A. L., & Lutz, R. J. *Career exploration and preparation for the special needs learner.* Boston: Allyn & Bacon, 1977.

Phelps, H. R. Postschool adjustment of mentally retarded children in selected Ohio cities. *Exceptional Children,* 1956, *23,* 58–62.

Porter, R., & Milazzo, T. A comparison of mentally retarded adults who attended a special class with those who attended regular school classes. *Exceptional Children,* 1958, *24,* 410–418.

President's Committee on Employment of the Handicapped. *One in eleven: Handicapped adults in america.* Washington, D.C.: 1975.

Razeghi, J., & Halloran, W. A new picture of vocational education for the employment of the handicapped. *School Shop,* 1978, *37,* 50–53.

Sabatino, D. A. *Neglect and delinquent children* (EDC Report). Wilkes-Baree, Pa.: Wilkes College, 1974.

Sabatino, D. A., & Mauser, A. J. *Intervention strategies for specialized secondary education.* Boston: Allyn & Bacon, 1978.

Sali, J., & Amir, M. Personal factors influencing the retarded person's success at work: A report from Israel. *American Journal of Mental Deficiency,* 1971, 76(1), 42–47.

Shalock, R. L., & Harper, R. S. Placement from community based mental retardation programs: How well do clients do? *American Journal of Mental Deficiency,* 1978, 83, 240–247.

Strickland, C. G., & Arrell, V. M. Employment of the mentally retarded. *Exceptional Children,* 1967, *34,* 21–24.

Thompson, J. F. *Foundations of vocational education: Social and philosophical concepts.* New Jersey: Prentice-Hall, 1973.

Tindall, L. W. *Vocational/Career education programs for persons with special needs in Wisconsin's vocational technical and adult education districts* (A part of project: Modifying regular programs and developing curriculum materials for the vocational education of the handicapped, No. 19001151147(A). Wisconsin State Board of Vocational, Technical, and Adult Education, Madison, 1977.

Tobias, J. Vocational adjustments of young retarded adults. *Mental Retardation,* 1970, *8*(3), 13–16.

U. S. Department of Labor, Bureau of Labor Statistics. *Occupational outlook handbook.* Washington, D.C.: 1978–1979.

Wallin, J. E. W. *Problems of subnormality.* Yonkers, N.Y.: World Book, 1917.

Weisenstein, G. R. Vocational education for exceptional persons: Have educators let it drop through a crack in their services continuum? *Thresholds in Secondary Education,* 1976, *2,* 16–17.

# PERSONNEL PREPARATION IN SPECIAL EDUCATION

Richard C. Schofer
*University of Missouri, Columbia*

M. Stephen Lilly
*University of Illinois, Urbana–Champaign*

This chapter is presented as a review of the literature on special education personnel preparation. Information is presented in two major sections: first, a comprehensive examination of teacher education in special education is presented, with the goal of characterizing both the quantity and the scope of professional literature in this area; second, the topic of special education cooperative manpower planning is discussed. This is a relatively new area of concern in special education, and published information is sparse; however the field abounds with unpublished documents.

The purpose of both major sections of the chapter is to provide an assessment of the state of the art in personnel preparation. The approaches to the two sections are somewhat different on several counts. Thus the first section relies on clearly articulated issues, while the second describes an emerging technology. The scope of the first section, of necessity, is extremely broad, since it covers the full gamut of the literature on special education teacher preparation. The second section, on the other hand, is focused upon a single issue in personnel preparation. It is hoped that the contrast between the two sections in this review will help to clarify a most complex area of professional endeavor—the preparation of personnel to serve students with exceptional needs.

## SPECIAL EDUCATION TEACHER PREPARATION:
## AN ANALYSIS OF THE LITERATURE

In this section, the literature on special education teacher preparation of the past five years will be presented and analyzed. The aim is to provide a systematic, as opposed to a complete, look at the literature, since this literature is voluminous.

It is often remarked, especially among university personnel, that it is relatively difficult to publish information on teacher education; journals are prone to give priority to manuscripts dealing with topics that are either more interesting or more scholarly than those of teacher education. The first step in the current review was, then, to determine the actual extent to which articles on teacher education have been included in the special education literature of the recent past. To make this determination, seven special education journals were scanned, and articles dealing with teacher education were noted and reviewed. Seven journals were used in the review:

*American Journal on Mental Deficiency* (AJMD)
*Education and Training of the Mentally Retarded* (ETMR)
*Exceptional Children* (EC)
*Focus on Exceptional Children* (FEC)
*Journal of Learning Disabilities* (JLD)
*Journal of Special Education* (JSE)
*Mental Retardation* (MR).

These journals were chosen because of their position of acknowledgment and respect among special educators, and because each has an established period of publication. In addition, one other journal was reviewed, even though it is in its first volume and has published only two issues. This journal, *Teacher Education and Special Education* (TEASE), was chosen for review because it is published by the Teacher Education Division of the Council for Exceptional Children, and it focuses primarily on issues concerning special education personnel preparation.

For the seven journals listed above, the last five *full* volume years were reviewed. In some cases, this meant that the period of review was January 1973 to December 1977, for others January 1974 to December 1978, and for others, September 1973 to May 1978. For the purpose of this review, the most recent volume of each journal reviewed was the last complete volume. No partial volumes of journals were reviewed.

In reviewing the journals for articles on personnel preparation, one obvious need was to define what is meant by "personnel preparation." Inclusion and exclusion boundaries had to be established in order to limit the size of this review. The following rules were adopted:

1). The review is limited to articles dealing with preparation (inservice and preservice) of teachers or support personnel (such as administrators or social workers). Articles dealing with training of parents or paraprofessional staff (including ward attendants in institutions) are excluded. Also excluded are articles focusing on doctoral level preparation of teacher educators or researchers.

2). Only articles dealing with issues in, programs for, or research on teacher education are included. Studies of teacher behavior as it relates to student achievement (which are often used as the basis for competency specification in teacher education programs) are reviewed elsewhere and are beyond the purview of this chapter.

3). Many articles deal with new roles for special educators in the schools. Unless these new roles are directly related to teacher education concerns, such articles are not included in the review.

As pointed out earlier, the first purpose of the review was to determine the actual extent to which articles on teacher preparation are included in the special education literature. Table 1 lists the number of teacher education–related articles in the last five volumes of the journals reviewed, with the exception of TEASE, for which Volume I information is listed.

It is interesting to note that 70 articles dealing with teacher education were found in the last five volume years of these journals, which would seem to contradict the claim that it is difficult to publish articles on teacher education. However, a closer inspection of the data indicates that teacher education is not well represented in the majority of journals reviewed. If the data from TEASE are removed from consideration, it can be seen that of the seven remaining journals dealing with general content in special education, two (ETMR and EC) account for 80 percent of all the articles published on teacher education. Of these two, ETMR has a special section on Teacher Education, which accounts for all of the articles listed for it. It appears that the probability of publishing an article on teacher education in the remaining journals is at best marginal, with the exception of FEC, which has a total of only eight to ten articles per volume. The remainder of the journals (AJMD, JLD, JSE, MR) have an extremely low percentage of articles dealing with teacher education.

In addition to tallying numbers of teacher education articles over the last five volumes of the journals under consideration, an attempt was

**TABLE 1**
**NUMBER OF TEACHER EDUCATION ARTICLES**
**IN SPECIAL EDUCATION JOURNALS**

| Journal* | Volume | | | | | |
| | R† | R-1 | R-2 | R-3 | R-4 | Total |
|---|---|---|---|---|---|---|
| AJMD | 0 | 0 | 0 | 1 | 0 | 1 |
| ETMR | 4 | 7 | 7 | 5 | 3 | 26 |
| EC | 3 | 7 | 6 | 3 | 3 | 22 |
| FEC | 1 | 0 | 1 | 1 | 1 | 4 |
| JLD | 1 | 1 | 0 | 0 | 0 | 2 |
| JSE | 0 | 0 | 1 | 1 | 1 | 3 |
| MR | 1 | 0 | 1 | 0 | 0 | 2 |
| TEASE | 10 | — | — | — | — | 10 |
| Total | 20 | 15 | 16 | 11 | 8 | 70 |

*Note.* All articles included in this table are listed in the reference section of this chapter, although not all are specifically cited in the text.
*See text for explanation of abbreviations.
†R refers to the most recent complete volume of the journal available, R-1 the second most recent, etc.

made to classify these articles according to content. Five categories were used for this classification, as follows:

1). *Conceptual article:* an article dealing with general or specific issues in teacher education that are presented without reference to either a specific training program or empirical data.

2). *Program description:* a description of either a full teacher preparation program, or a self-contained training sequence, with no data on program development or outcomes.

3). *Program description with developmental data:* a description of a teacher preparation program or training sequence, with data from developmental research.

4). *Program description with outcome data:* a description of a teacher preparation program or training sequence, with data on program effects, either on trainees or on students with whom trainees work.

5). *Teacher education research:* a report of data collection not specifically tied to a teacher preparation program or training sequence.

Table 2 presents a breakdown of the number of articles in each

## TABLE 2
## ARTICLES BY JOURNAL AND CATEGORY OF CONTENT

| Journal | Conceptual article | Program description | Program description/ development data | Program description/ outcome data | Research |
|---------|--------------------|--------------------|--------------------------------------|-----------------------------------|----------|
| AJMD    | 0 | 0  | 0 | 0 | 1  |
| ETMR    | 7 | 14 | 0 | 2 | 3  |
| EC      | 7 | 4  | 1 | 4 | 6  |
| FEC     | 2 | 1  | 1 | 0 | 0  |
| JLD     | 0 | 0  | 0 | 1 | 0  |
| JOSE    | 1 | 0  | 0 | 0 | 2  |
| MR      | 0 | 0  | 0 | 0 | 2  |
| TEASE   | 5 | 5  | 0 | 0 | 0  |
| Total   | 22 | 24 | 2 | 7 | 14 |

category for each journal, over the entire period of review. It should be noted that the first two categories of articles are conceptual and/or descriptive in nature, while the last three categories involve articles with some degree of data presentation. No attempt is made here to assess the quality of the data presented, although that is certainly a topic of concern to the authors.

It can be seen from Table 2 that 66 percent of all articles reviewed presented no data: 32 percent were conceptual articles and 34 percent were descriptions of teacher education programs for which outcome data were either not available or not included. Of the three journals with the highest rate of teacher education articles (ETMR, EC, TEASE), EC appears to have the best balance between empirical and conceptual material. ETMR appears to be heavily weighted toward data-free descriptions of programs, and TEASE is currently topically oriented with invited manuscripts, which minimizes the probability of receiving data-based articles for publication.

In order to provide a clearer picture of the types of articles included under each category, a brief review by category is presented below. Not all articles appearing in each category will be included in this review; the purpose is to present examples which will characterize the types of articles in the five categories.

**Conceptual articles**

Four general types of articles are included in this category. First, there are several articles dealing with general issues, historical patterns, and future trends in personnel preparation. A number of articles deal with Bureau of Education for the Handicapped (BEH) funding patterns (Burke, 1976; Burke & Saettler, 1976; Harvey, 1976; Saettler, 1976). Other articles deal with historical patterns and future trends in personnel preparation (Connor, 1976), and the need for increased consumer influence on special education personnel preparation programs (Reger, 1974).

A second type of conceptual article discusses models for the development of teacher preparation programs. Some of these articles are general in scope (Sheperd, 1975; Stamm, 1975), while others discuss specific approaches such as competency-based teacher education (Shores, Cegelka, & Nelson, 1973; Tawney, 1978).

A third class of conceptual articles focuses on personnel preparation needs in specific areas, such as resource teaching (Ostanski, 1975) and severely/profoundly handicapped (Brown & York, 1974; Stainback, Stainback, & Maurer, 1976).

The final area of conceptual articles relates to specific aspects of teacher education, while not being tied to program descriptions. Here we find topics such as practicum supervision (Walker, 1978), instruments for observation of student teachers (Cole, Kitano, & Rickert, 1978), and the use of simulation in teacher education (Wagonseller & Mari, 1977).

## Program descriptions

Because of the large number of teacher education program descriptions in the literature, no attempt will be made to review them in detail. Some program description articles focus on short-term training programs (e.g., Blumberg, 1974; Edgar, Baker, Harper, Swift, & Melseth, 1976; Witty, 1975). Others focus on specific aspects of teacher education programs, such as early practicum (Anderson & Hemenway, 1974), advocacy training (Berdine, Knapp, Tawney, & Martinson, 1975; Hamalian & Ludwig, 1976), or program evaluation (de Jung & Spence, 1975; Reid & Whorton, 1973). Finally, some articles present descriptions of complete programs for teacher preparation, often with detailed discussions of program development models (Berdine & Kelly, 1977; Brooks, 1975; Courtnage, Brady, Suroski, & Schmid, 1975).

## Program descriptions with developmental data

Only two articles in the literature reviewed report data on the development of teacher education programs, and in both cases the data relate to competency development. Meyen and Altman (1973) describe a competency validation study in which, as a part of the development of a program at the University of Missouri–Columbia, 100 competency statements were submitted to 720 special educators in 11 states. Competencies were rated on both importance and amenability to training; based on the outcomes, a set of competency statements for the training program was developed. Bullock, Dykes, and Kelly (1974) describe a similar competency validation study in developing a competency-based program at the University of Florida for projective teachers of the emotionally disturbed.

## Program descriptions with outcome data

The articles reviewed in this section all present some type of data on trainee performance or student performance as evidence of program effectiveness. The sophistication of the data varies tremendously from report to report and provides little generalizable information.

Some evaluation reports focus on short-term training or limited aspects of larger special education programs. As an example of the former, Cegelka and Tawney (1975) report on the Kentucky Experienced

373

Teacher Renewal Project, a competency-based inservice program offered through the University of Kentucky. Behavioral data were taken in participating teachers' classrooms two weeks prior to training, two months after training, and four months after training. While some positive change was evident at the two-month follow-up, the greatest change occurred at the four-month observation period, indicating a possible latency effect in teacher implementation of learned skills.

A single aspect of a special education training program was evaluated by Turnbull (1977). As a part of a course on mental retardation at the University of North Carolina, Chapel Hill, each student was required to form an advocacy relationship with a mentally retarded person in the community. At the end of the course, when asked to rate a number of course requirements, the advocacy requirement was the first choice of 54 percent of the students in the class, and the second choice of an additional 24 percent. Turnbull also reports that approximately 90 percent of the students continued the advocacy relationship after the course was completed.

In a very few cases, evaluation data on total teacher preparation programs have been presented in the literature. For example, Bruininks (1977) reports on the University of Minnesota training program in learning disabilities. This program attempts to combine the best features of competency-based and humanistic education. Bruininks describes the program in some detail, and reports that in a follow-up evaluation, principals rated program graduates higher than other teachers on eight general traits presumed to be related to teacher effectiveness. In addition, 42 program graduates employed as teachers for one year were asked to rate the 34 program competencies in terms of usefulness, and the mean ratings ranged from 3.4 to 4.9 on a 5-point scale.

Edgar and Neel (1976) report evaluation data on an education program for teachers of the mildly handicapped at the University of Washington. This report is significant in that competence was measured at three stages: (1) initial acquisition (during training); (2) proficiency (in practicum); and (3) maintenance (on the job, after completion of training program). The data show consistent decrements in competency application across the three stages for some skills. For example, 14 of 14 students successfully learned to collect performance data on student progress at the initial acquisition stage. Of these 14, 10 applied the skill in the practicum setting, and only 3 exhibited the skill in the actual posttraining work setting. These data should make us cautious in interpreting immediate outcomes of personnel preparation programs.

**Teacher education research**

Three major areas of teacher education research can be identified from the literature reviewed. The first area is competency development and validation for different roles in special education. Two studies of this type have already been reported, as a part of program development activities. Several teacher competency studies have been carried out, however, for the purpose of competency identification without specific reference to a given training program. Specific competency validation studies have been done in the areas of education for the trainable mentally retarded (Foos, 1976), crippled and other health impaired (Dykes, 1975), and mildly handicapped (Herr, Algozzine, & Heuchert, 1976). Strauch and Affleck (1976) have also validated competencies and roles for cooperating public school teachers. Redden and Blackhurst (1978) used a unique approach to developing and validating competencies to prepare elementary teachers for mainstreaming. In their study, 493 elementary teachers in schools with mainstreaming programs were asked to list three effective and three ineffective teacher behaviors related to instruction of special education students who were mainstreamed; 184 teachers responded, listing 828 behaviors. These behaviors were then translated into 32 competency statements which were validated by expert opinion.

A second area of teacher education research involves the analysis of teacher education programs in given areas of special education. For example, Hirshoren and Umansky (1977) surveyed all 50 states and the District of Columbia to determine the status of preschool special education certification. While only 12 states reported having a preschool certificate, 25 additional states and the District of Columbia have preschool teacher preparation programs in operation. In a different type of descriptive study, Brown and Palmer (1977) reviewed 223 BEH-funded projects which purported to be training in the area of emotional disturbance. Analysis revealed that only about 10 percent of the projects were training teachers of the severely emotionally disturbed, and the vast majority were focusing only on the elementary level. Such "archival" studies are now feasible, given the BEH data base on funded programs, and surely will increase in the future.

The final type of teacher education research to be reported here relates to the evaluation of specific courses or sequences of instruction. Two examples of such research will be cited. Renne and Blackurst (1976) compared three modes of instruction in the special education survey course: (1) lecture approach, (2) lecture approach with study guides, and

(3) programmed instruction. The students in the programmed instruction section learned more material than those in the other two groups, while student satisfaction was equal across all three sections.

In a study of teacher attitudes, Shaw and Gillung (1975) assessed the attitudes of 10 regular class teachers toward the handicapped prior to, immediately after, and three months following a course on mainstreaming. Attitudes improved as a result of the course, and the positive changes were maintained over a three-month period.

**Summary**

In general, it can be said that while teacher education concerns have been represented in the special education literature over the past five years, the nature of that representation is ripe for improvement. The vast majority of teacher education articles have been either conceptual presentations of data-free program descriptions. This is to be expected since special education teacher preparation has been in a period of rather rapid transition and data on new program developments have not come quickly.

It can be argued, however, that we are entering a new era, an era in which teacher preparation programs should be expected to have program evaluation and follow-up data as a matter of course. It is reasonable to expect that the number of program descriptions without evaluative information will be drastically reduced in the near future, and that the new focus will be on reporting and presenting evidence of programmatic successes and failures. The presence of good evaluation data is a mark of professional maturity within any field, and special education teacher preparation has reached a stage of maturity at which we can reasonably expect such data.

With regard to teacher education research, it can safely be said that little generalizable knowledge has been produced. The few studies that have been done are isolated and do not relate well to each other. Systematic research efforts are needed if we are to produce knowledge that will be of value to other teacher educators in special education. Only a handful of special educators in institutions of higher education are devoting themselves to systematic and prolonged research on teacher education. As the number of professionals thus engaged increases, so will the respectability of the field.

This section has been a review of the status of teacher education in the special education literature. We now turn to a specific topic too new and too fluid to be represented in the journals of our field, the topic of cooperative manpower planning.

## MANPOWER PLANNING IN SPECIAL
## EDUCATION: THE STATE OF THE ART

Although the term "manpower planning" is not new to the literature of many professions, its meaning varies greatly in scope, complexity, and impact from one field to another. In the United States the fields of mental health and vocational education have been particularly prominent in utilizing many of the strategies and technologies associated with manpower planning. As a federal agency, the Department of Labor has been the recognized leader in the area of manpower planning and forecasting in the United States. It has combined its resources with other governmental agencies to sponsor the Inter-Agency Growth Project to project economic output and employment needs for the United States. On the other hand, public education throughout the United States is not generally characterized by intensive manpower planning. Although most of the nation's educators realize that the projection of finances, teacher training and availability, vocational program offerings, and facility design and construction are greatly dependent upon the country's socioeconomic manpower needs, it is a fact that the educational community in the United States is decentralized and must react to a feedback system that is largely ex post facto (Schofer & McGough, 1976). Although substantial efforts are currently being made by many states relative to organized manpower planning in the field of special education, such efforts are just at the beginning stages.

In several other nations, particularly the Third World or developing nations, manpower planning is of paramount concern and is coordinated on a national basis (Organization for Economic Cooperation and Development [OECD], 1965). Since many of these countries make the general assumption of finite resources, they view sound manpower planning as vital to their survival. As a result, it is assumed by many that nations other than the United States may provide the future leadership for the establishment and implementation of sophisticated manpower planning systems.

### Background to special education manpower planning

Prior to the late 1950s, relatively few colleges and universities in the United States were committed to the preparation of special education personnel. The few colleges and universities involved in such training activities, for the most part, emphasized the preparation of teachers who would work with the educable mentally retarded in self-contained classrooms, usually in an elementary school setting. The number of colleges and universities offering preparation programs in other areas such as visually impaired, deaf and hard of hearing, speech impaired, and crippled and other health impaired, was comparatively small. Almost nonexistent in the late 1950s were training programs that emphasized such areas of concern as emotional disturbance, learning disabilities, moderately and severely handicapped, secondary-level handicapped, preschool handicapped, multihandicapped, adapted physical education, and special education administration. Such areas as emotional disturbance, learning disabilities, trainable mentally retarded, and special education administration began to flourish prior to the legislative movement which occurred in the middle 1960s.

One of the primary stimuli for college and university program development and expansion in special education has been, and continues to be, federal training assistance. Beginning with PL 85-926 (Graduate Fellowship Program in Education of the Mentally Retarded), as amended, and continuing to the present provisions of the Education for All Handicapped Children Act of 1975 (PL 94-142), many of our nation's colleges and universities have been able to improve and expand their special education training programs because of the financial resources made available from federal sources. State Education Agencies have assumed a major role in personnel preparation through the inservice training of special educators. They have also often been highly influential in identifying immediate and critical training needs in their respective states. Federal support has served to stimulate their involvement in training activities (Schofer & McGough, 1976).

In 1978 the BEH reported a minimum of 820 different training programs being offered by about 337 colleges and universities. This number represents substantial growth as compared to the small number of training programs operational in the 1950s. This growth is particularly significant when the inservice training efforts of State Education Agencies are also considered.

Without question, the marked growth and expansion of college and university training programs in special education has been highly beneficial to state and local education agencies by alleviating some of their manpower shortages. However, inherent in this growth has been the emergence of an unanticipated problem. For the first time, many states have begun reporting personnel surpluses in various areas of special education. In addition, it appears that many states have a proliferation and, at times, a seemingly unnecessary duplication of college and university training efforts in special education. Ironically, even though personnel surpluses and some program proliferation may exist in many states, there are still program areas (e.g., severely handicapped, vocational education for the handicapped, and preschool handicapped) in which insufficient personnel training may be occurring. Furthermore, there often appears to be an intrastate shortage of qualified personnel: i.e., even though a state might have a surplus of teachers of the mildly handicapped in its urban areas, the rural areas of the same state might be experiencing difficulties in attracting and/or retaining such personnel. One approach to alleviating such personnel problems has been to initiate a concerted state-wide manpower planning effort.

Although for many years several states have had some involvement with cooperative manpower planning in special education, the real impetus for such efforts occurred in 1974. At that time, the Division of Personnel Preparation, BEH, issued a statement encouraging each of the 50 states, the District of Columbia, and the 6 territories to establish special education manpower planning systems. This statement became known as the "BEH Directive on Cooperative Manpower Planning." Initially the Directive applied primarily to those State Education Agencies and colleges and universities that were making application for training funds under Part D provisions of PL 91-230 (Division of Personnel Preparation, 1974). However, with the passage of PL 94-142 in 1975, virtually all State Education Agencies came under the requirements of the personnel development sections [Sections 613 (a) (3) and 614 (a) (1) (c) (i)] of the Act relating to the "development and implementation of a comprehensive system of personnel development." As a result, the intent and purposes of the Directive have now become meshed with those of the personnel development sections of PL 94-142. This should, in time, considerably enhance the quality of cooperative personnel planning in special education: the Directive provided the initial impetus, while PL 94-142 provided statutory strength.

The personnel development section of PL 94-142 specifies that one of the major ingredients of a state's compliance plan (Annual Program Plan) should be the inclusion of "detailed procedures to assure that all personnel necessary to carry out the purposes of this Act are appropriately and adequately prepared and trained." In essence, this inclusion potentially amounts to a "comprehensive blueprint for personnel development" (Ballard & Zettel, 1978).

Since 1974 the primary vehicle for implementing special education manpower planning in each of the states has been the establishment of statewide cooperative manpower planning committees. It is through these committees that State Education Agencies, colleges and universities, local educational agency personnel, and other interested groups and

379

agencies have opportunities to examine the personnel needs and issues within a state and cooperatively develop plans of action for addressing those needs and issues. The existence of these committees not only meets the participatory planning requirements of PL 94-142, but can also serve, in varying degrees, to provide quality control agents relative to both preservice and inservice training within a state (Schofer, 1977).

### Status of manpower planning in special education as of 1978

In 1976, the Project on Cooperative Manpower Planning in Special Education, University of Missouri, Columbia, conducted a national survey to determine the status of cooperative manpower planning (Schofer & McGough, 1976). A second nation-wide status study was conducted in 1978 to determine the progress that had occurred in the various states relative to the establishment of special education manpower planning systems and compliance with the personnel development sections of PL 94-142 (Schofer & Duncan, 1978). The results of that study provide an overview of the state of the art of manpower planning in special education throughout the nation.

In total, there were 102 participants in this study: 53 State Education Agency representatives and 49 college/university representatives. Each of these 102 participants was acknowledged by the State Education Agency to be active in and knowledgeable about his/her state's manpower planning efforts. Responses to the survey instruments were received from each of the 50 states, the District of Columbia, Puerto Rico, and Guam. No response to the survey instrument was received from American Samoa, the Virgin Islands, and the Trust Territories.

Of the 53 responding states and territories, 42 reported that they had on-going state-wide manpower planning committees for special education. While some of these committees were in the formative stage, others were reported as having been organized and functioning for a number of years. Three of the committees reported some organizational activities prior to the 1974 BEH Directive on Cooperative Manpower Planning.

While membership varied, every committee had State Education Agency and college and university representatives. The criteria for selection of committee membership differed, but involvement and interest in handicapping conditions were the two criteria most often mentioned. The frequency of membership for various constituent groups is presented in Table 3. While most of the committees were characterized as advisory

**TABLE 3**
**MAJOR REPRESENTATION ON MANPOWER PLANNING COMMITTEES**

| Group | Percent of committees containing members from group |
|---|---|
| State Education Agency | 100 |
| Colleges and universities | 100 |
| Local directors of special education | 57 |
| School administrators | 57 |
| Parent's of handicapped | 57 |
| PL 94-142 State Advisory Committee Representative | 55 |

Note. While some state committees had state education agency and college/university representation only, other state committees had representation from as many as 12 different groups and agencies.

groups, over one-third of them had formed subcommittees and/or task forces with defined purposes, projects, and products (Schofer, 1978).

In most cases, balanced geographical distribution of membership within a state was achieved through the location of the agencies represented. Participation was through appointment by a state official (i.e., State Commissioner of Education or Director of Special Education), voluntary, or as a function of one's position with his/her respective agency. Twenty-five state committees reported that they provided compensation for a member's participation in committee activities; 14 committees did not, and 3 committees were in the process of determining whether compensation would be made. The compensation in every case was partial or full reimbursement of the representative's expenses. The expenses were usually met through utilization of State Education Agency–administered federal grant funds (Schofer & Duncan, 1978).

The Annual Program Plan has been described as the instrument which can be used to guide the states in their implementation of the requirements of PL 94-142 (Harvey, 1978). The respondents' perceptions of their manpower planning committee's input into the design of the personnel development sections of the Annual Program Plan ranged from feeling that their own state committee had had absolutely no input, to their committee's having written this section in total (Schofer, 1978).

381

While few of the respondents from the same state agreed exactly on their committee's input into the Annual Program Plan, they seemed to be in general agreement; e.g., one respondent might indicate moderate input while the other indicated little input. However, in six of the states, the participants' responses were exactly opposite: State Education Agency respondents felt their committee had considerable or moderate input, while the college/university respondents perceived the committee as having no input.

Of the states having committees, over one-half reported that their committees have documents delineating their purposes, goals, objectives, planned activities, and time-lines. Approximately 30 percent of the committees have constitutions or by-laws governing their operations. Very few committees are involved in yearly evaluation activities, although one-third of the committees indicated that they anticipated initiation of evaluation activities in the future. None of the committees reported that they required the signing of a cooperative agreement among members.

For the majority of the committees, special funding or a grant supports a portion or all of the committee's activities. It appears that Part D funds (PL 91-230) account for about 90 percent of this support. All of those committees receiving funding felt that it was critical to the implementation of their committee's efforts. Of the respondents from committees not receiving funding, many felt that funding would allow their committees to expand their efforts and activities.

Thirty of the 42 committees were found to be involved in data collection. Over half (57 percent) of these committees indicated that collection of data is done annually, with a variety of means of disseminating the resultant information to committee members, colleges and universities, local education agencies, and others. The type of data collected included a portion of all of the following types (Schofer, 1978):

1. Student enrollment by category statistics.
2. Professional personnel supply and demand information.
3. Pre- and inservice training program information.
4. University training program statistics.

The general reactions of the respondents to the BEH Directive on Cooperative Manpower Planning and to the personnel development sections of PL 94-142 were favorable. Some respondents noted that the full implementation of PL 94-142 is dependent upon the successful implementation of the personnel development sections. As shown in

Table 4, there was not general agreement among the respondents as to whether the BEH Directive on Cooperative Manpower Planning or the personnel development sections of PL 94-142 have had the greatest impact, thus far, on the development of manpower planning committees in the various states (Schofer, 1978).

In response to the request in the survey instrument to list the four major issues addressed by the committee during 1977–1978, the following were most frequently listed:

1. Inservice training programs.
2. Organization of committee.
3. Revision of certification standards.
4. Data collection.
5. Needs assessment.
6. Input to the Annual Program Plan.

When asked to respond to a question regarding their perception of the single most innovative activity that their committees have been

#### TABLE 4
#### PERCEIVED FACTORS IN DEVELOPMENT OF MANPOWER PLANNING COMMITTEES (FROM SURVEY OF MEMBERS)

| Factor | Percent of members |
|---|---|
| Personnel development sections of PL 94-142 were the sole factor | 4 |
| DPP/BEH* Directive was the sole factor | 9 |
| Neither was a factor | 9 |
| Personnel development sections of PL 94-142 were more of a factor than the DPP/BEH Directive | 17 |
| DPP/BEH[a] Directive was more of a factor than the personnel sections of PL 94-142 | 28 |
| They were equal factors | 33 |

*Note.* Data from Schofer & Duncan (1978).
*DPP/BEH: Department of Personnel Preparation, Bureau of Education for the Handicapped.

involved in since their inception, the following responses were predominant (Schofer & Duncan, 1978):

1. Data collection.
2. Preparation for, or implementation of inservice training.
3. Revision of certification standards.

Factors that would facilitate and those that might impede the successful development of cooperative manpower planning within a state were identified by the respondents in the 1978 survey. Those factors seen as contributing to the potential success of cooperative manpower planning can be summarized in these four categories:

1. *Funding:* Providing compensation (expenses) for committee participants, providing for paid staff, and paying for expenses such as newsletters were examples of how funding could be utilized to expand the effort of the committees.

2. *Clarification:* Precise understanding of the requirements of the rules and regulations of the personnel development sections of PL 94-142 and clarification of the structure, roles, and purpose of the committee, as well as the roles of the agencies and individuals involved in the committee, were stressed as necessary to the successful development of cooperative manpower planning. A clear understanding of the relationship of the BEH Directive on Cooperative Manpower Planning to the personnel development sections of PL 94-142 also appeared to be needed. Some states indicated little knowledge of or attention to the Directive while attempting to adhere to the regulations of PL 94-142.

3. *Input:* A broad base of input from many organizations and agencies involved with special education was seen as important for developing a representative cooperative manpower planning effort.

4. *Commitment and involvement:* Full involvement of significant professionals in the state was stressed as an important factor influencing the success of the cooperative manpower planning effort.

The lack of the "success" factors, as well as the lack of authority and time, were described as possibly impeding the success of cooperative manpower planning (Schofer & Duncan, 1978).

It is apparent that the quality and status of manpower planning in special education throughout the nation varies considerably from one state to another. Basic to the effectiveness of manpower planning is the establishment and implementation of well-organized and active statewide committees. It is in this dimension that more progress must be achieved. These committees, particularly those in the initial or early stages of development, need more assistance relative to group processing skills, goal setting, conflict resolution, and participatory planning techniques. In addition, because of the broad implications of special education manpower planning, it seems imperative that an increased emphasis be directed in the near future toward organized planning at the regional and national levels (Schofer, 1978).

With such components as Individualized Education Programs, due process procedures, and least restrictive environment, PL 94-142 may very well be a major factor in modifying many of the past and current practices of public education in the United States. To be sure, the personnel development sections of the Act will have great impact on all individuals and agencies concerned with the supply of professional manpower. This impact applies not only to college/university training programs, but to state and local education agencies as well. Each State Education Agency must submit an Annual Program Plan describing its participation under PL 94-142, and each of these programs must include a description of procedures for the development and implementation of a comprehensive system of personnel development. The primary focus of this comprehensive system of personnel development is on inservice training. However, when considering this comprehensive system, it is clear that states must also look at what is taking place in preservice training, inasmuch as the numbers and types of people being trained within a state at the preservice level will affect the nature of inservice training that is needed. In addition, the training resources that exist at the preservice level are usually critical for the creation of effective training programs (Schofer, 1977).

Since the personnel development sections of PL 94-142 have as a central theme the inclusion of inservice training, it is quite likely that inservice training will become "big business" in the years ahead. For the first time local school districts will have substantial amounts of money to provide inservice training to teachers and other related personnel (Schofer, 1977). The manpower planning committees that exist in most states within the comprehensive system of personnel development of PL 94-142 have the potential for mobilizing the training resources required for effective inservice training. In addition, many areas of possible conflict between colleges/universities, state education agencies, and local education agencies might be avoided through the proper utilization of such committees (Schofer, 1977).

Finally, effective manpower planning in special education involves much more than the mere gathering of statistics and determination of supply and demand ratios. It has as its major goal the provision of quality training at both the inservice and preservice levels. As the individual states develop and implement their respective comprehensive systems of personnel development under PL 94-142, this concern for and interest in quality should become paramount.

# References

Altman, R., & Meyen, E. L. Some observations on competency based instruction. *Exceptional Children*, 1974, *40*, 260–265.

Anderson, R. H., & Hemenway, R. E. Pre-student teaching practicum with exceptional children: A program description. *Education and Training of the Mentally Retarded*, 1974, *9*, 152–157.

Anderson, R. M., Dietrich, W. L., & Greer, J. G. Toward a noncategorical approach: Suggested course work for teachers of the retarded. *Education and Training of the Mentally Retarded*, 1976, *11*, 73–77.

Ballard, J., & Zettel, J. J. The managerial aspects of Public Law 94-142. *Exceptional Children*, 1978, *44*, 457–462.

Berdine, W. H., Cegelka, P. T., & Kelly, D. Practica evaluation: A competency based teacher education system. *Education and Training of the Mentally Retarded*, 1977, *12*, 381–385.

Berdine, W. H., & Kelly, D. Certification programs in trainable mentally handicapped. *Exceptional Children*, 1977, *43*, 455–457.

Berdine, W. H., Knapp, D. S., Tawney, J. S., & Martinson, M. C. Community action teacher training in special education. *Exceptional Children*, 1975, *41*, 495–496.

Berdine, W. H., Moyer, J. R., & Suppa, R. J. A competency-based student teaching supervision system. *Teacher Education and Special Education*, 1978, *1*(2), 48–54.

Blackhurst, E. W., & Wright, W. S. Learner-referencing student teacher evaluation. *Teacher Education and Special Education*, 1978, *1*(2), 55–65.

Blankenship, C. S., & Lilly, M. S. Essentials of special education for regular educators. *Teacher Education and Special Education*, 1977, *1*(1), 28–35.

Blumberg, A. Training special education teachers to use new methods. *Education and Training of the Mentally Retarded*, 1974, *9*, 78–82.

Brooks, B. J. Applied teacher training—A consumer based approach. *Education and Training of the Mentally Retarded*, 1975, *10*, 46–50.

Brown, G. B., & Palmer, D. J. A review of BEH funded personnel preparation programs in emotional disturbance. *Exceptional Children*, 1977, *44*, 168–174.

Brown, L., & York, R. Developing programs for severely handicapped students: Teacher training and classroom instruction. *Focus on Exceptional Children*, 1974, *6*(2), 1–11.

Bruininks, V. L. A humanistic competency-based training for teachers of learning disabled students. *Journal of Learning Disabilities*, 1977, *10*, 518–526.

Bullock, L. M., Dykes, M. K., & Kelly, T. J. Competency based teacher preparation in behavioral disorders. *Exceptional Children*, 1974, *41*, 192–194.

Burke, P. J. Personnel preparation: Historical perspectives. *Exceptional Children*, 1976, *43*, 144–147.

Burke, P. J., & Saettler, H. The Division of Personnel Preparation: How funding priorities are established and a personal assessment of the impact of PL 94-142. *Education and Training of the Mentally Retarded*, 1976, *11*, 361–365.

Cegelka, P. T., & Tawney, J. T. Decreasing the discrepancy: A case study in teacher reeducation. *Exceptional Children*, 1975, *41*, 268–269.

Cole, J. T., Kitano, M. K., & Rickert, D. C. Using observation instruments for the preparation and supervision of teachers. *Teacher Education and Special Education*, 1978, *1*(2), 40–47.

Connor, F. P. The past is prologue: Teacher preparation in special education. *Exceptional Children*, 1976, *42*, 366–378.

Courtnage, L., Brady, R., Suroski, A., & Schmid, R. Preparing competent teachers: A noncategorical competency-based teacher training model for special education. *Focus on Exceptional Children*, 1975, *7*(2), 6–12.

387

de Hoop, W. Multi-level preparation of special education personnel. *Education and Training of the Mentally Retarded,* 1973, *8,* 37–43.

de Jung, J., & Spence, J. Decision support model for program evaluation. *Education and Training of the Mentally Retarded,* 1975, *10,* 299–302.

David, W. J., & Fairchild, M. R. A study of noncategorical teacher preparation in special education: A self realization model. *Exceptional Children,* 1976, *42,* 390–397.

Division of Personnel Preparation, Bureau of Education for the Handicapped. U. S. Office of Education. *Cooperative planning for personnel preparation,* Washington, D. C.: Author, April 1974.

Dykes, M. K. Competency needs of special educators of crippled and other health-impaired children. *Journal of Special Education,* 1975, *9,* 367–374.

Edgar, E. B., Baker, S., Harper, C. T., Swift, P., & Melseth, S. An individualized inservice training program for teachers of the mentally retarded. *Education and Training of the Mentally Retarded,* 1976, *11,* 77–80.

Edgar, E., & Neel, R. S. Results of a competency based teacher training program. *Exceptional Children,* 1976, *43,* 33–35.

Fink, A. H., Glass, R. M., & Guskin, S. L. An analysis of teacher education programs in behavior disorders. *Exceptional Children,* 1975, *42,* 47–48.

Foos, R. A survey of competencies of teachers of trainable mentally retarded. *Education and Training of the Mentally Retarded,* 1976, *11,* 269–272.

Gerber, S. A., & Drezek, S. An interpersonal skills workshop for preparing special education teachers. *Education and Training of the Mentally Retarded,* 1977, *12,* 75–82.

Gillespie, P. H., & Sitko, M. C. Training preservice teachers in diagnostic teaching. *Exceptional Children,* 1976, *42,* 401–402.

Hale, S. A CBTE program for teachers of the learning disabled. *Journal of Teacher Education,* 1975, *26,* 257–260.

Hamalian, C. S., & Ludwig, A. J. Practicum in normalization and advocacy: A neglected component in teacher training. *Education and Training of the Mentally Retarded,* 1976, *11,* 172–175.

Hanninen, K. A., Coleman, T. W., & Parres, R. M. Anatomy of change: Curriculum revision in special education teacher training. *Exceptional Children,* 1977, *43,* 311–312.

Harvey, J. Future trends in personnel preparation. *Exceptional Children,* 1976, *43,* 148–150.

Harvey, J. Legislative intent and progress. *Exceptional Children,* 1978, *44,* 234–237.

Herr, D. E., Algozzine, R. F., & Heuchert, C. M. Competencies of teachers of the mildly handicapped. *Journal of Special Education,* 1976, *10,* 97–106.

Hirshoren, A., & Umansky, W. Certification for teachers of preschool handicapped children. *Exceptional Children,* 1977, *44,* 191–193.

Kelly, D. Using videotapes to evaluate student teaching performance. *Teacher Education and Special Education,* 1978, *1*(2), 37–39.

Kokaska, C., & Schmidt, A. Preparing students for the job market. *Education and Training of the Mentally Retarded,* 1976, *11,* 80–82.

Leone, P., & Retish, P. Affective differences among undergraduate students. *Mental Retardation,* 1977, *15*(2), 13–15.

Meyen, E. L., & Altman, R. Individualized instruction for pre-service teachers: An applicable competency based training model. *Focus on Exceptional Children,* 1973, *5*(1), 1–11.

Minkoff, J., & Sellin, D. E. College juniors' reactions to tutoring adolescent trainable retarded students. *Education and Training of the Mentally Retarded,* 1973, *8,* 146–149.

Nazarro, J. N. Innovation in teacher training: A conversation with Melvyn I. Semmel. *Education and Training of the Mentally Retarded,* 1976, *11,* 352–360.

Organization for Economic Cooperation and Development. *The mediterranean regional project.* Paris: Author, 1965.

Oseroff, A., Sander, B., & Connors, R. Field-based instruction: Outcomes, placement, and evaluation. *Teacher Education and Special Education*, 1978, *1*(2), 8–13.

Ostanski, J. New dimensions and considerations in the training of special education teachers. *Education and Training of the Mentally Retarded*, 1975, *10*, 117–119.

Prothero, J. C., & Ehlers, W. H. Social work students' attitude and knowledge changes following study of programmed materials. *American Journal of Mental Deficiency*, 1974, *79*, 83–86.

Redden, M. R., & Blackhurst, A. E. Mainstreaming competency specifications for elementary teachers. *Exceptional Children*, 1978, *44*, 615–617.

Reger, R. How can we influence teacher-training programs? *Journal of Special Education*, 1974, *8*, 7–13.

Reid, W. R., & Whorton, J. E. The first day. *Education and Training of the Mentally Retarded*, 1973, *8*, 44–45.

Renne, D. J., & Blackhurst, A. E. Adjunct autoinstruction in an introductory special education course. *Exceptional Children*, 1976, *43*, 224–225.

Russell, T., & Brown, L. G. An emerging model for training administrators of special education in sparsely populated areas. *Education and Training of the Mentally Retarded*, 1974, *9*, 209–215.

Saettler, H. Current priorities in personnel preparation. *Exceptional Children*, 1976, *43*, 147–148.

Sailor, W., Guess, D., & Lavis, L. Training teachers for education of the severely handicapped. *Education and Training of the Mentally Retarded*, 1975, *10*, 201–203.

Schofer, R. C. Cooperative manpower planning. In J. Smith (Ed.), *Personnel preparation and Public Law 94-142: The map, the mission and the mandate*. Washington, D.C.: Division of Personnel Preparation, Bureau of Education for the Handicapped, U. S. Office of Education, 1977.

Schofer, R. C. Cooperative manpower planning: A status study. *Teacher Education and Special Education*, 1978, *2*(1), 7–11.

Schofer, R. C., & Duncan, J. R. *Cooperative manpower planning in special education: A second status study*. Columbia, Mo.: University of Missouri–Columbia, Department of Special Education, October 1978.

Schofer, R. C., & McGough, R. L. *Statewide cooperative manpower planning in special education: A status study*. Columbia, Mo.: University of Missouri–Columbia, Department of Special Education, November 1976.

Semmel, M. I., & Englert, C. S. A decision-making orientation applied to student teaching supervision. *Teacher Education and Special Education*, 1978, *1*(2), 28–36.

Shane, D. G., & Van Osdol, W. R. Practicum—As a part of special education training programs. *Education and Training of the Mentally Retarded*, 1974, *9*, 74–77.

Shaw, S. F., & Gillung, T. B. Efficacy of a college course for regular class teachers of the mildly handicapped. *Mental Retardation*, 1975, *13*(4), 3–6.

Sheperd, G. Models for preparation programs. *Education and Training of the Mentally Retarded*, 1975, *10*, 193–196.

Shores, R. E., Cegelka, P. T., & Nelson, C. B. Competency based special education teacher training. *Exceptional Children*, 1973, *40*, 192–197.

Sontag, E., Bokee, M. B., & Burke, P. J. Special projects in personnel preparation—An overview of some programs designed to train personnel for the education of severely retarded children. *Education and Training of the Mentally Retarded*, 1974, *9*, 169–176.

Stainback, S., Stainback, W., & Maurer, S. Training teachers for the severely and profoundly handicapped: A new frontier. *Exceptional Children*, 1976, *42*, 203–210.

Stainback, S., Stainback, W., Schmid, R., & Courtnage, L. Training teachers for the severely and profoundly handicapped: An accountability model. *Education and Training of the Mentally Retarded*, 1977, *12*, 170–173.

Stamm, J. M. A general model for the design of a competency-based special education professional preparation program. *Education and Training of the Mentally Retarded,* 1975, *10,* 196–200.

Stowitschek, J. J., & Hofmeister, A. M. Effects of minicourse instruction on teachers and pupils. *Exceptional Children,* 1974, *40,* 490–495.

Strauch, J. C., & Affleck, G. G. Competencies for cooperating teachers in special education. *Exceptional Children,* 1976, *42,* 403–405.

Tawney, J. W. Explorations in the development of teacher competence. *Teacher Education and Special Education,* 1978, *1*(2), 66–76.

Turnbull, A. P. Citizen advocacy in special education training. *Education and Training of the Mentally Retarded,* 1977, *12,* 166–169.

Wagonseller, B., & Mari, A. Applications of the simulation technique as a training instrument for teachers and students. *Focus on Exceptional Children,* 1977, *9*(5), 10–12.

Walker, J. A. The practicum supervisor inches toward competence: Preliminary thoughts on a process. *Teacher Education and Special Education,* 1978, *1*(2), 14–27.

Whorton, J. A follow-up study of personnel trained in special education. *Education and Training of the Mentally Retarded,* 1975, *10,* 120–123.

Witty, E. P. Training to handle learning and behavioral problems in the regular classroom. *Journal of Teacher Education,* 1975, *26,* 135–138.

Yarger, S. J., & Schmieder, A. A. Teacher Centers and PL 94-142. *Teacher Education and Special Education,* 1977, *1*(1), 36–43.

# ROLE-MODEL COMPLEMENTS OF SCHOOL PSYCHOLOGY WITH SPECIAL EDUCATION

Ted L. Miller

*The University of Tennessee at Chattanooga*

Calvin O. Dyer

*The University of Michigan*

School psychology is an enigma to many special educators. The vagueness with which it is viewed by them may be related to the very wide range of tasks that psychologists in schools typically undertake. In a single day a school psychologist may be called upon to act as a psychometrician, a program evaluator, a counselor, a public relations specialist, or in several other very particular specialities (Bersoff, 1975; Gray, 1963). In this work the school psychologist often provides services to handicapped children and youth, and therefore special educators are in frequent contact with the profession. Understandably, special educators may tend to judge all school psychology as they have directly witnessed the professional activities of particular school psychologists. Certainly, few special educators have the time to consider the many services school psychologists might and indeed do provide. Thus the happenstance of abbreviated and perhaps selective experiences may promote an inaccurate concept of the many roles[1] of school psychology which complement special education services.

---

Thanks are expressed to Priscilla Mondt for her assistance in the preparation of the manuscript.

[1]The word *role* will be used throughout this chapter to denote the primary activity that the school psychologist might engage in. Thus, one whose primary activity is testing would assume the role of psychometrician. The word *model* will be used throughout this paper to represent more global constructs which may contain several role emphases. Thus, the clinical model might refer to any of the combined role functions of psychometrician, psychoeducational specialist, or counselor.

In many instances the most observed activity has the greatest probability of becoming the role ascribed to the psychologist. However, when special educators observe other activities being performed, or perhaps discuss these additional activities with colleagues, the mystery of what school psychologists do may deepen. Resulting ambiguity could readily be lessened by recognition that school psychology does not represent a unilateral role directed toward only a few activities. Instead, it more accurately denotes a broad range of professional actions that vary with circumstance and need. While special educators have tended to seek role designations by describing themselves in terms of the population that they serve and the settings within which they work (e.g., resource teacher for the learning disabled) or via the broad functions that they perform (e.g., special education administrator), school psychologists generally have not so categorized their roles. Perhaps special educators may now find themselves too well defined by restrictive, aging criteria, as is suggested by the move toward noncategorical teacher preparation. However, school psychologists continue to have their roles that complement special education misunderstood because of the many activities routinely performed under their title.

Resolution of this misunderstanding will not be easy. While this review is primarily concerned with school psychology, its purpose is not to offer another role possibility or to debate the value of one or more roles. Instead, the school psychology profession will be described as it has emerged in the literature and, more particularly, the emergence of school psychology's particular relationship with special education will be charted. Those areas where the professions of school psychology and special education have had mutually complementary role interests will be emphasized, and a projection of those areas where the growth of both professions demands close rapport will be offered. Accordingly, in the first section of this chapter the history of the field is briefly highlighted and a short review of current training and certification patterns is provided. In the next section some aspects of the many role responsibilities proposed for school psychology are discussed. The third section is concerned with the profession's self-evaluation of school psychological services as well as evaluations by special educators and other school personnel. The final section is a projection of the key components of change in future roles of school psychology from the standpoint of its continued complementary relationship with special education.

The chapter proceeds from the assumption that special education and school psychology are complementary in many of the responsibilities each discipline undertakes; that is, the professions are aligned in that they serve common goals, although their activities may differ substantially. This assumption is controversial, for there are views of school psychology which advocate the diversification of psychological services to the total school; i.e., the school beyond the boundaries of children and youth at obvious learning or social risk (e.g., Cardon, 1972). While logically sound, the authors regard this view as possessing pragmatic limitations. For example, Bardon (1976), in observing declining enrollments and other fiscal realities, has concluded that the number of school psychologists employed by the schools will in all likelihood not grow beyond some relatively optimal ratio of pupils to psychologists within the foreseeable future. By implication then, school psychologists must, despite their interest in other activities, continue to use their important skills with those children and youth who are deemed most in need. Very frequently these are the children and youth who are served by special education; therefore, a service relationship between the professions is inevitable.

School psychology's alignment with special education, as adherred to in this paper, is not a radical departure in the school psychology literature. Indeed it has been openly suggested for some time. Gray (1963) alluded to the necessity of such an approach, while Gallagher (1969) clarified the grounds for the relationship of psychology and special education: "[these disciplines] have always had a symbiotic relationship, because the psychologist was, and is, a necessary first step in any special education program" (pp. 219–220).

Other authors have discussed the school psychology–special education relationship at length. Lambert (1973) concluded that the traditional sources of school psychologists' influence lay in special education–related activities. Sabatino (1972), though critical of psychologists for the manner in which their work relationships with educators had developed, called upon the profession to acknowledge a genuine professional relationship with special education. Catterall (1972) clarified the economic ties between professions by indicating that over half of the finances for school psychology result from service relationships with special education. Quite recently, Ysseldyke (1978) cited eight potentially influential sources of change in school psychology that may require dramatic alterations in the profession's practice during the next decade. All eight points can be viewed as partially reflective of changes occurring in special education; five points seem to stem directly from special education.

In short, the profession of school psychology has had a long-term commitment to working with special children and, by extrapolation, with special educators. Since the public schools' commitment to handicapped children has now been mandated by federal legislation, it is reasonable to expect that school psychologists will figure prominantly in special education's newly affirmed responsibilities. Thus Meacham and Peckham (1978) asserted the status of school psychology at the three-quarter century mark as being "alive and well" (p.205). However, a statement in their paper seems to indicate the harbinger of this desirable conclusion: "Growth [of school psychology] seems to be related largely to the increase in special education programs throughout the United States . . . Recent Federal legislation, P.L. 94-142, could accelerate the process" (p. 195). Pragmatically, then, school psychology and special education are distinct yet closely linked specialities that are related because of their shared responsibilities to handicapped children and youth. It is from this position that the remainder of the chapter will proceed.

## OVERVIEW OF SCHOOL PSYCHOLOGY

### The inception of a profession

Activities that formed the basis for the foundation of school psychology can be seen within the evolution of modern psychology during the period 1875–1900. During this period European science, in recognition of the Darwinian thesis, openly promoted the recognition of continual, selective variation, hence the differentiation in living things. This insight did not go unnoticed by those associated with the infant science of psychology. The focus of mainstream study in psychology prior to 1875, and for some elements long afterward, had been devoted to ascertaining similarities among individuals. However, important as this was to prove to be, it was soon complemented by pleas to begin examining for the essential variations in man.

Of those individuals arguing the value of a study of individual differences, Francis Galton, an Englishman and a cousin of Darwin, must historically emerge as the prominant voice. Following his interests in individual differences, Galton pioneered studies of genius, the precise measurement of individual differences, and the use of statistics (particularly correlational techniques); he is also said to have invented, though not named, the first mental tests (Watson, 1963). The nature and intensity of this work led White and Harris (1961) to conclude that these efforts represent the activities that were to eventually provide a prototype for school psychology. Interestingly, inspection also suggests that Galton's efforts provided more than a few emphases for special education. Indeed, at one point in his *Hereditary Genius* (1892) he mentioned the work of

Seguin, an individual whose work must surely nominate him as a pioneer special educator.

Toward the end of the 19th century psychologist practitioners recognized the potential uses of measurement to promote services for school children with special needs. In the United States the first laboratory–clinic was established at the University of Pennsylvania by Lightner Witmer. Witmer's clinic was openly proclaimed as being devoted to child guidance, and, since individuals operating the clinic maintained close ties with public education, a major purpose of the clinic was to assist educators to solve school learning problems. Because of these ties the clinic is sometimes cited as the first example of psychology being applied to educational problems within the public school systems of the United States.

Two events occurred in the United States during the period 1896–1916 that are generally taken as instrumental in the foundation of school psychology. The first of these was the introduction of special classes into the public schools—an event signaling the beginnings of special education in this country. According to Bardon and Bennett (1974), this event was based upon both the recognition of individual differences and the increasing demands for universal education. The second major event was Louis Terman's (circa 1916) development of the Stanford Revision and Extension of the Binet-Simon Intelligence Scale (née Binet-Simon Scale of 1908). The rapid acceptance of Terman's product accomplished at least two things. First, it provided a then accepted confirmation of individual differences. Second, since the test had been fashioned from school-derived tasks, it was highly related to educational success. As a result, psychologists were soon able to use it in the process of accurately identifying individuals who could and could not profit from the special instruction then beginning to appear in the public schools.

Soon after these events, school psychologists began to appear, the first recorded use of the term being the title given to Arnold Gesell in 1915. Holt and Kicklighter (1971) have indicated that the State of Conneticut Board of Education granted the title to Gesell to "travel throughout rural Conneticut and examine children who were performing poorly in school. He consulted with school personnel, with parents and with child care agencies" (p.1). With the introduction of Gesell's work, school psychology can truly be considered as having arrived on the U.S. educational scene. However, from the outset school psychology did not develop in a nationally or even regionally consistent manner. To understand this one must recognize that there were few procedures or guidelines to follow and exchanges of information about school psychology were yet to come. Thus, Bardon and Bennett's (1974) statement to the effect that the profession's sporadic development was largely a result of professional determination through adaptation to local needs is quite logical. As a result, school psychologists even in adjoining school districts were often engaged in practices which were quite distinct, i.e., reflective of the systems' idiosyncrasies.

What was the case for districts must certainly have been more the case across the national perspective. Although activities, hence roles, varied considerably, it appears that school psychologists generally progressed from being psychometricians in the first period to, by the 1950s, becoming more clinically oriented professionals concerned with mental health issues. Later, as a result of the dramatic social changes of the 1960s, school psychologists began to combine the testing and clinical mental health roles to meet the demands of the period. In this combining of roles, school psychology began to integrate and use an ever greater array of information adopted from the parenting behavioral sciences. This tendency to adopt and use techniques from psychology and other behavioral sciences may be the basis for Bennett's (1970) conclusion that the specialty has been adept at modifying itself to the changing demands of society through the incorporation of knowledge from related disciplines. Whatever the case, it is certain that by the close of the 1960s school psychology manifested both the roots of the past and many new emphases accepted in response to the changing society. This has ultimately resulted in a diversity of thought that is reflected in the literature and within actual practice. Perhaps the one element that has remained most consistent is the profession's continued attention to the learning and behavioral problems of atypical children and youth.

### Training and certification

Today, two factors that greatly affect the roles pursued by the school psychologist are the training he or she receives and the certification standards by which he or she must abide. Together these factors greatly influence the activities that school psychologists may engage in. Issues in training have received more emphasis in the literature, but, increasingly, certification practices are being discussed. The following review highlights some of the major themes within these topics that may be considered very relevant to directing school psychology's role complements with special education.

*Training*

The first training program for school psychology is considered to be the one begun at the University of Illinois in 1953 (Cutts, 1955). Even before this date, however, training had been a subject of concern within the emerging field. The importance with which training was viewed is reflected in the fact that no less than three national conferences [the Boulder Conference (Raimy, 1950), the Thayer Conference (Cutts, 1955), and the Vail Conference (Korman, 1974)] have been held, and countless other state level conferences and national meetings have been much concerned with this topic. The following issues have dominated the general debate concerning training: (1) the (degree) level of training school psychologists; (2) the content or skills to be emphasized in training; and (3) the location of training, including internship settings. However, reports may be found on virtually every other aspect of training as well.

The number of statements providing descriptions of training of school psychologists shows no signs of diminishing and, since the mid-1960s, more than a few papers have appeared that describe some aspect of the then current status of training in school psychology (e.g., Bardon, 1964–65, 1968; Bardon, Constanzu, & Walker, 1971; Bardon & Walker, 1972; Bardon & Wenger, 1974; Brown & Lindstrom, 1978; Cardon & French, 1968–1969; French, Smith, & Cardon, 1968; Goh, 1977; Patros, Gross, & Bjorn, 1972; Silverman, 1969; Smith, 1964–1965; Tindall, 1964; White, 1963–1964). However, because such descriptions tend to become stale quite quickly, the following discussion is based largely on the more recent papers concerning the topic.

*Number of programs.* Goh (1977) concluded that programs for the training of school psychologists had grown in number from about 30 in 1961 to about 160 in 1974. Brown and Lindstrom (1978) reported an expansion of programs from 63 in 1964 to 143 in 1974. Bardon (1976) described school psychology programs as having grown from 79 in 1964 to 147 in 1973. Brown and Lindstrom (1978) indicated that by late 1977, 203 programs in U.S. colleges and universities were actively engaged in the training of school psychologists. Taking the number of programs in 1961 to be 30 and the current (1978) number of programs at 203, there are now over six times the number of training programs that existed less than two decades ago.

*Number of students and practitioners.* Bardon (1976) estimated that 5973 students were in training at all levels of preparation in 1974, a

397

number two-thirds the size of the approximately 9000 practicing school psychologists in the United States at that time. Since there is probably some overlap of practicing school psychologists and students in training, Bardon (1976) estimated that the number of students in training approached the population of school psychologists who have completed all training. Moreover, this trend shows signs of acceleration. A recent survey (Brown & Lindstrom, 1978) indicated that for the year 1976–1977 about 7450 students were enrolled, a figure over one-half the size of the estimated 12,226 school psychologists in active practice during the 1975–1976 school year (Meacham & Peckham, 1978). Clearly, both the number of students and the number of practicing school psychologists continues to expand.

*Location of training.* Brown and Lindstrom (1978) identified programs in 39 states and the District of Columbia; only 11 states reported no programs. Many states reported more than one program; California alone reported 26 training institutions, with New York, Pennsylvania, and Ohio next in order. Eight states reported only single institutions involved in training school psychologists.

The departmental affiliations of training faculty within higher education varies considerably among institutions. Brown and Lindstrom (1978) identified 822 persons as primary faculty, meaning that they contributed at least 50 percent of their faculty appointment to school psychology. Among the primary faculty, 253 were appointed within school psychology and 75 within clinical psychology. The remaining primary faculty affiliations were spread across eight other academic departments.

*Levels of training.* Goh (1977) mailed questionaires to 163 programs in the United States and four in Canada that were included in the publication *Graduate Study in Psychology for 1974-75* (APA, 1973) and/or listed in the summary by Bardon and Wenger (1974–1975); 97 questionaires were returned. This report produced the following observations: 26 percent of the schools offered master's level training alone, 7 percent offered post-masters specialist training alone, and 9 percent offered doctoral level training alone. Furthermore, 58 percent of the schools offered training at several levels: masters and specialist (26 percent), masters and doctorate (9 percent), and masters, specialist, and doctorate (16 percent). Of the masters degrees conferred, approximately 76 percent were arts and science degrees, with the remainder being in education. At the doctorate level 88 percent of the programs offered the Ph.D. but 39 percent either offered the Ed.D. or both Ph.D. and Ed.D. The Psy.D. was available at only one institution.

The above figures can be contrasted with another set of recent data. Brown and Lindstrom (1978) found 1774 students in training at the masters level, 3936 at what was termed the sixth-year level (two years of graduate study), and 1740 at the doctoral level. At least for new graduates, then, the school psychologist is trained at the sixth-year level about 50 percent of the time and at either the masters or doctorate 25 percent of the time. However, receipt of the doctoral degree tends to create options for employment in other than the public school setting (Brown, Sewell, & Lindstrom, 1977). Therefore, many doctoral level school psychologists do not enter the schools. As a result, the training levels within most school systems is below that which would be anticipated from the training levels of recent graduates.

*Training requirements.* Although the emphasis in training varies widely, some general conclusions can be reached. In one recent analysis of training, Goh (1977) identified 38 topical emphases which were then rated for importance on a 10-point scale by trainers representing 99 institutions. The three most important topics were assessment of learning difficulties, assessment of behavior and social problems, and psychoeducational assessment. These data were submitted to a principle components analysis from which nine factors were extracted which accounted for approximately 73 percent of the total variance. The nine factors and the variance that they accounted for were school based consultation (29 percent), educational assessment and remediation (11 percent), behavior modification technology (9 percent), psychological evaluation (5 percent), psychotherapeutic procedures (5 percent), quantitative methods (4 percent), community involvement (4 percent), professional roles and issues (3 percent), and psychological foundations (3 percent). Overall, the program trainers rated school-based consultation, educational assessment and remediation, and behavior modification technology as the most emphasized areas of training. Together the three topics accounted for about one-half of the variance. Community involvement, quantitative methods, and psychotherapeautic procedures were the least emphasized of the nine components. A multiple analysis of variance indicated that the relative importance assigned the nine components varied as a result of level of training, the affiliation of the faculty (e.g., psychology or educational psychology), and the length of a department's history. According to the results, consultation and quantitative methods tended to be emphasized more by doctoral programs and by those programs with longer history. Psychological evaluation was more highly emphasized by programs located outside of education.

A unique approach to the study of training in school psychology was provided by Burns and Rupiper (1977). Arguing that most of the available data on training was in fact only logical speculation, the authors reasoned that trends in training emphases would be reflected by a content analysis of textbooks used for school psychology. Seventeen textbooks covering the period 1960–1975 were identified and their content analyzed. From among these 17 textbooks, 46 percent of the total number of pages was contributed in the period of 1960–1965, 42 percent during the 1965–1970, and 12 percent during 1970–1975. A most striking feature of this analysis was the decline of page numbers for the last five-year period, a period of growth for school psychology.

The authors performed a content analysis of the materials in the texts. Twenty-five categories were determined and the number of pages contributed to each category were counted. Table 1 summarizes the resulting data obtained from Burns and Rupipers' (1977) investigation. As may be seen in the Table, the topic of assessment received the greatest emphasis, while six of the 25 categories received less than 1 percent emphasis. It is interesting to note that the topic of special education received as much emphasis as the topic of theories. This may suggest the importance given by trainers to the application of school psychology to special populations.

Burns and Rupiper (1977) drew the following conclusions from these data: (1) changes in publication interests had occurred during the period, which, presumably, reflected training interests; (2) the issue of "professional identity" (p. 338), which presumably equates to roles, had not diminished; (3) contrary to earlier predictions, there was a decreasing emphasis on research; (4) behavior modification techniques and all remedial activities were receiving increased attention; and (5) there had been a decreasing interest in group testing and counseling. Some earlier predictions about training trends in school psychology (e.g., a focus on research, a focus on prevention rather than remediation; for a review of these predictions see Bardon, 1964–1965; Silverman, 1969; Tindall, 1964) were not born out. Taken at face value, during the 15-year period 1960-1975, school psychologists in training became increasingly service oriented, more concerned with the roles they possess, less concerned with research, more behavioral in their intervention approaches, and more active in individual child study and remediation.

*Certification patterns*

Certification clearly affects school psychologists' roles and activities. This is accomplished in at least two ways. First, certification may reflect concerns that are in conflict with the philosophical view of what the school psychologist should do. Second, once the individual school psychologist has entered practice, certification requirements may exert specific role expectancies, as few school psychologists, understandably, are anxious to pursue activities that state certification doesn't recognize as within their professional domain.

Most states provide certification of school psychologists, but in a few states a licensure procedure is in effect. In many instances the school psychologist has an option to elect either procedure. Licensure procedures are usually administered by a State Board of Psychological Examiners, while certification is usually awarded by the State Department of Education. The latter procedure is more often elected, but, as Brown et al. (1977) indicate, either process represents "sanctioning credentials in order to allow the candidate to work as a school psychologist in a particular setting" (p.2). Generally, licensure allows a broader range of professional activity than does certification.

As is the case with training, the topic of certification has received much attention in the literature (Bluestein & Milofsky, 1970; Brown et al., 1977; Claytor, 1950; Graff & Clair, 1973; Gross, Bonham, & Bluestein, 1966; Hall, 1949; Hodges, 1960; Horrocks, 1946; Nelson, 1963; Newland, 1956; Sewell & Brown, 1976; Traxler, 1967). Many of these anlyses are now of historical significance only, thus the following review is largely drawn from the more contemporary references.

*Numbers of states certifying school psychologists.* As might be expected, the number of certifying bodies has increased dramatically. In the 21-year period 1946–1977 the number of states recognizing school psychologists[2] through certification increased from seven in 1946 (Horrocks, 1946) to almost all states and the District of Columbia in 1977 (Brown et al., 1977). Although seven states currently have fewer than one dozen certified school psychologists and one state apparently has none (Meacham & Peckham, 1978), every state but one seemingly has provisions for this professional specialty. Interestingly, the single exception (Michigan) provides for the approval of school psychologists through

[2]Terminology associated with the concept of role definition is important here. For example, five states refer to the profession as "school psychometrist," while many others have multiple designations. For the purposes of this chapter the authors assume that the terminology denotes roughly equivalent meaning across states.

## TABLE 1
## RESULTS OF PAGE ANALYSES USING CONTENT CATEGORIES ACROSS BOOKS AND TIME PERIODS

| Content Categories | Time Period | | | |
| --- | --- | --- | --- | --- |
| | 1960–1965 (percent) | 1966–1970 (percent) | 1971–1975 (percent) | Overall 1960–1975 (percent) |
| Administration & Organization | 9 | 4 | 0.7 | 6 |
| Assessment emphasis | 15 | 14 | 20 | 15 |
| Assessment, group | 1 | 2 | 1 | 1 |
| Behavior modification | 0 | 2 | 9 | 2 |
| Clinical personality | 12 | 9 | 6 | 10 |
| Community relations | 6 | 1 | 1 | 3 |
| Consulting | 3 | 16 | 6 | 8 |
| Curriculum Development | 0.8 | 1 | 0 | 0.8 |
| Ethics & Legal issues | 3 | 1 | 0.9 | 2 |
| Future trends | 1 | 4 | 6 | 3 |

| | | | | |
|---|---|---|---|---|
| History, current issues | 3 | 3 | 10 | 4 |
| Inservice training | 2 | 3 | 2 | 2 |
| Learning disabilities | 0 | 2 | 0.3 | 0.7 |
| Professional identity | 9 | 5 | 13 | 8 |
| Professional training | 6 | 0.8 | 4 | 4 |
| Remediation | 1 | 3 | 6 | 2 |
| Research issues | 4 | 3 | 2 | 3 |
| Resource materials | 0.3 | 1 | 3 | 1 |
| Sex education | 0 | 1 | 0 | 0.5 |
| Special education | 7 | 7 | 8 | 7 |
| Special populations | 3 | 2 | 0 | 2 |
| Teaching psychology | 1 | 0.1 | 0 | 0.5 |
| Theories | 5 | 12 | 2 | 7 |
| Therapy, general | 9 | 8 | 11 | 9 |
| Therapy, group | 2 | 2 | 0.7 | 2 |

Reproduced by permission. Burns, R.G., & Rupiper, O.J. Trends in school psychology as demonstrated by content analysis of school psychology textbooks. *Psychology in the Schools, 1977, 14,* p. 337.

403

the funding of special education programs within specific school districts.

*Certification levels and degree requirements.* Brown et al.(1977) indicate that 26 states possess a single level of certification while 22 have two or more. Five states require a bachelor's degree and graduate hours, 33 require the master's degree, 12 require the sixth-year program, and one requires the doctoral degree as basic entry requirements. In addition, six states require a teaching certificate.

*Course requirements.* Bluestein and Milofsky (1970) indentified 17 course topics that were required within state certification practices. Individual assessment techniques was the single most frequently required topic; the next five, in order, were developmental psychology, statistics, counseling, exceptional children, and measurement theory. The authors concluded that most students in school psychology were broadly trained and therefore exposed to some aspects of nearly all of the topics that they identified.

Graff and Clair (1973) found intellectual assessment to be the area of coursework most frequently cited, followed by coursework in tests and measurement. A three-way emphasis on statistics, counseling, and the psychology of exceptional children completed the top five requirements. It is interesting to note that both the Bluestein and Milofsky (1970) and Graff and Clair (1973) reviews concluded that the study of exceptional children was among the five most frequently mentioned topics.

Of all the training emphases in school psychology, the internship or practicum may be the least actually studied and objectively specified. While nearly all states require varying amounts of practicum, field experience, internship, or externship, the requirements vary widely from state to state and may be more or less stipulated. Perhaps the clearest statement that can be reached on this topic is that most school psychologists have some precertification practicum or internship experience.

*Summary*

The preceding sections have dealt with the training patterns and certification requirements of contemporary school psychology. Some conclusions about factors shaping roles in school psychology are evident. First, the school psychologist is trained at several levels and each level tends to specify certain characteristic skills. Second, the competencies associated with a school psychologist's role may be attained within a variety of different training backgrounds. Third, most states actively embrace the profession of school psychology, as judged from the fact that 80 percent of them have publicly funded training programs and almost 100 percent recognize school psychology through certification and/or licensure. Finally, although training at any one location may have unique features, most surveys have recorded an emphasis on formal coursework with prepares most school psychologists to work with handicapped populations and special education service units.

## ROLE MODELS IN SCHOOL PSYCHOLOGY

The roles of school psychologists may be described on the basis of several dimensions. For example, their roles can be analyzed from the perspective of (1) the target population for their services, (2) the primary location in which those services are delivered, (3) the goals or outcomes sought by the school psychologist, or (4) the particular professional skills that are emphasized. The number of dimensions that could be used to describe the role of the school psychologist may help to explain why it is sometimes difficult to make a genuine distinction between the role conceptualizations that school psychologists relate: Is, for example, the psychoeducational assessment model really different from the educational assessment model? Partially because of the vagueness of these dimensions, the authors are led to agree with Pielstick's (1970) comment that is unlikely that anyone will define the school psychologists' role, unless it is for a particular psychologist at a particular moment.

In reality, school psychologists assume many different roles. As was described earlier, Bardon and Bennett (1974) have concluded that general roles have been associated with time frames: Stage I psychologists were testers; Stage II psychologists were counselors; and now Stage III psychologists reflect both their educational tester and counselor backgrounds. However, this analysis certainly does not account for the variation in roles that exists. Bardon (1968) noted that the profession of school psychology has become more complex over the years—a phenomenon that would appear to be associated with the increasing complexity of the schools that they serve. Citing the trends of these changes, he concluded that what could be termed the school psychologists' goals were at least as important as their daily activities: "When people want to know our role, I do not think they want to know how we parcel out our working day; rather, they want to know what we are doing that is important and distinct enough to justify our being in the schools" (Bardon, 1968, p. 190). Our description of roles, then, will recognize the importance of the goals that the school psychologist is attempting to meet regardless of the particular activities he or she engages in. It will

405

deemphasize the description of day-to-day actions that are required and attempt to present a picture of the broad constraints that form school psychologists' roles.

In attempting to provide this description we will start with the assumption that school psychologists wish to engender change from within public schools through the application of principles of psychology. However, some authors (e.g., Lighthall, 1969; Medway, 1975), have deemphasized the importance of psychological skills to school psychology and emphasized instead techniques derived from other behavioral sciences (sociology). Other authors (Silberberg & Silberberg, 1971) have pointedly cast doubt on the value of a psychologist employed by the public schools and therefore under the jurisdiction of supervisors whose decisions may not readily be challenged. Still others have suggested that the school psychologists' basis for change ought to be through community mental health centers (Klosterman, 1974). However, despite those sporadic papers which question the value of school-based psychologists, most authors have found reason to support the concept of a school psychologist housed within the schools. Therefore, we will proceed from the psychologist-within-the-schools position advocated by Gray (1963) and others.

Gilmore (1974) concluded that the field of school psychology has been far more capable of defining what it is not than what it is and likened the field's anxiety over defining its role to that of an adolescent who is uncomfortable in answering questions as to who and what he or she is. Furthermore, Gilmore stressed the need for role models that reflect the combination of settings and situations within which school psychologists are to function. Like Pielstick (1970), he cautioned that a single model was inappropriate and suggested that major models could be categorized under the two headings of operations and sources. The term *operations* (or practices) refers to two dimensions: (1) the directness or indirectness of services provided, and (2) the degree to which a model is more service or science oriented. The term *sources* refers to the bases of the model according to each of three dimensions: (1) education or psychology as the primary parenting discipline; (2) adopted or developed, i.e., the acceptance of information from other disciplines versus the actual development of information; and (3) the model's relative concern for theoretical approaches or applied practices. The use of these five dimensions provides a sophisticated scale by which models can be compared.

Using the above framework, Gilmore (1974) analyzed the following five historically significant models: (1) the clinical model of Bardon (1965), which attempts to serve individual children through techniques developed in clinical psychology; (2) the psychoeducational model of Vallett (1963), which also attempts to serve children through individual work but emphasizes academic rather than emotional remediation and stresses diagnostic–prescriptive activities; (3) the education programmer model of Reger (1965), in which the school psychologist's activity is primarily associated with academic learning and the development of specific curricula for children; (4) the systems level problem solver of Gray (1963), which views problems and their solutions as being located in the context of an entire system; and (5) the preventative mental health model of Bower (1965), which stresses the activities of school psychologists as being oriented to prevention rather than toward primary remediation.

The ratings of these five models appear in Table 2. As may be seen from the table, the models vary considerably along the dimensions and thus show considerable diversity among the professional goals associated with each. There is little wonder then that role descriptions for school psychologists have been a source of considerable confusion. In summary, Gilmore's (1974) framework for analyzing models of school psychology appears to be capable of comparing most role-model emphases. As examples, consider the following cases in which diverse roles are stressed. In each instance note the degree of interrelatedness, hence synthesis, of role models that is possible within the framework of Gilmore's (1974) presentation.

Trachtman (1971) distinguished a conceptual difference between what a school psychologist should do and can do, and pointed out that school psychologists cannot accomplish every potential role suggested for them. Faced with this conclusion, Trachtman concludes that in addition to broad training in academic psychology, school psychologists should emphasize the skills in the clinical model. Cardon (1972) and Cowen and Lorion (1976) view school psychologists as adhering predominantly to the prevention model of Bower (1965); both suggest that the necessity for treatment according to the clinical models could be lessened with adequate prevention efforts. On the other hand, Bernstein (1976), Herron (1966), and Nickerson (1973) emphasize psychotherapy as an essential skill of the school psychologist.

Reilly (1974) proposes a combination of roles by drawing heavily upon systems interventions (e.g., Gray, 1963) and individual interventions (e.g., Bardon, 1965; Vallett, 1963). Bennett (1976) emphasizes the school psychologist's role in research, which in many respects may be seen as compatable with Lewis' (1974) program consultant and Granger and Campbells' (1977) program evaluator roles.

A number of authors propose variations of the systems level

# TABLE 2
## MODELS RANKED ON FIVE DIMENSIONS

| OPERATIONS | | SOURCE | | |
|---|---|---|---|---|
| **Direct** | **Service** | **Education** | **Adopted** | **Theory** |
| Clinical | Clinical | Ed. Programmer | Clinical | |
| Ed. Programmer | Preventative | System level | Preventative | |
| Psychoeducational | Ed. Programmer | | | |
| | Psychoeducational | Psychoeducational | | |
| | Systems level | | | Psychoeducational |
| | | | | Systems level |
| | | | | Ed. Programmer |
| | | | | Preventative |
| | | | Ed. Programmer | Clinical |
| | | | Psychoeducational | |
| Systems level | | Preventative | | |
| Preventative | | Clinical | | |
| **Indirect** | **Science** | **Psychology** | **Developed** | **Practice** |

Reproduced by permission. Gilmore, E.G. Models for school psychology: Dimensions, barriers and implications. *Journal of School Psychology,* 1974, *12,* p. 98.

model, i.e., a model which emphasizes recognition of events external to the child. Tracy and Sturgeon (1977) recognize the need for the school psychologist to assess and understand the system that provides psychological and educational services to the child or youth. Hyman and Schreiber (1975) and Mearig (1974) describe the need for child advocacy—a role in which school psychologists assume actions that benefit the school child by bringing selective pressures to bear upon a school system. Abidin (1972) stresses the need for consultation within the school to change the general rule systems under which teachers work, while McDaniel and Ahr (1965) emphasize inservice training. Finally, other articles view school psychology as the intersection of school and community (Brantley, Reilly, Beach, Cody, Fields, et al., 1974; Steinberg & Chandler, 1976), as a systems approach (Bergan, 1970), or as applied social psychology (Lighthall, 1969; Medway, 1975).

In summary, various roles appear to be expansions of the general model themes reviewed by Gilmore (1974). While some roles may actually be new, it seems that quite a few of the many proposed roles of school psychology are in reality only natural evolutions of a relatively few past emphases (Bardon & Bennett, 1974). Given the historical trend of school psychology to adapt roles to fit existing needs, it may be assumed that most of the models described by Gilmore (1974) and the many role implications suggested by the above survey are now represented to varying degree within active practice.

## Summary

Roles in school psychology have been presented in this section as largely aligned with five basic models. In practice, many school psychologists make extensive use of the concepts expressed in a variety of models and many practitioners are equipped to function across several models' requirements. In the past more than a few psychologists have presented a particular expertise which has been offered as a unique role. However, many of these roles seem to represent more the refinement of a basic model than a completely novel approach. Given this as an assumption, it seems possible to draw at least two conclusions about roles in school psychology. First, school psychology is not without internal cohesion; that is, it is not the ambiguous professional discipline that it is sometimes presented as being. Instead, school psychology actively represents numerous adaptive role emphases within, perhaps, five or so very definable models. Second, individual school psychologists routinely and legitimately approach problems in different fashions depending upon the goals of a specific situation. Logically, then, school psychologists should have some knowledge of a variety of models but be able to function through a particular model when its goals and the goals of a situation are aligned. In retrospect, a Trachtman's (1971) plea for broadly trained professionals seems quite valid.

Finally, two largely unanswered and provocative research issues emerge here. First, to what extent does training truly influence role or model adherance? Second, to what extent do the schools shape or accept particular role adherance? As we have seen here, there is reason to believe that training is a major determinant of role-model adherence although its precise relationship remains unknown. A summary of what is known of the issues concerning the second question is the major topic pursued in the following section.

## EVALUATIONS OF SCHOOL PSYCHOLOGY

Evaluations of the various roles and activites that school psychologists engage in can be considered from two perspectives described by Gilmore and Chandy (1973a, 1973b). Evaluation can result from among school psychologists themselves or it can result from the observations of professional persons outside school psychology. Some authors have offered support for self-determined evaluation (Dansinger, 1969; Gross & Farling, 1969; Roberts, 1970); others (Baker, 1965; Kirschner, 1971) have presented the advantages of external evaluation.

The assumptions behind each approach lead to the different emphases in the evaluations. The internal self-determined evaluation tends to assess professional behavior from the perspective of the psychologist or to describe the activities that school psychologists perceive themselves engaged in. There is less attention to justifying school psychologists and, perhaps, a higher degree of objectivity in describing their actual activities. The external type of evaluation, on the other hand, tends to focus more on justification for the school psychologist through the perception of other school professionals. In these evaluations the validity of the activities the school psychologist performs is determined by the values ascribed by their peers in associated professions. This section will be a summary of the results of Type I, or internal, and Type II, or external, evaluations of school psychologists.

### Type I evaluations

Although there are Type I evaluations that have been quite molecular in scope, e.g., evaluations in the administration of certain tests, this discussion will include only the more comprehensive evaluations, i.e., studies concerned with the more global aspects of school psychology.

Concern for the self-evaluation of the profession seems to be increasing. For example, Rosenfeld and Blanco (1974) discussed a case in which there was a judgment of professional inadequacy. They called upon the profession to establish and enforce more stringent standards. Silberberg and Silberberg (1971) reported their attempts to evaluate the profession and concluded that goals of school psychology could not be accomplished by an individual administratively bound to the school. Kirp and Kirp (1976) suggested that the profession of school psychology lacks self-determination inasmuch as it is unsure what it should or can do. This may be a critical point since the activities of the school psychologist are being challenged on several points of law, including confidentiality and due process (e.g., *Diana* v. *California State Board of Education, 1970; Larry P.* v. *Riles. 1972).*

To be useful, internal evaluations of school psychologists should be comprehensive and assess the total activities within which school psychologists function. Such evaluations should document the conditions and constraints under which school psychologists work. Perhaps, then, some negative external evaluations of school psychologists, "because an overworked school psychologist administers only a portion of IQ test battery" (Kirp & Kirp, 1976, p. 85), might be subject to reinterpretation. An example of the need for internal evaluations is contained in an important study recently reported by Meyers, MacMillan, and Yoshida (1978). In this study Meyers et al. thoroughly examined the allegation that the certification of educable mentally retarded students in California by school psychologists prior to the *Diana* and *Larry P.* cases was largely prone to error. The authors indicate that "the data permit a conclusion that the work of the school psychologists in the EMR placement was professionally competent, given the guidelines in effect at the time" (Meyers et al., 1978, p. 3).

It seems possible, then, that a failure to conduct thorough Type I evaluations could in many instances open the profession to allegations that are unfounded, untrue, or simply irrelevant. The failure just cited, perhaps motivated by a desire to change special education by legal mandate (Meyers et al., 1978) could and perhaps did leave school psychology in a libeled state. Fragmented Type I evaluations or Type II evaluations alone might have overlooked data which support the important conclusions of Meyers et al. (1978).

Some Type I studies have compared the relative value of the differing roles of school psychologists. Fairchild (1976) attempted an

411

examination of a consultant and traditional role. In this study, Fairchild found that he was able to respond to the requests for assistance from school personnel much more rapidly when following the consultant model (a Type I result); but when he also asked teachers to rate the value of each role on a contrasting scale (Type II), they rated both models highly and did not differentiate between them.

Keogh, Kukic, Becker, McLoughlin, and Kukic (1975) interviewed school psychologists from 58 school districts. Their 45-minute interviews included questions about training, responsibilities and activities, and views of assessment and testing. The data concerning the apportionment of their time are presented in Table 3. The authors' general conclusions included the following: (1) school psychologists were well-creditialed professionals who were satisfied with their work; (2) over one-half had training and experience as teachers; (3) affiliations with professional organizations were more often at local rather than national levels; (4) most of the school psychologist's time was spent in individual testing

**TABLE 3**

**SCHOOL PSYCHOLOGIST'S ESTIMATES OF PERCENT TIME PER WEEK SPENT IN PROFESSIONAL ACTIVITIES**

| Professional Activities | Hours per Week | | | | |
|---|---|---|---|---|---|
| | None | 1–5 | 6–10 | 11–20 | 20+ |
| Testing and Evaluation | 2 | 31 | 38 | 24 | 5 |
| Testing and Re-evaluation | 12 | 64 | 22 | 2 | 0 |
| Report Writing | 0 | 50 | 41 | 9 | 0 |
| Teacher Consultation | 0 | 50 | 34 | 16 | 0 |
| Classroom Observation | 9 | 81 | 10 | 0 | 0 |
| Child Counseling | 21 | 55 | 14 | 9 | 2 |
| Administration | 2 | 78 | 17 | 2 | 2 |
| Meetings | 0 | 96 | 4 | 0 | 0 |
| Parent Conferences | 0 | 78 | 22 | 0 | 0 |
| Supervising Psychometrists | 91 | 9 | 0 | 0 | 0 |
| Formal Research | 80 | 19 | 0 | 2 | 0 |
| Parent Education | 69 | 28 | 4 | 0 | 0 |
| Teacher In-Service | 55 | 43 | 2 | 0 | 0 |

Reproduced by permission. Keogh, B.K., Kukic, J.J., Becker, L.D., McLoughlin, R.J., and Kukic, M.B. School psychologists' services in special education programs. *Journal of School Psychology*, 1975, *14*, p. 144.

and related activities (e.g., scoring tests, reports); (5) in most instances very few tests constituted the usual repertoire of assessment; (6) most school psychologists expressed good relationships with educators; and (7) some psychologists felt that they needed further training.

Despite the fact that these and other direct evaluation studies have appeared, many Type I evaluations of school psychology could be classified as personal views, and therefore are subjective appraisals. Although more objective Type I evaluations are being generated (e.g., Bardon & Conti, 1974), the effectiveness of school psychologists' actions are currently measured in large part by the impressions from other professions, i.e., Type II evaluations.

**Type II evaluations**

The studies to be reported here are distinct from Type I evaluations in that the data predominantly represent the views of professionals other than school psychologists. They are similar in that they are often based on opinion or perception rather than direct objective data; however, these studies reflect the attitudes and values of associated professionals, and thereby provide some insight into the expectations that other educators hold for school psychologists.

A sizeable number of external studies have appeared. They report evaluations by school principals, teachers, and superintendents (Baker, 1965; Barclay, 1971; Dansinger, 1969; Giebink & Ringness, 1970; Gilmore & Chandy, 1973a, 1973b; Kahl & Fine, 1978; Kaplan, Chrin, & Chancy, 1977; Kirschner, 1971; Lesiak & Lounsbury, 1977; Medway, 1977; Perkins, 1964; Roberts, 1970; Roberts & Solomons, 1970; Schowengerdt, Fine, & Poggio, 1976; Styles, 1965). These reviews are grouped in the following paragraphs according to the educational affiliation of the respondents.

*Superintendents*

A few studies represent what is known of school superintendents' knowledge of and attitude toward school psychologists. Manley and Manley (1978) compared personal values and operative goals for school psychologists and school superintendents throughout Ohio. They found generally similar value systems between the two groups and overall agreement with respect to the emphasis they placed on goals of the school psychologist. Superintendents rated values such as ambition, obediance, and loyalty higher than did school psychologists and were also more inclined to emphasize goals that increase learning efficiency and community interaction. School psychologists seemed to be far more interested in what was termed a "positive mental health atmosphere" (Manley & Manley, 1978, p. 107) and in personal autonomy. They were in high agreement with superintendents that the traditional measurement emphasis of psychologists should be decreased, a point which is in conflict with the results found by Keogh et al. (1975). Manley and Manley (1978) described the results of their study as indicative of the fact that the role seems to be in a period of transition.

An extensive survey of school superintendents was undertaken by Kaplan et al. (1977) to evaluate school administrations' priorities for school psychologists. A 21-item questionaire was sent to all members (1100) of the Buckeye Association of School Administrators (Ohio); 418 members responded. The results indicated that superintendents rated the activities of diagnosis and child study as the highest priority, and research and evaluation of curricula as the lowest. These results are consistent with the Keogh et al. (1975) study of school psychologists' self-evaluations and the results of a previous study of administrators (Senft & Clair, 1972). However, it does not appear to be consistent with the Manley and Manley (1978) study, which found little support from superintendents for school psychologists serving in child-appraiser roles.

## Principals

Lesiak and Lounsbury (1977) compared elementary school principals' ratings of potential activities of school psychologists with those of psychological services supervisors on a questionaire originally devised by Kirschner (1971). Eleven of the 12 components were deemed valuable by both groups (only remedial instruction was not), with individual diagnostic work viewed as most important by both groups. Supervisors saw preventative programs, research, and inservice programs as more important than did principals. In turn, principals saw parental counseling and liaison between school and community as more important than did supervisors. These differences are generally in accord with the predictions one might make on the basis of the data offered by Manley and Manley (1978).

## Teachers

A study by Styles (1965) surveyed teachers' views about school psychologists' training and their resulting capacity to work with children. As a group, teachers tended to view school psychologists more as clinical psychologists than was warranted and to ascribe a greater knowledge of severe emotional disturbance to them than was actually the case. Teachers rated the average school psychologist's level of training quite accurately but were quite inconsistent in judging school psychologists' abilities to undertake specific tasks. For example, roughly one-third of the sample indicated that the school psychologist was fully qualified to conduct prolonged psychotherapy with individual students. When asked how school psychologists could be of most help to them, teachers responded as follows: (1) hold conferences with them regarding a specific pupil; and (2) provide written reports. Styles concluded that teachers did not hold exaggerated views of the school psychologist but maintained a view generally quite consistent with the clinical model described by Bardon (1965). The reader should note, however, that the study was carried out in 1963 and is thus quite dated.

Recently, Medway (1977) used a scale developed by Fairchild (1976) to have 15 high-contact (five or more professional encounters) and 15 low-contact (one to three professional encounters) teachers rate the activities of 15 school psychology interns. These data were then compared to actual logs kept by the interns. In general, the teachers were not aware of the service priorities of psychologists in the schools and attributed more interviewing, teacher consultation, and counseling duties to the school psychologist than was actually the case. In addition, the teachers greatly underestimated the time spent by psychologists in testing and report writing. Medway concluded that teachers generally do not recognize the proportions of time spent in specific activities by school psychologists. However, the teachers who had a greater number of opportunities to view the school psychologist were more often accurate in judging the many activities the latter engaged in. In summary, Medway's study shows how other professionals' perceptions of school psychologists may differ markedly depending upon the degree of interaction with them.

### Combined studies

A number of researchers have sought to compare perceptions of the school psychologist across the numerous professional affiliations within the schools (e.g., Miller, 1974; Waters, 1973). Of the many studies that could be cited, Gilmore and Chandy (1973b) will be reviewed as illustrative of the conclusions drawn from this type of study.

Gilmore and Chandy (1973b) conducted a study of teachers' perceptions of school psychologists. Experienced teachers anticipated more traditional activities, such as testing for special placement, while younger teachers expected more novel interventions. In the same study perceptions were obtained by school psychologists about their own activities. The psychologists tended to collect their data in the same manner regardless of the experience level of the teacher, but they seemed to use the data in a different manner depending upon the experience level of the teacher. Gilmore and Chandy also found that the value of the school psychologist was rated lower by teachers who had prolonged experience with them—a point at odds with the conclusions reached by Styles (1965). Gilmore and Chandy attributed this discrepancy to the fact that Styles surveyed special teachers who were probably better equipped to profit from school psychologists' information.

In the same study (Gilmore & Chandy, 1973b), principals were also contacted. Both principals and psychologists viewed the psychologist as a consultant more often than did teachers. Principals and psychologists also viewed the specialty as having greater knowledge of classroom management and children's abilities than did teachers. Principals and teachers both felt that the psychologists were more knowledgeable about teaching than did the psychologists themselves.

Gilmore and Chandy (1973b) emerged with three recommendations, two of which are germane to this section. First, school psychologists, teachers, and principals should, in effect, get to know each other better. Needs, expectations, and skills should be topics for long-term discussions. Second, future studies should concentrate more on measuring the actual behaviors of psychologists (a special case of the Type I evaluation) rather than simply the perceptions of psychologists and other professionals (many Type I and nearly all Type II evaluations).

**Summary**

It appears from the studies reviewed that school personnel do not have an accurate perception of the time spent by school psychologists in various activities and that their services are not as highly valued as they should be in some situations. It seems possible that their skills are not well utilized as a result. These conclusions lend support to the need for Type I evaluations as necessary for the field's development and Type II evaluations as necessary to assess the degree of acceptance of the profession in educational settings. There is a need for increasing the awareness within educational professions of the school psychologists' skills and the range of possible roles.

Sandoval and Lambert (1977) have proposed a procedure which could result in more comprehensive evaluations. Rejecting the traditional procedure of tallying tests administered and obtaining supervisor rating data, these authors proposed a procedure that includes multiple data sources: a vignette-based questionaire; a role-model questionaire; a services received questionaire; teacher interviews; and nonobtrusive sample measures. In short, a combination of these sources of information might well provide a more comprehensive Type II evaluation of the individual school psychologist. More effective Type I evaluation schemes await further research efforts.

## PROJECTION OF FUTURE RESPONSIBILITIES FOR SCHOOL PSYCHOLOGISTS

In this chapter we have examined the history of school psychology, explored the training and certification of school psychologists, and, finally, considered the roles of school psychologists through self-evaluation and evaluation by other educational personnel. Throughout this review it is noted that school psychology and special education are entwined and that there are few aspects of each which do not have some effect upon the other. Although separate and distinct, it is impossible to relate the history of one without reference to the other. There is little question that the futures of both will continue to be related as changes take place in public education which reflect the larger society, and, in turn, affect special education and school psychology. Failure to adapt to these changes would be, paraphrasing Eklund (1971), to follow the evolution of the dinosaur. Adaptation to change is the key to any profession's survival, and while special education is certainly not the only influence on school psychology, it may well be a primary one. Of necessity, then, professionals in school psychology must be aware of movements in the field of special education.

Referring to the effects of changes in special education upon the future of school psychology, Catterall (1972) affirmed the historical relationship of the two disciplines and suggested three particular areas to which school psychologists must be attentive. First, each school psychologist must examine his or her practices to determine which now have purpose and meaning and which may no longer be providing a useful service. Second, the school psychologist must actively consider adopting roles and models which will serve the educational system more broadly. Included in this recommendation is the facilitation of cooperation among the various disciplines. Finally, the school psychologist should be active in leadership and advocacy roles in order to have an influence on the directions of change in special education and the schools.

Catterall's (1972) remarks are appropriate and deserving of attention. The task that remains, however, is identification of changes that are anticipated for special education and the concomitant activities the school psychologist must prepare to engage in. Some of the future areas in which role–model complements will be crucial to both professions are identified below.

### Accountability

Of all the major thrusts anticipated in education for the 1980s and beyond, it seems clear that professional accountability must rank high. Recent articles (Saretsky, 1973; Sugarman, 1974) have emphasized accountability, or lack of it, in the school and the alternative—accountability through the courts. The press for accountability is justified and may provide the opportunity for all areas of education to meet the challenge of documenting change. This fact is especially true for school psychologists, for in many school systems there are no other professionals so well equipped to measure the sine qua non of school accountability—behavioral change. It is important to note, however, that behavioral change can be measured in multiple ways and that the methods of measurement should be comprehensive. Traditional procedures may need to be complemented by alternative measurement requirements and practices as accountability demands gather momentum.

Accountability in the change of children's behavior seems to include an increasing emphasis on the concept of ecology (e.g., Apter, 1977; Barker, 1968; Bronfenbrenner, 1977; Brooks & Baumeister, 1977; Rhodes, 1967; Rogers-Warren & Warren, 1977). The traditional emphases of psychoeducational testing and clinical intervention have been discussed in recent years, and some (Bersoff, 1971a) have likened many past practices to "institutional psychiatry" (p. 266), while others (Hayes & Clair, 1978) suggest that to continue in the process of the past could lead to the death of the profession. A review of school psychologists' perceptions of their role demonstrates a reluctance to work in settings beyond the school, as is necessary, for example, in consultation with parents and others in the community. The history of special education reminds us that parent and community support have been essential to the growth and development of special programs, and in many cases have dictated the success of programs. Therefore, school psychologists must increase involvement in homes, community centers, and other locations which have tremendous impact upon the behavior of children in schools. This, of course, demands the inclusion of new measurement practices.

Additionally, accountability will demand that school psychologists make further efforts to validate their professional worth. We have discussed this matter earlier and concluded that both Type I and Type II evaluations must continue, although Type II evaluations will almost certainly predominate in the forseeable future. Sandoval and Lambert (1977) provided some unique approaches for school psychologists which may well be a step toward external justification. By whatever means, however, it is essential that school psychologists come to be evaluated by criteria that support the expansion of their roles. As we have seen, many of these roles have special relevance and purpose for special education.

### Provisions of PL 94-142

The Education for All Handicapped Children Act of 1975 (PL 94-142) has received widespread attention since its enactment. Contained within the law are several "challenges and opportunities" (Kabler, 1977, p. 19) for school psychology within the next decade. The law is far ranging in implication and a thorough review of it is essential. In particular, it is very important that school psychologists note and consider the following issues.

*Least restrictive alternative.*

The implementation of this concept is mandated, yet there is reason to believe that the concept is not fully understood (Miller & Switzky, 1978). Therefore, increased emphasis must be placed on the follow-up of individuals who are placed in special settings—a task best suited to the skills of the school psychologist. The task is at once behavioral and legal and it is necessary for school psychologists to possess knowledge of both of these considerations.

*Services to all children and youth ages 3 to 21*

PL 94-142 mandated services to groups of children who in the past have generally not received the services of school psychologists because of the latter's limited (in practice) roles. Emphases have changed and school psychologists are now able to and indeed must expand and extend their services to all handicapping conditions covered by the act and, in the future, to students in greatly expanded age ranges. For many, this will require some training and experience, additional role responsibilities, and, perhaps, a reevaluation of personal and professional priorities.

*Nondiscriminatory testing*

Provisions in the Act emphasize the position that alternative data sources be included in obtaining information about children and that tests be scrutinized for their suitability of purpose. On the one hand, this is simply a good practice that the majority of school psychologists have emphasized for years. On the other hand, recent court decisions (e.g., *Merriken* v. *Cressman,* 1973) portend the application of standards to measurement that could legislate the preponderance of current measures out of existance. Thus the school psychologist could become trapped between an actual increase in the emphasis on measurement (accountability pressures) and a court critical of available procedures. Solutions will not be simple, and, as Bersoff and Miller (1979) have concluded, current solutions are stopgap; almost certainly, a part of the solution lies more in the legal and ethical process of test administration than in the technological refinement of measurement techniques.

## *The individual educational plan*

A key component of PL 94-142 lies in the expressed mandate to individualize instruction and to commit the essence of such a plan to paper for each child served. To become a meaningful process, the Individual Education Plan must be adroitly considered and developed. School psychologists' skills must be more actively engaged, and it will be necessary for them to take a very active role in the development of such plans rather than merely present data characterizing the child. It is at this juncture, sythesizing data to develop programs, that special educators and school psychologists have usually been least effective. It behooves us to emphasize collaborative efforts at this point.

## *Law and ethics*

Bersoff (1975) has noted the dilemma existing between professional ethical standards and legal requirements. Not all of these conflicts emanate from PL 94-142, but many are emphasized in this law. The key for school psychologists is to continually and carefully evaluate the guidelines within which they practice and to which they must adhere. The legalization of the school psychologist's world (Kirp & Kirp, 1976) does not seem to be reversing; indeed, one of the major professional journals directed to school psychologists (*The Journal of School Psychology*) has instituted a forum devoted to monitoring the influence of law on school psychology. Continued awareness on the part of the individual school psychologist seems to be prudent.

## The challenge of old practices and the accurate presentation of school psychology to special education

We begin this section with an observation: school psychology, doubtless for many reasons, has not presented itself well enough to special educators. Ysseldyke (1978) concluded that special education teachers possess only limited knowledge of school psychologists and as a group are becoming vocal in expressing their dissatisfaction with the profession. The following recommendations are offered as possible means for improving the situation.

### Provision of specific recommendations

Ysseldyke (1978) reports that teachers are frustrated with the generalities contained in most reports. Instead, teachers want specific information that can be used to design educational programs. In short, educators seem to want information relating to immediate concerns rather than a mere explanation of the presenting problem or a global analysis without intervention strategies (Atkin, 1978). Ysseldyke suggests that, as a group, school psychologists possess skills to accomplish this. Thus a priority for school psychologists is to examine those factors which will improve report writing or other forms of professional communication, and to make concerted efforts to evaluate the utility of the information that is provided to educators.

### Consultation, inservice, and community involvement

It is necessary for school psychologists to extend their role to actively include consultation. Consulting roles can potentially influence change over greater target areas, influence the heirarchy of schools top to bottom as well as bottom to top, and extend the school psychologist's role across the school; these factors are congruent with special education's current efforts to rejoin the school at large and the results of considerable empirical research.

For example, Heiny (1976) has noted that the community–parent influence upon children far exceeds that of the schools, and that our best efforts with school children are more often rewarded when we actively include parents in our efforts. Currently, the law mandates some degree of parental involvement, but perhaps this is not really sufficient. Successful programs of the future will almost certainly require a much higher degree of involvement with parents. The broadly trained school psychologist should be able to assist in these efforts.

### Alternatives to testing

A colorful description of school psychologists is that they can be identified by blisters on the left hand in which the Binet kit is carried and blisters on the right thumb and index finger from writing long reports. We might wonder as we enter the 1980s whether this particular model of data collection and dissemination is still as appropriate as it once was. The needs of special education have changed and the conceptual underpinnings of psychoeducational testing have been severely criticized (e.g., Ysseldyke, 1973). Recent articles in the school psychology literature (e.g., Kratochwell, 1977; Lynch, 1977; Sitko, Fink, & Gillespie, 1977) have demonstrated the value of systematic observation and described some techniques that are of use. These alternatives, or perhaps supplements to testing can be of inestimable value to school psychologists. They certainly may enable the professional to obtain more comprehensive data and, in the process, deliver a better product to educational consumers.

### Watching for trends in special education

Heiny (1976) has emphasized the fact that special education is not at all sure of its future directions and that a number of major philosophical as well as practical issues remain to be resolved. In short, school psychology has the opportunity to encourage the direction that special education will take by creating programs and policies that prove valuable to special education. School psychology and special education are, realistically, tied together, but this tie does not have to be a burden for either party. There exists in school psychology a vast potential for educational leadership (Lambert, 1973). This leadership, if encouraged to emerge, could benefit both professional groups.

## SUMMARY

The roles of the school psychologist of the future will continue to be varied and subject to the influences reported in this chapter. Whether these roles will be influenced more by the profession of school psychology or by other professions is a matter of speculation, but the liaison with special education will certainly continue. It is apparent that school psychology has no real parallel in public education, and that many of the roles it could serve have not yet been tried. Moreover, the profession has the potential to have a significant influence on special education, which, in turn, has the opportunity to promote immense change in all of education. A closer relationship would seem to benefit all parties and would be but a logical outgrowth of a shared history.

To return to roles, several points deserve emphasis. Bardon's (1968) demand to give attention to broad goals seems one very clear insight that should help dictate what school psychology might evolve to be. Gilmore's (1974) analysis of historical models seems to suggest that the profession's entity is construed largely within about five very basic role-model structures. Finally, Catterall's (1972) and Meacham and

Peckam's (1978) conclusion that special education is closely tied with school psychology points, we think, to some areas worthy of speculation. In the final analysis, the roles in school psychology will be what the professionals in it can create, and a part of that creation must take into consideration a close relationship with special education.

# References

Abidin, R. R. A psychosocial look at consultation and behavior modification. *Psychology in the Schools,* 1972, *9,* 358–363.

American Psychological Association, *Graduate study in psychology for 1974–75.* Washington, D.C.: Author, 1973.

Apter, S. J. Application of ecological theory: Toward a community special education model. *Exceptional Children,* 1977, *43,* 366–373.

Atkin, J. M. Institutional self evaluation versus national professional accreditation or back to the normal school? *Educational Researcher,* 1978, *7,* 3–7.

Baker, H. L. Psychological services; From the school staff's point of view. *Journal of School Psychology,* 1965, *3,* 36–42.

Barclay, J. R. Descriptive, theoretical and behavioral characteristics of subdoctoral school psychologists. *American Psychologist,* 1971, *26,* 257–280.

Bardon, J. I. (Ed.). Problems and issues in school psychology—1964; Proceedings of a conference on "new-directions" sponsored by the National Institute of Mental Health. *Journal of School Psychology,* 1964–1965, *3,* 1–44.

Bardon, J. I. Problems and issues in school psychology. *Journal of School Psychology,* 1965, *3,* 1–14.

Bardon, J. I. School psychology and school psychologists: An approach to an old problem. *American Psychologist,* 1968, *23,* 187–194.

Bardon, J. I. The State of the art (and science) of school psychology. *American Psychologist,* 1976, *31,* 785–791.

Bardon, J. I., & Bennett, V. C. *School Psychology.* Englewood Cliffs, N.J.: Prentice-Hall, 1974.

Bardon, J. I., Constanzu, J. J., & Walker, N. W. Institutions offering graduate training in school psychology, 1970–71. *Journal of School Psychology,* 1971, *9,* 252–260.

Bardon, J. I., & Conti, A. A proposal for evaluating the effectiveness of psychologists in the schools. *Psychology in the Schools,* 1974, *11,* 32–39.

Bardon, J. I., & Walker, N. W. Characteristics of graduate training programs in school psychology. *American Psychologist,* 1972, *27,* 652–656.

Bardon, J. I., & Wenger, R. D. Institutions offering graduate training in school psychology: 1973–74. *Journal of School Psychology,* 1974–1975, *12,* 75–83.

Barker, R. G. *Ecological psychology: Concepts and methods for studying the environment of human behavior.* Stanford, Calif.: Stanford University Press, 1968.

Bennett, V. Who is a school psychologist and what does he do? *Journal of School Psychology,* 1970, *8,* 166–171.

Bennett, V. C. Applied research can be useful: An example. *Journal of School Psychology,* 1976, *14,* 67–73.

Bergan, J. A systems approach to psychological services. *Psychology in the Schools,* 1970, *7,* 315–319.

Bernstein, M. Psychotherapy in the schools: Promise and perplexity. *Journal of School Psychology,* 1976, *14,* 314–321.

Bersoff, D. N. School psychology as "institutional psychiatry." *Professional Psychology,* 1971, *2,* 266–270.

Bersoff, D. N. Professional ethics and legal responsibilities: on the horns of a dilemma. *Journal of School Psychology,* 1975, *13,* 359–376.

Bersoff, D. N., & Miller, T. L. Ethical and legal issues of behavioral assessment. In D. A. Sabatino & T. L. Miller (Eds.), *Describing learner characteristics of handicapped children and youth.* New York: Grune & Stratton, 1979.

Bluestein, V. W., & Milofsky, C. A. Certification patterns and requirements for school psychologists. *Journal of School Psychology,* 1970, *8,* 270–277.

Bower, E. M. Reactions to the conference. *Journal of School Psychology*, 1965, *3*, 36–39.

Brantley, J. G., Reilly, D. H., Beach, N. L., Cody, W., Fields, R., & Lee, H. School psychology: The intersection of community, training institution and the school system. *Psychology in the Schools*, 1974, *11*, 28–31.

Bronfenbrenner, U. Toward an experimental ecology of human development. *American Psychologist*, 1977, *32*, 513–531.

Brooks, P. H., & Baumeister, A. A. A plea for consideration of ecological validity in the experimental psychology of mental retardation: A guest editorial. *American Journal of Mental Deficiency*, 1977, *15*, 37–45.

Brown, D. T., & Lindstrom, J. P. The training of school psychologists in the United States; An overview. *Psychology in the Schools*, 1978, *15*, 37–45.

Brown, D. T., Sewell, T. J., & Lindstrom, J. P. *The handbook of certification/licensure requirements for school psychologists* (Rev. ed.). Washington, D.C.: National Association of School Psychologists, 1977.

Burns, R. G., & Rupiper, O. J. Trends in school psychology as demonstrated by content analysis of school psychology textbooks. *Psychology in the Schools*, 1977, *14*, 332–340.

Cardon, B. W. School psychology for the total school. *Professional Psychology*, 1972, *3*, 53–56.

Cardon, B. W., & French, J. L. Organization and content of graduate programs in school psychology. *Journal of School Psychology*, 1968–1969, *7*, 28–32.

Catterall, C. D. Special education in transition—Implications for school psychology. *Journal of School Psychology*, 1972, *10*, 91–98.

Claytor, M. P. State certification requirements for public school psychologists. *Journal of Psychology*, 1950, *29*, 390–396.

Cowen, E., & Lorion, R. F. Changing roles for the school mental health professional. *Journal of School Psychology*, 1976, *14*, 131–137.

Cutts, N. E. (Ed.). *School psychologists at mid-century*. Washington, D.C.: American Psychological Association, 1955.

Dansinger, J. A five year follow-up study of Minnesota school psychologists. *Journal of School Psychology*, 1969, *7*, 47–53.

*Diana* v. *California State Board of Education*, No. C-67-RFP (N.D.Cal. 1970).

Eklund, S. J. *How not to train for obsolescence in school psychology: A position paper.* Unpublished manuscript, Bloomington, Indiana, 1971.

Fairchild, T. N. School psychological services: An empirical comparison of two models. *Psychology in the Schools*, 1976, *13*, 156–162.

French, J. L., Smith, P. C., & Cardon, B. W. Institutions offering graduate training and financial assistance in school psychology. *Journal of Psychology*, 1968, *6*, 261–267.

Gallagher, J. J. Psychology and special education—The future: Where the action is. *Psychology in the Schools*, 1969, *6*, 219–226.

Galton, F. *Hereditary genius*. London: MacMillan, 1892.

Giebink, J. W., & Ringness, T. A. On the relevancy of training in school psychology. *Journal of School Psychology*, 1970, *8*, 43–47.

Gilmore, E. G. Models for school psychology: Dimensions, barriers and implications. *Journal of School Psychology*, 1974, *12*, 95–101.

Gilmore, G. E., & Chandy, J. Teachers' perceptions of school psychological services. *Journal of School Psychology*, 1973a, *10*, 139–147.

Gilmore, G. E., & Chandy, J. Educators describe the school psychologist. *Psychology in the Schools*, 1973b, *10*, 397–403.

Goh, D. S. Graduate training in psychology. *Journal of School Psychology*, 1977, *15*, 207–218.

Graff, M. P., & Clair, T. N. Requirements for certification of school psychologists: A survey of recent trends. *American Psychologist*, 1973, *8*, 704–709.

Granger, R., & Campbell, P. The school psychologist as program evaluator. *Journal of School Psychology*, 1977, *15*, 174–179.

Gray, S. W. *The psychologist in the schools*. New York: Holt, 1963.

Gross, F. P., Bonham, S. J., & Bluestein, V. W. Entry requirements for state certification of school psychologists: A review of the past nineteen years. *Journal of School Psychology*, 1966, *4*, 43–51.

Gross, F. P., & Farling, W. A. An analysis of case loads of school psychologists. *Psychology in the Schools*, 1969, *6*, 98–100.

Hall, M. E. Current employment requirements of school psychologists. *American Psychologist*, 1949, *4*, 519–525.

Hayes, M. E., & Clair, T. N. School psychology—Why is the profession dying? *Psychology in the Schools*, 1978, *15*, 518–521.

Heiny, R. W. Renaissance or retreat for special education: Issues to explore before 1984. *Journal of Special Education*, 1976, *10*, 415–425.

Herron, W. G. Training school psychologists to do psychotherapy. *Psychology in the Schools*, 1966, *3*, 48–51.

Hodges, W. State certification of school psychologists. *American Psychologist*, 1960, *6*, 346–349.

Holt, F. D., & Kicklighter, R. H. (Eds.). *Psychological services in the schools: Readings in preparation, organization and practice*. Dubuque, Iowa: Brown, 1971.

Horrocks, J. E. State certification requirements for school psychologists. *American Psychologist*, 1946, *1*, 399–401.

Hyman, I., & Schreiber, K. The school psychologist as a child advocate. *Psychology in the Schools*, 1975, *12*, 50–57.

Kabler, M. L. Public Law 94-142 and school psychology: Challenges and opportunities. *The School Psychology Digest*, 1977, *6*, 19–30.

Kahl, L. J., & Fine, M. J. Teacher's perceptions of the school psychologist as a function of teaching experience, amount of contact, and socioeconomic status of the school. *Psychology in the Schools*, 1978, *15*, 577–582.

Kaplan, M. S., Chrin, M., & Chancy, B. Priority roles for school psychologists as seen by superintendents. *Journal of School Psychology*, 1977, *15*, 15–80.

Keogh, B. K., Kukic, S. J., Becker, L. D., McLoughlin, R. J., & Kukic, M. B. School psychologists' services in special education programs. *Journal of School Psychology*, 1975, *13*, 142–148.

Kirp, P. L., & Kirp, L. M. The legalization of the school psychologist's world. *Journal of School Psychology*, 1976, *14*, 83–89.

Kirschner, F. E. School psychology as viewed by supervisors of school psychological services. *Journal of School Psychology*, 1971, *9*, 343–346.

Klosterman, D. The role of the school psychologist in a community mental health center. *Psychology in the Schools*, 1974, *11*, 269–274.

Korman, M. National conference on levels and patterns of professional training in psychology. *American Psychologist*, 1974, *29*, 441–449.

Kratochwill, T. R. N=1: An alternative research strategy for school psychologists. *Journal of School Psychology*, 1977, *15*, 239–249.

Lambert, N. M. The school psychologist as a source of power and influence. *Journal of School Psychology*, 1973, *11*, 245–250.

*Larry P. v. Riles*, 343 F. Supp. 866 (D.D.C. 1972).

Lesiak, W. J., & Lounsbury, E. Views of school psychological services: A comparative study. *Psychology in the Schools*, 1977, *14*, 185–188.

Lewis, C. R. The school psychologist as program consultant. *Psychology in the Schools*, 1974, *11*, 294–295.

Lighthall, F. A. A social psychologist for school systems. *Psychology in the Schools*, 1969, *6*, 3–12.

Lynch, W. W. Guidelines to the use of classroom observation instruments by school psychologists. *School Psychology Monograph*, 1977, *3*, 1–22.

Manley, T. R., & Manley, E. T. A comparison of the personal values and operative goals of school psychologists and school superintendents. *Journal of School Psychology*, 1978, *16*, 99–109.

McDaniel, L. J., & Ahr, E. The psychologist as a resource person conducting inservice teacher education. *Psychology in the Schools*, 1965, *2*, 220–224.

Meacham, M. L., & Peckham, P. D. School psychologists at three-quarter century: Congruence between training, practice, preferred role and competence. *Journal of School Psychology*, 1978, *16*, 195–206.

Mearig, J. S. On becoming a child advocate in school psychology. *Journal of School Psychology*, 1974, *12*, 121–129.

Medway, F. J. A social psychological approach to internally based change in the schools. *Journal of School Psychology*, 1975, *13*, 19–27.

Medway, F. J. Teacher's knowledge of school psychologist's responsibilities. *Journal of School Psychology*, 1977, *15*, 301–307.

*Merriken v. Cressman*, 364 F. Supp. 913 (E.D. Pa. 1973).

Meyers, C. E., MacMillan, D. L., & Yoshida, R. K. Validity of psychologist's identification of EMR students in the perspective of the California decertification experience. *Journal of School Psychology*, 1978, *16*, 3–15.

Miller, J. N. Consumer response to theoretical role models in school psychology. *Journal of School Psychology*, 1974, *12*, 310–317.

Miller, T. L., & Switzky, H. N. The least restrictive alternative: Implications for service providers. *Journal of Special Education*, 1978, *12*, 123–131.

Nelson, W. H. Variations in patterns of certification of school psychologists. *Journal of School Psychology*, 1963, *2*, 17–33.

Newland, T. E. Formalized psychological services in state education programs. *American Psychologist*, 1956, *11*, 136–140.

Nickerson, E. T. Application of play to a school setting. *Psychology in the Schools*, 1973, *10*, 361–364.

Patros, P. G., Gross, F. P., & Bjorn, M. *A survey of institutions offering graduate training in the area of school psychology*. Washington D.C.: The National Association of School Psychologists, A72, No. 401, 1972.

Perkins, K. J. From identification to identity. *Journal of School Psychology*, 1964, *2*, 7–16.

Pielstick, N. L. The appropriate domain for the school psychologist. *Journal of School Psychology*, 1970, *8*, 317–319.

Raimy, V. C. (Ed.). *Training in clinical psychology*. Englewood Cliffs, N.J.: Prentice-Hall, 1950.

Reger, R. *School psychology*. Springfield, Ill.: Thomas, 1965.

Reilly, D. H. A conceptual model for school psychology. *Psychology in the Schools*, 1974, *11*, 165–169.

Rhodes, W. C. The disturbing child: A problem of ecological management. *Exceptional Children*, 1967, *33*, 449–455.

Roberts, R. D. Perceptions of actual and desired role functions of school psychologists by psychologists and teachers. *Psychology in the Schools*, 1970, *7*, 175–178.

Roberts, R. D., & Solomons, G. Perceptions of the duties and functions of the school psychologist. *American Psychologist*, 1970, *25*, 544–549.

Rogers-Warren, A., & Warren, S. F. (Eds.). *Ecological perspectives in behavioral analysis*. Baltimore: University Park Press, 1977.

Rosenfeld, J. G., & Blanco, R. F. Incompetence in school psychology: The case of "Dr. Gestalt." *Psychology in the Schools*, 1974, *3*, 263–269.

Sabatino, D. A. School psychology–special education: To acknowledge a relationship. *Journal of School Psychology*, 1972, *10*, 99–105.

427

Sandoval, J., & Lambert, N. M. Instruments for evaluating school psychologist's function and service. *Psychology in the Schools*, 1977, *14*, 172–179.

Saretsky, G. The strangely significant case of Peter Doe. *Phi Delta Kappan*, 1973, *54*, 589–592.

Schowengerdt, R. V., Fine, M. J., & Poggio, J. P. An examination of some bases of teacher satisfaction with school psychological services. *Psychology in the Schools*, 1976, *13*, 269–275.

Senft, L., & Clair, T. N. Iowa survey reveals principals' perceptions of school psychologists. *Newsletter: The School Psychologist*, 1972, *27*, 34–35.

Sewell, T. J., & Brown, D. T. *The handbook of certification/licensure requirements of school psychologists*. Washington, D.C.: National Association of School Psychologists, 1976.

Silberberg, N. E., & Silberberg, M. C. Should schools have psychologists? *Journal of School Psychology*, 1971, *9*, 321–328.

Silverman, H. L. School psychology: Divergent role conceptualizations. *Psychology in the Schools*, 1969, *6*, 266–271.

Sitko, M. C., Fink, A. H., & Gillespie, P. H. Utilizing systematic observation for decision making in school psychology. *School Psychology Monograph*, 1977, *3*, 23–44.

Smith, D. C. Institutions offering graduate training in psychology. *Journal of School Psychology*, 1964–1965, *3*, 58–66.

Steinberg, M., & Chandler, G. Coordinating services between a mental health center and public schools. *Journal of School Psychology*, 1976, *14*, 355–362.

Styles, W. A. Teachers' perceptions of the school psychologist's role. *Journal of School Psychology*, 1965, *3*, 23–27.

Sugarman, S. Accountability through the courts. *School Review*, 1974, *82*, 233–259.

Tindall, R. H. Trends in the development of psychological services in the schools. *Journal of School Psychology*, 1964, *3*, 1–12.

Trachtman, G. Doing your thing in school psychology. *Professional Psychology*, 1971, *2*, 377–381.

Tracy, M. L., & Sturgeon, S. The school psychologist as program evaluator: A comprehensive role in the 1980's. *Viewpoints*, 1977, *53*, 49–69.

Traxler, A. J. State certification of school psychologists. *American Psychologist*, 1967, *22*, 660–666.

Vallett, R. E. *The practice of school psychology: Professional problems*. New York: Wiley, 1963.

Waters, L. G. School psychologists as perceived by school personnel: Support for a consultant model. *Journal of School Psychology*, 1973, *11*, 40–45.

Watson, R. I. *The great psychologists: From Aristotle to Freud*. Philadelphia: Lippincott, 1963.

White, M. A. Graduate training in school psychology. *Journal of School Psychology*, 1963–1964, *2*, 34–42.

White, M. A., & Harris, M. *The school psychologist*. New York: Harper, 1961.

Ysseldyke, J. E. Diagnostic–prescriptive teaching: The search for aptitude–treatment interactions. In L. Mann & D. A. Sabatino (Eds.), *The first review of special education* (Vol. 1). New York: Grune & Stratton, 1973.

Ysseldyke, J. E. Who's calling the plays in school psychology? *Psychology in the Schools*, 1978, *15*, 373–378.

# SPECIAL EDUCATION IN WESTERN EUROPE AND SCANDINAVIA

Kristen D. Juul

*Southern Illinois University at Carbondale*

During the past two decades, considerable attention has been focused on innovative programs and services for the handicapped in Western Europe. Books, articles, and research reports have given scattered indications of laudable advances in education, rehabilitation, and other facets of caring for children and youth with special needs. However, a comprehensive picture is lacking. Much of the essential source material is contained in hundreds of publications in more than half a dozen languages. To produce an authoritative survey of special education in Western Europe will necessitate the close cooperation of a number of national and international experts. Such joint efforts are not yet in evidence, although some organizations such as the European Association for Special Education have made significant progress in that direction.

This survey on special education will mainly focus on nine countries in which the author has traveled and studied: they are Austria, Denmark, France, Great Britain, the Netherlands, Norway, Sweden, Switzerland and West Germany, or the German Federal Republic. The material is drawn from personal observations, interviews, and available literature. Much of the information is by necessity incomplete, and some has probably become outdated as a result of the very rapid changes in provisions for the handicapped that are taking place in all these countries.

In Europe, special education is generally defined broadly and reaches into and overlaps with allied fields such as psychology, psychiatry, rehabilitation, physical therapy, social services, housing, recreation, and even philosophy and politics. The British Warnock Report on the special educational needs of handicapped children and youth states the position clearly (Special Education Needs, 1978, pp. 6–7):

> Our concept of special education . . . extends beyond the idea of education
> provided in special schools, special classes or units for children with particular types
> of disability, and embraces the notion of any form of additional help, wherever it is
> provided and whenever it is provided, from birth to maturity, to overcome educa-
> tional difficulty.

The present exposition will to some extent rely on this comprehensive
definition.

## HISTORY OF SPECIAL EDUCATION

Special education has most of its origins in Western Europe. Many of
the systematic efforts to educate handlcapped children emanate from
the impassioned writings of the Swiss-French philosopher Jean Jacques
Rousseau. Pestalozzi (Heafford, 1967), who was Swiss, pioneered as a
teacher of orphans and other deprived and neglected children. Itard
(1962) and his disciple Seguin (Talbot, 1964), both French, devised
imaginative methods and materials to train the mentally retarded. The
Swiss-German Guggenbuhl (Kanner, 1964) originated a medical and
educational program for cretins. Epée and Sicard developed a sign
language for the education of the deaf, and Braille invented a written one
for the blind. During the first decades of the 20th century, the Italian
physician and educator Montessori (Standing, 1966) experimented with
new methods and materials of instruction for both normal and handicapped children. In Austria, Adler (1963) and Aichhorn (1965) brought
new concepts and approaches to bear upon the therapeutic education of
emotionally disturbed and socially maladjusted children. More recently,
the Swiss psychologist Piaget has had a significant impact on the
education of exceptional children.

An interesting phenomenon is the considerable number of Euro-
peans who have settled in the United States and then developed an
illustrious career in special education or an allied field. Later their
achievements have often had an impact on their native continent. From
Vienna alone came Bruno Bettelheim, Peter Blos, Rudolf Dreikurs,
Rudolf Ekstein, Carlo Pietzner, and Fritz Redl; from Germany, Charlotte
Buhler, Alfred Strauss, and Wolf Wolfensberger; and from Scandinavia,
Gunnar Dybwad and Ivar Lovas.

Since World War II the United States has led in many aspects of
services and programs for handicapped children and youth. American
leadership in special education theory, research, experimentation, and
writing is undisputed, and American publications in English and in
translation predominate in many bookstores and libraries. Numerous
American experts have been invited to Europe to teach, and thousands

of Europeans in special education and related fields have studied in the United States. One also finds a surprising number of American special educators and others in the helping professions who are living and working in Europe.

Other countries in the Western Hemisphere have also made their contributions to the current scene. The counterculture writings of Freire (1972) and Illich (1970) from Latin America have found a receptive audience among radical special educators, and the theoretical model of the Canadian psychoeducateur Guindon (1971) is applied in the training of child-care workers in England, France, and Switzerland.

Impulses from Eastern Europe and other communist countries have been comparatively limited. Two notable exceptions are Luria (1977) and Vygotsky (1965) from the Institute of Defectology in Moscow. Their theories and research have influenced such fields as learning disabilities, mental retardation, and speech disorders. With regard to therapeutic innovations, the conductive method in the treatment of cerebral palsy, developed by the Hungarian professor Petö (Cotton & Parnwell, 1967), has a following at least in England, Sweden, and West Germany. In rehabilitation, Hulek (1975), from Poland, has made many contributions in promoting international cooperation.

In the early 1960s American publications began to appear regarding positive developments in Europe. The proceedings of the Eighth World Congress of the International Society for the Welfare of Cripples (Taylor, 1960) contain many reports on advances in rehabilitation and special education. The same year, Taylor and Taylor (1960) produced a volume about special education for physically handicapped children in Western Europe. Shortly thereafter, President Kennedy sent missions to study and write about programs for the mentally retarded in Scandinavia and the Netherlands. Wolfensberger (1964a, 1964b, 1965) described his observations of many humane and innovative practices in the treatment of the mentally retarded in several countries. In 1968 Vail published a book on the mental health systems in Scandinavia, which had received much praise for the care given the mentally retarded, mentally ill, and criminal offenders. Faber (1968) recorded her impressions of programs for the mentally retarded in many lands, including Denmark, Great Britain, and Switzerland. The 1968 annual convention of the Council for Exceptional Children had a section on international aspects of special education which consisted of three papers on school programs for the handicapped in Europe.

In 1969 the President's Committee on Mental Retardation produced a report on changing patterns of residential care (Kugel &

Wolfensberger, 1969) that brought attention to the Scandinavian normalization principle and the ways it was being implemented. Linton (1971) published the first of a series of articles on the European educateurs, a new and effective type of professional in the service of maladjusted children and youth. Then came Clark and Clark's (1970) description of the Scandinavian services for the mentally handicapped, and Lippman's (1972) provocative comparison of European and American attitudes toward the handicapped. In his opinion, in Europe there is a more positive attitude toward the handicapped—a fact which is reflected in better services.

International perspectives were further broadened by the publication of a book, edited by Tarnopol and Tarnopol (1976), on reading and learning disabilities written by experts from 19 countries and a similar volume by Oyer (1976) about the hearing handicapped. Finally, two articles by Juul (1978) and Juul and Linton (1978) put the spotlight on progressive and innovative approaches to special education in Western Europe.

In the following sections an attempt will be made to describe some of the unique and interesting aspects of special education and other services to handicapped children and youth in Western Europe and Scandinavia. Special attention will be paid to those features that merit consideration and attention internationally.

## SPECIAL EDUCATION TODAY

The structure, administration, and support of special educational services differ greatly from one country to another and even within a country. Prosperous nations and affluent communities tend to have more provisions than those with less means. There are also differences in priorities. Thus, in West Germany, the federal government has little or no authority with regard to the public schools, and the individual states are quite uneven with regard to both legislation and financial assistance for services for school children with special needs.

In the Scandinavian countries for three decades the trend was in the direction of the centralization of authority at the national level. Relatively large segregated treatment centers were constructed for children in need of intensive and comprehensive care. However, in recent years this movement has reversed itself, and current laws favor more local responsibility, authority, and control.

In Scandinavia, the allocation of resources takes an interesting form. In Norway, for example, the guidelines recommend that about 10 percent of teaching hours in a school system be devoted to special education. It is common for regular teachers with some course work in special education to have release time to give individual or small group instruction to children with learning problems. For severely handicapped children, the government gives additional direct support.

In Denmark, special education is an integral part of regular education. There is no exclusive budget for the special programs, but there are suggestions as to the percentage of teaching hours that should be devoted to pupils with special needs. In the 1973–1974 school year this amounted to 14.4 percent of the amount of teaching time in Danish schools (Skov Jorgensen, 1975). There is also a sophisticated spectrum of services, ranging from resourreclasses to residential care. The more severely handicapped children stay in state institutions. The local school systems also run a number of residential schools. Some statistics may prove informative. Of the approximately 700,000 elementary-age children in the year 1973–1974, the following numbers and percentages received special education services:

| Type of special programs | Pupils | Percentages |
|---|---|---|
| State residential schools | 3,600 | .5 |
| Residential schools run by the local system | 700 | .1 |
| Special day schools | 3,900 | .6 |
| Special classes | 16,000 | 2.3 |
| Supplementary instruction in the regular school | 66,000 | 9.4 |
| Total | 90,200 | 12.9 |

The data indicate a cascade of services that reflect the need for special education. It is also worth noting that 3.5 percent of the school children are taught in segregated classes or schools.

Reliable statistics on the percentages of children receiving special educational services in most countries are hard to come by. In 1974 UNESCO published the results of an international survey. However, the data were incomplete or in conflict with information from other sources. The evidence available indicates clearly that Sweden has the highest proportion of children in special education. According to a 1978 report from the National Ministry of Education (Elowson, 1978), 19.6 percent of Swedish children receive some form of resource services, and 1.9

percent are in self-contained classes. To this can be added another one percent of children who are in special schools or other segregated settings.

On the basis of careful scrutiny of research data, the British Warnock Committee has recommended that the planning of services for school children should be based on the assumption that up to one in five children at some time will require some form of special educational provisions. This appears to be a goal that only Sweden has reached.

**Curriculum**

Special education in Europe tends to include not only the academic but also other aspects of the children's developmental needs. Physical, intellectual, emotional, social, artistic, and vocational experiences are woven into the daily activities. Excursions and travel are often part of the programs, and many schools have vacation facilities in the mountains, in the country, or by the sea. There is also much emphasis on tbe quality of the relationships between the teachers and the pupils.

An example is Witherslack Hall, a complex of three residential schools for behavior-disordered children in the Lake District in England. The director, Mr. John Horner, attempts to give the pupils the kinds of experiences loving and caring parents would provide for their children. The curriculum includes sailing, mountain climbing, and travel to other countries.

*Physical education and sports*

Physical education, creative movement, gymnastics, sports, and the outdoors have long been an intrinsic part of special education in Europe. The therapeutic value of sports in its multiple aspects was among others recognized by Guttmann (1976). As a physician, he worked at a spinal injuries center in England during and after World War II. In 1948 he started a sports festival for paralyzed veterans; it later grew to become the international Special Olympics.

Some interesting programs and approaches are briefly described below.

*Halliwick Method.* This innovative approach to recreation, re-habilitation, and personal adjustment was created in England in 1949 by James McMillan, an engineer in hydrodynamics. Working with physically handicapped children, he developed a method of swimming based on the physical laws regarding the behavior of nonsymmetrical bodies in water. Gradually, a comprehensive method and philosophy evolved that has as its aim perceptual improvement, character development, emotional adjustment, and social integration (McMillan, 1977). The Halliwick Method has won wide acceptance in Europe, particularly in Sweden, where the National Association for Movement Handicapped Children and Youth has done much to advocate it.

*Riding therapy.* Horseback riding as therapy was first recommended by Hippocrates (460–357 BC), known as the father of medicine. In recent years riding therapy has emerged as a significant movement in the treatment of handicapped children. One of the pioneers in this field was Elsebet Bödtker, a Norwegian physiotherapist. She recognized the values of horseback riding for children with handicaps, and in 1953 she established a riding school for disabled children. In 1973 the school hosted an international conference on riding therapy.

*Adventure playgrounds.* Adventure playgrounds were first developed in Denmark in the early 1940s and are now found almost everywhere in Europe. They were particularly conceived as an antidote to the increasing urbanization and the gradual loss of play space for children. This idea was later applied by Lady Allen of Hurtwood to children with special needs. In England, she founded the Handicapped Adventure Playground Association, and she has been the driving force behind the construction of such playgrounds in London (Handicapped Adventure Playground Association, 1974). Some application of the adventure playground idea can be observed in connection with many day and residential schools. The playgrounds range from elaborate permanent structures to "junk yards" where children can start from scratch and build what they like.

*Beitostolen Health Sports Center.* In 1970 the Beitostolen Health Sports Center began operation. It is situated deep in the legendary Jotunheimen mountains in central Norway. The founder and director is Erling Stordahl, who himself is blind. Years before, he focused attention on the health needs of the handicapped by starting an annual ski race through the mountains. Each year handicapped people come from all over the world to participate in the race.

The purpose of the Health Sports Center is to activate the handicapped and to inspire them to use the resources they have for physical, emotional, and social growth. The Center has a capacity of 60 clients, both children and adults. Their stay is usually about four weeks. A multidisciplinary staff of about 60 provide complete medical attention, physical therapy, and training in sports and outdoor activities. Some staff members work in the local communities to bring the clients in contact with sports clubs after they return home. At the Center there is a careful blending of different kinds of disabilities. Experience has shown that the clients tend to accept themselves better when they can compare their own problems with those of others and when they can naturally give a hand to others who need their help. The Center also provides space for the country's only graduate school for teachers in physical education for handicapped children. Considerable research is going on, and there is much emphasis on the dissemination of ideas on an international level. During this writer's last visit there were four Americans at the Center, for an extended stay, to study the program.

*Psychomotricity.* In France, movement therapy, or psychomotricity, has been studied and practiced for decades in therapeutic and special education. More than 70 years ago Dupré defined a syndrome called "motor debility" which was associated with a variety of developmental and behavioral disorders. Later, Wallon and others expanded the theoretical bases for a movement-oriented intervention. Guilmain originated a psychomotor therapy approach with brain-injured and severely retarded children. Similar procedures were later used with the mildly retarded, physically handicapped, and learning disabled children, and in cases of emotional disturbances and social maladjustment. A special profession called "reeducateur en psychomotricité" has evolved. The training consists of three years in a professional curriculum. In France there are currently eight colleges preparing these specialists, and close to 3000 graduates are serving in schools, residential centers, and hospitals. They usually work under close supervision by a physician.

Rigorous research evidence in support of this highly acclaimed therapeutic method is scant. Most of the investigations are clinical in nature. In one such study by Soubiran and Mazo (1965) regarding the progress in academic learning and psychological adjustment made by children subjected to psychomotor training, the authors maintain that 70 percent of the children made satisfactory progress both academically and in personal adjustment, 20 percent improved mainly in the latter area, and the remaining children showed little change.

It is interesting to note that this French contribution to therapeutic education is almost unknown outside the French cultural sphere. Apart from an article by De Ajuriaguerra (1968) in the first issue of the *Journal of Learning Disabilities* and a review by Egolf and Grunwaldt (1973) in the Swiss journal *Heilpädagogik,* this writer has come across no other references in English or in German.

*The arts*

Music, painting, weaving, sculpturing, theater, puppetry, and other formative and expressive arts often have an important place in curricular content. The specific art activities sometimes reflect national traditions. In Germany, orchestral music and group singing are favorite art forms. At the Schönbrunn School for mentally retarded children in Bavaria the pupils and the staff together have produced a record, *Schönbrunner Melodie,* with music from many lands and a record of a children's musical called "The Adventures of the Brave Benjamin" (*Kindermusical "Benjamin,"* 1978).

The Sogn School in Oslo, Norway, which is the educational section of the National Center for Child and Adolescent Psychiatry, does much with needlework, collage, and painting. A distinctive feature is one outside wall covered with washable panels which the young artists have filled with their creative endeavors. In this instance, the educational director, Unni Riise, is herself an accomplished artist and art therapist. She has recently published a book on art for children and youth with special needs (Riise, 1978).

Many schools and residential centers go to great lengths to surround the children with art and beauty. Some countries have laws requiring a certain part of the cost of construction to be spent on art. Consequently, one may find schools beautified with attractive murals, reliefs, statues, and other decorative work.

There is considerable literature available about music therapy. Geck (1977) has presented an informative survey of European trends, organizations, and publications, and Wolfgart (1971) has edited an international book of readings about the application of the Orff method with different types of handicaps. Orff is an eminent German composer wbo has developed new instruments and new instructional procedures to make it easier for children to learn music. In the English language, Nordoff and Robbins (1972) have reported about their therapeutic work and experimentation in several countries, and Alvin (1965) and Ward (1976) have given accounts of their extensive studies of the educational and therapeutic effects of music on exceptional children.

With regard to the other art forms, much less has been written. The existing literature, particularly within the realm of painting, is predominantly concerned with the explanatory and diagnostic values of the art productions rather than their therapeutic functions.

**Preschool education**

Preschool education and the care of the developmental needs of young handicapped children present a differentiated and complex picture. For example, compulsory school attendance starts in Great Britain at the age of five, in some other countries at six, and in Scandinavia at seven. There is a general absence of mandatory legislation for the education of young children with special needs. In addition, there is a strong sentiment that in the early years the parents should be the main educators of their children. However, there is frequently legislative encouragement of local and private initiative.

A good example is the lekotek, or toy library, movement. It was started in 1963 by Blid (1971) and Stensland Junker (1964, 1974), two Swedish parents of handicapped children. The purpose of these centers is to provide an evaluation of the children's developmental needs and then to instruct the parents on how to use toys and other learning materials to stimulate learning. There are currently over 60 lekoteks in Sweden, and many more in Denmark, Finland, Italy, Norway, and particularly England. Stensland Junker (1978) has also developed an infant test for early disorders that is used at the lekotek. It is called BOEL, and it gives information about psychomotor behavior, eye contact, and sound attention. The test is being used increasingly in some countries in routine screening for abnormalities in infants. The lekoteks are generally financed by service organizations or local government.

An outstanding nursery school is the Orthopedagogical Center in Amsterdam. It provides assessment, parental counseling, and a stimulating educational environment for about 40 multiply handicapped children from the age of three. Perhaps the most impressive nursery school in Europe is Sonderkindergarten "Schweizerspende." This special kindergarten was a gift to Vienna from Switzerland after World War II. It is located on the grounds of a park near the famous Schönbrunn Palace. The school accommodates 120 children from three to five years of age. Each class has 20 children, 2 teachers, and 1 aide. There are five groups of children with handicaps and one comparison group with normal children. Some rooms are furnished to provide experiences in daily living. A special minipool has been designed for aqua therapy, and sophisticated instruments are used for visual–perceptual evaluation and training.

Research about the effects of the integration of handicapped and normal preschool children has been going on in West Germany for a number of years. One demonstration program in Montessori-style classrooms has been conducted by Hellbrügge in a project sponsored by the University of Munich and the Max-Planck Institute for Psychiatry. The findings so far have been positive (Hellbrügge, 1977) but it has also been shown that heterogeneity in the classroom has its limits. The more handicapped and the older a child, the greater are the difficulties in integration (Speck, 1975a).

Germany can be considered the birthplace of preschool education. Froebel was the first educator to formalize public preschool education, e.g., in the kindergarten. The German Froebel Society, which since 1948 has been renamed the Pestalozzi-Froebel Society, celebrated its 100th anniversary in 1973. Froebel-oriented writing and research is considerable, and some of it has also been oriented toward handicapped children (Heiland, 1972).

The most effective intervention strategies with the preschool child in Europe lie in the medical fields. Most countries have free medical services and a mandatory health screening and reporting scheme for young children. The most efficient is probably the Swedish system. More than 99 percent of Swedish children receive their free, voluntary checkups several times during their preschool years. A computerized registry gives each individual at birth a permanent coded number with a health record which is available in a national registry bank. The health examinations include screening for vision and hearing deficits, mental development, and behavior disorders (Hersch, 1978).

In Austria, a multidisciplinary team steps into action as soon as there is a referral that a child may have problems. This team is headed by a "social pediatrician," a physician trained in the psychology and sociology of childhood disorders. As soon as a child is certified as being handicapped the parents begin receiving a state disability pension for the child. The team maintains continuous supervision of all the handicapped children in the district and sees to it that they receive appropriate services.

One intervention procedure which has had an immense impact in the treatment of cerebral palsied children in many countries is the Bobath Method (Finnie, 1975). It is based on the principles of neurodevelopmental therapy originated by Berth and Karl Bobath in England. The two essential elements of the method include early activation and the vital role of the parents in the daily handling and teaching of their child.

In England, a popular and expanding service is the health visitor program. The health visitors are specially trained nurses who are assigned

439

to a particular community or to a pediatrician. One of their many responsibilities consists of periodic visits to all homes with children to check on their health (Kahn & Kamerman, 1975). They are thus able to detect developmental problems in the early stages and to assist the parents in getting the right kind of help.

### Vocational training and employment

A visitor to Europe is sometimes struck by the many efforts that are made to prepare the handicapped for and to include them in the productive working force. An outstanding example is the Netherlands. In this country of 13 million people, about 60,000 disabled individuals are gainfully employed in sheltered workshops or under supervision on the open market. About 40,000 work in 200 sheltered workshops. Classified according to the nature of their disability, 35 percent are physically disabled, 25 percent are mentally retarded, 25 percent are mentally ill or severely emotionally disturbed, and 15 percent have social problems related to delinquency or acculturation. The total governmental expense is about one billion dollars, of which one-third is returned in the form of profit (Jonk, 1976).

Much emphasis is placed on vocational training. From the age of 12, the children with limited academic potential receive training in simple technical skills, and by the time they are 15 years old many are able to go into full employment.

In France, the Union Nationale des Associations de Parents d'Enfants Inadaptés (UNAPEI) has done much to find a place for the mentally retarded in society. The association runs almost 400 schools for over 31,000 moderately to severely mentally handicapped children and youth. Much of the curriculum is of a vocational nature. The UNAPEI has also developed a unique institution called Centres d'Aide pour le Travail (CAT), which can be translated as centers for aid in employment. There are presently 240 such centers and they serve about 15,000 handicapped. The number is rapidly increasing. This writer has visited the CAT in Dijon and will briefly describe some of its functions.

The intellectual levels of the clients range from moderately to severely retarded. The agency provides job training, supervises workers employed in factories, and conducts sheltered workshops for those unable to work in regular employment. It also manages several residences and plans leisure time activities. Some of the clients are employed in a packaging firm, some in a mustard factory, and some in a cosmetics plant. Actually, 20 of 200 employees in the cosmetics plant are mentally retarded; they work side by side with the others, all in white coats. Some of the young people serve as gardeners in the city parks and other landscaped areas. Others are receiving training as janitorial assistants in a large apartment complex. The most impressive parts of these programs are the competency and commitment of the educateurs that supervise them, the high functioning level of the clients, and the acceptance and even enthusiasm of the normal co-workers and employers.

In Geneva, Switzerland, the Society for the Vocational Integration of Adolescents and Adults has a vocational training program for about 130 young people who have completed their compulsory schooling. Seventy graduates are employed in one of the several workshops conducted by the society. One of these is operated in conjunction with a medical supplies company, and one is located in a concern producing fruit and vegetable specialties.

In Austria a unique organization called Jugend am Werk (Youth at Work) has been in operation since 1945. It was founded with the purpose of finding work and shelter for needy youth. It grew rapidly into a multipurpose agency which in three decades has served over 50,000 handicapped young men and women. Jugend am Werk currently operates a number of vocational training centers, sheltered workshops, and residential homes. All persons referred are subjected to careful observation and assessment with regard to their vocational inclinations and potential.

The Swedish government has made a large investment in attempting to increase the employability of the disabled. The AMU vocational training center in Uppsala is known internationally. The letters stand for a term which means "educating the work force." The facilities are outstanding, and the trainees have a choice of a number of different vocations. Some of the young people have already been trained in one field but are changing to another because of alterations in job opportunities. The instructors are carefully screened: the applicants need to have spent nine years in industry, one year at a teacher's college, and one year in vocational training.

**Folk high schools**

For almost 150 years the Scandinavian countries have had an unique educational institution called the folk high school. The purpose of this type of school is to help young people in their transition from adolescence to adulthood and to offer them an education in humanity and citizenship. A course usually lasts one year. Most of the funding comes from the public. The sponsoring organizations generally also give some financial support. The schools differ greatly in their curricula, philosophical orientation, and the type of students they attract. In recent years several schools have been designed to meet the needs of handicapped and disadvantaged young people. A couple of them will be briefly described. The best known is probably the Kjesäter Folk High School in Sweden (Zielnok & Kignell, 1975). It is run by the Swedish Scouting Association. It has a regular enrollment of 50 young people interested in the creative arts, 30 mentally retarded, and a variable number of deaf students; it also has a two-year training program for 30 recreation leaders. There are also shorter courses for Scout leaders for the handicapped. Follow-up studies of the mentally retarded show substantial improvement in self-concept and social adjustment.

Peder Morset Folk High School in Norway started operation in 1976. It is totally funded by the national rehabilitation services and is designed for 40 retarded and 24 nonretarded students; the latter are drawn mostly from applicants planning to enter the helping professions. The young people live in eight student houses. All have their own rooms, but in each house they share kitchen facilities and common rooms. Experience thus far has indicated that many of the handicapped need to remain for two years, as it takes them longer to develop the attitudes and social skills needed for more independent living (Heggland, 1977).

**Therapeutic communities**

Several therapeutic movements have sprung up that are based on drastically different conceptions of handicaps and normality. They are also sharply critical of traditional institutional and professional roles and practices and are searching for new ways of caring and curing. The best known is probably the group that has gathered around the British psychiatrists Laing and Cooper. Both view mental illness, and particularly schizophrenia, as the outcome of a persistent interpersonal conflict or double bind involving the patient and his family. They consider the patient the victim of a disturbance within the family, which in turn is the instrument of a pathological society in need of scapegoats. They see traditional hospitals as perpetuating and aggravating the degradation and dehumanization of the troubled person. In Kingsley Hall, London, Laing created a home where he and several other professional people lived with a number of schizophrenic individuals as a family (Gordon, 1971). Cooper (1971) tried a similar experiment on a ward in a mental hospital. Both have written extensively about their experiences, and they claim considerable therapeutic success. They combine their unorthodox practices with radical political ideas and a deep appreciation for the contributions the schizophrenic individuals can make to the rest of mankind, both through their unique visions and by serving as mirrors to a troubled humanity.

The second movement, L'Arche, or the place of refuge, was started in 1964 by Jean Vanier (Wolfensberger, 1973). In Trosly-Breuil, France, he built a small community where mentally handicapped and nonhandicapped adults could live and work together as families in a spirit of Christian love and mutual respect. In the past few years dozens of similar communities have sprung up on four continents. At a meeting in France in 1971 there were 14,000 people in attendance from 16 countries. This new dimension in human relationships has particularly attracted and affected teachers. The whole 1977 Fall issue of the prestigious Scandinavian special education quarterly *Nordisk Tidsskrift for Specialpaedagogik* was devoted to a description of a Danish l'Arche community, Niels Steensens Hus (Hviid, 1977). L'Arche is predominantly Catholic but is also attracting members of other religious denominations and creeds.

The anthroposophic movement is a third group that is offering new directions in alternative education and care. Anthroposophy, the wisdom of man, was started at the beginning of this century by an Austrian philosopher and educator, Rudolf Steiner. Steiner's educational principles, the Waldorf Method, were originally intended for normal children. They soon proved to have relevance with handicapped children as well. According to the anthroposophic view, the child's inner personality remains intact, regardless of the severity of his handicaps. He can be helped in his growth in a carefully designed setting where all his developmental needs are considered: they include close human relationships, multifaceted education with much attention given to art, music, movement, and drama; community participation; work; and worship. Proper medicine and nutrition are of central importance; most of the food is derived from biodynamic farming.

A special branch within anthroposophy is the Camphill movement. It was started around 1940 by Karl Konig. In 1939 he came to Scotland as a refugee from Nazi persecutions in Austria. Near Aberdeen he formed a village in which the mentally retarded villagers and the normal co-workers lived together on the basis of spiritual equality. Soon similar curative schools and villages for children were established in a number of countries.

In the anthroposophic schools there is considerable experimentation with novel forms of therapy in music, art, drama, role playing, and expressive movement. New and unique designs in architecture have also been introduced that have educational and therapeutic components incorporated in their structures (Grahl, 1970; "Healing Education," 1974; Pietzner, 1966; Weihs, 1971).

The anthroposophic schools are most numerous in Great Britain, the Netherlands, West Germany, and Sweden. Most of the children served are mentally retarded or multiply handicapped. However, increasingly the children referred are emotionally disturbed. In Scotland, a Steiner school has recently been established for this group; in southern Germany a center for young drug addicts has been active for several years; and in Sweden the anthroposophic facilities are much in demand because of their effective work with autistic children. The percentage of children served by these centers is still limited, however, they are having a considerable inspirational impact. An exhibition about the anthroposophic curative schools and communities in Sweden, held in Stockholm in 1976, attracted 35,000 visitors.

**Some special European concerns**

*School stress*

In Europe there is a traditional health and mental health concern which challenges the authorities both in regular and special education. It has to do with school fatigue and school stress, and in a broader sense the excessive demands school and home make upon many children. The *Überbürdung,* or over-burdening, problem was much discussed in medical and pedagogical circles throughout the 19th century, particularly in Germany. Sengling (1967) provides an excellent historical overview of the issue and also presents the findings from an investigation of stress symptoms among children referred to a child guidance clinic. About 30 percent of the young clients evidenced psychiatric symptoms as a result of excessive expectations.

The current intensity of the issue is reflected in the fact that in 1977 in West Germany, two major national conferences were convened and presided over by the Federal Minister of Education. The first meeting consisted of experts from medicine, psychiatry, psychology, and education ("Gutachten zum Problem," 1977). The second seminar had in attendance parents, teachers, students, and others directly involved with the problem ("Schulstress," 1977). The reports from both these deliberations include analyses of the factors causing school stress and practical measures to combat it.

*Mobbing*

In Scandinavia much attention is given to the phenomenon called *mobbing,* the process by which the weak and the different get excluded and picked and pecked on. Ever since Schelderup-Ebbe's discovery of the pecking phenomenon in Norwegian chicken coops in the early 1920s, the potential for this form of group behavior among humans has attracted the attention of Nordic psychologists. In 1973, Olweus published a comprehensive study of mobbing in the Stockholm public schools. He found that about five percent of children are victims of scapegoating and another five percent are leaders in initiating the exclusion. Subsequently, Pikas initiated an antimobbing project in the schools in Uppsala. The results have been published in English (Pikas, 1975). They are very encouraging and have become the basis for similar interventions in other schools and communities.

### Children of guest workers

The intensive industrialization during the postwar period started an influx of almost 15 million "guest workers" from southern Europe, northern Africa, and Asia. Most of them were unskilled and uneducated, and they have created immense social and cultural problems in the host countries. Many of the workers brought their families, which include four million children, half of whom are of school age. These children suffer from many academic, social, and emotional handicaps. Particularly difficult are the problems of language, culture conflicts, and national and personal identity. In some countries the educational authorities have made vigorous attempts to meet the needs of these children. In Sweden, where eight percent of the school population are foreign citizens, great efforts are made to support the children in maintaining their cultural heritage. This includes instruction in their home languages. In 1975 Swedish school boards employed over 1200 teachers who taught foreign children in 47 different languages (Chaib & Widgren, 1976). In West Germany, which has four million guest workers and families, similar measures have been reported ("Zweisprachiger Unterricht," 1977). Governmental authorities are also deeply concerned about the often deplorable conditions in which the children live and the relative failure of the schools and communities to help them (Dumrese, 1977).

## SPECIAL EDUCATORS

### Teacher training

There is considerable variation in the approach to the professional preparation of special education teachers in Europe. In some countries there are apparently few special requirements and licenses for teaching handicapped children, while in others the certification criteria are quite rigorous. Within the same country, there might also be more than one way in which teachers are certified. Thus West Germany is currently experimenting with several different training models at the 15 universities that prepare teachers in this field. Traditionally the program was entirely at the graduate level (Krohnert, 1972), but in the past few years several universities have introduced an undergraduate special education major (Speck, 1978). England and Wales have no uniform pattern of training teachers of the handicapped, and the great majority of the teachers of children with special educational needs have no additional recognized qualifications. There is, however, a comprehensive program of inservice training. The Warnock Report has presented recommendations for the future that include both a more systematic preparation of special teachers and the inclusion of considerable course work concerning handicapped children in regular teacher training.

Switzerland has half a dozen teachers' institutes, each of which has a special orientation reflecting the cultural diversity within the small nation (Kobi, 1973). The best known internationally is the Institut des Science de l'Education, Geneva, which for so many years has been associated with the name of Piaget. The country also has a coordinating agency, the Zentralstelle fou Heilpädagogik. It has the multiple purpose of uniting the efforts of the above centers to maintain high standards, improving curriculum, organizing inservice courses, and advising young people interested in special education.

In several countries specialization is entirely at the graduate level. In Scotland the training takes one year, and the candidates must have at least one year of teaching in the ordinary school (Blythman, 1978). In France, the requirement is one year of theoretical studies and a one-year practicum (Labregère, 1972). Instruction is provided in 3 national and 30 regional centers.

One highly regarded training facility is the State Graduate School of Special Education in Oslo, Norway. Since it is both an example of and a model for similar programs in the Scandinavian countries, a short description might be enlightening. The school has about 300 students, 22 full-time professors, 150 cooperating teachers, and about 50 part-time faculty. The latter includes leaders in specialized areas of expertise. Half of the funds for salaries go to these adjunct professors, and they have a very important role in the instructional program.

A prerequisite for acceptance to the Graduate School is a degree in elementary education or its equivalent. The admission standards at the teachers' colleges of education in Norway are high and are only exceeded by those for the colleges of medicine and law. Only about one-third of the applicants are admitted (Dullaert, 1978). The admissions procedures for the Graduate School are equally rigorous, and the percentage of applicants that are accepted ranges from 10 to 30. Work experience is important, and the average student accepted has more than six years of teaching, often with handicapped children. During their studies the students generally receive full teaching salaries, and upon the completion of their studies their pay is substantially increased.

The training program has three stages or parts. Part one takes one year. It aims at giving the students a broad general introduction to the field of special education. The candidates learn about the psychology of reading, diagnostic techniques, and teaching methods. The students practice in reading centers or in classes for the mildly mentally retarded. The graduates are certified to teach these groups. Part two takes another year. The students may specialize in one of five areas: the deaf and hard-of-hearing; the visually handicapped; speech pathology; the mentally retarded and brain injured; or the emotionally disturbed (Chazan, 1973). In 1976 a third stage was initiated. It takes two years and leads to a degree equivalent to the doctorate in the United States. The program gives the students research competence and also prepares them for leadership positions in special education.

### The educateur profession

An important European contribution to special education is a new profession—the *educateur*. The educateurs are a special kind of teacher or child-care worker with a broad range of competencies. They receive training in nonacademic subjects such as arts and crafts, sports, acting, photography, and leisure time management. They also become teachers of vocational subjects, supervise young people in vocational placements, work with parents, school authorities, and community agencies, and often assume the role of child advocate.

This profession is particularly well developed in France, where about 40 colleges provide training. The training program lasts three years, half of which is spent in practicum facilities. Selection procedures are rigorous, and all applicants are given academic and personality evaluations which generally include a psychiatric interview. The educateurs are well regarded and rewarded. Their salaries are higher than those of teachers. In 1978 the starting salary was close to the equivalent of $1000 per month.

Similar professions have evolved in other European countries but under different names. In West Germany they are called *Erziehers,* in the Netherlands *Orthopedagogues,* and in Scandinavia *milieu therapists*. However, in these countries they have generally not achieved the well-defined identity that they have in France. The opposite is the case in

Canada, where Guindon (1971) has developed a four-year training program for psychoeducateurs. In the United States, the reeducator or teacher–counselor model at Peabody College is partly based on the educateur concept. However, it is required that the applicants have prior certification as teachers. Other teacher training institutions in the United States are beginning to incorporate similar curriculum components, particularly in the preparation of teachers of behavior-disordered children.

## VOLUNTARY ORGANIZATIONS

Voluntary and charitable organizations have traditionally had an important role in the delivery of services to the handicapped. In some countries they continue to do so with a remarkable vitality. These nongovernmental bodies run schools, preschools centers, sheltered workshops, hospitals, hostels, group homes, old people's homes, and even professional schools. Some have publishing companies, information and counseling services, and legislative consultants. The public authorities recognize and encourage the contributions made by these agencies, and they receive substantial funding from the government.

In the German Federal Republic governmental responsibility and private initiative harmonize in an especially effective way. The largest of the service associations is the Catholic Caritas. It runs over 35,000 establishments for about one million clients. Lebenshilfe, the National Association of Parents and Friends of the Mentally Handicapped, has 45,000 children in 1150 day schools and nurseries, and 20,000 adult handicapped in 260 sheltered workshops and 1600 living in 80 hostels (Mutters, 1976).

Great Britain also relies heavily on voluntary organizations to carry out the tasks of serving the handicapped. This is done in close partnership with public authorities. A useful guide to the main national bodies in remedial and special education has been compiled by Sproule (1978). A unique Swiss innovation is Pro Infirmis. It is an umbrella organization which coordinates the work of a number of other specialized bodies serving the handicapped. It carries on a comprehensive educational program, publishes a journal, books, and brochures, and renders direct consultation to disabled children and adults.

In Austria, the Save the Children Society provides assistance to children with special needs. It runs homes and rehabilitation centers for youth with various types of handicaps. One of its special missions is to be available in crisis situations.

In Denmark, the Society and Home for the Disabled (1974) has been in operation for over 100 years. It owns four hospitals, eight orthopedic clinics, several children's homes, a boarding school, a vocational school, a workshop for the design and construction of orthopedic appliances and prosthetic devices, and a center for aids and equipment. The vocational school prepares the trainees for about 30 different trades. The Society also conducts an extensive international consultation and advisory service. The Swedish Scouting Association has backed the development of lekoteks as well as the Kjesäter Folk High School for the Handicapped. The Norwegian Red Cross has taken the initiative in the establishment of special schools and vocational rehabilitation centers. In Norway, the trend is for a new program to be initiated by concerned individuals or organizations. After the need as well as the viability of the program have been proven, the government often takes it over.

The ample governmental support for services to the handicapped has not adversely affected generosity or initiative in the private sector. In West Germany, a television campaign, "Aktion Sorgenkind," brings in about $15 million per year to equip facilities for the handicapped. In Sweden, a telethon collected $2 million in one day, and in Norway the "Rainbow Action" or campaign in 1976 created a fund in the amount of $3 million to build a rehabilitation center for the blind.

## NORMALIZATION AND INTEGRATION

The normalization movement has had a considerable impact on present programs and on plans for the future. Especially the principle of integration has become part of the "master plans" several countries have adopted as blueprints for the education of the handicapped in the years ahead. It is important to note that the special institutions will tend to continue as legitimate links in the range of services for the handicapped. In Great Britain, where boarding schools have a hoary tradition in the education of normal children, there is generally no strong objection to residential facilities for the handicapped. This writer recently visited two residential schools for behavior-disordered children referred by the educational authorities. The attractive buildings had previously housed exclusive boarding schools for the children of the very rich.

In West Germany some underlying problems have surfaced with the push for integration. Until a decade ago, the responsibility for the education and care of the handicapped had been largely assumed by religious and voluntary organizations. These schools were by their very nature segregated. Thus public school teachers and administrators had

had little if any experience in dealing with children with special needs, and they have therefore responded with some apprehension and resistance (Speck, 1975b).

In Denmark, a proposal for the administrative integration of the services for the handicapped has been passed into law and was put into effect on January 1, 1979. This implementation will not only mean decentralization of programs but a virtual dissolution of some of the national agencies that have served the disabled. The normalization principle involved, as expressed by Bank-Mikkelsen (1976), is that the handicapped are best served if they use the agencies available to ordinary people, unhampered by labels and categories. This change is generally hailed as a good step, but it is also viewed with concern by some dedicated professionals in the central institutions who fear that sometimes the local communities will not have the expertise to provide the quality of treatment some children require.

The normalization controversy has placed some special purpose schools in a crossfire of conflicting criticisms and demands from parents and politicians. A characteristic example is the Haug School in a wealthy school district in Norway. It was built in 1971 to serve about 130 physically, mentally, and emotionally handicapped children who could not be properly accommodated in regular schools. It is hard to imagine a more carefully planned, generously equipped, and competently run school. Nevertheless, for several years the administration has been under attack from parents who have been led by the controversy to expect too much both from their children and from the schools.

One negative aspect of integration has received scant public attention. It has to do with the impact on an institution when the less handicapped leave, and the more afflicted children who remain no longer have the friendship, support, and encouragement of their abler peers. It is this observer's opinion that the effects are detrimental both to the children and to the staff, who find themselves discouraged and less rewarded for their commitment and their efforts.

Research on the effectiveness of integrated over segregated education is either contradictory or inconclusive. The most positive results were found by Anderson (1973) in a British study on the integration in the regular schools of physically handicapped children with normal intelligence. It appears, in general, that the more handicapped the child the more disadvantages are associated with integrated schooling.

The heated and often unjustified attacks during the past decade against segregated education and the special institutions are beginning to subside. The controversy has led to an increased public awareness of their legitimate functions and to greater efforts to bring the special purpose facilities into closer contact and interaction with ordinary society.

## RESEARCH

The general picture with regard to research in special education is fragmented and unclear. The small size of most of the countries and the language barriers are formidable obstacles to quality research. In addition, considering the typically generous funding for the care of the handicapped, strikingly small amounts are set aside for scientific investigation. To explain this in part, many European experts assert that the quality of services for the handicapped is much more a moral than a scientific problem.

Nevertheless, interest in research is increasing, and in at least two countries the governments have commissioned research projects in connection with the making or implementation of new laws. In Great Britain, the Committee of Enquiry into the Education of Handicapped Children and Youth engaged several prestigious institutions and individuals to conduct some investigations before preparing its recommendations to the Parliament. In Sweden, the government solicited the cooperation of several university research institutes to conduct pilot projects before passing the new school laws in 1976. This research is continuing as the provisions of the law are gradually being carried out. Similar situations apply to delinquency research in the Scandinavian countries, where many of the findings and recommendations of the researchers are incorporated into their nation's criminal policy (National Institute of Mental Health, 1972).

A monumental but lopsided compilation of international research literature on handicapped children has been done by the National Children's Bureau in Great Britain (Dinnage, 1970, 1972; Pilling, 1973). Of the 2436 annotated entries, 1235 are from Great Britain, 1070 from the United States, and 131 from other countries.

Under the auspices of UNESCO, an international review of the present situation and research trends in special education was published. In this volume, Stukat (1973) has contributed an informative and detailed analysis of research in the Scandinavian countries.

The most comprehensive research study involving handicapped children presently in progress in Europe is probably the National Child Development Study in Great Britain. It consists of a periodic follow-up of all the 17,000 children in England, Scotland, and Wales born during a certain week in 1958. So far there have been follow-up studies at the ages 7, 11, and 16 (Davie, Butler, & Goldstein, 1972; Fogelman, 1976; Pringle, Butler, & Davie, 1966). A research project scheduled to be completed in late 1978 concerns the employment behavior of 18-year olds. Many of the findings of the studies have been used in the national planning for children and youth with special educational needs.

The greatest strength in European research lies in the area of prevalence or incidence studies of handicapping conditions. In addition to the investigation mentioned above, Great Britain has also contributed the famous Isle of Wight survey (Rutter, Tizard, & Whitmore, 1970), in which the total 9- to 11-year-old population on the island was examined for physical, mental, and emotional disorders. A comparison study of the incidence of psychiatric disturbances in a London borough (Rutter, Cox, Rupling, Berger & Yule, 1975) rendered the findings that twice as many children in the metropolis had emotional problems as compared to children in a less urbanized region.

Similar research in Sweden (Jonsson & Kälvesten, 1964), West Germany (Thalman, 1971), Norway (Lavik, 1976), France (Chiland, 1973), and other European countries indicates that between 10 and 30 percent of school children have adjustment difficulties of sufficient severity to justify therapeutic intervention.

A towering authority in the much neglected field of dyscalculia is the Swedish psychologist Magne (1975). In numerous studies he has explored the many aspects of difficulties in the use of numbers. In Norway, Gjessing (1978) has for many years conducted investigations on dyslexia. Both authors find that a significant percentage of learning disorders can be traced to failures in instruction.

A unique Swedish study (Gustafsson & Stigebrandt, 1972) consisted of a detailed comparison of regular and special classes with regard to what and how the teachers taught. In most of the dimensions measured there were no differences. The findings have provided an explanation of why special class placements have failed to show any improvements in student performance. They have also raised questions about the adequacy of teacher training in special education and the justification for special classes.

## CONCLUSION

In this short review we have attempted to present the most distinctive features of special education in Western Europe and Scandinavia. It is in reality a highly diverse, variegated, and constantly changing situation.

There are many contrasts and discrepancies between the ideals and the realities in the delivery of services. At the same time there is an almost palpable presence of a positive acceptance of the rights of the handicapped, which bodes well for the growth of programs in the years ahead.

# References

Adler, A. *The problem child.* New York: Capricorn Books, 1963.

Aichhorn, A. *Wayward youth.* New York: Viking Press, 1965.

Alvin, J. *Music for the handicapped child.* Oxford: Oxford University Press, 1969.

Anderson, E. M. *The disabled school child: A study of integration in primary schools.* London: Methuen, 1973.

Bank-Mikkelsen, N. E. Administrativ normalisering. *S. Å. - Nyt,* 1976, *15*(9), 3–6.

Blid, E. *Leka, öva, lära.* Stockholm: Bonniers, 1971.

Blythman, M. The training of teachers for special education in Scotland. In W. B. Dockrell, W. R. Dunn, & A. Milne (Eds.), *Special education in Scotland.* Edinburgh: The Scottish Council for Research in Education, 1978.

Chaib, M., & Widgren, J. *Invandrarbarn och skolan. En nyckelfraaga for Europe.* Stockholm: Wahlström & Widstrand, 1976.

Chazan, M. Special education for maladjusted children and adolescents in Norway. *Journal of Child Psychology and Psychiatry and Allied Disciplines,* 1973, *14,* 57–69.

Chiland, C. Pratique quotidienne et recherche d'une etude longitudinale. *L'Information Psychiatrique.* 1973, *49,* 671–675.

Clark, M. J., & Clark, K. *Scandinavian programs for the mentally retarded: How they work.* Washington, D.C.: U.S. Department of Health, Education and Welfare, Office of Education, 1970.

Cooper, D. *Psychiatry and anti-psychiatry.* New York: Ballantine, 1971.

Cotton, E., & Parnwell, M. From Hungary: The Petö method. *Special Education,* 1967, *54,* 7–11.

Davie, R., Butler, N. R., & Goldstein, H. *From birth to seven.* London: Longman, 1972.

De Ajuriaguerra, J. The theoretical bases of psychomotor rehabilitation of children. *Journal of Learning Disabilities,* 1968, *1,* 42–52.

Dinnage, R. *The handicapped child. Research review* (Vol. 1). London: Longman, 1970.

Dinnage, R. *The handicapped child. Research review* (Vol. 2). London: Longman, 1972.

Dullaert, J. Norwegian elementary school teacher preparation. *Phi Delta Kappan,* 1978, *59,* 462–463.

Dumrese, J. Über die Hälfte der Ausländerkinder ohne Hauptschulabschluss. *Informationen—Bildung, Wissenschaft,* 1977, *3,* 36–39.

Egolf, H., & Grunwaldt, P. Die französische "Psychomotorik"—ein Verfahren einer Leibeserziehung mit Behinderten. *Heilpädagogik,* 1973, *42,* 264–273.

Elowson, F. *Rapport angående specialundervisning i Sverige.* Stockholm: Skolöverstyrelsen, 1978.

Faber, N. W. *The retarded child.* New York: Crown, 1968.

Finnie, R. *Handling the young cerebral palsied child at home* (2nd ed.). New York: Dutton, 1975.

Fogelman, K. (Ed.). *Britain's sixteen-year-olds.* London: National Children's Bureau, 1976.

Freire, P. *Pedagogy of the oppressed.* New York: Herder and Herder, 1972.

Geck, M. *Musikterapi.* Stockholm: Wahlström & Widstrand, 1977.

Gjessing, H. G. *Lese-og skrivevansker. Dyslexi.* Oslo: Universitetsforlaget, 1978.

Gordon, J. S., Laing, R. D.: In search of a new psychiatry. *The Atlantic,* 1971, *227*(1), 50–66.

Grahl, V. *The exceptional child. A way of life for mentally handicapped children.* Spring Valley, N.Y.: The Anthroposophic Press, 1970.

Guindon, J. *Les étapes de la rééducation des jeunes délinquants et des autres.* Paris: Editions Fleurus, 1971.

Gustafsson, B., & Stigebrandt, E. *Vad kännetecknar undervisning i hjälpklass.* Göteborg, Sweden: Pedagogiska Institutionen, 1972.

Gutachten zum Problem "Überbeanspruchung von Schülern." *Informationen—Bildung, Wissenschaft,* July 1977, 123–127.

Guttmann, L. *Sports for the physically handicapped.* Paris: UNESCO, 1976.

Handicapped Adventure Playground Association. *Adventure playgrounds for children.* London, 1974.

Heafford, M. R. *Pestalozzi.* London: Methuen, 1967.

*Healing education based on anthroposophy's image of man.* Stuttgart: Freies Geistesleben, 1974.

Heggland, R. Folkehogskole for psykisk utviklingshemmede. *Vaar Rett,* 1977, *8*(4), 2–3.

Heiland, H. *Literatur und Trends in der Fröbelforschung.* Weinheim, West Germany: Beltz, 1972.

Hellbrügge, T. *Unser Montessori Modell.* München: Kindler, 1977.

Hersch, S. P. Sweden's approach to health screening for preschool children. *American Journal of Orthopsychiatry.* 1978, *48*(1), 33–39.

Hulek, A. *Rehabilitation of the disabled and other social services.* Warsaw: Polish Scientific Publishers, 1975.

Hviid, J. Hvem er handicappet? En bog om en alternativ livsstil. *Nordisk Tidsskrift for Specialpaedagogik,* 1977, *55,* 237–366.

Illich, I. *Deschooling society.* New York: Harper & Row, 1970.

Itard, J.-M.-G. *The wild boy of Aveyron.* New York: Appleton-Century-Crofts, 1962.

Jonk, A. *Sheltered employment in the Netherlands.* Mimeographed paper, Industrial Medicine Department of Public Health, 1976.

Jonsson, G., & Kälvesten, A. L. *222 Stockholmspojkar.* Stockholm: Almqvist & Wiksell, 1964.

Juul, K. D. European approaches and innovations in serving the handicapped. *Exceptional Children,* 1978, *44,* 322–330.

Juul, K. D., & Linton, T. E. European approaches to the treatment of behavior disordered children. *Behavior Disorders,* 1978, *3,* 232–249.

Kahn, A. J., & Kamerman, S. B. *Not for the poor alone: European social services.* Philadelphia: Temple University Press, 1975.

Kanner, L. *A history of the care and study of the mentally retarded.* Springfield, Ill.: Thomas, 1964.

*Kindermusical "Benjamin."* Krailling, West Germany: Itonmusik, 1978.

Kobi, E. E. Einige Hinweise zur Situation der Heilpädagogik in der Schweitz. *Heilpädagogik,* 1973, *42,* 4–6.

Krohnert, O. Teacher education in Germany. *Special Education,* 1972, *61,* 9–11.

Kugel, F. B., & Wolfensberger, W. (Eds.). *Changing patterns of residential services for the mentally retarded.* Washington, D.C.: President's Committee on Mental Retardation, 1968.

Labregère, A. *Adaptation et éducation speciale en France.* Paris: Ministère de l'Éducation Nationale, 1972.

Lavik, N. J. *Ungdoms mentale helse.* Oslo: Universitetsforlaget, 1976.

Linton, T. E. The educateur model: A theoretical monograph. *The Journal of Special Education,* 1971, *5,* 155–190.

Lippman, L. *Attitudes toward the handicapped: A comparison between Europe and the United States.* Springfield, Ill.: Thomas, 1972.

Luria, A. R. Cerebral organization of conscious acts: A frontal lobe function. In L. Tarnopol & M. Tarnopol (Eds.), *Brain function and reading disabilities.* Baltimore: University Park Press, 1977.

Magne, O. *Matematiksvårigheter.* Stockholm: Sveriges Lararforbund, 1975.

McMillan, J. Personal communication, 1977.

Mutters, T. Services for the mentally retarded in West Germany. *Retardation,* Spring 1976, 1–3.

National Institute of Mental Health, Center for Studies on Crime and Delinquency. *Crime and delinquency research in selected European countries.* Rockville, Md., 1972.

Nordoff, P., & Robbins, C. *Therapy in music for handicapped children.* New York: St. Martin's Press, 1972.

Olweus, D. *Hackkycklingar och översittare. Forskning om skolmobbing.* Stockholm: Almqvist & Wiksell, 1973.

Oyer, H. J. *Communication for the hearing handicapped. An international perspective.* Baltimore: University Park Press, 1976.

Pietzner, C. *Aspects of curative education.* New York: The Anthroposophic Press, 1966.

Pikas, A. Treatment of mobbing in school: Principles for and the work of an anti-mobbing group. *Scandinavian Journal of Educational Research,* 1975, *19,* 1–12.

Pilling, D. *The handicapped child. Research review* (Vol. 3). London: Longman, 1973.

Pringle, M. L. K., Butler, N. R., & Davie, R. *11,000 seven-year-olds.* London: Longman, 1966.

Riise, U. *Form og forming. Barn og unge med spesielle vansker.* Oslo: Universitetsforlaget, 1978.

Rutter, M., Cox, A., Berger, M., & Yule, W. The prevalence of psychiatric disorders. *British Journal of Psychiatry,* 1975, *126,* 493–509.

Rutter, M., Tizard, J., & Whitmore, K. *Education, health and behavior.* London: Longman, 1970.

Schulstress-Ursachen und notwendige Konsequenzen. *Informationen—Bildung, Wissenschaft,* December 1977, 239–242.

Sengling, D. *Das Problem der Überforderung im Kindes und Jugendalter.* Weinheim: Julius Beltz, 1967.

Skov Jorgensen, I. *Specialundervisning i Danmark. Skolepsykologi,* 1975, *12,* 348–354.

*Society and Home for the Disabled.* Copenhagen: Vanførehjemmets Bogtrykkeri, 1974.

Soubiran, G. B., & Mazo, P. *La réadaption scolaire des enfants intelligents par la reééducation psychomotrice.* Paris: Editions Doin, 1965.

*Special educational needs. Report of the Committee of Inquiry into the Education of Handicapped Children and Youth.* London: Her Majesty's Stationery Office, 1978.

Speck, O. Analyse der Möglichkeit gemeinsamer Unterrichtung "behinderter und Nichtbehinderter." *Lehren und Lernen,* 1975a, *Heft 5,* 17–25.

Speck, O. Zur Gegenwartslage und bildungspolitischen Diskussion im Erziehungswesen für Behinderte in der Bundesrepublik Deutschland. *Zeitschrift für Heilpädagogik,* 1975b, 26, 205–213.

Speck, O. Personnel preparation: International comparisons. In A. H. Fink (Ed.), *International perspectives on future special education.* Reston, VA.: The Council for Exceptional Children, 1978.

Sproule, A. Remedial and special education: A teacher's guide to the main national bodies. *The Times Educational Supplement,* September 22, 1978, *3299,* 48–49.

Standing, E. M. *The Montessori revolution in educadion.* New York: Schocken Books, 1966.

Stensland Junker, K. *The child in the glass ball.* Nashville, Tenn.: Abingdon Press, 1964.

Stensland Junker, K. A center for play habilitation as an indispensable part of the medical and educational care of handicapped and sick children. *Paediatrician,* 1974, *3,* 315–320.

Stensland Junker, K., Barr, B., Maliniemi, S., & Wasz-Hockert, O. BOEL Screening: A program for the early detection of communicative disorders. *Audiology,* 1978, *17,* 51–61.

Stukat, K. G. Sweden and other Scandinavian countries. In *The present situation and trends of research in the field of special education.* Paris: UNESCO, 1973.

Talbot, M. E. *Edouard Seguin: A study of an educational approach to the treatment of mentally defective children.* New York: Teachers College Press, 1964.

Tarnopol, L., & Tarnopol, M. *Reading disabilities: An international perspective.* Baltimore: University Park Press, 1976.

Taylor, E. J. *Rehabilitation and world peace.* New York: International Society for Rehabilitation of the Disabled, 1960.

Taylor, W. W., & Taylor, I. W. *Special education of physically handicapped children in Western Europe.* New York: International Society for the Welfare of Cripples, 1960.

Thalman, H. C. *Verhaltensstörungen bei Kindern im Grundschulalter.* Stuttgart: Ernst Klett, 1971.

Vail, D. J. *Mental health systems in Scandinavia.* Springfield, Ill.: Thomas, 1968.

Vygotsky, L. S. *Thought and language.* Cambridge, Mass.: M.I.T. Press, 1965.

Ward, D. *Hearts and hands and voices. Music in the education of slow learners.* London: Oxford University Press, 1976.

Weihs, T. J. *Children in need of special care.* London: Souvenir Press, 1971.

Wolfensberger, W. Some observations on European programs for the mentally retarded. *Mental Retardation,* 1964a, *2,* 280–285.

Wolfensberger, W. Teaching and training of the retarded in European countries. *Mental Retardation,* 1964b, *2,* 331–337.

Wolfensberger, W. General observations on European programs. *Mental Retardation,* 1965, *3,* 8–11.

Wolfensberger, W. (Ed.). *A selective overview of the work of Jean Vanier and the movement of L'Arche.* Toronto, Canada: National Institute of Mental Retardation, 1973.

Wolfgart, H. (Ed.). *Das Orff-Schulwerk im Dienste der Erziehung und Therapie behinderter Kinder.* Berlin-Charlottenburg: Carl Marhold, 1971.

Zielnok, W., & Kignell, E. Behinderte belegen Kurse an einer schwedischen Heim-Volkschule. *Lebenshilfe,* 1975, *14,* 98–104.

Zweisprachiger Unterricht für Kinder ausländischer Arbeitnehmer. *Informationen—Bildung, Wissenschaft,* 1977, *3,* 44–45.

# SPECIAL EDUCATION IN POLAND AND THE SOVIET UNION: CURRENT DEVELOPMENTS

Ivan Z. Holowinsky
*Rutgers The State University*

The purpose of this chapter is to review the current status of and developments in special education in Poland and the Soviet Union. In order for those developments to be understood they have to be viewed in terms of past practices as well as current political realities. While it is generally difficult to interpret educational developments abroad, it is especially difficult to review educational developments in Eastern Europe. As stated previously (Holowinsky, 1973, p. 287):

> a survey of special education in Eastern Europe is complicated by such factors as unavailable source material, inadequate translations of terminology, problems in the interpretation of classification systems and obscurities due to the absence of common criteria such as standardized intelligence and educational tests.

No attempt will be made in this chapter to review comparative terminology and classification in the field of special education in Eastern Europe. However, in order to have some general understanding of this topic, the interested reader is referred to previous publications by this author (Holowinsky, 1973, 1974, 1976).

The present review will focus upon relevant research, curriculum developments, and personnel preparation, essentially for the past five years (1973–1978), in Poland and the Soviet Union. Since there are distinct historical and cultural differences between Poland and the Soviet Union, special education developments in those two countries will be viewed separately.

## RELEVANT RESEARCH

### Poland

In Poland research in special education is published primarily in *Szkola Specjalna (Special School),* an offical quarterly publication of the ministry of education. The journal also publishes review, survey, and

459

methodological articles. In order to highlight the types of studies published in *Special School,* a sample of current research by Klimasinski (1974), Panczyk (1975), Maszczak (1975a, 1975b), Blaszkewich (1974), Bukowski (1976), Pawlikowska (1977), and Maszczak (1978) will be reviewed briefly.

Klimasinski (1974) investigated application of Piaget's theory of mental development to the psychological examination of the blind. The study raised the following question: "Does the mental development of blind children progress in the same fashion as that of children with normal vision, since it is known that spatial perception plays a very important role in the formation of mental representations?" Since those born blind are by definition lacking spatial perception, the study attempted to investigate the degree to which this defect affects their development of concrete operations. The sample for this study consisted of 78 youngsters, 7 to 17 years old and blind since birth or prior to 5 years of age. The children were required to place nine sticks, 12–28 cm in length, in descending order from the longest to the shortest. Those who completed this task satisfactorily were instructed to place additional sticks, 17, 19, 21, and 23 cm in length, at appropriate places in the sequence. The children who were unable to place the initial nine sticks in sequential order received an easier task. They were asked to place in sequence five sticks 12, 16, 20, 24, and 28 cm in length. It has been suggested by Inhelder (Klimasinski, 1974) that 60 percent of children with vision can perform the above tasks at 7 years of age, and by 8 years of age the performance is nearly 100 percent correct.

Results of Klimasinski's (1974) study showed that blind children performed such activities significantly less successfully than children with vision. Only at 14 years of age were 100 percent of the blind children able to complete the sequence. Even at this age, the blind children were unable to complete the task of inclusion of new elements into the existing sequence.

Panczyk (1975) investigated laterality in a sample of 697 mildly retarded children selected at random from among 3436 elementary special school pupils. The author had used, for comparison purposes, estimates from the literature that indicated that 50 percent of the general population are right handed with definitely dominant left hemisphere, 5 percent are left handed with distinctly dominant right hemisphere, and the remaining 45 percent have various degrees of mixed dominance. In the present sample it was found that 36.2 percent of the girls and 29.8 percent of the boys were right handed, 24.2 percent of the girls and 21.2 percent of the boys were left handed, and 39.6 percent of the girls and 49 percent of the boys were ambidextrous. In regard to the preference for lower extremities, 31 percent of the girls and 26.1 percent of the boys showed preference for the right leg, 8.1 percent of the girls and 11.9 percent of the boys showed preference for left leg, and 60.9 percent of the girls and 62 percent of the boys had mixed laterality. The study concluded that a delayed process of laterality is a characteristic among the mildly retarded.

Maszczak (1975a) studied etiological factors in deafness. The author surveyed the total population of elementary schools for deaf children in Poland during the 1972–1973 school year. In Poland deaf children are classified as either deaf or hard of hearing. Deaf children are further subdivided into the profoundly deaf (who neither hear nor understand language) and the moderately deaf (who hear and understand language, but only with strong hearing aids). Children who hear and understand language when it is spoken loudly are labeled as hard of hearing. Maszczak surveyed 3015 children with hearing difficulties, among whom 2216 were identified as deaf and 799 as hard of hearing. In the majority of children the onset of deafness was identified during infancy or the neonatal stage: 1750 were deaf since birth and 1034 became deaf between 1 and 2 years of age; only 231 became deaf after 3 years of age. The following were identified as the most prevalent etiological factors contributing to deafness: heredity and prenatal causes in 498 cases, ear infections in 459 cases, and meningitis in 433 cases.

Utilizing the same sample, Maszczak (1975b) reported on the physical development and proficiency of deaf mentally retarded children. Deaf mildly retarded children comprised about 8.7 percent of the deaf children surveyed in Poland in the 1972–1973 school year. The level of physical development of deaf mentally retarded children was inferior to that of both deaf children and hearing children of average intelligence. The physical proficiency of deaf mentally retarded girls was found to be superior to that of deaf mentally retarded boys.

Blaszkewich (1974) reported on the self-evaluation of graduates of special schools. The survey included 500 graduates of special schools for the mentally retarded, both basic and vocational. Most of those surveyed remained single (355), and 87 percent of the respondents indicated that they had no difficulty with their present jobs.

Bukowski (1976), using a sample of 40 severely retarded children (19 boys and 21 girls), investigated factors which enhance the popularity of a child within a group. Using sociometric assessment techniques, Bukowski divided the group into more popular and less popular children. Behavioral attributes of both groups, as determined by children, were ascertained. Popular children were described as looking well, friendly,

461

helpful, usually smiling, and having a good disposition. Unpopular children were described as unkempt, aggressive, short-tempered, clumsy, and behaving in a peculiar manner.

Pawlikowska's (1977) research conducted in the Institute for the Blind in Krakow. The sample consisted of 43 children (24 boys and 19 girls) 8 1/4–18 years old. The study investigated perceptual properties of the Braille alphabet. It was determined that the most difficult symbols were those for *L, K, R, F, T,* and *D*. The most difficult combinations were *K* following *L* or *R*. The difficulty, for example, with *LK* is related to the number of points as well as their gestalt, which has a difficult perceptual structure. The author concluded that there are letters in the Braille alphabet that are difficult to read, not so much because of their individual characteristics, but because they are difficult to perceive when they are combined with other letters.

Maszczak (1978) reported on the somatic development of deaf children in Poland using the same sample as in the reports described above (Maszczak, 1975a, b). General findings of the study were as follows: (1) "adolescent spurt," or accelerated development, was somewhat slow in comparison to the general population [norms for the general population as indicated by Trzesniowski (1961) and Wolenski (1977) were employed]; and (2) the mean height and weight of deaf children was lower than that of hearing children. The study, however, also points out the importance of environmental findings related to the above differences.

## Soviet Union

In the Soviet Union research in special education is published in *Defectologia (Defectology),* an official publication of the Academy of Pedagogical Sciences of the USSR. Most of the research published in *Defectology* is related to mental retardation and sensory disorders; some examples are reviewed here.

Rayskaya (1976) and Akinshchikova, Yeremeyeva, Verlinskaya, and Tysianchniuk (1976) reported on characteristics of oligophrenic children. Rayskaya (1976) reported that patients with Turner's syndrome revealed borderline intelligence with weaknesses in the area of visual–motor integration. Personality structure in Turner's syndrome individuals was found to be marked by psychological infantilism. Akinshchikova et al. (1976) surveyed intellectual functioning in children with sex-linked chromosomal aberrations. Their sample included 46 school-age children (20 with Turner's syndrome, 20 with Klinefelter's syndrome, and 6 with trisomy of chromosome X). Subjects with Turner's snydrome manifested adequate verbal intelligence with below average performance intelligence. Klinefelter's syndrome youngsters manifested both verbal and performance intelligence within average range. Subjects with trisomy of chromosome X were of borderline intelligence.

Peresleni and Sagdulayev (1975) investigated the performance capacity of mentally retarded children during the regular school day. They were pursuing leads provided by earlier research that had shown that the performance capacity of children declines toward the end of the school day, manifested by an increased quantity of errors; this is related to lowered concentration of attention. The purpose of their study was to compare the performance of mildly retarded youngsters to that of average elementary-age children. Their subjects included 84 children attending grades 2–6 of an auxiliary school. Two tasks designed to measure work capacity were presented at the beginning of the school day, again after the second lesson, and again at the end of the school day. The first task consisted of crossing out the letter $a$ from the reading page. The second task consisted of crossing out the letter $a$ in all cases except after the letter $n$. The study revealed significant differences in the number of errors between the control group and the oligophrenics at each grade level.

Bgazhnokova (1975) reported on role expectations among 110 mildly retarded children attending grades 4, 6, and 8 of an auxiliary school in Moscow. She found that their role expectations became more realistic as they matured.

Karpova, Karpov, and Isayev (1977) found that the reading disabilities of oligophrenics cannot be accounted for simply on grounds of their intellectual inadequacy. Studying a sample of 14 oligophrenics, 8–12 years of age, they obtained the following results:

|  | Oligophrenics | Controls |
| --- | --- | --- |
| No. of fixations per 100 words | 351 | 173 |
| No. of regressions | 134 | 39 |
| Average length of individual fixation (sec) | .46 | .27 |

Interesting data on a twin study in oligophrenics have been presented by Lilin (1978), Who reported on Bertyn's data. Bertyn collected data on 189 pairs of twins among 5109 pupils of 32 auxiliary schools. He identified 143 sets of twins in which one or both twins were diagnosed as oligophrenic; 38 percent of the monozygotic and 35 percent of the dizygotic twins had one or both parents who were oligophrenic. Mothers were more frequently oligophrenic (50.3 percent) than fathers (21.6 percent).

Levels of spatial orientation skills in mentally retarded adolescents were investigated by Abbasov (1977). This study surveyed 126 mildly retarded children, 8–16 years of age. General problems were noted with spatial orientation. The children had difficulty in following spatial positions. The author suggested that mentally retarded children should be taught spatial orientation through direct concrete activities within the environment, e.g., hiking. The children should be asked to describe their hikes verbally as well as draw them on paper.

Since studies on projective techniques are very rare in the Soviet literature, it is of interest to note that Albrecht (1976) reported on the emotional profile of oligophrenic adolescents utilizing the TAT. The test results suggested that the subjects have infantile personality structures and are preoccupied with animals. Albrecht's study also suggested some relationship between levels of retardation and type and degree of emotional maladjustment.

Rostiagaylova (1977) reported that the psychological characteristics of hydrocephalic children vary considerably depending upon the degree of the organic insult. In serious forms of hydrocephalus one may notice cerebral palsy, mental retardation, and sensory and other psychopathological disorders. In less serious forms, intellectual functioning may remain within the average or borderline range of intelligence. The children in her sample were lacking in goal-directed, task-oriented behavior.

Interesting observations on developmentally backward children who are not mentally retarded are presented in an article by Markovskaya (1977). She repeats observations offered by Vlasova and Pevzner to the effect that developmentally backward children in most instances manifest inadequacy of the central nervous system. Their degree of underdevelopment varies depending upon the character and the age of onset of the neurological insult they have suffered; it ranges from a mild, more or less undifferentiated form to complex conditions which require differentiation between oligophrenic and organic dementia. She suggests that a proper differential analysis of various forms of developmental backwardness requires investigation of higher cortical functions. She warns, however, that questions concerning the relationship among higher cortical functions (memory, perception, spatial organization, and speech), encephalopathic defects, and other intellectual and emotional variables have not been sufficiently resolved.

Yavkin (1975) investigated clinical characteristics of first-grade underachievers from families of chronic alcoholics. The survey included 119 children from 75 families. Among the parents, 4 were mentally retarded, 1 had epilepsy, and 73 had a history of various forms of educational difficulties. Among the children, 17 were mentally retarded, 19 had various emotional disorders, 15 suffered from minimal cerebral dysfunction, 23 were physically underdeveloped, and 153 presented various types of educational difficulties.

Kozakov (1975) described an interesting utilization of two instruments as aid in helping the blind to recognize colors in the environment. The instruments are known as a "thyphlospectroscope" and a "color informer." The thyphlospectroscope demonstrates to the blind the distribution of light within the color spectrum. The color informer enables blind people to discern colors in their environment. In this instrument a photoelectrical cell picks up light energy and changes it, depending upon its frequency (color), into sounds of various frequencies. Colors are indicated as follows: white, even sound frequency; red, lower frequency; blue, higher frequency. Thus, hue is indicated by the pitch of the sound. With the help of the color informer, a blind person can auditorily recognize such colors as red, orange, yellow, white, and blue.

Techniques of intellectual assessment of preschool children with defective speech were reviewed by Umanskaya (1977) in a study based upon observation of spontaneous symbolic play. The sample consisted of 200 preschoolers diagnosed as allalics and mentally retarded. Attention was paid to collective play as well as group play. The examiner was interested in the following: (1) selection of toys, (2) appropriate use of toys, (3) organization and sequence of play, (4) role playing, (5) stability of attention, (6) fantasy, (7) verbal communication, and (8) reason for termination of the play. It was observed that the spontaneous play of intellectually backward children is reduced to stereotyped repetitions of activities previously learned with elements of creativity and planning absent.

A study by Shklovsky (1976) was concerned with the question of speech dominance in stuttering. The sample consisted of 147 stutterers (mean age 24 years) whom 105 were males and 42 females; of this total number 136 were right handed, 6 left handed, and 5 ambidextrous. Words were presented to the pupils' right and left ears separately. The results revealed a lack of relationship between stuttering and mixed dominance. Left handedness, ambidextrousness, and right or left hemispheric dominance for speech were all found to be etiologically unrelated to stuttering.

The vocational and social adjustment of former special school students was reported on by Karvialis (1975) and Agavelian (1974). Karvialis (1975) surveyed 645 graduates of auxiliary schools, 238 graduates of schools for the deaf and hard of hearing, and 324 graduates of schools for the blind. It should be pointed out that boys outnumbered girls nearly two to one (63.6 percent boys and 36.4 percent girls) among the graduates of auxiliary schools. However, the breakdown among deaf and blind pupils according to sex was nearly equal; 49.7 percent males and 50.3 percent females among the deaf, and 51.9 percent males and 49.1 percent females among the blind. The family status of the graduates was as follows: 73.2 percent of the auxiliary school graduates remained single; among the deaf and blind, 35.4 and 36.4 percent respectively, remained single. In Agavelian's (1974) survey of 100 graduates of auxiliary schools (60 males and 40 females) it was found that the most frequent reason for job changes on the part of the graduates was difficulty in adjusting as team members. Forty-six graduates were employed in vocational areas similar to those for which they had been trained, and 54 were employed in areas other than those for which they had received vocational preparation in school.

Yeremenko (1977) reported on research efforts combined with pedagogical work. In the Kiev auxiliary school ($N = 10$) there is a concentration of research upon physiological and psychopathological mechanisms of the behavior and cognitive activities of the mentally retarded children. In the Department of Defectology of the Scientific Research Institute of Pedagogy of the Ukrainian SSR experiments are being conducted in the area of individualized instruction. Further research efforts are being considered by the Department in such areas as education and training of developmentally backward children and the severely and profoundly retarded, training of the mentally retarded at home and in preschool facilities, and education of deaf children with intellectual subnormalities.

The Soviet Union is also increasing its emphasis on abnormal child personality research. Yashkova (1978) described a conference which took place in the Institute of Defectology of the Academy of Pedagogical Sciences in April 1977. It was devoted to problems of the psychoeducational aspects of personality.

## CURRICULUM DEVELOPMENT

### Poland

Special education efforts in Poland go back to the early 19th century. The Institute for the Deaf-Mute, the first special school in Poland, was organized in 1817 (N.N., 1978).

In the 1945–1946 school year Poland was reported to have 53 elementary special schools for the mentally retarded, blind, deaf, and socially maladjusted. The pupils served by these schools totaled 3700. There were no programs reported for chronically ill, disabled, partially blind, or hard of hearing pupils (Kotlarski, 1973). The data provided in 1976 show spectacular growth for special education in Poland (Kur, 1976). From 1958 to 1973, 104 new special schools were built. Using the 1950–1951 school year as a baseline, this represents a fourfold increase in preschool education services and a fivefold increase in elementary special education. During the 1973–1974 school year, there were 5073 children attending special preschool programs and 102,944 attending elementary special schools. Currently (1977–1978) special education in Poland provides a variety of services to children with visual defects, auditory defects, mental retardation, chronic illness, poor health, learning disabilities, emotional maladjustment, and borderline intellectual capacity. Polish handicapped pupils currently are educated in special preschool facilities, special elementary schools, special vocational schools, residential boarding schools, and therapeutic facilities, and also receive home instruction (Belcerek, 1977).

The nature and the role of special education in Poland has been discussed by Doroszewska (1973), Hulek (1977a), and Lipkowski (1977). Doroszewska (1973) insisted that special education, in order to achieve the status of a distinct discipline, should answer the question as to how (with what methods and with what techniques) to achieve pedagogical goals with handicapped children. She has also suggested that special education should function in an interdisciplinary arrangement with medicine, psychology, sociology, and educational technology. In a similar vein, Hulek (1977a) has suggested that special education should be identified as "therapeutic pedagogy" *(pedagogica rehabilitacyjna)*. Lipkowski (1977) observed that special education ranges from mild and moderately handicapping conditions to profound and multiple handicapping conditions, and from preschool education to geriatrics. Basic to the success of special education, he observed, is the detailed diagnosis and knowledge of the handicapped individual. Since therapy involves working with children who have biological defects, as well as those who are ill and disabled, he suggested that the more precise definition of special education should be "orthopedagogy."

Polish special educators are currently concerned with issues of integration or mainstreaming. Hoffman (1978) identified three stages in special education services: (1) separate self-contained programs, (2) partially integrated programs, and (3) completely integrated programs. Hulek (1977a) maintained that the success of mainstreaming efforts

467

depend upon the quality of regular schools: the higher the level of services and education in regular schools, the better are conditions for the mainstreaming of the handicapped.

Recently a movement has been underway in Poland to reorganize the special education curriculum. Hulek (1977b) formulated some recommendations for the development of a 10-year curriculum for exceptional children. He suggested that special attention be paid to both the etiology of handicapping conditions and individualized instruction. In 1976 the Ministry of Education, in cooperation with the Institute of School Programs, suggested the following sequence of special education programs:

0–3 CA    Home care and parent counseling.

3–7 CA    Preschool for the handicapped.

7–17 CA    Special schools for the chronically ill, those with motor defects, the socially maladjusted, blind, visually handicapped, deaf, hard of hearing, educable mentally retarded, trainable mentally retarded, socially maladjusted mentally retarded, blind mentally retarded, and deaf mentally retarded.

17–19 CA    Special vocational schools or sheltered workshops.

Under this plan, a typical curriculum for the educable mentally retarded includes the following fields of study: social and natural environment, language, music, crafts, history, geography, social behavior, arithmetic, natural sciences, vocational training, and physical exercise.

Training and education of the deaf in Poland has been described by Nowak (1974) and Nowak and Slowinski (1977). The training of deaf children in the Warsaw school district began in 1951. Special schools for deaf preschoolers opened during the 1956–1957 school year, and 80 children were enrolled in the program. In 1966–1967 two classes for deaf mentally retarded children were established. During the 1973–1974 school year three facilities for deaf children in the Warsaw district were educating 330 children, of whom 75 were in preschool programs for the deaf mentally retarded. Novak and Slowinski (1977) noted that education of the deaf-blind has a long tradition in Poland, dating back to 1938. Rehabilitation of deaf-blind adults began in 1969. Communication was noted as the most difficult aspect of training. An innovative method (to Polish educators) of teaching the alphabet to the deaf-blind was developed; it uses a three-dimensional tactile alphabet that can be placed on the palm of the subject.

The growth of facilities for the education and training of the profoundly handicapped in Warsaw was described by Kowalczykowa

(1974). The first school for the profoundly handicapped in Poland was established in 1963. In 1973 there were six self-contained facilities, three "life-skills" schools, and three special preschools, serving a total of 420 profoundly handicapped children. In 1973 the first Special Olympics was held in Warsaw. Kowalczykowa further noted that improvements are needed in such areas as (1) development of the register of profoundly handicapped children, (2) further development of training centers, and (3) organization of after-school care.

Concern for education and training of the developmentally disabled within Poland has been noted by Blaim, Sawa, and Pultorak (1974), Nartowska (1975), and Roszkiewicz (1976). Blaim et al. (1974) described a program of treatment for dyslexic children in a day-care hospital. Day-care hospital treatment for dyslexic children first opened in Poland in 1968. Prior to entering the program, the children were evaluated by a child study team that consisted of a pediatrician, a special educator, a clinical psychologist, and a physical education instructor. Good results obtained with dyslexic children were attributed to the following factors: special individual psychotherapy, change in school environment and methods of teaching, simultaneous treatment of various other defects, and involvement of the child's home environment in treatment.

Nartowska (1975) identified three main reasons related to educational failures: (1) methodological inadequacies such as poor organization and methods of teaching; (2) social reasons such as adverse conditions in the home and school environment, and (3) individual reasons such as adverse psychomotor development. Roszkiewicz (1976) elaborated upon the psychological and educational aspects of the concept of "mental dullness," defining mental dullness operationally as intellectual potential within the IQ range of 80–89.

Considerable attention is presently being devoted to the vocational preparation of retarded and handicapped youngsters. The basic vocational special schools have served both resident and commuting population (Sledzinski, 1974). They offer basic training in such areas as tailoring, plumbing, and carpentry. However, not all handicapped youth take advantage of this opportunity. Berling (1975) complained that, in Wroclaw school district, 663 youngsters graduated from elementary special schools in 1971, but less than 50 percent continued their studies in special vocational schools.

The status of vocational education for the handicapped has been described by Karwowski (1976). Vocational training of the handicapped was relatively at a standstill prior to 1956, when only 50 special vocational schools trained 4169 youngsters. In 1973 there were already 80 such schools, and 12,673 youngsters were trained. More progress has been noted since 1973. At present there are 129 special vocational schools distributed as follows: for the mentally retarded 111, chronically ill 2, orthopedically handicapped 1, deaf 11, blind 3, and visually handicapped 1. However, 32 percent of handicapped children still do not receive any vocational training. Las (1975) reported on social activities of vocational special school graduates. His sample consisted of 120 graduates of special schools. Approximately 50 percent of graduates of those schools continued their specialized vocational education. The report emphasized, among various concerns, the need to teach graduates how to utilize better their leisure time activities. The study also suggested that those graduates who were socially more active also demonstrated better job stability.

Special education problems in rural areas have been discussed by Szymanski (1975). As an example he discussed a rural county with a population of over 92,000. Prior to 1965 there was not a single special school nor special class in the whole county. A recently conducted survey revealed 128 children in need of special services; however, only 37 children were getting some form of special help. The rest were at home without any provision for special services.

**Soviet Union**

The special education curriculum in the Soviet Union has recently increased its emphasis on preschool education of the handicapped. The Council of Ministers of the Soviet Union decided as of January 1975 to improve education, vocational training, and care of individuals with defects of mental and physical development (Provotorov, 1975). Its recent 5-year plan (1976–1980) emphasizes the development of various early childhood facilities, as well as improvement in the training of teachers for residential schools of the mentally retarded. Since 1976 a class limit of 12 has been set for children with auditory, visual, and speech defects and 16 for mentally retarded classes.

Aleksandrovskaya and Boitsova (1974) discussed the elaborate procedures that have been developed for early identification and registration of mentally and physically handicapped children. Developmental abnormalities are noted at the time of birth in the delivery room. Subsequent assessment is conducted in a child clinic at the place of residency of the parents. Data on the infant are registered on a chart known as "History of Infant Development." This chart is transferred into the child's day-care or kindergarten, where a new chart is added, known as "Individual Child's Chart N 26." In addition, every child who has a chronic illness or developmental defect is recorded on the control chart of the hospital survey. The authors noted that, as a rule, pediatricians and physicians indicate illnesses on the charts, but not developmental defects. Among older preschoolers speech defects are most frequently noted, followed by visual and motor defects. In some major cities of such Soviet Republics as Russia, Ukraine, and Byelorussia, compulsory examinations of all 3-year-old children are required. Children are examined by an otolaryngologist, a neuropathologist, an orthopedic surgeon, etc. The authors also suggested that problems of the identification and assessment of abnormal children, as well as the type and nature of the medicopedagogical help available to them should become part of the curriculum for training educators and physicians.

The spread of preschool education of the handicapped in the Soviet Union can be determined by the following data. Filkina (1977) reported that in 1970 there were 700 preschool groups in the Soviet Union in which more than 11,000 atypical children were educated. Information provided as of June 1976 listed 1580 preschool facilities with 49,648 children. In addition, facilities were created for 5900 more atypical children. For example, in Uzbekistan, from 1971 to 1976, the number of preschool facilities increased fourfold (Filkina, Morozova, & Moronova, 1976). Inservice training is provided for medical personnel interested in preschool education.

In view of the Soviet's traditional dislike for the use of standardized psychodiagnostic tests, Yassman's (1975) report on a symposium devoted to psychodiagnostics is very interesting. A paper presented by Lubovsky at the symposium argued for the appropriate use of quantitative data and statistical analysis to help determine qualitatively unique characteristics of developmental disabilities. The decision of the symposium participants to petition the Executive Council of the Soviet Psychological Association and the Academy of Pedagogical Sciences for permission to develop theoretical and practical approaches to psychodiagnosis deviates from the traditional Soviet position. A similar trend is noted in a book written in 1974 by Zamsky (reviewed by Belkin, 1975). The author, while still critical of psychometrics, nevertheless acknowledges that the long campaign against pedology prevented the development of legitimate attempts to determine the parameters of childrens' psychological, physical, and social development.

Yeremenko (1976) described differential instruction in auxiliary schools. He distinguishes between an "individual approach" and "differential instruction." While the individual approach represents application of the same program to every child in the same class, under differential education every child has a tailor-made program and utilizes educational material commensurate with his or her potential. The principles of differential education have formed the basis of experimental education in many auxiliary schools of the Ukrainian SSR since 1967.

Speech stimulation and language training programs for the handicapped have drastically increased since the 1976–1977 school year. The speech and language curriculum originally included 4 hours per week of speech training; it has now been increased to 18 hours. Slezina (1976) has described the speech training of deaf school children as being aimed at the maximum utilization of their auditory potential.

The education and training of severely and moderately retarded youngsters has been described by Kuzmitskaya, Maller, and Tsykoto (1976). This study reported on the progress of moderately retarded adolescents (15–17 years old); in one-third the condition was caused by Down's syndrome. All the youngsters in this sample were able to commute within the neighborhood, make small purchases, help with household chores, etc. The authors concluded that under appropriate home conditions, and with specialized training, it is possible to train even severely retarded children. In a second article Kuzmitskaya (1977) described a curriculum for trainable mentally retarded youngsters with a focus on nine areas: (1) personal communication (how to pay attention, greet someone, use a telephone, know one's own name and the names of the immediate members of the family, etc.); (2) orientation to place (house and street number, public transportation, etc.); (3) occupations of people in towns and villages; (4) commerce (stores, clothing); (5) food preparation; (6) available health services; (7) post office, telephone, telegraph, and radio; (8) recreation (movie, theater, television, parks, circus, holiday); and (9) the working day, wages, and salaries.

Formakova (1974) discussed the education and training of children suffering from a complicated form of oligophrenia. She defines this condition as oligophrenia complicated by severe personality and character pathology. Such children have poor impulse control, do not follow instructions, have a tendency toward aggressive outbursts, and expect immediate satisfaction of their demands. It is difficult to educate such children in a public school setting and home instruction is suggested. She sets up several behavioral objectives for such a child and recommends that parents adhere to them in detail. The parents are instructed to expect a child to systematically observe daily routines including self-help activities and daily physical exercise. The child should be expected to independently perform a variety of activities.

Gavor (1976) described educational programs for the handicapped attending auxiliary boarding schools. Such schools are usually responsible for providing services to mentally retarded youngsters within a five-county area. Various means are used by these schools to communicate with the parents of the children attending them: these include newspaper articles, exhibits, open lectures, parents' assemblies, and visitations. As a rule, parents visit the school once a month. Home visits by the school's staff members enable them to become familiar with the social, cultural, and material aspects of the family.

The development of special education services in the Moldavian SSR has been described by Ivanitsky, Bukun, and Konstandoglo (1977). Since 1976, the following child study teams have been in existence: inhouse medicopedagogical committees, which usually serve one school building; regional committees; state appeals committees; and state defectological consultation committees. During the 1970–1971 school year, a special education program was organized at the Kysheniv Pedagogical Institute. In 1974 a Department of Special Education was established, and one year later evening and externship courses were organized for those teachers already employed in special schools. It is anticipated that some special education services will be provided in all republics of the Soviet Union by the end of this five-year plan. For example, it is anticipated that by 1980, 26,000 children in the Kazakh SSR will profit from special education services (Machyhyna, 1977).

## PERSONNEL PREPARATION

### Poland

Special education personnel preparation in Poland has a long history. June 1, 1974, was the half-century mark since the formation of the Special Education Section of the Polish Teachers Association (Kirejczyk, 1975). In 1922 the National Institute for Special Education was formed in Warsaw under the leadership of Maria Grzegozsewska. Since 1973 special education teachers have been prepared at eleven universities and teachers colleges; both full- and part-time studies are encouraged at these institutions (Belcerek, 1977).

In accordance with the decision of the Council of Ministries dated April 2, 1976 (Dryzalowska, 1976), the name of the National Institute of Special Education was granted to the Graduate School of Special Education. The main task of the school is to train special education teachers and educational therapists. Special educators are also trained at the Graduate School of Education in Krakow (Baran, 1974). The school offers masters degrees in four areas of special education: mental retardation, auditory disorders, chronically ill and physically handicapped, and socially maladjusted. It opened in the fall of 1964 and by the spring of 1973 it had issued 313 diplomas of program completion, 213 master's degrees, and 101 specialists certificates.

In 1977 the Polish Ministry of Education began to provide post-graduate studies in special education at the Graduate School of Special Education in Warsaw. The purpose of these postgraduate studies is the further education of active special education teachers who have master's degrees but are lacking specialized preparation. Areas of study include (1) deaf and hard of hearing, (2) chronically ill, (3) socially maladjusted, and (4) diagnosis and assessment. For example, a three-semester sequence of studies for teachers of the socially maladjusted includes 143 hours of lectures and 157 hours of practicum. The following content areas of studies are included: special pedagogy, etiology of social maladjustments, psychology of social maladjustments, therapeutic education, methods of education, methods of rehabilitation, elementary criminology, law, speech, correction, and remediation of children with educational difficulties. Most of those who attend postgraduate studies are part-time students.

Hulek (1978) explained that special education teachers in Poland essentially come from two backgrounds of preparation. Some become teachers by entering four-year teacher training programs after graduation from a high school. Others enter the university with a subject matter background and experience in teaching and then are prepared as special educators. Not all special education programs have well-trained teachers. In 1978 Kowalczykowa reported that only 90 percent of the faculty in preschools for the blind and deaf had specialized training. In other types of preschool facilities only 30–40 percent of teachers have specialized training, but it is anticipated that by 1980, 70 percent of faculty at all types of preschool facilities will have specialized training.

Tomasik and Zabczynska (1975) published a follow-up of graduates of the National Institute of Special Education (since 1976 known as the Graduate School of Special Education). For many years, it was the only institution that trained special educators in Poland. The survey was based on 212 questionnaires collected in 1974; among the respondents 99 were full-time and 113 were part-time students. Categorized according to their fields of specialization, 134 completed training in working with the mentally retarded, 36 with the socially maladjusted, 22 with the chronically ill, 18 with the deaf and 2 with blind. The survey revealed that 150 (70 percent) of the graduates were females; 40 percent of the graduates were employed in special schools and 45 percent in elementary schools.

Hulek (1978) listed improvements in special education services for the chronically ill and socially maladjusted; cooperation with social workers, psychologist, recreational instructors, and physicians was cited as among important needs for the future development of special education.

In the spring of 1978 the special education team of the Pedagogical Science Committee of the Polish Academy of Sciences formulated updated guidelines for special education. Among their recommendations were the following (Hulek, 1978):

1.  A student should first become familiar with normal children and on this basis should be trained how to deal with handicapped children.

2.  Future teachers should know how to cooperate with various agencies and institutions outside the school.

3.  Teachers should continue their education after graduation from the university by attending postdiploma programs and various courses.

**Soviet Union**

In the Soviet Union special educators serve two groups of children: (1) those in special schools for the blind, deaf, oligophrenic, visually impaired, auditorially impaired, neurologically impaired, and those with speech defects (Machyhyna, 1970); and (2) those who attend auxiliary schools. At the present time, both special and auxiliary schools are employing teachers with 2 years of pedagogical preparation. Some teachers have specialized defectological training and many are graduates of the inservice programs offered by defectological institutes (Minasian, 1970).

A brief historical perspective on the development of special education teacher training programs in the Soviet Union has been provided by Zhivina (1974). Current developments in the field of special education in the Soviet Union date from 1959. At that time the total training of a special education teacher lasted for five years and emphasized student teaching or practica (24 weeks). The curriculum was reorganized into a four-year program in 1963, with the following emphases: in the first year of study, an introduction to defectology, physics, chemistry, biology, anatomy, and historical materialism; in the second year, psychopathology, psychiatry, neuropathology of children, political economy, and geography; in the third year, pedagogical psychopathology, developmental psychopathology, and a practicum; and in the fourth year, public education in the Soviet Union, sexual psychopathology, a clinical praticum, and political education (Zhivina, 1974).

The importance of defectological training has recently been underscored by the formation of a Council of Defectology within the Ministry of Education of the USSR (Usanova & Shakhovskaya, 1976) as well as the formation of medicopedagogical committees include pathologists. At this time, medicopedagogical committees are not yet mandatory in all republics of the Soviet Union.

Efforts are continuously being made in the Soviet Union to achieve better teacher training methods, revise curricula, and improve the quality of faculty members in defectological departments. In February 1975, the first all-union congress of instructors in defectological departments took place in Shayanlay (Lithuanian SSR). The congress emphasized the following (Kortseva & Shakhovskaya, 1976): (1) preparation of specialists in the area of preschool education of the handicapped; (2) improvement in field work, practica, and supervised student teaching; (3) independent projects and independent studies; (4) medicopedagogical cooperation in the preparation of teacher-defectologists as well as cooperation between physicians and teachers; and (5) exchange of instructors between various universities and institutes.

In September 1975 a conference at the Moskow State Pedagogical Institute was devoted to upgrading the qualifications of faculty members teaching at defectological departments of universities and pedagogical institutes (Usanova & Shakhovskaya, 1976). As one of the proposed improvements in curriculum the study of genetics has been introduced.

An attempt has been made do improve the student teaching and practica of undergraduate defectology students. For this purpose a special committee was formed during the school year 1975–1976 under the auspices of the Ministry of Education of the USSR (Shakhovskaya, Usanova, & Ushakova, 1977). Symposia, correspondence, courses, and workshops are organized by the committee in order to improve the professional development of defectologists. The main emphasis has been upon an enhanced relationship between theory and practice. There are also correspondence courses which are intended primarily to benefit teachers who are already functioning as special educators (Usanova & Shakhovskaya, 1976).

In order to provide defectological training for the broad spectrum of special educators, the University of Defectological Sciences was established in Kiev in 1972. The course of study at this "university without walls" extends for 2 years and covers such areas as education of the mentally retarded, speech pathology, and education of the blind ( "The University," 1975). The largest program at this university is in the area of mental retardation.

## INTERNATIONAL CONFERENCES ON SPECIAL EDUCATION

Relatively new developments in the field of special education in Eastern Europe are joint conferences which bring together representatives of the Communist bloc countries (Cisek, 1975; M. R., 1977). The first such conference took place in 1961 in Moscow. It was devoted to educational methodologies and educational research. The second conference took place in 1974 in East Berlin. It discussed problems of personality development within communist countries. The third conference took place in 1977 in Warsaw. Participating in it were representatives from Bulgaria, Czechoslovakia, Cuba, Mongolia, East Germany, Romania, Hungary, Vietnam, the Soviet Union, and Poland. Its main topic was the role of the educator in the personality development of children and youth. The conference emphasized that the nature of school in the communist societies is changing from primarily an instructional institution to a place of concerted ideological effort. It was emphasized that teachers should possess a Marxist orientation and "accepted" value systems. The conference decided to pay special attention to the process of selection of candidates for the teaching profession.

## CONCLUSION

In conclusion, it is possible to make some generalizations about special education in Poland and the Soviet Union. Since education in both Poland and the Soviet Union, as in any other communist country, is highly centralized, it enables researchers in the field easy access to large samples of the population. However, with few exceptions, most of the studies reviewed in this chapter did not employ rigorous statistical methodology.

In the field of curriculum development in Poland one is impressed by the rapid growth of services and the very broad definition of special education from preschool to geriatrics. A new 10-year curriculum is being implemented at present. It is of interest to notice the rather specialized approach of Polish educators: they envision separate programs for the blind mentally retarded, deaf mentally retarded, and socially maladjusted mentally retarded. At the same time there is concern for and discussion of the mainstreaming of the educable mentally retarded.

In contrast to Poland, in the Soviet Union special education is narrowly defined in the traditional sense as education of the mentally retarded (oligophrenopedagogy), blind (thyphlopedagogy), deaf (surdopedagogy) and those with speech disorders (legopedagogy). The problems of the socially maladjusted are not considered within the domain of special education. There is, however, an increased emphasis in the Soviet Union on preschool education of the handicapped; a registry of all handicapped and potentially handicapped is maintained. Of considerable interest is the apparent reassessment within the Soviet Union of the negative attitude toward standardized testing. On the other hand, there is presently an increased emphasis on political indoctrination of teachers within the Soviet sphere, as indicated by joint conferences of special educators from all communist countries.

# References

Abbasov, M. G. Level of some spatial orientation skills in mentally retarded school children. *Defectologia*, 1977, *1*, 38–43.

Agavelian, O. K. Several apsects of social and vocational adaptations of auxiliary school graduates. *Defectologia*, 1974, *1*, 62–68.

Akinshchikova, G. I., & Yeremeyeva, A. I., Verlinskaya, D. K., Tysianchniuk, S. F. Experimental study of intelligence in children with sex-linked chromosomal aberration. *Defectologia*, 1976, *6*, 16–22.

Albrecht, E. Ya. Emotional sphere in oligophrenic adolescent under psychic decompensation. *Defectologia*, 1976, *4*, 38–44.

Aleksandrovskaya, M. M., & Boitsova, O. S. Organization of early identification and registration of mentally and physically handicapped children. *Defectologia*, 1974, *6*, 3–9.

Baran, J. Training of special educators in the Graduate School of Education in Kracow. *Special School*, 1974, *3*, 257–261.

Belcerek, M. Organization of special education in Poland. In A. Hulek (Ed.), *Therapeutic pedagogy*. Warsaw: State Scientific Publications, 1977.

Belkin, A. History of education of mentally retarded by K. S. Zamsky. *Defectologia*, 1975, *3*, 93–95.

Berling, Z. Preparation of mentally handicapped youth for social life. *Special School*, 1975, *1*, 48–54.

Bgazhnokova, I. M. Reasoning operations in mentally retarded students in the process of actualization of knowledge. *Defectologia*, 1975, *3*, 24–29.

Blaim, A., Sawa, B., Pultorak, M. Results of dyslexia treatment in day care hospital. *Special School*, 1974, *4*, 309–318.

Blaszkewich, R. Self evaluation of the graduates of special schools for the mentally retarded. *Special School*, 1974, *1*, 26–35.

Bukowski, M. Social position of severely handicapped child within his peer group. *Special School*, 1976, *1*, 23–32.

Cisek, D. International conference on the educational programs for special educators (Warsaw, December 5–7, 1974). *Special School*, 1975, *2*, 55–60.

Doroszewska, J. Special education in the service of the handicapped. In A. Hulek (Ed.), *Rehabilitation of the disabled in Polish Peoples Republic*. Warsaw: State Medical Publications, 1973.

Dryzalowska, G. M. Grzegorsewska Graduate School of Special Education. *Special School*, 1976, *2*, 80–81.

Filkina, L. M. Actual size of social pre-school upbringing of atypical children and several problems of its further development. *Defectologia*, 1977, *1*, 3–11.

Filkina, L. M., Morozova, N. G., & Moronova, S. A. Social preschool education of atypical children in Uzbekisten. *Defectologia*, 1976, *6*, 78–84.

Formakova, A. I. Individual upbringing and training of children with complicated form of oligophrenia. *Defectologia*, 1974, *2*, 55–59.

Gavor, I. I. Work of auxiliary boarding school with parents of students. *Defectologia*, 1976, *3*, 72–78.

Hoffman, B. Individual and social aspects of development and interpretation in special education. *Special School*, 1978, *3*, 163–169.

Holowinsky, I. Z. Special education in Eastern Europe. In L. Mann & D. Sabatino (Eds.), *The first review of special education*. Philadelphia: JSE Press, 1973.

Holowinsky, I. Z. Preschool education and research in the Soviet Union. In L. Mann & D. Sabatino (Eds.), *The second review of special education*. Philadelphia: JSE Press, 1974.

479

Holowinsky, I. Z. Functional centers hypothesis: Soviet view of learning disorders. In L. Mann & D. Sabatino (Eds.), *The third review of special education*. New York: Grune & Stratton, 1976.

Hulek, A. Mainstreaming systems of special education. In A. Hulek (Ed.), *Therapeutic pedagogy*. Warsaw: State Scientific Publications, 1977a.

Hulek, A. Some remarks on work connected with curricula for ten-year schools in the field of special education. *Special School*, 1977b, *4*, 270–271.

Hulek, A. *Personnel preparation: International comparison*. Paper presented at the First World Congress on Future Special Education, Sterling, Scotland, June 1978.

Ivanitsky, A. I., Bukun, N. I., & Konstandoglo, I. F. Development of defectology in the Moldavian, SSR. *Defectologia*, 1977, *5*, 38–43.

Karpova, A. N., Karpov, B. A., & Isayev, D. N. Investigation of eye movements of oligophrenic children during reading. *Defectologia*, 1977, *5*, 25–33.

Karvialis, V. Yu. Families of former special school students. *Defectologia*, 1975, *4*, 28–34.

Karwowski, J. Vocational education for handicapped children. *Special School*, 1976, *2*, 5–14.

Kirejczyk, K. Half century of activity of the Special Education Section of the Polish Teacher's Association. *Special School*, 1975, *1*, 7–18.

Klimasinski, K. Application of Piaget's theory of mental development in psychological examination of the blind. In H. Larkowa (Ed.), *Psychological problems in rehabilitation of the disabled*. Warsaw: State Medical Publications, 1974, 114–118.

Kortseva, I., Shakhovskaya, S. Problems of improvement of special teacher's training. *Defectologia*, 1976, *1*, 87–91.

Kotlarski, M. Organization of specail education. In A. Hulek (Ed.), *Rehabilitation of the disabled in Polish Peoples Republic*. Warsaw: State Medical Publications, 1973.

Kowalczykowa, J. Facilities for education and training of profoundly handicapped in Warsaw in the period 1963–1973. *Special School*, 1974, *3*, 230–234.

Kowalczykowa, J. About the necessity of education of children with developmental disabilities. *Special School*, 1978, *2*, 94–98.

Kozakov, A. A. Application of photoelectrical instruments presenting color information to the blind. *Defectologia*, 1975, *1*, 71–75.

Kur, W. Current needs and potential for training and care of the mentally retarded rural children. In A. Hulek (Ed.), *Problems of the disabled and other handicapped in rural areas*. Warsaw: State Scientific Publications, 1976.

Kuzmitskaya, M. I. Preparation of trainable retardates to practical life (home and social adaptation). *Defectologia*, 1977, *5*, 89–91.

Kuzmitskaya, M. I., Maller, A. R., & Tsykoto, V. H. Experimental education of severely retarded children in auxiliary schools. *Defectologia*, 1976, *6*, 26–31.

Las, H. The evaluation of social activity of elementary special school and vocational special school graduates in the opinion of various organizations. *Special School*, 1975, *1*, 33–45.

Lilin, Y. U. Twins and oligophrenia. *Defectologia*, 1978, *2*, 74–77.

Lipkowski, O. Special education and other sciences. In A. Hulek (Ed.), *Therapeutic pedagogy*. Warsaw: State Scientific Publications, 1977.

Machyhyna, V. F. Appropriate selection and staffing as an important link in the work of special schools. *Defectologia*, 1970, *1*, 3–7.

Machyhyna, V. F. Progress of special education in the Kazakh SSR. *Defectologia*, 1977, *4*, 4–9.

Markovskaya, I. F. Neuropsychological analysis of clinical modifications of developmental backwardness. *Defectologia*, 1977, *6*, 3–11.

Maszczak, T. The time of onset and etiology of deafness of children as revealed by cross-sectional research in the school year 1972–73. *Special School*, 1975a, *2*, 31–37.

Maszczak, T. Physical development and efficiency of deaf mentally retarded children. *Special School*, 1975b, *4*, 25–28.

Maszczak, T. Somatic development of deaf children in Poland. *Special School*, 1978, *1*, 16–25.

Minasian, A. M. Education of handicapped children in the Armenian SSR. *Defectologia*, 1970, *1*, 25–34.

M. R. Third conference of educators from communist countries. *Special School*, 1977, *4*, 296–297.

Nartowska, H. Development disturbances as reason for failure in learning. *Special School*, 1975, *2*, 5–15.

N. N. 160 years of Institute for Deaf-Mute in Warsaw. *Special School*, 1978, *1*, 65–66.

Nowak, J. Training of deaf children in Warsaw district. *Special School*, 1974, *4*, 346–352.

Nowak, J., & Slowinski, J. Problems of the education of the deaf-blind. *Special School*, 1977, *1*, 51–56.

Panczyk, J. The problem of limbs lateralization of slightly mentally handicapped children. *Special School*, 1975, *3*, 33–42.

Pawlikowska, G. Studies of perceptual determinants of readability of Braille characters combinations. *Special School*, 1977, *2*, 100–119.

Peresleni, L. I., & Sagdulayev, S. A. On intellectual performance capacity and disorders in various forms of oligophrenia. *Defectologia*, 1975, *3*, 29–35.

Provotorov, V. P. Another evidence of Party's care for children and adolescents with mental and physical impairments. *Defectologia*, 1975, *3*, 3–7.

Rayskaya, M. M. Special structure of the defect under sex chromosome mosaicism. *Defectologia*, 1976, *1*, 37–45.

Rostiagaylova, L. I. Psychological characteristics of hydrocephalic children. *Defectologia*, 1977, *6*, 25–30.

Roszkiewicz, I. Psychological and educational aspects of mental dullness. *Special School*, 1976, *2*, 33–38.

Shakhovskaya, S. M., Usanova, O. N., Ushakova, I. P. Student-teaching and practicum of undergraduate defectology students. *Defectologia*, 1977, *2*, 84–90.

Shklovsky, V. M. Hemispheric speech dominance in stuttering. *Defectologia*, 1976, *1*, 20–32.

Sledzinski, W. Some thoughts about vocational education of mildly retarded youngsters. *Special School*, 1974, *2*, 147–149.

Slezina, N. F. Special training of deaf school children under new conditions. *Defectologia*, 1976, *5*, 57–66.

Szymanski, T. The problem of county children in need of special care. *Special School*, 1975, *14*, 47–51.

The university of defectological knowledge (editorial chronicle). *Defectologia*, 1975, *6*, 91–92.

Tomasik, E., & Zabczynska, E. Graduates of the National Institute of Special Education and the life situation. *Special School*, 1975, *4*, 28–39.

Trzesniowski, R. *Physical development and efficiency of Polish youth*. Warsaw: NK, 1961.

Umanskaya, N. M. Techniques of intelligence assessment in preschool children with underdeveloped speech. *Defectologia*, 1977, *2*, 64–72.

Usanova, D., & Shakhovskaya, S. Need to accomplish preparation of teacher–defectologists. *Defectologia*, 1976, *2*, 86–90.

Wolenski, N. *Human development*. Warsaw: State Science Publishers, 1977.

Yashkova, N. Research conference on abnormal child personality. *Defectologia*, 1978, *1*, 78–86.

Yassman, L. New developments in psychodiagnostic methods. *Defectologia*, 1975, *2*, 89–94.

481

Yavkin, V. M. Clinical characteristics of failing primary-grade regular school pupils from families of chronic alcoholics. *Defectologia,* 1975, *3,* 35–44.

Yeremenko, I. H. On differential instructions in auxiliary schools. *Defectologia,* 1976, *4,* 56–63.

Yeremenko, I. H. Conditions and perspectives of scientific research in the field of defectology in Ukrainian SSR. *Defectologia,* 1977, *5,* 12–20.

Zamsky, Kh. S. *History of the education of the mentally retarded.* Moscow: Education Publisher, 1974.

Zhivina, A. I. Major stages of development of special education teacher training in the USSR. *Defectologia,* 1974, *2,* 68–75.

# Index